John Montague

A Poet's Life

John Montague
A Poet's Life

Adrian Frazier

THE LILLIPUT PRESS
DUBLIN

First published 2024 by
THE LILLIPUT PRESS

62–63 Sitric Road,
Arbour Hill,
Dublin 7,
Ireland
www.lilliputpress.ie

A CIP record for this title is available from The British Library.

Hardback ISBN 978 1 84351 910 2
eBook ISBN 978 1 84351 925 6

Lilliput gratefully acknowledges the financial support of the Arts Council / An Chomhairle Ealaíon.

Set in 11pt on 16 pt Adobe Garamond Pro by Compuscript
Printed and bound in Sweden by Scandbook

To Thomas Redshaw

CONTENTS

ACKNOWLEDGMENTS

'What about Tom Redshaw?' John Montague asked in May 2015 when we first discussed my undertaking to write his biography. We would work on it together, I said.

In fact, Tom and I did collaborate from beginning to end. Redshaw was not just Montague's bibliographer and the most productive scholar of his poetry, he was a Montague family friend from the late 1960s onward. He is himself at work on a biography of Liam Miller, publisher of The Dolmen Press, so the two of us were up to our elbows in many of the same archives. The collaboration deepened our friendship and gave us both pleasure. This biography is rightly dedicated to Thomas Dillon Redshaw.

The biography of a recent contemporary largely depends on the quality of the archive and the reports of witnesses. Montague was a careful record-keeper of his own writing life. Through most of his mature life, he kept a daily diary in which he recorded not just appointments, addresses and the like, but also ideas for stories and drafts of poems. When the composition of a poem moved to a full-sized page, he often spelled out models, listed possible themes, and gave advice to himself. Various drafts would normally go into a folder, along with newspaper clippings, reviews, photographs and other materials related to the poem. The folders themselves would usually be stashed within the covers of a published volume of his work.

Although poetry itself does not often bring in significant royalties, research libraries will sometimes spend a considerable sum to acquire the papers of a prominent poet. Montague sold his archive in four tranches: in the 1970s to the University of Victoria, British Columbia; in the 1980s, to the State University of

New York at Buffalo; and in the 1990s to the National Library of Ireland. The remainder of his papers went to University College Cork.

These archives contain not only his working papers but his correspondence. The age of serious letter-writing is now in the past. In his time, Montague kept up exchanges about works-in-progress with a number of scholars and writers. Chief among these are the letters to and from Barry Callaghan, Barrie Cooke, Donald Fanger, Serge Fauchereau, Thomas Kinsella, Liam Miller, Timothy O'Keeffe, Thomas Parkinson and Richard Ryan. These are sometimes letters of five, ten, or fifteen pages of seriously considered writing (Montague often made several drafts of his letters, and left some important draft letters unsent). I am grateful to Fanger, Fauchereau, and Ryan for making available to me their own files of Montague correspondence, and to the libraries that hold the letters of the other correspondents.

For a candid understanding of Montague's personal life, I am beholden to his companions who have either allowed access to their letters in Montague's various archival collections, or themselves provided letters and diaries, and afterwards replied to my questions, particularly Susan Patron, Elizabeth Sheehan and Janet Somerville.

The insight of Montague's closest friends over the years was often my guide. Barry Callaghan, Serge Fauchereau, Richard Ryan, Philip Brady and Tom McGurk met with me for interviews, sometimes on several occasions. Thomas McCarthy, by publishing his own journals (both in excerpts and in a book), has enriched everyone's understanding of the poet; McCarthy also responded helpfully to my enquiries. Other Cork writers lent assistance, particularly Nuala Ní Dhomhnaill, Patrick Crotty and Greg Delanty, who sat down for extensive interviews.

For family history, I largely relied upon Andrew Montague, the son of the poet's brother Turlough. Resident in Fintona, and with immense local knowledge, he was scrupulous in his assistance. He made it clear that if this biography were uninformed or inaccurate, it would not be his fault. He located key official documents as well as telling me things that had never been written down. His sisters Dara and Sheena, and his brother Turlough, as well as his cousins Peter and Mary, also contributed.

Montague has three surviving widows, Madeleine, Evelyn and Elizabeth. Each took me in hand and told me how things had been and where I had made a mistake. Evelyn gave me three afternoons of serious conversation. Elizabeth prepared a personal memoir, in addition to granting an interview and answering many enquiries. They all offered notes on the complete draft. I tried to show John as they saw him, as well as how he imagined them. The daughters of John and Evelyn, Oonagh and Sybil Montague, contributed by interview, telephone and email.

My friend and neighbour, the poet Eva Bourke, lent an ear if I felt the need of a reality check on some matter. She read the manuscript in draft and asked the right questions. Martin Carney, my father-in-law, born about the same time as Montague, read the chapters as they were written, and gave his honest opinion of the man and of the unfolding story. Sometimes he was able to illuminate for me a bygone aspect of Irish life, such as the mating customs of Irish dance halls or the teaching practices of national schools. Kevin Barry, Professor Emeritus of University of Galway, did a friend's duty in reading early sections and giving me a green light to continue.

My literary agent (and long-time friend) Jonathan Williams involved himself with this book to a remarkable extent. He had also been the agent for John and Elizabeth Montague. He knew the entire literary scene I was attempting to describe. He put me in touch with a number of witnesses I may otherwise never have found. When the manuscript began to take shape, he read drafts and made scores of notes, three times. I have tried not to let him down.

There are many to thank. The distinguished witnesses who took the time to help include the following (no doubt, I have accidentally failed to credit some others): Jennifer Airey, Guinn Batten, John Behan, Richard Bizot, Eva Bourke, Kevin Bowen, Kevin Barry, Jodi Boyle, Anthony Bradley, Phil Brady, Rory Brennan, Tom Burns, Christopher Cahill, Caroline Callner, Matthew Campbell, Cliodhna Carney, Martin Carney, Eiléan Ní Chuilleanáin, Frances Clarke, Mary Conefrey, Evelyn Conlon, Valerie Coogan, Liadin Cooke, Patricia Coughlan, Vincent Crapanzano, Katharine Crouan, Jacques Darras, Howard Davies, Margaretta D'Arcy, Alex Davis, Gerald Dawe, Seamus Deane, Greg Delanty, Louis de Paor, Máirín Ní Dhonnchadha, Tony Carroll, Denis Donoghue, Lelia Doolan, Theo Dorgan, Stephen Ennis, Peter Fallon, Serge Fauchereau, John FitzGerald, Ger Fitzgibbon, Michael Foley, Lawrence Fong, John Wilson Foster, Roy Foster, George Frazier, Joe Gagen, David Gardiner, Alessandro Gentili, Seán Golden, Fiona Green, Nicholas Grene, Eamon Grennan, Christopher Griffin, Elizabeth Grubgeld, Brendan Hackett, Gerry Harty, Elizabeth Healy,

Jefferson Holdridge, Alannah Hopkin, Brendan Horisk, Frank Horisk, Barry Houlihan, Ben Howard, Catherine Howell, Destiny Hrncir, Marian Janssen, Pierre Johannon, Dillon Johnston, Colbert Kearney, Suzanne Keen, Aidan Kelly, Patsy Kelly, William Kennedy, Frank Kerznowski, Thomas Kilroy, Jane Kramer, David Lampe, James Larkin, Brian Lawlor, Catherine La Farge, Adrienne Leavy, Conor Linnie, Mary O'Sullivan Long, Edna Longley, Michael Longley, Frances Lynn, Sean Lysaght, Rory MacFlynn, Jim MacKillop, Derek Mahon, Dennis Maloney, Liam Mansfield, Lara Marlowe, James Maynard, Thomas McCarthy, Bill McCormack, Hubert McDermott, Lucy McDiarmid, Hugh McFadden, Avice-Claire McGovern, Paula Meehan, Frank Miata, Conor Montague, Paul Muldoon, Helena Mulkerns, Deirdre Mulrooney, Gerry Murphy, Patsy Murphy, Eoin O'Brien, Peggy O'Brien, Dáibhí Ó Cróinín, Cronan O Doibhlin, Eamon O'Donoghue, Colette O'Flaherty, Timothy O'Grady, Seán O'Laoire, Mary O'Malley, Ed O'Shea, Paul Perry, Lionel Pilkington, Laetitia Pollard, Christopher Reid, Christopher Ricks, John Ridland, David Rigsbee, Clíona Ní Ríordáin, Maurice Riordan, Frank Rogers, Jim Rogers, Seamus Rogers, Richard Ryan, Elizabeth Sheehan, Frank Shovlin, Tony Skelton, Janice Fitzpatrick Simmons, Jordan Smith, Gerard Smyth, Janet Somerville, Rod Stoneman, Steven Stuart-Smith, Gary Snyder, Eoin Sweeney, Colm Tóibín, Emer Twomey, Irving Wardle, Robert and Rebecca Tracy, William Wall, Barbara Weiner, David Wheatley, Mark Wormald, Nina Witozek, Vincent Woods.

I am grateful for the professional help and courtesy of the special collections' staff at the following libraries: John J. Burns Library, Boston College; The Poetry Collection, University at Buffalo; Shields Library, University of California at Davis; Cambridge University Library; James Joyce Library, University College Dublin; Boole Library, University College Cork; Rose Library, Emory University; James Hardiman Library, University of Galway; National Library of Ireland; Brotherton Library, Leeds University; Elizabeth Dafoe Library, University of Manitoba; Maynooth University Library; Library of the State University of New York at Albany; McFarlin Special Collections, University of Tulsa; McPherson Library, University of Victoria; Reynolds Library, Wake Forest University; Library of the University of Washington in Seattle.

For permission to quote from Montague's archive I am grateful to Elizabeth Montague, his literary executor, and for permission to quote from his published works, to Peter Fallon of The Gallery Press.

PRELIMINARY CONSIDERATIONS

Not long after beginning to work on the life of John Montague, eight years ago, I was asked Why are you writing about *him*? Why not Seamus Heaney? Isn't he more famous? A little snort of laughter might have been heard on the slopes of Parnassus, whether it was John elbowing a ghostly Seamus in the ribs, or the other way round. Not to detract from the merits of Seamus Heaney, as gentleman or poet, but there are advantages to John Montague as a subject for a literary biography.

His course in life offers a full view of post-war poetry, not just poetry in Ireland, but a vantage-point on modern poetry in America, Britain and France. Do you know the parlour game 'Six Degrees of Kevin Bacon?' The actor was in everything, or next door to it. Montague is the same among poets. Allen Ginsberg? In 1955 Montague was in Medieval English class with him at Berkeley, just a month before the first reading of *Howl*. Harold Bloom? Montague was his classmate at Yale University in 1953, when Bloom talked endlessly and with rabbinical profundity.

At the Iowa Writers Workshop, the other student poets included Robert Bly, W.D. Snodgrass, Philip Levine and James Dickey; one of his instructors was John Berryman. In Berkeley, he had an affair with a woman running an art gallery; one of the artists she represented was 'Jess', who turned up at her dinner party with his partner, the poet Robert Duncan.

Poetry, of course, is not a matter of who you know. That's the point made by Patrick Kavanagh's poem 'Epic': 'I have lived in important places, times/ When great events were decided,' such as a neighbour shouting, 'Damn your soul!' as another farmer raises a potato spade in anger. Nonetheless, Montague's nose for cosmopolitan literary life makes for a narrative that illuminates not just his own poetry, but modern poetry in general. When important things were just breaking into flower, he was often a witness, a participant, a change agent, sometimes even the leading contributor. That was in New Haven, Iowa City, Berkeley, Dublin, Paris, Cork city, Belfast and New York. Particularly in his home country, he was a path-breaker.

2

To write a proper literary biography you need more than just a writer of interest. It is necessary to have the materials, the traces of works-in-progress, living witnesses, observers in the past who left memoranda, and a full archive of correspondence. Where Montague is concerned, the evidence is there. Conscious of what Yeats's archive looked like (from Allan Wade's 1955 edition of the *Letters*), he became a professional curator of his own papers. He kept letters he received, and drafts of many that he sent. Then he sold off his so-called 'complete archive' not once, or twice, but four times. Poetry had in that period acquired status; it was, to borrow a phrase from T.S. Eliot, the definition of culture.

When Montague was starting off in university, serious literature was rising towards this peak of prestige. In America the GI Bill sent veterans to college. To help them, in the late 1940s Harvard's president Robert Maynard Hutchins created a Great Book publishing scheme. The seeds of Western Civilization – recently rescued from Nazism at the cost of fifty million lives – were thought to be found in literary works: the best that has been thought and said. From the early 1950s, partly due to the nature of New Criticism, lyric poetry acquired the highest status of all literary forms.

In a cultural parallel of the Marshall Plan, a group from Harvard, often led by Jewish literary critics and writers like F.O. Matthiessen and Saul Bellow, set up the Salzburg Seminar in Austria. This was meant to be an introduction for Europeans to the new post-war world: a high-minded combination of American literary modernism with constitutional democracy and free speech. Montague was a scholarship boy at this seminar in the summer of 1950. In his own words, he became a 'fellow-traveller' of these American anti-communist liberals.

From the mid-1950s he kept up a number of literary correspondences – chains of letters back and forth that may be ten pages long. On his own side, Montague would often do an outline, and then a first draft, before producing a legible and coherent fair copy of the letter posted. Some of his key correspondents were the following:

Donald Fanger, met at Berkeley in the 1950s, later Harvard professor of the European novel;

Serge Fauchereau, French critic and cultural historian;

Robin Skelton, English poet, magician, anthologist and Yeats scholar, later professor at University of Victoria in Canada;

Thomas Kinsella, fellow Dolmen Press poet and rival;

Tim O'Keeffe, London editor and publisher, at MacGibbon and Kee;

Thomas Parkinson, poet, historian of Beat poets, and Yeats scholar at University of California, Berkeley;

Barrie Cooke, Anglo-American painter long resident in Ireland;

Richard Ryan, Irish poet and diplomat;

Liam Miller, printer and publisher at The Dolmen Press;

Barry Callaghan, Toronto poet, journalist and editor of *Exile*.

Montague's letters are occasions for self-examination, with point-by-point plans for improvement. A biographer would never have access to such hours of self-invention if the letter had not been written, and having been written, saved.

The poet was himself a magpie, snatching up bits and pieces to make his nest bigger and bigger, but the eggs over which he brooded often took a long time to hatch. He collected preparatory materials – newspaper articles, photographs, phrases written on a bank statement or bus ticket, false starts. He kept all these bits and pieces in a sheaf, and would go back over them time and again – in pencil, ballpoint, or fountain pen. 'What is the point of this?' he might ask himself, or 'Why not end this here?' An early habit was to list two or three models for the work in progress, often the work of a contemporary, such as Charles Tomlinson, Thomas Kinsella, Robert Lowell, or Robert Duncan. He kept abreast of what his contemporaries were doing.

Montague is a peculiarly conscious and scholarly poet. He sometimes states the intended theme of the poem on the manuscript page. On occasion, he would then cross it out, and suggest to himself a different theme; he had misunderstood his own poem in progress – it was going somewhere else. Composition is fluent, molten, bubbling, sometimes going to sleep for months or years, before reawakening and erupting again. It is not uncommon in the case of a Montague poem for eight or ten years, even fifteen years, to pass between a poem's first appearance in a notebook and its publication in a volume. 'All Legendary Obstacles' was eleven years in the making from first to last.

In the archive, one may see the poet at work. That is the meat and drink of a literary biography.

3

At the origin of Montague's poetry is his motherless loneliness as a small boy in Garvaghey, County Tyrone, away from parents and brothers, enduring a stammer that arose suddenly and mysteriously. Although he turned out to be a bright lad, coming at or near the top in several subjects in national scholarship competitions, the doors to many professions were closed to him simply because of his inability to speak up. He was not going to be a priest, a barrister, a medic, or any public-facing occupation. All through university he never spoke in class.

The laborious perfection of a spoken utterance is the very definition of poetry. Montague came to see that he could sort out his feelings by way of meditation, organize his thoughts, then fix them word by word on paper. This was the medicine for what ailed him. It was also a way of making himself intimately understood, first to himself, and perhaps some day graspable and attractive to another.

In the lecture rooms of University College Dublin and around the portico of the National Library, any student with a taste for verse could sense the loitering ghost of James Joyce. Someone like them – Catholic, Irish, nearly penniless, but bookish – had from this very place begun a journey to recognition as a hero of European letters. Dublin was beginning to see the traffic of American professors looking for clues on to how to understand Joyce. They were noticed in the pubs and bookshops, people like Hugh Kenner and Richard Ellmann. And asking about Yeats too; in fact, especially Yeats. To be a poet in ways only the elite could completely appreciate, that would be a very fine thing, and evidently not impossible for an Irishman.

But how was one to do it? Nowadays, a person could apply for instruction in a writing programme, or buy a how-to manual in paperback. In the late 1940s, when Montague was becoming serious about his poetry, there was just one guidebook, and it was a most eccentric one. Published at Faber by T.S. Eliot, *The White Goddess* addressed itself specifically to young men who wanted to know how to write a great poem. There was only one way to do it, according to this book. Robert Graves had boiled down the story of Yeats's life into a formula. The secret was to fall in love with a woman not your wife, a woman in whom the

Moon-goddess has taken up residence. This superior, whimsical being will break your heart to pieces. You will try but you will never master her, yet she will give you the training and experience you require to write a great poem. In her you will encounter the tragic, beautiful mystery of life itself.

The White Goddess was a formative book not just for Montague, but for Thomas Kinsella, Michael Longley, Derek Mahon and Ted Hughes, and for Sylvia Plath and Anne Sexton among the women poets of the period. Many Americans – Robert Creeley, Robert Duncan, and W.S. Merwin, for instance – moved to Majorca to be near to the cliff-dwelling bard and trickster. Montague himself made the pilgrimage in 1963. And in 1975, he brought the old man for a grand tour in Ireland, the country in which Graves had first learned to walk and to speak English.

The Muse theory is no longer on the recommended reading list for young poets; far from it. Apart from the fact that it equates the poetic life with serial adultery, it is difficult to say which contemporary sin it most indulges: idealizing a woman or objectifying her. No educational treatise could be more sexist. It directly told women not even to try to be poets. As for the critique that the apprehension of a woman by a Muse poet is always superficial, one would have to investigate the case poem by poem. The original Gravesian notion of the Muse is founded in awe and curiosity about the other. Many outcomes are possible.

When the women's movement got underway – the seventies in America, and the eighties in Ireland – poetry continued to play a key role. Lyric self-expression was a central activity of feminist 'consciousness-raising sessions'. But the path to which Robert Graves had pointed as the only road to take was closed. The story of how one Gravesian male poet dealt with this triumphant feminist critique makes for an interesting chapter in literary history.

4

One other dimension of Montague's poetic practice that became more clearly visible as a result of biographical research was the role of magic. When he was a visiting writer-in-residence in the mid-1960s at UC Berkeley, Montague was asked to give a public lecture on Yeats. In the course of his remarks, he struck a condescending note, like that of W.H. Auden, concerning 'the pitiful, the deplorable spectacle of a grown man occupied with the mumbo-jumbo of magic and the nonsense of India'. Robert Duncan, sporting a cloak, with many rings on his fingers, rose to indignantly defend the centrality of magic to all great poetry. Montague was delighted by this apparition of a present-day necromancer. He followed up the subject in his friendship with Duncan, who brought him around to bookshops specializing in the occult in San Francisco. Montague added his name to their mailing lists.

The magician side of Yeats's practice was also cultivated by Montague's friend Robin Skelton. He rose to a position high in the echelons of West Coast warlocks, who, wearing pentagrams, milled about the colleges of Vancouver as well as San Francisco. A glance at a list of Skelton's dozens of non-fiction books indicates how his interest shifted from scholarship to creative writing manuals and finally to handbooks on magic. In Montague's *Collected Poems* he too often builds his lyrics on the fundamental speech-acts that underlie magic spells, what J.L. Austin called 'performatives': sentences that don't say what they are doing; they do it. They bless, curse, apologize, promise, name, lament and command. A ritualized performative can make things change: bring about peace, sleep, sexual desire, consolation, or terror.

For that period, this interest in the lost magical powers of speech was not particularly eccentric. Many poets educated themselves about archaic paths into the depths of human experience – through dream, myth, drugs, music, even choric movement. *Technicians of the Sacred* was the title of a popular California anthology of such approaches. In *A Slow Dance* the poet-figure certainly takes the shape of a shaman. That is also true of Seamus Heaney in the contemporaneous *North*, of Ted Hughes in *Wodwo*, and of Galway Kinnell in *The Book of Nightmares*. Robert Graves himself consulted with Carlos Castaneda after the publication of *The Teachings of Don Juan*, and came away with his own small stash of peyote buttons.

5

One Modernist who loomed large over the post-war generation, but has since sunk into the waters of academic Lethe, was Ezra Pound. His *Pisan Cantos* had won the first Bollingen Prize for American Poetry in 1949 at the time Montague was starting an MA on Austin Clarke. On his list of books bought in 1951, one is *The Poetry of Ezra Pound*. There Hugh Kenner begins what he completed twenty years later in *The Pound Era*, the argument that Ezra Pound was the key to twentieth-century modernism, someone without whom there would have been no *Waste Land*, and maybe no *Ulysses* either. Without Pound, Robert Frost may have otherwise gone unnoticed by the mandarins and William Carlos Williams remained out of touch with artistic developments beyond New Jersey. Even Yeats got a second life, and broke free from the Celtic twilight, Kenner observed, after a sharing a cottage one winter with Pound. Hugh Kenner tended to overlook Pound's antisemitism and the obviously treasonous character of his wartime conduct; he also failed to admit just how boring and truly bonkers were the economic ideas that choked up the pages of the middle *Cantos*. But he did highlight two things about Pound that continued to interest Montague.

The first is that it is still possible for a poet to aim for the historic capstone of a major career: the epic, a poem containing history. In the last dribs and drabs of *The Cantos*, Pound would admit that he had failed: 'I cannot make it cohere,' even though, he grumbles, 'it does [somehow] cohere'. That left it to a younger writer to write a long poem that was neither boring nor insane and clearly did cohere. Montague pondered several possible models (e.g., the Mississippi novels of Faulkner, as well as Goldsmith's *The Deserted Village*), and began the poem in May 1961. It took him eleven years to complete *The Rough Field*. But he had in that time learned how to write a long poem as a symphonically orchestrated sequence of lyrics in various modes with a set of guiding mythic images. Having learned to do it, he wrote one after another: *The Great Cloak*, *The Dead Kingdom* and *Border Sick Call*. This is a mighty achievement.

The second thing Montague picked up from Pound is that a literary movement does not come to pass by accident – a few people of talent happening to be born around the same time in one locality. There is, necessarily, a role for the impresario, the caller of meetings, the editor of anthologies, the reviewer of contemporary works. Yeats himself excelled in these roles from the 1890s, but Pound – particularly as depicted by Kenner – was the exemplary cultural activist. When confined in an Italian concentration camp, Pound became aware of the grotesque failure of his own political plans, but he was still proud of his cultural work: 'to draw from air a live tradition/this is not vanity'. That is a phrase often quoted by Montague.

When Montague returned to Dublin after his five years in the USA, he found it 'dead as doornails'. Along with Liam Miller, Montague took upon himself the role of kicking it back into life. The flowering of The Dolmen Press, the launching of a new generation of Irish writers in *The Dolmen Miscellany*, the novelty of public poetry readings, the establishment of Garech Browne's Claddagh Records, the spoken word recordings of Clarke, Kavanagh, Montague, Heaney, Kinsella and others, the avant-garde vibrancy of the Lyric Theatre's magazine *Threshold*, which quickened back into life many Ulster writers and made a place for new ones, the Planter and the Gael tours of John Hewitt and Montague, the creation by means of his Faber anthology of a bilingual back story for contemporary Irish poetry, the Irish Studies department at UCD – John Montague had his long and pointy beak in all these activities.

Taken all together, they make up a 'Second Irish Revival'. That is not a name given in retrospect, so that after sixty years we can say, 'In the 1960s, there began to be a real cultural renaissance in Ireland.' That was the name Montague gave it beforehand. The phrase occurs again and again in his correspondence with, among others, Liam Miller, Robin Skelton and Donald Fanger. There is a certain special skill in being a mover and shaker, and part of it is the ability to take pleasure in the flourishing of others. Montague had that special skill. The lonely boy without his family always wanted to be part of something bigger, something both happy and prosperous. He brought it to pass not just in Dublin but in Cork too.

6

One key aspect of contemporary poetic practice had no root in Irish society at large: personal candour. Montague encountered the more confessional side of the lyric early on, in 1955 at Iowa, where his classmate W.D. Snodgrass was beginning to write the poems published in *Heart's Needle*. That was the book that inspired Robert Lowell, and later Anne Sexton, to write poems of psychological crisis.

Montague rose to the challenge of this more candid way of writing, but he altered it. He treated his own case not simply as that of a patient in the course of therapy, but in the diagnostic manner of W.H. Auden, as symptomatic of cultural neurosis on a national scale.

He created a form of autobiographical quest narratives with a political aim; the importance of this invention is underappreciated. Long ahead of the public acknowledgment of such issues, he wrote personally about abortion, divorce, alcoholism, domestic violence and clerical abuse in education. In this way, he offered to others release from a painful past. His ambition was not just to be a poet, but to be a healer.

7

A few words must be said about the technical problem presented by this particular biography – that I knew John Montague myself.

I first met him, along with Garech Browne, in the Bailey pub in Dublin in 1973, and again in Cork in 1977 for a published interview. He began to spend the winter semesters in upstate New York in the late 1980s, near where I was teaching, so we met frequently thereafter. Our paths later crossed in Galway, Dublin, Cork and Nice.

While it is helpful to personally know your subject, in a scholarly biography the narration usually does not have a first-person dimension. Compare the situation to a film. You have seen the movie, but you do not know what the face of the cameraman looks like. He was by definition always there and always out of shot. I could not be the objective, scholarly third-person narrator up to the year 1973, or 1977, and then suddenly pop up, crossing in front of the camera, so to speak. That would be not only unbecoming but a technical mistake.

So I put a factually based scene into the first chapter in which John, at the very end of his life, tells me about a key incident in those years, the day at Garvaghey primary school when he first suffered his speech impediment. The reader will be unlikely to reproach me for having passed along his words. After appearing in the first chapter, it does not seem quite so strange that I should later sometimes reappear in the role of witness and reporter.

One further drawback of a biographer being a friend of the subject would be that you would find it hard to reveal things about him that were true but discreditable. In John's case, however, I knew he would want me to pay particular attention to what some would keep hidden, just as he had done. I simply had to follow his example of ruthless intimacy and maintain a pitiless fidelity to the blizzard of specific data that is a personal life, in pursuit of a portrait notable for the intimacy of its apprehension. That is what I owed him.

It is easier to tell the truth about your subject if your real purpose is to tell the story of how the life turned itself into the achievement of the poetry. The poetry is above the poet, and in terms of public interest if in no other way, the poet is above the teacher, the lover, the father, the husband and the brother. John conceived of himself as the parent of the being that brought the poems into existence; he, at all times, served that growing child. He dedicated his life to becoming the author of his books. There is a cost in that, one paid by himself and others. A biographer cannot be blind to the harm, or hide it from the reader, but ultimately, one has to remember that the reason a book is being written about John Montague is that he wrote the poems. Otherwise, this long intrusion into his private life would be unjustified.

What I did not have to do is to act like a manager in a human resources department, and weigh the complaints filed about the subject against the sum of his credits, or imagine that, in his shoes, I would have lived his life better than he did. My goal has to be to capture his life story in its uniqueness, and, at the same time, to quote Samuel Johnson, to reveal 'the uniformity in the state of man': that 'we are all prompted by the same motives, all deceived by the same fallacies, all animated by hope, obstructed by danger, entangled by desire, and seduced by pleasure'.

Adrian Frazier, September 2024

GARVAGHEY, COUNTY TYRONE:
HIS PRIMARY SCHOOL

ANCHOR LINE—T.S.S. "CAMERONIA"

Figure 1: The Cameronia

I

Not long after the three boys were put on board the *Cameronia*, on 5 May 1933, Johnnie, the youngest, aged four, came down with measles. He was taken from third-class quarters to a bed in the infirmary, a compartment stinking of disinfectant. He was not suffering all that badly; he felt special, pleased by the attentions he was getting. A woman on board, missing her own child left behind in America, came to bring him caramels in the evenings. The ship's doctor gave him coloured cards from his cigarette packs; Johnnie played games with them on his counterpane. He did not miss the days on deck with his older brothers, Seamus, eleven years old, and Turlough, nine. The sight of the heavy sea on the first day was a fright. Years afterwards, however, he would sometimes dream of another voyage, one shared by all three brothers.[1]

Bound for Liverpool, the *Cameronia* slowed after rounding Malin Head in Donegal and sounded its horn at the mouth of Lough Foyle on 10 May. A tender came out to receive the Irish passengers.[2] From third-class accommodation they disembarked: nine housewives, three of them with children, several labourers, a cook, a grocer and a 56-year-old man retiring to Bunbeg, County Donegal, plus the three Montague brothers. At the port of Derry, two different parties were waiting for them.

In New York, following the death of the boys' uncle John Patrick Montague from liver disease a month earlier, Jim and Molly (Carney) Montague quickly decided that they could no longer take care of their three children. Jim would have to find paying work, and Molly, often ailing, suspected even of having tuberculosis, could not manage the household on her own. Their prospects were poor. The Great Depression hung over America. There was no relief there. They would have to arrange to foster the children out with family back home in Ireland.

Before his death, Uncle John had been the breadwinner for the extended family at 56 Rodney Street in Williamsburg, Brooklyn. An enormously popular fellow, he met emigrants off the boat in New York. Playing his fiddle, he welcomed them back to his drinking parlour – 'speakeasy' was the term for it during the Prohibition years. Patriotic, piously Catholic and charismatic, John was the heart of a little community of emigrants from Tyrone, cousins, in-laws, former neighbours, Irish civil war refugees from Ulster.

On 10 April 1933 the mourners bundled into funeral coaches following the hearse that carried John slowly from the Church of Our Lady of Good Counsel out to St John's Cemetery in Long Island: his brother-in-law Tom Carney and wife, Eileen, Bridget and Catherine Quinn, the McGarrity brothers, James and John, several Caseys, McLaughlins and McRorys.[3] Times had been hard; they looked as if they were about to get harder.

The plan was that the oldest son, Seamus, would lodge with his maternal grandmother, Hannah Carney, the widow of an auctioneer and spirit merchant in Fintona and herself a sound businesswoman. She ran a private loan business (funding Catholics who could not get bank mortgages, in order to buy land).

She also rented out cottages in 'the back lane'. When they were infants, she had helped care for Seamus and Turlough, before Molly left to join her husband in America in 1928. Hannah Carney agreed by post to take the oldest, but just the one. What about the other two? They could go to Jim Montague's sisters in Garvaghey, Brigid and Winifred ('Freda'). They lived nine miles from Fintona in the old two-storey family house, alongside the Omagh Road. Neither was married. They would be glad to make a home for the two lads.

Maybe no one explained these plans to the boys themselves – how they were to be shared out between the Montague aunts and the Carney grandmother.[4] At the pier in Derry, faced with separation from Seamus, Turlough kicked up a fuss, and refused to go with Aunt Brigid and Aunt Freda. He wanted to return with his big brother to Fintona, the town where he had been born. He got his way, and Hannah Carney wound up with Turlough too.[5] The two aunts, contented with their sole prize, closed around the bewildered smallest boy.

That was how John Montague ended up growing up apart and alone from both his parents and his two brothers from the age of four.

2

Figure 2: Aunt Freda Montague and Johnnie, 1933.

After Brigid and Freda made the trip from Derry back to Garvaghey, snapshots were taken. In a photo in front of the little Austin 7, Freda stands behind Johnnie, her hands protectively on his shoulders. Already shaping up to be a tall, slope-shouldered lad, pale-skinned and with the characteristic squinched yet radiant look about his eyes, he is wearing a white, short-pants 'onesie' with a scalloped collar, nearly sleeveless. He had been wearing it since leaving Brooklyn.

He came with one other outfit, too big for him as yet, woollen knickerbockers with matching jacket and leather brogues, nothing like the clothes of other children around Garvaghey.

The other snapshot shows Johnnie and Aunt Brigid on a grassy hillside behind the house. There is a note in Brigid's hand on the back of the photograph: 'Johnnie had been rolling down the hill & wanted me to do the same' (there being no brothers to play with).

Under her black headscarf, Brigid wears a pleasant, affectionate wry grin, her arm encircling Johnnie's waist. Looking at the pair of them, a person wouldn't need to be told they were family: nearly all the Montague features are there, narrow face, high cheekbones, aquiline bone structure, though here Brigid alone has the nose John would have to grow into, and their russet colouring cannot be seen in a black and white photograph.

Figure 3: Aunt Brigid and Johnnie in Garvaghey.

The local school at the top of the hill was still in session in the middle of May, but the boy had only turned four at the end of February, and was just getting over measles. He had but newly arrived in a strange place. Classes could wait until autumn. Now was a time for rest and play.

For his room, they gave him the place of honour, the bedroom of his grandfather and namesake.[6] John Patrick Montague had died in 1907, aged sixty-seven, leaving his widow with nine children. In addition to James and John, the brothers who had gone to Brooklyn, and Brigid and Freda still on the farm, his heirs included Tom, in 1906 a student at St Patrick's College, Armagh, but in 1933 a Jesuit priest in Australia, and Anne, Kate, Mary Agnes and Teresa.[7]

Old John Montague had been a Justice of the Peace, no common thing for a Catholic in the Unionist north. He was also betimes a teacher, farmer, Belfast businessman and Redmondite supporter of moderate parliamentary nationalism. His funeral was a big event in County Tyrone: ten priests gathered for the obsequies, a dozen Justices of the Peace and solicitors, and postmasters from across the region, along with various branches of the Montagues and all the householders along the Broad Road.[8]

Figure 4: John Montague, J.P. (1840–1907) and family. The poet's father, James, is seated on the ground, to the left.

He left £900 at his death (about €130,000 today), but his 117-acre property was tied up in an unusual will.[9] It was the Irish custom to leave the house and farm to the oldest male descendant, in order to ensure the survival of the family plot of land, but John's will provided that each of his children was entitled to bed and board in the house that he left to his wife. Apart from Brigid and Freda, by 1933 the inheritors of old John P. Montague had scattered. Anne married a Mr Sheridan, and lived seven miles up the hill in Altamuskin; Kate had become Mrs MacKernan; Mary Agnes had a family with John O'Meara in Abbeylara, County Longford; Teresa was a nun in a convent. If family fortunes had fallen, or spilled out over the earth, they might gather and rise again. The two aunts cherished great hopes for little Johnnie, the new master.

Johnnie did not know any of this yet. The strangeness of his situation overwhelmed his powers of understanding. But he was, he later judged, 'patient as an archaeologist'.[10] He observed little things that 'he had to grow old to understand'.[11] There were ancient-looking books in the room, photographs on the mantelpiece, a trapdoor into the attic. He could overhear the grown-ups down in the kitchen. There would be time to explore. Mysteries awaited him.

He was put to bed after his six o'clock supper, in a large old wooden bed. The hours of summer daylight are long in Northern Ireland, much longer than New York; it doesn't get dark until after 10 pm in May. John later recalled lying disconsolately 'watching the fading lights on a group of slight spiky pines' opposite his window. The silence would creep across the lawn, the shadows of the pines coming inch by inch into the room. Above his bed hung a picture of his grandfather; there was another of the Holy Family. A rushy St Brigid's cross was tacked on the wall. Outside, there was no honk of taxi or ding-ding-ding of the trolley he had known in New York, just 'the curious whisper of the wind'.[12]

He did not settle easily. He had night terrors for years. When he began to try to write poetry in college, he often tried to get at that eerie witching hour of the summer evenings in early childhood. One unpublished draft was evidently patterned after 'Time Was Away' by Louis MacNeice:[13]

> The door swung open and the window darkened,
> And I looked up without knowing why:
> The door swung open and a hinge creaked,
> What was behind the door and why?
>
> The door swung open and I looked up,
> Hand unsteady, causing a blot:
> The door swung open and something touched the latch
> And something moved in the passage which
>
> Was there and yet not alive.
> A shadow climbing a rickety stair,
> A ghost in the cellarage with its unheard cry,
> A slight suspiration – terrible, shy.
>
> And the cat looked up from the saucer of milk,
> Her slight eyeballs moving like glinting silk,
> Across the floor moving on trembling pads
> White, white mouth open and delicate cry.

As in the room and behind the door
The dark things moved, gross as a boar
Horned and heavy and with triplicate heads
The thin crying of evil in the night outside.

3

When morning came, there was much about the Montague home place to interest a boy. In the farmyard behind the house was a byre, a long turf shed, stalls, a manger and a chicken coop. The Montagues kept a horse called Tim. Johnnie stared at the great lip slurping water at a tank. The horse's big barrel sides were scarred with the welt of the leather harness. Dropping his head, Tim nibbled at a dock leaf.[14]

Johnnie's aunts had a dairy cow too, and Freda milked it morning and evening; that was worth watching. Up on the hill a flock of turkeys grazed. When Freda came out of an evening to feed the fowl, she would shake corn in a metal pail and the turkeys came 'zooming over the hedges ... thirty of them, red-faced and sharp-beaked with flapping uneven wings ... landing on their splayed claws to come running full tilt across the level ground'.[15] The ducks in the farmyard scattered to make way for them, then crowded back in to peck the corn sprinkled over the ground. A farmyard was a place of wonders for a child straight from Rodney Street, Brooklyn.

The house itself turned out to be not just a farmhouse. It was a post office and lending library too. Brigid, with her wire-rimmed spectacles, was the qualified postmistress, her literacy a service to the whole community. 'White-haired, gaunt as a rake, she stood in her little office among the weighing scales and postal regulations, indicating where his or her mark should go.' She patiently listened to callers' tales of long-drawn-out family quarrels and offered her 'sweet assurance'.[16]

Others came to buy odds and ends from what had been, in earlier decades, a flourishing shop. One family still came regularly – 'one or other of seven nearly identical children lugging a basket as big as himself across the fields' – because they had quarrelled with the new grocer, a more up-to-date business, half a mile up the hill. Although the post office and shop were meant to close at three in the afternoon, people came at all hours and were never turned away.

While Brigid was postmistress, Freda was honorary librarian; the house was a branch of the Carnegie Library for County Tyrone. A hundred books came each quarter and were arranged 'in wooden cases with hasps like pirate trunks'. Inside were treasures – sixty volumes of fiction, twenty juvenile and twenty general knowledge. Once ranged on the half-empty shelves, they began to smell, the boy thought, like the meagre groceries, sweet and musty, with damp on the bindings. By the time he was ten, Johnnie had become a serious bookworm and those who came to borrow a volume consulted him as unofficial deputy librarian – at least on all categories besides love stories; they were Freda's department.[17]

Borrowers asked, 'Is there any love in it? Your aunt said the last was good, but there was damn all love in it.'

'There's plenty this time,' Johnnie would say, hedging.

'Is it good love or the other sort?'

'The other sort,' he would answer, just guessing what it was they were after.

Several local boys recall Freda as being a 'tough woman', even 'sharp, harsh, dictatorial'.[18] Brigid was gentler; she was a great one for the prayers. Young Frank Horisk would come in to borrow a book, and he just had to wait until Freda saw fit to come in from the kitchen. After sizing up the customer, she would put a book on the counter and say, 'There … Take that – that's for you.' He had no other say in the matter. Of course, when it came to little Johnnie, once he took up reading, he had the run of the shelves.

There was a story behind Freda's love of love stories, and her grumpiness. In her twenties, she had been a popular lass – a Gaelic Leaguer, 'girl courier of Cumann na mBan', step-dancer, amateur actress and pianist; she was a prize-winner at nationalist fleadhs.[19] Even into the time after Johnnie joined the household, she would take the stage at local concerts to sing an Irish ballad and dance a hornpipe. Every Sunday she played the organ in church and also took charge of the choir.

In the early 1930s Master MacMahon, the teacher in Roscavey, used to call in to borrow a book, and then stop to chat with this talented girl. Her hopes of matrimony were soon pinned on Jim MacMahon.

Before Johnnie's arrival, Brigid and Freda let their father's old bedroom to a tenant. They had mortgage payments due monthly; every little bit of income helped. When a new teacher arrived for Garvaghey school, she took the room, an attractive woman with a fine singing voice, named Celia. After the pretty lodger was moved out to make room for Johnnie, Celia was seen in the neighbourhood on the arm of Jim MacMahon. Indeed, Freda raged that the Garvaghey schoolmistress was to be found lying in ditches with Master MacMahon, 'all the ditches of the county'.[20] It was bad enough for Freda to lose her chance at wedding one of the few educated gentlemen of the parish, but to have him stolen from under her nose, and by a schoolteacher ever-afterwards present in Garvaghey village, not a big or populous place – that was a bitter gall. Freda's ill-starred romance was another thing not explained to little Johnnie.

4

As the months of summer rolled on, Johnnie was allowed the run of the farm. He would go up with Freda and the little collie to bring the milk cow to the barn. Later, he might walk up alone with the dog and watch over the cattle. Around 1950, when he was beginning to write poetry, he described one of those lonely moments of childhood when he was dreaming by himself. Never published, it reads like a hitherto undiscovered poem by Patrick Kavanagh:[21]

> The spot where I lay in the furze bush
> And read about spaceships and watched people pass
> …
> Rattle of lorries on the road passing at night
> Dog sitting by the grassy verge in the twilight
> The kind of love you feel moving in the byre
> Where the chickens cheep and the hens settle themselves
> The light dim in the kitchen from a candle on the sideboard
> The ducks quacking in expectation of food.
> In all these sounds you have accompaniment.
> Soon will be the time of milking and foddering.

A boy alone in the house, he wanted more 'accompaniment' than his dog and the barnyard fowl. Across the Broad Road, he could see Austin Lynch and his brother Gerard. He would like to go barefoot with them on hot days up the Broad Road to Kelly's shop and get a candy for a halfpenny; he too would like to stick his toes in the bubbling tar. Opposite, there were the rundown stables of Broughan House, a former halt on the Dublin–Derry coach road.[22] It would be fun to climb through those places with the Lynch brothers, or go down to splash in the Garvaghey river.

Yet his aunts were slow to let him mingle with the other children in the townland. It was not just that he was too young, or that he did not yet know his way about. They thought him a class above the locals and destined for great things.

Nonetheless, they could not but give him more rope as time went by. Aunt Freda dated his acceptance of Garvaghey as home, and her acceptance of him as a villager, from the time he raced back to the house, late and out of breath, saying he had been 'keppin' the cows, who had taken fright because somebody 'coped' a cart.[23]

In September he started attending Garvaghey Primary School, up the hill, on the south side of the Catholic church. There is a photograph of the schoolboy dated June 1934, at the end of his first year.

With the black cat in his arms, his curls brushed out and hair parted, he is wearing the woollen short pants, matching jacket with flapped pockets and knee-socks that had come with him from Brooklyn to County Tyrone.

He made a friend at school, a girl, to judge by 'A Love Present', a story in which she is called 'Mary'. He was allowed to play with the children of her family; they owned the new shop at the crossroads.[24] Mary was the eldest and on her account Johnnie accepted as his pals her puffy-faced little brothers. He fancied her swinging pigtails, and teased her, and believed she liked him back. By the time the school inspector made his visit, both were picked out as prize students. The teacher put them through their paces. In the classroom skit, she was Little Red Riding Hood and Johnnie got to play the wolf.

The following school year, Johnnie came down with something in his chest. For a month he was kept at home. The novelty of being sick soon wore off and he waited for a visitor; he waited for Mary. Finally, Freda called upstairs that someone had arrived to see him. He hung over the banister to see if it was Mary. It wasn't. It was a girl from the back of the class, a child from a labourer's cottage. She had often waited like a spaniel after school in the hope of talking to him.

'Tell her to go away,' the boy cried out.

The grown man saw, in pain, his 'arrogant, precious little spirit',[25] the prince of his aunts' dreams.

5

It is impossible, decades later, to do justice to the experience of a small child. Here, the story of John Montague's first years arises from a few public records, such as passenger manifests, stray mentions in old newspapers, some surviving snapshots, recollections by his surviving neighbours and family lore. Over and above these are Montague's own efforts to recapture in words the self he possessed upon first becoming conscious. His experience was such as to make him ask the questions, Who am I? What am I? For answers, he was alert to clues in his surroundings. He also looked inward. Interiority was darkness, mystery, rich in possibilities. At certain junctures later in life, a window appeared to open between things outside and things inside. These rememberable moments arose for him as 'spots of time'. During certain favourable hours, he could mentally go back to Garvaghey and watch things happening as if he were still there, but his former self remained other, to a degree incomprehensible. The boy in the past was holding, metaphorically speaking, an antique Persian brass lamp. Even so, the genie inside it, the active magic, if present, was hidden.

What returned to him were often occasions of shock: the terror of lying alone in bed in the endless evening twilight; the first consciousness of shame upon doing wrong to another; stabs of loneliness and a longing to run with others and be just like them; the looming presences 'like dolmens' of the old people in the village; a consuming alertness to the quick alterity of different embodied beings, horses, dogs, the white-mouthed cat, barnyard fowl, aunts.

In practice, this search among scenes of childhood for the medicine for one's soul follows the example of William Wordsworth.[26]

> There are in our existence spots of time,
> That with distinct pre-eminence retain
> A renovating virtue, whence, depressed
> By false opinion and contentious thought,
> Or aught of heavier or more deadly weight,
> In trivial occupations, and the round
> Of ordinary intercourse, our minds
> Are nourished and invisibly repaired …

For Wordsworth, these renovating sources existed in childhood, not afterwards; and among scenes of nature, never in towns or cities; and when one was alone with one's self, not with a gang of others. All this came home to John Montague. Garvaghey was the cradle of his selfhood.

If Montague was a lifelong Wordsworthian, he also grew to be a citizen of the age of Freud. For Freud, it is often not the radiant spots of time from the past, but the blank areas of the unconscious that shape the self. What we do not recollect, and cannot, may like a dark star cast its gravitational force over our course in life. People's 'childhood memories', Freud believed, are mainly formed much later, around puberty, in a complicated process of remodelling, analogous to the process by which a nation constructs legends about its early history.[27] These so-called childhood memories take the form of scenes – tableaux – but the pictures do not really show the past; they screen it from view. Something falsely recalled, magnified out of proportion, masks yet another memory, one of greater emotional importance, difficult to face.

Montague accepted the importance, for the sake of one's mental health, of recovering the reality of what happened in childhood. It is often shame, sometimes about matters of sex, at other times about class, poverty, unbelief, unmarried female pregnancy, contagious sickness in the family, or physical disabilities, which cause families to repress painful truths. As a result, a lot of the emotional history of the Irish people is obscured. Daniel Corkery spoke of 'the Hidden Ireland' as rural Gaelic-speaking communities that persisted into the eighteenth century; but there is another sort of hidden Ireland, one made up of all the subjects culturally deemed secret and locked behind walls of silence and shame. In his mature poetry, Montague gave direction to his sequences and short stories by turning them into quest romances of a particularly therapeutic kind, in pursuit of revelation of the hidden.

The last time I talked with John Montague, in early October 2016, two months before his death, was in a hotel in County Derry, before his return with his wife Elizabeth to Nice, France.[28] His voice was breathy, hoarse, nearly inaudible, but his mind was sharp. He had, he said, been trying to hunt down in the Linenhall Library, Belfast, a copy of a book he had been asked to read from in Garvaghey School. He had a picture in his mind of the page, how the print was laid out and the Victorian line drawing that illustrated the passage. He had written a poem about it long ago, 'Obsession'. It was most important that he locate the book.

When the schoolboy was moved to the senior side of the Garvaghey School, the headmistress, Celia MacMahon, told him to stand and read out a passage to the class; she had heard tales from his previous teacher of him being precociously literate.[29] He stared at the page. He knew the meaning of the words, but not the experiences described – they were, he recollected, disturbing, scary, sexual. In his 1967 verses on this moment of recurrent terror ('Obsession'), he writes:[30]

> Once again, the naked girl
> Dances on the lawn
> Under the horrible trees
> Smelling of rain
> And ringed Saturn leans
> His vast ear over the world;
>
> But though everywhere the unseen
> (Scurry of feet, scrape of flint)
> Are gathering, I cannot
> Protest. My tongue
> Lies curled in my mouth –
> My power of speech is gone.

Trembling in the classroom, he tried to tackle the passage, but the first syllable stuck in his mouth. He bobbed his head, craned his neck to spit out the words. He flung himself at it again, but failed to break through to speech. The other children watched him struggling, the top boy in the class struck dumb. Mrs MacMahon told him to get on with it. But he couldn't. That must have been how it was, the minute, the hour, the day he lost his ability to speak freely.

He wanted me to know that Mrs MacMahon was a beautiful woman, and dressed well, in form-fitting clothes. Her singing voice was entrancing. It may be that she had teased him about the remaining traces of his Brooklyn accent, or his woollen outfit from New York, now too small for him; he was not sure about that. Maybe she had it in for him, on account of the high and mighty pretensions of the Montagues in the Lilliputian hierarchy of Garvaghey; or because of the old feud with Freda and her rancid gossip. He was ignorant of that background when he was a little boy.

Mostly, it was the passage itself: how could she ask a little boy to read a thing the like of that?

Like what? I asked.

He wasn't sure. He had had no luck in tracing the volume. What was certain is that that woman had ruined his life.

6

A stammer is a medical mystery. One out of five of those who are afflicted are men. No one knows why women are spared more often than men. There is no consensus about why it suddenly comes on a person. An audience is required for its appearance. It is something that happens to a person in public, when one cannot do the simple, ordinary thing: speak. A power that has been with one since early childhood has suddenly vanished, and one is left gasping, lost, a babbler again.

People with the stigma are liable to a number of obvious bad consequences: anxiety about public performance, general social phobia, fear of impotence, a depressed outlook, avoidance of certain professions, dread of being teased and rejected. A schoolboy with a stammer knows he is going to be seen by classmates as stupid, strange, nuts, not a whole man, a freak, looney, 'handicapped'. Boys have a large vocabulary for the condition.

Professional therapists recommend various tricks or treatments. Not one of them is certain to bring relief; there is no sure cure. It would be difficult to become a successful lawyer, politician, journalist, or professor if one could not speak readily in public, so a stammer often narrows the sufferer's outlook in life.

For a person who comes to feel his life's destiny is to be a poet, it is a specifically professional stumbling block. Over the last century, the way in which a poet appears before the world, and a means by which he or she (if famous) earns money, is by giving public readings. It would happen to John Montague over and over – not always, not predictably, not even most of the time, but often – that he could not read his own poems in public, no matter for how long and strenuously he tried. He just couldn't get the first word of the first printed line out of his mouth, though he could discuss in an easy offhand manner the background to a poem. It was weird and upsetting to everyone in the room. People did not like to look, did not like to be made to look, but they could not decently get up and leave the room, with their distinguished guest undergoing a crisis on the platform.

Yet the stammer did not turn out to be an insuperable barrier for Montague. He went ahead and became a poet, a professor and a public figure. Over the decades he often got it under control, but he never mastered it. He became famous. Invitations came from all over the world to fly him out – to France, Germany, Italy, Japan, India, Australia, up and down North America--to give a public reading from his work. Often, things went beautifully; sometimes they turned out disastrously. Those accumulated debacles on stage in crowded theatres took a toll. The instantaneous reversal of fortune, from the anticipated celebration of the ego to imprisonment within a parody of himself, from printed eloquence to sounds spitting unintelligibly from his lips, repeated time and again from past nightmares – it was hideous, ruinous, pitiful. When he was eighty-seven years old, he had to admit it had been so.

7

John's third wife Elizabeth (Wassell) Montague took another view of the cause of the stammer. Elizabeth is a novelist, and she is also double-dyed in the discourse of therapy. Both her parents were New York psychiatrists. Living with John for his last twenty-three years, she knew the subject well. It would be foolish not to take her opinion seriously. In a message written jointly with John, Elizabeth said:[31]

> I wonder if John might have seen or read something which he then placed over that schoolroom scene, a kind of pentimento, or perhaps that dancing girl and her brother was a story he himself composed? His imagination was always so rich and fertile. In any case, his mother returned from America and called on him at just about the same time as the traumatic classroom episode, and so I also wonder if Celia MacMahon may be a stand-in for the mother.

As he settled in to life in Garvaghey, Johnnie's imagination did run wild. He wondered how it was he came to be there. And why had he been born in America? Why did his uncle, father and mother leave Tyrone? Why was he, after coming from Brooklyn, not brought up by his grandmother in Fintona with his two older brothers? When his mother returned from Brooklyn at the end of September 1935, why did she not collect him straight away and bring him to

Fintona?[32] Something about him, or about her? He had floating, vague answers to each of these questions, or no answers at all.

One of Montague's most fraught memories – or screen memories – was of not being loved by his mother and being given up by her, as unwanted. He brought this up in conversations and in broadcast interviews. It is the climactic scene in 'A Flowering Absence', from his sequence *The Dead Kingdom*. That poem begins with the poet 'rehears[ing] a time/when I was taken from a sick room:/as before from your flayed womb./And given away to be fostered/wherever charity could afford.' 'All roads wind backwards to it/' he concludes, 'An unwanted child, a primal hurt.' The poem traces his stammer to an ineradicable doubt about whether he was loved by his mother.

Yet, obviously, the poet cannot have remembered events from the hours and days right after his own birth. The scene he 'rehearses' is one that he has imagined, constructed out of hints from stories he later heard from older family members. The spirit in which he imagines that he was placed in the hands of a wet nurse – that is, that he wasn't wanted, that his mother spurned his presence first in her womb and after his birth too, that she wished she had never become pregnant a third time – is a sob story projected back into the past. The fact of the matter (which the poem allows, but does not emphasize) is that his mother had been too sick to care for him. She had had a hard birth and had suffered a prolapse of her womb.[33] He would not have survived without a wet nurse. It is just as reasonable to imagine that loving relatives – his father, his uncle – desperate to ensure his survival, hurried in search of help and that his mother, not indifferent to this emergency, anxiously awaited word of their success in finding someone to nurse her newborn son.

So that creation myth is not logical, but it is authentically psychological. Many have had at least momentarily the feeling, *My mother does not love me*, or, nearly as mortifying, *She loves my brother/sister more*. It is one of the most disturbing thoughts one can have. Montague had especially good grounds for this nauseating fear, since he was reared apart from his mother from the age of four and began to create his sense of himself and his informative past while still, in a certain sense, a motherless boy. It is just that his bitterness and self-pity (and subsequent search for proofs of love from other women) arose from an imagined scene in his infancy.

At the end of his time, Montague was still going back to the well in Garvaghey for autobiographical poems. Remarkably, in one of these re-approaches to origins, unpublished in his final collection, *Second Childhood*, the poet revisits a scene from the time of his mother's return from Brooklyn to County Tyrone. It is a prose poem entitled 'A Lost Mother':

> In the middle of my loneliness, my aunts asked me to come home early from my wanderings, because I was to have a visitor. Who? I wondered to my dog, but in obedience did not venture beyond our little Garvaghey river, where I threw stones at the rabbits on the opposite bank.
>
> The atmosphere in the kitchen was solemn. An armchair had been brought in from the parlour, and in it was seated a serious lady, dressed in black or some other sombre colour: who could she be? But after a few moments, I faintly recognised her as someone I had once known. I hung back, unsure, since I both knew her, and did not know her. And my aunts clearly had dubious feelings about this glum creature, a source of unwelcome ceremony, compelling them to delay the chores which beckoned endlessly: they had had to make tea, and serve it in cups, not mugs as they did for the farm labourers, along with small ladylike biscuits instead of our customary sturdy arrowroots.
>
> How did I feel when I was told she was my mother? And how did she feel, sitting stiffly in her out-of-place town clothes? She had brought me presents: large American coloured pencils, and Mickey Mouse and Donald Duck comic books. Mickey and Donald had been receding for me, less real than the rooster in the farmyard and his attendant hens. But what I remember most, as I try to replay the scene, is the stifling atmosphere of sadness. Did she try to kiss or, even worse, hug me? I would have hidden behind the skirts of Aunt Brigid. Had she come to reclaim me? I would never know, except that I had swiftly decided I was for my hovering aunts and against this gloomy stranger, feeling the trouble she was causing. And my dog was whimpering at the door.
>
> So I was relieved when she was gone. Wasn't I?

This was not the only time he recalled the visit of his mother to collect him from Garvaghey with a view to bringing him to live in Fintona. In an interview with the *Sunday Independent* in April 1984 he made the visit the inception of his stammer:[34] 'Then one day [in Garvaghey] he was called in from the field.

A woman was standing with his aunt. "This is your mother, John." He ran back to the field, unable to understand why she could be back in Ireland and not want to stay with him. This was the start of a stammer that even still sometimes creeps up on him.'

In October 1985 on a visit to his Brooklyn birthplace, he recalled for a *Newsday* reporter the same event: 'My mother came back in 1937 [actually September 1935]. I was called in from the field to meet a woman I didn't recognise. She had sweets. I didn't want to have anything to do with her. She was dressed in black; she smelled of a small town. The mother I wanted should smell like Brooklyn.'

To the *Sunday Independent*, he says she did not want to stay with him; to *Newsday* that he did not want to live with her. Plainly, he was not certain how to describe what had happened.

In his prose poem, at eighty-seven he opens the door to one of the closed rooms of childhood and puts questions to his boyhood self, a self that has not yet learned to speak of such things. Everything is preserved in that room, as in a diorama. How does that little boy standing there feel? How does that woman, a grass widow, feel? She is dressed in black, as if in mourning, and brings sweets, as if to court his affections. But he will have nothing to do with her. Had she tried to take him in her arms, he would have felt, he says, repulsion, a physical sense that she was alien, did not smell right, as if, at the level of the limbic system, the infant had never been imprinted by its mother. The mother–child bond had never formed, or it had been snapped for him, perhaps for her too.

So if this scene represents the true state of affairs, then he was not unwanted. He was instead wanted by three women, Molly, Brigid and Freda. As in the judgment of Solomon, there is a court of judgment about the possession of a child, but the burden of choice is reversed: the child is asked to decide because the women couldn't cut him in two. And he chose.

What then becomes of the primal hurt? Perhaps it is that in this crisis, although wanting to have a mother and to be loved by her above all, he could not himself instantly give love. He could not perform the act just then expected of him; he had lost all appetite for her embrace. All he had to do was run across the kitchen and bury his face in her skirts. But he shrank from her.

At the end of his life, Montague had got to the point of thinking he was in fact a lucky man, not at all like Job in the Bible with every reason to curse God and die, but blessed both in the many who loved him and in the place he was reared, which in itself had been like a mother to him. It took him nearly nine decades, but God has been good to us if at the end of life we can look back, survey the damage and finally be at peace with what had gone before.

8

In the Montague archive at the National Library of Ireland there is series of draft verses entitled 'Ledger', an imagistic narrative from the period after he first lost the power of speech. His aunt tells him that he'll need to go up to the new shop at the crossroads and get some things no longer found on their dusty shelves. He hangs his head in 'strangled assent'. With her list of items, he legs it up the Broad Road to Kelly's, then waits in the back corner of the shop until the other customers have left before he approaches the counter. After one stab at gasping out a word, he pushes his list forward for the shopkeeper to fill. He turns his eyes up to where the Calor lamp lights up a circle on the flitches of bacon hanging from a rafter, then to the tins on the high shelves. Thinking of the sentence he could not get out of his mouth, a roaming, over-rich sense of verbal possibilities builds up:

'all those words
lost/
stuck/
queuing/
ledgered/
totting/
adding up/
in my head'.

At every poetry reading in later life, the draft concludes, after being lavishly introduced to a throng of listeners, he was suddenly 'haunted/tormented/dogged/ driven by' that silent boy.[35] He halted before the possibilities. Entrammelled in never-ending hesitations. he could not embrace a single choice.

He was not wholly exiled into a lonely speechlessness. His aunts sent him to carry messages to those who could not make it to the post office, to Ally Owens, for instance, when she became too old to collect her pension. After breaking a stick from the hedge to swipe at weeds and flowers, he would dash up the road towards her cottage, and on the way back might stop to explore an old lime kiln. On pension day Jamie MacCrystal, who always sang to himself but without any tune, would tip him a penny. He long remembered delivering books to Minnie Kearney, the embodiment for him of the Cailleach, the wise old woman of Irish folklore. She lived up a broken path in a hillside cottage with a dog, a goat in the bedroom and often a litter of pups in the corner.[36] She liked to try to inveigle the lad into some chat. She teased him that his aunts were wasting their time trying to turn him into the image of his Justice of the Peace grandfather.[37] To Minnie he carried parcels from the lending library of her favourites, love stories from the *Red Star* serial. He even wondered later if it had been she 'who cut the wound of poetry into my youth'.[38] He brought their monthly benefit to the O'Neills, a blind family who lived miles from the Garvaghey post office.[39] Although a mostly silent messenger, he was observant and came to know the people of his Tyrone parish; he felt their shadows pass into him. He was a constituent of his community.

As for Garvaghey School, he remained affrighted by the daily demand to speak up in class. It may be that it was Aunt Freda who put the blame for his stammer on her nemesis, Celia MacMahon. His aunts imagined the affliction could be cured by sending him to another school. In September 1938 he enrolled in Glencull Primary, nearly three miles east along the Broad Road. There the head teacher was Harry McGurren.[40] Stammer or not, he was impressed by the schoolwork of this clever and literate new boy. Before Montague left Glencull in 1941, Master McGurren would be suggesting that he get Aunt Freda to order in copies of classics, such as *War and Peace* and *Crime and Punishment*, things that did not often turn up in Tyrone lending libraries.[41] He knew how to feed the boy's unusual appetite for knowledge.

Figure 5: Montague revisits Glencull School, County Tyrone.
BBC Radio Magazine, *October 1971.*

With a certain inevitability, classmates gave the stammerer the nickname 'Nuts Montague'. He treated it as a joke, acting the maggot, as if his whole presentation of self were a deliberate clown show. Yet, according to a schoolmate, they had to respect his academic ability. They begged him to write essays for them, and, no fool, he charged them for doing so.[42]

His aunts saved the prodigy's copybooks; he in turn safeguarded them until they finally came into the possession of the University College Cork Special Collections. A dozen essays survive, from before September 1939 to a year or so later.

The first, 'I Win a Prize', is childishly innocent of self-consciousness about its vanity and of how pathetically he exposes his desire for a reunion with his brothers:

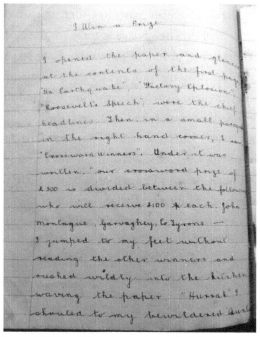

Figure 6: 'I Win A Prize', school essay by John Montague.

I opened the paper and glanced at the contents of the first page. 'An Earthquake', 'Factory Explosion', 'Roosevelt's Speech', were the chief headlines. Then, in a small paragraph in the right-hand corner, I saw 'Crossword Winners'. Under it was written, 'Our crossword prize of £500 is divided between the following who will receive £100 each. John Montague, Garvaghey, County Tyrone –.' I jumped to my feet without reading the other winners and rushed wildly into the kitchen waving the paper. 'Hurrah,' I shouted to my bewildered aunts.

'I have won a hundred pounds.' After a while my aunts succeeded in quieting me and learned of my success. A month later, the postman came up to our door and handed me a letter. With trembling hands I opened it and found in it a cheque for a hundred pounds. In I dashed and showed it to my no less excited aunts. I could hardly eat my dinner so excited I was.

My parents would only accept fifteen pounds each and when I had bought my relations presents, I still have sixty-five pounds. I decided to bring my two brothers and myself on a trip to the continent for it was the beginning of the summer holidays and I would have plenty of time.

The three boys take a steamer from Belfast to Italy, past Land's End and down the French, Portuguese and Spanish coasts to Gibraltar, then over to Italy (high marks for geography there). They board a train to Venice, then take a ride in a gondola. Seamus, with an Italian phrase book, orders their dinner in a restaurant. They visit the Alps, the Vatican and the art museum in Milan. Upon his return, classmates at Glencull School gather around, and the hero tells them (no stammer mentioned) of ancient and modern Italy.

It is difficult not to see in this first fiction a portent of the poet's later hang-up over prizes. Often enough when he was mature, it was a rival who won a literary contest: Thomas Kinsella, Seamus Heaney, or another. There were all too many good poets in the Ireland of his time. The importance of the prize redoubled for him when he did not win it, as a token of personal bad luck, merit overlooked, perhaps on account of him being unable to speak up for himself. The prize, if he had won it, would have been a metonym of all wish fulfilments.

A second story (*à la* Jules Verne) tells of the sons of a great English inventor, who has constructed a plane that will travel one thousand miles per hour. A £70,000 purse is put up if the plane can fly around the world in twenty-four hours. The two boys pilot the plane on behalf of their missing-in-action father, but an armed stowaway forces them off course over the Sahara. The lads thrillingly overcome the villain. On their return, a letter from King George V awaits them at an English airfield; gold medals for bravery too. The end of the story seems strange now, in light of Montague's politics as an adult, but as an approval-seeking schoolchild in Unionist Northern Ireland, he was a right little loyalist and British patriot, as well as a lonely boy who wished his unknown father were a hero in a time of war and that he was joined in fellowship with his brothers.

'Winter 1940' asks, when the northern sky is lit over Belfast, if Ireland will be invaded, then used as a staging post for a German attack on Britain. The fourth essay describes an earlier era when 'people watched the struggle for supremacy between great powers', the Battle of Waterloo. That was settled in Britain's favour and to the benefit 'of all free peoples', a schoolboy's echo of Churchill's wartime speeches.

In a fifth essay, the writer identifies with the character of 'Jim Smith', a child from London evacuated to a country village because of the Blitz. Jim, separated from his parents, is placed in a small farmhouse with kindly country people. One of them takes him along to visit a forge when the farm horse is to be shod. The child gazes at the raised hearth, the bellows, a donkey tied to the wall, and the smith hammering out an iron shoe on the anvil. In a kind of inverse of 'The Deserted Village', people have returned to rural life, and the Tyrone countryside is a realm of wonder to a city boy.

9

Young master Montague never treated his brothers to a pleasure cruise, but he was sometimes reunited with Seamus and Turlough. In the summer of 1937 his mother brought all three boys for a holiday in Bundoran. They were joined by Molly's brother Tom Carney and his wife Eileen, residents of Queens, New York. A photograph taken by Aunt Eileen survives of Molly with two of her sons outside a shop in the seaside Donegal resort. In another snapshot from this holiday, Johnnie is pictured on the strand between his mother and Uncle Tom Carney.

Figure 7: Turlough, John and Mary (Molly) Montague, Bundoran, 1937.

The days with his mother in Bundoran go unmentioned in the multitude of Montague's memorials of childhood, but another aspect of summer holidays is often recalled: the spells with his O'Meara cousins either in County Longford or in Garvaghey. The O'Meara children were from the Montague side of the family, children of Aunt Mary, a sister to Brigid and Freda.

One of the essays in the school copybooks, 'A Ride in a Motorcar', turns a drive to Longford into a boy's adventure story. Uncle John O'Meara, a teacher, had locked up the national school in Abbeylara, County Longford, before heading for the family's customary three-week summer visit to Garvaghey. Once in Tyrone, Master O'Meara remembers that the parish priest had planned for two dances to be held in the Longford school. He will have to drive the 74 miles back and open it up. Young Johnnie comes along for the ride. As they cross the border, he sees that the trees are beginning to leaf out; the fields are full of orchards coming into bloom. It is an idyll of life in the Free State, a country not at war. The grown man would return to that motif in 'This Neutral Realm', a section of *The Dead Kingdom*.

When with the O'Mearas, Johnnie was delighted to be in a family with two boys and a girl around his own age. Brendan O'Meara, later a station master in Laragh, County Cork, remained a friend for life. With John O'Meara, Jr, the younger brother who later settled around the home place in Garvaghey, the poet would have a more complicated relationship: 'they were friends until they weren't'. Mary Agnes O'Meara was the oldest, a pretty girl, with Montague features.[43] She is the focus of a piece of comic autobiography, 'Above Board', published in *A Love Present*. It is centred on her 1941 visit to Garvaghey during Johnnie's last summer before he headed off to St Patrick's College, Armagh. Coming from a convent school, sixteen years old, Mary Agnes has 'sprouted, with all the signs of young womanhood'.[44] Soon, John becomes unaccustomedly popular with the older boys of the townland. In the evenings, they come round to play cards. He senses that they are angling for his pretty cousin, and in the finale, fancying himself a knight from the age of chivalry, he upsets their wicked schemes.

From about the time of Johnnie's arrival in County Tyrone, John O'Meara Snr took upon himself the role of caretaker of the Garvaghey household. Freda and Brigid had depended on American remittances to meet payments on an old family debt, but these stopped in April 1933 when their brother John died in Brooklyn. On 8 December that year John O'Meara stepped forward as the one man of the extended family still in Ireland. He lent his wife's sisters £250, at

6 per cent interest, with the farm as collateral.[45] Out of the small income from the post office and lending library, the two women were unable to meet the payments on this loan. Two years later John O'Meara registered a judgment in the High Court and assumed, in return for his loan, partial ownership of the farm. A month later he lent Brigid and Freda another £200. That debt was not discharged for more than fifty years. In the end, after Freda and Brigid had died, John O'Meara's son would be the one who owned the farm, the next young master of the home place.

IO

The future Freda and Brigid saw for Johnnie was not as a local farmer or postmaster. Customarily in nineteenth- and early twentieth-century Ireland the oldest boy might inherit the farm, the brightest boy go into the Church (then the route to status, ease, and sometimes, by a complex social necromancy, wealth) and the third son, if intelligent, would become a teacher, guard, or civil servant; perhaps even at the outside try for one of the professions, law or medicine. The other young males, unless they made a lucky marriage to a woman of property, were likely as not to look for day work at hiring fairs. Better yet, they would emigrate. As for the daughters of a family, their pick of futures was more meagre still: marriage, the convent, nursing, school-teaching, or emigration, frequently into domestic service. A hilly farm was not for their nephew with his academic promise. Besides, Brigid and Freda did not really own the farm; John O'Meara held the mortgage.

For glory by way of the Church, there was family precedent. Rev. Michael Montague (1773–1845) grew up locally in Errigal Ciaran parish. At the time he was born, Catholics were suffering under the Penal Laws, which barred them from education, public office, the professions and significant property ownership. Public worship in their own churches was prohibited. Most of the ancient cathedrals of the country had been reconsecrated as Protestant.

In Altamuskin, above Garvaghey, there is in a bowl-shaped glade beside a mountain stream with a rough altar stone below the trees. That was where the Montagues went to Mass on Sundays in the eighteenth century. Even in John Montague's childhood, once a year at Christmas, the Garvaghey parishioners made a candlelight pilgrimage to this wild sanctuary. Michael Montague took his first communion there.

Once the Penal Laws were relaxed (reform began in 1778), Michael Montague and his brother John were among the first to take advantage of the new opportunities. The two boys were educated at Clare Castle Seminary, County Armagh. John Montague became the parish priest of Dungannon. Michael went for further study to the Royal College of St Patrick, Maynooth, the first seminary established by parliament for the training of priests in Ireland. He entered the college upon its opening in November 1795 and remained there until his death fifty years later. In 1801 he was appointed professor of logic. He became bursar in 1816 and president in 1834. In his October 1845 obituary in *The Freeman's Journal,* he is called 'the father of the college … it was built by him'.[46] By then Maynooth was the largest Roman Catholic seminary in the world.

According to family lore, it was through the Rev. Michael Montague that money came to the Altamuskin Montagues. He had had a salary and few expenses during his lifetime. With the inheritance, the Montagues were able to descend from the hilltops and buy little farms along the road in the valley. Ultimately, John Montague JP had the two-storey house built, with a slate roof, a rarity for a Catholic's dwelling; people of that faith ordinarily lived in thatched cottages, with walls of field stone or sod.[47]

In Freda and Brigid's own time there was not just the pious example of their brother Thomas, a Jesuit priest working in an Australian college, but their cousin, Cardinal Joseph MacRory (1861–1945). He was Archbishop of Armagh. MacRory's father was a farmer in Ballygawley, and his mother Rose was a Montague.

The two aunts brought Johnnie at age ten to meet Cardinal MacRory. They pushed him forward to read from the family copy of MacRory's edition of *The Gospel of St. John* (Dublin: Browne and Nolan, 1900), long shelved in Johnnie's bedroom. The boy looked up at the 'broad and smiling peasant face' beneath the tasselled red cap.[48] This time, he did not stammer. The elderly aunts then kissed the cardinal's ring.

While Seamus and Turlough were students at the Christian Brothers school in Omagh (before entering UCD and Queen's University Belfast, to study medicine and law respectively; the three Montague brothers were all exceptional students), it was settled that Johnnie would go to St Patrick's College, Armagh, under the shadow of Cardinal MacRory's cathedral. St Patrick's was a clerical training college. Two-thirds of the graduates became priests.

Figure 8: Cardinal MacRory, 7 October 1930.

II

From the Carneys Johnnie learned about the rebel tradition in his family. Molly's two brothers, Frank and Tom, had both been in the Irish Volunteers and saw service near the capital.[49] Molly told her sons that when she and their father married, the couple spent their honeymoon in Dublin. She visited her brother Tom, then interned at the Curragh.[50] In the morning when Jim Montague slipped out to daily Mass, bullets were flying in the streets. During their stay, Molly said, her brother Frank, 'one of Michael Collins's men', took part in the Bloody Sunday operation to assassinate British agents. He was arrested, according to Montague's elegy to his grandmother Hannah Carney, in the family kitchen and carried off to Ballykinlar Internment Camp.

Molly had a good story too about her time in the Cumann na mBan, the Sinn Féin auxiliary for women. She was, she told her children, commissioned to carry a message to an IRA officer in Mountjoy Prison. She hid the paper in her boot. When the prison guard searching visitors told her to remove her footwear, she was sharpish – No, no, she'd taken too much trouble that morning to lace them up, now to have to do it all over again. That did the job. He let her pass.[51]

Upon the signing of the Treaty and the release of prisoners, there was no sweetness of victory for the Carney brothers. The Government of Ireland Act (1920) granted independence to the twenty-six counties of the Free State, but Tyrone was one of the six counties constituting a new federation, Northern Ireland. Always a cold house for Catholics, after Partition the North became more sectarian still. As for people like the Carney brothers, veterans of the IRA, there would be no jobs or council houses, not for the likes of them. Frank emigrated to England and joined a medical practice in Chester. Tom and his wife, Eileen, settled in Queens, New York. The Carney household in Fintona, bereft of its menfolk, took hard against the new Ulster dominion.

From hand-me-down stories on the Montague side of the family, Johnnie gathered that the emigration of his father and uncle had also been, in effect, political exile. He told interviewers that his father had joined the IRA in 1916, and like his Carney uncles, had seen service through the Troubles. A republican on the run, he had been forced to flee the country.[52]

Figure 9: St John's Castle, Ballygawley.

When John Montague was going to school and university, his father was living alone back in Brooklyn. He was a nickel-pusher in a cage, selling subway tickets. Whatever money he had left over from his own upkeep, he sent home for his wife and children; it was never much. At night he sought oblivion in drink. Montague's poetry, particularly *The Rough Field* and *The Dead Kingdom*, does not shy away from these realities, but 'Stele for a Northern Republican' is, as the title indicates, a commemoration to a veteran of past wars. National service is set against personal failure. It balances accounts by rehearsing his father's own tale of derring-do – Jim Montague, still in his twenties, slips out of the Redmondite's house to join others in burning St John's Castle in Ballygawley. Another time, after an IRA ambush, a wounded policeman is brought in to be nursed by his sisters on the kitchen floor.

Did all this really happen? The poet is hesitant to trace with a historian's rigour his father's part in 'the holy war to restore our country'; he lets it pass.[53]

The burning of 'Big Houses' was a broadly social and even festive event in the period: tenants gathered over the hours to watch the fire burn down and to carry off furniture, and Jim might have been on the scene without having been among the conspirators who packed the entrance hall with bales of straw, poured petrol through the rooms and ignited the blaze.

Apart from the instance of St John's Castle, there is some independent evidence that Montague boys from some branch of the family had a serious scrape with the local constabulary. But was it Thomas, James and John Montague of Garvaghey? In January 1921 the B-Specials, loyalist police reserves, raided a Sunday night dance at Ballygawley. It was, they suspected, some sort of Sinn Féin meeting. They told the fifty young people to raise their hands and line up along the wall. During a search for weapons, a constable fired a shot; more weapons were discharged. Among those wounded in the skirmish were three constables and three civilians named Montague. But while both Jim and John Montague later told stories of being Irish rebels, they never told one of taking a bullet from the B-Specials.[54] Nor does the poet ever speak of this particular episode of sectarian harassment.[55]

When John Montague first published 'Stele for a Northern Republican' in *The Honest Ulsterman* in May 1970 and later when he told an RTÉ interviewer in December 1977 that his father had been forced into exile because he was in the IRA, his picture of the family past may have had more to do with the time of recollection, during a second 'Troubles' (1966–98), than with the specific events that led up to his father's departure in October 1923. A civil rights campaign for equal employment, secret paramilitary actions and detention without trial were all once again the daily news of life in Northern Ireland. Montague presents himself then as someone whose family history is politically relevant. But evidence has yet to appear that either James or John Montague was ever in regular, or irregular, military service. They may have all along been law-abiding constitutional, Redmondite nationalists, like their father, the Justice of the Peace.

12

Seamus and Frank Rogers told a different story of what caused the Montague brothers to leave Tyrone.[56] The Rogers brothers are cousins of the Montagues. Their great-grandmother was the sister of John Montague's great-grandmother, the wife of the Justice of the Peace. The Rogers remember the poet's uncle John being described as a good fiddler and local *bon vivant*. Jim sang at dances and was a demon for practical jokes. In a photograph of the brothers from the early 1920s, Jim and John look like gay blades, in spiffy clothes, not like hillside farmers; in another, Uncle John, sporting a high-crowned trilby and wearing riding boots, is accompanied by his greyhound.

According to Seamus Rogers, in late 1921 the Montague boys got swept up in a money-making scheme. It had to do with a war, but not the Anglo-Irish War, then ending, or the Irish Civil War, soon to begin. This scheme had to do with the war between Turkey and Greece, declared in 1919. How could it happen that the Montagues, or any Irishman, would have anything to do with that?

Many Irish newspapers carried a story from August 1921 that the Greek government was offering £45 a horse, and wanted up to 10,000 horses in total, to meet the needs of their war in Turkey.[57] The Greek army had lost battles in Anatolia in January, March and August 1921, in spite of superior manpower. This large order was sensational news for Irish farmers. They had been deeply involved in breeding horses for the battlefields in France, but when the Armistice was signed in 1919, the price of horses crashed. Irish breeders had a huge stock on hand, all still requiring feed. The Laverty brothers in the Moy were organizing the purchase and shipping of horses for the Greek army.

In order to cash in on what appeared to be a sure thing, all Jim and John Montague needed was capital. On 14 December 1921 they registered a charge of £700 against the family farm, payable on 1 May, only five months later.[58] Remember, the deed for that family farm was still restricted by the terms of John Montague Snr's will; several of his daughters were still living there. The two brothers also borrowed £134 from Francis Rogers in Beara, the father of Frank and Seamus, who passed on this information.

But it was fast becoming too late to help the Greek Army. The last battle would be fought on 26 August 1922. Each army had about 200,000 men, but the Turks had five cavalry divisions and the Greeks just one. The Greeks in this last battle suffered 50,000 casualties and were driven out of Anatolia. The Irish horses had not arrived in time. When Laverty's shipments of 1700 arrived at Piraeus, they were no longer wanted; the Greek government was in no position to pay. The Lavertys were bankrupted. The hopes of the Montague boys went up in smoke.

On 26 May 1922 Brigid Montague took an action in the County Court against the estate of her father in order to secure the farm against repossession by the bank, on account of the brothers' lien going unpaid. Payments on the mortgage were made, month by month through the 1920s and early '30s, in remittances from Brooklyn by John, the poet's uncle. His whole reason for going to America had been to get the money to pay off this debt.

It is hard to know if the poet ever got wind of the bad bet on the horse market and how it led to his father's emigration. The poet's widow never heard him speak of it. However, if you listen closely to the drunken talk in 'The Last Sheaf', a *Rough Field* poem about an evening spent with old friends in Kelly's Bar, Garvaghey, you can catch what is possibly a passing reference to it:[59]

> [T]alk expands, in drunken detail.
> 'I said to him'; 'He swore to me.'
> With smart-alec roughness Henry
> Rakes up our family history:
> 'Was it patriotism, or bankruptcy?'

The answer to the question is that of course John and Jim Montague were patriotic, but it was bankruptcy that caused them to go to America. They had to get jobs, in order to save the family house for their sisters, Brigid and Freda. In the end, they made good their debt, if at a heavy emotional cost to themselves and their children.

13

In his story 'The Letters' (1991), John Montague depicts himself as a schoolboy stumbling upon the truth about his parents, or a part of it.[60] One Sunday, he pretends to be sick and stays home when his aunts go to Mass. He wants to read a book left behind by an O'Meara cousin, *Sexton Blake and the Pearl of India*. He knows it is kept in a high cupboard. Standing on a stool, he lifts out the book, and then sees behind it a bundle of letters with American stamps. What was this? Proof maybe of the existence of a man he could barely remember, his father. No, the letters were from his Uncle John. They gave news of his parents:

> You asked how things are going between 'the couple.' I wish you hadn't because I'd rather not think about the whole thing. You know I don't think much of him [that is, Jim, the poet's father] and events have borne me out. After she came out with the two boys, he pulled up his socks and got a job in a grocery business but lost it because of

some carelessness. They ... seem to quarrel all the time, since he is at home. He comes over to me looking for help but what can I do? He is my own brother but if I can work and drink, why not him?

The boy opens another envelope. He reads how rough his mother is on his father, how unreliable Jim is, that he can't keep a job, or stay sober. Molly has begun to look down on the whole Montague side of the family.

The last letter touches on John's own infancy:

I regret to say that I have bad news to report from here. She is sick again and in fact has not been really well since the birth. I must say Jim is marvelous with the baby. To see him crooning to it (he still sings quite well) makes me like him all over again ... I do my best for them but I have not been feeling myself lately ... I told him that if anything happened to me he should think about sending them all home again.

Helena Mulkerns told me that she was in the East Village in 1993, at a New York club for Irish-Americans called Sin É, owned by the singer Jeff Buckley. On the night there was a staged reading of this story by a young Brian F. O'Byrne (later a well-known film actor). The poet himself was in the crowd. At the close when the applause rose, Helena looked at John. He was choking back dry sobs, like the character in the story reading that last letter. The wounded little boy was never far from the grown poet.

14

There was one farmer in Garvaghey in whose footsteps John Montague followed: Barney Horisk. He bought a small farm in the area in the mid-1930s. Soon he was appearing in amateur drama performances, often in the same cast with Aunt Freda.[61] He did not have many years of school, but he was clever. He published newspaper articles, one for instance on 'fair days' of the past. In the evenings neighbours would drop in to sit by the fire and listen to his tales of old times. His memory was a marvel.[62]

After departing for college and then university, Montague would give Barney Horisk a detailed account of his progress in life by way of a Christmas letter. On returns home, he never failed to check in with Barney, his channel to the ongoing life of the community. He made lists of turns of phrase used by Barney and his wife Kitty:[63]

> She's an old haverel.
> Ah now. Go down the lane.
> A man past bein' ignorant.
> Mrs Murray's hedge was black with clothes.
> Barney McKillion wanting a cart to assemble the parts of the plough.
> Old curiosity box, mind your prayers and your own business.
> A class of a bee with a red tail.

After marriage, Montague would bring his wife (each of the three) to meet Barney Horisk, as if to seek his blessing. In *The Rough Field*, Barney is the rooted voice of the place:[64]

> 'I like to look across,' said
> Barney Horisk leaning on his *sleán*
> 'And think of all the people
> Who have bin.'
> Like shards
> Of a lost culture, the slopes
> Are strewn with cabins, deserted
> In my lifetime…

Barney Horisk was a virtual father for Montague, but he was also a divining rod back to the Garvaghey wellsprings, a chronicler of events in the lives of the local people.

Garvaghey was essential to Montague's sense of self, but he spent only seven continuous years there. He arrived when he was four years old and left for St Patrick's College, Armagh, when he was eleven. The landscape, the history, the ancient monuments of Knockmany and Sessilgreen, the particular inhabitants standing like dolmens around him, the streams and trees and plant life – the whole *habitus* of the barony of Clogher inform Montague's sense of what is meaningful and beautiful. The poet went back to Garvaghey and his memories of childhood as to a well.

One of his earliest signature poems is 'The Water Carrier' (1961), a poem that would play a part in the progress of Seamus Heaney's poetry.[65] There Montague recalls his chores around the house in the 1930s. Everything about the twice-daily task of fetching water – the two buckets, one of them enamel; the two sources, a pool in the river and a spring channelled through a rusty pipe, the boy balanced between the brimming pails, the bramble path, the smell of berries in the brambles – each particular is carefully poised into a balanced design. The details of daily life in memory become radiant with unforced symbolism. These acres, he realizes in the poem's conclusion, are the living source of the poetry it is in him to write. But he also acknowledges that that source is 'half-imagined and half-real'. To fight free of fantasy and keep in touch with the reality of the community, he relied on Barney Horisk, along with his aunts, the Lynch boys and the people at Kelly's shop and pub.

15

About a month before he died, John Montague was having a nap at his apartment in Nice, France, when he awoke and called to his wife.[66] Elizabeth found him curled up in bed. He asked her if she would put her arms around him. In his dream, he had returned to a time he was to be sent to a Gaeltacht for Irish college. No, he told his aunts, he wouldn't be sent away, not for anything, not again.

A priest had been coming by Glencull Primary to offer after-school classes in Irish. Now he had organized a group trip to Donegal. How could Brigid and Freda let down Father So-and-So? They made Johnnie cycle through the rain to tell the priest himself.

At eighty-seven years old, John was reliving that nightmare. But, he told Elizabeth, that was one of the moments that made him a poet. It was a maxim for him that it is in the broken places that poetry flourishes.

It was not many weeks later in 1941 that he would have to leave home anyway. He had been groomed by his aunts, and singled out by teachers, as a candidate for the clergy. Now he had been awarded a County and College Scholarship to cover the cost of his education at St Patrick's College in Armagh, a training college for priests. At summer's end he tried to put off his departure, but finally he had to go. This chapter of his life was over.

DOING TIME IN ARMAGH AT
ST PATRICK'S COLLEGE

I

More than forty years after he left Garvaghey for St Patrick's College, John Montague began to excavate his 'Time in Armagh'. Like a prison sentence served in the distant past, it lay numb inside him, 'the least conscious time of my life'. In the 1980s, in order to awaken his memories, he went to two gatherings of the Past Pupils Union. Out of the blue he wrote to old schoolmates. 'Do you remember', he wrote to one, 'how I came about six weeks late, and cried for the whole first term?'[1]

The dormitory had three long rows of beds, one along each wall, the other down the middle, a chair's width apart; forty boys to a room. If one boy got a cold, they all got it. If one boy, homesick, was crying, they all had to listen to him. The dormitory was a good breeding ground for silliness and cruelty. There was another Montague, no relation, named Terence; he hated Gaelic football and school even more; he was called 'Dopey'.[2] Tormented, he was taken from school to another St Patrick's, the Dublin mental hospital. John Kennedy was 'Buns'; everyone forgot how he came to be stuck with this tag. Iggy Jones, quick on the pitch, was 'Sticky'. John Montague, the stammerer, became 'Screwy'. Are boys just cruel, or did the school make them so? That is what the sixty-year-old poet wanted to find out in writing the sequence *Time in Armagh* (1993).

Figure 10: Dormitory; St Patrick's College, Armagh.

The Vincentian priests who ran the place did not teach their students to play tennis or to swim; athletics was Gaelic football and Father Maron's lessons in boxing. Professional boxing was at peak popularity. Before he left Garvaghey, Johnnie himself followed the news of the championship bout between Joe Louis and Billy Conn (18 June 1941).[3] So did his father, Jim, back in Brooklyn. As a present, he sent Johnnie a punching bag to hang up in the byre. Johnnie called over the Lynch brothers, but they were so rough, he decided he had best take part as referee, not a contender for the crown.[4]

At St Patrick's it was not playful combat among friends, but a hierarchy instituted by means of violence, or the threat of violence. Bigger boys took it out on the littler ones. For instance, one might jab a new boy with a Sacred Heart pin during Mass, just when he couldn't cry out.

Boys of the same size and class did not often come to blows.[5] One 'spectacular brief fight' in the classroom between Buns Kennedy and Jim Devlin – 'the silence of anger/transformed with the thud of punches,/swift, brutal, the drip of blood'[6] – appalled everyone. Is this what was pent up inside the student body? 'Clear up the mess,' the master said, 'and get back to your lessons.'

The muddy outdoor playing field was their tiny but true coliseum. The priests were keen for Gaelic games.[7] Football was compulsory. With fifteen to a side, they needed every boy to be togged up. On the cold pitch the pecking order was established. Montague admired those classmates with talent for the game, but he hated it. He grew to be big enough to stand his ground, but something loose in the knees, and unwieldy about his long legs, made him a poor sprinter (though always a ready walker over country lanes). This was a competition in which he was destined to come hindermost.

The truly spectacular open displays of violence at St Patrick's were on the part of the Vincentian priests. The head of school was Rev. J. Roughan, 'all too rightly named'. He kept a large selection of canes, and, when the time came to punish, would do some test swings through the air in order to choose the best. The unfortunate student was then made to hold out his open palms and keep them still. The priest would bring the rod down, once, twice, and on and on, up to a maximum of ten strokes. The cane was understood to be an essential pedagogical tool of instruction. It left a memory that lasted.

2

St Patrick's College, Armagh, was not just sport and sadism. The poet and broadcaster Tom McGurk, an alumnus, thought highly of the lay teachers. Good scholars, they might have taught at Queen's University Belfast, but being Catholics, they wound up in Armagh. He particularly remembered Jerry Hicks in English, and Seán O'Boyle, who taught Latin and Irish. The same two teachers are recalled with gratitude by Paul Muldoon.[8] Hicks would hunt up still surviving speakers of Irish in the hills of County Tyrone and collect folksongs for the BBC archive. A singer himself, he put out a record with Gael Linn. Later on, he would lead Muldoon's class through Montague's poem, 'The Trout'.

Seán O'Boyle passed along to students the story his own father told him, that 'With the Treaty, we Northerners had been sold like bullocks at the Smithfield Market, but so long as music and literature survive, we will survive too.'[9] What was not taught in the Protestant schools was the very thing that would save Northern Irish Catholics – Irish poetry, stories and songs, and a sense of their own ancient past in the land, all omitted from the British curriculum.

During the years he was at St Patrick's, Montague did not get swept up by the national enthusiasm of these two teachers. In Johnnie's opinion, O'Boyle taught them a lot more Irish than they needed for the state exams.[10] Somehow, though, the rhythms of the poems from their school anthology, like the south Armagh aislings sometimes sung to an air by O'Boyle, 'beat in the back of [his] mind'. Twenty years later, he realized that if he was going to be an Irish writer, he had better learn more Irish. He wrote to Seán O'Boyle looking for help.[11] Montague's subsequent volume of translations from the Irish, *A Fair House* (1972), carries a tribute to his old teacher.[12]

After publishing *Time in Armagh*, Montague realized that he had not done justice to the teachers, particularly the lay teachers. He would not have come top in the province for state scholarships had they not prepared him so well.

Admittedly, he was a born 'dab' or 'swot'.[13] If examinations had been a sport, Montague would have been a star athlete. In 1946 he came 1st in Northern Ireland in Latin, 2nd in English and 5th place in history. At the time, however, he counted among 'the emotional shames of school' 'the poor substitute of mental superiority for athletic skill'.[14]

3

Following the revelations of the Murphy Report (2009), people might assume that all Catholic boarding schools in Ireland were rife with what used to be called 'the English vice', schoolboy homosexuality. But it was not everywhere the case that the particular harm of Catholic schools was priests molesting boys, or boys raping one another. Thomas Kilroy, when writing his version of Wedekind's *Spring Awakening, Christ, Deliver Us* (2010), consciously refocused the drama on cruelty, rather than sex. That was a deliberate reflection of his own Irish experience in the early 1950s. When Montague went about revisiting his experience at St Patrick's College, Armagh, he inquired of former classmates if they recalled sex between boys, or between teachers and students. He himself couldn't: 'I remember no real sexuality, homo or otherwise, though when [P*** O***] fell in love with Frank Lenny, I was shocked. Or jealous?'[15]

Here he allows for the possibility that he himself may have unconsciously fancied the future Auxiliary Bishop of Armagh, and, also, that there were, so to speak, 'unreal sexualities' bred up within the walls of the school. Frank Lenny came even higher in the estimate of the Vincentians than young Montague. He was not just impeccable academically; he was a natural for the holy vestments. Wearing white gloves and a satin surplice, Head Prefect Lenny led the file of students as they walked behind the cardinal in Armagh Cathedral, carrying the long rippling red train.[16] The authorities of the college spotted one of their own in Frank Lenny and made him their pet.

In his final year Montague was made a prefect too, but he then failed to demonstrate an equal eagerness to join the ranks. When pressed about choosing a seminary for his next step, he asked for time. Maybe a university would be better; he could see a bit of the world, just to make sure he had a calling.

Were you in, or were you out, of the society of initiates? Homosexuality and the Catholic clergy were zones of secrecy, where things were said in code, or not at all. Everything joyous about sensuality lay under a blanket of suppression. The boys were never unclothed around one another; they wore their shorts even in the showers. An institution full of males, and only males, but the penis remained hidden.

4

Montague himself was not unacquainted with homosexual acts. One day when he was not much more than ten years old, he met Gerald Lynch as he was carrying water from the spring. Lynch called him aside into Sarah Bailey's ruined cottage, then a shelter for cattle. From there he led him down to the bank of the Garvaghey river. The older lad explained to him about sex, an explanation that was more show than tell:[17]

> Soon he was unbuttoning his dungarees to unleash the red, swollen shape of his cock, the skin of which he began to work up and down with his hand. There was a jerk & the carnal smell of sperm sinking into the moist grass/to smear the grass. I can barely [describe] the shock of the scene ... I could not see the relation between his prick, and the slender pencil he made me produce. It could throb too/ become inflamed/, and rise, but it was more than a year before in the room next to my aunt, I felt my body change. As the seed shot out, the sibilant sound of my aunt's prayers came from the next room, and my aunt seemed to sense something, for she halted in her prayers to call out: Are you all right?

For several years, the two boys used to meet by the river for such sessions. Afterwards, they would lie side by side in the grass, talking about women. Sometimes, one might pretend to be the girl, so the other could play at 'bulling the cow'. What they knew of 'love', they learned from the animals in the fields. The idea, Montague says, never entered their heads that they might become one another's beloved. As soon as the older Lynch boy located an amiable girl, he was off after her, leaving his friend behind in the house with his two aunts.

This tale of 'first learning a mystery, as everyone must', was drafted in the form of a prose memoir in 1968.[18] In the 1990s Montague returned to the draft materials, and put the episode into verse for 'The Current', published in *Smashing the Piano* (1999) when he was seventy years old. Perhaps a general surrender of secrets (and smash-up of proprieties) might in the end prove helpful to the young.

5

On the way home, at vacation time, from St Patrick's, Montague could not but see the signs of war. Once, delayed at Dungannon between buses, he came upon a small prisoner-of-war camp. A German came out of a Nissen hut to hang his socks on the barbed wire.[19] A bigger detention camp was built outside Armagh. At recess, St Pat's students could go there as to a zoo.

From mid-1942 American troops began to arrive in Northern Ireland.[20] Heavy-duty trucks and even tanks rolled by the Montagues' house on the Broad Road. By early 1944, there were 120,000 GIs in Northern Ireland, mustering for D-Day, with a headquarters in Knock Na Moe House, Omagh, just a few miles to the west of Garvaghey.

In Fintona 5000 US soldiers were housed in Nissen huts on the lawn of Browne-Lecky's Big House at the edge of town. Business was booming in the family pub because of the incursion of soldiers. The market town had always had a certain reputation – witness the saying, 'I was never married but I once spent a night in Fintona.' Townswomen rejoiced, Johnnie later wrote, over the arrival of so many men in fresh uniforms.

Montague admitted, that as a boy, he at first 'loved the War'.[21] He kept track of events through newspapers, and then, on a special map, moved pins to mark the progress of armies. His maternal grandmother, Hannah Carney, was also excited by news from the Continent, especially when it was bad news for the British. A diehard republican, she got her side of the story from 'Lord Haw Haw' (William Joyce), via German radio broadcasts.[22]

> 'D'ye hear him; the English are getting it this time,' she enthused to some poor GI slumped over his drink: 'He'll slap it up them!' Polite, uncomprehending, they agreed with her unholy glee as she retailed Joyce's supercilious exaggerations.

Johnnie's own sense of glee left him on the nights Belfast was bombed in the late spring of 1941. The students of St Patrick's were evacuated at night to newly dug bomb shelters alongside the football field. Huddled in the mud, they saw one plane cross low over the trees. Everyone waited for the shudder and the flash. Afterwards, like the others, Johnnie thanked the Blessed Virgin Mary that he had been saved.[23]

6

On the Easter holiday in 1944 John came home to see a production of Lennox Robinson's *Professor Tim*. Aunt Freda and Barney Horisk were in the cast; three different priests handled direction, production and lighting.[24] On the way back to Garvaghey from Mahon Hall in Ballygawley, the car carrying Freda, Barney and Johnnie was waved to a stop by men in black uniforms holding red lamps. These were B-Specials, a voluntary, part-time constabulary. The members were Protestant shopkeepers, tradesmen and farmers, active one night each week. They would patrol only in groups, a sergeant and eight or ten constables. They carried guns. On this night, Barney Horisk knew well who they were and what they were doing – harassing Catholics on the way home from an 'Irish' entertainment. Montague remembered Barney roaring out of the car window at the leader, 'George Allen, stop acting the clift! Are you being paid to not recognize your neighbours? Away and fight Hitler, where you're needed.'[25] (A 'clift' was a fool.)

More and more, Montague spent his free time in Fintona, rather than with his aunts in Garvaghey. Partly, he came a-courting his mother. One poem depicts him teasingly untying her apron strings as she's busy at the cooker, causing her to turn:[26]

> 'Don't come again,' you say, roughly,
> 'I start to get fond of you, John,
> and then you are up and gone' …

He also wanted to hang around with his older brothers, on the chance of being taken up by them, like one of the family. Over and above these motives, there were in Fintona some girls of his own age.

His first romance was with a girl he sometimes calls 'Maura Canavan'. The poet was fond of blooms of bog cotton ('canavan') and the association stuck.

Maureen Campbell was her real name. She was the niece of Johnnie's Aunt Eileen Carney, and lived directly across the street from Carney's pub on Main

Street, Fintona. The pair found one another at an Irish festival in Ballygawley. They set to kissing on the way home, right at the bridge opposite the RUC barracks in Fintona.[27] It would not have been like Montague to forget these details – his first kiss was between a *feis* and an RUC Barracks. Another day, they walked to burnt-out St John's Castle and lay in the overgrown demesne, squeezing kisses on one another's mouths until their lips were sore.

In the years afterwards, Montague's mother in every letter to her son included a bit of news about Maureen Campbell – still single; not just single but likely to be left on the shelf; now has a boyfriend; boyfriend went away to war; she's moved to the USA; she's become engaged, soon to be wed in Fintona; husband turns out to be from Poland; Maureen now the mother of a son.[28] Johnnie was not asking for these bulletins, but she knew he would want to know. You don't forget a first love.

When he was Senior Prefect at St Patrick's College, at night, once he had checked that the boys in the dormitory were not chattering away, or weeping with homesickness, he went back to his own cot to write love letters to Maureen Campbell. He searched for phrases in praise of her small ears, her fragrant hair ('Absence').[29] More and more, it struck him that what was missing from the Vincentian system of life was the presence of women, therefore of tenderness.

7

The stammer never let him alone. Back in Garvaghey on holiday, he was asked to assist as altar boy at a funeral. The moment came for him to recite from the service, and he got stuck, stuck and stuck again, until the parish priest took over. Smart he might be, but how was this boy to become a clergyman?

Prefects rotated the duty of serving at the altar of Armagh Cathedral. When Montague's turn came around, he bribed another boy with a Mars Bar to do it for him.[30] Dean Roughan noticed the dodge. The dean believed he knew just the way to educate the boy out of his stammer. Summoned, Johnnie was asked, Did he want to be caned, or serve at High Mass the next week? Take your pick.

High Mass was a singing Mass. It was no problem for a stammerer like Johnnie to sing. It was just speaking that presented a problem. He could sing like a lark.[31] He took the second option.

As a last resort, his aunts sent him to a speech therapist in Belfast. Montague turned this experience into the sequence 'Speech Lesson' (2011), with the refrain *Will I never, ever speak again?*[32] Week after week, he rode the train back and forth for his appointments. In a consulting room near Belfast City Hall, a young Englishwoman pushed down at the base of his chest:

'Young man, learn to speak from your diaphragm:
Many merry men marched many times.'
…
She presses down, again and again:
'Consider our King: he broadcasts, stammering.
So let the wind whistle through your lungs.
And read poetry aloud, it can be such fun!'

It was a thrill to be touched by a woman, but the stammer remained.

8

A family conference was held in Fintona about Johnnie's future. If he were not to be a priest, then what would he do? Where would he study? Like his brother Seamus, he had won a Tyrone County prize for his examination results. Seamus had gone south to University College Dublin, and done medicine, while Turlough was studying law at Queen's University Belfast. It appeared that Johnnie, who had a gift for words but not for speech, was likely to turn out to be some sort of writer. Seamus's friend Ben Kiely from Omagh, just starting out as an author, was finding openings in Dublin: the newspapers, theatres and publishers were all there.[33] So it was settled: Johnnie would follow his oldest brother to UCD.

During his last term at St Patrick's, Johnnie began to slip out to watch films whenever he had a chance. On his trips to Belfast for speech therapy, he took in a picture before getting the train home. One Sunday afternoon in the Armagh cinema, before the main feature, he watched a newsreel of Allied soldiers forcing an entry into a German concentration camp. A door opened upon horrors. Starved prisoners, unable to stand, pleaded. One seemed to Johnnie to mew like a cat. He hallucinated voices rising from the black and white pictures, 'an ululation, terrible, shy'.[34] All he could think to do that afternoon was to go back St Patrick's College and kick a football through the air.

First the Holocaust, then the Atomic Bomb – the shock of total war was registered by that generation of writers; they would struggle for ways to make sense of it.

3

UNIVERSITY COLLEGE DUBLIN
AND HIS FRATERNITY

I

It was arranged that seventeen-year-old Johnnie would go into the same digs where Seamus Montague had stayed when at UCD: Mrs Crinion's house on Chelmsford Road, Ranelagh, a mile south of the lecture halls on Earlsfort Terrace.

The room was not large and it had to be shared with another, a lad named McCaughey from outside Fintona, in his second year, but not much wiser about life in Dublin than Johnnie.[1]

In September 1946 Aunt Freda first brought John across the border to Longford for a stopover with the O'Meara family before the two boarded a bus to Dublin, where Freda delivered her boy into Mrs Crinion's hands.

2

Mrs Crinion's house was on the list of accommodations approved on behalf of UCD by the Dean of Residence (who visited twice a year). He had been approved by Monsignor John Horgan, Dean of Philosophy, who in turn had been approved by Archbishop John McQuaid from the Bishop's Palace in Drumcondra.[2]

University College Dublin esteemed itself as a particularly Catholic university. Legally, under the Irish Universities Act of 1908, it had become part of the non-denominational National University of Ireland, including the former

'Queen's Colleges' in Cork and Galway, UCC and UCG. In the view of its president, Michael Tierney, however, UCD was 'first among equals' in the NUI. It claimed descent from the 'Catholic University of Ireland', established under Cardinal Newman in 1851 as an alternative both to the godless Queen's Colleges and to Protestant Trinity College.

In 1944 Archbishop McQuaid's Lenten Pastoral declared that it would be a *mortal sin* for a Catholic to disobey the already-existing ban on attendance at Trinity, so, just to survive, the 350-year-old university had to rake in more tuition-paying students from England and Northern Ireland. President Tierney himself kept up 'a truceless cold war' with Trinity.[3] UCD aimed to be *the* national university.

The UCD buildings off St Stephen's Green were crowded, though the entire student body by present standards was small – 2–300 men; 800 women (the UCD student population in 2021 was 33,284).[4] The numbers were spread across many faculties – not just Arts and Science, but Veterinary, Medicine, Education, Engineering, Commerce, Agriculture, Architecture and Nursing schools. About 20 per cent of the student body was clerical. The front rows in lecture theatres in Arts were often entirely occupied by nuns in full religious habits. Other seminarians were visibly scattered through the rows of desks.[5]

Half the students planned to emigrate immediately upon graduation, including 78 per cent of those in medicine.[6] A student of Roger McHugh answered the question, 'Why Did You Come to UCD?' with these Byronic rhymes:[7]

> What inclination sent us o'er these borders?
> Holy Matrimony? Holy Orders?
> …
> Where do we go from here? A question nervous!
> The ESB, the Bar, the Civil Service;
> Some will win heathens on a foreign mission,
> Some win rich wives (and so, farewell, ambition!)
> Some o'er a dwindling Empire watch will keep,
> Some go to jail and some into the Sweep,
> Most will grab parchment, slake their thirsty throat,
> And make a bee-line for the English boat.

3

Between his stammer, his growing up in the countryside and his coming from the North, Montague felt himself an outsider three times over in his first years at university. The insiders were the city boys from fee-paying schools, like Blackrock College and Belvedere College, and the girls from Loreto. They were often the offspring of those who had fought in, or benefited by, the War of Independence, people with connections to Fianna Fáil or Fine Gael, the parties that sprang from the two sides of the Civil War and now agreed about almost everything except as to which party should hold office.

Those on the rise jostled for places in the debating societies, the chief arenas for the ambitious. Charlie Haughey, future *capo* of Fianna Fáil, was already established in 1946 as the auditor of the Commerce Society. He ran the Monday-night meetings with a much-admired autocratic energy.[8]

Yet the club with the highest status was the Literary and Historical Society. The 'L&H' met on Saturday nights in the New Physics Theatre. One would have to come early to get a seat, or even a place in the aisle.

This debating society had a heralded past: it was set up by Cardinal Newman. James Joyce had given talks there on Ibsen and Mangan. Tom Kettle made his mark at the L&H debates before being elected to Parliament. Brian O'Nolan ('Flann O'Brien') first tasted the pleasures of immediate applause when he aired his wit in heckling the appointed lecturer.[9]

The year before Montague started university, Anthony Cronin made a bid for leadership of the L&H. Ordinarily, the auditor was a person of supreme poise, with an armoury of high-flown verbiage. Whatever the question of the day, the auditor held to one of two lines of thinking: Fianna Fáil or Fine Gael. Cronin, from Enniscorthy and a Blackrock graduate, took a third course, that of the Labour Party.

In debate, Tony Cronin gave an impression of one unacquainted with practised eloquence but driven by disillusionment to speak the truth. He was a clever verbal boxer, drawing his man in – then sarcasm was his right cross and pained sincerity his left hook. In one staged attack on the presiding auditor, he made a motion to elect Jim Larkin (1874–1947) as the vice-president of the L&H.[10] To honour this hero of the Dublin Lock-out was fitting for reasons both sentimental and patriotic. The founder of the Irish Labour movement was dying at the time. But to elect him vice-president would be a poke in the eye for each of the two established parties. The motion split the L&H. The following year Cronin barely missed being elected auditor.

It is worth taking the time to examine Cronin's point of view, for he was a leader among the young UCD intellectuals. In his first year at the university he read Flann O'Brien's *At Swim-Two-Birds* and was struck by the portrait of the *Oblomov*-like life of the UCD students. Humorously incapable of taking any serious life decisions, they were pedantically intelligent but listless, with a serious commitment only to ridicule, small bets on horse races and cadging pints of Guinness. After himself drifting from architecture to law, from economics to history, for Cronin *At Swim-Two-Birds* was a sudden, unhappy look in the mirror.

At the same time, the novel came to his rescue: it suggested a way of living in Ireland, a viable attitude to the place. When, many years later, Cronin came to write the biography of Brian O'Nolan, he expounded upon this attitude. The post-Free State generation had lost faith, the biographer explained, in both Church and Motherland; they knew in their bones that each was a failure; the economic and cultural life of the new state was barely ticking over. They remained irritably aware of James Joyce as a forerunner. He had sat in the same lecture halls and stood, like them, chatting in the portico of the National Library on Kildare Street. However, they could not, like Joyce, fly free of the 'nets' of nationality, language and religion. That was not a way of living in Ireland, but a reason for leaving it. Yet to doubt the Church openly would break one's parents' hearts. As for the Free State, even if one had come to despise the fatuous, self-regarding and often self-dealing leaders of the country, it was unthinkable that one would want the British back in power.[11,12]

Actually, this was not the particular double-bind of Brian O'Nolan. He was never anything but an orthodox Catholic. And, as Cronin had to admit, O'Nolan thought that Ireland, whatever its shortcomings, was 'as good a place as anywhere else'.[13] But it was an accurate analysis of Cronin's own painful disappointment with 'Emergency' Ireland. In his editorial for *The National Student* in December 1946, he wrote:[14]

> There is in fact no intellectual life worth mentioning in this College at this time, no communal excitement about ideas and their application to life, art, and politics .... Talent and self-sacrifice are so often rewarded with exile or poverty, the whole nation has been given over, as to a devil of despair, to the belief there is no future in idealism.

The magazine's advice to new students was,

1. Never go to lectures: 'They waste the time of students, the energy of staff and the money of the College';
2. Spend no more than half an hour two or three mornings a week at university.

The *At Swim-Two-Birds* remedy for depression was to regard literature itself as a mode of being, 'an in-joke, a badge of superiority and a freemason's clasp' between those who secretly knew that the Catholic Ireland to which they all conformed was a hollow show.

4

To anyone with a stammer, a debating society was a special kind of hell. However, as a first-year student, Montague sometimes looked in on the L&H. The attitudes of Cronin and his followers puzzled him. Obviously, neutrality during the war had made life in the Free State dull, inert and vaguely afflicted with guilt; elsewhere, so many millions of those-not-Irish were dying to defeat Hitler. Yet all that most Catholics in the North wanted was to be part of the Free State. So what if education, hospitals, orphanages, indeed, the administration of the whole social system, had been handed over to the Church? Compared with the system set up by their hostile Protestant neighbours at Stormont, that seemed just fine.

The scholarship boy from County Tyrone certainly attended lectures. After the lectures, he went to the library. There he took careful notes, steadily, over his three years at college. One could win a money prize by coming first in an exam. Montague won five of them and graduated with overall 'Firsts' in English and history. Yet prize-winning was not his ultimate aim. It was the result of his avidity, his intelligence and his search. But his search for what?

Montague became aware of James Joyce as a UCD forerunner late in his first year, when, at a meeting of the English Literature Society, he heard Brendan Dillon (later a prominent diplomat) give a paper on *A Portrait of the Artist as a Young Man*. On reading the novel, Montague was shocked by what seemed like a psychiatric casebook on his own condition. 'Now at last I had been shown what was wrong with me, what was wrong with us.'[15] The critique of Catholic education was particularly troubling; troubling and awakening. Yet *The Portrait* also encouraged him to see literary endeavour as a form of individual heroism on an international scale.

His next move was in the footsteps of Joyce (and Oscar Wilde, George Moore, Samuel Beckett and even Brendan Behan): to go to France, doorway to self-discovery. In the late summer of 1947 Montague went with another boy, a student from Derry, to gather in the grapes, the *vendange*.[16] The two students cycled alongside the bruised hedgerows of Normandy, awed by the white crosses of the freshly dead soldiers in the fields.[17] The boys started off with just £15 sterling between them, but at Château Thierry, Haut de France, they were paid the equivalent of ten shillings a day for three and half weeks and shared a daily bottle of champagne. After hitchhiking farther east to Geneva, they returned to Paris, where Montague hoped to find, he recalled, 'a Black mistress, like Baudelaire's Jeanne Duval'. Instead, a Dutch friend led the Irish lads to a gay nightclub. Montague wanted to have sex, but not, at that time, that kind.

By 1947 he had begun writing poems. The earliest were 'spontaneous overflows of powerful feeling', scribbled immediately into school copybooks while on the bus back to Tyrone, bursts of elation as 'all the world/Careers through my senses like music'.[18] In one unmeasured screed, he thinks of his verses as prayers, something he pays back to God in gratitude for the 'gift of youth'. He devotes his attention not just to the 'fat customs man' at the border, but to the 'creases around his knee' and the way his shadow moves along the stone wall, before the bus rumbles on.[19] A Joycean 'haecceity' was holy, those properties by virtue of which a particular thing can be described as this and not as anything else.

Another motive for making verses was to release into written words his vastly verbal consciousness, trapped inside by the stammer.[20]

> One of these days, yes, someday I'll sit
> Myself, a pen, a white slip of paper
> And crack the world with a word
> And then can even be silent again
> Satisfied as sunshine on grass.
>
> I have no lover
> Nor can I trust my mouth
> With friendship …

> I'd talk my way past Peter
> And storm the gate of Hell

He wrote verses longing for love, and one stab at a poem, incomplete, to a 'gentle/lovely/lonely girl' with whom he had walked along the avenue below the autumn trees, before winter put an end to this romance that was just possibly all in his imagination.

In Dublin he sought an escape from loneliness by going to ballrooms. There were many: the Gresham Hotel ballroom on O'Connell Street, the Four Provinces on Harcourt Street and the National Ballroom in Parnell Square (now partly the Irish Writers' Centre) – but when Bill Fuller opened the Crystal Ballroom at 22 South Anne Street in 1948, that became Montague's favourite.

Figure 11: The National Ballroom, Parnell Square, Dublin, part of which is now the Irish Writers Centre.

It had a revolving glittering sphere suspended above the dance floor, casting 'a shimmer over our city faces'. The band would cycle through dance numbers: slow waltz, fast waltz, samba and polka. Montague fancied himself an expressive fellow on the dance floor, 'flexible, erratic and lithe'.[21] According to ballroom etiquette, a man could ask any girl to dance, no chat-up required, so long as she was not part of a couple. If he got the nerve to request a dance, she would find the grace to accept – that was the decorum. After several turns with the same partner, a man might ask permission to walk the lady home at the end of the evening. There was no kissing in the dance hall (or drinking of alcohol either), but there might be on the way home, 'plastered against a wall'.[22]

One of Montague's early attempts at a poem arises from his search for female companionship in the ballrooms:[23]

> Dance as often as dance you can
> Till spring shakes her pert blonde head, and starts your life,
> Agile as an acrobat, light on her heels as a cat,
> In sweater and shorts, breasts moulded like apples,
> To shatter your frail illusion of glass into fragments
> The sky-high sob of the trumpet tone lifts one stranded on the ebb
>   tide of pain.

Had he been reading Swinburne? There are three more unrevised stanzas, as the poet commands himself to sing, wonder and dream, each as often as he can. It's forced, wilful and finally 'stranded on the ebb tide'.

The poems he polished and sent for publication to *The National Student* were not so gauchely transparent. They were mannered studies in versification and poetic attitudes, adaptations of W.H. Auden, Stephen Spender or Rimbaud.[24] In them, a new determination to learn his trade is plainly legible.

5

In the steeplechase of young poets at UCD, Pearse Hutchinson (1927–2012) was first out of the gate, with Tony Cronin making a run on the inside. While still a student at Synge Street School, Hutchinson had poems published in *The Bell*.[25] Another fast-starter was Hutchinson's Synge Street schoolmate John Jordan (1930–88). As a teenager, Jordan had been involved in a sophisticated correspondence with the London drama critic James Agate, printed in Agate's published diaries.

Jordan published poems alongside those of Pearse Hutchinson in *The National Student*, where Tony Cronin ran the editorial board. Hutchinson mimicked Gerard Manley Hopkins, and Cronin followed Auden as closely as he could. The early verse of John Jordan was like that of an accomplished actor ad-libbing a monologue in a Jacobean tragedy – impressive, but hammy. In fact, some of his poems managed to recognizably take off Micheál Mac Liammóir's self-presentation in daily life.[26]

Montague ran into John Jordan along with Denis Donoghue (1928–2021) in his classes in English literature. Both were well read and formidably intelligent individuals. He sought out Pearse Hutchinson on his own. Pearse put him on to the work of Austin Clarke. Compared with the others, the scholarship boy from Tyrone was a late starter as a college poet, but by 1949 he too was sending poems to *The National Student.*

Figure 12: Montague on O'Connell Street, Dublin, in college scarf.

6

Tony Cronin, Pearse Hutchinson, John Jordan, Denis Donoghue and Thomas Kinsella: this was Montague's cohort, his fraternity. Through their long lives, these literary figures would remain at all times aware of one another. How am I doing compared with him? And as a group, how do we stand up? As Montague puts it in *Company: A Chosen Life:*[27]

> … we are cast as in a constellation with our contemporaries, whose passage across the skies encourages or disturbs us, with the whole pattern only gradually becoming clear.

They never knew whether they would get a hand up or a snub from one another. The first they expected as their due but were often enough stung by the second. There was point-scoring and begrudgery aplenty down the decades. One didn't want to see one's mate get 'above himself' but you did want to be part of a golden generation.

Denis Donoghue, ever the high Catholic, viewed Montague, with his nights in ballrooms and poems in the college magazine, as being very 'worldly'.[28] His own 'unworldly' activities were concentrated on singing lessons with Royal Irish Academy of Music Professor Brian Boydell, 'whose voice and general tone he copied', according to Colm Tóibín – a Cambridge-inflected, Anglo-Irish tone.[29] Donoghue foresaw his own field of future accomplishment as stretching far beyond the boundaries of Ireland and his Dublin contemporaries. He regarded modern Irish literature as a hole-in-corner affair.

Montague tried to befriend John Jordan, like himself a star student, but, woundingly, Jordan stood 'aloof, arrogant'.[30] Even over time, Jordan 'failed to acquire a liking' for Montague.[31] Jordan's affiliations were with Micheál Mac Liammóir and Hilton Edwards, the actor and manager of the Gate Theatre.

Figure 13: Micheál Mac Liammóir, as Hamlet.

One evening after rehearsals, the two chatted with the younger actor about the nature of male–male sexual relations. On a later occasion, they took Jordan round to the gay bars of Paris.[32] The Tyrone lad stood well outside this charmed circle.

7

The two senior poets in the Ireland of the 1940s were Austin Clarke and Patrick Kavanagh. Neither had much of a reputation in Britain, much less America, but they were celebrities in Dublin. A UCD graduate himself, Clarke dressed like a cleric, black suit and on his head the broad-brimmed black hat of an Irish country priest, with a mournful look on his face as he took his seat in the Palace Bar, where the *Irish Times* journalists drank in the afternoon. He reviewed poetry for *The Irish Times*, usually unenthusiastically, and had an arts programme on the national broadcaster, a steady if small-paying job.[33]

Figure 14: Austin Clarke.

In the early 1930s Kavanagh had walked in his patched work clothes all the way to Dublin from his farm in Inniskeen, County Monaghan. This was an ostentation: he had other clothes and ways to travel, but he aimed to make an impression upon AE, editor of the *Irish Statesman*, and he succeeded.[34] In the mid-1940s, stalled in Dublin, he kept himself going by means of a regular column in Peadar O'Curry's *Catholic Standard* (writing as 'The Ploughman'). When Ben Kiely retired as that paper's film critic in early 1946, Kavanagh took on that job too, pontificating at four guineas a week.[35] His main goal was to finish his novel *Tarry Flynn*, published in 1948 by Pilot Press, but, although a masterpiece, it failed to bring the immediate rewards of a rich wife and fat royalties on which the poet had banked.[36]

Figure 15: Anthony Cronin and Patrick Kavanagh, 16 June 1954.

Kavanagh detested Clarke and viewed his Radio Éireann gig as a national injustice. Clarke did his gloomy best to ignore this rude man from the bogs, but he began to spit fire when Kavanagh published 'The Gallivanting Poet' in the November 1947 issue of *The Bell*. This was an all-out attack on F.R. Higgins (1896–1941), a Protestant and late friend of Clarke's. Kavanagh said the poems of Higgins were phony, and anyway, 'Protestant poetry is un-Irish.' A letter to *The Irish Times* objected to Kavanagh's insults as tasteless (there being, piously, nothing worse than not to be Irish, unless it was to be Protestant). Higgins was by Irish reckoning but recently dead, six years, and he had relatives still living in Ireland, the letter complained. Kavanagh's published answer to this letter was that not just the poetry of Higgins, but of Clarke too, was phony, phony because it was deliberately Irish. 'Poetry is not Irish or any other nationality,' he declared – a head-spinning yet sensible broadside against Clarke's 'Irish mode' of Gaelic prosody in English verse.[37] In a follow-up piece for *The Bell*, Kavanagh laid waste to every other poet on the horizon – Frank O'Connor, John Hewitt, Valentin Iremonger – all the regular contributors to the magazine. He was really enjoying himself.

In revenge, *The Bell* sent out an interviewer to take the measure of the man from Monaghan:

> Seated at the same cafe table as Mr Kavanagh, one is constantly conscious of … the Elemental. A great root-hand shoots across the table to the toast-dish, casting a thunder-cloud shadow on the cloth. P.K., without warning, suddenly crosses his legs, jerks the table a good two feet in the air, cups and dishes a jingle-jangling, and continues the conversation as if no earthquake had occurred.

Apart from his having no table manners, the interviewer sees Kavanagh as a plough horse: 'the great equine head, the scobed nostrils, the great grey eyes of Man's Second Best Friend'.[38]

Paddy Kavanagh, ploughman, bully, Catholic mystic and true literary genius, held court in McDaid's pub, off Grafton Street. There he permitted the UCD graduates to buy him drinks:[39]

> 'It's five pounds to talk to me today.'
> 'Paddy, it's usually a pound. Even on a bad day.'
> 'But it's a black day for me. Hand over or feck off.'

Cronin, Jordan and Hutchinson became regulars at his table. Cronin gives a mercilessly comic description of the scene in *The Life of Riley*, where McDaid's is called 'O'Turk's' (the den of Irish young Turks):[40]

> The cardinal principle there was gurrierdom. Here not success, but unsuccess, was looked upon with favour. Here the man who made a hames of it and continued, whatever the obstacles, to make a hames of it, was the man of fashion. Hence O'Turk's had a high proportion of beggars, and of successful and well-to-do beggars at that, not ordinary, common or garden, public-house touchers. There had to be a history of sacrifice or misfortune or oddity to qualify. One should be a wit, but maladroit, and unable to hold any permanent employment.

'The atmosphere of thievery and chicanery' made this pub, Cronin explained, inhospitable to any 'well-brought-up girl'. Like a pen for buck goats, there was a rich male stink about the place that put it at the farthest distance from the atmosphere of the parental home.

A curiosity about Kavanagh's young hangers-on in McDaid's is how many of them were homosexuals – Jordan, Hutchinson, Dickie Riordan, James Liddy and (on occasion) Brendan Behan – though in Kavanagh's view the last was no hanger-on, more an enemy, even the Antichrist.

With Kavanagh spread like a temperamental monarch on his pub throne, the regulars did their best to keep him in good humour. Yet he could be kind. One day Liddy was confiding in the poet, and Kavanagh leaned over and whispered consolingly, 'You're bent, but you're not as bent as Jordan.'[41]

Montague was not shy of a pint, nor homophobic, and he enjoyed drinking with writers. Inevitably, he put his nose into McDaid's. A young writer could hardly not do so (though Kinsella nearly managed).[42] The new magazine *Envoy* was edited on the premises. But the courtiers in McDaid's when drunk could get very rough and fall suddenly upon a maladroit lad with a stammer, just for laughs. The cesspool aspect of the place also put off an ambitious young writer. Montague did not look with favour upon unsuccess.

8

On a Tuesday evening at 7.30 pm in his room at 103 Beechwood Avenue, Ranelagh, Montague was tuned into Austin Clarke's Radio Éireann programme when he heard his own name announced. He was the winner of a poetry competition! How exciting it was when two of his own poems, 'A Dainty Pianist' and 'Wonder', were read on air. Even his aunt in Longford chanced to hear the programme.

Part of the prize was having the poems published in *The Dublin Magazine* for July 1949. 'Wonder' is yet another verse composed on a CIE bus headed to Tyrone, but in this case the spontaneous effusions have been 'recollected in tranquillity' and subsequently fitted into roughly metered lines, woozy with word-play:[43]

> I sat on a staid country bus
> Soft moving through road cut fields
> Half listening to town-bound housewives' morning hum,
> My senses slipping, as a drowsy coma steals
> Across the frosty awareness of my mind.
> Then suddenly startled, I was awake, to find
> That there was a race between bus and sun,
> Jumping and jolting across a series of slender hills,
> And filling the window frame with freckled light.
>
> Once on a swerving corner caught
> On wheel rims we seemed to gin,
> Rocketing past purple hedges, while the even
> Roll of the sun ran right through fern soft mist
> To horse-neck level drawn again.
> Then a hill hid us. I blinked.
> Voices stumbled around me. The engine snored.
> But I could remember, and would still remember
> The O! tender sheer splendour of the sun.

Every writer remembers the thrill of first public recognition. Austin Clarke, Montague concluded, must be a person of great literary discernment. Upon the completion of his undergraduate degree, he decided he would do an MA on Clarke's poetry.

Clarke's work was certainly worthy of study, but at the National Library, Montague could find little on it, nothing at all by an Irish academic, just one piece by the Irish-American John Kelleher of Harvard. The new MA student would put this neglect to rights: 'It's a bloody disgrace that genuine, unbiased criticism of Irish writing (especially poetry) only comes from abroad.'[44]

Given the attitude of Kavanagh & Co. to Radio Éireann's Irish poet, it was a dangerous thing to undertake a research project on Austin Clarke. As friends would sometimes warn him, Montague could be gormless in his schemes for self-advancement. Just treating authorship as a career was anathema to the McDaid's crowd.

9

Montague accepted he would have to work for a living while doing his MA. Ben Kiely offered to ring up the editor of the *Catholic Standard*, Peadar O'Curry. Montague then went round to his former UCD professor of medieval Irish history, Aubrey Gwynn, a Jesuit.[45] Did he perhaps recall his classmate at Milltown Park seminary, Thomas Montague, SJ? That was his uncle! Now Johnnie was looking for work in journalism. Would it be too much trouble for the professor to put in a word with the *Standard*'s editor? With that stroke, Montague recalled, he was 'home and dry'.[46]

O'Curry tried him out with some book reviews and a film column. His first signed article, published on 18 November 1949, was a review of Walt Disney's *Melody Time*. Montague (who loved Mickey Mouse) showed his religious and academic bona fides by quoting from 'a very fine Catholic cinematic magazine' in French, and name-checked nearly the entire back catalogue of Disney films. A-plus work, high-spirited and highfalutin. To this Ulster Catholic, there was nothing to complain about in the multitude of strings connecting Church to university, to business, even to government in the Free State. You just needed to know how to pull them.

The job as *Standard* film critic had once provided Kavanagh with an essential trickle of shillings.[47] Yet his condescension to a rival and popular art form irritated the newspaper's film-going readers. Kavanagh made hobby horses of his resentments: film was not a real art form like poetry, actors (however brilliant) were just tradesmen, and there was nothing at all good on at present. 'I don't suppose many readers would blame me if this week I had actually given the go-by to the cinemas, or used some other peg upon which to hang my point of view', he wrote on 1 July 1949, continuing, 'The weather is really wonderful ....'

That article was the breaking point for the editor whom Kavanagh nicknamed 'Petty Curry'. He fired the poet.[48]

Various writers took up the column in the following three months. They cautiously signed off by means of Gaelic pen-names or untraceable initials. When Montague got the job, he proudly spelled out his byline. This was a piece of cheek Kavanagh would surely never forget.

10

Barney Horisk in Garvaghey thought Johnnie's articles in *The Standard* were too highbrow and told him so.[49] From the viewpoint of the general reader, he was right, but Montague's reviews remain intelligent, lively journalism, even now recognizably first-rate stuff.

He took seriously the fact that he was writing for a Catholic newspaper. On the whole, the Church was suspicious of Hollywood, not just as a rival mass entertainment, but, if not vigorously censored, a grave temptation to sin. Montague made the case that film was the Seventh Art, a new part of God's creation, quoting the French critic P.F. Quesnay: 'The cinema has been born for us, it is more than an art, it is a new language, a means of expression that our century has been seeking for a long time already.'[50]

Montague treated the films of John Ford as the oeuvre of a great modern artist, and him a good Irish Catholic too.[51]

Like his UCD friends, he was deep into English and French Catholic writers – Graham Greene, Evelyn Waugh, Charles Péguy and François Mauriac, along with the philosophy of Jacques Maritain. On an itemized list of his recent book purchases appear both *The Modern Thomist* and Jean-Paul Sartre's *The Psychology of Imagination*.[52] The post-war sense of the absurdity of life, which for Sartre was the foundation of existentialism, these Catholic intellectuals saw as evidence of the fall of man and original sin. Only out of the condition of utter loss might one hope to encounter the 'appalling strangeness of the mercy of God' (Montague's phrase).[53]

In December 1949 Tony Cronin argued in a review that Waugh was the best of all the Catholic writers, and *Brideshead Revisited* was his finest book, but still it was a failure. Why? Cronin's formulation was roundabout, but clear enough: 'It could be suggested that the fault is in the Catholic conception of the nature of the universe.'[54] Sin existed – that was obvious; but God and salvation just as obviously did not. Montague regarded Cronin's public crisis of faith with alarm.[55] He literally feared for his friend's soul. He himself aimed to display the possibility of being at once an intellectual and a Catholic.

On his earnings from the *Standard*, Montague moved to two large, draughty rooms in an old Georgian house on Seville Place, near the Five Lamps, a popular haunt of prostitutes on the east side of the Amiens Street railway station.[56]

Figure 16: 103 Seville Place.

One night he in lay in bed unable to sleep as engines pulled lengths of coaches through the night. He worried over the condition of his soul:[57]

> The saints look down from the Irish walls
> Onto a world that lies in the dark.
>
> Every man chooses his smaller self:
> Every man breaks down the poet in himself;
> Breaks his soul down till it is small enough to stop a hole
> And can keep the wind away.

These unfinished verses were dedicated to Francis Stuart, 'dreary captain without a helm.' Husband of Maud Gonne's daughter, Iseult, Stuart had broadcast Nazi wartime propaganda from Berlin. In his 1949 novel *Redemption*, crime was seen in the light of Catholic apologetics, the Graham Greene formula that vice (or in Stuart's case, treachery) may induct a person into a spiritual elite.

At the time, Montague accepted as valid these paradoxical problematics of 'the perilous belief in God'.[58] *The Third Man* (showing at the Savoy) he celebrated as not just a Christian but as a Catholic film, because, he explained to readers of the *Standard*, Graham Greene's screenplay really concerned the religious crisis of an ordinary man (played by Joseph Cotton) wanting to do the right thing, but finding himself caught between war victims and a smiling American villain profiting off black-market penicillin (played by Orson Welles). Director Carol Reed then created a motion picture of a post-war Vienna 'hurt grievously, the raw nerves quivering, the movements of its people jerky and afraid'. As a study of spiritual conflict, the movie had, Montague claimed, 'all the incalculable effect of great artistry'. Unlike Cronin, he still held out the hope in early 1950 that Catholicism could enable a valid personal response to the horror of war and its aftermath.

II

In 1950 Montague applied to the Harvard Seminar in American Studies, then in its fourth year of operation in Salzburg, Austria.[59] The only Irish applicant, he was accepted, and to his relief, offered financial assistance. He had to take a leave of absence from his job with the *Catholic Standard*, but he was at the same time offered a commission to report on the Conference of Catholic Cinema, part of the 'Anno Santo' celebrations in Rome, when six million people made a pilgrimage to pray for peace.[60] Using these two events as fixtures, he planned a poor man's version of the European grand tour, departing before Easter and a return in September.

Following a cheery farewell interview with northerner Seamus O'Kelly in the 21 March 1950 *Irish Times*, he got the boat to Holyhead.[61] A Shakespeare festival in Stratford-upon-Avon was his first stop. He stayed over for a few days in Paris to watch double features of the latest films, then boarded the train to Salzburg. A letter published in *The National Student* reflects on the Austrian celebrations of Good Friday, which left him 'to wonder on an ancient miracle, perhaps atavistic, perhaps the only all-resolving truth, now an un-plucked thorn in our daily flesh':[62]

> This day they say a man has died
> And I counted the trees by the water's edge
> And found them three.

One a shrivelled stump suckled by no sunlight
Others laughing with foliage
And water sleeping behind.

That 'water's edge' in line two is the lakeside outside Schloss Leopoldskron, the eighteenth-century palace that housed the Salzburg Seminar. Visible on the horizon was the mountain where Hitler once had his holiday home, the Berghof.

Before the war, the palace had been the home of theatre impresario Max Reinhardt. In 1947 his widow made it available to three former Harvard University graduates for a kind of academic Marshall Plan. The approximately 175 students came from many countries, including Germany, but not one from Franco's Spain or the Russian-controlled areas of Eastern Europe. Salzburg was a central base for the US forces of occupation. Jeeps and army trucks filled the streets. The seminar itself was obviously a form of American 'soft propaganda', although funded by charitable donations, and not the CIA. 'We have come here', the Harvard Americanist F.O. Matthiessen gravely declared, 'to enact anew the chief function of culture and humanism, to bring man again into communication with man.'[63] The lecturers, many of them Jews, tried to demonstrate, by the way in which they taught, the US constitutional values of free speech (e.g. criticism of racial injustices in America), religious tolerance and equal suffrage for all.[64]

There were lectures in varied aspects on American life: Sociology, Industrial Relations, Poetry and the Psychology of the Adolescent. Montague attended afternoon discussions of works by Whitman, Emerson, Dreiser, Faulkner and Henry James.[65] Matching himself against European graduates, their training with his, how did he come off?[66]

Pretty badly, I'll admit: for the average Irish student is far behind in fluency of languages, humility before achievement or just plain *savoir vivre*. He is gauche, eager perhaps, but more arrogant and precious than his counterparts abroad.

In Ireland, literary criticism was gossip plus personal flair, not logical analysis. Montague realized he had a lot to learn.

He was lucky in his American lecturers. Henry Nash Smith would show up in 1955 as chair of the English Department in the University of California,

Berkeley, where he awarded Montague a teaching fellowship. Karl Shapiro, one of the poets on the staff, became editor of blue-ribbon journals, which in time took Montague's poems for publication. Saul Bellow, future Nobel Prize-winner, led discussions on the American novel. Randall Jarrell, the stellar American poet and critic, introduced students to *The Waste Land*, as well as to the work of Wallace Stevens and Robert Lowell.[67] In contemporary letters, there were no more impressive names than these. The American seminar was meant to extend a helping hand to post-war Europeans; it was certainly a benefit to one young Irish poet.

After six weeks in Salzburg, Montague passed through Vienna in June for Herbert von Karajan's Bach festival, in the company of Seán White (then doing an MA at UCD, later to edit *Irish Writing*). The pilgrim next made his way to Rome for the Anno Santo celebrations. The Italian heat was overwhelming: 'I staggered around the city like a poisoned pup.'[68] He was very slow to find a way to write about his sweltering visit to St Peter's. 'Rome: Anno Santo' was not begun until 1954, and the poem was finished only in 1958.

The delay may have had to do with his not being able to face how he felt. Being swept up in the sweating mass of 'ignorant Irish on pilgrimage' disturbed him: the whispering nuns, the crowds of Irish matrons in nun-like black, farmers from 'stone-fenced fields', all of them telling rosaries and marching towards the Pope as to a 'Godhead': their fervent devotions repelled him, but he did not like to say so.[69] The poem is not a farewell to faith, but it is ironic about Catholic belief. After his return to Ireland, he stopped going to Mass.

Where Tony Cronin had been, he now found himself.

12

It is possible that at this time Montague was passing through another crisis, one concerning his sexual identity. Before he left Dublin on his *wanderjahr*, he had been 'walking out' with the daughter of an Irish civil servant, and he would resume doing so upon his return. In his diaries he calls her 'Sally'. In *A Chosen Light* (1967) she appears as 'Virgo Hibernica', a kind of Diana figure in the Wicklow woods on Sunday morning strolls. He believed himself to be in love with her but was granted very few kisses over 'six years of insignificant suffering'.[70]

Before Montague left Dublin on his 'grand tour', Brendan Behan – the two were fast friends, both stammerers, though Brendan vanquished his affliction – gave him the address of an old-fashioned bordello in Paris, one where, in the atmosphere of a drunken dinner party, any kind of love was possible. In 1962 Montague thought he might write about his night in the brothel, but only in a 'carefully censored' manner.[71] *Company* (2001) turns it into a light literary anecdote:

> ... Brendan gave me several addresses in Paris – I used only the first, a Monsieur Pierre, patron of a café in the rue Jacob, but it was a humdinger. I found myself drinking champagne with Pierre and a shell-shocked ... Belgian – Presently, Monsieur Pierre conducted us to a 'good house', where we got more than bed and board for a long weekend. The Belgian veteran presided over the Sunday dinner, with whores to the right and left of him, and the Madame at the other end. As the rough red flowed, we grew merrier and merrier, like characters in a Maupassant story, dancing and singing ...

The story told in *The Lost Notebook* (1987) conveys a more disturbing encounter with sex. It takes up the narrative of Montague's 1950s travels after Rome. In Florence he is running out of money. An American girl he had noticed in the Uffizi Gallery, and failed to impress, takes pity on him and lets him sleep on the floor of her room. Soon enough, he is in her cot. Yet while she knew all about sex, he knows nothing, and she at first refuses to help him; he could not even find her vagina: 'You little Irish Catholic prick,' she mutters. He is shocked by her language.[72] Eventually, she becomes his instructress.

As they grow closer, he learns that she aspires to be a successful painter, like her brother. She left America to get away from her family. Her parents quarrelled constantly, so she sought refuge in her brother's bed. One time, the Irish boy takes the American girl from behind. It leaves them both distrait. He asks, Is that what your brother did to you? Yes, she says. Her brother was gay, and made her satisfy him with her mouth too; later he pimped her to gallery owners. The Irish boy is horrified, and piteous. The present-day narrator concludes that, when young, he had failed his American friend. Her needs were genuine, and his own 'constrictedness' as an Irish Catholic was just what frustrated her.

Montague returned to Ireland by way of Paris. That summer John Jordan was in the city in the company of Micheál Mac Liammóir, Kate O'Brien and others. Jordan was between one boyfriend and another. The newest was Jozef, a penniless Dutchman he had met near the Sorbonne. On 1 August 1950 the two went to a gay bar, and who should appear but Jordan's UCD classmate:[73]

But my God, Paris, Paris, anything can happen. Last night too, sitting in the Royal with Jozef and Daniel Monroe, I met John Montague, who had suffered from the apparently monstrous *crise de nerfs* with Donal and John Good. M. confesses himself queer, which is not surprising. Still the sniggering prurient approach to sex. Dublin will be a nice hotbed of neurotics in September.

It is possible that when Montague ran into Jordan in such circumstances and 'confessed himself queer', he was just being arch, ironic. Ulstermen often say what is the polar opposite of the truth as a deadpan joke. It is also possible that in the era of Spender, Auden and Isherwood, Montague thought that to be a poet was to be a homosexual, so he would give it a try, like Jordan, Behan and Hutchinson, and see if he could enter their charmed circle. Yet it is more likely that he was going through a period of genuine ignorance, doubt and immaturity in relation to his own sexuality.

Later in his life, Montague was not homophobic. Even when married and having earned a reputation as a skirt-chaser, he would sometimes propose to young male friends that they join him for a roll in the hay.[74] He did not take offence when refused or appear embarrassed. Sometimes he no doubt did find a welcoming partner. But in 1950 he could not be quite so light-hearted; sodomy was still a crime.

Heterosexual relations were difficult for him too. Even after losing his virginity, he was not easy about intercourse with willing women in Ireland. In a 1962 draft autobiography, he gives this self-diagnosis: 'The seminary and the homosexual imbalance in his generation at the University had made him into a lecherous prude. Girls who knew the score dropped him quickly for sharper men' – 'sharper' meaning just men who knew how to perform sexual intercourse, a secret in the years before pornography, and knowledge difficult to unlock before the legalization of contraception.[75]

He eventually found a friend in Dublin, 'Suzanne', a nineteen-year-old woman from the Sudetenland. Her family had fled to Ireland ahead of the Russian occupation. She promised her mother to save sex for marriage, but she was as curious as he was. In her bed under a big bolster, they did all the things that couples do, apart from intercourse, 'even mild sadism'.[76] They were together from autumn 1950 through the next calendar year. They might have had a future together as husband and wife, but, he reflected, what then? He probably would have hung on for a post at UCD, then, tired of this life, betrayed her with others. He had not even been able while keeping company with Suzanne in 1951 to give up walking out on Sundays with the 'Virgo Hibernica'.

Suzanne, bewildered by his lack of commitment, made up her mind to return to Germany in January 1952 ('wisely fecked off home to Berlin').[77]

Around the same time, his cool middle-class muse Sally – who kept the indecisive, two-timing Montague in hope until then – broke the news that she had accepted a proposal from another gentleman. Eleven years later, still feeling guilty, Montague drafted an unpublished farewell poem, 'For Suzanne':[78]

> Often with me, that hour when
> We said goodbye at the bar
> And I saw for the last time
> In your eye my power to hurt
> You. Easy to say it was
> Neither of our faults
> Caught in the long ignorance of youth
> But yours was the braver choice.
> Today under the tall tree
> I accepted the hard truth
> Of my self-indulgent past
> Separate love and life
> Wherever you are, I salute you.

13

Montague's dilemma in the early 1950s was whether to be a poet or a scholar. His immediate future as a journalist ended in October 1951 with his contribution to the symposium 'The Young Writer and *The Bell*.' He spoke ill of the motherland, 'absorbed in its political and religious catch cries and witch-hunts', then added that the mother-and-child debate had almost made him ashamed of being an Irish Catholic.[79] Some readers were impressed with him for speaking out, but not Peadar O'Curry, editor of the *Catholic Standard*. He sacked him.

On his Austin Clarke project, he had made no headway at all during his European travels, possibly for fear of those in McDaid's. Unable to get government funds himself, Kavanagh had been roused to satire when a university graduate had gone abroad on public money:[80]

Because he's got the practical knowledge;

And that is why he has been sent
To travel on the Continent,

To bring back the secret of great arts
To Kerry and remoter parts,

To spread in Naas and Clonakilty
News of Gigli and R.M. Rilke.

Safer to change his MA topic to Irish prose!

Montague wrote articles on George Moore and William Carleton, published in *The Bell*, in August 1951 and April 1952 respectively. He particularly identified with Carleton, a local favourite of Ben Kiely too:[81]

> For a youngster living on the edge of the Clogher Valley the stories of William Carleton were not fiction but fact; gradually one learnt the genealogy of the various houses, gathered a hint of the intricate law-cases and local feuds, saw Orange drummers practising before a tin-roofed lodge. There were people still alive who could remember Anne Duffy, the original of all his idealized heroines, the blind fiddler Micky MacRory, and in a famous fight at a barn-dance only thirty years before the two whole townlands battered away at each other until dawn was breaking, and there were no more untouched skulls. Clamping turf in an upland bog, one could see, across the cramped heathery hills, the double-wooded swell or saddle of Knockmany, the mountain which haunted all of Carleton's work.

He then bundled together the essays, added an introduction and submitted them for an MA. Written with an unspeakably greater amount of dash and intellectual spirit than is customary for a postgraduate dissertation, it would not have been surprising had this stylishness got the back up of Professor John Jeremiah Hogan. The degree was, however, not only awarded without fuss, but Montague was given a First.[82]

Still in pursuit of an academic career, he decided to go for the 'Travelling Studentship', a competitive scholarship that enabled an Irish student to study at

Oxford or Cambridge. It was known that John Jordan was competing for this award too; he had begun studying in January.[83] In May 1952 Montague started reading English literature from Anglo-Saxon onwards. The October test would have three broad questions and one special subject. He knew that Jordan was doing Shakespeare and that, as an actor, he had an incomparable knowledge of drama. Montague chose to focus on Milton's *Paradise Lost*, unconscious preparation, he later reflected, for writing his own long poem.[84]

When the results were announced in the autumn, Jordan had carried the day. For Montague, this was a 'galling defeat'.[85] He had so often before come first in examinations. Now the walls of Dublin seemed to echo with rumours of his failure. The £100 bursary for second place was little comfort. He nearly had a breakdown.

But the 'defeat' did not put an end to his academic ambitions. At the end of 1952 he contacted Roger McHugh (of his lecturers at UCD, the most sympathetic) to inquire about the offer of a Fulbright Fellowship for study in the USA.

What would have become of Montague had he won the Travelling Studentship and gone to Oxford? Anything is possible, from being thereafter warmly welcomed as a poet in England (rather than received coldly, as would be the case), to not writing poetry at all. Perhaps coming from a republican Catholic background, he would have felt so alienated in Oxford he would have turned around and left, or suffered a breakdown. Or he might have settled in, and gone on to a university professorship, perhaps in a UK department of French. Maybe he would have wound up like John Jordan, an Oxford-educated alcoholic on a part-time lecturer's salary at UCD, writing book reviews for the Dublin daily and weekly press. Whatever Montague's future would have been, his mature poetry would probably not have had the same American dimensions.

14

All through these two years of graduate study in Dublin, Montague was also writing poems, and short stories too. Archives hold dozens of the poems in draft. Often, the author has visibly returned to the pages, improving a line or noting too-obvious echoes of contemporary poets. W.R. Rodgers, Auden, MacNeice and Yeats are the most frequently spotted. Sometimes, the page indicates that he had deliberately set out to match a key poem by a contemporary. For instance, the lofty perspective and controlled stanzas of the following verses are Montague's take on Auden's autobiographical 'In Praise of Limestone':

I
From Ulster, that bitter fragment of an indolent island,
Where the cattle crop neat grass, cut well to boundary,
A mouldering farmhouse, with snail trains of silver damp,
The glitter of dew-webbed rushes, and ordered lorries
Sweeping past on a well-tarred road,
Everything ordered, austere and secure,
With the clipped speech of broadcloth men sure
Of their markets, their methods of ploughing,
Except when a flag waved at a meeting
Its fictitious challenge of self-justifying patriotism.

II
There my first lesson in intolerance and countering reserve,
The things that should never be said,
The idiot on the platform mouthing rubbish
To feel more important, bangin[g] his head
Like a drum to bring force to the argument;
While the evening light glittered
On the ghostlike pines in the plantation
And the small boy watching saw day die
From the private platform of a four-poster bed.

III
To Dublin, the delicate smoke-chaning city
Perched on a river, with gulls quarrelling in the sky,
A city full of half lights and gentler voices,
With the hills creeping close, to hang
Like ripe plums outside a student's window;
Walking the streets in those early days
Almost believing in the dream
Of being slightly less unhappy
Of being home for a time in a marginal city.

IV

Today, leaving the city, climbing further inland,
To where from a hilltop the sea and city appear
Like first vision of beauty: now at last
Scales drop from my eyes, seeing less
The fernlike uncurling of mist, the streets
Where clear voiced children rejoice among
Broken buildings, then the saturated air
Which over the slight country diffuses
Like a kind and evasive despair.

The writing, if journalistic, is fluent and lucid, but the poem loses its confidence at the close. Although he tried three different endings, he could not find within himself a satisfactory resolution at that moment, in art or life.

'Seville Place' is a biographically interesting draft. It paints a picture of his lodgings during the months of exam preparation:

Always at the same hour I awaken,
To begin living. Eight o'clock …
The rain falls lightly on the window …

I reach out, switch on the wireless
To keep myself awake. 'This is the News.'
Another day's pattern of comment and event,
News and interviews. A man is dead,
A sea-plane crashed on the Scottish coast:
A hated politician has given up the ghost.
American threatens, Russia warns,
Some Asian tribe has taken up arms:
Frontier troops have been alert all night:
A society girl has sold her charms
In lawful marriage.

I slide onto the floor-boards,
Move to the window and draw the curtains.
Cyclists move on the damp surface of the street
With precision, as on a conveyor belt,

Houses look dull and blind-eyed.
In the station, the train puffs
A frail design of smoke
Which forms, reforms and melts.
It slithers noisily on its tracks.
Eager to be at work.
And so, without much more fuss, or lazy
Glutting of the eye, I slowly put on my clothes
Claiming myself, not valuable perhaps,
But the only fact we cannot reject
Is having been born.

His subsequent marginal notes (in many different inks) point out echoes of Delmore Schwartz and E.E. Cummings – and he could have added Auden and MacNeice – and fairly ask: 'Precision, but to what point?'

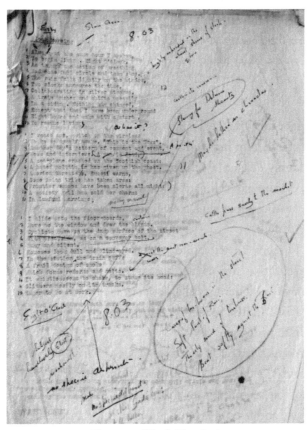

Figure 17: 'Bleak Morning'.

Some poems he sent out for publication. *The Dublin Magazine* took an imitation of Robert Graves, 'In Her Service' (the first appearance of the concept of the Muse in Montague's work).[86] *The Bell* printed 'Daily I Awake' in March 1952, and two more in October of that year. As *Bell* poetry editor, however, Tony Cronin was a difficult barrier for Montague to get over. Kavanagh, co-editor of poetry at *Envoy*, would have none of Montague at all, although the other co-editor, Valentin Iremonger, 'sneaked' one past the 'angry' bard.[87] Overall, given the amount of work he was doing, he was discouraged by rejections in Dublin. Disappointment prodded him to write these self-consciously Yeatsian verses:[88]

> Having been taught to hate
> Whose gift only runs to gentleness
> Having been taught to strike
> Whose only wish was tenderness
>
> I turn from all, and place
> My power against all, and
> Lay their little names
> Down on the bitter streets

15

Montague longed for a friendly literary mentor, a big brother. Valentin Iremonger (1918–91) became that for him and, with his wife, Sheila, gave him an occasional place at the family dinner table. Their Sandymount home was a refuge from 'the ingrown, discouraging climate' of the McDaid's crowd.[89] Sheila was great at affectionately teasing Montague, a civilizing practice that helped to put him at ease with womenfolk.[90]

Valentin, formerly an actor, and a pal of Roger McHugh, had won the AE Memorial Prize in 1945 for his first poetry collection. Reviewers noted that he was *au courant* with Modernist English poets. He had a post in the Department of External Affairs. In his capacity as ambassador to London, he would later be a genuine help to Montague.

It was Iremonger, fed up with his co-editor at *Envoy*, who wrote the brilliant but deadly portrait in *The Leader* (11 October 1952) that set off the Kavanagh libel trial. A memorable sentence from that piece – 'Mr Kavanagh's mind, when he abandons poetry and fiction, is like a monkey house at feeding time' – may not be entirely fair or accurate, but it was close enough to hit home. The subsequent libel suit that Kavanagh hoped would make his fortune was nearly the end of him, a courtroom crucifixion.

16

Peadar O'Donnell commissioned a short story for *The Bell*. In a session of brainstorming, Montague listed possible subjects. His fertility of invention is striking and so is the way he looks to Tyrone for his material. Here is a sample from a longer table of topics:

> Adultery with a married girl.
> The teacher who fancied himself a dramatist ... Writing criticism for the papers and engaging in religious controversies and drinking himself to an early grave. His greatest need was for an audience. Contempt for people.
> The mad priest, crooning to himself at the fire, dunghill to the eyes ...
> Met the wee girl at the chapel, then fear of being caught.
> Badminton, golf, the dog, the show.
> Love with a Protestant or foreigner.
> Boxing in the back garden – with brothers. Once with bare fists and broken table.
> The nest of pullulating spinsters, closing the door, so people cannot see them, in ragged jumpers and with blotched faces.
> The lonely man in the farmhouse; you came on people like that, afraid and withered and lonely.
> The gypsies and the cycle after dark; the drive after the pictures at Glencull.
> Come to the door of the pub and watch across the street; the young men lounging opposite, and the way they decreased in number each year. Escape with her to London.
> The sailor Tony home from the sea; any girl would come out with you and the back of the car was always there, or the alleys, or the haycart over the bridge. Didn't have to wear a girdle.

As a 'Note to Self', he wrote on the same page: 'The innocence you detested for its awkwardness was better than your intelligence.' Yet his treatment of his mother's hometown, Fintona, was harsh. Even in his own estimate, his first tale 'The New Enamel Bucket' was 'a masterpiece of sheer mean sordidity'.

The only excuse for it was its 'monumental accuracy'.[91] Published much later in his collection *The Death of a Chieftain*, it is a story of a stunningly bleak pub crawl in a small Ulster town.

This one was not right for Peadar O'Donnell and *The Bell*. Next, Montague wrote a story about a student uprising at a college very like St Patrick's in Armagh. Conceptually, the story was perhaps suggested by Jean Vigo's famous French film *Zéro de conduite* (1933), but the resistance to the tyranny of teachers by the Irish seminary boys is more subtle and less spectacular. 'That Dark Accomplice' depicts the students, at first offering cunning resistance to a raw new dean, being at last tricked into submission by his priestly guilt-trip. Peadar O'Donnell, after a look at a first draft, offered £15 for it (a decent price). 'That's it,' Montague agreed. 'And there'll be lots more.' But on further reflection, 'the pull of the Mass rock' caused O'Donnell to spike the final version of the story.[92] One mustn't criticize the clergy.

On the one side there was the vindictiveness of the Dublin poets; on the other side Catholic censorship. John Montague felt boxed in. He was happy enough to board the *SS America* for New York on 16 July 1953, a Fulbright Scholar bound for the doctoral programme in English at Yale University.

Figure 18: SS America *(1954).*

4

YALE, IOWA WRITERS' WORKSHOP, BERKELEY AND MADELEINE DE BRAUER

I

John Montague sailed for New York just a year after his father James T. Montague had finally returned to Ireland from that city. He had long forgotten his father's face. From what he heard, he built up a 'vague but flattering image ... of a red-haired young man who sang occasionally at dances and was a demon for practical jokes'.[1] An old fellow in Garvaghey once stunned Johnnie by answering another's question – What will this boy become? – with 'a blackguard, like his father before him.'[2] Was his father not a good man?

Maybe twice a year, a letter would arrive from Brooklyn. One that came in 1946 expressed sorrow that Johnnie had not felt himself called to the priesthood. *Poor sweet old man!* Montague thought.[3]

A year later, in 1947, the three sons made a concerted appeal (they each wrote a letter and sent them all together) for their 57-year-old father to retire from taking tolls for the New York transit system and come home to Fintona. He made no answer.[4] Seamus and Turlough next wanted to send Molly over to bring him back; they would provide the steamship tickets. Turlough lived with his mother and helped manage the pub – he also kept a little office in the snug, where he did legal business. However, in 1952 he was planning to get married and to build a house of his own. Turlough wrote to his father that not only did he hope he would come home for the September wedding, but that he would remain to take his place in the family home and business. That appeal succeeded.

The three boys drove all the way down to Cobh, County Cork, to meet the Cunard liner bringing their father home. Then, down the gangplank he came: 'A small dumpy man/with a hat/That look at the rain withershins,' and just one small suitcase after all his years abroad.⁵ 'Something in me began to contract,' Montague recalled, 'and also to expand.'

On the long drive north over small roads, they stopped at pubs for reunion pints, and once to listen to Johnnie's 7.15 pm broadcast of a book review on Radio Éireann. It was good of his two older brothers to allow Johnnie this moment of precedence. Secure in their own professional lives, doctor and lawyer, they were able to take pride in his success: speaking, on air – the stammer publicly overcome.

That Christmas of 1952 in Fintona, John Montague remembered as his happiest. All of them for once together, at midnight Mass.

2

The following July, during his passage to New York, Montague drafted three poems on ship's stationery.⁶ He may have been heading off to join a class of top graduate students, but on board *SS America* he was behaving like a poet.

Molly's brother Tom Carney and his wife Eileen met him at the boat on 14 July 1953. Before John left to explore the country, Tom bought him a new American suit, fit for a businessman.

Montague – always a keen traveller – set out to see America, beginning with the nation's capital. Postcards of the Lincoln and Jefferson memorials were drafted for his parents and brothers but never sent. For a long time after his arrival in America, he did not communicate with his family back home.

From Washington DC he got a bus to Richmond, Virginia, home of Edgar Allan Poe. He had not before thought of what it would be like to find whole cities inhabited mostly by African Americans. There were very few dark-skinned people at all in Ireland. A drive over the Smoky Mountains brought him to Chattanooga, Tennessee. He took the tour to Oak Ridge, a city built by the federal government to develop the atomic bomb – a frightful place, where a weapon was industrially conceived that could end all human life. The notion ate away at him. A drive along the Mississippi brought him to St Louis, where he saw a melodrama staged on a paddlewheel riverboat. In Chicago, Lake Michigan astonished him: 'like a ferocious Indian sea'.

Everywhere, he witnessed with envy the physical freedom of the young Americans: they all seemed to have been taught how to swim; throughout the summer they took to rivers, lakes and pools. In general, he confessed himself amazed.[7] It was a fearful lot to take in.

3

The Yale English department in 1953 was a world-power's research centre for literary studies. The scholarship of its faculty fused three streams of thought: T.S. Eliot's Anglo-Catholic high humanism, the Southern Agrarians' rural anti-modernism and the Vienna School of European philology. The European philologist René Wellek (along with Austin Warren) synthesized these elements in *Theory of Literature* (1949). The popular name for the approach to poetry was 'The New Criticism', as made actionable by Cleanth Brooks and Robert Penn Warren (two Southern Agrarians who had moved from Louisiana State University to Yale) in their popular textbook *Understanding Poetry* (1938).

A simplified version of the approach is that a student need not know a great deal about the life of the author or the historical context in order to analyse the unity and coherence of the 'verbal icon'. What was necessary was to focus on tropes such as metaphor, irony, paradox and ambiguity. The approach put interpretive ingenuity at a premium. In fact, this simple version of The New Criticism did not exclusively prevail in the Yale graduate programme. In Montague's time, students were expected to see a work in light of all that could be known about it, but also to employ the new technical vocabulary and to rate difficulty and verbal density as literary virtues. The poetry of Robert Lowell realized their aesthetic: extravagant Shakespearean rhetoric, obscure, yet with hints of deeper Catholic meanings, everything a broken allegory, but one with no key, and held together by a display of personal neurosis.

A page of course options survives from Montague's first meeting with his academic advisor. The first semester offered seminars in Renaissance literature with Louis Martz and in Augustan literature with Maynard Mack. Perhaps, his advisor noted, Montague should just audit these, rather than take them for credit – those professors 'would probably work you very hard'.[8] A better choice for this Irish lad might be Frederick Pottle's seminar on Samuel Johnson. In semester two, Montague chose 'Development of Twentieth-Century American Literature' with Norman Holmes Pearson, a correspondent of Ezra Pound's.

He would be the one to convince a sceptical Montague of the literary importance of *The Cantos*. Of all his courses, he liked best the one with Robert Penn Warren on Faulkner's novels.[9]

4

It is difficult to determine just when things began to go wrong with Montague's year at Yale. In his private notebooks years later, he himself never really got to the bottom of it.

Right off the bat he felt ill at ease in his American businessman's new suit. The other male graduate students wore tweed – old-fashioned farmer's weave in Ireland, but in the Ivy League, the academic's uniform. Many of the brightest students, male and female, were Jews. The zeal of Harold Bloom in full spate was unforgettable but also intimidating.[10] How could an Irish lad from the countryside keep up with these high-flyers? They were the next generation of leading literature professors across the United States.

He was not accustomed to a Socratic method of teaching, with a teacher asking questions, and putting students on the spot to answer, then following up with more questions about the answer. Nor had he any experience of presenting the thesis-driven argumentative paper, concocted to stimulate classroom debate. With his stammer he was, in his own discouraged phrase, like 'the deaf mute with flow signals'.[11] Montague never spoke up in class during his year at Yale. Not once.

Even outside of class, he could find few with whom to talk. An exception was Leonora Leet. Her specialism was Jacobean drama. Finding out that he wrote poems, she asked to see them. She freely showed respect for his gifts, and affection for him too. After a night together, she surprised him with 'a Jewish deli breakfast: herrings and smoked salmon and rye bread'.[12] Leonora wrapped him in a 'hot embrace' at a New Year's Eve party, but Montague recalled the night as a disaster. Not her fault, but he was estranged. He did little afterwards to close the distance between them.[13] He also had a brief crush on a Greek student, memorable for his curly black hair.[14]

Mostly he stayed in his room, campus housing, 2773 Yale Station. Letters from Ireland piled up unanswered. He drafted replies and then let them lie, unposted. To an English friend, the poet Kenneth McRobbie, he wrote,

'First, as to facts, I am having a very hard time here.'[15] He reached out to Tony Cronin, but with diffidence, 'if you feel like answering, O.K.' After flattering Cronin on his talent as editor of *The Bell*, he came to the real point of the message: he had not found America easy – 'you feel lost'.[16] He apparently did not send this letter either.

On St Patrick's Day 1954 he tried to find his own people by going to a dance sponsored by the Tyrone Men's Association. There he ran into a man from Fintona, Maurice Donnelly, still 'a pushy little politician', so no fellowship to be found there. Alone again in his dormitory, he encountered life only through daily newspapers and radio broadcasts. The headlines were always alarming: bulletins regarding the nuclear stand-off with the Soviet Union and the battles in Korea. A slight hysteria appears in an unsent letter from late March 1954, this one to Brigid and Freda Montague:[17]

> Also, and this is what is making me care less and less – things are going to blow up in a few years. The effect of the second World War was unbelievable – but the [waves] of fear & doubt are going to increase. America has the ugliest cities in the world, but lovely lakes, mountains: and the most intelligent people.
>
> I sometimes see all Garvaghey in my mind's eye, but of course I cannot go back, even to Ireland, for very long, for that matter. I want to be where things are happening ....
>
> De Valera is probably right in keeping Ireland out of the twentieth century but the young people will not stay ....
>
> My love to all. What is wrong with me, of course, is that I have had too little happen to me in Ireland: you can't write about a country that is sleeping peacefully while the whole globe is on fire.

The globe was not in fact on fire yet. But Montague had come to inhabit a state of fear. A draft poem from this period is entitled 'Storm Coming Up':[18]

> A car wiper working against the fretful snow,
> News of the latest trial and the winning horse,
> Troops are landing or the commission's report is through
> These are normal things, and set the heart at rest.

> Buying a bargain in a cheaper store,
> Watch that the shopman does not fool you, though.
> With purchases walking through the snow;
> These are normal things, and set the heart at rest.
>
> We begin with the given to which the heart responds
> Trace love back to its origins
> And back
> Are driven to confession of our sins
>
> The radio suggests one new form of fear:
> The total terror and eclipse are here;
> Atomic mushroom may flower anywhere,
> But these are normal things, and ask us not to care.

The ironic refrain does not in any way 'set the heart at rest'. American normality was nightmarish – capitalism just a daily man-against-man conflict. The Cold War policy of the USA meant containment battles all over the earth. Montague was undergoing not just 'culture shock' but terrifying alienation in New Haven.

As the academic year went on, he observed his classmates at Yale pairing up. Perhaps he too might take that path? But things did not turn out well when he attended a dance at Vassar, the elite women's college in upstate New York. On a calendar page for 23 April 1954 he reproached himself:[19]

> Badly dressed, a failure in love: conscious of estrangement, unwilling
> to learn your own method: In the wrong society: looking for a Vassar
> girl to marry: Catch yourself on, big boy, and begin all over again ….

The mood of terror and depression pervades draft verses from late April or early May 1954:[20]

> The people mope and moan before the television set
> The blue lilac dangles, and the flowered dogwood,
> Alive in the Quadrangle: all night the frightened student
> Turned in his bed ….

What happened to Montague, the frightened student turning in his bed, that sent him off into a nervous breakdown?

One of his later efforts to understand this upsetting period focused on a brief time in the city:[21]

> First weeks in New York … Greenwich Village but afternoon in New
> York hotel – strip house – queer bar. Greyhound Bus Station. Hard
> not to feel depressed.

He entered into a danger zone, 42nd Street style, and he had not come out unaffected.[22] In his notebooks, Montague compares this experience with *Lunar Caustic*. Malcolm Lowry's novella is an inside account of a psychotic break, with full hallucinations.[23] Lowry, terrified, romanticized this 'season in hell', comparing himself with Rimbaud and Baudelaire.

Montague was not in pursuit of a literary experience of madness. Yet in his silent room, voices were speaking, not his own. In 1963 he recalled the period in some verses in his notebook:[24]

> It all comes flooding back
> That wild unhappiness
> A mechanism … thrust
> Off balance, out of gear,
> By the loneliness, the casual sensuality
> Of the great city. Broken also
> By the memory of my father in that place.

This is still a more analytical view than he was able to take during the crisis. Then he was not so much concerned about the proper functioning of a mental mechanism, as with the condition of his soul. Two years after his disillusionment in Rome, he began to believe that his suffering was a result of sin. He went to confession and received the Eucharist.[25]

5

In the spring of 1954 Montague, just a shadow of himself, learned that he would not be asked back to Yale for a second postgraduate year. Norman Holmes Pearson looked after the Fulbright Scholar to the extent of arranging a scholarship to the University of Indiana School of Letters in June and July. This was no ordinary summer school. John Crowe Ransom, Richard Blackmur,

Leslie Fiedler, Richard Wilbur and William Empson, stars of modern poetry and literary criticism, were on the staff.

Montague had a room in a dormitory and a job as a busboy (waiter's assistant) in the cafeteria. More than half of the students were women. Two became lasting friends: Margo Fanger and Mary McAllister.[26] Margo and her husband, Donald Fanger, would encounter Montague again a year later at the University of California, Berkeley.

Mary was the daughter of Thomas J. McAllister, a prominent Irish-American member of the Democratic Party and a federal judge in Michigan. Mary's red-haired sister Claire McAllister, a poet, had been living in Dublin in 1951/52. Several splendid portraits of her survive from that time, painted by her companion Patrick Swift. Mary invited Montague home to meet her parents in Grand Rapids, Michigan, the first of several friendly visits through the years.[27]

Things were looking up, but what would his next step be? Go home or stay in America? He wrote to Professor John Kelleher at Harvard, asking for help. Might there be some sort of post available for a fellow Irishman around Boston? There was no answer. In Bloomington, he went along to the School of Letters cocktail party.[28] Using a ripe Ulster accent, Montague recited for John Crowe Ransom and William Empson Kavanagh's 'Stony Grey Soil'.

'You shouldn't return to Ireland just yet; stay in America a while,' Ransom proposed. 'Go on to the Iowa Writers' School.' Ransom rang the school's director, Paul Engle, to arrange an assistantship for Montague.[29] Not until midsummer was it fixed that the next leg of Montague's American odyssey would take him farther west.

6

Figure 19: John Montague, passport photograph, 1954.

Nearly every English-speaking university now has a writing programme, but in 1954 the Writers' Workshop in Iowa City was not just pre-eminent, it stood alone. The concept was simple: bring in master craftsmen (and women) to be the instructors, rather than professors of literature. Then make the students' own writing the text for discussion, rotating round the room, so each class member has a turn in the spotlight. The draft poem or story is examined as a work in progress, with the aim of collectively identifying its value and possible routes to its improvement.

One feature of the practice at Iowa was odd, though often replicated. At the start of the year students were divided into writers of poetry and writers of fiction, as if those were two types of people. Obviously, some writers do both. Robert Penn Warren (an early visiting instructor) won Pulitzer Prizes for his novel *All the King's Men* (1947) and for two collections of verse (1958 and 1979). Montague himself wrote both stories and poems. At Iowa he was classed with the poets, but also took courses in fiction.

In September 1954, looking around at one another that first week in the post-war Quonset hut, the new students could not know who would wash out, and who would be the next Robert Lowell. There was a lot of talent in the room. Constance Urdang (a key person in the Washington University – St Louis – writing programme of the 1970s) was there, and her future husband, Donald Finkel. Gertrude Buckman, first wife of Delmore Schwartz, and one of Lowell's lovers, was in the class. The men included Robert Bly, W.D. Snodgrass, Bill Dickey, Philip Levine, Robert Mezey, Lucien Stryk and Peter Everwine. In semester two, Donald Justice was both convenor and student. If you know anything about twentieth-century American poetry, you will see right away that this class was stacked with dynamite. These writers would blast off from Iowa in many directions, anchoring new writing programmes all over the USA.

Many were then entangled with Robert Lowell. He had been an instructor in 1953/54, and in the 1954/55 academic year appeared for a reading and a workshop session. Lowell had all the gifts, and not just his old Boston family inheritances. He was stupendously intelligent, Harvard-educated in English, French, German and Classical literatures, and committed to the seriousness of a poet's calling. If his commitment took him into nervous breakdowns, so be it. If it meant never settling, just travelling like a troubadour, he was not put off. Achievement of the best poems possible was his aim in life. That was, he believed, worth all the sacrifices (by others too, the martyrdom of friends, wives, children). Since there was little money in the sale of poetry in twentieth-century America, it could be difficult to sustain one's confidence in this pursuit over a lifetime, yet Lowell's confidence was never shaken. He took on the full weight of the job in the ancient sense, as servant of society, its unacknowledged conscience. His reward, he hoped, would be to be remembered with the great poets who had been his guides.

The sense of vocation is captured by Lowell in his tribute to John Berryman:[30]

> Yet really we had the same life,
> the generic one
> our generation offered
> (*Les Maudits* – the compliment
> each American generation
> pays itself in passing):
> first students, then with our own,
> our galaxy of grands maîtres,
> our fifties' fellowships
> to Paris, Rome and Florence,
> veterans of the Cold War not the War –
> all the best of life ...
> then daydreaming to drink at six,
> waiting for the iced fire,
> even the feel of the frosted glass,
> like waiting for a girl ...
> if you had waited.
> We asked to be obsessed with writing,
> and we were.

There might be troubles with alcohol, he allows, and adultery too ('a girl'), but one thing was constant: the obsession with literary greatness. That was the big lesson when Lowell was teacher. What does poetry require of you? Everything; all you've got.

Yet the young poets at Iowa were not all contented to be cast in the mould of Lowell's 1950s' style – dense, allusive and hieratic. Bly tells a story of catching Lowell's attention during his spring visit to Iowa. He managed to get the poet's advice on a lyric Bly had written after a drive through Maryland with its huge trees. The poem began and ended with the line 'With pale women in Maryland.' Lowell asked, 'Do you know which county you were passing through in Maryland?'

'No,' Bly replied.

'Well, you could find that out, then go there; or go to a library and find out details of the history of that county. That's what I do. In that situation, I look up all the historical facts I can, find out who founded that county, what sort of crimes took place, who introduced the tobacco farming and so on. Then as I rewrite, I try to get as many of those facts as I can into the poem.'[31]

Bly concluded that if that was how it was done, he was in the wrong business. He instead renewed his belief in the significance of images as they first arose in the mind, put down one after another, without the filling out of a stanza, no transitions either. Eventually, this would be known as the 'Deep Image' school of poetry.

W.D. Snodgrass was also wrestling with Lowell's influence. He had been alarmed by Randall Jarrell's sinking compliment, 'Snodgrass, do you know you're writing the very best second-rate Lowell in the country?' What was wrong, Jarrell said, was that he had packed his poems with too many intellectual fireworks, as if that were the point. At Iowa Snodgrass began to tell a story in verse, the story of losing his daughter in a divorce. The verses were still formally conceived, but the content was unguardedly intimate. Lowell at first did not like this new work – 'tear-jerking stuff',[32] but later he came around to the way Snodgrass had put his life on the line in the poems published as *Heart's Needle*. They showed Lowell the way to *Life Studies* (1959) and what M.L. Rosenthal named 'Confessional Poetry'.

Philip Levine was not entangled with Lowell so much as with John Berryman. In Levine's first year at Iowa, 1953/54, Lowell ran the workshop in one semester, Berryman in the other. Levine had come to Iowa after working in Detroit auto factories, and he wanted to find a way to incorporate American voices within verse, to make the eloquence and song-like qualities of workers' speech audible. He was a proletarian aesthete, genuine in both dimensions. His target was not entirely alien from Berryman's play with the voices of 'Mr Bones' and the narrator in *The Dream Songs*.

Even more inspiring for Levine was the example of William Carlos Williams, and his emphasis on the American (as opposed to the English) language, although lines like 'They feed, they lion, they lion feed,' came from his own sonic laboratory.[33]

Lowell, with his greedy beast of a brain, was not unable to learn from younger writers. In time, especially after a reading tour of the West Coast, he would himself go in the direction of W.C. Williams, looser metres, more personal story-telling and greater engagement with the reader.[34]

7

In October 1955, settled in his University of Iowa dormitory, before going to bed for the night, Montague typed out a page of advice to himself, acting as his own father so to speak:

> Annotate, like F. Scott Fitzgerald, my entire past life.
>
> Decision: this is a mad world and may plunge into war anyway; therefore, try to produce a book of poems; plan stories equal to Hemingway's for Paris magazines; develop and annotate my critical attitude; do not at any point take on too much; that's about all, so good night; except to plan the theme of that short and rather scabrous first novel.
>
> Do not try to live through events too often ...
>
> The failure to correspond to myself; *je ne suis pas pédéraste*; not of necessity, anyway ...
>
> Keep hours like any clerk – Conrad and Joyce and all – nearly everyone had another job. Valéry, Joyce, Mauriac, Greene.
>
> Lowell's poems can be equalled.

He did not want another year of failure, idle in the dorm, no extended relationships, a broken-off romance with a boy and no headway on his plan to be a great writer. He set his sights on measuring up to Robert Lowell.

Montague's immediate plan was to produce for workshop discussion 'my Quaker Graveyard in Nantucket', his version of Lowell's 1947 effort at writing a canonical poem.[35] It is a long elegy for Lowell's cousin Warren Winslow, killed at sea during World War II, but it never mentions the war, or his cousin either. Warren Winslow is even more absent than Henry King is from Milton's 'Lycidas', the poem whose allusiveness and big music Lowell emulates. Instead, he gathered materials from Thoreau about a shipwreck on the Maine coast, all kinds of tropes and scenes straight out of *Moby-Dick*, Bible episodes, Jonah in particular, a hoard of Yankee fishing jargon and a soundscape from Hopkins's 'The Wreck of the Deutschland'. Lowell compacted these disparate materials into a hammering, honking sequence of stanzas of very dark import. Oddly for an elegy, it is not at all consoling. Still, people had to take off their hats to Ambition personified.

In writing 'Soliloquy on a Southern Strand', Montague did not borrow language from Lowell's poem, but he did take a tip about the method of approach, and he did aim to be impressive. Both poems are haunted by a troubled faith in God.

'Soliloquy on a Southern Strand' is the dramatic monologue of an ageing Irish Jesuit priest on a beach in Australia. Montague's mask is his Uncle Thomas. He had letters from Thomas; he knew the voice. His own life matched up with his uncle's: both were raised on the farm in Garvaghey, singled out for the priesthood, sent off to a seminary and then found themselves exiled in a distant land, faith shaken and alienated.

He massed his material in big stanzas of blank verse, rhymed irregularly, as Lowell had done, though the American poet went for a more startling, hectic variety. Montague's poem usually seeks the sad ease of Uncle Thomas's spoken voice. Elsewhere, it reaches for the *O altitudo* note of early Lowell:[36]

> What here avails my separate cloth,
> My darkling self, whose meaning contradicts
> The primal drama they enact in play?
> …
> Is this the proper ending for a man?
> The Pacific waves crash in upon the beach,
> Roll and rise and inward stretch upon the beach …

No one talks that way. 'Soliloquy on a Southern Strand' is impressive, as student work. 'Montague,' Randall Jarrell might well have said, 'do you know you have succeeded in writing a second-rate imitation of Robert Lowell?' The truth is: that is not easy to do.

In April, when the poem was up for examination in the workshop, Montague recorded the comments. It was pointed out that the picture of Ireland was sentimental. Montague thought to himself, *That's okay: it's the effect of the old priest's nostalgia, not mine.* Another student gave the view that, with just a bit more work, this draft could turn into a major achievement. But W.D.

Snodgrass observed, 'This is not the real poem.' There was another poem behind it, one that Montague had not yet succeeded in writing.[37] That other poem would presumably confront his religious doubts with vigour, rather than weakly conclude:

> No martyrdom, no wonder, no patent loss:
> Is it for this mild ending that I
> Have carried, all this way, my cross?

8

At Iowa there was pressure on the student poets to hit a mark, that of the poem publishable in a contemporary periodical. This pressure may have both accelerated changes in Montague's poetry and sent it off course. A consideration of a draft poem before and after Iowa suggests this possibility.

Before coming to America, Montague had experimented with free association. Rising from sleep in 1953, he scribbled down memories of his aunts in Garvaghey, and worries about violence in his parents' marriage:[38]

> The house of aging women; assuming the day's load; night gown; the emotional shames of school; the poor substitute of mental superiority for lack of athletic skill; sharing childhood secrets, the separation; the coldness between them; something hidden and jeering; family chronicle; the invalid in the house, no room for gaiety, neither had its place for the irrelevant grief of the young …. Coming along the end of the lane a wee fox terrier came flying out and took a lump out of him and before the night they had to smother him between two bedticks. A woman carrying a child, fat and fretful. A wife hunting her husband in speakeasys and he refusing to go for your bum of a brother and laying him cold with a bottle and he met him with two black eyes.

On the other side of the page, he dashed off verses about his childhood terrors when put to bed early in summertime:

> Children are afraid in the night, hearing the clock talk
> As though to itself, and the shadows peck at the window
> The lost birds crying under the shelter of branches

The drip drip of water and something moving that
Could be alive like a rat or a mouse but has no place
And inhabits the dark without reason:
Lying in beds the young and the sleepless hear
The murmur of walls when dimensions are hidden
And fear the absence of clear light and the family gods
That can be touched with a finger, the darkness
Has taken them all and gives no answer.
The clouds are plentiful outside and stars
Put their eyes to chinks to watch the turnings
Of a nervous earth; the window forbids the starlight
And the person doubting the dark that drains
Him like water touches himself to feel substance
Suspicious of the integrity of the blind eye
Searches with sensitive fingers for bone of himself;
Outside the moon glowers like a rustic but
In man's four-walled dwellings fear rustles
Under and over the stairs. Only where lovers
Entreaty to combat the dark, turn to each other,
And build a new light of limbs interweaving;
And even they must turn separate or hear in the night
The rhythm of another's breath and feel the
Darkness coming in around them alone.
When they sleep, still ceaseless the spiders
Move in the darkness and the woodwork creaks
And the watchdog twitches in his sleep crying
After game on hills, he never could run,
Better to turn aside and sleep again rather
Then test the fury of darkness with the strength
Of the eyelid. Night is as old as the hills
And the child will aways cry at the thing
That never comes up the stairs.

Taken together as text and subtext, the two passages convey Montague's childhood anxiety, the causes of it and what he hopes would bring him relief (a loving partner). It is a rough draft, but one distinguished by truth to personal experience.

Three years later, Montague came back to these verses and pared them into three neat stanzas. Entitled 'Nursery Story', the poem appeared in *The Nation* on 1 February 1958:

> Children learn the first lesson of fear in the night,
> Hearing the clock talk as though to itself,
> The lost birds crying under the creak of branches,
> The *drip-drip* of a water-tap, and something moving
> That could be alive, like a rat or a mouse,
> But inhabits the dark without reason.
>
> Islanded in the night, the young and the sleepless hear
> The slight edge of the curtain twitching and shifting
> And rubbing the dark, the murmur of walls
> When dimensions are hidden, and suddenly fear
> This absence of clear light, and the family of objects
> That can be touched by a finger:
>
> Golliwog with gross eyes dead in a corner,
> Jack-in-the-Box who murdered Jack Horner,
> Cinderella betrayed by the giant ogre,
> Sinbad-the-Sailor with the great Roc on his back,
> Stridently calling, and Tom the Piper's son,
> Fleeing in fear from a grotesque father.

The workshop-driven changes have turned the free-associative verses into a publishable magazine poem, period verse in the contemporary idiom. At the same time, they depersonalize, delocalize and make literary what was a freshly grasped lump of psychic material belonging to an orphaned lad in County Tyrone. The life has somewhat gone out of it. The 1950s' cult of universality, irony and loaded Shakespearean pentameters did not best suit Montague's gifts, although he published in top American magazines a number of good poems in that manner.

9

The vital thing for Montague about Iowa is that it made his generation known to him, in the persons of both his teachers and fellow students. Later, he would ask young aspiring poets, 'Who are your contemporaries? You must identify your contemporaries.'[39] Throughout his life, he kept an eye on the ongoing work of Iowa classmates.

Distinguished contemporary poets visited Iowa regularly. At one workshop, Louis MacNeice picked out for admiration Montague's 'Irish Street Scene, with Lovers', a MacNeician snapshot.[40] The most impressive visit was by William Carlos Williams. Williams had suffered strokes in 1951 and '53, and he was only recently resuming public appearances.[41] His right arm was partially paralyzed, and his old stammer was worse than ever. Montague could sympathize with his struggle to make himself understood.

In the seminar, Williams selected for discussion drafts by Snodgrass and Montague.[42] When he came to Montague's draft, it was to make the point that while it was good, it was not written in the American line. Williams's great cause was to root out American mimicry of the English literary voice. When Montague read out the poem, the old poet realized: this man is not an American! And his face fell. After the class, he apologized.

That evening Williams gave a reading at the Old Capitol in Iowa City. Fumbling in his speech and slow, he was mocked by some students. Afterwards, Montague went to congratulate him, sensing he needed it. Williams turned and put his arm around Montague, and said, 'Poet! Poet!' Montague felt this to be not just good-heartedness, but also a kind of christening, something momentous. It preceded a long, life-changing apprenticeship.

He took the point that it was false for Americans to mimic Englishness. They must write in an American grain. But just what exactly would be the *Irish* grain? What was that measure? That became his quest.

10

'Whenever I call you on the phone,' Robert Bly asked Montague one day, 'why does a woman's voice answer?'

The most important thing that happened in Iowa, the most important thing perhaps that had so far happened in Montague's life, happened in the autumn of 1954 when he met another international student, Madeleine de Brauer.

It is strange to speak of falling in love as an 'aporia', yet, for a biographer, such an episode is often simultaneously important and perplexing. The two people spend their time alone, out of sight of historical witnesses. They communicate with one another, verbally and non-verbally. However, they do not put it down on paper; they're together all the time, and busy. They make themselves naked to one another. They lose their shame. They grant one another the right to do as they please. They arrive at a feeling of complete mutual understanding. But all that is at that moment coming to pass they keep secret until they are sure of themselves as a couple.

There is no archival record of Montague's first months with Madeleine. One can only assume it was with them what falling in love is for others, important and mysterious.

Still, it may be observed that before the autumn of 1954 Montague was a lonely young man, troubled in his sexuality, just getting back on his feet after a nervous breakdown. By the time the school year ended, June 1955, he was a man in love, full of dreams for the future and ready to set out with his beloved on adventures in Mexico. The thing that happened to him, one has to conclude, was Madeleine. She made a sick boy better.

Figure 20: Madeleine de Brauer, Iowa City, 1955.

In one volume of his autobiography *Company*, Montague recalls that in Iowa, 'I met a titled young Frenchwoman with an eager grin and golden-brown eyes, called Madeleine de Brauer ... and [we] soon moved into a small wooden house together, something quite unusual in the Grant Wood American Middle West of that time. I think we got a kind of fool's pardon as eccentric, sex-mad foreigners in those repressed Eisenhower years. ...'[43]

Madeleine had been born in a château – Bellozanne, in Normandy. She was a direct descendant of Maréchal d'Avout (1773–1820), one of Napoleon's generals, a figure with a part in Tolstoy's *War and Peace*. Her family of seven were French nobility, with castle, servants and lands. From her letters, a reader can see that she was, these things apart, a person of intelligence, grace and sparkling humour. She had gone to America both to teach introductory French and to take classes in the history of English literature. You'd think she had the world to choose from, but she settled her favour on this aspiring poet from an Ulster farm.

That summer they set off together for Mexico, with the Aztec ruins for a destination. In her scrapbook from the journey, you can see her affection for Montague in the shots she framed with her Kodak. He is posed in silhouette, in profile, alone and lost in thought. She poeticizes the poet.

Figure 21: Montague in a restaurant by the sea, Mexico, by Madeleine de Brauer, Summer 1955.

Figure 22: The poet, after breakfast in the hotel, reading, by Madeleine de Brauer, Mexico, Summer 1955.

He is an object of beauty in her eyes. And how much did John Montague wish to be a woman's object of beauty! Even more, he had 'a mind, a sense of humour, a command of language' that was 'totally enslaving for the girl [Madeleine] still was then'.[44] How wonderful to be so beheld by a woman of Madeleine's discernment. It was the making of him.

Theirs was a literary Mexico. They came armed with the works of Malcolm Lowry, Graham Greene and D.H. Lawrence. While there, Montague made clippings from local newspapers in preparation for writing the short story 'Death of a Chieftain', not finished until 1963. The story bears the marks of his current reading, along with his subsequent friendship with the Guinness heir, the Hon. Garech Browne.

That summer in Mexico was blissful, to judge by Madeleine's scrapbook. Yet at the summer's end she left John in Berkeley, California, and went to the University of Illinois in Urbana.[45] When they had made their academic plans in early 1955, they had not yet agreed to remain a couple. She was pursuing a higher degree in English literature, and he had decided to resume study for a PhD. But once they parted, they found themselves longing for one another and in a hurry to be together again.

II

In the Berkeley English department Montague was assigned as a research assistant to Professor Thomas F. Parkinson (1920–92). The son of a plumber and union organizer in the Bay Area, Parkinson was a liberal activist committed to social justice. He had won a poetry prize as a Berkeley undergraduate, and he continued to publish poems in parallel with his scholarly work. More than anyone else in the English department, he was a fellow traveller with practising poets in the area, such as the poet-anarchist Kenneth Rexroth, Robert Duncan and later, the Beat poets (he wrote the first book on Beat poetry). When Montague met him, Parkinson was working on a study of W.B. Yeats, the first to examine closely the manuscripts and to make observations about Yeats's compositional practices. *W.B. Yeats: Self-Critic* would appear in 1961, followed by *W.B. Yeats: The Later Poetry* in 1964. Montague was lucky in this assignment to a scholar-poet like himself. The two quickly became fast friends.

In an American doctoral programme, years of coursework were required before one could even begin a dissertation. Some of the requirements had little appeal for those of a literary disposition. In his first semester, Montague took three courses. In Anglo-Saxon, one of his fellow students was Allen Ginsberg, a former student of Lionel Trilling at Columbia University, freshly arrived in California. Their professor was determined that the students first learn the grammar of Anglo-Saxon. Neither Montague nor Ginsberg was happy about this.

His second course was not pleasing either. The professor employed the course as an extension of his research project, a linguistic atlas of California, mapping those places that used the word *tap*, as opposed to those that used either *faucet* or *spigot*. One day after class, Montague and another Fulbright scholar, Muriel Thomas from New Zealand, confided their disappointment to one another. They were joined by a third member of the class. Montague remarked that he was really enjoying a book he was reading in his third course (perhaps Tobias Smollett's *Humphry Clinker*). The student responded, 'Enjoyed? I haven't *enjoyed* a thing I've read for years. I consider that a matter of maturation.'[46] This humourless and disapproving attitude was widespread in a discipline that was newly ambitious to be recognized as a serious branch of *Wissenschaft*.

The third course was a different story altogether. It was Ian Watt's 'The Rise of the Novel', to give it the title of Watt's classic study published in 1957. A fellow student in that course was Donald Fanger, an American Jew from Los Angeles. Fanger would go on to a brilliant scholarly career in Russian and European literatures, with posts at Brown, Stanford and finally Harvard. Montague and Fanger struck up a friendship that became important to each of them. By means of long and deeply serious letters, they used one another as sounding boards over the next thirty years.

12

On 7 October 1955 Tom Parkinson brought Montague to a poetry reading. The invitation read:[47]

> Six Poets at the Six Gallery. Kenneth Rexroth, M.C. Remarkable collection of angels all gathered at once in the same spot. Wine, music, dancing girls, serious poetry, free satori [sudden enlightenment]. Small collection for wine and postcards. Charming event.

This was the famous reading that launched the San Francisco Poetry Renaissance and made 'Beat' poetry the culture news of the year. Jack Kerouac did not himself recite, but he collected donations for gallon jugs of wine, then passed them around. He sat on stage, facing the audience and 'giving out little wows and yesses of approval and even whole sentences of comment with nobody's invitation but, in the general gaiety, nobody's disapproval either'.[48] The master of ceremonies was the dean of Bay Area poets, Kenneth Rexroth. The six poets were Rexroth, Michael McClure, Philip Lamantia, Philip Whalen, Allen Ginsberg and Gary Snyder. Ginsberg recalled:[49]

> We were all writing idiomatic verse; everyone was interested in Kerouac, and it was an accumulation of the San Francisco West Coast Bohemian-Anarchist-Modernist tradition, as well as the New York impulse or energy that we brought, and Kerouac's obvious genius which [Robert] Duncan appreciated and so did Rexroth.

Ginsberg, by then fairly drunk, did not take the podium until 11 pm. His one text for the night was *Howl*, the profane outcry in long biblical lines, written just weeks earlier. Montague recalled the moment in *Company*:[50]

> Then Ginsberg stood up, and I heard a different Allen from the shy, shrewd student of Anglo-Saxon. He began quietly, but his voice lifted into incantation as he came to the Moloch passages, an apocalyptic vision of the tall towers of San Francisco, written under the influence of hallucinogens:
>
> Moloch whose eyes are a thousand blind windows!
> Moloch whose skyscrapers stand in the long streets like endless
> Jehovahs! Moloch whose factories dream and croak in the fog!

At the end of a line, the audience would shout, 'Go!' as at a jazz club when a saxophonist is riffing. 'Go, man, go!' The audience joined in. Ginsberg was in seventh heaven.

This was no ordinary poetry reading. Soon the six poets were branching out, headlining events around the Bay Area. Poetry readings became happenings, wild festive events for young rebels. Sometimes the poets accompanied themselves with little Asian bells and drums, as if the performance were a Buddhist ritual. Dancing girls and satori were frequently promised. Sometimes, the poet stripped naked in a hyper-literal metaphor for honesty. Costumes became theatrical. Poetry readings were hip. The craze spread from the Bay Area eastward from city to city.

Ginsberg, the master impresario, with an inspiring belief in the genius of his friends, ran a publicity campaign on both coasts for 'Beat poets'. Without overstatement, *Howl* was the score for a cultural revolution. Its patron saint was William Carlos Williams: 'To me,' Ginsberg wrote, 'Williams's "open form" meant "open mind" … I had a much larger agenda,'[51] – like a not-so-humble Jesus saying of John the Baptist, 'To me, baptism is more than a dip in the river.' Ginsberg saw himself in revolutionary terms.

A few weeks later, after the first reading of *Howl*, Ginsberg dropped out of Berkeley to become a full-time poet-activist.

After October 1955 Thomas Parkinson began to organize not just another reading like the one at the Six Gallery, but a re-enactment of it (staged on 18 March 1956 at the Town Hall Theatre, Berkeley). In the course of things, Montague, then living in Parkinson's basement on Cragmont Avenue, recalls that he came along to Ginsberg's cottage and met the people hanging around at 1624 Milvia Street, Berkeley. Later he obtained mimeographed copies of *Howl* to share with Dublin poets. But in the mid-1950s, he himself did not get on board the Beats' bus. The Ginsberg and Robert Duncan practice of rapid and unrevised composition – 'First Thought, Last Thought' – was alien to his own habits of slowly licking a poem into shape. For him, a single short lyric might be years in arriving at its full articulation. Anyway, in 1955, psychologically speaking, Montague was not ready to 'let it all hang out'; he was still getting back on his feet and settling down.

13

The Berkeley graduate programme was demanding. Over the academic year, Montague wrote few enough poems, and those were ironic snapshots of American life, alienated, from an exile's point of view.

His main writing energies went into his seminar papers. Donald Fanger kept copies of a few of these. One on the American Puritan revivalist, Jonathan Edwards looks at its subject from a carefully defined European Catholic point of view. Edwards and the Puritan tradition were being taken very seriously in those years by professors of American literature, but to Montague, Edwards was the sort of character one might find in Portadown, a New World Ian Paisley. He kept him at arm's length, as provincial and inhumane.

One surviving seminar paper he wrote was for Mark Shorer's class in fiction and presented to the class on 20 March 1956. Fanger found the paper both brilliant and hilarious; he treasured his copy ('I will never forget Shorer's face registering your lines about his winding up in the lap of DH Lawrence).'[52] Written with great brio, the essay compares Smollett's *Humphry Clinker* with Joyce's *Ulysses*. Montague's thesis concerns Shorer's own schematic history of fiction. New Criticism, Montague notes, is now attempting to analyse the novel:[53]

> I find it disquieting that the two most persistent and able critics of the novel form so far, Dr Leavis in England, Mr Shorer in America, have both made their discriminating pilgrimage – their pilgrimage toward discrimination – only to end in the lap of D.H. Lawrence. It is as though, having long starved their sense of redundancy, of excess, in admiration for purity of form, craftiness of technique, they stagger to the end of their way feeling a need for some total abandonment. It is as though Allen Tate were suddenly to announce that Robinson Jeffers is, after all, the greatest poet of the century: there is nothing to prepare us for this.

In learnedness, this is exquisite. The tone is elegant, but consciously undiplomatic; there is not the expected amount of salaaming. And those comparisons – was he raising a laugh at the expense of the teacher? Shorer protested.

Montague created difficulties with figures of authority in the academy. Something in him refused to play the game, although he showed that he could have done it if he had cared to do so. Years later, he summed up the situation for Fanger:

> As you know, I have always had trouble with the academics: they resist (even Shorer) my wild theses (which are generally right, but if they refuse to see it, I refuse to prove it, brick by brick), my refusal to deal with the obvious … and my general passionate proselytizing for my vision of life. And, of course, the skimping of details.[54]

He still had not shed his old ambivalence on the question: poet or professor? He entered one top graduate programme after another, but then found the company of unliterary academics to be repellent. He could not help signalling that he did not belong among them.

14

The chief preoccupation of John Montague in 1955 and 1956 was Madeleine. At every break in the academic calendar, they travelled across the vast country to be together. At Thanksgiving (the fourth Thursday in November), they met in Taos, New Mexico, the last home of D.H. Lawrence. This was a happy combination of romance with literary tourism. For the Christmas holiday, Madeleine was to come by train all the way from Chicago to San Francisco.

That December day, as Montague waited at the station, there was a hard winter rain. On the news, bulletins arrived of flooding in the valley.[55] The train was terribly late, and Montague shifted from station to bar, trying to picture where in the continental wastes – to him 'the long imaginary plain' – her train might be. When she finally arrived, the two kissed, and wept, and were unable to speak.

It took Montague ten years to complete his much-admired poem about that experience, 'All Legendary Obstacles'. He once suggested to an interviewer that 'the Orpheus Myth comes into it'.[56] That may be so, but the poem also draws together loneliness, an inability to speak, reunion and a woman's love, all dynamic elements in Montague's psyche. He is 'still unable to speak', but loved:

> All legendary obstacles lay between
> Us, the long imaginary plain,
> The monstrous ruck of mountains
> And, swinging across the night,
> Flooding the Sacramento, San Joaquin,
> The hissing drift of winter rain.
>
> All day I waited, shifting
> Nervously from station to bar
> As I saw another train sail
> By, the San Francisco Chief or
> Golden Gate, water dripping
> From great flanged wheels.
>
> At midnight you came, pale
> Above the negro porter's lamp.
> I was too blind with rain
> And doubt to speak, but

> Reached from the platform
> Until our chilled hands met.
>
> You had been travelling for days
> With an old lady, who marked
> A neat circle on the glass
> With her glove, to watch us
> Move into the wet darkness
> Kissing, still unable to speak.

Like a beautiful reprise of a scene in a 1940s movie, the final 'camera shots' are first of the old woman in the carriage and then, from her point of view, a fade-away vignette of the hero and heroine vanishing in the distance – poetry and cinema technique married.

For the Easter break in 1956, the pair met in Denver, Colorado. At Christmas, after Madeleine's long train journey, Montague had proposed, putting the question as if he were an Ulster farmer: 'Well, should we take out a licence to breed?' Joking apart, the couple meant to start a family.

Montague composed a letter in the best French he could manage, asking Madeleine's aristocratic parents for their daughter's hand. By 22 April 1956 his own mother, Molly, received news in Fintona of the engagement. Always comically quick to see the sorry side, she did not actually say, 'Marry in haste, repent at leisure,' or directly allude to her own sad marriage, but Molly did advise them in writing to consider matters carefully before taking the final step.

The two spent the summer in Berkeley, while Montague was teaching a class. Tom Parkinson and his wife Ariel entertained them on Cragmont Avenue, their house in the hills, and became, along with the Fangers, the couple's best friends. There were regular Sunday dinners together. Tom wanted them to stay on at the university. Once they had children, John and Madeleine thought, they might like to return to California to settle down. But John first wanted to reconnect with Ireland and to establish himself as a writer.

Their plans were to marry in Normandy, then settle in Dublin. Although there were no jobs on offer at UCD (Montague asked), by 20 July 1956 Roger McHugh found him a post with Niall Sheridan at the Irish Tourist Board, as editor in the publicity department.[57] Madeleine's natural gifts made her employable anywhere. Montague would be returning to Ireland, a married man with a job.

5

BAGGOTONIA AND HIS FIRST TWO BOOKS

I

When John Montague first began to keep company with Madeleine de Brauer in Iowa, even after she explained that her grandfather the Duc d'Auerstadt's home was not so much a house as a château, he could hardly have fully taken in the reality of Bellozanne.[1]

Figure 23: Bellozane, home of Madeleine de Brauer's family in Normandy; postcard.

On 5 September 1956 Madeleine collected John from the boat at Le Havre in a Simca sedan, and drove him down past Rouen towards Gournay-en-Bray, before turning into the entrance to Bellozanne: two four-storey towers rose on the ends of a three-storey mansion, seven stately windows across. To the east was a set of buildings, three sides around a square, several times larger than the main house. To the west were outbuildings for horses, cattle and the general necessities of a great estate. It was a lot to reckon with.

In his diary entries published in *Poetry* (Chicago) in December 1956, Montague admits that it was hard at first to keep track of all the members of the de Brauer family. There were four generations present to greet him, the youngest eight years old, the oldest eighty.[2] The afternoon meal was five courses, served over hours, with conversation about international affairs in Egypt, the Soviet Union, Ireland, England and America, led by Madeleine's mother.

John was rescued by Brigitte, Madeleine's young niece, who took him to see the horses and the rabbit hutches, where fifty rabbits were being fattened for the table. A multitude, everywhere.

And it was his plan to bring the daughter of this estate to live in Dublin! He was worried.[3]

At the wedding ceremony on 18 October, when it came to the moment of truth, Montague was stricken by his stammer. He could not get the little word *oui* out of his mouth. '*Dites yes. C'est la même chose,*' the charming old Abbé Looten whispered, and John escaped the difficulty.[4]

Figure 24: Wedding photograph, 18 October 1956; John Montague, Madeleine de Brauer Montague and in the background Madeleine's father, Léopold de Brauer. After the ceremony, Madeleine remarked, 'How strange to be called Madeleine Montague.' 'My poor girl,' John replied, 'it is almost as bad as Malachy Mulligan.'

In fact, so far as his stammer was concerned, marriage meant a new day for Montague. The assurance of Madeleine's love proved to be the best remedy yet for his performance anxiety. The stammer never went away entirely, but it grew less wild, malevolent and dominating. It was half-tamed, like a troublesome household pet.

For a honeymoon, the couple returned to their custom of literary tourism and spent two weeks in Normandy visiting the birthplaces of Flaubert, Proust and Gide. Montague's habit of mind was to turn towards the scenes of childhood in order to locate the springs of creativity. Illiers-Combray (Proust's 'Balbec') was, he thought, a poor enough town, though not so poor as Garvaghey, nor so plain as Fintona, but, still, 'one must use what one can'.[5] He must of necessity settle back into his own life. While at Illiers-Combray, the pair drew up a list of possible names for their first child, should it be a boy.[6]

Montague had been writing every day since leaving California – the travelogue for *Poetry*, journal entries and drafts of poems, one about ghost soldiers in the mists of Normandy, another inspired by Irish emigrants boarding the boat at Cobh,[7] and a third triggered by 'the red alcoholised faces' of Dubliners. He had always been a – 'graphomaniac' is not the right word, because his drive to articulate was a cure, not an illness – but perhaps 'scriptophile' fits, a person who liked to get things right by means of words. It was as if he wished never to lose a thought. Whenever he opened his notebook, he left a trace.

Yet to establish himself as what he was, Montague realized he must publish, and to publish he had to finish drafts and send poems out to editors. Madeleine was a help in keeping him to this resolution. She drew up a ledger with something like double-entry book-keeping, to record what titles he had sent out, when, to whom and what the result had been. On 18 October, before the couple arrived in Ireland, *The Irish Times* printed 'Irish Street Scene, with Lovers', the poem Louis MacNeice had admired in Iowa and which Montague had first drafted in 1952. He was making a fresh start.

In Dublin the newlyweds booked into the Abbotsford Hotel at 72 Harcourt Street, with a view out the back windows of Iveagh Gardens. They lodged there in the first week of November while searching for a place to let. The news in the hotel lobby was all about the Hungarian Revolution, a week in progress when the Montagues came to Dublin. On 4 November the Soviets invaded to suppress the move to self-determination. At the same time, Anthony Eden was attempting to deal with a crisis in the Suez.[8] These events fed into verse:

Honeymoon

I heard of the Hungarian Revolution
in a hotel in Harcourt Street –
The Abbotsford, after Walter Scott.
I had just returned to Ireland

Driving from the cobbled docks
in an atrophied Ford V-8
with my French wife who stared
at the gulls sliding down from the sky

Every hour the lounge was crowded
to hear the latest communique from Suez
or Budapest, strident voices
of uncertainty, as pitiless [as] history

Sunday we escaped to walk
the Howth cliffs. But nightmare
pursued, the spectrum reduced
to mournful reds and blacks

the sea a melancholy track
to march upon. All conquering
love seemed nowhere
near, only a herring gull

pointing a way to new,
frail possibilities –
of truth, of deception?
where we skirted

a chaos of fiercely
demanding water, gnawed rocks,
to emerge, like accomplices,
raw-eyed, hands tightly joined.

With its European armies, sea of history and lovers on the brink, Matthew Arnold's 'Dover Beach' lies behind the poem, but the voice is not that of Arnold. It is not 'in the English grain', or the American either. The short shuttle of quatrains, the descriptive reportage and ease of speech take the verse farther from elaborations of Auden and Lowell and a step in the direction of Montague's own contemporary European idiom. Thanks were due to William Carlos Williams.

Montague did not, however, realize that this was his opening and for several years kept writing poems in an urbanely ironic, formally tight and syntactically elaborate manner, from the W.H. Auden school of cultural commentary.

2

They found a basement flat at 6 Herbert Street, down the road from the Pepper Canister Church on Upper Mount Street, just to the west of the Grand Canal. The family residence of Walter and Bettie Doyle-Kelly, it was a five-storey red-brick house, built in the early nineteenth century. The basement flat had just one main room, where the couple 'ate, read, worked and slept'.[9] There was a small back bedroom, which they imagined could one day serve as a nursery. In the meantime, it was fitted out with a bed for guests.

Figure 25: 6 Herbert Street, Dublin; entry to basement flat.

In the 1950s 'Baggotonia' was taking shape as Dublin's bohemia, and John and Madeleine had moved to the heart of it. The area east of St Stephen's Green and Government Buildings was stocked with Georgian houses, broken into flats. The rents of basements, attics and carriage houses to the rear were affordable.[10]

The country's writers, artists and publishers were concentrated within a few blocks of one another:

> Patrick Kavanagh, writer, 62 Pembroke Road
>
> Thomas Kinsella, poet, Percy Place, adjacent to the Grand Canal
>
> Garech Browne, founder, Claddagh Records, Quinn's Lane, mews attachment off Pembroke Road
>
> Brendan Behan, writer, 15 Herbert Street
>
> John Montague, poet, 6 Herbert Street
>
> Alan Simpson and Carolyn Swift, directors, Pike Theatre, Herbert Lane
>
> Patrick Funge and Jo McGrath, Lantern Theatre, 127 Lower Baggot Street
>
> Leland Bardwell, writer, 33 Lower Leeson Street
>
> Hayden Murphy, editor, *Broadsheet*, 10 Herbert Lane
>
> Patrick Scott, painter, 30 Upper Mount Street
>
> Liam Miller, editor, The Dolmen Press, 94 Lower Baggot Street
>
> The Dolmen Press, 23 Upper Mount Street
>
> Camille Souter, painter, 37 Upper Mount Street
>
> Patrick and Elizabeth Hickey, Design Studio, 21 Upper Mount Street
>
> Patrick Pye, painter, 41 Upper Mount Street
>
> Bord Fáilte (Montague worked there), or Fógra Fáilte, Mount Street Crescent
>
> Patrick Kavanagh, in the last years of his life, canal end of Upper Mount St, along with Leland Bardwell, writer
>
> Leslie MacWeeney, painter, 11 Mount Street
>
> Richard Murphy, 11 Upper Mount Street

Figure 26: 'Baggotonia', from 'Atlas of Georgian Dublin'. The 'x' midway up on the right is at the top of Herbert Street; Merrion Square is top centre; Trinity College is at the top left; St Stephen's Green bottom left.

John and Madeleine would soon run into many of these characters. The first they encountered was Brendan Behan, their neighbour at 15 Herbert Street. Introduced to the bride, Behan asked if he might put a finger in her mouth:[11]

> 'Bite, daughter,' he cried, 'bite as hard as you can, on the knuckle.'
>
> A surprised Madeleine did as she was instructed, until Brendan's face whitened.
>
> 'Jaysus, girl, you're a fine specimen, and may you have fine children. But,' he continued, his eyes narrowing with mischief, 'do you know what you've gone and done? You've married an Ulsterman. A grand girl like yourself, you'd expect a bit of appreciation and affection. But all you'll get from one of that lot is a pair of cold feet in the bed.'

They both loved Brendan. You would go to him as to a play, the best you'd ever seen.

Within weeks, Montague met Liam Miller (1924–87), publisher of The Dolmen Press.[12] Miller was then employed as draughtsman in Vincent Kelly's architectural firm on Merrion Square, and in his spare time he was running his imprint out of a garage in Glenageary.[13] In 1957 he would leave his job in the architect's office and become a full-time publisher, with the printing works established in the basement of 23 Upper Mount Street, just 150 metres from Montague's residence on Herbert Street.

Ever since his childhood in Mountrath, County Laois, Miller had loved theatre and, second to theatre, books, not just reading them, but, while still in his teens, keeping a ledger of author, title, publisher, typeface and binding. He admired the Arts and Crafts style of Lily and Lolly Yeats at The Cuala Press (1908–46). In 1951, after starting work in Vincent Kelly's firm, he and his wife Jo decided they would teach themselves the printer's craft and design books of Irish poetry. His first was Sigerson Clifford's *Travelling Tinkers: A Book of Ballads*.

Soon Liam Miller began to collaborate regularly with Thomas Kinsella. By March 1952 he had designed, set and printed Kinsella's *The Starlit Eye*, followed by *Three Legendary Sonnets* (1952), *The Death of a Queen* (1956) and *Poems* (1956). These were artisanal books in small printings. However, when Montague first met Liam Miller, he was beginning to prepare a fully 'professional' collection by Kinsella, *Another September*.[14]

In 1955 Dolmen had also published Richard Murphy's *The Archaeology of Love* (two hundred copies) and a private printing of *Sailing to an Island* (thirty-five copies), paid for by Murphy's wife, Patricia Avis.

While away in America, Montague regarded Dublin, with its back-biting and hard-drinking literary community, as a graveyard for poets, but in his absence two intelligent young poets, Kinsella and Murphy, had surprisingly launched their careers there. Meanwhile, his own little boat was not yet seaworthy. This was disconcerting. He had thought his literary position in Ireland would have been strengthened by his American graduate studies, but he was faced with the fact that he had been left behind, particularly by Thomas Kinsella. A year later, after it was announced that *Another September* was the Poetry Book Society selection, Montague sent this statement of his position to Tom Parkinson:[15]

> Naturally I'm raving with jealousy [about Kinsella's prize], but smile like a villain .... All that is left to me now is to plunge in and produce a book to pull the balls off the lot of them. My plan is to get Liam Miller working on a small book, about 18 poems, for the Autumn, while I circulate a larger mss among the English publishers, for Spring 1959 ....
>
> The ice is breaking in Ireland; I'm striving to be part of the new fleet; resistance [is] breaking down. Five years ago I had them all flat on their backs with my juvenile brilliance and wordy skill. Takes time to come back. Never go away is the moral, not physically, but in the literary sense. Keep your big dirty thumb in the pie.

In the books pages of *The Irish Times*, Montague was confronted with another rival. His UCD classmate Denis Donoghue had established himself as Ireland's critical arbiter of modern letters, a position that Montague thought would suit himself. Donoghue wrote his reviews emphatically as a professor, with contempt for un-academic standards. Yet some of his views seemed not just pompous but absurd. According to Donoghue, Yeats as a subject was dead; everything worth saying about him had already been said.[16] In another article, echoing an eccentric enthusiasm of Hugh Kenner's, Donoghue trumpeted Wyndham Lewis as one of the top two or three authors of the twentieth century.[17]

In 19 January 1957, not three months back in Ireland, Montague contributed a letter to the editorial page of *The Irish Times* that Denis Donoghue was unlikely to forgive or forget. The letter laughs at the professor's pedantry and points out mistakes of fact and judgement in Donoghue's review of *The Vanishing Hero* by Seán O'Faoláin. It concludes with a lesson in good manners: the UCD lecturer should not have been so high-handed with someone like O'Faoláin, who was, after all, 'a practitioner of the art he is discussing'.[18] Donoghue was proud and lofty and judged literature by the highest Eliotic standards. He looked down on all but all writers. He certainly did not see a practitioner, *per se*, as his equal, much less his superior. This was an upsetting letter for him to read, knowing that all Dublin was reading it too.

A few days before this letter was published, Montague went to a party hosted by the Irish-American poet Ned O'Gorman. Donald Davie, then a lecturer at Trinity, was among the guests. Montague respected *Purity of Diction in English Verse* (1952) and *Articulate Energy* (1955), and he wanted to get to know their author. At the party, the two gossiped about Hugh Kenner (already alert to Montague's work, according to Davie). Montague offered to help Davie get his own poems read by the editor of *Poetry* (Chicago). Davie longed for American recognition. Right after the party, a warm letter from the TCD lecturer arrived at 6 Herbert Street. But Montague then learned that Davie was best friends with Denis Donoghue. Whoops! Once Davie had seen the 'master job of butchery' in *The Irish Times*, Montague guessed that the two of them would not have 'social relations in the future'.[19] He was right about that.

At a stroke, Montague had made two powerful enemies. Donoghue would before long be the Professor of English at UCD, in charge of who got jobs there. Davie was the most active (and sharp-tongued) reviewer of poetry in the British newspapers, where one day Montague's *Poisoned Lands* would fall into his hands.

3

Montague's job at Bord Fáilte Éireann began in January 1957. He was paid £750 a year (about €22,000 in 2022). He was fortunate in his boss, Niall Sheridan (1912–98). In the 1930s Sheridan was the classmate and friend of Brian O'Nolan, Denis Devlin, Donagh MacDonagh and other UCD bright sparks. He is the original of the character Brinsley, the narrator's interlocutor and drinking partner in *At Swim-Two-Birds*.

Under Niall Sheridan's administration, work got done, but 'it took its own sweet pace'.[20] Sheridan had a column in *The Irish Times* offering tips on horse races. When the bell sounded and the horses were off, the staff in the tourist board gathered around a radio. It was a point of honour and dignity in the Ireland of that time to accept that drink and horses were matters of the highest importance. If you didn't accept that, there was something wrong with you.

The job in the publicity department required Montague to fill in occasionally at ceremonial events that Niall Sheridan could not be bothered to attend, where a bishop or sometimes even a cardinal made the opening speech and a minister or Dáil deputy made another. He also got the chance to accompany a delegation of French journalists visiting Galway.[21] And when Tom Parkinson came to Ireland, with a commission to do an article about Ireland for *The Nation*, Montague was his guide. They were in Newry just a day after the IRA bombed its post office and bus station:[22]

> It is a salutary experience now and again, to see one's country through the eyes of a reasonable foreigner. I had fought hard all week to present [to Tom Parkinson] an image of the new Lemass Ireland, reasonable, hard-working, anxious to take its place among the responsible nations of the world. But Ireland kept letting me down: whenever we entered a pub the inhabitants seemed to burst into song, chair legs were splintered, and police walked in. We were arrested in Newry as IRA men, and nearly stripped at the border by Customs. And everywhere we went we met Brendan Behan, who greeted us with cries of 'Americans, Go Home.'

However, taking old friends round the country was not Montague's daily duty. His regular work was to update the *Ireland Guide*. He found it tedious.

Elizabeth Healy, later editor of *Ireland of the Welcomes* (the Bord Fáilte magazine), recalled that in the eyes of the other staff, Montague appeared to be a very European, cosmopolitan character. She herself was 'younger than her age, raw, callow'. 'He teased me mercilessly, but he was never cruel. We got to get along.'[23] When Montague published his story about Bord Fáilte in *Death of a Chieftain*, she and all the other staff were tickled pink – it said everything that they themselves dared not say about the place.

The job did sometimes affect his work as a poet. It encouraged him to see Ireland from an outsider's point of view and to pictorialize it. On occasion, he turned research for the tourist board into holidays with Madeleine. They visited Achill Island, the coast of Kerry and the lakes of Killarney. These resulted in poems, but some of them – like 'Kenmare Bay' and 'A Footnote on Monasticism' in *Poisoned Lands* – are patently the verses of a visitor and inhabit the genre of the picturesque.[24] Seamus Heaney, perhaps ill-advisedly influenced, would himself be led astray to publish work of this kind in his first two collections, as if on a retainer from an Irish heritage society.

4

In 1958 a string of house guests made use of the back bedroom at 6 Herbert Street. Nelson Algren (1909–81) came to take the measure of Dublin in March. Algren's usual beat was the streets of Chicago. His novel about a heroin addict, *The Man with the Golden Arm*, won the National Book Award in 1949 and, like *Walk on the Wild Side* (1956), was made into a successful film. John and Madeleine had read *The Mandarins*, Simone de Beauvoir's novel featuring her affair with Algren, and they looked forward to meeting the original man himself.

When Algren showed up on the steps, Montague pretended to know nothing about the invitation. Algren's subsequent account in *Who Lost an American* (1960) captures Montague's 'fly' Ulster irony:[25] 'We don't want your Coca-Cola culture around here. Go away.'

'Let him in, John', Mrs Montague suggested; 'A button is missing on his waistcoat.'

'Can you sew in a doorway?' Mr Montague asked her.

'We won't be able to warm up the house for half an hour,' she pointed out.

'Won't you come in?' Mr Montague invited me.

Montague then brought Algren off to McDaid's to meet Ireland's 'poet of the way it happened and the way it is', Patrick Kavanagh. As a topic of conversation, Algren mentioned a recent book on depopulation in Ireland. 'A sad thing to think that the Irish are vanishing.' 'Too good to be true,' Kavanagh retorted. Montague next took the Chicago novelist to meet Brendan Behan. On the way, Algren remarked, 'Say, that looks like a palm tree there.' His Bord Fáilte guide explained, 'That is because it *is* a palm tree.'

The conversation with Behan covered the topics of homosexuality, the border and national literature. Behan on sex: 'If a man is horrified by another's sins … it is because he is uneducated, inexperienced and a hypocrite. Certain things must be restrained in the world for our convenience – but for convenience only. Why can't we let it go at that?'

On the border: 'We've been banjaxed,' Montague said. 'Fughed,' Behan explained, 'from a height.'

On national literature: 'The first duty of a writer is to let his country down. He knows his own people best. He has a special responsibility to let them down.'

In late September 1958 John and Madeleine welcomed Clancy Sigal and Doris Lessing to their small back bedroom. Sigal was a Marxist from Los Angeles and boyhood friend of Donald Fanger. Aiming to become an author, he had come to London and wound up in a tempestuous affair with Doris Lessing at 58 Warwick Road. That relationship would be dramatized in Lessing's classic novel *The Golden Notebook* (1962). 'Saul Green' (Clancy Sigal) is a faithless American rascal, but the heroine Anna is finished with Englishmen. They are 'rude to their wives, unable to give pleasure, bullying, selfish, indifferent to their children, eager to marry a young secretary', not real men at all.[26] With Clancy, the sex was fierce.

Madeleine and John brought the Leftist pair to James Plunkett's suitably revolutionary *The Risen People* at the Abbey Theatre. The next stop was a genuinely proletarian writer and ex-convict too, Brendan Behan. Behan and Lessing did not hit it off: she was always serious; he was usually joshing. The Dublin visit was not a rollicking success. Doris did not go in for a drunken bash in a pub and disapproved of the Irish life-is-a-joke attitude. From Dublin, the two couples went back to London together, where they attended the opening of Behan's *The Hostage* at the Royal, Stratford on 14 October 1958, a revolutionary play of a different kind. 'Appallingly lovely,' Montague reported; it was a stage version of that old-fashioned European bordello to which Behan had sent Montague in 1950.[27]

In December Donald and Margo Fanger, in London previous to a research trip to the Soviet Union, visited the Montagues for eight days over Christmas, 1958. By that time, John and Madeleine had received devastating news. When, after their marriage, months passed with no sign of a pregnancy, Madeleine consulted with medics. In her girlhood, she had had a burst appendix. Her father was then serving at the front in World War II and could not promptly give the parental consent necessary for surgery. The conclusion of the doctors in 1958 was that the result of that incident was the blocking of her fallopian tubes. It was unlikely that she would ever have a child.[28]

Upon receiving this frightful news, the couple retreated together to the small back bedroom once conceived as a future nursery. This is the unstated occasion for the poem 'That Room':[29]

> Side by side on the narrow bed
> We lay, like chained giants,
> Tasting each other's tears, in terror
> Of the news which left little to hide
> But our two faces that stared
> To ritual masks, absurd and flayed.
>
> Rarely in a lifetime comes such news
> Shafting knowledge straight to the heart
> Making shameless sorrow start –
> Not childish tears, querulously vain –
> But adult tears that hurt and harm,
> Seeping like acid to the bone.
>
> Sound of hooves on the midnight road
> Raised a romantic image to mind:
> The Dean riding late to Marley?
> But we must suffer the facts of self;
> No one endures another's fate
> And no one will ever know
>
> What happened in that room
> But when we came to leave
> We scrubbed each other's tears,
> Prepared the usual show. That day
> Love's claims made chains of time and place
> To bind us together more: equal in adversity.

5

They had to rethink their future. What were their prospects? Madeleine had been studying for her *agrégation*, the competitive examination for the French civil service, but had failed twice. Meanwhile, she was highly esteemed in her job at the French embassy in Dublin. She clearly had organizational and diplomatic gifts and could succeed in many spheres. (For Montague, it was live or die in just one, literature.)

Life in Dublin – especially the pub culture – held little attraction for Madeleine. She did enjoy the company of the remnants of Ireland's aristocracy, like John Godley, Lord Kilbracken and the Honourable Garech Browne, as well as its new elite, such as Michael Scott (architect) and Dorothy Walker (art critic). Todd Andrews, a leading public figure, respected Madeleine and confided in her. But, all things considered, she preferred Paris and the proximity of her extended family.

John had begun reading towards a doctoral dissertation on Oliver Goldsmith for Professor J.J. Hogan at UCD. His chief aspiration, however, was to be a poet and fiction writer. He regarded his Bord Fáilte work as an annoying distraction from his poetry, scholarship and literary journalism.

It was decided between the pair of them that John should in time leave Bord Fáilte and then finish the dissertation; six months of work should do it.[30] With a PhD, he would be able to apply for university posts, whether in Ireland, France or the USA. The degree would enable them as a couple to move freely in the world. Yes, it was true, as John wrote:[31]

> Some who travel light
> May feel deprived
> Of all the love that weighs
> On other people's lives

but if, regrettably, they were not to have children, they should take advantage of not being tied down. If John really did wish to make the most of his gifts as a writer, then let him do just that. Eventually, they could get a place to live in Paris, where Madeleine could find a proper job. She would support him, if his royalties as an author fell short.[32] She offered him his liberty to become what he was, in an act of belief in him.

6

A diversion from these grave matters occurred on 19 February 1959. Madeleine went along with Garech Browne (1939–2018) to the Sibyl Connolly fashion show on Merrion Square.

Garech was the first-born son of the 4th Baron Oranmore and Browne (of Castle Macgarrett, County Galway) and his second wife, Oonagh, daughter of Ernest Guinness. He was a young scamp, intelligent but wild. He had run away at age fourteen from his Swiss boarding school by forging a telegram from his mother, requesting, on account of an emergency, his immediate return home. Lately, he had discovered a passion for being Irish, particularly for traditional music, and hand-woven tweeds too (these passions lasted to the end of his life). He became a popular subject for news items about the eccentricities of the former Ascendancy. Most recently, he had made headlines by running off with the eighteen-year-old 'raven-haired daughter of a forest worker in Roundwood', working as second housemaid in Luggala, the eighteenth-century Guinness hunting lodge in County Wicklow.[33]

At the fashion show, a *Daily Express* reporter mistook Madeleine for that second housemaid of Luggala. When a photographer closed in, Garech tried to flee and wrapped Madeleine's stole over his face, but one hack tore it away while another took a photograph. It was celebrity harassment, aimed at a junior member of the Protestant Ascendancy.

The experience was horrible, but Montague was delighted. Here was material for a libel suit, the Irish writer's classic chance to strike it rich. All Madeleine had to do was testify to being herself, Madeleine de Brauer, never a pantry maid from Roundwood, County Wicklow, but the granddaughter of the Duke of Auerstaedt, Bellozanne, Normandy. Montague could then take the stand as the indignant Catholic husband – his wife was no Guinness hussy.[34]

Before this courtroom drama could be enacted, a difficulty arose. Lord Kilbracken, friend of both the Montagues and Garech Browne, was at work on a long piece for the *Daily Express* about the Soviet Union, entitled 'A Peer behind the Iron Curtain'. Bankrupting the paper was not in his interest. He and John had a row. In the end, the Montagues agreed to settle for a relatively small amount.

With their winnings, Madeleine (the only driver in the family) bought 'a glossy new Ford Prefect'. For his part, John invested in starting a company with Garech Browne, Claddagh Records; he bought fifty one-pound shares.[35] Garech and his brother Tara had been travelling around the country with a tape recorder, looking for the best traditional musicians. John's own interest was in the spoken word. He hoped to make records of Kavanagh and Austin Clarke reading their poetry.

The launch of Claddagh Records took place on 12 December 1959 in Garech's converted coach house in Quinn's Lane, off Pembroke Road. The first record was of Leo Rowsome on the Uileann pipes. Among the guests were Margaret Barry (Traveller and traditional singer), Brendan Behan, Michael O'Gorman from Bord Fáilte, and 'Quidnunc' (Seamus O'Kelly) of *The Irish Times*.[36] It was a proper hosting of the forces in Baggotonia of traditional music, contemporary poetry, Wildean wit, Anglo-Irish patronage, state-sponsored bodies and high-class arts journalism.

A few weeks later, some in this crowd gathered again in Wicklow for Christmas at Luggala. Lord Kilbracken, Claud Cockburn and Peter O'Toole joined the house party.[37] Festivities were broken up on the night of Christmas Eve when Miguel Ferreras Aciro, Oonagh Guinness's new husband, fell upon Brendan Behan, out in the courtyard, drunk and singing 'Adeste Fideles'. From an upstairs window, John saw Brendan lying on the ground and Miguel kicking him. He ran downstairs to intercede. Miguel gave as his reason for the attack that Brendan was a queer and a paedophile. That was partly true (he enjoyed sex with women too), but no secret. Brendan nonetheless was often invited to Luggala as a prized house guest. It is possible that Miguel, a violent man, was triggered by Brendan's warning that if he did not treat Oonagh well, the IRA would come after him.[38]

'A curious contrast to quiet scholarly activities,' Montague reported to Tim O'Keeffe, his editor at MacGibbon and Kee.[39]

7

In early 1958 Madeleine was at work in the commercial counsellor's office of the French embassy when a tall man entered and asked for her help in translating a letter. It was written on artist's paper and signed with little stars: 'Jean Cocteau'. The French artist wished to thank the addressee, Morris Graves, for using the Duchess of Windsor as an intermediary in introducing Cocteau to the American poet Theodore Roethke, of whom 'dear Auden' had so often spoken. What a constellation of glittering names![40] This was someone her husband would surely want to meet.

Morris Graves (1910–2001) was a celebrated American painter from the Pacific Northwest, a Modernist mystic, his fame in the USA preceding that of the Abstract Expressionists. Graves remembered, he said, hearing of the poet Montague from his Seattle friends, the poets Roethke and David Wagoner.[41] Before long, John and Madeleine, and Morris and his companion Richard Svare, were regularly in one another's company.

For the past few years, Morris Graves had been living in the West of Ireland, but in September 1958 he bought Woodtown Manor for £2,000 [approx. €50,000 in 2022 money].[42] This was an early eighteenth-century, seven-bay country house on twenty-three acres in the hills above Dublin. It was a bargain but a wreck. A crew of twelve men were hired to replace the roof, plumbing and heating, dig ponds, wall them in stone, channel water courses to make a gurgling music and build up terraced gardens. Graves put his genius and wealth into making beautiful homes.

Morris Graves's friend Nancy Wilson describes her first impression of the interior when the work was done:[43]

> I stood in the drawing room doorway and saw the utter inspired magic of the far end of the room; those painted and scratched grey-green-brown-blue ovals in the centres of the shallow recesses beside the bay; the sharp beautiful surprise and focus of that amazing wooden headdress (African) with its muted cerise, orange black and blue steps; the firm silhouette of the man and horse; the Chinese sage; the smell of the bowl of apples and the burning peat ... This is truly an inspired creation.

John and Madeleine were regular guests, as were Ricki and John Huston, the Hollywood director.[44] After Madeleine's father Léopold died, her mother Marguerite came visiting, and Morris had a tea party for them all.

Over the Christmas holidays in 1959, while Morris and Richard were in New York for an exhibition of paintings, the Montagues moved into Woodtown Manor. John was supposed to be at work on his Goldsmith dissertation, but he put the better part of himself into a lyric appreciation of Woodtown Manor and of the Zen-like aesthetic of Morris Graves, who loved to draw and paint just such small birds and creatures as are named in the poem:[45]

> Here the delicate dance of silence,
> The quick step of the robin,

The sudden skittering rush of the wren:
Minute essences move in and out of creation
Until the skin of soundlessness forms again.

Part order, part wilderness,
Water creates its cadenced illusion
Of glaucous, fluent growth;
Fins raised, as in a waking dream,
Bright fish probe their painted stream.

Imaginary animals harbour here:
The young fox coiled in its covert,
Bright-eyed and mean, the baby bird:
The heron, like a radiant italic,
Illuminating the gospel of the absurd.

And all the menagerie of the living marvellous:
Stone shape of toad,
Flicker of insect life,
Shift of wind-touched grass
As though a beneficent spirit stirred.

II

Twin deities hover in Irish air
Reconciling poles of east and west;
The detached and sensual Indian God,
Franciscan dream of gentleness:
Gravity of Georgian manor
Approves, with classic stare,
Their dual disciplines of tenderness.

Madeleine reported on the situation to Tom Parkinson. The letter is characteristic of her writing – nearly every sentence has its chuckle of intelligent humour:[46]

> Now John has a great desire to write to you. But he is very long about these things and has to make spiritual preparations. So I thought I would write first to send you the most ardent love the American Post Office can bear ....

We spent three weeks in Morris Graves's Manor, magnificent, spacious, silent, just before winter came. He came back (from the States, as I expect you know) just in time to save me from commuting on a sleigh. His America sounded brilliant, anxious and glittering. John felt very provincial and a bit downcast. But I, brought up as you know along lean Spartan lines, taught from the cradle never to complain, told him like a Victorian Governess that by the time he was Morris's age he might deserve all the glory.

With luck and D.V. [*deo volente*, 'God willing'] by the end of this month, John will be at mid-thesis. Also a new book of poems must be stacked in typescript ....

There have been Poetry Readings, at which Mrs Yeats Junior played the harp and sang shrilly during the intervals. John was very brilliant ... at any rate, that's what most people thought, and he first among them. But I can't decently blow his trumpet, if you see what I mean (this quite virtuously, and none of your dirty double-entendre).

8

Once back in Ireland, Montague got in touch with his old UCD contemporaries. In October 1957 Pearse Hutchinson visited 6 Herbert Street and left carrying a number of books from Montague's library – *Under the Volcano*, *Howl*, *Nausea* and collections of poetry by Philip Larkin and Edwin Muir. Montague noted the loan (to his distress, the Malcolm Lowry novel was often recalled but never returned).[47]

Certain books were more than texts for Montague and more than mementos too: he wrote in them and used them as file folders for letters, clippings and drafts. They are the chief organizational unit in his archive. After Hutchinson died in 2012, John tried to find out if his *Under the Volcano* was hidden among the possessions of the deceased.

When Madeleine's father died in December 1957 and she was away in France, Montague hit the pubs with Hutchinson and Behan. One night after closing time (10.30 pm), Hutchinson borrowed money from Montague to buy carry-away bottles of stout; then, living it up on Montague's banknote, hailed a taxi to go to Behan's house:[48] At 4 am Mrs Behan finally chased them out. John described the aftermath in a letter to Parkinson: 'Pearse soddenly grumbled and began fumbling for the remaining bottles. 'Leave us a few for the morning in the name of Jesus,' says Brendan.

'But I paid for them,' says Pearse. Altercation; Pearse breaks bottles on the wall, spattering the Behan mansion with dung brown porter stains.

'In the name of Jaysus,' says Brendan, 'I had to puck him one in the mouth. He stood there cursing so I shoved him out (*oratio obliquy Brendanibus*) and he still cursed so I came out with me hand out, to apologise, and he reached out, so I pucked him good and hard in the teeth: an old trick.'

Sodden Pearse, riveted in blood, falls on Herbert Street.'

It is like a page out of Anthony Cronin's *Life of Riley* (1964) or *Dead as Doornails* (1976) – drunken male mayhem in the city of Dublin.

Tony Cronin was not in Dublin when Montague returned from America. He became literary editor at *Time and Tide* (1956–58). In Chelsea, he fell in with the hard-drinking bohemian set around George Barker, including Elizabeth Smart, Patrick Swift and David Wright. The group started a journal entitled *X*. Cronin (under the pseudonym 'Martin Gerard') provided its literary commentary. He promised to be honest, which turned out to mean brutal, intelligent and with a sharp eye for his subjects' weak spots. In the second issue, Cronin's 'A Child's Guide to Two Decades' is borne onward on a tide of apparent hatred for the persons representing the Movement, Confessionalism and University Dons; that is, every poet within sight except his friends in *X*, plus Patrick Kavanagh.[49]

Montague, after meeting David Wright in Dublin, submitted a half-dozen of the best poems from *Poisoned Lands* for publication in *X*. Not one was taken. A disappointment. When asked by Tim O'Keeffe if Cronin was a 'friend' of his, Montague replied: 'I couldn't say whether friend or enemy, and I don't especially care. Behind the opinions and the malevolence, he's a pretty dull mind and has very little real writing ability, except in destruction. I imagine I'll be "a friend" of his if I become known.'[50] Ouch! 'Formorian fierceness of family and local feud' was not confined to the hinterland of County Tyrone.

The first few years Montague was back in Dublin, John Jordan (another college classmate) was still living in Oxford; he returned to an Assistant Lecturer post at UCD only in September 1959.[51] Earlier Montague crossed paths (and swords) with Denis Donoghue, still doing doctoral work at UCD.

A year and a half after Montague's *Irish Times* January 1957 letter of correction, Donoghue, still smarting, brought up the subject on the same editorial page. A controversy had sprung up after Donoghue declared at the UCD Summer School that it was important to study the works of Yeats and Joyce, because, except for those two, modern Irish literature was 'virtually dead'.[52] People like Synge, George Moore and AE never mattered; on the present scene there was no one, the UCD lecturer announced.

Some still-surviving writers, including Monk Gibbon and Patrick Kavanagh, wrote in protest. Donoghue then explained that a newspaper was no place to debate important literary questions. For instance, although John Montague had previously queried his claim that Joseph Conrad influenced William Faulkner, when Donoghue had later come across a book by an American academic that bore out this claim, he decided to let the matter pass, because *The Irish Times* was not the proper medium for such a discussion. (This is a classic example of the rhetorical figure *occupatio*, deliberate talk of a subject you say you cannot talk about and, to top it off, in the very newspaper in which you say you cannot talk about it.)

Donoghue evidently meant that it would be best to hash out his differences over Faulkner's style privately with Montague or in an academic journal. Instead, the conflict was continued in open air. On 12 February 1960 a poetry reading was held in the Eblana Theatre. One hundred and eighty people showed up to listen to Máire Mhac an tSaoi, Patrick Galvin and Montague recite their work. Two days later at the same venue, there was a discussion of modern Irish poetry, featuring Denis Donoghue, Father Burke-Savage, A.J. Leventhal and Donagh MacDonagh (co-editor of *The Oxford Book of Irish Verse*).[53] Was Irish literature 'virtually dead'? The notes in Montague's diary about this event may record what he said on the occasion, or simply what he wished he had said: 'Argument with Denis ... I might respectfully say that Kenner, Davie and yourself – three super-academics – might not be the best judges of contemporary poets.' Those three scholars rated Charles Tomlinson as the top contemporary poet in the English language. Montague himself thought Tomlinson's poems, while estimable, appealed only to the literary-minded; he felt no warmth in them.

Montague preferred, he explained, writers like W.D. Snodgrass, who turn their attentions to 'this pain that is more than I can say'. Who were those writers?

In rank order, 1. Lowell, 2. Snodgrass, 3. Kinsella, 4. Larkin. And as for the T.S. Eliot version of modernism, which meant the rejection of contemporary life – a view shared by Tomlinson, Montague did not believe that any longer. Literary modernism was not necessarily anti-modernization. 'My approach: not to refuse experience, but to face it … As [D.H.] Lawrence did.'[54] 'I take my *Tao* from whom I can,' and at present, he was inspired by the life and art of Morris Graves.[55]

Yet Montague treated Denis Donoghue respectfully. Their dialogue, he told Denis was for him, and he hoped for Denis too, 'helpful, not destructive'.[56] In June he sent him a group of new poems and later warmly thanked the UCD lecturer for his observations.[57]

9

The Dolmen Press published Montague's *Forms of Exile*, a collection of twenty-four poems, in January 1959. Most of these were written while in America, or earlier. The title was intended to be pluri-significative: 'Exile from Ireland, from God and belief, from everything, only the art work shapes the continued sense of nothingness.'[58]

No reviewer pondered it in such terms. His UCD classmates Pearse Hutchinson and John Jordan each offered faint praise; John Hewitt a cautiously judicious welcome.[59] The most sensible response the book received was in a letter from his Yale friend Leonora Leet. 'Soliloquy on a Southern Strand' was, she said, 'truly great', and she was won over by 'The Sean Bhean Bhocht', but many of the others she did not like:[60]

> 'Nursery Story' has a great opening but then the poem deteriorates into stereotyped poetic superiority. I became convinced of something … a feeling of exile is not a viable emotional attitude from which to produce poetry. For I think you succeed not when you are feeling exiled but only when you are warmed by sympathy, even if it is the sympathy for another exiled being (as in 'Soliloquy'). I think you generally fail when you are speaking in your own voice. Then you become the self-conscious, sensitive, superior poetic type and the poetry assumes an adolescent tone.

Severe criticism, but, Montague realized, from a perceptive friend. He would learn from it.

Montague's poetry caught a fresh breeze when, as an offshoot of her Lyric Theatre Company in Belfast, Mary O'Malley started a new literary magazine, *Threshold*. Mary was an advocate of Yeats and of poets' theatre in general.[61] Roger McHugh suggested that she recruit Montague for her journal.[62] He promptly offered non-fiction prose, a short story and poems. His report on the Irish national election of March 1957 appeared in the second issue. The snapshot of de Valera came close to the edge of what was acceptable:[63] '[O]ld men, perhaps veterans, gazed in rapture at their old leader, a gaunt, stiff-backed sacerdotal figure …. The bony face, the dry, quiet voice wove their spell over the enormous crowd; but the question remains, can such a shrewd master of political tactics really believe in the antique Carlylean dream he proposes as an ideal from every platform?'

Sometimes, in Mary O'Malley's view, Montague even went beyond what it was prudent to publish. She cut this descriptive bit from the picture of 'Dev': 'beak-nosed and nearly bald: a sacerdotal heron'. Montague was sore about the censorship but delighted that in Northern Ireland there had come to be an outlet for contemporary writing. In August Mary O'Malley enrolled him as a literary advisor to the magazine. Could he get Kinsella to submit poems? Bumping into the poetry-writing civil servant on Baggot Street, Montague did just that. He also got his friends Tom Parkinson and Pearse Hutchinson to contribute to the third issue. He persuaded people to subscribe and made gifts of subscriptions to friends and family. He held forth at a fund-raiser at the Shelbourne Hotel.[64] In the long term, he planned to buck up *Threshold*'s poetry editor, John Hewitt, by undertaking a serious critical appreciation of Hewitt's decades of generally unnoticed work.[65]

When Montague had called on Mrs W.B. Yeats, she urged him 'to put a bomb' under people.[66] He was good at that. It was a Poundian gift, and not mere vanity, to gather 'from the air a live tradition'.[67] Montague always longed to be part of something bigger than himself.

Along with Austin Clarke and Laurence Lerner (Queen's University), Hewitt was a judge for the first May Morton Poetry Competition in 1960, with a prize of £50 (€1500 in 2022 currency). Literary competitions were a novelty in Ireland. There were 136 submissions. Montague placed his bet on a poem with a theme relevant to the North.

On his return to Garvaghey after being abroad, Montague had begun work on a poem inspired by Minnie Kearney ('Maggie Owens'), the woman heavily wrapped in shawls who lived up in the hills along with her dogs and a goat, and would, when as a boy he brought her mail, and romances to read, tell him stories of the faeries.[68] Only the title of the poem, 'The Sean Bhean Bhocht' (Poor Old Woman), suggested he was seeing her as an archetype. Otherwise, it is descriptive of a particular person, someone who I well as imposed herself on his imagination. 'My feeling is for the weak,' he had correctly realized, when trying to identify for himself the nature of his talent.[69] It may be that she is a stand-in for Brigid and Freda Montague, the aunts who raised him, childless older women, who lived on their own, without husbands.

He was proud of the accomplishment. It just missed being the last poem included in Lennox Robinson and Donagh MacDonagh's *The Oxford Book of Irish Verse* (1958).[70]

Some unused lines in his drafts led him on to a fuller way of addressing his first world, a gallery of representative figures, 'Like Dolmens Round My Childhood'.[71] The characters were the real people of Ireland, for him the essence of the country, the faces in which he had first encountered it, but they were passing or had passed away, and with them, their way of life was lost, but he felt that, if ancient, they remained permanent parts of his being, and could no more go away than a dolmen could stride off over the horizon. They would always stand over him.

A main impulse of modern Irish poetry was culture shock, the result of late but then rapid modernization. It was inspired by the sudden change from a rural, sometimes Irish-speaking, usually folk-Catholic way of life, to something modern, educated, industrialized and town-centred. The young went off to university, and, after graduation, when they looked back, their origins had been transformed. The first world had vanished. The sickness of heart known as 'nostalgia' is central to poets like Seamus Heaney and John Montague.

The scholar Robin Skelton, after reading a draft of 'Like Dolmens ...', suggested adding the image of a 'man-trap', to indicate that Montague was a captive of his ancestry. No, Montague explained:[72] 'I harrow up my lineage, first because they haunt me, and to create a work of art is a form of exorcism: they become separated and permanent forms. Also, secondarily, a form of self-understanding. But no urge to escape .... The Presences for me are not a man-trap, but Fates, Inevitabilities.'

The key that connects the old people to the dolmens, things that pass away to things that are immemorial, is a specific culturally marked identity achieved over time. There are, in fact, among the megalithic remains of County Tyrone, few if any dolmens,[73] but the area has many circles of standing stones and a remarkable passage tomb on the top of Knockmany Hill (popularly understood to be sacred to the goddess Anya or Áine), overlooking the barony. Montague did experience a moment of vision after a climb up Knockmany, when he saw the Clogher Valley, all its little farms and its varied Neolithic monuments, as one single form of life, with a pre-Catholic spirit of place. By a personal rite of initiation, he felt himself to have been enlisted into the company of those who belonged there, a devotee of the ancient goddess of the mountain. Between the goddess Anya and Maggie Owens, he saw an essential connection. The quasi-religious aura of the experience is indicated by the hieratic solemnity of the verses.

Figure 27: 'Anya's Tomb', Knockmany Hill, County Tyrone. Photographer R. J. Welch; Ulster Museum postcard. The chambered tomb is now enclosed.

In April 1960 it was announced that 'Like Dolmens Round My Childhood' was the winner of the May Morton Memorial Prize, one of the rare times when Montague would come first in a literary competition (not a decisive matter; Joyce won no competitions in his lifetime). The poem proved to be a breakthrough into the 'lean parish of [his] art'.[74] On 22 May 1960 he went to Belfast to accept the prize and give a reading, televised on BBC Ulster. Afterwards, he boarded a bus to Garvaghey. Just as when he was in college, a bus ride opened up a vein of lyric meditation.[75]

> Poem, On the return to the Broad Road
> return to a destroyed rural culture
>
> Catching the bus at Smithfield
> Chilly, bright, that bleakness ...
>
> Only when I crossed into Tyrone
> That someone spoke to me:
> An ex-soldier talking of vice in Dungannon ...

His pen flowed on, page after page.

> All of life as the exile songs say
> Is saying farewell, but it is not every day
> One says goodbye to a way of life.

In these inklings, he had found his theme for a poetic sequence on an epic scale. 'Bleak' is identified as the key tone in the palette. He finds its beginning and end too: first, taking a bus; at last, trying to say goodbye to the place. From the start, he knew he would call it 'The Rough Field', an English translation of *Garvaghey*, from the Irish *Garbh Acaidh*. He thereafter went about the business carefully. Not for twelve years would he bring the book to a conclusion. Over time, history would come to inhabit the poem, especially 'the Troubles'.

10

For his second book, Montague found a London publisher: Tim O'Keeffe (1926–94), of MacGibbon and Kee – Doris Lessing's then publisher. Born in Kinsale, County Cork, though raised in England, O'Keeffe had a particular interest in Irish writers. In May 1959 he extended a hand to Brian O'Nolan ('Flann O'Brien'), offering to re-publish *At Swim-Two-Birds*, forgotten since its first 1939 printing.[76] That proving a success, he brought into print *The Poor Mouth* (in translation), *A Hard Life* and, posthumously, *The Third Policeman*. It is thanks to Tim O'Keeffe that Brian O'Nolan was first widely known as someone other than 'Myles na gCopaleen', the popular humourist in *The Irish Times*.

O'Keeffe liked Montague and was keen on his prospects. On 24 December 1960 he recommended the firm take him on, not just for *Poisoned Lands*, but for his career:[77]

> These are John Montague's poems which I think should be published. He comes via [the literary agent] AD Peters, to whom I sent him last year, and I gather that Nelson Algren has recommended the collection – Can we offer £75 on account of a flat 10%? Montague is shortly off to Paris to finish a collection of short stories (he had one in the recent Faber collection) and he is someone of great promise. Besides stories and a novel that he has worked at, he also has a scholarly study of Goldsmith which could be useful on the lit. crit. side of the list ... He's a quite brilliant character – the best academic record of his year at university – and I'd guess that Paris could put him right on his feet. He had a plummy job in Dublin but resigned it to write full-time. All the Irish pundits – Frank O'Connor, Behan, [Brian O'] Nolan, Iremonger – are behind him and he's got the kind of ambition that won't be content with being buttered up in Dublin ... I am sure that we will be getting a really solid body of work from him in the future.

Montague had had to give Liam Miller £40 to get *Forms of Exile* into print, while Tim O'Keeffe gave him an advance of £75. The amounts are not life-changing, but, as signals, they were important.

Key poems for the collection were written in the spring and summer of 1960, once he had written 'Like Dolmens Round My Childhood' and won the May Morton Prize. These included 'Woodtown Manor', 'Wild Sports of the West', 'Poisoned Lands', 'The Mummer Speaks', 'Auschwitz, Mon Amour' and his signature poem, 'The Water Carrier'. Some were clearly inspired by the new impulse to recover by means of art a lost or dying way of life in County Tyrone. The lyric territory covered is sometimes like that found in the early poetry of Patrick Kavanagh, but the views taken are politically edgy and stylistically self-conscious.[78] They are not the poems of a student in an American postgraduate writing programme, but they are those of someone who has come home from one.

Montague summarized his intentions for Jack Sweeney, the curator of the Poetry Library at Harvard University and a steady supporter:[79]

> As I plan the book, 'The Mummer Speaks' is supposed to preface the lot and define the purpose as 'a purging lament of bad times.' Release comes from accepting and even mocking ('Poisoned lands') the fact of evil, stylizing it so that it seems past and unreal ('Newsreel'), and turning towards the healing powers of art and love ('Woodtown Manor' and a few others). Thus, the whole book will be sculpted into themes but also part of a movement, ending in a series of [Robert] Gravesian satires (i.e., 'The First Invasion' & 'Regionalism') which have, I hope, the gaiety of complete amusement.

II

On 23 September 1961 Valentin Iremonger hosted the launch of *Poisoned Lands* at the Irish Embassy in Grosvenor Square, London. Anthony Burgess and Louis MacNeice were among the guests.[80] But, as far as Montague was concerned, these good auguries were swept aside the following Friday by Donald Davie's review in the *New Statesmen*:

> An Irishman who writes in English, who knows he is probably addressing more non-Irish readers than Irish ones, is tempted to use a tourist's eye, as I think John Montague does. In fact, he explicitly presents himself as *déraciné* from the Irish scenes he writes about. Fair enough. And he has his nostalgia well in check, holding the balance even between the gain and the loss of the uprooting. This means, though, that we see these Irish images through the clear but distancing and diminishing lens of some globe-trotting Guggenheim Scholar's Leica.

The slant is informed by Davie's inside knowledge – that Montague had been on a fellowship (Fulbright, not Guggenheim), worked at the Tourist Board and left his Irish publisher for an English one. The review covers the poems carried over from *Forms of Exile* (a member of the editorial board at Dolmen, Davie had examined these poems earlier), and ignores the new work in *Poisoned Lands* on the vanishing way of life in County Tyrone. That he should speak of Montague as explicitly declaring himself *déraciné* shows that he overlooked 'Like Dolmens Round My Childhood'. Perhaps Donald Davie didn't read the new book at all.

But Davie is also superior and cutting about each of the four collections he covers in this review; that was his nature. His main point, if snidely phrased, is similar to the fair-minded criticism from Leonora Leet of *Forms of Exile*.

Authors suffer when they get a poor review. Denis Donoghue was nettled by Montague's critique in *The Irish Times*. He was still writhing from the sting in his own letter to the editor six months later.[81] Yet Montague's torment from Davie's slight was over the top. He drafted at least three replies – one indignant about mistakes of fact, another elaborately ironic in its praise of Davie's talent for putting down Irishmen too big for their boots and a third that was unguardedly plaintive: 'Your review was the most unkind single incident that has happened to me since I started writing.'[82] Other reviews of *Poisoned Lands* followed in the autumn of 1961 and were generally positive, from Bernard Bergonzi in *The Guardian* ('excellent poet'), G.S. Fraser in *The Times Literary Supplement* ('impressive plain and sober honesty') and Robin Skelton in *Critical Quarterly* ('savage candour'). But all that Montague remembered of the book's reception is that first stinker from Donald Davie. It left him with a permanent impression that from the start he was never treated fairly in the English press.

6

THE DOLMEN MISCELLANY AND THE SECOND IRISH REVIVAL

I

According to Richard Murphy, it was at his suggestion, when he was living a few doors away at 11 Upper Mount Street, that Liam Miller should organize a group reading by the three young poets he published. A reading by just himself, Murphy suspected, would hardly raise a crowd.[1] Liam Miller had plenty of experience in putting on plays at the Abbey and Lantern theatres; he knew how to stage an event. He booked the ballroom of the Royal Hibernian, a grand old hotel, now demolished, that once stood on Dawson Street, opposite Molesworth Street.

Then Liam Miller obtained the co-sponsorship of the Irish Academy of Letters (founded by Yeats) and secured Peadar O'Donnell, former editor of *The Bell*, as chairman for the event. A well-designed invitation card was printed by the Dolmen Press in red and black and posted to a select audience of one hundred and fifty. The guest list was a kind of honour society: if on it, you belonged to Dublin's literary elite. A press release sent to the Dublin daily papers, accompanied by author photographs, included captions notifying the public that each of the poets had already won a major prize. It is always helpful in raising an Irish audience to have the stamp of international approval.[2] Liam Miller made it obvious that the whole thing was to be a classy event.

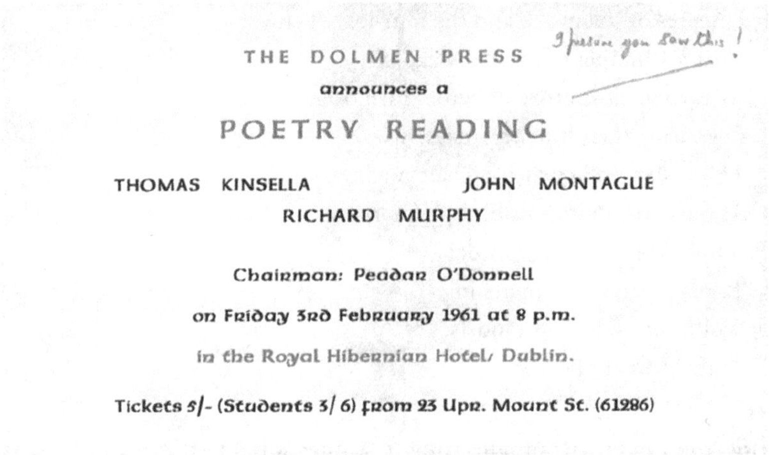

THE DOLMEN PRESS *I picture you saw this!*

announces a

POETRY READING

THOMAS KINSELLA JOHN MONTAGUE

RICHARD MURPHY

Chairman: Peadar O'Donnell

on Friday 3rd February 1961 at 8 p.m.

in the Royal Hibernian Hotel, Dublin.

Tickets 5/- (Students 3/6) from 23 Upr. Mount St. (61286)

Figure 28: Invitation to Royal Hibernian Hotel reading, designed by Liam Miller.

On the night of 3 February 1961, arriving at the hotel, the poets met a throng in the lobby. Three hundred chairs had been arrayed in the ballroom in a half-circle facing a platform. There was still not enough room, even standing room, for all those ready to pay five shillings to attend. More than a hundred were turned away. Kavanagh appeared in good time, came to the door of the ballroom, coughed loudly to make his presence known, then declined to enter.[3] Yet many from the older generation, including Padraic Colum, Donagh MacDonagh, Austin Clarke and Thomas MacGreevy, appeared delighted that something new was coming to pass. It was a field day for literary people.

Montague, haunted by the stammer, wanted to go first and get it over with. He had made a list of a dozen poems, all written since *Forms of Exile*, key breakthroughs into 'the lean parish of his art', like 'The Water Carrier' and 'The Mummer Speaks', poems that would soon come to mean so much to Seamus Heaney. He also read for the first time in public what would be a blazon for this trio of poets, 'Old Mythologies', published two weeks later in *The Times Literary Supplement*.[4]

> And now, at last, all proud deeds done,
> Mouths dust-stopped, dark they embrace,
> Suitably disposed, as urns, underground.
> Cattle munching soft spring grass —

Epicures of shamrock and the four-leaved clover –
Hear a whimper of ancient weapons,
As a whole dormitory of heroes turn over,
Regretting their butchers' days.
This valley cradles their archaic madness
As once, on an impossibly epic morning,
It upheld their savage stride:
To bagpiped battle marching,
Wolfhounds, lean as models,
At their urgent heels.

Drafting the poem, Montague sought 'a new sort of strictness & control: a measured sympathy, an iron jaw'.[5] That control is conveyed in the periodic first sentence, with the main clause delayed and several times suspended by punctuated apostrophes. It is the utterance of a highly cultivated person, cod-Yeatsian in its hieratic manner, arch and cheeky about the earlier generation of warriors, with those witty anachronisms – 'a whole dormitory of heroes' and 'Wolfhounds, lean as models' prankishly distancing himself from his legendary forerunners. The bloody-minded Gaelic ancestors are seen as at once ridiculous and glorious. This is the university-educated post-war intelligentsia slyly cocking a snook at the shamrock-and-four-leaf-clover clichés of the revolutionary generation.

A young Tom Kilroy heard in such poems the generational voice, after 'the slide of the population from the fields into the streets', so that few were what their fathers had been, or lived where they were born. An 'iron grille' had dropped between father and son. 'Social displacement is the common lot of the modern Irishman and his poet, the poet who most sensitively records this predicament, is John Montague.'[6]

After reading a few poems from his list, Montague 'got away as soon as possible' and left the stage to a stocky man in a suit, Thomas Kinsella, not yet wearing a beard. Kinsella was a great believer in his own genius. His unbroken, pre-Seamus Heaney string of victories in poetry competitions confirmed his opinion. By day, he was a senior civil servant employed in T.K. Whitaker's Department of Finance. The department's Programme for Economic Expansion in 1958 spelled the beginning of the end of de Valera's dream of rural Catholic autarky. The only way out of a situation in which 75 per cent of young Irish people had to emigrate, it argued, was for the government to seek foreign investment for industrial development.

Kinsella was the new style of Irishman foreseen by T.K. Whitaker, one who, as a newspaper noted, didn't drop anchor each afternoon in McDaid's pub but boarded an airplane with poems in his briefcase as he went to London to collect the Guinness Prize for Poetry.[7] For a yardstick of social change, recall that Kinsella's father and grandfather had worked at Guinness's. In the Royal Hibernian ballroom, Kinsella read the lengthy meditation 'A Country Walk' while himself walking up and down the platform with country calm.[8] Mary O'Malley, down from Belfast for the event, sensed from his confident performance that Kinsella was lengths out in front of his contemporaries.

Richard Murphy concluded the programme. He was born in Milford House in County Galway and grew up in Sri Lanka where his father was Mayor of Colombo. Murphy went to boarding school at Canterbury, then Wellington College, before attending Oxford University. At present he was living in a flat at 11 Upper Mount Street, Dublin, while shipwrights on Inishbofin restored his recently purchased *Ave Maria*, a Galway hooker built in the 1920s. Murphy represented himself in publicity stills wearing a white Aran sweater, the Connemara captain of the *Ave Maria*. Montague and Murphy were uneasy with each other. One had grown up in a Tyrone village but thought of himself as a Catholic chieftain; the other was born in an Anglo-Irish property but now presented himself as a native Irishman.

Murphy read, Montague recalled, for what seemed like hours. He recited the entirety of 'The Last Galway Hooker', a sensitively researched, blank verse history of his boat, from its construction in the Claddagh, through its ownership by a fisherman, a priest and an old fisherman from Inishbofin, before coming into Murphy's delicate hands. It harps on the vintage Yeatsian theme of the alliance of the 'nobility' and the 'peasantry' in Ireland; a 'marriage' Yeats called it, speaking figuratively. Aside from the reverently detailed respect for Irish culture, there is a subtextual resonance in the poem: the boat is always called 'she', and the successive owners are all lone-wolf males. When Murphy read out a line about 'anti-fouling her bottom', nervous laughter rippled through the auditorium (the line was later cut). The long poem was 'a pretty solid piece of work', Montague had to admit, yet it seemed 'a bit like Richard himself ...

ponderous, often boring, but finally impressing one by its doggedness, and the amount of honest work that has gone into it'.⁹

Richard Murphy did not just work at his poetry; he put into effect strategies for its advancement. He brought Charles Monteith, poetry editor at Faber and from an Ulster family, on a fishing trip off the coast of Connemara. Later, Murphy was invited to join Faber's elite poetry list; he was the first Irish poet of his time to enjoy this status. He befriended Ted Hughes and Sylvia Plath, the star couple of contemporary British poetry, and had them as guests with him in the West. When Theodore Roethke came to Dublin, he looked up Montague (usually the first point of contact for American writers). Montague brought Roethke around to meet Mrs Yeats, and then introduced the American poet to Murphy and other local writers. In his autobiography *The Kick*, Murphy reports, 'I decided to try to entice [Roethke] from the literary pub life of Dublin and invite him across to the west coast. Ambition prompted me: aged fifty-two, [Roethke] was then at the height of his fame. I thought he might help me to find a publisher in America, if he were to stay on Inishbofin for a few weeks and sail on my boat.'¹⁰ Montague wrote to Kinsella, 'What was lacking in Irish verse until recently was proper ambition, professional preoccupation with the job.'¹¹ These were not lacking in Richard Murphy. 'A bollocks, but, by dint of ambition & harsh common-sense, [he] produces the goods.'¹²

At the end of the evening in the Royal Hibernian in his concluding remarks as chairman, Peadar O'Donnell suggested that all three young men ought to be immediately inducted into the Irish Academy of Letters, a generous applause line.¹³ Not many days later, O'Donnell did more than that. Calling Kinsella, Montague and Liam Miller to a meeting in the Gresham Hotel, he offered to advance them money to start a literary magazine, featuring the new generation in Ireland. Montague was to be general editor, Kinsella poetry editor and Miller publisher. Before the month was out, O'Donnell supplied Montague with an honorarium to get started, and a few months later, handed over 'a moderately decent block of money' to pay contributors.¹⁴ After dozens of suggestions for a title were rejected, the one-off publication wound up being called *The Dolmen Miscellany of Irish Writing*. It would be a generational statement.

2

In a study of the dynamics of collaborative circles, Michael Farrell identifies regularities in five artistic and intellectual movements.[15] His examples range from the French Impressionist painters in the 1870s and '80s to the Fugitive poets in the American South of the 1930s (Robert Penn Warren, Allen Tate and others). It is fairly easy to match up the 'Second Irish Revival' that began that evening at the Royal Hibernian Hotel with Farrell's conclusions.

Successful movements typically begin when a 'gatekeeper' in a 'magnet place' selects ambitious young friends eager to achieve success. Previously, they have been marginalized by an existing kingpin. The group normally has at its centre a charismatic leader. For instance, in the first Irish Literary Revival at the beginning of the twentieth century, the 'magnet place' was Coole Park in County Galway, Lady Gregory's estate house, and the 'charismatic leader' was W.B. Yeats. Other typical roles, according to Farrell, belong to the kingpin outside the group, the lightning rod within, the scapegoat who marks the borderlines of acceptability, and the peacemaker.

In the case of the second Irish Revival, the kingpin was Patrick Kavanagh. He was the undeniable poetic genius of the country, now socketed into the corner of McDaid's pub. He had plenty of followers, including Cronin, Liddy, Jordan and Hutchinson, but the three Dolmen poets wanted to break loose. Thomas Kinsella was at the start the group's leading writer, but was he charismatic? More a solitary figure. In fact, he did not particularly like to see himself as one of a group, even if it were conceded that he was first among equals. Richard Murphy fits the part of the scapegoat, since, while for sectarian reasons his inclusion proved that there was not a religious test for membership, his being kept at a distance when he so much wanted to join demonstrated the survival of sectarian and class prejudice underneath the primacy of good work.[16]

Montague, as editor, was an all-purpose operative and facilitator. Creative movements soon break into collaborative pairs, Farrell states, but Montague shared drafts of works-in-progress with many contributors to the *Miscellany*: Kinsella, John McGahern, Aidan Higgins, Valentin Iremonger – others too. Thanks to his experience at Iowa Writers' Workshop and his witness to the Beats' moment of origin, he was a believer in the benefits of collective creativity.

The stages of development according to Farrell include 1) quest for self-definition, 2) rebellion against the previous generation, 3) concerted creativity,

4) group presentation (such as a published anthology), 5) separation, in which the more and less successful break away from one another, and 6) reunion. In February 1962 these developments, with variations, lay in the future.

Because of his focus on internal group dynamics, Farrell underestimates external factors. For instance, had Peadar O'Donnell not handed over the pounds sterling, there would not have been a *Dolmen Miscellany*. The generational self-awareness and collaborative enterprise that arose from that single volume may have been postponed or never made manifest.

By coincidence, in March 1961, just a month after the Hibernian reading, Anthony Cronin ridiculed O'Donnell in 'Getting Wurred In', an excerpt from *The Life of Riley* published in *X*. The old Republican proprietor (called 'Pronsios') kept giving Associate Editor 'Riley' (Cronin) unwanted advice, particularly about the responsibilities of his generation. To the young man, it was all old hat. In fact, in the early 1950s, O'Donnell, an old-fashioned Marxist, had exhorted Cronin to get 'wired in' to the historical moment of Irish society and bring it to consciousness. He insisted that a special issue of *The Bell* be dedicated to younger writers.[17] But there weren't among his old UCD classmates, Cronin judged, others worth publishing. Still, O'Donnell insisted. The star turn in that issue, 'Young Writers and *The Bell*', was the essay by Montague. But ten years later, things had changed. Not only were there more writers of clear accomplishment on the scene, there was a readership.

Mary O'Malley reported, excitedly, on the Hibernian reading to John Hewitt.[18] She was tempted to invite the trio of poets to repeat the event in Belfast at the Lyric Theatre. But, she concluded, with her best effort, she could gather only a small audience, maybe fifty, nothing like what she estimated to be the five hundred or so crammed into the ballroom of the Royal Hibernian. Those circumstances would change, change utterly, once the Civil Rights marches and sanguinary missteps by the British army brought worldwide attention to Ulster. Then Seamus Heaney, Michael and Edna Longley, James Simmons, Medbh McGuckian, Ciaran Carson and others around Queen's University would sprout up in Belfast, a whole new branch of the movement.

Montague was awake to the fact that the numbers who bought tickets to the Royal Hibernian meant that a new audience had come to exist in Dublin since the war, often university educated and hungry for a contemporary expression of their own existence.[19] This made all the difference. The Irish Film Society, he noted, had two thousand members. That population wanted to stay in Ireland, not to emigrate, and they wanted something better than imported entertainments. This audience would be there for future readings, plays and new fiction; films too. It made the Pike Theatre (off Herbert Lane) and the Lantern Theatre (on Merrion Square) possible. It made starting a journal, such as *Poetry Ireland*, conceivable. Without a sufficient audience, there would have been no second Irish Revival.

3

In late January 1961, just before the Royal Hibernian reading, Montague was laid up in a Belfast hospital, under the care of Mary O'Malley's husband, Dr Pearse O'Malley. He had been suffering from an ulcer in his intestine for months; a cough too. He claimed that it was all the fault of his doctoral dissertation (the consumption of spirits had nothing to do with it). The ulcer was treated in Belfast, but the improvement was temporary. For several years, he suffered relapses. Tests at the hospital also identified scarring of the lungs, apparently from a childhood dose of tuberculosis.[20]

After the reading, Montague returned to the North to attend an anniversary Mass for his father in Fintona. James T. Montague had died in November 1959 after seven years back in Tyrone. On the train from Dublin Montague began to meditate a poem on his 'cold mad father', 'odd man I hardly knew', another instance of travel to a funeral in the North sparking the poet to confront his origins. A 'note to self' suggests he experiment with Richard Murphy's style in the depiction of a small village, and W.D. Snodgrass's freely autobiographical manner in dealing with a painful family situation.[21] He continued working at the draft about his father's return (ultimately entitled 'At Last') into March 1961. Once that poem was completed, the pair were not yet done with one another. Montague was haunted by the old man's ghost in these unfinished verses from 1963:[22]

> Inside me sometimes I feel
> A man trying to get out –
> My drunken father.

> He came into a room where I
> Hammered on a typewriter, and
> Sitting down, began to lay the fire.

'I might have been happy with my hands.'
Life can so hammer one into a shape
One cannot begin to know.

Just so, I have seen my father go
Back, and drink at the springs
Of his youth, like someone crazed.

Montague stayed on in Fintona after the commemorative service to spend a few weeks with his mother. Madeleine was already in Paris searching for an apartment. If the convalescent son hoped to be spoiled by mothering, he didn't know Molly. He reported to Mary O'Malley:

If you are tempted to think I am melancholy or a little bit hypochondriac you should meet my mother: she (almost proudly) told me that she hadn't been well since I was born. As a matter of fact, she gave a blow-by-blow description of my birth to a group of us as we sat drinking one night: I have the impression that all Fintona has, at one time or another, been on a guided tour of my mother's womb. However, I find it funny, in a macabre sort of way, like singing in a graveyard, so we drank together and looked at TV (she takes in about three plays a night), and when a telegram came from my wife wondering why I wasn't in Paris, our mournful little idyll ended.

Figure 29: Molly and John Montague, c. 1956; photograph by Madeleine Montague.
Madeleine complimented Molly on how well she had raised her boys, now a doctor, lawyer
and scholar. She replied in a rough Ulster tone, 'They were bright and they were straight.'
'No love lost,' Madeleine reflected (letter to AF, 7 January 2023).

4

Before moving to France, Montague typed up a complete draft of his dissertation on Oliver Goldsmith. He had worked on it intermittently since 1957. In those three and a half years, he had also completed two collections of poems, a few short stories and many book reviews. He held a full-time job at the Tourist Board until May 1959, when he resigned this pensionable post. As mentioned earlier, he and Madeleine agreed that with the move to Paris John would become a full-time writer. But 'the price of freedom exacted by a generous but far-seeing wife' was to get the PhD as 'insurance'.[23]

Unlike today's dissertation protocol of monthly meetings with a supervisor, Montague had two consultations with Professor Hogan, one after he had an introduction and outline (November 1959), and another after he had written chapters two and three (April 1960).[24] He published Chapter One, 'The Tragic Picaresque: Oliver Goldsmith, the Biographical Aspect', in the Spring 1960 issue of *Studies*. The final two chapters were hard work, but by February 1961, fulfilling his promise to Madeleine, he submitted the dissertation.

In Paris before him, Madeleine found an apartment at 11 rue Daguerre. It was in a row of artists' studios, built around 1910, set in a courtyard off a market street near Denfert Rochereau, just above Montparnasse. Like their Herbert Street home in Dublin, it was basically one large room. There was an inset balcony and loft, a wall of bookshelves (the former tenant was a Greek philosopher), a shower, and silence. Apart from glass in the doorway and front, it had no window; a skylight illuminated the space in the daytime. Other ateliers in the courtyard belonged to a sculptor, a Japanese picture-framer, a commercial artist and the poet Claude Esteban and his wife, Denise, a painter. It was a community of craftspeople.[25]

The couple were unable to take possession until the last week of June. In the meantime, they found lodging in a new high-rise at 5 rue Mathurin-Régnier, west of Montparnasse. It was from there that Madeleine set off to her new job at the Patronat, the organization of French employers, and Montague sat down to work as an independent author. 'I must begin to run my poetry like a business,' he told himself.

His ambition was to build up, part by part, the long poem *The Rough Field* as a companion in Irish literature to *The Deserted Village* and Kavanagh's *The Great Hunger*, but he knew this could not be rushed and would require that he expand his poetic technique. In the short term, he aimed to produce a 'condition of Ireland' short-story collection, with a focus on Ulster.

He hustled to keep up with other writerly obligations. Correspondence with each of the contributors to the *Dolmen Miscellany* had to be undertaken, and once begun, sustained. His publisher, MacGibbon and Kee, employed him part-time as an advisor. This entailed evaluating manuscripts, recruiting new authors and building up the Irish list. In time, it would also result in him becoming the unacknowledged compiler of *The Collected Poems* of Patrick Kavanagh. He fielded reviewing assignments from *The Guardian*, *The Irish Times* and *The Spectator* (which ultimately offered him a salaried post as literary editor). His annual contract as the 'Paris Correspondent' of *The Irish Times* committed him to surveys of the French scene.

Amidst this work-to-deadline, Montague continued to interrogate himself in his notebooks and poems about what his distinctive aesthetic should be. This question was further explored in serious back-and-forth correspondences, sometimes running to hundreds of pages, with Thomas Parkinson, Robin Skelton and Donald Fanger, and, from Ireland, with Barrie Cooke, Aidan Higgins, Thomas Kinsella, Liam Miller and John Jordan. These exchanges involved commentaries on works-in-progress and the sketching out of long-range plans.

Montague was aware of the gossip, some of it from Richard Murphy, that he lived off his high-born French wife, had an expensive apartment in Paris and spent his time womanizing.[26] In fact, he worked hard as a writer, but he did not make a great deal of money at it. Here is his own tally for 1963:

£126 from *Irish Times*
£60 partial advance on stories
5 reviews for *Spectator*
2 reviews for *Guardian*
Poems in *Poetry Ireland*, *Irish Times*, *Carleton Miscellany*, *Threshold*
Reading Fee from Manchester
Preface for Barrie Cooke's exhibition catalogue
Translation fee for German publication of short story
Approximate total: £460

This sum is about €10,000 in present-day money, hardly enough to support oneself in central Paris or Dublin. In the early 1960s, one was paid for the publication of one's poems, stories and articles (not always the case now). A few authors chanced to publish a truly profitable hit or even brought to pass a series of commercially successful novels. Yet to be a 'man of letters' was hardly viable in the late twentieth century. Poetry could be treated as a business (that is, approached in a professional way), but it was not a profitable one.

5

Montague never lost the study habits learned at St Patrick's College, Armagh. At the start, even of a poem or letter, he gathered research materials (often clippings from newspapers), identified models for what he aimed to do and made outlines. He would characteristically jot down advice to himself, often simply vows to do something this time that was really great. As he jokingly admitted to Tom Parkinson, 'You must remember that to get the Montague engine off the ground, even an inch, requires coaxing and boasting. My bibliographies are incitements to action, shrill cries of the Montague bird warming itself up.'[27] Writing for him was an elaborately premeditated act.

Before settling down to his stories, he re-read *Dubliners* and George Moore's *The Untilled Field*. He noted that in *Dublin's Joyce* (1955) Hugh Kenner argued that *Dubliners* was an intricately planned book. '[A] new *Dubliners*, 50 years after' wouldn't come about by chance. He may have derived from Kenner's interpretation of Joyce's stories the anti-heroic practice of making his protagonists weak versions of himself, what he might have been had he taken another path in life. Joyce's literary style was, Montague felt, 'too strict'; those of O'Connor and O'Faoláin 'too bouncy and free'. The features of his own stories, he hoped, would be deadpan satire and frightful honesty. 'These must go beyond the usual Irish stories – there must be pain and savagery in them.'[28]

He had one in the bank already, 'That Dark Accomplice', intended in 1952 for *The Bell* (its depiction of a priest had scared off Peadar O'Donnell). It had since been published in *Threshold*, included in the *Faber Book of Irish Short Stories* and translated into German. The first new one, finished in April, was 'The Parish of the Dead'. It arose from the funeral of a Montague aunt who had heard the banshee when his Uncle John died in Brooklyn. More a thoughtful vignette than a story, it exhibited the obsession with obsequies in the Ulster countryside. Looking at it, Montague feared that his toil over the dissertation had made him 'too analytical, too intellectual for story-writing'.[29] Published in the *Oberlin Review*, the story was left out of *Death of a Chieftain*.

In May he hit his stride with 'The New Enamel Bucket', a title derived from 'The Water Carrier', the poem about the pure springs of life in his parish. In the story, it becomes a symbol of townie impurity. Two farmers, one of them driving some cows, meet one another going to the fair in Fintona (called 'Moorhill'). The older farmer gets a good price for his stock and, after buying a white enamel bucket for bringing drinking water from the spring, inveigles the younger into 'going on the piss'. From one pub to the next they go, picking up loafers on the dole, who themselves never buy a round, but coddle their host. The old farmer gets sillier and meaner with every drink he takes and nearly succeeds in starting a fight with a large Protestant gentleman. The others drag him off to the lowest dive in town, where barman and customers all speak in the lingo of cowboys-and-Indians movies. Now rat-arsed drunk, the hangers-on play soccer with the enamel bucket. Put out of this last pub, they pummel the young farmer, too drunk to defend himself, just for sport. The old farmer finds him crumpled on waste ground and washes the blood from his face with water from the now battered and leaky enamel bucket.

The story carries with it the inside knowledge of one whose family operated a bar in Fintona ('The Poet's Pub'). It betrays the sordid side of life in the Carney/Montagues' home place. While it is in the nature of writers to sell out secrets and expose their families to embarrassment in front of the neighbours, the author's mother and brothers were not best pleased by the publication of *Death of a Chieftain*, and they let him know it.[30]

By September, while accompanying Garech Browne to the Venice palazzo his mother had rented for the season, Montague was well into 'The Cry'. He had high hopes that he would 'explode the whole province of Ulster in the most trenchant stories Irish literature has ever known' (a fine example of his use of boasts 'to get the Montague engine off the ground').[31] He had in his sights sectarian B-Specials, the cowed Ulster Catholics and 'the whole attitude of local Protestants'.

Peter, the protagonist, is someone like himself, who has gone off to university. Now a successful journalist in London, he has come home to visit his parents in a town that is, again, undeniably Fintona. One night, Peter hears a cry in the street. Looking out the bedroom window, he sees black-caped policemen mercilessly kicking a man on the ground. Up and down the street, others are at their windows, watching. One even tells the police to stop, for God's sake. 'Keep your bloody nose out of it, will ye?' one shouts back. 'Do you want to get a touch too?'

The next morning Peter is determined that something must be done. In a curious anticipation of Seamus Heaney's metaphor in 'Digging', his father asks, 'What the hell are you going to fight them with …? A pen-nib? … A fat lot of use that would be against a machine gun.' His parents are both from republican backgrounds, but they've been cowed. Peter goes about his business like an investigative reporter, tracing the identity of the victim, interviewing his family and consulting with the civil authorities, but gradually he realizes that these people do not want his kind of help. His own mother begs him not to publish the article he's writing: 'It's me and [your father] will have to live here if that thing appears, not you.' Finally, even the village simpleton has a message for Peter, scribbled on a wall, 'Nosy Parker go home' (meaning London).

Twenty years later, 'The Cry' was still strong stuff for Ulster. Derek Mahon's dramatization, scheduled for production in County Antrim in 1983, was interfered with by the local B-Specials; who also vainly threatened to sue the BBC.[32]

6

The production of short stories stalled in the autumn of 1961. In July Montague had gone back to Dublin for his dissertation *viva*, the oral examination before a panel of assessors. Plans were afoot for book publication by MacGibbon and Kee. He had no reason to believe there would be any trouble. But after consultation, the examiners informed him that he had not yet passed. Some revision would be required.

They did not like the comparisons between Goldsmith and twentieth-century writers like T.S. Eliot and Ezra Pound; this was not properly historicist. He sometimes stated his own literary vision; that smelled to the examiners of subjectivity. Frequently he declined to prove his claims brick by brick. He skipped over the academic necessity of making plain what was obvious.[33] All told, there was not, they assured him, a great deal to do. Three months should be plenty of time, and he could then send in the final draft by post.

No doubt, this hemming-and-hawing of 'old farts' was annoying, but it was also commonplace. Often, corrections are required before conferral of the degree. But Montague was shocked to the core. Where was the praise? He left the meeting bewildered and angry. He cried out to authorities of church and state, confessing his indignation to Ambassador Iremonger, to Father Donal O'Sullivan, chairman of the Arts Council, and Father Burke-Savage, editor of

Studies (which had published a chapter of the dissertation).[34] There was no way he could break from the composition of his book of stories in order to spend three months making changes to the dissertation that were not even improvements. 'To go off my writing path to placate them would be sheer madness.'[35] But was he going to just let all that academic work go to waste? He dithered.

Figure 30: Scraps left over from Montague's dissertation on Oliver Goldsmith.

Montague never did resubmit his Goldsmith dissertation, though the chapters were eventually published one by one in periodicals. Still, he got, if not a PhD, a lot of other things out of the work. Goldsmith was a sympathetic role model, a stammerer from up the country like himself, a chronic student but not a dyed-in-the-wool scholar, with a sweet gift for good work in almost any type of writing he tried, newspaper columns, fiction, song, play or long poem. His talent for literary society (friend of Johnson, Garrick and Reynolds) was itself amiable. Goldsmith's 'state-of-the-nation' pastoral – 'The Deserted Village' – remained for Montague a viable literary ideal. Goldsmith is the secret key to the variety of Montague's own career as a writer.

7

Four months after the shock of his dissertation *viva*, Montague managed to get three different stories started, but they then all got stuck.[36] A year later, he was still moving paragraphs around in the same drafts.[37] Only in the late spring and summer of 1963 did he find his confidence again.

All the way back in January 1961, he had begun to collect news clippings and make notes for a story about the New Economic Programme and his work experience at Bord Fáilte. Not until a year and a half later, August 1963, did he put the final touches to 'A Change of Management'. Its protagonist, John O'Shea, is a mid-level, unambitious employee in his tenth year at Bord na h-Ath Breithe (the National Renaissance Board). He likes his easy-going boss (modelled on Niall Sheridan), but a 'new broom' is sweeping into this state-sponsored organization, a man named 'Clohessy'.[38] He has worked abroad at multi-national corporations. Clohessy is patriotic, but he has no truck with the old ways, contemptuous of unambitious, pensionable civil servants settled like lice in the pelt of the body politic.

The protagonist's crony, named 'Cronin' (after Anthony Cronin) detests this new man, precisely because he has just 'what you need to get on in this country':

'You mean energy?' John O'Shea asks.

'I mean neck; pure, unadulterated, armour-plated, insensitive neck.'

If put in charge, people like Clohessy will 'murder us with activity! Factories owned by Germans, posh hotels catering to the international set'. The T.K. Whitaker vision of the new Ireland is not for Cronin. He quits his job to keep from being fired. But John O'Shea thinks maybe it would be best to get in under some competent manager like Clohessy and give his best, 'was it such a criminal thing to wish to lead an ordinary life?'

Two of the last stories to be written were indirect tributes to Madeleine. 'A Ball of Fire' is not successful in representing the creative work of a painter (even though Montague was friends with many contemporary artists), but it does make the point that the main difference between the artist-protagonist and the sour old widower next door is that the artist has a very good person for a wife, even though he hardly realizes what she means for him.[39]

Madeleine is the outright model for the heroine of 'An Occasion of Sin', a French woman, open-faced, at ease with herself and the world, who has been living six months in Ireland with her husband. She finds it hard to bear the gloom of the country. For relief, she bathes in the sea in Sandycove, near the Forty Foot. As she changes into her swimsuit, the Irish bystanders watch her carefully. They themselves have a contorted way of getting clothes off and suit on, without ever being naked in between.

In the summer student priests come to the beach. They ask her questions about the book she is reading, about Paris, simple conversation. A man then walks over and tells her that she must not talk to these boys, they are student priests. Finding the reproach ridiculous, she vents to her husband, but he admits he can see the man's point – she could be 'classed as an occasion of sin'. Her husband, she is shocked to learn, is just as odd as the rest of the Irish.[40]

The narration in 'An Occasion of Sin' is first-rate, but looking over his collection with an editorial eye, Montague was not satisfied.[41] In editing *The Dolmen Miscellany*, he had come to see prior to book publication the novels of John McGahern and Aidan Higgins. Compared with the sentence-by-sentence originality of *The Barracks* and *Langrishe, Go Down*, the writing in *Death of a Chieftain* was that of the finest journalism, suitable for a vivid 'state of the nation' story, but not something new in the art of fiction.

Yet looking with envy over his neighbour's fence at the Modernist stylistic furniture over there, Montague was in danger of undervaluing his own writing. 'Journalistic' had become a high critical pejorative, signifying 'superficial', 'hackneyed' and 'materialist'. But one of Montague's strengths, built up over time by means of disciplined practice, was the hunt for a level of factuality in both prose and verse. The result is his own combination of Auden's cultural psychoanalysis with W.C. Williams's guiding adage, 'No ideas but in things.' Montague's stories were based on a wide-ranging study of newspapers and periodicals and his own intelligent observation of people. He then brought to their realization a commitment to clarity, rather than to the impasto of lyricism or the comedy of character, as was typical of the Irish story at the time.[42] He did something new with his fiction.

On 24 September 1964 *The Irish Times* greeted *Death of a Chieftain* as indeed equal to *The Barracks* and a landmark of the 'new Irish Renaissance'. At the launch in London, three astonishingly intelligent and beautiful women were there to congratulate him – Edna O'Brien, Carolyn Kizer and Ricki Huston.[43] It nearly made him giddy. Although pleased by the attention and public praise, Montague was not entirely convinced of his own achievement. He swore to do better in future.[44]

8

Montague had met neither John McGahern nor Aidan Higgins before editing the *Miscellany*, but, a keen follower of the latest literary magazines, he spotted their first publications. Once he solicited a contribution, meetings followed.[45]

Montague was 'thunderstruck by the beauty and power' of *The Barracks*. After reading draft pages in September 1961, he showed McGahern some of his own fiction. The work was clever, McGahern allowed, but he felt that it 'slide[s] off from facing the experience'. At Iowa Montague learned not to be defensive about criticism. Several months later, in his journal, he posed the question, Why did he never write about love? And then he started 'That Room', the poem quoted earlier about himself and Madeleine getting news of not being able to have a child together. Below the first draft, he commented, 'This would satisfy McGahern,' and then counselled himself, 'Really bear down on it.'[46]

In their exchanges about editing the excerpt from *The Barracks*, Montague passed on news that *Encounter* was publishing a group of his poems. McGahern admitted that he was surprised to feel glad of Montague's news, instead of jealous. It reminded him of a 'beautiful thing' in Yeats's *Autobiographies*, the poet saying, 'If we don't know each other and share in each other's triumphs,' this generation of writers will be worse off.'[47] Good advice, if hard to follow. Yet a degree of mutual goodwill may be what is needed for a literary movement to take wing.

Montague was struck by the stories of Aidan Higgins in *Felo de Se* (published by John Calder in 1960). 'Some of the writing is brilliant,' he enthused to John Jordan, 'and he is marvellously free from any of our taboos and fears. The only thing that troubled me was the technical opacity: stories meandered or splayed out. Despite the great wit and intelligence, I felt cheated, finally. Anyway, he's a considerable number of cuts above buttermilk, and I will try to get something from him [for *The Dolmen Miscellany*].'[48]

Higgins offered an excerpt from his work-in-progress, *Langrishe, Go Down*, the best book he would ever write. He accepted line edits from Montague and in return, gave his own impressions of *Poisoned Lands*. The 'news-headline' poems were not to his taste, but he liked 'Old Mythologies' and, particularly, 'The Water Carrier', as the type of thing he wished to do himself.[49]

That mutually fruitful relationship continued for nearly ten years. Sometimes Higgins turned to Montague for help with how to translate from French, or with questions about a detail in European history, as if the poet were to be his editor and research assistant for ever. That was annoying, but also normal writerly self-absorption.[50] Once, Higgins unnerved the poet by saying he did not think Montague had the right amount of belief in his own greatness (this was never a problem for Higgins). Montague's own self-assessment in July 1963 was, 'I am not yet, but could become, a major writer.'[51] Each of the two was, at bottom, a needy boaster. Turn-and-turn-about, they shared current reading and private schemes for cutting-edge literary success.

That generation of writers, in America as well as Ireland (post-war existentialists who took literature as the highest human value), had a priestlike arrogance in their quest for public prestige. To excel, to be better than others, was their ruling passion. Literary performance became a male sport, a trial-by-contest where there had to be losers. Aidan Higgins sometimes seemed especially vigilant to finger the losers. He would demonstrate contempt for them as fakes, failures, impotent beings. But in the Higgins–Montague correspondence from the 1960s (not afterwards), mutual respect shines through. The reputation of Tony Cronin, former UCD star and an ongoing source of anxiety, often served as a burnt offering in the cause of forming a more perfect union between the two writers. Both Montague and Higgins were proud to be close to Samuel Beckett, their hero in the cause of Literary Style. A few times, the three met for drinks in Paris. In the company of young Irish writers, Beckett could be convivial, avuncular and even helpful with publishers.

Thomas Kinsella had no doubts about his own importance. In November 1959, he took to painting historical frescoes. Madeleine tartly remarked, 'It is unexpected; he thinks himself a great man, I am given to understand.'[52] Everyone was given to understand the same. Montague was a believer, as he stated in a review in the August 1959 issue of *Poetry*. He began to match up his own efforts to Kinsella's achievements. 'Poisoned Lands' was consciously patterned after 'Thinking of Mr. D'.[53] As far as Kinsella was concerned, there was no rivalry. He tried to be polite, but he did not in fact treat his friend as an equal. He could not understand why Montague, if he were a true poet, would spend time editing the *Miscellany*, gathering the poems of Kavanagh, or writing short stories. The insinuation stung.

Montague had a deep desire to honour the father figures of his generation. When he tried to recruit Kinsella to do an essay for the *Miscellany* on the outburst of late poems from Austin Clarke, Kinsella was honestly sceptical: 'In general, [Clarke] wasn't good enough for his technique when it was good, and lost control over his technique when he started speaking like a major man.' Austin had 'a general lack of the gift of communication'.[54] Brutal.

Yet Kinsella generally trusted Montague's critical judgement. Montague's strong edit of 'A Country Walk' was 'a great help'. In January 1962 and, getting no answer, again in February, Kinsella asked if Montague would do the same for 'Downstream', a lengthy work-in-progress. Montague was reluctant. In his own work, he was following up hints in William Carlos Williams, and it seemed to him 'a pity, when we were halfway towards finding a verse close to speech, to lapse [like Kinsella] tiredly back into the old Tennysonianisms'. But he allowed there should be room for a poetry such as Kinsella was then writing, 'in the great line, rich, encrusted', and his own emerging aesthetic, 'a naturalness, like breathing'.[55] When Montague did look at the draft of 'Downstream', he sensed a 'willed effect, as if [Kinsella] were driving the poems and not vice versa'.[56] Still, he suppressed these reservations for the time being and offered reader's notes of a kind to make the poem better in the form in which it had been undertaken. Kinsella was grateful, yet he kept publicly silent about the help he had received.[57] There was no *il miglior fabbro* gesture of thanks, such as T.S. Eliot made to Pound for his reconstruction of *The Waste Land*.

By late 1962 Montague was reacting even more strongly against Kinsella's 'extravagant vein of love' and the imagery of 'swans and dew'. Rather than Kinsella's 'synthetic conflagrations of language', Montague wanted instead to put 'the real thing' into poetry. He was spurred to have a fresh go at the long-pondered 'All Legendary Obstacles', treating it like a simple chapter of romantic autobiography.[58]

The tension between the two writers came to a head one day after Christmas 1962, at the DBC (Dublin Bread Company). Montague had taken a few morning whiskies with the novelist Kate O'Brien before the encounter; these loosened his tongue.[59] He let out his resentment over how much he gave Kinsella – reviews, line edits, a supportive correspondence – and how little he got in return. It stuck in his throat, he admitted, that Kinsella kept winning one prize after another, while he himself was on a 'run of ill luck'.[60] He honestly did not like Kinsella's current style: it was obscure, clotted, pretentious and churned out in service of a stanzaic scheme. Kinsella rose to the defence of his poems. In the present historical situation, he argued, true literature had to be difficult and obscure, like the work of Joyce or Pound.

No, no, Montague returned, modern poetry 'can be real, without difficulty, with an openness of heart', like D.H. Lawrence's poetic sequence 'Look! We Have Come Through!'.

The two poets up to this meeting had had a fruitful friendship, but so much plain speaking made a difference. Afterwards, Montague felt both apologetic, especially about having been half-cut with spirits, and defensive. Ultimately, he did want to create distance in a relationship in which he had not been treated as an equal. Like anyone, he aimed to make his own mark. That did not excuse the fact that his critique of Kinsella had been one-sided. So far, he knew that he himself had failed to go as deeply as Kinsella 'in investigating the grounds of my own life'.[61] No question, Kinsella was a serious writer.

As for Kinsella, he bristled and asked if were not possible that he had won prizes because his work was good (leaving unstated that Montague hadn't because his wasn't). Later, he made peace. He humorously pleaded, 'In mitigation of my selfishness ... I am, in fact, a bastard in many, many ways,' but he said, in the case of Montague's poetry, his lack of generosity 'originates in lethargy rather than cunning'.[62]

In the long term, it may be that Montague's critical outburst at Kinsella's early style had something to do with the subsequent turn in Kinsella's career as a poet. Obscurity would still feature in the collections that followed, but Kinsella turned his back on the lyric sweetness and strict formalities of the early, prize-winning books. There were no more swans on the water in *Notes from the Land of the Dead* (1972) or *A Technical Supplement* (1976). His attitude to his early collections soured, and he echoed Montague's reservations.

9

These rivalrous male friendships raise the question: Where were the female contributors to *The Dolmen Miscellany*?

the Dolmen

miscellany of Irish writing

editor	John Montague
poetry editor	Thomas Kinsella

BRIAN MOORE	Preliminary Pages for a Work of Revenge, *story. page* 1
THOMAS KINSELLA	A Country Walk, *poem.* 8
AIDAN HIGGINS	Helen Langrishe Goes Home, *extract from novel.* 12
THREE POETS	Pearse Hutchinson. 27 James Liddy. 31 Richard Weber. 34
JOHN JORDAN	First Draft, *story.* 36
RICHARD MURPHY	The Cleggan Disaster, *poem.* 46
JOHN MONTAGUE	The Sentimental Prophecy: A study of *The Deserted Village.* 62
VALENTIN IREMONGER	Poems and Translations. 80
JOHN MACGAHERN	A Barrack Evening, *extract from novel.* 84
JAMES PLUNKETT	Ferris Moore and the Earwig, *story.* 95
REVIEWS	103

1962

DUBLIN	The Dolmen Press
LONDON & NEW YORK	Oxford University Press

Figure 31: Table of Contents, Dolmen Miscellany of Irish Writing.

It had a strong line-up, no doubt, but there are a dozen men and not one woman. Thirty years later, far and away most new Irish writers were women. In 1961 it is true that not so many contributors to the leading literary magazines were female. Still, Edna O'Brien was nearly the same age as Montague, a year younger, and she had published her first book, *The Country Girls*, in 1960. As a literary scout, Montague cannot have missed that event. Since he included a short story by the solid James Plunkett, why not one from Mary Lavin? She was a presence in Dublin and regularly published in *The New Yorker*. Or something from Kate O'Brien, but to Montague, Kate O'Brien was a kindly auntie figure, not a contemporary. Basically, there is no better explanation for the exclusively male line-up in *The Dolmen Miscellany* than the blind sexism of the period and the get-ahead ambition of each of the males involved, particularly the editor. In regard to writing, Montague at the time had eyes only for men.

In his part-time post as literary advisor for MacKibbon and Kee, on top of doing reader reports on manuscripts, Montague provided advice on new acquisitions. He suggested that Tim O'Keeffe find out about British rights to works of James Baldwin and Louis Simpson. Repeatedly, he advocated that the publisher be the London distribution point of Bay Area writers, particularly Gary Snyder and Robert Creeley.[63] 'The trouble with the Beats is that no one bothered to find out who were the real ones,' and those were, for Montague, Snyder, Creeley and Robert Duncan.[64]

The most important acquisition that Montague inspired was William Carlos Williams, then almost completely unknown in Britain. O'Keeffe got the rights to the *Collected Earlier Poems*, *The Selected Poems*, *The Collected Later Poems* and *Pictures from Brueghel*. Williams was properly set before the transatlantic reading public by MacGibbon and Kee as a major contemporary poet in the English language.

O'Keeffe and Montague next set their sights on a big London edition of the poems of Hugh MacDiarmid, but the plan to feature the great Scottish poet fell through.

There has been confusion about Montague's role in the publication of *The Collected Poems* of Patrick Kavanagh, even after Antoinette Quinn's 2001 biography of the poet illuminated the matter.[65] Here are the facts. In 1961 Tim O'Keeffe was in the George, a Soho tavern, listening to poet and broadcaster W.R. Rodgers and Montague merrily talking about the poems of Kavanagh. They each recited from memory their favourites. Rodgers did a ripping rendition of 'Shancoduff' in a true Northern accent.[66] After his success with publishing Flann O'Brien, O'Keeffe decided, Why not go after the man from Monaghan?

On 20 November 1961, well-watered in the Plough tavern in Bloomsbury, Kavanagh agreed to accept an advance on the volume. However, he clearly was going to do little himself by way of collecting the poems. Montague proposed John Jordan or Tony Cronin for the job, but Cronin had moved to Spain. Anyway, he was on periodically frosty terms with his old mentor. It came down to the fact that O'Keeffe trusted Montague. Arm-twisting, the publisher wheedled, 'this was your idea in the first place!'.[67] Montague was worried – his relations with Kavanagh were 'fraught and unfriendly' – but he agreed to cooperate behind the scenes.

Thirty years later, when Montague's role was revealed, Martin Green complained that actually he was the one who deserved credit for the selection; Montague had done next to nothing.[68] Indeed, to supplement *Come Dance with Kitty Stobling*, Green, then a publisher in O'Keeffe's office, made three trips to Dublin to prise loose further poems.[69] So Martin Green did his part. In July 1962 after O'Keeffe had the sum of Green's efforts typed up, he posted the manuscript to Montague.[70] Still, the gathering did not include Kavanagh's volumes from the 1940s, *The Great Hunger* and *A Soul for Sale*, which were essential. After foraging in the National Library of Ireland, by December Montague added in poems from the *Irish Statesman*, the *Dublin Magazine*, *The Bell* and *Arena*. In January and February 1963 Montague's painter friend Barrie Cooke continued the hunt through periodicals and sent whatever he came across.[71]

In ordering the contents, Montague aimed to reveal a pattern, 'from satire to confession, and finally acceptance', an implied narrative widely noticed by readers.[72] The image of the contemplative sage finally at peace with life was a fiction, a well-meant effort to rehabilitate a broken father figure in his old age. Little thanks did Montague get for it.

Figure 32: Paul Durcan and Tim O'Keeffe, launch of Patrick Kavanagh's Collected Poems.

When the collection was published in September 1964, Kavanagh was chuffed by the sparkling notices of the lifework of 'the best living Irish poet'. A few months later, he reviewed Montague's short stories, *Death of a Chieftain*, in *Hibernia*. He gave the book a real kicking, from first to last:[73] 'John Montague's stories are a curious business. They appear to be made from prefabricated material taken from all sorts of fiction and I would say particularly women's magazine fiction. And never was any writer so eager to be "with it". Every move is right. ...' Unrelenting abuse continued to the end. And this from a revered father figure! The shame of it! Nearly every literate person in Dublin then read *Hibernia*.

In his notebook that December, Montague made three entirely different attempts at a reply, before settling on one brief, lofty and insincere letter to the editor: 'I would rather not engage in the Donnybrook side of literature. Still, the authentic note of baffled jealousy was sweet to hear.'

While the wound was still raw, Montague sought advice in Paris from Samuel Beckett and his friend Con Leventhal. 'Don't answer!' Beckett hissed. 'They're not worth it!' But Montague, humiliated, was panicking; he simply had to do something. 'If I felt like that,' Beckett sternly replied, 'I'd give up writing.' Besides, Irish literature is of no interest to anyone, the older writer declared; its authors were the most insular of all the writers on the planet.

In his notebook, Montague urged himself to become more like Beckett, a person who doesn't care about what anyone thinks, a man of no feeling.[74] That was never going to happen. Montague was a sensitive beast, even an oversensitive one. Besides that, for a score of reasons, he did care about Irish national literature.

10

Montague's discipleship to D.H. Lawrence was not particularly eccentric in the 1960s. Aside from the large annual paperback sale of his novels, Lawrence was then regarded by British and American scholars as both the last in the 'great tradition' of English novelists and a major international Modernist.

Montague loved the stories, the travel writings and particularly the lyric sequence 'Look! We Have Come Through!'. 'Try to make myself into a Lawrentian,' was a note to self in May 1961: 'fluent', 'capable of many things', 'a presence'.[75] Ever the active agent of literary trends, a month later Montague was explaining in *The Irish Times* the fruitful potential of Lawrence for contemporary writers: 'It is a matter of openness to experience, as in the case of the American poet, William

Carlos Williams; for delicacy of response, seen, for instance, in Lawrence's animal poems. Already this attitude has flowered in an extraordinary way, in the recent poems of the young Yorkshire poet, Ted Hughes; in the later poems of Theodore Roethke.'[76] For the next several years, Montague would urge himself to transcend his own sense of shame and 'let oneself go, be natural – the Lawrence mood'.[77]

The Lawrentian project of self-liberation was something that Montague had in common with the painter Barrie Cooke. The child of an English father and American mother, Cooke attended Harvard University and, among his classmates, enjoyed the companionship of poets Donald Hall, Frank O'Hara and John Ashbery. He had an ear for poetry; he could tell what sounded right and what was off-key. Ted Hughes was one of Cooke's best friends, a relationship rooted not just in exchanges of poems for pictures, but in fishing trips together.

Cooke moved to Ireland in 1954, then studied for a year with German Expressionist Oskar Kokoschka. On his return, he joined the Independent Artists, along with John Behan, Camille Souter, Brian Bourke and Patrick Pye. Pye was the one, in that Baggotonia hothouse, who introduced Montague to Cooke. By April 1961 the two had a cracking correspondence underway, with each providing the other with a detailed education in their respective artistic aims.

Cooke could be very funny. He dashed off cartoonish self-portraits, one of a three-headed Cooke handing out copies right, left and centre of Montague's *Poisoned Glands* [*sic*].

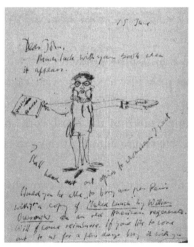

Figure 33: Barrie Cooke to John Montague, handing out copies of 'Poisoned Glands', 15 June [1961].

His letters were signed with absurd aliases: 'Lemuel Gulliver', 'Pico della Mirandola', 'Alfonso Osorio', etc. When he got wind of the supposedly well-funded *Miscellany*, he wrote:[78]

> What is this I hear about an Irish magazine? ... You must have drawings and all that sort of thing in it. And interviews ... And long articles on me with expensive colour reproductions. What about slip-in, fold-out, LP Gramophone records (2' diameter) with all the staff reading their work in turn. Good first number. That's the way to attract the rich and the rich are the way to attract the bra-and-corset ads, Dunsk Danish pot-ware, crystal doorknobs for Rolls Royces, Galerie Musk (agents for Lao Pi, Moo Wao Zam, Hoo Choo), Boutique Minuette – reproductions of Icelandic XVI c. armoires, Period Hoslaf III. Don't accept any adverts for anti-vivisection, beer, Faber & Faber, or gardening. What will it be called? *Tastebud? Tomorrow?*

Cooke made several visits to Paris and 11 rue Daguerre. And whenever Montague was in Ireland, he tried to save a few days for a trip to the Cooke household, whether in County Clare, or later in Kilkenny, to watch the painter at work in his studio. Montague would be just the person, Cooke decided, to write an essay on his work. He wanted a poet, not a journalist, dealer or academic to give verbal expression to what he was doing with paint. For an Independent Artist, this was not unusual. Rarely were painters and writers ever so in tune with one another. The initiative typically came from the artists and was returned fourfold by the writers.

Montague, always the A-plus student, wanted first to master the bibliography. Cooke not only provided him with a reading list (John Berger, Kenneth Clark and others), but used the correspondence to personally explain in detail the ongoing importance of the brushwork and colouring of certain European great masters. He taught Montague how to talk about painting. His letters are brilliant.

The electrical point of contact between the two artists was their Lawrentian relationship to the female other as a source of wonder, terror, power and life. When Barrie Cooke was living in County Clare, he became fascinated by the Sheela-na-Gig in Kilnaboy Chapel – a pagan image carved in stone, too magically potent for medieval Catholics to abandon from their spiritual lives. But whatever did it mean? Cooke couldn't say, but he was astounded by it. For his April 1962 show at the Ritchie Hendriks gallery in Dublin, he did a number of works in which the earth is Sheela, or Sheela is the earth. He wanted to show Gaia as a living, wondrous being, with female cycles, rhythms of life and death, terror and desire, the female spirit of this living Earth. If Montague were to do the catalogue essay, Cooke felt he had to see these Sheela-na-Gigs.[79]

> The most successful are fired terracotta figures that I have mounted on a ground of plaster and painted. They will need a deal of explaining I can guess – a large catalogue preface by a Carmelite nun …. They are, peculiarly, much less sensual (in the *luxe*, calm, *volupte* way) than a lot of my stuff. I suppose they have to be for the subject to be borne. A spread-eagled woman has got to be [hardened?] somewhat – given a little stud farm chastity. I have used real (Burren) bones in 2 of them, set into the plaster and gravel too. (This all sounds too goddamn modish but I really don't think they are … I have used plaster & stones & gravel for simple, nineteenth century, illusionist purposes – I want them to <u>represent</u> rocks & gravel). Despite squatting pose they have … a cruel, regal, prehistoric air.

Figure 34: Kilnaboy Venus, a Sheela-na-Gig in County Clare.

Once he had seen the exhibition, Montague agreed to write the essay (published in *The Dubliner* in March 1964).

This contact with Cooke's 'imaginarium' triggered a complicated development in Montague's poetry. After a May visit to County Clare, during which he saw the 'Kilnaboy Venus', he wrote some verses below the title 'The Hag of the Mill':

> In that landscape of castle
> On the cathedral door at Kilnaboy
> That gross and grinning head
> Flat as a turd,
> Hands splayed in its sex.

The poem, with eyes like fingertips, begins to look candidly at the Sheela-na-Gig, but darts away, disgusted.

When Montague returns to the composition a month later (21 August 1962), 'The Hag of the Mill' draft morphs into a meditation on Minnie Kearney, the Cailleach in Garvaghey who was the subject of 'The Sean Bhean Bhocht' and a stanza of 'Like Dolmens Round My Childhood'. She was, he came to believe, the one who 'cut the wound of poetry into my youth':[80]

> The dark face turns towards me
> Seeking what? solace? ...
>
> Why should my life be
> fastened to this frieze
> of ancients of which
> she is the strangest figure of all
>
> a scene as blasted as
> anything in B[eckett]: the bare
> windswept hills behind

Pinned to this notebook page is a clipping from an English newspaper about a 61-year-old woman who was gagged by an intruder, then died of fright. Montague added a later clipping from the *Ulster Herald* reporting another assault on an old woman. A 48-year-old labourer broke down an 85-year-old spinster's door, dragged her across the floor and threw her on the bed. It was the fourth offence of the kind by the accused, Jim McKillion, a man from around Garvaghey. The judge sentenced him to a fine of four shillings, to cover for the damage to the door. Montague's horrified, ironic note at the top of the clipping is 'The Story of Miss MacSorley's Door!'[81]

Soon Montague was on the scent of what would become a different poem altogether, 'The Wild Dog Rose'. It is an effort to get past misogyny, past gynophobia too, with its root in unease over female difference and panic at woman's precedence in the order of life. There was a lot to cross over, both a feeling of abandonment and a fear of engulfment.

The poem's speaker is in Garvaghey, paying a visit to Minnie Kearney. This time, the boy must hold the frank gaze of the old woman and hear out her story, a story so terrible he wants to push it away. It will be the last time he sees her alive. By and by, she wanders into telling him of being assaulted one night when a drunken rover from the hills broke into her cabin. In an act of total listening, Montague lets her voice take over the poem. It is a time of learning for him, a chance to come into a greater capacity for empathy.

Montague was a long time getting the right ending to the poem (which was not published until 1970). The third and final section honours the old woman's pantheistic devotion to Mary, a folk Catholicism that by then the poet had himself left behind.

Back in 1960 Montague received a letter from Aunt Freda, which mentioned that Aunt Brigid was losing her memory, but still prayed often. He then wrote two lines on a scrap of newspaper:[82]

> Petals of a watery red, with a weak white heart,
> Nature's offering, not ours: frail, untrained.

He kept these lines for many years. Ultimately, he transferred the association from Brigid Montague to Minnie Kearney, the speaker in 'The Wild Dog Rose' and explicated the image of the heart-shaped petals:

> And still
> the dog rose shines in the hedge.
> Petals beaten wide by rain, it
> sways slightly, at the tip of a
> slender, tangled, arching branch
> which, with her stick, she gathers
> into us.

'The wild rose
is the only rose without thorns,'
she says, holding a wet blossom
for a second, in a hand knotted
as the knob of her stick.
'Whenever I see it, I remember
the Holy Mother of God and
all she suffered.'
　　Briefly
the air is strong with the smell
of that weak flower, offering
its crumbling yellow cup
and pale bleeding lips
fading to white
　　at the rim
of each bruised and heart-
shaped petal.

One of the best poems John Montague ever wrote. And its 'First Mover' was the Kilnaboy Venus.

II

Paired with the Lawrentian quest to cast off the false and find the true self was a discipline of experiment in line and stanza. Montague's Iowa classmate Robert Bly, in Paris for a time, gave him useful advice. Bly and James Wright had had a fruitful method of collaboration, in which they 'used to help each other by "cutting the tails off" poems', in pursuit of the concision of Chinese lyrics.[83] In Paris, Bly did the same for Montague.

With his English-major habits of mind, Montague had a tendency to moralize his poems and felt it necessary to wind up with a 'meaning of life' statement, almost like the epigrammatic couplet at the close of a Shakespearean sonnet.[84] Upon arriving in Paris, he noticed in the windows on rue Jacob a radiometer, little fans of mica spinning in the stream of light; they were for sale as an executive's desktop ornament. He was drawn to write about the image, but he was not sure what for him its significance was. Possible titles included

'Message from Paris' and 'School of Pain'. Or was he just feeling at sea in the French capital? How should he moralize this? An early 21-line draft ended:

> Casting its light over unhappiness,
> Ceaselessly flashing its tiny signals
> Not of help, but of neutral energy.
> Minute windmills of the infinite
> They generate their own force
> Merely by turning. They present
> All the challenge of the pointlessly delicate,
> The prettily/pettily/intricate, just by being.
>
> Such indifference murders me!
> I stare at them until I am drowned,
> Deaf, dumb, lost; gone past seeing.

Bly snipped off everything after 'neutral energy', a third of the whole. He also chopped out dispensable words in the pentameter lines. As a result, the lines of the published poem vary from two beats to five. Montague was staggered: 'I think this [revised poem] gains in the energy of the form, but I'm not sure it offsets the loss of the general moral ... or is it lost?' What was left of his draft was implicitly self-referential, a poem about the art of poetry. Montague let Bly's changes stand and then began to pay heed to the image-based, free-verse aesthetic behind them.[85]

For the emerging collection he accumulated a group of 'artistic credo' lyrics, including '11 Rue Daguerre', which carries the title phrase 'a chosen light'. Another is 'A Bright Day', which celebrates light and clarity as values in Montague's aesthetic. One word in a key line gave Montague trouble: the writer's goal was 'saying something as X as possible'. For 'X' he considered numerous options: *calmly*, *clearly*, *luminously*, *exhaustively*, *rigorously* and *precisely*. All of them suit his aim. He settled on 'luminously'.

'A Bright Day' (dedicated to John McGahern) was one of Seamus Heaney's favourites. He 'loved it for its art, at once delicately tentative and utterly surefooted, but even more for what the art affords, a sense that the veil has trembled, that the glass we see through darkly has been momentarily and uncannily made clear'.[86]

12

In the summer of 1963 Montague had a choice between two job offers: literary editor of *The Spectator* or poet-in-residence at the University of California, Berkeley. Madeleine made the decision for him. She did not want to move to England, and she knew that in early 1964 her job would take her to the United States, so she could spend a few weeks in California, 'Long enough,' Montague wrote to Parkinson, 'she says to clear anyone out of my bed, darn my socks and repair any social blunders I may have made in the first two months.'[87] In fact, she did not darn his socks.

En route to California, he stopped in New York to give a reading with Desmond O'Grady at the Poetry Centre (O'Grady: 'It was [a contest]. I won').[88] In the following days the writer Patric Farrell brought Montague across town to meet, first, Marianne Moore and, next, Mrs Kermit Roosevelt.[89] Montague also called on his American agent, Sheldon Meyer, then looked up Padraic Colum, Beckett's chum George Reavey, the short-story writer Grace Paley, *The New Yorker's* Jane Kramer and her husband, Vincent Crapanzano (friends from Paris), and two anthologists, Donald Allen and Oscar Williams. Before leaving, he attended a reading by James Dickey at the Poetry Centre. Montague worked the city as if he were running for political office.

At Berkeley, his teaching duties included a literature course and a creative-writing workshop. On the weekends, according to *Company*, Tom Parkinson brought him along to San Francisco, where Parkinson was carrying on with a young woman. At a loose end, Montague wound up in bed with her room-mate. It was 'Big Tom', Madeleine's dear friend, who initiated John into the furtive practices of adultery. When his San Francisco bed partner began to consult, for the sake of variety, chapters of the *Kama Sutra*, she scared off the Ulster lad. That was Montague's first extra-marital affair. There would soon be others.[90]

Madeleine came for a week or so in early March. She had, he recalled, tutored him 'in the French style of marriage, where affairs were considered a natural way of letting off steam, and might even be good for the couple'. Once Madeleine left, he sent her a letter saying her visit showed 'me who I am, and where we both stand (immutably) and how my present world joins our past'.[91] In fact, although he was unaware of it, he was standing at the edge of a cliff in the middle of the night.

During Madeleine's visit, something occurred that led to Montague's poem 'The Blow' (section two of 'Loving Reflections'). He slapped his wife on the cheek. Why? Truths were 'upturn[ed]/Too near the bone', but what truths is not said. The blow was sudden, smartly given. Confused, Montague then wondered if he should apologize. Falling back on D.H. Lawrence, he concluded that whatever deed has sprung from passion must be good:[92]

> Hypocrisy
> Is not love's agent,
> Though our fierce awareness
> Would distort instinct
> To stage a mood.

Lawrence makes a poor couples therapist. He and Frieda regularly battered one another, to the bewilderment of friends. Their fights were horrible, but not, it seemed to onlookers, a matter for the police, because he was an under-sized, weak-chested person; Frieda was more than his equal. Madeleine had no such advantage. It was apparently Montague's characteristic oversensitivity to humiliation that led to this slap. Then he conceitedly justified the mistake in verse. This was a step into the beyond – dangerous territory.

13

For the students in Montague's writing workshop, *The Selected Poems* of Robert Graves was required reading.[93] Not so much remembered now for his poetry as for his novels, Graves was a major figure for young post-war poets.

A variety of acolytes made the pilgrimage to Canallún, the seaside house Graves built on a cliff near Deyá, Mallorca. W.S. Merwin even took a job as tutor to the Graves children in order to be close to the poet, before being dismissed for sleeping with one of the old man's muses, Judith Bledsoe.[94] During his own stay on the island, Robert Creeley sketched a splendid verbal portrait:[95]

> He is a long man, not too heavy. A long heavy face, blue eyes with greyish curly hair … almost like Dylan Thomas. His mouth is full, somewhat babyish, big though, and apt to look undetermined. His nose strong, heavy again. In profile he is apt to look somewhat cruel or priggish. Most of the fineness, or most mobile & intelligent part,

occurs around his eyes & forehead. The rest is sensual. He walks with a sort of antagonistic thrusting movement, never too easily, i.e., he always strides. He is impatient out of nervousness, and his voice has a desperate edge to it, and again nervous. He speaks in rushes. He can, at times, be utterly kind, and he is always, I think, well-intentioned. But he is a very damn blind & closed man. Hence, one must not trust him.

Counted among the old poet's followers were Ted Hughes, Thomas Kinsella, Robert Duncan, Derek Mahon and Michael Longley.

The attraction was as much to Graves's *The White Goddess* (1948) as to the poems themselves. After the war, there was a flocking of young men toward 'great literature', not just because of the GI Bill in America, but, after the horrors of war, a felt need for a new humanism. Graves's so-called 'historical grammar of poetic myth', published by T.S. Eliot at Faber & Faber, was the only creative-writing handbook on the market. In it, Graves codified the poetic life of W.B. Yeats into an arcane *vade mecum*.

The first page addresses itself directly to young men who want to be great poets; poetry, like war, is taken to be a 'boys only' endeavour. There is just one way to do it, Graves explains; you have to learn the ancient magical language of poetic myth that is at the heart of every great poem. It is also necessary to submit yourself entirely to the Moon goddess, or Muse, as she takes up temporary residence in a particular mortal woman. You cannot possess your Muse or marry her, he tells his novice readers, but you must fall in love with her and hold nothing back. Your education is to be by way of suffering, through sacrificial encounters with a mind unlike your own and better than your own.

The majority of the rest of *The White Goddess* is taken up with a bewildering exegesis of the earliest Welsh poetry, in quest of an ogham alphabet of trees, supposedly the druids' secret for immortal verses. Those chapters had no influence at all, but the opening pages about the Muse had Pied Piper-like power over male children of the post-war period, and some female children too – Sylvia Plath and Anne Sexton were deeply influenced by *The White Goddess*.

Although as early as 1952 Montague dedicated himself to the Muse in schoolbook fashion by means of the hyper-Gravesian stanzas of 'In Her Service',[96] he was so promiscuous about his devotions to forefathers that Graves did not then become a predominant influence. Before their dates of publication (perhaps in hope of an endorsement), Montague posted the texts of *Forms of Exile* and *Poisoned Lands* to Mallorca. Graves was good enough to write back each time with commentary on particular poems – but he did not provide blurbs.[97] He appreciated Montague's Apollonian perceptiveness and clarity, but believed he needed to channel the Dionysian frenzy of Suibhne, the mad medieval Irish poet. In *Poisoned Lands*, Graves welcomed the 'wildness and controlled stress' of 'Like Dolmens Round My Childhood' and offered line-edits for 'The Last Invasion'.[98] Montague was a natural hero-worshipper. Getting such kindly attention from Robert Graves was thrilling. He told his friends about it each time he received a letter from the mentor in Mallorca. Graves welcomed a visit (he was used to receiving pilgrims). In September 1963 Montague and Madeleine made the trip so that John could pay his respects.

Oddly, while there, Montague drafted his poem 'Beyond the Liss', a quirky fable in the manner of Graves, about an old hunchback who walks the roads at twilight and, hearing music, puts his head over a hedge to spy on female faeries dancing. Was this fable triggered by meeting the lustful old rhymester with his retinue of young muses?[99]

Up to 1964, Montague had not himself put the Muse theory into practice as a licence for lechery. Still, his most profound human experiences, he realized, came from opening himself to a woman, particularly to the crone figures of Minnie Kearney, Freda and Brigid Montague and his mother, Molly. Right after Madeleine left Berkeley, Montague looked over his recent poems and discovered 'an absence of pressure'. He was 'taking the easy way'.[100] Was he just manufacturing versions of life with routine expertise? He should undergo a passion like that of the unwillingly crucified. He should put himself at risk.

That makes his subsequent affair with a visiting lecturer in Berkeley appear to be calculated. In fact, his relationship with 'Lena' (not her real name) blindsided him. She knocked him completely off-balance. Lena was a brilliant Jewish woman engaged to a man who, along with his siblings, would have a remarkable creative life. She became a scholar internationally esteemed by her peers. In 1964 she happened to be spending a research year in Berkeley. At the end of the semester her plan was to marry and live in England.

Neither John nor Lena was prepared for the fury of their coming together. In 'her sexual audacity', Lena seemed 'an embodiment of some primal force', like 'Kali or Coatlicue'. To put it like that is to interpret experience according to the Robert Graves formula, with his teaching that it would be through a particular woman that a male poet might come into contact with archetypal life forces. In fact, John was swept away by Lena herself, her personal force of mind, character and fearlessness.[101]

In early April he tried out a poem with an American setting, from a young husband's point of view. The speaker is alarmed by an 'innocently vulpine howl of happiness' from his wife; he feels as if he were yoked to a different species. On 13 April Montague thought himself lost in a dark tunnel. Love was such a 'disruptive force'. This was more than he had planned for. On 24 April, as Lena lay in a 'soft, exhausted sleep', he had a flashback to the summer of 1950 in Florence, when he learned from a young American painter about sexual intercourse, and sodomy too.[102] Again, he had met a woman who dominated him. She could look right into him. She told him that she could see behind that famous smile of his that everyone loves. She was a witness to his essential sadness, the distant hurt in his eyes. What he was was a damaged child.[103]

In *Company*, Montague admits he fled for a time from the relationship. After as little as three weeks with Lena in the borrowed Berkeley apartment of a Vancouver schoolteacher, he went north to see James Dickey at Reed College and then, moving farther up the country, he gave a reading at the University of Washington, hosted by Carolyn Kizer. Montague and Kizer liked one another. He treated her as an honorary male. The pair shared both poems and news about their private lives. On 5 June, back in Berkeley, he wrote to 'Dear Carolyn', 'you golden-haired scoundrel', to say he was happy for her sake that she had gotten away for some days with her lover. He himself was 'trying to delicately terminate my affair here, so that we can both move back into our chosen lives'.[104] It would not be that easy.

On 7 June Montague tried to make light of his entanglement with Lena in some never-finished verses addressed to Madeleine. They were an obvious attempt to reassure himself that everything was all right and his life had not been fundamentally altered. He was safe; they were safe. After a few days with another woman, he began, he found himself turning back towards Madeleine with tenderness, like a bird to its nest. He was pleased with what they had between them – the few demands Madeleine made of him, or he of her, beyond 'the minimal bonds of decency/To keep a marriage going': 'To behave well towards relatives/To endure each other's friends.' It is like a marriage-contract scene in a play by William Congreve, the negotiation of an unorthodox private treaty between two individuals. It is also whistling in the wind.

After leaving California in mid-June, Lena wrote to John in Paris, secretively, using Liam Miller at Dolmen and the *New York Times* journalist Charles Monaghan's Paris address as letter drops. She had tried to reach Montague by telephone before he left Berkeley, hoping to hear his intimate little Irish stammer once again but she was half-glad not to have reached him. The pair of them needed time apart to manage their lovesickness. She was busy with preparations for her September wedding, an event in the Boston social calendar. However, she would, in hope of news of him, read *The Irish Times* concealed inside her copy of *Jewish Chronicle*.

As their private correspondence continued over the summer, Montague found himself haunted. Old and new loves melted into one another during intercourse. He had nightmares of being left by Madeleine. He suffered recurrent terrors of abandonment. How right he was to draw back from Lena's fierce love! She did not belong to him. Remember, he told himself, there were things about Lena not to his liking – her breasts, her shoulders, her recklessness.[105] In his poem 'Coatlicue', he depicts himself as the goddess's unwilling but chosen victim, recoiling from her 'small,/squat body', 'swart/small breasts', as if she were a living Sheela-na-Gig and he had played no willing part at all in their affair.

Beyond Lena's saucy sense of humour and literary intelligence, she wielded a disconcerting power over Montague. He must fight against it. 'Learn to be cruel,' he scolded himself, and put a stop to this relationship. Still, before the launch of *Death of a Chieftain* in late September, he invited Lena to come along to the event at the Irish embassy in London.

From his subsequent notebook drafts and notes to self it is clear that Montague believed Lena had become a type of muse for him, a dark, frightening imago, one that released a new kind of poetry. From beyond his ego, she had entered into him and, painfully, made him bigger, different from what he had been. She must therefore be understood as a gift, he reasoned. In spite of all his past talk of D.H. Lawrence, this was the first time that sex had been a mode of understanding for him, a means to fresh knowledge.[106] Before he returned for his second spell in Berkeley, he sent Lena a packet of new poems. While admitting that she had a personal investment in the idea of his work having been improved by his acquaintanceship with her, she honestly believed these poems were better than anything he had done before. There were fewer commonplaces, fewer sickly-sweet phrases. And she was happy to be playing a part, even as a dark lady.

One of the key poems that came out of the affair with Lena was 'The Gruagach'. It is another fable of the Robert Graves type, based on a Celtic folklore figure. Lost in a valley, simple herdsmen are alarmed by the sight of a 'brute-thighed giantess'. Their guide assures them, That is just an illusion. They have projected images of their own 'dirty and misshapen selves' into the mountain mists. So the herdsmen wait. A clearing of the mist then reveals the female curve of the mountain, her 'Bleached ribs of rock'. The vision that closes the poem, half-miracle, half-reality made manifest, is inspired by Barrie Cooke's Sheela-na-Gigs, in which the woman is the earth, and earth is a woman. You can deny that anything supernatural occurred and say that it was all in the dirty minds of the men, but these simple herdsmen have been changed, they believe, as a result of something outside themselves.

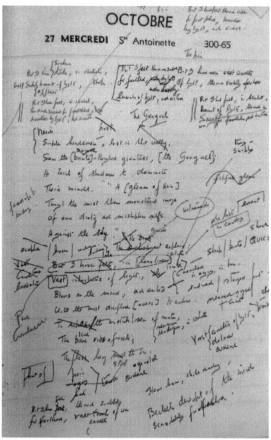

Figure 35: Draft of 'The Gruagach', 27 October 1965. Buffalo.

14

When John Montague left Paris in mid-January 1965, going away alone for his second stint at Berkeley, he felt uneasy about his marriage. He had worked hard over the previous several years to construct a life around the choice he and Madeleine had made to be together. He took comfort in their orderly and sky-lighted studio, their beloved cats, their mutual trust and their seclusion off the courtyard with its grafted cherry tree, a wedding symbol.

In the course of writing the poems for *A Chosen Light*, he had fashioned an aesthetic of grace, order and control. He cherished a passage from Camus: 'When you have once seen the glow of happiness on the face of a beloved person, you know that a man can have no vocation but to awaken that light in the faces surrounding him, and yet we are torn apart by the thought of sadness, which, by the very fact of being alive, we cast into the hearts we meet.'[107] What if the couple's hold on happiness was slipping away?

He hated to think it was his own fault. In a tiny script, on the back of a torn piece of cardboard, full of foreboding, he drafted his poem 'Postscript':[108]

> My love, while we talked
> They removed the roof. Then
> They started on the walls,
> Panes of glass uprooting
> From timber, like teeth.
> But you spoke calmly on,
> Your example of courtesy.
> Compelling me to reply
> When we reached the last
> Syllable, nearly accepting
> Our claims positions, I saw that
> The floorboards were gone:
> It was clay we stood upon.

Perhaps the poem should have been entitled 'Prophecy'. Already in 1965, he envisioned their divorce.

Once in California again he wrote to Madeleine of his loneliness and unease. Was he going to have another nervous breakdown as at Yale?

I had a real moment of panic. You know the symptoms, galloped stomach, mad bouts of sleeplessness, jitteriness that reduces the psyche to a harp-string. There are natures that have an inbuilt discipline, like yours. People like myself need some kind of outside formality, especially at times like these. I wonder if my background has not something to do with it; and the removal of religion has now left a void.[109]

He had best buckle up, because he was in for a fast ride. He had returned to Berkeley at peak 1960s. The Free Speech, Free Love and Anti-War movements were in full swing.

7

THE BERKELEY RENAISSANCE AND THE FREE
LOVE MOVEMENT

I

For his second turn teaching at Berkeley, rather than bunk with Tom Parkinson in the Berkeley hills, Montague took a room at the four-storey Hotel Carlton, conveniently situated at the crossroads of Durant and Telegraph Avenue, just a block down from the university.

At the entrance to the campus on Bancroft Way, recruitment tables lined the sidewalk. Hawkers handed out leaflets inviting one to find Jesus, to integrate schools, to guarantee free speech, to legalize marijuana, to relieve poverty in Africa, to join a Buddhist meditation group, to end racism, to ban the bomb, to stop the war in Vietnam, to liberate women, and many other causes not heard of in the students' hometowns.

Passing by a litter of leaflets, Montague followed the promenade under the Sather Gate, over Strawberry Creek and up into Sproul Plaza, the central quadrangle of the old university, bounded by Sproul Hall (the administration building), the Student Union with its array of open-air tables, the new eight-storey Barrows Hall to the east, and farther up to the west, Wheeler Hall, vast home of the English Department, where Montague was assigned the office of Brendan Ó hEithir, then on sabbatical.

Stretching away from the old quadrangle towards the foothills were the new 'centres' for science, business and technology, the industrial plants of the 'knowledge factory' envisioned by President Clark Kerr in *The Uses of the University* (1964). Knowledge had replaced, Clark Kerr explained, oil, coal and manual labour as the main driver of human progress. The path to the future was for the research 'multiversity', guided by a new managerial class, to take money from business, the military-industrial complex, the state and its student customers in order to produce, on contract, what would profit the nation.

Kerr's nationalist-utilitarian vision of the university ultimately prevailed across the Western world, but, upon first publication, his book was met with shock by the thousands of students of humanities and social sciences at Berkeley. Rebellion against Kerr's redefinition of the purpose of higher education animated the leaders of the Free Speech Movement.

The active conflict began when the dean of the university ordered the removal of the speakers' tables at the gateway to the university. Taking advantage of this authoritarian move, Jack Weinberg promptly made a speech criticizing Clark Kerr's servile conception of the university's role in society. On 1 October the information tables were provocatively set up right in the quadrangle on Sproul Plaza. When Weinberg, arrested, went limp in the style of non-violent protest, and was placed in a police car, the students organized a sit-down protest. Why was he charged? Weinberg was asked. 'It seems that certain – certain of the products [of the 'knowledge factory'] are not coming out according to standard specifications [meaning himself].'

Mario Savio, the movement's charismatic orator, climbed on top of the police car in his stockinged feet – so as not to damage public property – and made a speech, then another student climbed up to speak, then another, each limited to three minutes. The crowd grew from twenty, to fifty, to hundreds, to more than a thousand. For thirty-two hours Jack Weinberg sat alone in the back of the police car, protectively surrounded by students, before negotiations with the Dean's Office brought a temporary end to the protest.[1]

Figure 36: Students in Sproul Plaza, Mario Savio giving a speech from roof of a police car, 1 October 1964.

Publicly embarrassed, the Dean's Office tried to handle the situation by expelling a handful of protestors, only to bring about an 'I am Spartacus!' response, in which hundreds of impenitent students demanded to be treated in the same way. On 2 December Joan Baez gave a free concert on Sproul Plaza, leading the crowds in a chorus of 'We Shall Overcome'. Mario Savio then gave his famous speech from the steps of Sproul Hall:

> I ask you to consider: If this is a firm, and if the board of regents are the board of directors; and if President Kerr in fact is the manager; then I'll tell you something. The faculty are a bunch of employees, and we're the raw material! But we're a bunch of raw materials that don't mean to be …. We're human beings!
>
> There is a time when the operation of the machine becomes so odious, makes you so sick at heart, that you can't take part! You can't even passively take part! And you've got to put your bodies upon the gears and upon the wheels … upon the levers, upon all the apparatus, and you've got to make it stop!

Over 1500 students then followed Mario Savio into Sproul Hall for a sit-in. This stopped the business of the university altogether. It also captured the attention of national television. Edward Meese (later President Reagan's attorney general) called in 600 police officers to drag out the passively resisting students – 770 were arrested.

Montague's mentor Tom Parkinson, as mentioned the son of a labour organizer, was the first faculty member to make common cause with the students in the Free Speech Movement, but by the end of the semester a large majority of the faculty voted against the administration, in favour of the free political speech being permitted on campus.[2]

Things had not settled by the time Montague arrived in early February 1965. A few weeks later, a young radical from New York drifted onto campus holding forth a notebook page on which he had written 'F U C K.' A policeman spotted him, and the young man was charged with an offence against the local obscenity laws and taken away in a patrol car. In solidarity with that single protester, representatives of the Free Speech Movement held an obscenity rally on the steps of the Student Union. The forbidden word was shouted over the public address system time and time again and chanted in chorus by the crowd. Montague, watching, briefly recorded the event in his diary. Strange, in Dublin, that word was used two or three times in every sentence and nobody noticed.

Then he went back to Hotel Carlton to experiment with a poem in the short-line metric of Robert Creeley.

2

Montague's post at Berkeley required him to offer three courses: a first-year Shakespeare course, an undergraduate writing class and a postgraduate poetry workshop, enough to keep a teacher busy and more than the tenured faculty's load.[3] Gary Snyder, an adjunct in the English department at the time, had the same teaching assignment. Montague's diary for February shows that the two were soon in touch and making common cause. On the weekend, the Irish poet rode on the back of Snyder's motorcycle across the bridge to his house at 479 Green Street, in North Beach, San Francisco, a couple of miles from the City Lights Bookstore and little more than a mile from Ghirardelli Marketplace. On top of being a poet, Gary Snyder was a back-to-the woods revolutionary, cutting-edge ecologist, anti-consumerist prophet and Zen spiritual teacher. He had comrades and plenty of followers, male and female. Jack Kerouac gives a lively picture of Gary Snyder as 'Japhy', hero of *The Dharma Bums*. In an early scene, the utterly uninhibited Japhy illustrates for a friend the esoteric discipline of Tantric sex. Kerouac captures the weird, charming, pedantic side of Snyder:[4] 'This is what they do in the temples of Tibet. It's a holy ceremony, it's done just like this in front of chanting priests. People pray and recite Om Mani Pahdme Hum, which means Amen the Thunderbolt in the Dark Void. I'm the thunderbolt and Princess is the dark void, you see.'

Figure 37: Montague in yoga position, reading The Dharma Bums, *Berkeley, 1965; Photograph taken by Carole Smith; Carole to JM, 27 April 1966.*

Snyder encouraged Montague to shed his hang-ups by participating in an orgy. One needed to get past shame, hypocrisy and conceit to write in the simple sincere voice of the new poetry. An orgy was a step too far for this Ulster Catholic, however. Montague did make friends with Carole, a young woman from Los Angeles studying Buddhism with Gary Snyder. After sharing a companionate bed for a night in March, Montague left Carole with some verses in which he experimented with enjambement, looking for 'the way Gary gets energy into the line'.[5]

> North Beach mornings
> Waking to a white tower
> That has been erected overnight;
> The eye follows the curve
> Of the hills as we take
> Morning coffee …

In North Beach, people were preternaturally relaxed about having sex, as easy as drinking coffee together or writing a poem. It seemed unreal. Irish culture in the twentieth century was built on sexual self-control. Men did not normally marry until they were the age of grandfathers. Unmarried women were imprisoned in Magdalene laundries if they fell pregnant. The Irish conception of public morality was narrowed to one sin, sex, so that 'violence, perjury, deceit in business were all treated as venial' and drunkenness was not regarded as a vice at all.[6] The culture shock of 1960s' California was dizzying for an Irishman.

Montague aimed to make his courses into 'a species of intellectual adventure'.[7] It was a period in the cultural life of American universities in which young people looked for meaning in poetry, or rather, looked to poetry for meaning, because other repositories of value were failing (pastors, politicians, parents). It was not to Gary Snyder alone that young Californians attributed the status of a shaman. Many of the poets of the Berkeley Renaissance were the next thing to rock stars – Allen Ginsberg, Joanne Kyger, Robert Duncan, Jack Spicer, Philip Whalen, Lew Welch, Tom Parkinson too and others – they all had a special status in the new youth culture.

The young Irishman himself acquired a small number of admirers. One young woman trailed him from class back to his office and hung daisy chains on his doorknob (in that gesture, Madeleine spotted the opportunity for a *double entendre*). The student asked if, as teacher, he would be so kind as to liberate her from her virginity. Thomas Parkinson, no saint in respect of staff-student affairs, warned his young friend to be careful. Perhaps Montague did become more discreet, at least with undergraduates, but by the second week of March he had cause to warn himself in his diary about promiscuity. He sermonized himself in an Irish penitential manner: it was demeaning to operate through just one part of one's being, and that the lowest part. But it was difficult not to do what for the first time in his life was freely permissible – casual sex for the sake of pleasure and friendship.

The free-love spirit thrived briefly in American cultural history – after the pill, before the outbreak of AIDS and when a main interpretation of women's liberation was the freedom of women to have sex when, how and with whom they wished, without obligation. Key to the concept of liberation was freedom from being male property in marriage and family. Self-ownership, with all the consequences of equal rights under the law, was the goal. It was as if, Montague reflected, the women had all been reading Robert Graves' 'She is No Liar'. This poem is in praise of a woman who, in a spirit of self-determination, writes off a night's love:[8]

> She is no liar, yet she will wash away
> Honey from her lips, blood from her shadowy hand,
> And, dressed at dawn in clean white robes will say,
> Trusting the ignorant world to understand:
> 'Such things no longer are; this is today.'

During these months, Montague discovered that he really liked making love and, to his surprise, was even complimented on his efforts. This was the first physical activity for which he appeared to show some talent.[9]

Over the course of the semester, he slept with seven different women. While in the company of Berkeley Buddhists and orientalists, he was taught to reflect that, by means of these affairs, he was communing with Parvati, the Hindu goddess of love and devotion. She is often represented as having many heads, some lovely and feminine, others at least half-male, because bearded or moustachioed, or old and grey-haired, still more with the trunks of elephants, or lions' whiskers, every one of them smiling peacefully. Parvati is the gentle, nurturing face of earthly life. A new concept altogether for the boy from Garvaghey.

3

With one woman that semester, Paule Anglim, Montague forged a lasting friendship. The two truly enjoyed one another's company. They often had dinner and took trips together out of town. By birth a Québécois, Paule Anglim became a leading dealer of contemporary art in San Francisco. One of the artists she represented was the collagist Jess Collins, life partner of poet Robert Duncan. In March 1965 Paule planned a dinner party at her house across the Golden Gate Bridge and then arranged for a car to collect first Montague and then Duncan and Collins, so that the two poets would have a chance to get to know one another on the way to the party.

Montague was already a great admirer of Duncan's poetry. Before arriving in Berkeley, he had formulated the hope that, by sitting at Duncan's feet, he could acquire something of his fierce artistic belief in the holiness of the imagination.[10] As a practising visionary, Robert Duncan was the most Yeatsian of all contemporary poets. Montague had his doubts about some of the more recent, seemingly endless dithyrambic political poems, but he was impressed by the figure Duncan cut. When Duncan read a poem, his voice was 'ecstatic with electricity', his head and body quivering. He dressed the part too, with clothes not off the rack – full-sleeved shirts with extra broad collars, pastel in colour, closed by a purple tie or a large fluffy bow. Like Robert Graves (one of Duncan's heroes), he wore rings that supposedly possessed magical powers of protection. With the 'saucy cock of his head with its brash combed-up pompadour', Duncan was a full-on fop and a major Romantic poet too.[11]

Robert Duncan was a monologist. In a literary person like Montague, he found an ideal listener who, unwearied, could follow every move in Duncan's fantastical dialectic. Duncan venerated the great poets of the past, from ancient Greeks like Pindar, through the Romantics Blake, Shelley and Keats. He was deliberately eclectic and conceived of all great literature as the communal property of poets, from which one borrowed freely and returned one's own best thoughts to this spiritual bank. Like Carl Jung and Robert Graves, he saw the world through archetypes and the gods of dead religions. His poems, he believed, came from outside himself, whether from the spirit of ancient poets, the collective unconscious, or somewhere else beyond the world of the human ego. The poem was entrusted to one from without oneself.

Among contemporary American poets, Duncan was the most successful in making use of the example of Ezra Pound. Unfazed by an indictment for treason that had hung over the head of Pound, Duncan honoured his patriotic protest against the failure of the United States to live up to its original principles. The nation had betrayed itself to capitalism and military expansionism. Angered by the Vietnam War and the armed suppression of youth culture, Duncan carried on Pound's tradition of protest. He poured everything into open-form book-length sequences, with ode-like variable lyrics. And like Yeats, Duncan was a deep diver in esoteric libraries.[12] With his encouragement, Montague was soon on the mailing list of an occult bookstore in San Francisco. He began to adapt for the purposes of poetry some of the speech acts of magicians: the charm, the spell, the blessing, the prophecy and the invocation of spirits.

Duncan's signature poem, 'Often I am Permitted to Return to a Meadow', began as a lyric outburst of rage against an English critic who dismissed Pound's work.[13] He drew upon Jewish Gnosticism for the image of the field of Macphelah, burial ground of Adam, Eve and Abraham, and therefore the Garden of Eden. That image was melded with one of the square Roman field, which traditionally included an ancestral tomb, hearth, dwelling and tutelary spirits at the boundary wall. This Kabbalistic complex underlay the page on which Duncan composed, a field upon which sounding verses could be projected in lines determined in their length by a lungful of breath. Rather than justifying his lines along the left margin, or employing a fixed pattern of indentations, sometimes Duncan (like Charles Olson) distributed the lines over the whole page to register an effect of complex syncopation, a method called 'Composition by Field'.

Being past pilgrims to Mallorca, both Montague and Duncan talked of Robert Graves and *The White Goddess*. Duncan had been inspired by Anaïs Nin; he was her pet in New York City in the late 1930s and early '40s. But his primary muse was H.D. (Hilda Doolittle), the Imagist poet and long-time friend of Pound. For six years Duncan had been engaged with his *H.D. Book*, a tribute to the role women played in literary modernism and a workbook for his own evolving aesthetic. Now he was reading his book's proofs. That was literary catnip for Montague; he was twitching with curiosity. After the party, he wrote to Duncan asking if, when the two met again at Philip Whalen's reading, he might, as Duncan had offered, have a look at those proofs. Please? He would feel honoured.[14]

When Madeleine came for a visit to California, John brought her to meet his new friends Robert and Jess; he knew she would find the pair a treat.[15] Like Morris Graves and Richard Svare, the couple were gifted homemakers. They had put aside the promiscuous and wandering life of some homosexuals, pushed to the outlaw margins of society. Jess and Robert over time assembled beloved pieces of furniture, often Victoriana, trouvailles of totemistic value, their own dining customs and personal rituals of hospitality. They made a home for themselves. Robert Duncan explained that 'loyalty is to the household' (he allowed himself promiscuity beyond its walls).[16] As film-maker Stan Brakage, a former housemate, observed: 'They were people living out the peculiarities of their lives as a triumph, rather than an abyss.' John and Madeleine Montague were curious about models for a non-traditional, companionate marriage. They respected the social innovations driven by creative homosexuals. As an homage to their household, Montague sent Robert and Jess a copy of his next book: 'I call it *A Chosen Light* after our studio, another hearth.'[17]

While in Berkeley for his second stint of teaching, Montague was able to steady himself by visits to the household nearby of Robert Tracy and his wife, Rebecca. Robert Tracy, a professor of English, was a friend of Donald Fanger and later of Seamus Heaney; he joined the Berkeley faculty in 1960.[18] Montague became a frequent guest at the Tracy's dinner table. He was particularly partial to Rebecca's 'Hangtown Fry', a mining-camp specialty. The Tracys put on a fine dinner party whenever Madeleine came to visit, with the Parkinsons and Fanger's old friend, the novelist Chester Aron and his wife, Marguerite, as guests.[19] The friendship carried over into family visits to Ireland and Robert Tracy's books and articles on modern Irish literature.

4

'Vietnam Day', the enormous 'teach-in' on the Berkeley campus, was not a single day; it ran from 21 to 23 May. Thirty-five thousand people came to hear a line-up of anti-war campaigners – Dr Benjamin Spock, Norman Mailer, Buddhist Alan Watts, comedian Dick Gregory and lots of others. The procession of lecturers was broken up by crowd-pleasing appearances of comedians, agit-prop performers, folk singers like Phil Ochs and the poets of the Berkeley Renaissance.

Montague was touched when he was invited by the local poets to take part.[20] He read at 12.30 pm on 21 May. It is not known how he read, or what he read.

Poets like Duncan, Snyder and Allen Ginsberg had written chant-like, rousing, rhetorical poems of a type to be declaimed to a sea of people. Montague had not, not yet. He could have read 'The Siege of Mullingar', a public poem styled after Yeats's 'September 1913', in which he hailed the first appearance in Ireland of the spirit of the 1960s (written after a wild *fleadh cheoil* in June 1963).[21] It was a ringing, prophetic, declamatory poem, the verse accompaniment to Whitaker's 'First Programme for Economic Expansion', because it was a hymn to the end of the old Ireland and to the birth of the new. But what did that poem have to do with B52s bombing the Vietnamese? The Vietnam Day experience made Montague want to go back to Ireland, away from a political context in which he had no say, to one where he might make a difference.[22]

By the time of the Berkeley Poetry Conference (12–24 July), Montague had returned from California to Europe. It brought together in person the New York and California contributors to Donald Allen's anthology *The New American Poetry* (1960). However, before Montague's departure, Tom Parkinson, a chief organizer of the conference, hosted parties for many of the poets. The Irishman was in the swim of things at these events. In mid-June Montague exhausted himself at another week-long poetry festival in San Francisco, which featured seven invited poets, winding up with a reading by Bill Dickey, a classmate from the Iowa Writers' Workshop.

So many big readings! Nineteen sixty-five was a year of the hosting of battalions of poets, both in festivals and at academically serious conferences. Amazingly, these events drew crowds. In June, Lena sent John a detailed report on the International Poetry Incarnation, an extravaganza staged at the Royal Albert Hall, London. It had a paying audience of seven thousand. Allen Ginsberg, Pablo Neruda, Alexander Trocchi and Andrei Voznesensky whooped it up with Michael Horowitz and other English poets, not always in mutual admiration. The event triggered the experimentalist British anthology *Children of Albion* (1969). With the help of Lena, Peter Whitehead, the director of music videos for Pink Floyd and the Rolling Stones, filmed the readings in a suitably idiosyncratic cinematography. Between the camera lens and the poet at the microphone, a stoned young woman dances with herself.[23]

Upon his return to Ireland, Montague was invited to the International Poetry Festival at the Belgian seaside town Knokke le Zoute. On board his flight from Paris to Brussels, Montague jotted down notes for the introduction to his reading. The sight out of the plane window of all the criss-crossing motorways, and of post-war planned cities with their ring roads, gave him a thought. A new religion had taken the place of Christianity – worship of the automobile. Everything was sacrificed to this idol: historic cities, Sunday strollers, the countryside, even the air people breathe. He worked himself up into a proper anti-capitalist, environmentalist rant, just like a Berkeley poet.[24] This moment of perception lies behind his 'Hymn to the New Omagh Road' in *The Rough Field*.

In Knokke he was impressed by the manly Slavs – poets who had been threatened by police and some of them jailed – in Hungary, Yugoslavia and Poland. The 'complicated melancholy' of Czeslaw Milosz was particularly striking, as if he bore the weight of history on his back.[25] A poet's work was necessary and, if you did it right, it could be dangerous.

5

Over the spring and summer John had often been in correspondence with Lena.[26] They arranged to meet up at a Soho apartment on 1 September, after the Belgian festival.

The hours the couple spent together left Montague in the days afterwards with black dreams and sexual hallucinations. He struggled with verses under the guiding titles 'The Pale Light', 'Succubus' and 'Medusa'. The drafts depict the encounter as the nightmarish reappearance in his life of an archetypal female figure, with ashen breath and snake-like hair. Her presence 'Rears the genitals' and 'Tears away all/I had so carefully built – /Position, marriage, fame.' After a night of turning and turning in bed, 'the hiss of seed' 'Is the whimper of death being born.'[27] The death of what? His social life? The death of his seed? The death of a foetus? Alongside the draft lines, Montague put to himself the question: 'Am I a complete bastard?'[28]

Montague tentatively confided in Barrie Cooke: 'I saw Lena in London. Although I am not in love with her, we are connected. Under force of circumstances, we did something that frightens me a little. Perhaps I will be able to tell you about it someday. I don't think we can go any further ...'[29] It is unknown what that frightening thing they did together was. John and Lena's journey together had not, in any case, come to an end.

In early October Montague flew to Dublin to read at Spike Milligan's event at the Abbey Theatre, a night of poetry, jazz and singing.[30] A letter from Lena awaited him at Liam Miller's house.

A baby had been conceived. Her husband doubted it was his own. He proposed she obtain an abortion.

The news overwhelmed Montague. He walked up and down the rainy streets of Dublin trying to compose an answer. She had had an abortion before; a second might be the death of her, he feared. Anyway, the pregnancy might not come to term. If it did, could she not still have the child and stay married? He could not think it out clearly. It was her decision, but if she wanted to write again, or talk on the phone, he let her know he would accompany her through the experience, but remotely. He made no offer to leave his wife and make a life with Lena. He did not want to do either of those things.

A day later, he drafted 'Coming Events', a prose-poem about Gerard David's fifteenth-century painting of a man being flayed.[31]

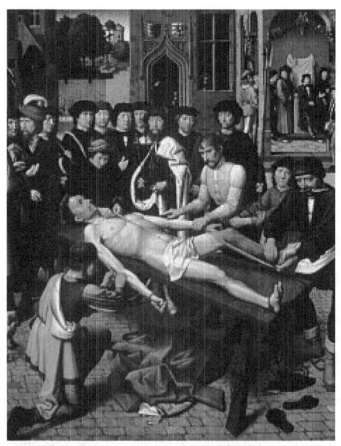

Figure 38: Gerard David, The Judgment of Cambyses: The Flaying of Sisamnes *(1498).*

He could not change his religious background, he reasoned to himself. It was just a fact that he had been raised as a Catholic. Abortion, he had been taught, was a crime against life. He had to absorb what he himself had done and expiate his own sin over time for the rest of his life. In the future, like Robert Frost, he must learn to keep this trouble down, 'under the surface, where great griefs belong'.[32] No one must know, but him, Lena and her husband.

In late October Lena sent him what was not so much just an angry letter as a letter reflecting on her anger. Neither her husband nor her lover was doing what she wanted; neither supported her. They left her to decide, but they gave her only one door to walk through – abortion. One would not raise another man's child; the other would not leave his wife to be a father to the child he sired and that she still wanted to bear. They were alike, both conventional and hypocritical; the only difference between them was that the Irishman had a spoonful of fake charm. What Lena had to do was repugnant to her.

Montague felt the force of this letter. He worked his way through a succession of draft replies. He refused to fall into recriminations or to deny his part in what had become a fiasco. At the time, he was in Garvaghey visiting Aunt Brigid, then in the Omagh hospital. He walked up to the churchyard and paused before the headstones of his ancestors. He imagined there another small stone, that of his newly conceived son, never to be born.

The letter that he finally managed to send she found gentle and comprehending, though she pointed out to him the patriarchalism of his interest in the survival of his name and the continuation of the family homeplace. Still, she knew she could not expect him *not* to be a man and an Irish Catholic. That's what he was.

As it happened, the crisis slowly brought her closer to her husband. Honestly, even though each could see awful things in the other, they felt bound to one another. Besides, Lena was unwilling to choose the 'martyrdom' of a single woman's life and sole parenthood. In closing, she thanked Montague for the poem to his 'Dark Muse', 'The Gruagach'. She treasured it. She still retained a Muse's pride in co-authorship.

By 17 November it was all over. Yes, she agreed she would like to talk with him, and she agreed to his proposal that they should not see one another, not for a very long time. There was nothing left to hide, and nothing left to desire.[33]

6

It was the domestic custom of John and Madeleine at 11 rue Daguerre to read one another's post when one of the two was out of town. In that way, they were open with one another. However, John had arranged for Lena's letters to be routed through other addresses than his own in Paris and Dublin, so as to keep that single correspondence private. But the affair did not remain secret. In the middle of the crisis over Lena's pregnancy, there is a note to Madeleine in John's notebook: 'Why have you taken to reading my notebooks, Pussycat?'[34] It is uncertain whether Madeleine also picked up one of the blue aerograms sent by Lena, such as the heart-rending letter about the abortion described in the poem 'Special Delivery'. Somehow she became aware of the seriousness of the affair, and he knew that she knew.[35] It weighed on both of them.

The tender constraint between the couple is the painful theme of 'A Private Reason', begun in July after Montague's return from Berkeley. He and Madeleine walked around the ornamental lakes at Versailles, not speaking of what was on their minds, but behaving beautifully, with courtly Gallic dignity.[36] The poem admires that traditional form of life, but from the point of view of an outsider, and one aware of all the wild sorrow that goes chokingly unspoken by those who stick to their customary roles.

'A Private Reason' is a poem like 'That Room', not just in being a sad love poem to Madeleine, but in being intimate without betraying privacies. It is for the biographer to do that.

7

Part of Montague's reaction to the abortion went into one of his best poems, 'Courtyard in Winter'. Its impetus was the suicide of Joan Wardle, the ex-wife of the theatre critic Irving Wardle. After the Wardles split up, she had become a friend of Montague's, possibly a lover. The two men met at the Falstaff pub in Paris in 1964. Irving was worried about Joan.[37] She seemed disturbed and beyond his reach, now that they were apart. What did Montague know about her present state?

With Joan, John had had, he told Irving, a 'very deep' conversation, but, as he writes in the poem, he 'never/Managed to ease the single hurt/That edged her towards her death.' A year or more later, in the autumn of 1965, while hobbling through the crisis with Lena, he was shocked to learn that Joan had killed herself a few months earlier (by pills, not by gas as in the poem; there's a Sylvia Plath subtext to the wintry scene as well). Suicide and abortion seemed alike, tragically final outcomes for persons who could not solve a passing problem, mistaken actions taken in cold and dark times, just before dawn.

The poem's counsel is just what Montague had vainly been telling himself: the saving power of discipline, endurance and kindness. It was what Madeleine had taught him and here, in a poem about another woman's suffering, he regards it as, for himself, a lifesaver. Beyond that lesson, 'A Courtyard in Winter' falls back on childhood touchstones, a boy bringing messages from the post office to lonely people in the hills, pure water fetched from its source and trust in a true community. It is a poem that can bear comparison with the great meditative elegies of W.B. Yeats. A very high standard.

8

The Californian trend of poetry festivals – like Civil Rights demonstrations – came to Belfast too. Montague registered the significance of the line-up for the Belfast Festival in November 1965: 'It dawns on me that there is, very definitely, a take-over bid in the North.'[38] He alerted Liam Miller, who was preparing small editions for Montague and Kinsella – *All Legendary Obstacles* and *Wormwood*. 'What about another big [Dolmen Editions] reading in the Spring? Some kind of general programme in which (at the time of publication) I could read *All Legendary Obstacles*, Liddy and the bards could perform, Austin [Clarke's] Claddagh record could be launched, and Seamus Heaney's fare down could be paid.' Regarding Heaney, he added, 'We must try and enlist this colt, before we have a Rival Renaissance going full blast in Belfast, with both sides <u>doomed</u> to failure.'

Montague quickly drew up a proposal for a biennial 'Living Poetry Festival' to be held in Dublin:

a. <u>Performances</u>

The Lantern Theatre Company have in their current repertory a full-length play by Austin Clarke, <u>The Moment Next to Nothing</u>; a short play, <u>The Viscount of Blarney</u>; and have in preparation Austin Clarke's <u>Cervantes</u>.

Plays by Yeats and other plays in verse by Irish dramatists could be presented. Perhaps one of the Gaelic Theatre Companies could present a poetic play in verse …

b. Readings

1. Reading of Austin Clarke's poetry (and press conference for Claddagh record)
2. Reading of poems from the Old Irish, with translations
3. A reading by three Irish poets (possibly John Montague, Thomas Kinsella, Richard Murphy) [added in pencil: Seamus Heaney]
4. Reading by a guest poet from abroad (possibly Robert Graves ... or MacDiarmid, & MacCaig)
5. A reading by poets in Irish
6. A reading by young poets writing today

Other Events.

1. Poetry and Ballads ... presented by leading singers
2. Irish poets set to music (pencil: Ó Riada)
3. A lecture on Austin Clarke's work (pencil: by John Jordan)
4. A discussion, bilingual possibly, of Poetry in Ireland today (pencil: Martin Ó Direan)
5. The Poet and 1916, an illustrated lecture
6. A poetry competition or a prize

Support from Arts Council, Cultural Relations Committee, Bord Fáilte, business interests, publishers, booksellers and universities.

The ambition here is large and generous, with poetry variously allied to music, song, bilingualism, scholarship, education and history. Montague wanted to nurse along the young 'Second Irish Revival' but he also wanted to secure (as opposed to 'Ulster poetry') an All-Ireland movement, even an 'archipelagic' one that included the Scots and Welsh. At the core, he was an anti-Partition Irish republican.

Montague maintained a careful watch over the rise of Seamus Heaney. A dedicated file of clippings was kept up to date, going back to the 1963 newspaper appearance of 'An Advancement of Learning' and 'Churning Day'. Montague examined that poem as if he were marking a student paper. Its title was very literary, perhaps too much so, Montague commented in the margin. 'Ever-disgusting' was an awkward, redundant modifier of 'rodent'. However, the last line stopped him in his tracks: 'the pat and slap of small spades on wet lumps'.

'Hopkins through [W.R.] Rodgers, only <u>better</u>,' the teacher exclaimed. Here was a student who surpassed his masters.

In December 1964 Montague clipped 'Digging' from the *New Statesman*. Like McGahern, Heaney 'keeps right to the object'. Montague edited out some words, looking for something leaner, less square and block-like. Yet 'Digging' conveyed 'perfect arrogance, and a programme'.[39] It was like a thesis statement at the beginning of a ground-breaking dissertation. This student had passed to the next level.

The two Ulster poets met in Belfast in June 1965 at a fundraiser for the Lyric Theatre. Mary O'Malley organized a poetry reading by Padraic Colum, John Hewitt, Roy McFadden, Kinsella, Montague and 26-year-old Seamus Heaney. Thereafter, work by Heaney began to show up everywhere that Montague himself was publishing – *The Listener*, *The Irish Times*, *Threshold*, *Kilkenny Magazine* and *Hibernia*. In January 1966 Montague wrote to Tim O'Keeffe, 'That man seems to be following me, the way I follow Kavanagh, although I plan to be sweeter-tempered with him.'[40] Montague did not want to stop the burgeoning young Derryman; he wanted to make common cause with him.'I mean this – we must contact the Belfast group at its apex,' he told Liam Miller, 'which does seem to be Heaney.'[41]

In spite of such foresight, it was already too late. After meeting Montague in Belfast, Heaney did submit a collection of poems to Dolmen on 16 September 1964, but, not having heard promptly from Liam Miller, he then received an offer from Charles Monteith, the Antrim-born editor at Faber. So, Heaney asked Dolmen for his manuscript to be returned on 2 March 1965.[42] *Death of a Naturalist* turned out to be a bellwether publication; the rest of the herd followed the buck ram. A number of the fine poets from the North would thereafter be published in London by Faber: Paul Muldoon and Tom Paulin, just to take the first cohort; others would follow. Dolmen was not in the running for the new voices from the North.

When Montague read Faber's edition of *Death of a Naturalist* in May 1966, he felt a bit sick: the resemblance to his own work was so close. Heaney had turned what he had borrowed into a formula, then spun off variations at a geometrical rate of increase. It was, Montague said at the time, like someone 'walking on my grave', an ominous metaphor from a poet who was still just thirty-seven years old.[43]

The sensational public reception of *Death of a Naturalist* would lead the way to celebration of the 'Ulster Renaissance'. The 'Second Irish Revival' as a 'brand' would vanish like snow off a rope.

9

The Tyrone poet was going in the other direction, from London to Dublin. While Montague remained a MacGibbon and Kee author, his growing friendship with Liam Miller made him wish to do a small collection, in a limited edition, with The Dolmen Press. This would be 'the most integrated group of poems yet to come from [his] pen'. He meant the autobiographical sequence to compare (in form) with D.H. Lawrence's *Look! We Have Come Through!*[44] The title came from the poem to Madeleine he had finally managed to finish, 'All Legendary Obstacles'.

Excited about the commission, Miller envisioned a design of 'chaste elegance': a tall, slender page, with plenty of margin, italic type of just one size.[45] Barrie Cooke was recruited to do an ink drawing for the cover. Montague wanted an image of 'mournful fleshliness'. What Cooke came up with nearly frightened off poet and publisher. The relation of the hips, male and female, to one another, and the suggestive use of heavy cross-hatching, were felt to be sensational. It undeniably depicts two naked figures interlocking, not the usual cover for an Irish publication. Overall, Montague was impressed, particularly by Liam Miller's achievement: 'an exceedingly handsome book'.[46]

Figure 39: Barrie Cooke, drawing for All Legendary Obstacles, *1966.*

Some of the lyrics in *All Legendary Obstacles* arose not from John's relationship to Madeleine but from the affair with Lena, such as 'The Gruagach' and 'A Charm'.[47] There were others among the poems he was feverishly writing in the autumn of 1965 that were just as intense, honest and intimate, but he kept those out of the book. For the time being, they seemed unprintably personal. Later, they would be gathered into a section of *Tides* (1970) entitled 'The Pale Light'.

Alluding to the sets of prayers in the Rosary, Montague thought of the poems in *All Legendary Obstacles* as 'The Glorious Mysteries' (dedicated to the Virgin) and the *Tides* group as 'The Sorrowful Mysteries' (concerning the agony and crucifixion of Jesus). The grandiose comparison is self-mocking, at least half-ironic about his hopes of revelation by means of sexual experiences.

10

Montague had left Berkeley with the desire to re-engage with Irish life. Once again Professor Roger McHugh came to his aid. There would be a place for him in the new UCD Department of Anglo-Irish Literature, headed up by McHugh.[48]

John Jordan was already on the staff at UCD. The two former classmates remained anxious about precedence. Jordan stopped in to 11 rue Daguerre in the autumn of 1965 to sniff out what courses Montague intended to teach at UCD and, by the same token, to establish his prior claims. The visit got Montague's back up. He let Roger McHugh know that it was essential that if he were to come to UCD, he be appointed at a rank at least equal to that of John Jordan. This seems a trivial matter, but it was excruciatingly important to each of them. In some ways, Montague was a true academic.

In late January Montague gave a lecture at Earlsfort Terrace, with both John Jordan and Roger McHugh seated among the students in the auditorium. They were there to evaluate him. It went well and he was offered a post, but at the rank of assistant lecturer. Nothing higher was possible. His pride wounded, Montague havered over accepting.[49]

He had already gone about re-establishing his Dublin connections by lunching variously with Todd Andrews, Michael Scott, Dorothy Walker, Father Donal O'Sullivan and other key figures in the cultural establishment. He had also rounded up international contributors to *A Tribute to Austin Clarke on His Seventieth Birthday*. Liam Miller was well advanced with its design. Other aspects of Montague's grand programme for a biennial Irish poetry festival had not been funded, but in May there would be launches of the Dolmen editions of Kinsella and Montague, as well as a birthday celebration for Austin Clarke. He had begun to stir things up in Ireland. A post at UCD would provide a base to continue these efforts. However, he noticed that many writers had left Ireland for other countries – Kinsella, Aidan Higgins, John McGahern, Tony Cronin, Pearse Hutchinson, even Kavanagh for much of the time. Dublin seemed a bit empty.

Meanwhile, his engagement with cultural life in Paris had quickened. He and Madeleine had become friends with the famous print-maker Stanley William Hayter and his beautiful Irish partner Désirée Moorhead. They were just a ten-minute walk away at 36 rue Boissonade, in the 14th arrondissement.

Over the holiday season of 1965 Hayter proposed a collaboration. He would do a series of multicoloured engravings of the sea, and John could write poems in accompaniment. Soon, Montague's mind was reeling with images of rigging and polyps, currents and deliquescence. He immersed himself in Melville's *Moby-Dick.* Hayter's knowledge of physics and chemistry gave the poet a new take on the sea: life-and-death as a continuous organic process. Writing the imagistic, philosophical lyrics of 'Sea Changes' became Montague's way of coming out of the chaos of melancholy that resulted from the aborted child and the death of his Aunt Brigid. He dealt with the nature of existence through sea images, without the self-protective devices of irony and ambiguity, or any hint of personal confession.[50]

Montague's friendship with the young French critic Serge Fauchereau was also deepening. In April 1965, Serge, a schoolteacher in the provinces on a trip to Paris, met Robert Bly and John Ashbery in a hotel on rue Jacob. Bly suggested, since Serge was so interested in poetry, that he look up John Montague at 11 rue Daguerre.[51] Soon the two were engaged upon a serious literary correspondence, long scholarly aestheticizing letters, in which they hatched plans for trans-cultural publications. Serge busied himself with translating poems and stories by Montague for *Les Lettres Nouvelles.*[52] A long-term project was Fauchereau's book about modern poetry in English. There was no better local guide to this subject than Montague. Serge always had the energy not just to conceive of big projects, but to bring them to fruition.

An anthology of modern French poetry was Montague's own new enterprise, with translations by James Dickey and himself. MacGibbon and Kee in London and Grove Press in New York were on board as publishers. Montague estimated that the job would take at least three years (as it turned out, he was still working on it when he died). Serge Fauchereau could be counted on as adviser to the selection of writers and on the accuracy of the translations. The grand purpose of the anthology was to bring the two literatures, English and French, so united in the first flush of modernism, back into conversation with one another.[53]

In May 1966, while reading Richard Loftus's *Nationalism in Modern Anglo-Irish Poetry*, John reflected in a letter to Serge on the opposing pulls he felt, to Irish poetry, and to world poetry:

> I am reading with great interest Loftus, a healthy, thoughtful work ... Myself, though I feel intensely – all too, as Joyce said – Irish ... I have no theories about the country except a desire to preserve what seems individual and best in it, just as I would if I were a Catalan. I feel more anxious to go back, even to re-learn my Irish, but I also feel the opposite desire, to slowly understand as much of our world (France and America my special areas, so to speak) as possible. I refuse to make a case out of it ... Neither a dramatic expatriate, nor a little Irelander; the dichotomy seems to me dated.[54]

This was one his first efforts to articulate his conception of a post-nationalist 'global regionalism'.[55]

Ultimately, he wanted the post at UCD, especially after an outbreak of violence in Belfast over Easter 1966, clashes between Ian Paisley's followers and republicans celebrating the fiftieth anniversary of Easter 1916. This was a conflict in which Montague felt he had a stake.

Madeleine was instrumental in talking John down off his high horse. He accepted an appointment for two quarters a year, January to May (Madeleine: 'With six weeks holiday in the middle – no wonder the Irish are so ignorant!').[56]

Montague's new post at UCD did not put an end to his transcultural ambitions. By the end of the first semester he had booked the Lantern Theatre for talks by Serge Fauchereau and Michel Deguy. Deguy was a poet, professor of literature at the Sorbonne and editor of *Les Temps Modernes*, the magazine founded by Jean-Paul Sartre. In Dublin he explained the situation of the contemporary French poet, while Fauchereau gave a French critic's view of Irish poetry. Montague translated.[57] The funding for the event was scant, so the French visitors were accommodated on various couches and single beds of Montague's ramshackle attic apartment (borrowed from poet Richard Weber) at 13 Anglesea Street, Temple Bar.

*Figure 40: Lantern Theatre reception, 24 July 1967; John Montague,
Serge Fauchereau and Michel Deguy.*

II

Upon Montague's arrival in January 1967 to teach at UCD, he had John Berryman on his hands much of the time. Before coming to Dublin for a year (September 1966 to June 1967), Berryman had written to Montague asking for help in finding a house for himself, his wife, Kate, and his young daughter, Martha. Montague had the poet initially booked into the Majestic Hotel, across from the United Arts Club, and asked Liam Miller to take over the job of house-hunting. Berryman was delighted with the Georgian buildings just outside the doors of the Majestic on Fitzwilliam Street, where the 'Eighteenth Century lives on and on'. Inside, while he was sinking one martini after another, 'The Irish converse about practical questions,/& about finding us a house fast' ('Dream Song 307'). 'The Irish' would be Liam Miller and John Montague. Within a week, the Berrymans moved into 55 Lansdowne Park, Ballsbridge.[58]

Montague harboured doubts about the confessionalism of Berryman's *Dream Songs*. Berryman always imagined himself as the loser in a winner's country. 'There is something *voulu*, a willed disorder in his work,' Montague wrote to Serge Fauchereau in December 1966, as if Berryman actually desired to be a *poète maudit*, whereas surely one ought to be forcibly driven 'beyond the gentility principle', not seek out that state 'with a cold intelligence …

deliberately'.[59] Like a down-and-out criminal singing the blues, Berryman is generally aware of the damage done by his life, yet that awareness is a cocktail of self-pity. As a role model for a young man, he wasn't the best.

After spending more time with the spectacled, great-bearded poet, however, Montague found him 'as splendid and generous a figure as one might meet'.[60] The two men each had a 'rare gift for communicable literary hero worship'.[61] The American had come to Ireland because it was, he thought, 'the chief lion-breeding place'. 'I bow gently to my superiors ... Swift, Yeats, Joyce' ('Dream Song 307'). Berryman did drink a lot. 'Even more than I do,' Montague admitted. Berryman had settled into Jack Ryan's pub, just a five-minute walk from the house he rented. It served him from morning until night as office, lecture hall, podium for poetry recitals and reception room. Within a few months, he had written seventy-five 'dream songs' in the place.

In the autumn his companions had often just been the pub regulars, but from January on, Montague brought people to meet the great man, like Denis Donoghue and Nuala O'Faolain.[62] A real performer, halfway between vaudeville and Shakespearean actor, Berryman loved an audience.

A hard-living, hard-working poet named John Berryman
achieves sudden—and deserved—renown

Figure 41: John Berryman in Dublin. Life Magazine, *21 July 1967.*

In January Kate Berryman pulled Montague aside to tell him that something had to be done. She could not bear any longer the drunkenness and personal disorder. Toward the end of the month, Berryman was committed to Grangegorman, the black, granite, early-nineteenth-century buildings formerly known as the Richmond Lunatic Asylum. The forced period of calm and sobriety, even if brief, was a help. After his release, Berryman and Montague resumed their 'long weird conversations'. 'He is, surprisingly enough,' Montague reported, 'a very sweet man & almost too scholarly.'[63]

Just before Berryman's departure from Ireland, Montague organized a reading for 19 June 1967 at the Graduates' Club, St Stephen's Green. In his introduction to the evening, Montague said this would not be a solemn event, but an entertainment. Maybe this was not the best opening. The audience could not keep quiet. Berryman read 'Dream Song 312' about coming to Dublin to have it out with the 'majestic Shade' of W.B. Yeats; he had brought with him his family, his homage and his soft remorse. 'Begod, I'll blast ye!' was cried out, more than once.

Thomas Redshaw, then an MA student at UCD, was in the audience. He recalled that the first-name familiarities of Dublin bohemia, and the presence of several people with the forename 'John', allowed things to go sideways. When Berryman began to sing and whisper the dream songs, one hand grasping manuscript pages, Kavanagh barked, 'Speak up, John!' John Jordan tried to hush up Kavanagh, but made so much noise doing so, someone said, 'Shut up, John' (meaning Jordan). Hearing this, Berryman stopped and gazed out over his glasses. Montague rose to plead for quiet. 'Shut up, John' was then aimed at him. Once again, Kavanagh interrupted, Jordan protested and Montague gestured reprovingly. 'Go on, John,' someone up front finally instructed Berryman and the reading staggered on to the end of evening.[64]

At the intermission several members of the UCD English Department made a group exit, led by Denis Donoghue. They may have been disgusted by the general rowdiness, or perhaps they left in protest at the recitation of 'Dream Song 4', focused on a lady's 'compact & delicious body' as she fills up at dinner 'with chicken páprika'. 'What wonders is she sitting on?' the speaker asks himself. The departure of the UCD academics added to a shambolic scene.

'Appalling manners' was the judgment upon the audience of *The Irish Times* reviewer.[65] 'We have disgraced ourselves again,' Montague declared from the stage, echoing the declaration of Yeats (remembering the *Playboy* riots) to the audience rioting at O'Casey's *The Plough and the Stars*. All said, the night could not have been more memorable.

Passing through Paris some days later, Berryman visited 11 rue Daguerre. Somehow, the great-bearded man got through the outer door and into the courtyard, where he rumbled the poet Claude Esteban: '*Ou est le poète*

Irlandais?' Claude called at John's door to say, 'There's an American Moses asking for you.'[66]

Serge Fauchereau remembers being present that afternoon. They cast fortunes with Tarot cards. One went missing, and a search was undertaken for the lost card. Berryman rose from his chair to find that he had been sitting on it. The card was the Black Knight, Death. Berryman was shaken. How could he not take it as a sign?[67]

12

A Chosen Light had been in preparation with MacGibbon and Kee since September 1966. Montague was weak with anxiety over the deliberations of the Poetry Book Society; this collection could not fail, he hoped, to be a 'Choice' or at the very least 'Recommended'. It meant such a difference in the number of copies sold and, of course, in the recognition of merit. Tim O'Keeffe did his best to help – he had lunch with the Society's secretary, Eric White, even though he didn't like the man.[68]

Louis le Brocquy was commissioned to do a drawing for the cover. He offered two. One was an ink-brush sketch of Samuel Beckett, to accompany 'Salute, in passing, for Sam' (*A Chosen Light*). The other was of male and female torsos, 'to suggest in very simple terms an interior life'.[69] That image was reproduced on the dust jacket.

Figure 42: Louis le Brocquy image, cover A Chosen Light (1967).

When autumn 1967 came round, the Poetry Book Society announced that its 'Choice' was a collection by Thom Gunn and its 'Recommendation' one by Elizabeth Jennings. In raging grief, Montague wrote to Tim O'Keeffe: 'My conviction grows that the whole English literary structure is rotten …. They just can't recognise feeling in verse anymore.'[70] There is, of course, no shame in coming second to Thom Gunn, and Elizabeth Jennings was an honoured member of the Movement group of poets, with deep ties to the English literary establishment.

Part of Montague's problem with English competition juries may be revealed in the response of a young Michael Longley to the collection. It had been pointed out to Longley that Montague was taking a hint from the American Black Mountain poets (like Robert Creeley and Denise Levertov): simple diction, understatement and a metric close to speech. Longley accepted that Montague was a poet of the first rank and a maker of beautiful love poems, but he just could not help but feel certain things necessary to poetry of lasting greatness, such as complete pentameter lines, stanzaic resolution, not slant but true rhymes and a strong climax, were often missing from his poems. Was this a result of accident or inability? The poems just did not sound right to Longley. Why would you want 'a low-pitched style' that 'seeks exactness'? Was that sufficient? Why not pitch high and go for richness?[71]

Montague wrote about his troubles to Thomas Kinsella, not perhaps the ideal grief counsellor on the matter of poetry prizes. He usually won them. His *Wormwood* – a collection of eight short poems – had just received the Denis Devlin Award, beating out Kavanagh's *Collected Poems*. In Montague's opinion, this was an absurd injustice. Kinsella replied that he himself could see the jury's decision as a just one. As for prizes, Douglas Sealy was probably right, Kinsella thought: 'the Montague tone does not immediately arrest, but grows to convince'. 'You choose words of minimum connotations nearly always, 'usual words' that don't insist or direct.'[72] Readers can miss what is happening. Fair comment.

13

In mid-November Montague set out from Paris for the Belfast Festival, stopping in Dublin to collect Thomas Kinsella, who was also giving a reading there. If the Revival had moved North, then North they would have to go.

On 17 November Derek Mahon came up to the house of 'Padraic Fiacc' (the poet Joe O'Connor) to tell him that, according to reliable gossip, John Montague was soon going to be in the Gin Palace. Would Fiacc come along and introduce him? When they arrived, several poets were passing around their first collections of poems. In the Belfast literary scene, there was always a lot of drink, some sharp elbows, then forced laughter and quick comebacks. When James Simmons gave a copy of *Late but in Earnest* (1967) to Longley, he brushed him off: 'Thank you, Jimmy, though it's not my kind of poetry.' Seamus Heaney, buoyant with the reception of *Death of a Naturalist*, was, Fiacc noted, 'dressed in so much tweed with his feet up on the table he was almost a caricature of himself'. His friends were already calling him, in ball-busting mockery of his good fortune, 'Famous Seamus.' Heaney was editing a series of 'Festival Pamphlets'. Once Seamus had a few drinks, Fiacc asked him why he had not returned his poems if he did not intend to use them. 'Joe,' Seamus grinned, 'why don't you opt for a posthumous reputation?'[73] Laughter all around, in which Fiacc was compelled to join.

14

The Belfast Festival was hardly over when news arrived of the death of Patrick Kavanagh, age sixty-three. There was then a mighty rallying of poets for the obsequies. Hundreds of local people and many from Dublin too gathered in Inniskeen, County Monaghan. John Montague was one of the four poets asked to read at the graveside.[74] It is a good thing Paddy did not know what was going on above ground. That man Montague reading 'In Memory of My Mother'! So succession passes, through strangest hands.

8

PARIS IN '68 AND THE MEETING WITH
EVELYN ROBSON

I

For his second year of teaching at UCD, after failing to find a decent flat, Montague lodged at Woodtown Manor, high in the hills above Dublin, with Howth visible in the distance on the far side of the city.

In June 1965 Garech Browne, then twenty-six years old, bought the artistically restored house and grounds from Morris Graves.[1] The Guinness heir made the move from a mews house off Fitzwilliam Square on Montague's advice: 'Garech with a mansion would be a great thing,' John explained to Liam Miller. Garech 'will have to grow up to the house, rather than the reverse'. He often spoke to other friends about Garech in this paternalist way. Kinsella thought Montague was wasting his time with an idle young lord, but it was Montague's long-term project to 'turn G.B. into a useful citizen'.[2]

Garech, or his chauffeur, would drive from *fleadh* to *fleadh* in search of the best traditional musicians. Typically dressed in London-tailored, pepper-and-salt Connemara tweeds with *báinín* waistcoat, cinched at the waist with a *crios* and with his long broom-coloured hair tied back by a ribbon, Garech would manifest himself at these country festivals like an otherworldly avatar of a native Irishman. He was, however, more than a dandy. He spent the time to become a connoisseur of Irish folk music. His Claddagh Records was founded in November 1962, with Montague as a director and The Chieftains as the 'house band'. The company led the way to the current worldwide popularity of Irish traditional music.

Garech's first goal for Claddagh was to record Leo Rowsome on the uillean pipes. Another part of the scheme, however, was Montague's own pet project: to capture before it was too late the voices of Austin Clarke, Patrick Kavanagh, Samuel Beckett and Hugh MacDiarmid. Imagine if one could hear the voice of Shakespeare, or Wordsworth reciting *The Prelude*! It was not too late to record present-day masters for the sake of future generations. Next, Montague wanted to introduce young Irish poets like himself to a record-playing public. At first, though willing to bankroll spoken-word records, Garech was slow to do anything else to bring them to pass. In early 1964, just as Austin Clarke was being taped, Garech let drop the news that he was taking a trip to China. Montague sent a scolding letter from Paris. The boy was abandoning his 'proper task', work that 'might give him his place in the world'.³ Garech postponed the trip.

On their drives to hunt up locally renowned traditional musicians, Montague himself got an education. Garech brought John to hear Joe Heaney before the *sean-nós* singer moved to America in 1965. When Joe Heaney, standing, gripped the back of a wooden chair, his head forced back by song, and gave vent to a sense of racial loss, Montague's mind returned to his lonely uncle and namesake who died in Brooklyn.⁴ This train of thought led to 'The Country Fiddler', dedicated to Garech Browne.

Montague had never known wealth before, apart from his visits to Madeleine's Bellozanne. Year after year Garech put him on the guest list for Christmases at Luggala. Eighteen or twenty would be seated in the dining room, wearing black tie and evening gowns. Like his mother, Oonagh Guinness, Garech enjoyed collecting interesting people – 'like rings on his fingers', Richard Ryan remarked. Some of the holiday guests might be barons like John Godley, Lord Kilbracken, or Guinness connections by way of marriage, such as Lucian Freud, but Garech took pleasure in eccentricity and genuine talent whatever the person's social class. Brendan Behan had been a family favourite at Christmas. Garech had not just a Claddagh business relationship, but a deep, long-lasting connection with Paddy Moloney of The Chieftains, a Dubliner not himself to the manor born. The actor John Hurt was another long-time friend. Garech had known Eddie Delaney, the sculptor, since boyhood; Delaney's father tended the beehives at Castle MacGarrett, the County Mayo estate of Garech's father, Lord Oranmore and Browne. Montague added further to the glittering host at Woodtown and Luggala by bringing along over time special guests such as Robert Graves, Hugh MacDiarmid and John Berryman.⁵

Although Garech ran away from school well before graduation, he became a serious reader. By following his own untaught nose into arcane byways, he built up an odd, precious and large library of rare books. Many of its treasures concerned Asian religions. When poems like 'Konarak' (named after the Hindu Sun Temple in India) began to show up in Montague's work, that was partly due to the library of Garech Browne.[6] The faces of those in the temple frieze at Konarak wear expressions of bliss, as their bodies twist in Tantric couplings. The image crystallized certain ideas of sensuality Montague had encountered in California and rediscovered on the bookshelves at Woodtown.

2

Garech's own love life underwent frequent revolutions. When John took up residence at Woodtown Manor in January 1968, Garech was extricating himself from his affair with Tessa Prendergast Welborn, the dress designer and inventor of the bikini. She got it in her head that the Irish poet was to blame for her relationship troubles. A Jamaican by birth, Tessa left 'little ju-ju signs on the stairs' to spook the Ulsterman. At dinner, from across the table she gave him what he took to be 'the evil eye'.[7] But the break-up was not John's doing, nor just the result of his bad example. Garech had been using his older friend as a scapegoat. In fact, the young lord was secretly well along into his next relationship (about which, John was in the know). Soon, Garech and Tessa each abandoned Woodtown Manor, and John was left on his own, to be looked after by Garech's butler, his meals prepared by the butler's wife.[8]

The empty house was lonely. Montague was soon indulging in his own hospitalities. The composer Seán Ó Riada joined him on some nights. A person of sizzling intelligence, Ó Riada, after graduating from University College Cork, had been a director of music at RTÉ and the Abbey Theatre. In 1961 he founded Ceoltóirí Cualann, an ensemble of traditional musicians, plus harpsichord, to play his original 'traditional' compositions. He was at the cutting edges of both Irish folk and European Modernist music and a sharp reader of poetry too. By the time of his orchestral composition for the film *Mise Éire* (1959), Ó Riada already was in music what Kinsella and Montague were trying to be in poetry, an Irish ethnic Modernist at peak form.

In 1963 he moved his family of seven to the Gaeltacht in west Cork. So thereafter, when in Dublin he needed a place to stay he was welcomed at

Woodtown by Montague. Yet even by Dublin standards, Ó Riada was a difficult drunk. In early 1968 his death by drink at age forty was just three years off.

Ó Riada took the small room off the return of the stairwell, and Montague had one of the main bedrooms on the upper floor. Together, the two men set out on a day trip to the Hell Fire Club, four kilometres across into the Dublin mountains. It is possible that Garech Browne brought them there in one of his horse-drawn antique carriages; he then had a passion for dressing up in a coachman's outfit, with hat, cape and whip, and driving about the country roads.

In the early eighteenth century the speaker of the Irish parliament, William Conolly, had a hunting lodge built on the top of Montpelier Hill. In defiance of superstition, it was raised right on top of a passage tomb, possibly constructed out of its despoiled stones. After Conolly's death, the lodge became the Hell Fire Club, founded by a man known to practise magic. Hell Fire Club members earned a reputation for gambling, debauchery and hard drinking. According to folklore, a stranger once joined their game of cards. When a player bent down to pick up a dropped card, he saw that the stranger had cloven hooves. Seán Ó Riada told John he himself was acquainted with magic; he had second sight too.

Since the 1950s Montague had toyed with the idea of a play or story about Buck Whaley, a member of the Hell Fire Club in the late eighteenth century. With a house on St Stephen's Green, Whaley was a rake in pre-Union Dublin. When it came time in 1800 to vote on the Act of Union (which entailed the surrender of parliamentary independence), Buck Whaley cynically accepted bribes from both sides. Progress on the play was held up by the author's uncertainty about its protagonist. Was this courageous rapscallion a hero? Bar the dissipations, a man of promise, like Garech Browne? Or just the representative of a parasitic class that had lost all sense of decorum?[9] At a minimum Montague needed to decide if Buck Whaley was a bad man or a good one. 'Whaley's Leap' remained unfinished.

3

At the beginning of the year Montague continued his conversation (by post and in person) with Barrie Cooke. The intimacy of the two men's exchanges appears more typical of what is reputed to be possible between women friends. What was each man's particular sexual identity, in all its specificity? And how did that connect with his creative work? These questions were raised directly by Robin Skelton's complaint by letter that the poems of *All Legendary Obstacles* were too physical. He found them embarrassing. Was there disarray in Montague's personal life, he wondered? After a look at Skelton's message, Cooke observed that:

> We are probably both less sensual than we may appear from our subject matter. Neither of us are as sexual as [Ted] Hughes who does not write about sex except indirectly (and there of course it's all sex) and we do. Hughes was shocked as well as delighted by my nudes – shocked because he felt that in art you shouldn't be so direct. I think however that I am probably more sensual than you – in the feminine, animal meaning of it.[10]

As a poet Ted Hughes preferred private meanings to be smuggled under the deck, unknown even to the captain of the ship. In life and love, however, he was aggressive. He had been a hunter since boyhood – he thrilled to the chase, the capture and the kill. That is the kind of man he grew up to be. Hughes and Cooke also loved fishing, a matter of stalking, persistently presenting the lure and then making fast one's prey. Montague was neither fisherman nor hunter.

So, what kind of a man was he? For all his introspection, he admitted to Cooke, 'I know very little about my deepest impulses, or not until long after … One's clarity has cost a lot.'[11] Could he be a 'cold sensualist', a rake?[12] That did not seem to fit; he was no Buck Whaley. Nor was he an atheist libertine of the French stripe. He truly enjoyed the company of women and, when excited by mutual affection, he sought an accord with his companion.

His trouble was, he speculated, that he had grown up in the countryside where the coarsest brutality was the rule in conversation. When men talked together about a woman, there was nothing gentle about their language, no courtesy at all. They would speculate if she would prove a 'good stall', or 'a fine ride'; best of all would be 'a bucker'.[13] A 'hard man' would always be trying 'to get a leg over'. In each idiomatic phrase, the woman is a horse to be mounted and broken for service. The whole dehumanizing discourse had been harmful to him, he suspected.

Another theory he entertained was that his middle-aged randiness sprang from his not having had children. He was left with a surplus of affection, which he spent on women to whom he was not married. Still another possibility was that the only way to get the 'SS Montague' (his poetry) out of dry dock was to put to sea in search of a new love.[14] Perhaps he was like the singer-songwriter who renews his or her repertoire by means of romantic tumult, recurrent experiences of desire, jealousy and heartbreak. A settled life was contrary to the troubadour's *déformation professionnelle*. He posted on his UCD office door Yeats's adage *Myself I must remake*.[15] But starting a new life could end up making a mess of the old one.

One afternoon in John Ryan's pub, The Bailey, Montague was in a group carousing with Garech Browne dressed in his coachman's regalia. A twenty-year-old girl from Hollywood, California, entered the bar and joined the group. Susan Hall was on a 'term abroad' scheme set up by W.R. Rodgers, then a writer-in-residence at Pitzer College in Claremont, California. In *The Pear Is Ripe*, Montague recalls her appearance: 'she had a milk-white complexion, and long black hair inherited from her Crow grandmother. That glossy hair falling in panels on either side of her large-eyed face, along with her miniskirts and flat shoes, gave her the innocent look popular at that time. Yet, also in keeping with the times, she was sexually adventurous.'[16] How quickly the American spirit of Free Love had crossed the Atlantic!

Susan had already taken the architect Frank Barry (father of novelist Sebastian Barry) as a lover. He was an early Dolmen poet and married to the Abbey actress Joan O'Hara. Susan turned the heads of others too. American women stood out in the Dublin of the 1960s, Richard Ryan recalls. They were often tanned, athletic, with freshly shampooed hair; they shaved their legs; they had contraceptives. On top of that, Susan was exceptionally intelligent, vibrant and open to experience. She revelled in the attention she got in Ireland. She even 'brushed a fan' across the face of 22-year-old Ryan.[17] Her dash through Baggotonia set off alarms among wives, but Eddie Delaney's wife Nancy, after hearing about Susan from the painter Michael Farrell, found upon meeting her she was a 'nice little girl'. In fact, she envied the way Susan played the field. She herself had never got the chance.

Montague courted the young Californian for all he was worth. By mid-February, Susan was a sleepover guest at Woodtown Manor.[18] At first, Montague told himself she was just a 'naïve teenybopper', but such stereotyping was mere defensiveness. He was, he later admitted, already half in love with her. He tried to make himself present in her life as often as possible, just to keep Frank Barry and others at bay. When Susan returned to her flat on Pembroke Road, Frank would call. She could not turn him away. The way that man made love – it almost made her pass out. Montague did not care for that bit of information.

He brought Susan along to visit Barrie Cooke's new home, a former mill on the Nore river in Kilkenny. They also travelled together to Cúil Aodha in west Cork and called into Seán Ó Riada's family. When Montague gave a reading in Belfast, Susan came along. She even accompanied him to London, where they slept at Martin and Fiona Green's house, a Chelsea mark of honour. That London visit was a lot of 'technical trouble' to take over a passing fling, Nuala O'Faolain remarked to John.

He was making Susan into his 'official girlfriend'.[19] But he remained absurdly jealous, anxious in particular that she might return to Frank Barry while John made a visit home to Paris. He was still more upset upon finding that she had done so.[20] He was in a ridiculous position. What right had he, a serial adulterer, to ask a single young woman to be faithful to him? He felt helpless and weak. Susan told him she would make him strong, as strong as she herself was, by virtue of her belief in him. He wanted more reassurance than that. What promises could they make to one another? That he should always wish her well was her request. She promised in return that he could count on her 'always to turn up, sooner or later, for life, until you let me & yourself down'.[21] It is an intelligent response; it leaves her free, is as much threat as promise, and remains open to her own interpretation.

He liked to look upon her body in bed. The poem 'Life Class', ostensibly about a painter's model, was started at this time. It is an itemizing, voyeuristic poem from a male point of view (a French genre called a *blazon*, in which a woman's parts are panegyrically catalogued top to bottom, bottom to top). The poem's inquiry comes up against the impossibility of knowing the real life of the woman whose physical appearance and private parts fascinate him. What did she have that he so much desired? Two things, in Susan's case: one that he had lost for ever, youth; and a second that he could never have: the capacity to bear children. Plus, she was smart, beautiful and indomitable.

4

On Friday, 15 March 1968, Susan Hall was in the audience for a night of poetry organized by the 'UCD Poetry Workshop'. Much has been written about Philip Hobsbaum's 'Group' workshop, run out of Queen's in Belfast, where Seamus Heaney's industry was first on display. Richard Ryan set up something comparable at UCD. The college cohort at this period would include poets such as Eamon Grennan and Harry Clifton. The workshop convened sessions on poems-in-progress, set up readings and published a broadsheet. On this evening W.J. McCormack ('Hugh Maxton'), Hayden Murphy and Pearse Hutchinson read, along with several student poets. Montague concluded the programme. He performed well on the night. The elaborately ironic West Coast-influenced 'Hymn to the New Omagh Road' was given an airing, but Nuala O'Faolain's favourite was 'Premonition', still in draft form.[22]

This poem was based on a 'lucid dream' in which the speaker beholds his beloved as she is stabbed again and again by another. Impossible to say for sure just who the beloved is, or even what the sensational scene of male helplessness and female suffering implies. It could as easily be a metaphor for what he himself was doing to Madeleine as what Frank Barry was doing to Susan, or something else altogether. Lots of Montague poems have connections with films; this one belongs with late-night horror shows.

Two days later, St Patrick's Day, a Sunday, there was a GAA match at Croke Park, Ulster versus Leinster, a fixture of interest to a man from Tyrone. Afterwards, John and Susan went to The Bailey, the late Patrick Kavanagh's haunt after he was put out of McDaid's for not settling his bar debt. On this 17 March The Bailey's proprietor, John Ryan, put Kavanagh's death mask on display. The clientele then promenaded down Baggot Street to celebrate the new commemorative bench on the bank of the Grand Canal, before returning to the pub. Montague reported on the occasion for *The Guardian*.[23]

The crowd in the Bailey doubled in size when the celebrants arrived from the wedding of Harden Rodgers to John Jay. Harden, the daughter of W.R. Rodgers, was a junior lecturer in English at Trinity College Dublin and a close friend of Montague's. Later, there was a poetry reading by Derek Mahon at the Lantern Theatre on Merrion Square. From Montague's point of view, it was 'a real pet of a day', almost 'too much happiness'. Poetry for once was at the centre of life, publicly celebrated on the national holiday.

At the end of the night, under a moon just past full, John brought Susan back to Woodtown Manor. Later, she threw on his black dressing-gown before a trip to the washroom. She passed Seán Ó Riada on the landing. When Montague followed after her, Ó Riada, drunk, uttered a kind of curse: 'All your womenfolk are possessed by death, save one. You are in extreme danger.'[24]

Susan was afraid of Ó Riada; she knew he thought ill of her. He had told her so. In a book on magic, John had read that those threatened by a curse should draw a circle around themselves and then remain within its protection. John performed this ritual. As a piece of theatre showing goodwill, Susan was grateful for it. All night long a big wind whirled around the house, and she cradled herself in his arms.[25]

Montague started several poems about Susan arising from the nightmarish end of St Patrick's Day 1968. The curse of Seán Ó Riada left its conservative Catholic mark on Montague's image of the young Californian. The poem quoted in *The Pear Is Ripe*, which describes Susan's appearance in John's black dressing gown, concludes with a line spoken from Ó Riada's doom-laden point of view: 'How pretty you look,/Miss Death!'[26] In his subsequent self-mythologizing, Montague looked back on his affairs with Lena and Susan as a period in which he was courting death, the Dark Lady.

Another trace in the *Collected Poems* of the affair with Susan is 'Closed Circuit'. The title may derive from Samuel Beckett's blackly comic *Murphy*. Character A loves Character B who loves Character C who loves Character A; so, 'Love requited is a closed circuit.'[27] The poem is the bitter residue of Montague's middle-aged jealousy after tangling with a free, independent young American.

At the end of the UCD term, Montague returned to Paris, then in upheaval with the worker-and-student rebellion of May 1968. Susan made a short furtive visit to him there before her 11 June flight home. When that day came, it was Frank Barry who took her to the airport.[28]

A year later when Susan came to visit the Montagues in the rue Daguerre, she was newly married and accompanied by her husband, René Patron, a restorer of rare books. The couple settled in Hollywood, and Susan became a public librarian. She began to write for young readers and turned out to be a successful, Newbery Award-winning author.

5

At the beginning of May 1968 Montague left Paris to attend Barrie Cooke's exhibition in Dublin, then headed north with Garech Browne to meet Seamus Heaney and members of the Group at a Dungannon arts festival.[29] The next stop for the two poets was Belfast in order to tape *The Northern Muse*, their Claddagh spoken-word record. On his return trip to Paris, Montague stopped over in Brighton for several days with Robert Duncan.[30]

While he was away, life in Paris had been turned on its head. The upheaval began in the following way. On 2 May its dean closed the new suburban University of Nanterre. It was his hope to contain an unruly student rebellion, but he triggered a concatenation of events that with astonishing rapidity took the shape of a revolution.[31] The Nanterre students, locked out and enraged, showed up in the city centre on the Left Bank at the Sorbonne, where fellow students joined them in a sympathy strike. Classes were suspended. Students took possession of university buildings for an anarchic experiment in direct democracy. Boulevards were barricaded. Paving stones were ripped from the streets and hurled at riot police. The student protesters were attacked with batons and rushed off to suddenly overrun hospitals. Workers, some already on strike at Billancourt Renault factory, occupied aviation and automobile factories around the country. A general strike then shuttered banks, schools, post offices, as well as general industries. Ordinary civic life came to a crawl. Petrol was rationed, shops were emptied by hoarders, panicking smokers made a run on Gitanes and Gauloises, television stations stopped broadcasting, and telephone callers could not get through.[32] The national theatre was seized by students, who delivered political harangues from the stage. Everyday life in Paris had become something else altogether.

The students in the streets were violent, fun-loving, unreasonable and programmatically insolent. Walls became billboards for graffiti laced with a ludic Nietzschean poetry, adding a frisky, feral new chapter to the noble history of French maxims.

* *Soyez réalistes, demandez l'impossible.*
Be realistic, demand the impossible.

* *On ne revendiquera rien, on ne demandera rien. On prendra, on occupera.*

We will claim nothing, we will ask for nothing. We will take, we will occupy.

* *Soyons cruels!*
Let us be cruel!

* *La révolution est incroyable parce que vraie.*
The revolution is incredible because it is real.

* *Il est interdit d'interdire*
It is forbidden to forbid.

* *La barricade ferme la rue mais ouvre la voie.*
The barricade closes the road but opens the way.

* *Le patron a besoin de toi, tu n'as pas besoin de lui.*
The boss has a need for you, you don't have a need for him.

* *L'émancipation de l'homme sera totale ou ne sera pas.*
The liberation of humanity will be total or it will not be.

* *Cours, camarade, le vieux monde est derrière toi!*
Run, comrade, the old world is behind you!

To adult onlookers, these kids – males unlike men, with long hair; women in trousers with short hair – seemed like irritating children on spring break, too bored to study, not behaving like proper men and women. However, it disturbed Parisian parents when their kids were beaten with truncheons and carted off to hospitals. The police, and thus the state, forfeited public support through the bloody, organized fury of its repression.

By the end of the month President de Gaulle was not to be found in France. Had he fled? In fact, he was visiting a NATO base in Baden-Baden, Germany, to make sure he had the backing of generals for a military crack-down, should his offer of 25 per cent raises for workers and a new election fail to bring an end to the unrest.

Upon de Gaulle's return to France, the student demonstrations vanished like smoke. Was it just because of the cold heavy rains that swept over Paris at the end of May? Or was it that the students, unlike the workers, had no demands that could be met? As Sartre observed, they wanted everything and nothing. They insisted on radical freedom – freedom from work, boredom, examinations, wars, monogamy, landlords, hierarchies of every kind.[33] On 23 June de Gaulle won re-election in a landslide. The month of May in retrospect appeared to have been a carnival, not, as it had once seemed, regime change in action.

Montague promised an eyewitness assessment to Todd Andrews, former IRA revolutionary.[34] Andrews was proud of the black Uzbek hat, just like Brezhnev's, given to him by a Russian leader, but his current revolutionary sympathies did not extend further. He had been the boss of a succession of Irish state-sponsored bodies, for fuel, transport and broadcasting.[35] During the turmoil of May 1968 Todd Andrews was particularly concerned about his friend Madeleine Montague, as the Patronat (the employers' organization where she worked) was a target of the demonstrators and a key partner in de Gaulle's plan for the pacification of the workers.

Montague's hope was different: he wanted to pick up tips for starting 'A New Ulster Revolution'. The secret of the Paris students' success, he noted, was surprise. From start to finish, who was behind it all should be a mystery to the authorities. The underlying and unacknowledged resentment of the population must suddenly manifest itself, once the touchpaper was set alight by marches and strikes. Montague did not mark as an indispensable factor that the rebel leaders were violent. Paris officials had been actively provoked – disobeyed, cursed, challenged, insulted, threatened, even roughed up – so that they would call in the police, thus unmasking the violence that maintained present-day social structures. That was the Situationist road map for the events of May 1968.[36]

After the first week of June, Montague flew back to Dublin to appear on Andy O'Mahony's programme on RTÉ. To the dismay of Todd Andrews, Montague spoke up in favour of the students. As in his poem 'Boulevard St Michel' (published in *The Irish Times*, 15 June 1968), he saw the destruction as 'cleansing'. The rioters' 'freedom and terrible joy' was thrilling. The Panthéon in flames brought a kind of 'religious awe' back to the experience of the ordinary citizen. Irish students should themselves wake up and notice what needed to be overhauled in the Irish state. Nonsense, Todd Andrews wrote to Madeleine.[37] These international student rebellions were contagious, spreading from country to country. Irish students did not need that kind of encouragement from the country's leading poet. Anyway, what did young people in Ireland have to complain about? Look what had come to pass – there was now a sit-in at UCD. The idea that the young knew better than the old was absurd. He knew that from his sons; they had nothing like his own knowledge and judgment. 'If there's any bullying to be done, I am going to be the bully.' Todd Andrews supposed Madeleine would see things the way he did.

6

In late June and early July, Montague tried to mine a new vein in his poetry. Partly inspired by the students, he dared himself to be more honest about his desires, even if it meant taking risks. He looked to the example of Sylvia Plath. He admitted to himself a 'blank hunger' for Susan Hall.[38] With respect to Madeleine, he felt at once guilty and angry, yet was also conscious that he had no reason to be angry with her. Through drink, he had tried to not let his right hand know what his left hand was doing. He essayed a comparison of himself with their tomcat who limped home with a torn ear after nights on the prowl, while Madeleine waited at home, then on his return cleansed his wounds and made a fresh bed for him – a feeble stab at domesticating his infidelities.[39]

How much damage had he in fact already done, he wondered, both to himself and to Madeleine?[40] He wanted to be honest with her, but his quoting of T.S. Eliot's lines 'I that was near your heart was removed therefrom' was a classic case of using the passive voice (and a literary allusion) to escape personal responsibility.[41] Yet to be more explicit was to be crueller. In his diary, he rehearsed a direct request to Madeleine for sexual freedom:[42]

> Can you accept my multiple life? Having no children leaves me free, as I am at this moment, to prowl. Sex between us will die away. Tell me, what you really feel about it? I need this to bring me to the boil. I would not have been able to write abt. you except for [Lena] … How much pain there is in it for you. Esteem I have for you.

He saw signs of ageing in Madeleine, then hated himself for having noticed them. Sleepless, he felt her hot body next to him at night, a cap over her curlers, lightly snoring. She must also sometimes turn over in bed and see his greying hair, his drink-reddened eyes, his rancid teeth. The mere fact of ageing, with no children, was failure in life. In a dream recorded in his notebook, John, Lena and Madeleine were all at a party. A country person, pointing at them, spoke of 'those who have no children and could well afford them'.[43]

At heart he knew Madeleine was better than him. He got drunk and made a fool of himself, time and again, like one of those round-bottomed bottles you push over that then, rocking, rights itself. She was steady, sensible, with her feet on the ground, yet still sensitive. Over the years she had become like a mother to him, a really kind mother, for whom a grown man like himself was a child to be indulged.[44] He was spoilt, as he had been by his aunts. But he was not happy.

7

The date 20 July 1968 is a significant one in the life of John Montague. He was alone in the flat at rue Daguerre when a young woman arrived to interview him for a university magazine doing a special issue on English-language writers living in Paris. She was Evelyn Robson, an extraordinarily beautiful student from Nanterre, a suburb of Paris.

Her father, Stanley Robson, was a handsome American Jew born in Brooklyn, the son of a schoolteacher. He had been admitted to the University of Virginia, but never attended; the war broke out. The head of a platoon that landed on D-Day, he had crawled over the mutilated bodies of his men to make his way up the shore. Of that platoon he was one of the only survivors. He was never the same afterwards. Sometimes he sought escape from his demons through drink. He could be violent to his wife and his daughters too.

In the jubilation after the Armistice, he and Evelyn's mother, Denise, had fallen in love. She was from a Protestant family named Baugatz, immigrants to France from Silesia generations earlier, after Prussia's war against the Hapsburg empire. The family prospered and had a small manor house, as well as a place in Paris. French anti-Semitism being what it was, they looked down on Stanley. The marriage had ended when his wife, having had enough, changed the locks.

Even before doing English literature at Nanterre, Evelyn was fluent in the language. In 1964 she had worked as an au pair in Ireland. She was, like John

Montague himself, an admirer of Oliver Goldsmith's poem 'The Deserted Village'. That is partly why she chose to work for a family in a small town in the Irish midlands. She loved the area. During that year in Ireland, it happened that she had once seen John Montague on Irish television.[45]

Interviews are occasions of a certain permissible intimacy. The interviewer has a licence to be curious, even nosy. Of course, interviews do not always wind up with love-making. This one did. Afterwards, they went to see Ingmar Bergman's *The Hour of the Wolf*, then had dinner at Le Lotus du Vietnam.[46]

John promptly began to consecrate Evelyn's appearance in his life with a poem, 'A Dream of July'. Straightaway, he saw the young student as a mother figure, the Greek goddess Ceres, embodiment of summer and fruitfulness. Yet, at the poem's end, he also casts her as a Gravesian moon goddess, thus a Muse:

> Ceres, corn goddess,
> Mistress of summer,
> Steps sure-footed over
> The scythed grass.
> Her abundant body
> Compounded of honey
> And gold, the spike
> Of each nipple
> A wild strawberry –
> She raises to the
> Moon the pale gold
> Mask of her face.

This is not playing by the rules of *The White Goddess*. According to that text, a poet's muse is not the mother of his children, or even his wife, but the unpossessable procreator of his poems. That misprision gave Montague pause for reflection a few years later, but in July 1968 he was enraptured.

Evelyn went along with his ardour, he sensed, a little reluctantly. She was a young girl 'dissatisfied with her mythic burden'. The fates did not place that burden on her; he did. She had been 'fulfilled in spite of herself'. He rushed things, painting word pictures of raising a family together in Ireland, long before he was actually ready, psychologically, to leave Madeleine.

Four days after meeting Evelyn, however, he already sensed he was at a crossroads. Yet he hesitated. There was 'No choice which does/not make me ache/with regret.'[47] He did not so much remain at the crossroads, as take both paths at once, without confronting his own duplicity.

Figure 43: Evelyn Robson.

In the last week of July, John and Madeleine went south for a holiday with Louis and Anne le Brocquy. Ripped away from his new infatuation, John sulked. In a hot room buzzing with mosquitoes, the two, quarrelling, stood awkwardly on the bed springs, squashing the insects against the walls. Madeleine got worked up enough to give a John a piece of her mind:[48]

> The wall around all the squashed bodies of insects.
> Not man enough to disguise your feelings.
> If you are unhappy, the world can no longer go round.
> We were doing well until you came …
> Don't darling me, then tear me down.
> I always thought there was a deep-down trust.

Alone with Louis le Brocquy's work all around him, John felt like he was in 'a real little truth chamber'. He had to admit he was doing harm to his wife. Her 'helpful goodness had surrounded him so much he did not even recognize it'. She was satisfied with little in the way of attention, yet he still failed to give her that little.[49] He was shocked by himself: 'Have I never really swallowed suffering? Or learnt to love?'[50]

Figure 44: John Montague and Louis le Brocquy on the coast near Nice.

8

In late August, back in Paris, Montague worked at his edition of the *Faber Book of Irish Verse*, contracted for in early 1967.[51] He decided to tackle 'The Hag of Beare', a ninth-century Gaelic lament by a legendary old nun. This classic had often been put into English – among others, by Kuno Meyer, Augusta Gregory and Frank O'Connor – but it fell right into the lap of Montague's current concerns. The poem's underlying motif of the changes of the moon was already the theme of his work-in-progress, *Tides*. The lyrics of that emerging collection had all been inspired by particular women: Lena, Susan, Madeleine, Evelyn, his mother, Molly, and his dying Aunt Brigid. Through his version of the Gaelic poem, he could conceptualize in totality a gendered form of life. The Jungian, archetypal mode of understanding human life is not so highly esteemed today as it then was, but in this translation, Montague, who so recently was berating himself for his failure to empathize with particular women he was hurting, gave universal voice to a lifetime of female suffering and pleasure, and particularly to the woe of old age. No matter how many moons have passed, his old woman of Beare has a spirited, unrepentant, heroic take on life; she is as tough as can be.

In the second week of September he came to Dublin to give a reading at the Living Art Exhibition, before going onward to County Clare for the Merriman School. In *The Irish Times* Donal Foley gave an account of Montague's impromptu reading of 'The Hag of Beare' at the Aberdeen Arms Hotel in Lahinch:[52]

> The early hours of this morning witnessed a totally unscheduled but artistically irreproachable contribution to the programme from John Montague. In a crowded hotel lounge at Lahinch, the Tyrone poet delivered a new and as yet unpublished translation of 'The Woman of Beare' to an audience which, in utter silence, strained at his every syllable. As the words, in a voice which combined the declamatory manner with quiet and personal hesitancy, spun out the story of the old woman who had seen everything and knew everything, old in wisdom and slightly battered in virtue, the poem and the people listening to it fused into an event of the deepest human significance.

From County Clare, Montague was called away to Tyrone, where his Aunt Mary Agnes O'Meara lay dying in the old Montague family house, now owned by John O'Meara. The O'Mearas' Abbeylara homestead was no longer, as in his schoolboy holidays, a house of noisy children. On the final time Montague stopped in Longford, just the sound of two old people was to be heard there, saying the rosary in damp rooms.

Bedridden in Garvaghey, Mary Agnes no longer wanted food. Her husband had brought her water from the well, she told John; he thought it would do her good. A sheet of tin was always kept over the old well. Its water tasted sweet, a smell of green running through it. The drink did do her good, she said, just as her husband told her it would. But it did not keep her from dying a few days later. It is not hard to imagine how affecting this scene was for the poet. It brought together a deathbed, a crone, a well and a last drink fetched by a beloved man.[53]

9

On 14 November 1968 Richard Ryan (his father having been a successful oddsmaker, he had a car of his own) collected Montague from Dublin airport and brought him to the Claddagh recording studio, where Garech Browne was supervising the taping of the great Scottish poet Hugh MacDiarmid (real name: Christopher Murray Grieve). For the same reasons that Montague admired the work of the modernist poet and painter of partly Welsh origin, David Jones, he revered MacDiarmid's poetry. The two brought together literary modernism, Celtic fringe nationalism and experiments with the long poem.[54] That evening Montague brought the old master along to a 15 November debate over the proposed merger of Trinity College and UCD. There was an audience of three thousand. Montague rose to introduce MacDiarmid to the crowd. The message the white-haired communist poet, dressed in a kilt and grey coat, then delivered to the students was full-throated support: 'Whatever your aims are, you cannot make a worse mess of it than your elders have.'[55]

During their days together at Woodtown Manor, Montague admitted to MacDiarmid that looking at his own royalty accounts made him despondent. The books of Kinsella, Heaney and even Richard Murphy were widely sold, but he was having a hard time getting a hearing. MacGibbon and Kee, his UK publisher (MacDiarmid's too), was heading for the rocks. Even the shops in his native Northern Ireland did not carry Montague's books. MacDiarmid was consolatory: 'When you begin, you think you're mad, then you think you're a minority; in the end, you're a majority.'[56] Just wait, he advised; the long poem, once complete, would make a difference in Montague's standing.[57]

The latest sections of *The Rough Field* were hewing towards the Scottish master in the degree of their political engagement.[58] Through Dolmen limited editions, Montague issued sections as they were written. He wanted them to be interventions in Irish public life. 'Hymn to the New Omagh Road' – an environmental protest poem, printed in May 1968 – was sparked by Montague's distress at a road improvement scheme between Omagh and Ballygawley (where a vast roundabout was constructed). Bulldozers scraped away the verge along the Montague family property, destroying trees and hedges for miles; ancient roadside springs were paved over.

The title of the collection is sarcastic. Its genre is not really a hymn, but a satire on the contemporary religion of the automobile. Montague had collected clippings from machinery manuals and economic impact studies. Excerpts, with only slight revision, were put into a balance-sheet format. Ecological losses were described in original verse, but utilitarian gains were documented by means of the prose excerpts. Montague sometimes made much of the fact that many other Irish poets were treating the countryside as a timeless idyll, while his eyes were open to how much rural life was changing. Yet 'Hymn to the New Omagh Road' is no less sentimental for taking the form of pained irony rather than nostalgic pastoral.

The Bread God is a second experiment in form. Again, Montague collected raw materials in print form – an anti-papist newsletter circulated by an Orange organization, a pamphlet on the dedication of the Cardinal MacRory Memorial Park, official correspondence of the Belfast Grand Lodge, pages from *Songs and Poems of Tyrone* (ed. Felix Kearney) and family letters from Thomas Montague SJ. The fanciful cover page of the Dolmen edition suggests that the form of the poem is a radio broadcast on the history of Errigal parish, periodically interrupted by a pirate station with a very different programme of sectarian hate.

JOHN MONTAGUE

the
BREAD GOD

¶A lecture/with illustrations in verse/on the recent history of the church in the ancient parish of Errigal Kieran/already referred to in the Annals of the Four Masters as being a monastic centre twelve centuries ago.

¶ Listeners are warned that reception may be interfered with by pirate stations, but every effort will be made to provide undisturbed contemplation

DOLMEN EDITIONS

Figure 45: The Bread God, *cover; printed December 1968.*

A sequence of lyric vignettes of Christmas Mass at a country chapel is broken up by the prose excerpts, the simplicity and purity of folk religion thrown into relief by shouts and drumbeats of Protestants on the march.[59]

Montague's pride in his family's Catholicism, along with his sense of historical injury, emerge best in the delicate half-rhymes of 'Penal Rock: Altamuskin'. This glade was one his favourite spots in the parish, where local Catholics gathered when eighteenth-century Penal Laws outlawed Catholic churches and clergy [see Figure 9]:

> To learn the massrock's lesson, leave your car,
> Descend frost-gripped steps to where
> A humid moss overlaps the valley floor.
> Crisp as a pistol-shot, the winter air
> Recalls poor Tagues, folding the nap of their frieze
> Under one knee, long suffering as beasts,
> But parched for that surviving sign of grace,
> The bog-latin murmur of their priest.
> A crude stone oratory, carved by a cousin,
> Commemorates the place. For two hundred years
> People of our name have sheltered in this glen
> But now all have left. A few flowers
> Wither on the altar, so I melt a ball of snow
> From the hedge into their rusty tin before I go.

Liam Miller experimented with typefaces, paper, inks and layouts for these artistic limited editions (now sometimes worth €300 a copy). However, Montague felt a simple broadsheet would have been more to his purpose. A notice in *The Irish Times* was sniffy about the 'large format with rubrics and uncial headings'. Worse yet, the reviewer, Douglas Sealy, usually appreciative of Montague's work, did not like Paisleyite propaganda in a clash with verse.[60] Cubist collage was not, in Sealy's view, an acceptable kind of poetry, just evidence of unfinished work.

Back in April 1968 Montague had arranged for a wider circulation of 'Hymn to the New Omagh Road' by way of *The Irish Press*, but ten months passed and still the books editor, David Marcus, had not put the sequence into print. 'Damnit,' Montague complained, 'it is meant to be popular poetry.' Now reviewers would not make sense of *The Bread God* because they had not earlier been introduced to his Modernist aggregate method by 'Hymn to the New Omagh Road'.

He wanted to achieve like Ezra Pound the open form of a 'poem containing history', but a national poet stood at a disadvantage. In terms of formal innovation, he could not go faster than his society did. *The Irish Press* reviewed the new sequence with 'not a mention of what the poem was about, or its technique, just a smack at Liam [Miller]. Meanwhile, Ulster tears itself to pieces …. Crucify me, somebody, or tear off my buttons for love. EEK!'[61]

10

Events in the North kept Montague on edge. In June 1968 there was a civil rights protest in County Tyrone after an unmarried Protestant woman (and member of a Unionist party) was granted public housing over the heads of the many Catholic families on the waiting list. The only thing new about this injustice was the protest against it. In October the Royal Ulster Constabulary attacked a follow-up civil rights march in Derry; one hundred were injured. A few days later a student march from Queen's University Belfast was blocked by Ian Paisley and his followers. In January 1969 'People's Democracy' organized a march from Belfast to Derry. These marches, though advertised as peaceful, were particularly provocative in the Ulster context. There, Protestants might seasonally stage triumphalist parades along historic routes of conquest, right into the shatter zones of Catholic communities. For Catholics to march was turning the tables and felt to be a threat to Protestant supremacy. On 4 January off-duty RUC members armed with iron bars, bricks and bottles attacked the People's Democracy marchers at Burntollet Bridge; it was a battering of the unresisting.

A few months later Civil Rights organizers planned to resume this interrupted march from Burntollet onward to Derry. When the government banned them from doing so, there were riots in the Bogside, a Catholic neighbourhood just outside the walls of Derry. The RUC then met passive resistance with truncheons. One protester was beaten to death on 19 April 1969. Montague's personal sense of belonging to Tyrone intensified with each day's news.

Montague asked Richard Ryan if he would drive north for a few days. They stopped for dinner in the Fintona home of John's older brother Turlough, a successful lawyer, now with a large family and a house overlooking the golf course, formerly the grounds of the Browne-Lecky estate. In the courts Turlough represented Catholic tenants in cases against the Northern Ireland housing authority. He was a key source of information for John about Ulster politics.

John envied Turlough and Bridie their large family and solid standing, yet he felt (perhaps incorrectly) that they belittled his own achievements. In reaction, John recycled jokes about Fintona:[62]

> What is the height of confusion? Father's Day in Fintona.
> What is the main tourist attraction in the Fintona area? The Ballygawley Roundabout.
> I was never married but I was twice in Fintona.

If you are proud of having become, although a Catholic, widely respected in the town, as Turlough was, such jokes are irritating.

In the view of Richard Ryan, Turlough's wife Bridie looked down on the bohemian aspects of John's life – his lack of a steady job, his heavy drinking, his never paying his own way, always short of pocket money, his long hair, his going-about with young people, probably with girls too. He was a bit of a disgrace. Bridie had little time for his airs.[63] Richard Ryan, who looked up to the poet, was startled by this lack of standing within his own family.

On a dusky winter afternoon in the Poet's Pub, Main Street, Fintona, Ryan met John's 'tiny and cranky' mother, Molly. When John took himself off to the gents', Molly, thinking it was Richard who had left the room, started 'giving out yards' to her son, about all the many mistakes he had made in his life.[64] Her son Seamus, the doctor, was her favourite and Turlough her mainstay; Johnnie was the black sheep.

Still, Montague saw himself ever more in light of the place in which he was reared. He was both in the tribe and outside it, like, he fancied, a shaman. For a contemporary poet to think of himself as some sort of witch doctor, or of herself as a witch, was not outlandish in 1969: Robert Bly, Galway Kinnell, Sylvia Plath, Anne Sexton, Seamus Heaney and Ted Hughes understood themselves in that light too. An anthropological take on life was current. Reading Carlos Castaneda and eating peyote buttons were contemporary poetic practices.

Montague might have stopped being a Mass-going Catholic, but he was wide open to potential spiritual experiences. When he climbed up Knockmany with Richard Ryan, it was for him a pilgrimage to the goddess Anya. Among the trees on the mountain top, John began a dance-like step as if to a drum. He aimed to throw himself into a trance, in preparation for a journey to another time and another world. Chanting, he raised his arms to the trees – beech, Scots pine, birches, hazel and oak – all murmuring in the wind, a kind of roaring of whispers.[65] Louder and louder he chanted, while Richard, the bashful initiate, started to imitate his movements. Something important was being forced into being. Later Montague reported to Richard that in a vision he had seen the men who lived at Seskilgreen in 3000 BC, cousins to the mysterious neolithic people of Newgrange. Then he got a message from the goddess Anya, resident spirit of saddle-backed Knockmany. This experience led to the foundation poem of Montague's 1975 collection *A Slow Dance*:[66]

> With a body
> heavy as earth
> she begins to speak;
>
> her words
> are dew, bright,
> deadly to drink,
>
> her hair,
> the damp mare's
> nest of the grass:
>
> her arms,
> thighs, chance
> of a swaying branch
>
> her secret
> message, shaped
> by a wandering wind
>
> puts the eye
> of reason out;
> so novice, blind,
>
> ease your
> hand into the
> rot-smelling crotch

of a hollow
tree, and find
two pebbles of quartz

protected by
a spider's web:
her sunless breasts.

Richard Ryan, the 'novice' of line 18, did in fact put his hand inside the bole of a hollow tree and found there two large, smooth reddish-white pebbles. He showed them to friends in Dublin – blood-streaked talismans of Ulster.[67]

There had been real magic up there on the mountain for Montague, his companion believed. In a 2016 letter to the old poet, which arrived just days before his death, Ryan recalled the time that 'you invoked the power of poetry on your behalf, in that place commanding the surrounding countryside in which you had struggled to find meaning for it all, those childhood years, and later to find a voice with which to express it'.[68] Montague's late poem 'Return' (dedicated to Ryan) wonders aloud if that mountaintop hour had been a decisive event, when he ceremonially took upon himself the role of spokesman for a people and a place.[69]

II

Montague was certainly in an excitable state of mind. On 15 March 1969 he read his poems in the United Arts Club, Dublin, along with Richard Ryan and Seamus Heaney. When it came to be his turn at the rostrum, he set his diary and other papers down on the floor at the feet of John Jordan.[70] In the hubbub at the end of the performances, Montague suddenly noticed they were gone. He went into a panic; people could not help but notice his distress.[71] In the days afterwards, he suspected a number of different Dublin poets of having made off with his private papers. His daily calendar did not just record appointments. In minuscule handwriting, Montague also used it to keep a dream diary, draft poems, sketch out stories and record snippets of conversation. It was his workbook. He was particularly concerned at the loss because of recent references to Ricki Huston – she had been killed in a car accident on 29 January 1969. In his diary, Montague had jotted down thoughts by way of getting started on an elegy. He did not want Ricki Huston, or himself, or the pair of them to become the stuff of Dublin gossip.[72] They had never been lovers, but someone might think so from his notes. Utterly discomfited, he appealed to anyone he met who happened to have been at the United Arts Club on the night. Would they please help him recover his property? Two months later, while Montague was in the USA, the poet Hayden Murphy returned the diary and papers – which had been mischievously stolen – to the Dolmen office in Dublin, putting to rest a period of high anxiety for Montague.[73]

From mid-April through May, Montague travelled from one university to another in North America on a whistle-stop reading tour: Wesleyan, Brown, Rhode Island University, Providence, New York University, Columbia, Bucknell, Illinois (Chicago), Purdue, Wisconsin (Milwaukee), Minnesota, Toronto, Buffalo and Canisius College, NY. He lingered in Chicago, in order to establish a business relationship with Michael Anania, editor of The Swallow Press. An agreement was reached for the publication of John's next collection, *Tides*, for spring 1971.[74] With Anania's help, John appeared on the Studs Terkel radio show in Chicago, reading to listeners' approval, 'All Legendary Obstacles'. It seems that he also had a rendezvous with Susan Hall Patron. He wrote to Donald Fanger that he had 'lived out the last few days of my first real affair with someone young, half my age.' 'Poets are renewed through women, though I am suspicious of Gravesian exaggerations.'[75] Susan afterwards sent him a letter (untraced), declining in future to serve in the role of Muse or light of love.

12

Back from the USA, Montague was not long in Paris before he left again. His official purpose was to lecture on Beckett in a Dublin summer school (11 and 12 August) and give a reading with Brother Antoninus, the Catholic Beat poet, at the Merriman School in Ennis (25 August). However, he had other reasons for being in Ireland: his parallel engagements with the Troubles and with Evelyn Robson.

In mid-August, while sectarian riots spread from Derry to Belfast, where Protestant gangs burnt out Catholic homes, neighbourhood by neighbourhood, Montague joined the 'National Executive' of an ad hoc 'Citizens' Committee'. It released a statement in support of Taoiseach Jack Lynch's statement that the Republic 'could no longer stand by and see innocent people injured'. But what else could they do besides stand by and complain? A public meeting was held by the Citizens' Committee on 16 August 1969 at the suitably Republican venue of the Dublin GPO.

In the struggles of that time, this ephemeral organization carried little weight, but Montague was willing to try anything to help. He believed that 'Brits Out' and a United Ireland were the solution. He was as yet unable to conjure up a more diplomatic, even-handed proposal, such as Richard Ryan would explore with counterparts when working at the Irish embassy in London, in the run-up to the Anglo-Irish Agreement (1985).

On 24 August Montague travelled to County Tyrone to take part in a Civil Rights march from Coalisland to Dungannon. It turned out to be a terrifying experience; he was 'nearly beaten up twice'. The visit gave rise to a rhythmic impulse:[76]

> Cries of pain & hate
> CRIES
> Cries of loss & terror
> CRIES
> Cries of Christ Crucified
> By Christ

Written on the back of a Citizens' Committee flyer, these lines were the beginning of 'A New Siege', dedicated to Bernadette Devlin, the 21-year-old Queen's University student from Tyrone who had been elected to a seat in the Westminster parliament.[77] When the British army entered Derry and put the Bogside under siege in the second week of August, Bernadette Devlin had taken the side of the Catholic residents. She was arrested on 13 August for incitement to riot.

His 'new muse', Montague swore to himself, must be 'the face of human suffering'.[78] As with the two recently published sections of *The Rough Field*, he gathered preparatory materials, such as an *Irish Times* photograph of soldiers guarding the Derry Guildhall while Ian Paisley addressed a thousand supporters. He kept near his desk during composition a *Time* magazine photograph of a striker bleeding on the pavement while a policeman continued to beat him.

Although begun in a spirit of agitation, 'A New Siege' was continued with studied care over the course of a year. The format was laid down early: a shuttle of two to three beat lines, with a strong caesura, like a medieval Anglo-Saxon poem (Ted Hughes noticed this ancestry).[79] Into the shuttle of phrases, Montague wove quotations from earlier sections of *The Rough Field*. Other phrases read like news headlines, teletype bulletins, Blake's 'Proverbs of Hell', or the Situationist slogans on the walls of Paris in 1968. The word 'lines' was further used to mean frontiers, scars, bands of enemies, fault lines in rock and routes of travel. Most of all, the word suggests energy vectors in the process of life. 'A New Siege' grew from being a protest poem into a vision of history from the perspective of physics (credit to William Hayter).[80] It is also a summary of motifs in *The Rough Field*, inspired by events that erupted long after that poem's beginning.

On 12 August 1970, having finished the section, Montague returned north to Armagh Women's Prison. Bernadette Devlin was being held there after her conviction for incitement to riot. Two policemen waited in the prison yard. Montague climbed the steps and rang the bell. Could he present to the prison governor a copy of *A New Siege*? Permission denied, the door was slammed shut. Montague then declaimed the poem from the prison steps.[81] He was half-aware of the absurd side of his demonstration. The two policemen were snorting with laughter; 'The Teigs must really be in trouble,' he imagined them saying to one another, 'if this is all they have to send into battle.' But he was chuffed that there were also reporters and press photographers at the scene.

Just the previous month, on 11 July 1970 in his televised address to the nation, Taoiseach Jack Lynch had, with credit to the author, quoted prominently from *A New Siege*: 'Old moulds are broken in the North.' Montague's verse campaign was getting noticed.

13

Evelyn spent 1969/70 as an instructor in the French department of University College Galway. It is a safe bet that whenever Montague was in Ireland, he was, in addition to other things, seeing Evelyn.

Madeleine, no fool, and acquainted with his correspondence, tried to warn John of trouble ahead. While he was in Ireland, she wished he would not 'scatter [his] brain and best feelings on unworthy objects': 'Your generosity of imagination … lend[s] marvellous trappings to shadowy virtues, tinselled charms, cowslips.'[82] This tiptoeing yet condescending admonition failed to alter the course of events. No doubt, Madeleine elsewhere addressed the problem more directly, but things had gone too far to turn back without harm to someone. A poem of this period addresses a 'lady' who makes 'stern and strange' demands: she wants him to 'sacrifice' another. But that, the speaker protests, would be like 'chopping my left hand/to appear before you/waving the bloodied/circle of the stump/as my only offering.'[83] It is not certain whether this poem springs from Madeleine demanding that he give up Evelyn, or Evelyn demanding that he leave Madeleine. By 1970 they were both part of him.

Over the winter holidays in 1969, Tom Parkinson, on a sabbatical year abroad at the University of York, visited the Montagues in Paris.[84] John confided to his old mentor that he was thinking of leaving Madeleine, then marrying Evelyn. He wanted to have a child. He knew Evelyn could be difficult, but he felt a deep, telepathic connection to her. Yes, there was a lot to be said for having one wife through all one's days, in a relationship enriched by years of memories, but he did not think he could go on as he was, living a double life, cheating on Madeleine. It was tearing him up and was harmful both to Madeleine and Evelyn.

After his return to York, Tom Parkinson wrote John a straightforward letter. He began by saying that he knew he was risking their long friendship, but he had to say that he believed John was making a terrible mistake.[85] Evelyn would not always be young and beautiful, and John could not even be sure that she would actually bear him a child. No, what he advised was that John and Madeleine should adopt a child. The advice did not go down well. To John's ears, it was like a curse had been uttered over his future with Evelyn. Also, Tom, a chronic adulterer, played the part of a hypocrite. The friendship was never the same afterwards.[86]

Yet all was not easy in John's relationship with Evelyn. She was, Barrie Cooke observed, 'beautiful, angry and awkward'.[87] At a restaurant in Paris she grew impatient with Frank Kersnowski (writing a book about Montague) and was rude.[88] At the Odeon Theatre, she blew up when an American made a noise during the performance. John, who cultivated his relationships with scholars, scolded her for being hysterical, as if she had been a child, and he, her father.[89] She was only nasty through insecurity, he believed. She had had a hard time as a young girl. Her father, whom she loved, had been an old-fashioned disciplinarian; he punished the children physically. As Evelyn got older, she fought back. Theirs had been an intimate but injurious relationship.[90] Evelyn's mother assured John that with the security of marriage and the steadying duties of motherhood, Evelyn would become less tempestuous. There grew to be a compact between the couple: Evelyn accepted that she needed care, and John promised to provide it and to heal whatever ailed her.[91]

Conversely, Evelyn's stormy nature was part of her attraction. John dreaded their fights, but admitted to Richard Ryan that 'I might well like Evelyn's bitchiness because it responds to, or matches, something predatory in myself: she may not only be my favourite sparring partner, but this seems to release something in me. After a mostly up-and-down week in London, I wrote 'The Hero's Portion' by her side in the train coming back.'[92] She gave him access to primal emotions, both of violence and lust. Everything was about the poetry. If he were finally to conclude that Evelyn was good for his poetry, then, given his ultimate devotion to the work, that would decide matters. But he was not yet sure of the future.

What would their life together be if the pair of them moved to Ireland? She was often getting in fights with people at work. Rather than taking her side, John stood back and diagnosed a 'persecution complex'. How would her combative sensitivity go down in Ireland, he wondered, 'where people are only too ready to answer back'? 'The question is whether I can make her phobias manageable, or whether they will stir the demons in my own hatch, so that we sting each other to exhaustion and spiritual death.'[93]

14

Robin Skelton, another Montague mentor, was Evelyn's advocate. In May 1970 he spent a week that he very much enjoyed in her company in Galway and Dublin, then brought her to the airport for her return flight to Paris. Afterwards, the two kept up a rapid-fire correspondence, as he sent her half-flirtatious poems, and she solicited Robin's help in advancing her relationship with John.[94] Two important letters must be quoted at length. Told by Robin what a wonderful woman Evelyn was, John replied:[95]

> A quotation from Master Graves (PARIS REVIEW interview): 'As a rule the Muse is one whose father has deserted her mother when she was young and for whom therefore the patriarchal charm is broken, and who hates patriarchy. She may grow to be very intelligent, but emotionally she is arrested at the age of fourteen or fifteen.'

An almost perfect description of the Lady Evelyn, although as I copy it out I see the differences. But it explains why one has to live through a ritual series of storms, rebukes, assaults: the struggle against the male principle has to be re-enacted every so often, in a most infantile form. And then all is clear and loving ....

But I am glad that you were able to see that there is something there. At her best, she has a kind of intuition which I find rare; at her worst, she is a real pest who can convert even someone so mild as myself into a total brute ....

**A basic problem: 'Never marry the muse' didn't someone say? She seems to be one. And perhaps the person one lives with should be a gentle critic, not a disciple .... To live with E. would be to live in myth, her intuitions are so strong.

Skelton's advice was just as emphatic as Parkinson's had been, but the very opposite:[96]

I have seen you [at home with Madeleine] psychologically wither and writhe, become small, become little boyish (an evasion I know in myself from the far past) ... and I have seen the counter-movement when you are [not in Paris], and when the strong-thewed lines, the tough words, the vivid biting words, more nearly match the person that was the medium for them ....

I believe neither in the matriarchal nor the patriarchal system, but in a partnership of energies directed at the one goal, whose ever it happens to be: Yeats/George; Marian Evans/Lewes; William Blake/|Catherine – the word matters more than them ....

As for Evelyn, I have known her for 300 years or so; as a consequence, I know too much to be anything but partisan .... When I first saw Evelyn at Woodtown, you remember you asked me what I thought of her? I said 'perfect'. The way she thinks is so much the way poetry thinks.

I think she should have your children.

I know, I trespass. I walk on thin ice .... We have our own childhood to make parentage chancy, our own parents to make fatherhood a gamble ....

But look at those hips! Ceres, I said.

Still, John temporized. He took the flat next to 11 rue Daguerre, so that he and Madeleine could continue in a sort of bicameral marriage. She was often away at weekends with a friend; he spent those times in Evelyn's nest. In the late summer of 1970 the Montagues holidayed together with the le Brocquys in Nice, but on their return, John left with Evelyn for a week in England. They drove around Thomas Hardy country, then called on Ted Hughes's house in Devon (he had moved). Evelyn, now with a job in the US embassy in Paris, got a flat in Montparnasse at 20 rue Duroc, only a ten-minute drive from 11 rue Daguerre. In October 1970 after reading a biography of Ezra Pound, who, while writing *The Cantos* in Rapallo, had gone back and forth between Olga Rudge and his wife, Dorothy, Montague began to think maybe a *ménage à trois* would be manageable.[97]

15

By October 1969 Montague was readying his next collection of poems for publication, but he was not happy with the promotion and distribution sides of MacGibbon and Kee. The publisher had been absorbed into the media group Granada. Tim O'Keeffe was being pushed out. Without O'Keeffe in the firm, John felt he could no longer influence the overall list, as he had done in the cases of Patrick Kavanagh, Patrick Boyle, Maurice Leitch, William Carlos Williams and Hugh MacDiarmid. In order to force the issue, Montague made demands. He asked for a revised edition in paperback of *A Chosen Light*, his next collection *Tides* to be priced more affordably, preparations to be made for his anthology of modern French poetry and all his current titles to be regularly supplied to Irish bookshops.[98] Yet his past sales had not made him so valuable to MacGibbon and Kee that he could make ultimatums.

Jeremy Lewis, an editor with André Deutsch, was keen to sign him up, but Montague decided instead to consolidate his writings with The Dolmen Press (Oxford University Press handling UK distribution).[99] Liam Miller was willing to reissue *Poisoned Lands* (revised), and he was the obvious choice to publish *The Rough Field*, having printed its sections as chapbooks. On 14 January 1970 Montague asked Liam Miller if he would be able to take on *Tides* and all his other work in future.[100] Miller was game, and by 3 March 1970 was already preparing to print *Tides*. At the end of April proofs arrived in Carbondale, Illinois, where Thomas Kinsella was hosting an American Conference of Irish Studies meeting.

16

On 3 October 1970 Eavan Boland reviewed *Tides* in *The Irish Times* as 'undoubtedly [Montague's] best work so far'. However, she mistook the story underlying the lyrics to be a romance of one true love, rather than, as was the case, the turbulent record of a man metaphorically lost at sea, promiscuously tossed hither and yon.[101] *Tides* arose from some poetic centre other than his ego and revealed aspects of himself of which he had not before known and found 'hard to face': impulses that were harsh, voyeuristic, predatory, insecure, or allied to the death instinct.[102] The book, either on account of, or despite, its unguarded intimacy, continued to be welcomed. It was a 'Recommendation' of the Poetry Book Society. And for once an English newspaper awarded Montague the laurels. With *Tides*, Peter Porter wrote in *The Guardian*, Montague showed himself to be better than Seamus Heaney, Michael Longley, or Derek Mahon.[103] The 'horse-race' view was frequently pernicious for all the contemporary Irish poets and particularly for Montague, but it was pleasant for once to come first.

Figure 46: The Dolmen Press edition of Tides *with cover illustration by Stanley W. Hayter, 1970.*

FLIGHT TO CORK, FATHERHOOD, AND
THE ROUGH FIELD

I

The main feature of the May 1970 American Conference of Irish Studies, hosted by Thomas Kinsella in Carbondale, Illinois, was the symposium on 'Ulster Now'. Tim Pat Coogan, J.C. Beckett, Seamus Heaney, Mary O'Malley and Montague were the panellists, an over-representation of nationalists; only Queen's University Belfast professor Beckett was a Unionist. When Mary O'Malley complained of J.C. Beckett's bias against the ethos of the Republic, the historian was indignant. It was only being disinterestedly objective, he declared, to assert, along with John Hewitt, 'this is our country also, nowhere else; and we shall not be outcast on the world.'[1] Seamus Heaney spoke up to smooth ruffled feathers with a 'faults on both sides' line of argument. The writer's duty, he said, was first to be critical of his own community, not to stir up trouble with the other side.

Montague did not agree. Beleaguered Northern Catholics had to have someone to speak up for them. Ever since the Anglo-Irish War of 1919–21, they had been abandoned by their co-religionists in the Republic while being treated as second-class citizens in the Six Counties. Asked what future he saw for the province, he quoted the prophetess Fedelm in Kinsella's recently published translation of *Táin Bó Cúailgne*: 'I see it crimson, I see it red.'[2] The American academics were shocked. How could he say something so awful? Montague repeated that he foresaw a 'river of blood'.[3] For the remainder of the conference, some participants steered clear of him as a dangerous character.

That spring Mary O'Malley invited John to edit a 'Northern Crisis' issue of *Threshold*. When he solicited contributions from Ulster writers, he 'ran into a monstrous block'. 'Surely this is a case for journalists,' some said.[4] Others excused themselves by saying either that they felt too intensely to say anything in public, or that they were weary of the whole thing. Only John Hewitt was quick to rise to the occasion. However, Derek Mahon, Michael Foley, Tom McGurk and Brian Moore all ultimately contributed, along with Seamus Deane (draft passages for *Reading in the Dark* [1996]) and Seamus Heaney, who was represented by the politically indirect but important poem 'The Tollund Man'. Of all the contents, Montague's 'A New Siege' stood out for being electric in its direct connection to events.

Brendan Kennelly hated Montague's poem and told him so – just the stuff of leading articles and platform slogans, the TCD lecturer argued, not real poetry, which should be personal and universal. Montague was making the mistake of following in the footsteps of Austin Clarke, whose crabbed satires would soon be forgotten. A better guide was Patrick Kavanagh, with his belief that the cycle of life in a small parish provided all that was necessary for artistic validity. In a heated self-defence, Montague declared that each section of *The Rough Field* was just as personal as his love poems and just as rooted in his locality. Behind the current period of history there was a great change beating, which was bound to affect the imagination, just as the French Revolution affected the Romantics. Did Kennelly not pick up the reference to William Blake in *A New Siege*?[5]

The bruising exchange continued into October: 'Don't give me all that academic blather metaphor,' Kennelly wrote:

> Your political verse is literal, prosaic and eminently forgettable, a childish response to a nasty provincial squabble. It will be remembered for its various and ardent dedications to enthusiastic young women – another fetching example of your naivete. You appear to suffer from a sort of disease of dedication, a passion to offer your fragments to whomever will accept them.

These jeering remarks refer to Montague's letter to *The Irish Times* of 29 August 1970. It was Montague's practice to use the *Irish Times* letters page to promote his present endeavours, and this letter laboriously explained why *A New Siege* is dedicated to Mary Holland (a journalist covering the North) in the *Threshold* publication, but to Bernadette Devlin in the Dolmen edition. Kennelly had lost his temper: it was clearly ridiculous to insinuate that these two eminent figures were Montague groupies.

The bitterness ran deep. Kennelly was an anti-Modernist Romantic; Montague, a Romantic Modernist. They were each doing an anthology of Irish poetry, Kennelly for Penguin, Montague for Faber.[6] They both taught contemporary poetry, Kennelly at TCD, Montague at UCD (with whom Kennelly's wife, Peggy O'Brien, had done an MA in 1968, a factor in their face-off). No doubt, Kennelly sensed that Montague had no time at all for his poetry. Kennelly was Kerry, Montague Tyrone. It was head-banging male rivalry on every front, poetry played like rugby.[7]

2

The Arts Council of Northern Ireland saw an opportunity to further its objective of 'education through mutual understanding' in the *Threshold* pieces by Montague and Hewitt. The previous year, it had funded a circuit of poetry readings featuring Michael Longley and Seamus Heaney, called 'Room to Rhyme'. The programme was even-handed, one Protestant and one Catholic, but sectarian balance was not emphasized, as it would be by the title of the second tour, 'The Planter and the Gael'. In November 1970 Hewitt and Montague went round towns in the Six Counties, beginning with Ian Paisley's home town, Ballymena. It was a travelling exhibition of the possibility that the two traditions could be friendly partners. People were invited to come together to hear out 'the other side'. A typically conciliatory poem was Hewitt's sonnet on how his great-grandmother, after handing out bread over the half-door to a passing beggar, caught Famine fever and died: 'that brief confrontation, conscribed me of the Irishry for ever'.[8] One hundred and fifty people turned out in Omagh at the Royal Arms Hotel, where Montague read poems set in the Clogher Valley and leaned hard on his identity going back four thousand years in the place, an obviously untraceable genealogy to Stone Age Tyrone. Hewitt, while professing himself one of the colonists, spoke up for how people in the North should think themselves lucky in having not just one tradition but two.[9]

Figure 47: From left, Barney Horisk, Kitty Horisk, John Montague, woman and child unidentified, John Hewitt, and Davy Hammond, Garvaghey, November 1970.

The tour was judged to be a success. So the Arts Council sent the two poets out a second time in April 1971, but by then the conflict had become more violent, and the success was not repeated.[10] It was past time for people to be paying eight shillings to attend an inter-faith poetry reading.

3

Seán Lucy invited Montague to deliver the 1971 Thomas Davis Memorial Lecture and proposed its title too, 'The Impact of International Modern Poetry on Irish Writing'. Lucy was the son of an Irish-born British army officer, who served in both world wars and later retired to an active civic life in Cork city. After himself serving in the army, then teaching in England, Seán Lucy returned home as the UCC professor of English, on the strength of his book about T.S. Eliot.

Montague's 9 April 1971 initial Thomas Davis Memorial Lecture was a masterful survey of the relations of Irish poets to European and international writing throughout the twentieth century. With chastening clarity, it dealt with Yeats, MacNeice, Denis Devlin, Austin Clarke and others. Overall, he explained, Irish poets had little or no standing internationally, Yeats included. The Irish were too caught up in themselves. Even in England, recent Irish poets, MacNeice apart, did not count for much.

Irish poetry was currently, Montague judged, healthier than at any time since the beginning of the century, but it remained provincial. Most Irish poets still wrote 'as though Pound, Lawrence and Williams had not brought a new music into English poetry'.[11] This was a clear swipe at the iambic pentameter conservatism of both the Belfast Group and the Trinity classicists, as well as an advertisement for himself.

Lucy was delighted with the lecture. In Cork he had been hearing good things about Montague from Seán Ó Riada, lecturer in music. It was the hope of Seán Lucy that the city should again become a cultural centre, as it had been in the time of his father's friends O'Faoláin, O'Connor and Daniel Corkery. There were signs of new growth. Seán Ó Tuama was now running UCC Irish-language seminars almost like writing workshops and the poet Seán Ó Ríordáin had been appointed writer-in-residence at the university. Things were looking up. In May 1971 Lucy asked if Montague would care to join the English department, at least for a year or two.[12] He could be part of a rising wave.

Montague was looking for an escape from Paris and from his marriage. He had put out feelers to Robin Skelton for a position in the University of Victoria, British Columbia, and to Tom Parkinson for a return to Berkeley. These requests pending, he was not yet ready to commit to Cork.

The two met again in August 1971 when John showed up with Evelyn at the Yeats summer school in Sligo. Lucy, a poet himself, read along with James Simmons, Michael Longley and Montague at one session. One of the Northerners, seeing Montague in the front row, was jumpy before going on stage. 'How the fuck am I going to talk with that long nose cocked up at me and those steely blue eyes boring into me?' Lucy was surprised at the 'fiercely mixed feelings of the "second generation" of Ulster poets towards their ex-patriate elder brother and exemplar, Montague'.[13] Neither Simmons nor Longley in fact saw Montague as an exemplar, much less a brother, but Seán Lucy was beginning to do so. He again urged Montague to give Cork a try. It might suit him and Evelyn as a place to settle.

Two months later, the two were pallbearers in the funeral of Seán Ó Riada. Thirty priests, a group of poets and Charles Haughey gathered for the ceremony. In the wake house, Ó Riada's widow said to Montague: 'Seán told me a lot about you. It's time for you to come home.'[14] A deal was struck with Seán Lucy, and Montague accepted a temporary lectureship at University College Cork, beginning in January 1972. On his return to Paris, he did not go back to the rue Daguerre, but moved in with Evelyn. The break had begun.

4

To read Madeleine's letters just before and for the months after John's departure from Paris tears a heart to shreds. They are full of love, anguish, understanding and desperate competitiveness. In November 1971 she wrote: 'My dear, you are leaving me without being convinced you are right, thinking only that any step back would be defeat. You are leaving me & starting a new life without enthusiasm ….' She left the door open for his return.

John had appealed to her that Evelyn, however volatile, had become essential to him as his muse. This carried no weight with her. She argued that he could not stake 'a claim on someone else's mind & psyche'. What John aimed to do was a 'sin', feeding like a parasite on a woman's spirit – a trenchant critique of the Robert Graves theory of poetic inspiration.[15]

The Christmas holidays in Paris were hell for John, Madeleine and Evelyn, and for the worried mothers of both women. Before he left for Ireland in January 1972 John collected his suitcase, packed by Madeleine, then wrote to her from Cork:[16]

> Looking at my carefully packed case, and realizing with how heavy a heart it must have been done, I feel sad that I am causing so much pain to someone of whom I am so fond, and can only plead that for the time being I am torn by emotions which I only partly understand myself. A poor plea, perhaps, and far from the kind of human dignity and control you respect so much, but maybe in Ireland I will be able to calm down, to come to terms with the tensions which are racking me. Anyway, if it is of any comfort to you, I am not proud of my hurtful words or actions towards you, whom I would not wish to offend, and hope you will forgive me. Especially as I know you wish me only good: even at your expense – what greater gift of heart can one expect? … Know that I will not give up lightly what we have taken so long to construct.

While the letter as a whole is well meant, the future tense in the last sentence is soft-heartedly meretricious. He had already long ago given up on what the two of them had constructed.

John carefully studied each of Madeleine's letters over the next year, annotating some of them, in a search for signs of her evolving state of mind.

He asked Désirée Moorhead, Bill Hayter's partner and a Paris neighbour, for a report on how Madeleine seemed to her.[17] Anguished and strangely surprised by John's departure, Désirée replied. There was little let-up until Christmas 1972, when Madeleine took the initiative and sent John back her wedding ring. In a dignified, unreconciled and angrily sad letter, she asked him in the future not to lie about what they once had made together, which he had foolishly brought to an end. This request from Madeleine – 'Don't betray our truth' – planted the seed for one of Montague's best poems, 'Herbert Street Revisited', the only kind of reparation it was in him to make.[18]

As for Madeleine, she raised her spirits for a final act of graciousness. She sent John the gift of a large silver ring, representing a gannet with its wings spread, nearly two inches across. It was inscribed 'Soar above pettiness to the realms of happiness.' He took it as an act of pure generosity, a blessing on his freedom of action and a command to make the most of his life. He wore it afterwards as a talisman and his private symbol, particularly whenever he had to make a public performance.[19]

5

Evelyn, with a job in Paris, visited Ireland when she could get away. The plan was for her to move permanently after Easter. On 30 January 1972 she was with John in the Ormonde Hotel, Dublin, when news of Bloody Sunday came on television. Twenty-six unarmed protesters were shot when the British army opened fire on a demonstration in the streets of Derry. The next day, Montague met Kevin O'Sullivan (a Columbia University professor) and Kinsella in a pub on Baggot Street. They brooded over what was to be done.[20] Both the North and the Republic were in an uproar.

Two weeks later, with Evelyn by his side, Montague joined an Enniskillen march led by Bernadette Devlin at which seventy-four protesters were arrested. In court, they were represented by John's brother Turlough.[21]

On this trip north, John introduced Evelyn to his brothers, but not to his mother. She was in Enniskillen hospital, and the shock of a son getting divorced might, he feared, finish her.[22] On their visit to Ederney, County Fermanagh, Seamus Montague had been telling John and Evelyn of a recent discovery – Uncle Frank Carney had served time in the Curragh detention camp! – when John changed the subject ... he intended to get a divorce. Seamus's jaw dropped. 'Well, Johnny, we can live this down too.' From the family's point of view, divorce was as shameful as a prison sentence. And in fact, contrary to his prediction, Seamus never did forgive John.

Turlough, the middle brother, told John his only course of action would be an appeal to the Vatican for an annulment. There was no other divorce 'we could recognize', we being not just Catholics in general, but his family in particular. Without an annulment, any child John might have with Evelyn would be, Turlough alarmingly declared, 'born a bastard'.[23] Turlough's family loved Madeleine. She had been wonderfully kind to them. They did not know Evelyn at all. In the long run, they could never really accept her, try as they might. The children mourned their Paris auntie.

During Evelyn's ten-day visit to Ireland in February 1972 she was often ill. She could not keep food down. John tried to nurse her, but it became clear that she required full-time care. Evelyn returned to her mother's house in Paris, where doctors diagnosed viral hepatitis. A month of bed rest was prescribed, followed by three months' convalescence on a strict diet. It was not yet safe for her, John concluded, to start a family.[24]

6

Montague enjoyed 'the rivers, the hills, the pure air' of Cork city. He was also surprised to find that he was happy to be back in a classroom. At UCD, Berkeley and Vincennes, he had taught eighteenth-century literature, modern Irish writing and poetry workshops; now he was assigned a lecture course on the Romantics.

Nuala Ní Dhomhnaill and Patrick Crotty, among his first students, remember the impact of the arrival of the poet in the department.[25] The syllabus and nature of instruction at UCC were then old-fashioned. Typically, a lecturer put on a black gown, stood at the podium and read out the day's lesson from notes. One nun on the teaching staff paid exclusive attention to the theological doctrine of each literary work. Another lecturer played tapes of himself reading out chapters of eighteenth-century fiction, and he was not a man particularly good at recitation. Seán Lucy put effort into his performances, but they were stagy. So the standard of teaching in 1972 was not high; it got better later.

Montague was a fresh breeze. He did not write out his lectures and did not wear a robe. He entered the lecture hall carrying the class text, John Hayward's

Nineteenth Century Poetry: An Anthology, then read out a poem, thoughtfully rather than dramatically, and made impromptu inter-linear comments. He drew connections with other poems, ancestors or descendants, rivals or companions. The poems were alive to him, part of a vast and animated society of poems. He invited questions and comments from students and listened to them carefully. The main force of his teaching was his example. Here was a highly intelligent person, obviously learned, and apparently sane, who thought poetry was the most serious subject in the world.

It gave Montague pleasure to provide a Parisian shock to the provincial and still very Catholic student body. He gossiped about Wordsworth's affair with Annette Vallon in France, and his having left her with child. The same poet's 'Nutting', Montague explained, was not just about an autumn harvest; it was a story of sex in the woods, very erotic indeed. One young woman asked him if he could please stop using the word 'erotic'. Wouldn't 'passionate' serve just as well? Complaints were made to the head of department. Seán Lucy rose to the occasion by setting up a formal debate as to whether or not 'Nutting' had anything to do with sex.[26]

7

On 8 May 1972 Claddagh Records organized a benefit poetry reading of a decidedly political cast. It was staged in Clonard Hall, part of a monastery on the Falls Road, Belfast. On the night, Kinsella read his ripping, indignant broadside 'Butcher's Dozen', blasted out in response to the Widgery Report's whitewash of the British army's role in Bloody Sunday. Montague chanted 'A New Siege' to battle music by The Chieftains – 'The March of the O'Neills'.[27] Seamus Heaney, just back from California, read some poems too, but he had nothing to offer like those hard-hitting performance pieces. He was worried by what his fellow poets were doing. Why excite such a crowd, at such a time, in the heart of Catholic Belfast? The reading could cause a riot.

Later Heaney felt shut out by Kinsella and Montague. They believed he took a soft line on Unionists and avoided political statements mainly because that served his London-alert literary ambition. He himself thought that the fact that Montague and Kinsella did not have to live in the North, and returned south after their readings, had made them reckless.[28] Anyway, Heaney wrote a few weeks later, 'It would wrench the rhythms of my writing procedures to start squaring up to contemporary events with more will than ways to deal with them.'[29]

Even if aligned politically and united by their concern about the rise of Seamus Heaney, Kinsella and Montague were not getting along. Far from it. At Seán Ó Riada's funeral in October 1971, Kinsella, celebrated for his version of the *Táin Bó Cúailgne*, disparaged Montague's translations from the Irish in *A Fair House*, published by Cuala Press. On the same occasion, Kinsella attacked Garech Browne for bringing along The Chieftains just to 'gain mileage from Ó Riada's dying'.

Montague drafted a long letter of remonstrance, objecting to Kinsella's bigotry with respect to Garech and his class. The way Kinsella had spoken of the Ulster Protestants at the memorial service for Louis MacNeice was shocking – people like Michael Longley and Derek Mahon, as if they were Trinity boys and only that. At the Ó Riada funeral Tom had asked John if the militant Protestant Edmund Spenser, being a religious bigot, could possibly have written good poetry. Montague turned the point of the inquiry right back to Kinsella. Ask yourself, being what you are, could you do so? But, yes, Montague continued, of course a bigot can write great poetry 'because poetry makes greater demands on him than his daily self'. As for Kinsella's 'daily self': 'You have a powerful, limited, nearly solipsistic nature which makes communicating with you worse than difficult.' 'I respect your experience of the void, but wish it were not so strident and absolutist; others have been there before you, from Rochester to Sartre.'[30] Hard-hitting words. Montague did not like being second fiddle at The Dolmen Press, and he was fighting back.

He had high hopes for *The Rough Field*. It had been twelve years since, on a bus down from Belfast, he had had a vision of both the beginning and the end of his sequence about Garvaghey. He went about the job carefully, waiting until he had acquired the techniques to represent the different sides of his subject. Originally, that subject had been the decline of a traditional way of life in Ulster, focused on the lives of locals, alongside the multigenerational experiences of his own family. Poring over his materials, he gradually went deeper into the damaged or unfulfilled personalities of his father and uncles. The poem swelled to encompass the decline of the Gaelic order, the colonization of Ulster by the British and the neutral Free State. When the sectarian conflict blew up in the late 1960s and the British army entered the scene, Montague rose to the occasion and incorporated current events into the final sections, so that upon publication it appeared to many readers to be a compelling explanation of the way things were. *The Rough Field* had gone from being a reflective meditation, along the lines of

'The Deserted Village' (but Modernist in form), to a literary kind of news, not wholly unlike Norman Mailer's *The Armies of the Night*. Montague had surprised himself by doing something remarkable. He feared no one would notice.

With the help of Robin Skelton and Liam Miller, a table of contents was established during a long session in the Majestic Hotel, Fitzwilliam Street, Dublin, in May 1971, but then Miller turned his attention to other matters, particularly his hot-selling edition of Kinsella's *Táin*.[31] Montague grew impatient. A year went by before a first set of proofs was ready in June 1972. Publication was set for 26 October, then put back to 10 November. Yet at readings scheduled for that month in the UK, copies were still not on hand for sale.[32] In the first week of December, Montague, panicking, checked with *The Listener*, *The Guardian* and *The Spectator*. Review copies had not been received from Oxford University Press, Dolmen's UK distributor. On the telephone to the OUP office, he was 'crusty', and a member of its editorial staff complained to Liam Miller of Montague's importunity. In trying to serve as his own public relations man, Montague was driving himself demented, on top of being a nuisance to those in the book trade.

In Ireland, *The Rough Field* got a lot of help from friends and a warm welcome on its publication. Seamus Heaney interviewed Montague on RTÉ in October, ahead of its release. Benedict Kiely generously heralded its publication in *The Irish Times*. Father Burke-Savage agreed to publish an article by Thomas Redshaw in *Studies*, which laid the critical groundwork for examination of the poem.[33] Liam Miller organized a reading with four voices in the Peacock Theatre, Dublin, with music supplied by the Chieftains, and the whole thing was broadcast in two parts by RTÉ. Brendan Kennelly looked past old quarrels with the author and wrote a thoughtful review in the *Sunday Independent*.[34]

> *The Rough Field* is such an attractive poem. It never loses sight of the fact that history is made from the lives of men and women ... It is a very unusual poem in that it reminds our violent age that a gentle view of the world is still possible and desirable. The poem tells us that we can cope with the horrors of history if we substitute calm meditation for blind and frenzied action.

In March 1973 Eavan Boland conducted a long follow-up interview for *The Irish Times*, focused on the book's unfurling impact.[35] Overall, its publication was treated as an event of national importance in Ireland.

The reception in England was sometimes chilly. The *TLS* review was snide. Anonymously written by a young Terry Eagleton in a stilted, donnish manner, it was dismissive not only of Montague but also of Seamus Deane's first collection, *Gradual Wars*. (Eagleton later became a public admirer of *The Rough Field* and a Field Day companion of Deane's.)[36] Nonetheless, Londoners showed up in droves on 8 July 1973 for a choric reading of the poem at the Roundhouse in Chalk Farm. Many were turned away for lack of seats. Seamus Heaney, Ben Kiely, Patrick Magee and Tom McGurk (all with Ulster voices) joined Montague and The Chieftains in the performance, filmed by Liam Miller's son. Unfortunately, although well notified, Oxford University Press again failed to provide books for the event. Montague, touchy about his English standing, continued to believe himself snake-bit with bad luck.

Seamus Heaney wryly agreed that he himself 'had the lion's share of good luck' while the Tyrone man had 'a gift for taking the wooden spoon' (the prize for coming last).[37] Heaney's *Wintering Out*, published by Faber at the same time as *The Rough Field*, took all the prizes that year. In hindsight, that appears questionable as a consensus view. Many of Heaney's poems had been developed from a hint from Montague's 'A Primal Gaeltacht' about Irish place-names in the North (Brian Friel also ran with this idea in his play *Translations*).[38] Heaney, given his fascination with etymology, was able to make much of Montague's observation. His inscription on a gift copy of *Wintering Out* is cheekily competitive:[39]

> For John Montague
> Here comes the last mummer
> shadowing Seán the Hunchback
> squeezing into the hedge
> of the rough field.
> Poor Teagues turn their heads
> back from the rock.
> Sweeney cocks an ear
> somewhere in the fens.

The cryptic message was not hard for Montague to decode. 'The Last Mummer' is Heaney's persona in *Wintering Out*; 'Seán the Hunchback' is Montague's persona in *Beyond the Liss*, where he is in pursuit of Robert Graves. The needling joke is that now Heaney shadows Montague, just as Montague did Graves. He is staking his own claim on the poetic territory of the *The Rough Field*.[40]

On the title page of *Wintering Out*, Montague scribbled, 'the auld copycat'.[41]

8

In early 1973 John and Evelyn went over to London for a poetry reading, part of the UK publicity campaign for *The Rough Field*. Before they boarded the *Inishfallen* to sail from Cork to Swansea, Evelyn bought a pregnancy test at the local chemist. During the crossing, the two learned that they were going to be parents. Arriving that evening in London 'high and happy', they called in to see Aidan Higgins in Muswell Hill.[42]

What happened next was the stuff of subsequent rumour. It appears that, upon hearing their news, Higgins said, Great, let's celebrate. But Montague, as usual, had arrived without a bottle, expecting others to provide. The house was flat out of drink. Higgins had been taking speed and drinking heavily.[43] He suddenly turned hostile. Was he just triggered by the way Montague had crashed in upon him, or had he been spoiling for a fight for some time? There were angry words and Higgins took a swing and clipped Montague on the jaw. Next, a loud fracas, pushing and shouting, alarmed the neighbours. Evelyn told them there was no need to call the police. She begged John to come away, and they left.

That put an end to a long relationship between two ambitious *confrères*, each trying to get ahead in the race for fame, happy enough to help one another because one was a prose writer and the other (mainly) a poet. Meeting a few years later in the house of Seamus Heaney, Higgins apologized to Montague. He said drink was to blame for the out-of-the-blue 'puck on the gob'. But the hatchet was not truly buried. In reviews, Higgins subsequently was niggardly about Montague's work. Worse yet, he sometimes boasted to literary friends about the time he had bested the poet in a straight-out fist fight. Fed by gossip, the one-punch unpleasantness became a legendary contest of champions. In fact, neither Higgins nor Montague was ever much of a brawler.

9

Oonagh Montague was born on the last day of August 1973. Evelyn teasingly praised John for his great courage in remaining in the room throughout the forceps delivery. Robin Skelton was asked to be the child's godfather and Désirée Moorhead her godmother, in honour of the roles each had played in helping along John and Evelyn's romance.[44]

The couple had found an idyllic place to live, Fortview, a former coastguard cottage on Roche's Point, County Cork. They took up occupancy a few weeks after Oonagh's birth. It was a spectacular site, a curving lane with a row of two-storey houses on one side, the sea cliff on the other, and at its end a whitewashed lighthouse. The foghorn would sound in the night, and when the winds blew, foam 'scudded over the house like snow'.[45] John romanticized the first family household, particularly in the last poem of *The Great Cloak*, giving the collection a novelistic, happy ending. Like Yeats's tower, Fortview was fine as poetic symbol but not so practical as a dwelling, particularly for a young mother just home with a baby, and no shops nearby. Evelyn, after a happy pregnancy, was overcome with postnatal depression. One poem in *The Great Cloak*, 'When the Wind Blows', takes the shape of a lullaby to send away the ghost of her harsh father, so that she may safely rock in the arms of another man, her husband. The next-to-last poem is a plea for peace in this 'long-sought house' after one of her explosions of fury. John and Evelyn were glad of what they had, but it was not just bliss at Roche's Point.[46]

Figure 48: Montague in local near Roche's Point.

Gradually Evelyn took up the threads of life again. She had done a bit of writing before, covering John's trip to an international writers' conference in Struga, Macedonia ('When Poets Transcend Cold-War Politics', *The Irish Press*, 5 October 1972). During their trips together to London, she and John had come to know Antony Rudolf and Daniel Weissbort, poets and editors, just starting families like themselves. In early 1974 Weissbort commissioned Evelyn to guest-edit an issue of *Modern Poetry in Translation*, focusing on Celtic poets.[47] She was well able for the work and could do it in intervals of caring for her child.

Near Roche's Point was Shanagarry, the country house (built around 1820) owned by the printer and scholar René Hague and his wife Joan. She was the daughter of Eric Gill, the great English sculptor, letter-cutter and print-maker. Gill never took the trouble to reconcile incest with his daughters with his vision of a strictly Catholic way of life. He was a charismatic, lusty, hyper-patriarchal, mystic genius. At Gill's Catholic artists commune at the Capel-y-Ffin Monastery, Wales, René Hague (an ex-seminarian) married Joan Gill, while Joan's sister Petra became engaged to the poet and artist David Jones (she subsequently married another). The Eric Gill clan remained close long after the death of the patriarch. Hague latterly spent much of his energy on explications of the writing of David Jones and an edition of Eric Gill's engravings.

Life at Shanagarry had something of both an old-fashioned marriage and the Eric Gill commune. The couple reconstructed Gill interiors – 'pewter plates on a Romney Green oak dresser' – and carried on his sacramentalist habits of life.[48] René and Joan appeared happy in their gendered division of labour; 'there was no spikiness or pulling in different directions'. It was for René to write the books, bring in the money, bake his special pies and read bedtime stories to their children (this last activity was earlier in the marriage). Joan made the bread, minded the children, cooked, gardened, milked the cow and did all the washing.[49] While patriarchal, René Hague was kindly. If John said something that stung Evelyn, René would reproach him: 'No, that was sharp, John.'[50] Montague bowed to his wisdom. Both Evelyn and John were under the spell of Shanagarry. It was their retro sixties ideal, with an arts-and-crafts pedigree.

Montague credited Hague and David Jones, along with Kathleen Raine, another of that set, as spiritual guides. Kathleen Raine (1908–2003), a wise mother figure in the eyes of John and Evelyn, was a wonderfully strange character.[51] Widely read as a schoolgirl in the history of English literature, she did

Natural Sciences at Cambridge. Upon graduation, she agreed to a companionate marriage to a Classics lecturer, Hugh Sykes Davies. That ill-conceived compact was followed by marriage to Charles Madge, sociologist and communist. In time, Madge took up with Stephen Spender's wife, then Kathleen joined the household of a wealthy widow at Rock Hall, Northumberland, a retreat for several poets and artists, including David Jones.

Kathleen's last great love was for a gay man, the travel writer Gavin Maxwell, whose own undying passion was for an otter named Mij. After house-sitting for Maxwell in 1956, Kathleen was deemed responsible for the death of the otter, sundering the completely one-sided love affair. She bought a house at 47 Paulton Square, Chelsea, and offered bounteous hospitality to writers, scholars and mystics, including, after 1969, John Montague. Like W.B. Yeats (along with William Blake, a god to her), Kathleen Raine took very seriously anything in which anyone had at some time believed. It was all true. She was a bright lady deep into the dark arts.

John may have first heard of Kathleen through Liam Miller (kindred spirits, as devout Yeatsians). The Dolmen Press was planning a publication of her poems. But it was Robin Skelton who brought Montague around to meet her in person in December 1969.[52] Thereafter he was a regular caller at 47 Paulton Square whenever in London. Kathleen Raine became an important figure in his life.

In the same year, John began to visit Raine's friend David Jones in whatever nursing home the old World War I veteran was at the time laid up.[53] Jones had suffered a stroke and then a fall, requiring a hip replacement. He was never fully back on his feet roaming the world. It was good of Montague to keep paying respect to the convalescent poet, largely forgotten by British literary culture. In 1970 Montague brought Garech Browne and Paddy Moloney along in an attempt to convince Jones to record *Anathemata* for Claddagh Records. To Montague (as to Auden and Eliot), it was one of the greatest long poems of the century. On that occasion, Jones enjoyed hearing an Irish air played on the tin whistle, but he did not fancy himself a performer and declined to read for posterity. Still, Montague kept up his visits, and after each meeting he made notes of the conversations. To him, the remarks of David Jones carried great portent. Years later he put them into verse lines, often revised them and finally published them in his last collection of poems as 'The Great Bell', part of his own testament.

10

In the autumn John sent his brother Turlough a formal birth announcement of Oonagh's arrival and added a stinging reproach. Turlough's wife Bridie, John complained, had visited Garvaghey and told Freda Montague that John had left Madeleine and was living with another woman in Cork. John would not again be welcome, she reportedly had said, at Turlough's house in Fintona.

John was in a volatile state, made worse by a poisonous mixture of shame and pride. He was explosively defensive of Evelyn whenever she was ill-treated by Catholics around Cork, on account of her being French, or very young, or unmarried. At the same time, as if ashamed, John was concealing Evelyn's existence from his mother and aunt in County Tyrone.

The birth of Oonagh was momentous. It justified in his mind all the trouble and heartache he had caused by his infidelities and divorce. Happily, Madeleine had found a partner of her own, Serge Mottuel, who by his first wife had a young daughter in need of mothering. Everything was working out well. He had been right all along. But if he was so right, why could he not tell Molly and Freda about the birth of Oonagh? He later gave this reasoning to Turlough: 'Although what I have done will be commonplace in the Ireland of your children, I see no point in disrupting the peace of the older generation, who have lived by a different code.' But this moral complexity and historical relativism did not put him in a strong position to be lecturing others. 'I hope that you, Turlough, will see that [Bridie] does not repeat the performance with our mother, which would be even more unwise, in view of her state of health.'[54]

Turlough was not going to take this quietly. He was every bit as bearishly sensitive about attacks upon his wife as John was. Bridie was not an idle tattler; she was a qualified pharmacist who did locums in towns across south Tyrone and had a professional reputation for confidentiality to maintain. On 8 November 1973 he replied that the tone John had taken in his letter was 'unworthy of anyone with a soul'. Whoever said that Bridie had gossiped to Freda was a 'liar'. John was obligated 'to proceed to the source and say for Bridie and me LIAR'. In fact, he continued, word of John's present arrangements had some time back spread throughout the parish from various sources, including Turlough himself, but not from Bridie, who was no gossip.

Only a day or two after Turlough's letter arrived, the telephone rang at Fortview. John's cousin Brendan O'Meara was on the line, and he had bad news. John's mother had died at the Erne Hospital in Enniskillen. People were gathering for the funeral in Fintona.

In the face of the death of their mother, it might have been hoped that the differences between John and Turlough would seem of little account, but they were too recent and too raw, and both men had their pride. It is a long way on little roads from Roche's Point to Fintona, and John himself was not a driver. He arrived late. Typical, Turlough thought; always neglectful of the most important duties. Each brother felt insulted by the other. John poured out his grief in a letter to Madeleine. She replied:[55]

> As for you and your family, my dear, how can you be surprised? You taunted them, and they answer back in their own way, the way of society fending for its young. You know of course that it will happen again, as it will to me, as I pursue my own course.

Good advice, but the best advice is sometimes the hardest to follow. The two brothers prolonged their quarrel into the settlement of their mother's estate (gross assets: £7,000). In May 1974 John stood in immediate need of a few thousand pounds in order to make a down payment on 25 Grattan Hill, a small Georgian terraced house. Turlough, as trustee, had advanced Seamus Montague his share of the estate, but he did not take the initiative to offer John his portion. He wanted first an apology to Bridie from John, or at least some kind of answer to his last indignant letter.

Each brother next took half-steps in the direction of reconciliation. John credited Turlough for his loyalty to Bridie, but gave particulars for why he believed she had indeed upset Freda the previous summer with her talk of John's affairs. John laid out further grievances too, but closed with an affirmation of brotherly affection. As a peace offering, it was not much but it was something. Turlough answered with equal courtesy and equal reserve, and advanced £2,000 to John for the Grattan Hill house.[56] Between the brothers, there things sat.

II

On 13 March 1974, seven years after its commissioning, Montague's *Faber Book of Irish Verse* was launched at the National Gallery of Ireland in Dublin. It was remarkably different from earlier anthologies of Irish poetry. For one thing, it did not begin with poetry in English in the sixteenth century, but with poetry in Irish from the sixth century. One third was translated from Irish into English. The translators, from the nineteenth century onwards, were poets with a body of work in English, so that the anthology gave a picture of a national literature in which the first language of Ireland had for a long time inter-animated its verse in English, making Irish literature on the whole distinct from British literature. Rather than dying away as a once-but-no-longer enlivening stream, the Irish language is shown to be again flowing strongly through the work of post-Free State Poets, most of whom were taught Irish in school. Montague assisted in producing this effect by soliciting new translations from his contemporaries, and himself putting into English some classic Irish poems. Overall, Montague's anthology is in line with the thesis of Thomas Kinsella's argument about the 'Dual Tradition' in his December 1966 keynote address to the Modern Language Association (quoted by Montague in the opening paragraph of his introduction). The anthology scants the achievement of nineteenth-century English poets in Ireland, raises into view the long tradition of poetry in Irish, and features both the Modernist and Gaelic-conversant poetry that followed the Irish Revival of Yeats and AE.

Denis Donoghue may have been partly right when he stated in an unfriendly review of the anthology (he pretended to be programmatically against poetry in translation) that Montague had a political agenda, perhaps having to do with the Troubles.[57] Donoghue could not find evidence for that particular agenda; there wasn't one, but there is a decided emphasis on the natural and normal lustiness of the ancient Irish and the long tradition of Irish poets' celebration of love. This emphasis is clearly a critique of the Jansenist, Church-dominated culture of the Republic. Augustine Martin noticed this intention: 'The theme of eros weaves itself among the other themes – nature, war, holiness, learning, love of country, grief of exile.'[58]

Some reviewers complained about the inclusion of Robert Graves (the recent Oxford Professor of Poetry was commonly regarded as English).[59] Graves himself had been happy to contribute. His grandfather was the Bishop of Limerick, and his father, Albert Perceval Graves (1846–1931), had been born in Dublin, wrote poetry and edited anthologies of Irish poetry, before settling in Wales. But the point of Robert Graves being wedged into the table of contributors is that he is the key to the whole thing. The anthology includes a remarkable array of ancient poetic forms: epigrams, curses, triads, ballads, *caoiní*, praise poems, elegies in abundance, songs, satires, lullabies, prayers and oaths. To Robert Graves, all poetry drew its strength from such primal speech acts. The disciplined forms of tradition had magical powers and key social functions.

Those primal speech forms were a continuing strength of Irish poetry. Contemporary writers behaved like twentieth-century *filí* with still-active duties to their tribe. They gathered at wakes of elder artists, like MacNeice, Kavanagh and Padraic Colum. The poets present in Cúil Aodha for the funeral of Seán Ó Riada were as essential to the ceremony as the thirty priests (Kinsella, Heaney and Montague all wrote long elegies for the composer). When protesters were shot down in Derry, Kinsella rushed to raise a cry. Slow, sad funeral marches for a communal cortège were produced by Seamus Heaney in *North*. Battle hymns were printed as broadsides by Montague. When a prize was offered (although no longer by a tribal chieftain), they lustily battled to win it. Their loves were celebrated in songs. Michael Longley, James Simmons and Derek Mahon published satirical verse letters to one another. Overall, there was a rapid stealing back and forth of motifs amongst contemporaries. A vibrant, competitive masculine culture of poets, like a bi-sectarian bardic college, had come into being. This was momentous.

A self-contradictory bit in the introduction to the Faber anthology gives the game away. In its third paragraph, Montague brings up an illustrious aspect of early Irish poetry – that there had been a succession of strong women poets. He then repeats some words of doctrinaire Gravesianism: 'Psychologically, a female poet has always seemed an absurdity, because of the necessarily intense relationship between the poet and the Muse.'[60] (A woman poet with a male muse was for Graves imponderable.) The anomaly could be explained, Montague continues, by the fact – not entirely accurate – that in early Ireland there was no discrimination against women poets.[61] This observation assumes that the flourishing of female poets was a good thing about ancient Ireland. Then would it not obviously follow that discrimination, not the lack of a muse relationship, was the reason for the underperformance and under-representation of female voices in more recent times?

For his own anthology, from his generation onwards (poets born after 1920), Montague selected twenty-one males and just two women. Had one of his aims for the anthology been gender balance, for the earlier decades he could have included Dora Sigerson (just as interesting as Seamus O'Sullivan), or picked Sheila Wingfield in place of the Californian Robinson Jeffers. It is difficult to think of contemporaries whose work by 1970 surpasses that of the two women he included, Eiléan Ní Chuilleanáin and Eavan Boland, but Montague could have found female poets already just as accomplished as the youngest men added, Paul Murray and Gregory O'Donoghue. It is surprising Montague overlooked Máire Mhac an tSaoi and the early work of Nuala Ní Dhomhnaill.[62] Perhaps those two poets were left out on account of writing exclusively in Irish. Today, anthologists would be obligated to find close to an equal number of men and women poets, even if new translations were required.

In hindsight, the *Faber Book of Irish Verse* is a monument to a masculinist period that would soon be brought to an end by a then undetected, but huge, gathering wave of contemporary poetry by Irish women. Montague's generation had created a remarkable revival, one of significance in the history of poetry in English, but in a major respect, the representation of women, it was lifeless.

UNIVERSITY COLLEGE CORK AND
A RISING GENERATION OF POETS

I

In April 1974 University College Cork appointed John Montague to a permanent and pensionable post as lecturer. It was gratifying to find himself welcomed by the city and the university. He proudly announced the news to his brothers, men with professions.[1] Now he needed a home for his family. However, paying for one required something in addition to his salary as a junior lecturer and the £2,000 legacy from his mother.

At a Canadian Association of Irish Studies conference in late March, he learned of a summer school post at the University of Buffalo. It was, by Irish standards, a handsomely paid job of work, $2799 for a six-week term. An Irish lecturer's starting salary was roughly £4000 a year. Going to North America to supplement his salary from then on became a pattern in Montague's life. He wryly compared himself to itinerant labourers who traditionally took the boat from Ulster to Scotland for seasonal work in the fields.

At the end of June 1974, after four weeks of marking UCC examinations, John left Evelyn, Oonagh and the family cats behind at Roche's Point and headed off by himself to Buffalo. The plan was for Evelyn to close up Fortview, organize the move to their new home at 25 Grattan Hill and then fly to Buffalo with Oonagh to join John in the third week of July.[2]

Lodged in a bare room in a vacant student dormitory in downtown Buffalo, John was irritable. Right away, he began missing his wife and daughter. In his absence, Evelyn tackled John's correspondence and kept him up to date:

Among what I found open was the proof of 'Wheels Slowly Turning' that Gregory [O'Donoghue] and I corrected and returned to the Lyric Theatre, also a rather nasty note from [illegible name] saying that he was unwilling to pay £40 for your article, and a letter from an old flame in need of some re-kindling: Nuala O'Faolain. I wouldn't mind some re-kindling myself. I miss you very much. The house feels empty and Roche's Point different.[3]

John, hearing that the landlord was asking Evelyn to vacate the cottage before the close of the rental period, composed a stern rebuke on university stationery. At the time, he was a worried, hard-working, protective father.

The time in Buffalo became easier after he made friends with a young professor of medieval literature at Buffalo State College, David Lampe. He found a television for John's dormitory room and, after Evelyn arrived, a playpen for Oonagh. John was a frequent dinner guest at the Lampes' home, where the two children began to think of him as an 'errant' but interesting uncle.[4] It was a shame, Lampe thought, that here was an important Irish poet in town, and no one else paid any heed to the fact, so he organized a poetry reading at Buffalo State for 4 August 1974. The event, well-advertised, drew a good crowd, including the poet James Wright. For the next thirty years, Lampe continued to organize poetry readings, over one hundred of them between 1974 and 2008, thirteen featuring Montague.[5] As an associate of White Pine Press, Lampe saw into print several American editions of Montague's prose and poetry.

On their return from Buffalo to Ireland, for the last week of August John brought Evelyn and Oonagh along to Newcastle House, a country-house hotel near Ardagh, County Longford, where a bicentennial Goldsmith Summer School was being held. In view of his lectureship at UCC (and hope of promotion), Montague took up on Evelyn's behalf a project that Madeleine had often urged him to complete: his thesis on Goldsmith. Talbot Press, a venerable Dublin imprint, had been acquired by the Smurfit Publishing Group.[6] They wanted Montague's Goldsmith for their revived list.[7] The summer school served as a forcing house for turning his dissertation fragments into chapters of a book for a general readership. Montague gave not just one lecture but two. Seamus Heaney chaired Montague's first session, 'A Sentimental Prophecy', and Ben Kiely did the honours for 'Goldsmith's Zoo'. A third section of the dissertation, 'The Philosophical Vagabond', appeared in the July issue of *Ireland of the Welcomes*. However, the Talbot Press Goldsmith book never came out – whether because the author procrastinated, or the publisher retreated, is unknown. It is a strange fate for a dissertation that was certainly publishable when first submitted in 1961, but Montague was primarily a poet, not a scholar. Most of his attention in 1974 and '75, apart from that taken up by teaching, went into the poems he was writing for *A Slow Dance*, *The Great Cloak* and *The Dead Kingdom*. All three volumes were on the boil: the first two mostly done and the last just undertaken in the summer of 1974.

2

The new family home at 25 Grattan Hill in Cork was in a nineteenth-century terrace of houses built on a steep slope overlooking Kent Station and the marina across the River Lee. The poet Thomas McCarthy (b. 1954), one of Montague's UCC students and a practised gardener from Cappoquin, County Waterford, eventually made improvements to the sharply rising area behind the house.[8] It was not long before more young poets from Cork also found their way to 25 Grattan Hill.

Along with Patrick Crotty and Nuala Ní Dhomhnaill, there were other student poets at UCC when Montague joined the staff in 1972. New ones seemed to show up each year. Maurice Riordan (b. 1953) had been a schoolmate of Crotty's at St Colman's College, Fermoy.[9] The pair of them had a precociously intense interest in literature. Riordan would do graduate work at McMaster University in Hamilton, Ontario, before blossoming as a poet during the 1990s in England. Crotty had the gift of an extraordinary memory for poems; he took a festive delight in recitation. Montague tended to typecast the flock of poets. He had, McCarthy recalls, 'a very academic, categorizing frame of mind'. He saw himself as Exile Poet, Robert Graves as White Goddess Poet and Heaney as Farmer Poet. Among his students, McCarthy was the Gardener Poet and Pat Crotty was the Critic.[10]

Over the next several years, Montague would now and then ask Crotty to stop by Grattan Hill. Once Pat reported for duty, the two would look at drafts of John's poems – for the revised *Poisoned Lands* (1977), *The Great Cloak* (1978) and *The Dead Kingdom* (1984). John listened to what his student had to say; he was receptive, not argumentative. After an hour and a half, they would go down the hill together for a pint.[11] If he had ever had any doubts, these sessions gave Crotty good reason to trust his own faculties, and that was all to the good, but he began to feel that Montague colonized the minds of others. There was something extractive about his interest in people.

A somewhat different point is made by Gregory Delanty, five years younger than Crotty. When he was sixteen or seventeen, Delanty, the son of a printer, was writing poems to his girlfriend. He began to imagine they were very fine poems. The editor of a city newspaper told him there was a poet living in Cork, a real poet, and he had a house on Grattan Hill, number twenty-five. Delanty found the house, and a tall man answered the door. Yes, he was John Montague. Greg said he had some poems he wanted him to read. All right, Montague replied, write down your address on this piece of paper, and after I look at them, I'll send you a letter. No, no, young Delanty replied. He wanted to have an opinion on them straightaway. So, Montague welcomed him inside and accepted the hand-written pages. After reading for a while, Montague said, Well, you have some talent. Greg Delanty recalls that, though the meeting lasted little more than twenty minutes, it meant a lot to him.[12] But as he got older, and saw more of Montague, Delanty began to be wary. 'He would say things that hurt you … he kept feeling for the point, the painful spot, and he didn't stop until he found it.' That needling, investigative Tyrone intelligence made him someone to watch out for. When sufficiently annoyed, Delanty fought back. It may be that that is just the response Montague aimed to provoke.

Among the books he gave the younger poet to read, one was the first edition of *The Norton Anthology of Modern Poetry* edited by Richard Ellmann and Robert O'Clair. Delanty read everything from cover to cover, including the letter that John left inside from Richard Ellmann apologizing for John's exclusion. It was a softback edition, and later Delanty had his father casebind it in the Eagle Printing Company for Montague.

The first student poet Montague lit upon after his arrival at UCC was Gregory O'Donoghue. He tended to dress all in black, like a character in a story by James Clarence Mangan. O'Donoghue's father, Robert, was literary editor of the *Cork Examiner*, so Greg had a leg up on the other young poets in access to books and literary news. Montague was impressed in the spring of 1972 when he saw him reading John Berryman's *77 Dream Songs*. After O'Donoghue passed that volume on to Nuala Ní Dhomhnaill, she realized for the first time that 'one could confront the pain of one's life through poetry'.[13] Clearly, something was already stirring in Cork when Montague arrived on the scene. In May 1972, on the lookout for a new generation of poets in Ireland, Montague wrote to Serge Fauchereau that he believed he had found some. Gregory O'Donoghue, he hoped, might replace Richard Ryan (by then in the Irish Embassy in Japan) 'as my spur and insight into a newer thing'.[14] He was not looking to manufacture protégés, but to harvest something fresh for the sake of his own work. One final poem was added before the *Faber Book of Irish Verse* went to print, a dream song in Cork dialect by Gregory O'Donoghue.

Himself in his mid-forties, Montague liked the company of these rollicking students just half his age. Mostly he met them either at 25 Grattan Hill or in public houses, not at UCC. A number of pubs enjoyed his custom – the Western Star, Ma Henchy's, Nancy Blake's – but Montague's favourite haunt was the Long Valley Bar, which was done up like the inside of a ship.[15] Its proprietor Humphrey Moynihan dressed in a white butcher's apron and wore a tie; he was a thin, long-nosed fellow. In his eyes, the poet was a man on his own level. He treated this customer like a co-owner. With the presence behind the bar of Mrs Moynihan, the Long Valley was untypical of Irish pubs in the 1970s in being not entirely a male precinct. Once Nuala Ní Dhomhnaill left with her husband for Turkey in 1972, with the exception of Catherine Phil MacCarthy (UCC 1973–76), most of the Cork poets of that decade were male (this would change in the following years). The lads knew to look for Montague in the Long Valley.

There Montague made himself approachable, or else joined in whatever fun was going on. He did not stand rounds, or return the favour of a drink, but he showed curiosity in people. Eamonn O'Donoghue, later a prominent eye surgeon, sensed that Montague was 'on a mission'. He was trying to feed the fire he found burning when he came to Cork. 'He would put a book your way he thought might be useful to you.'[16] First, he would suggest the title, then, after a time, he would locate a copy and pass it over the ornate table at the Long Valley. Lots of times, he loaned books of contemporary poetry that simply could not be bought in Cork, particularly collections of American and international poetry.

Sometimes he would give tips to young poets, like a trainer talking to a jockey. One day late in the month of May, Montague advised Tom McCarthy to go barefoot in the summer, just for the sake of his poetry; doing so would heighten his sense perceptions.[17] The younger man was shrewd enough to realize that the suggestion was not preposterous: Montague's own poems were not just visually descriptive; they registered odours, textures, temperatures and soundscapes. A poet was meant to be sensually open to experience. McCarthy's published journal is littered with such stories that begin, 'I met John Montague in the Long Valley ...' and follow with a lesson. Montague was a more committed teacher in the pub than he ever had been in the lecture hall. One gained from him a sense that poetry was a difficult, exalted and mysterious craft, but fundamentally, part of the fun of life, its essential interest.

Montague did not keep up a professional demeanour or police the barrier between teacher and student – far from it. And he did not hide what may be called his human qualities – his vanity, jealousy, priapism, sense of injury and streak of silliness. Often enough, he 'didn't do himself any favours' by his behaviour.[18] Seamus Heaney was one of the first of many poets that Montague invited to Cork, and it was good for students to be introduced to his work, but their teacher did not conceal from the young poets his 'wild and intense' resentment of Heaney's uninterrupted success. He thought there was some sort of clever trick or phony appeal behind it all. He also fretted that Heaney was stealing from him; Heaney's gain was always Montague's loss.

The young Seamus Heaney had a huge appetite for poets, eating up one after another – Hopkins, Lawrence, Frost, Kavanagh, Hughes, Lowell and Montague – and, in the course of digestion, he let out little burps of verse, fragrant of his most recent meal. This was perfectly normal in the growth of a true poet, but it was not always pleasant if you were the meal. After reading *Wintering Out*, Tom McCarthy recorded in his diary that 'Pat Crotty and I have to be careful not to talk of Heaney when John is around. It seems to me that Heaney will be famous forever, and we in the South will have to accept the fact.'[19] McCarthy accepted that fact a lot sooner than Montague did, whose reservations boiled down to simple envy of Heaney's popularity.

Yet Montague's human flaws did not make him a less important figure. There is a defensiveness in recollections by some Cork poets. They say they were never acolytes; they were well along in their own development before meeting Montague. This is perhaps partly a reaction against Montague's subsequent tendency to take credit for the flowering of poetry in Cork after his arrival. And instances of actual imitation are in fact rare, but there must have been something catalytic about Montague's participation in the local literary scene.

Theo Dorgan, in the class behind Crotty, Ní Dhomhnaill, O'Donoghue and Riordan at UCC, explores the matter at length in a memoir entitled 'The Influence of Anxiety'. Dorgan elucidates respects in which he is not like Montague (much anxiety, very little influence), but he also records his gratitude for the hospitality of John and Evelyn at Grattan Hill. The student poets were a provincial bunch of youths, but:

> ... we were made welcome in that house, made feel at home. If the bills and mundane correspondence ended up on the kitchen table, while reviews, letters of invitation and other insignia of the advanced literary life were left lying on the hall table, we might have seen the small vanity of it, but we sensed ... that this was John's way of signalling to us that there was a literary world beyond the provincial bounds of our damp and foggy city, that he belonged out there, and that we, too, however peripherally, had an engagement with that wider world through our common, if uneven, commitment to the craft.[20]

3

While Montague did not require the young to bend the knee, he was himself disposed to pay homage to older writers. As with the elaborate celebrations prepared for Austin Clarke's seventieth birthday, he went out of his way to organize ceremonies in which a master poet was honoured for a lifetime of achievement. For the second week of December 1973 he brought about a visit to Cork and Dublin by Hugh MacDiarmid and his wife Valda. MacDiarmid, thanking Montague afterwards, said the Cork audience was not just large but the 'most responsive I've had anywhere'. The appearance on Gay Byrne's talk show was also gratifying.[21] The MacDiarmid visit had a further significant consequence: Patrick Crotty wound up doing a UCC thesis on the Scottish master and then spent a good part of his life editing the collected works.

Once he was made permanent at UCC, Montague invited 79-year-old Robert Graves to give a reading. Accepting the offer, Graves remarked that the last time he had been in Ireland was 1918, when he played rugby for the Welch Fusiliers against Limerick city.[22] The visit of Robert Graves was not the typical engagement in which a speaker flies in one day, gives a reading and flies out the next. Graves was an ailing, forgetful old man, and in the company of his wife, Beryl, he was planning a stay of twelve days. Montague called upon all the skills he had acquired at Bord Fáilte to schedule the visit: he arranged for a welcome party at the airport, national press coverage, a television appearance, a reading in the Peacock Theatre, Dublin, as well as the one at UCC, the release of a recording by Claddagh and a stay at Luggala, Garech Browne's Wicklow estate. He rolled out the red carpet.

People began to arrive at the UCC reading well before eight o'clock on 12 May 1975. They filled the lecture hall, then the corridors and hallway. By eight, the line of those wishing to attend reached down the road.[23] Seán Lucy did the introduction. Graves settled his eyeglasses, held by a silver chain, and turned the pages of a book, then looked up, bewildered. Oh, he said, I have brought the poems of Robert Frost ... an old friend of mine. He next took up a sheaf of manuscripts and read from that. Between times, Graves talked of the hold Ireland had upon him; it was the country in which he had learned to walk and talk. At the close of the reading, Montague joined the poet on stage and proposed a vote of thanks, saying, 'This is an extraordinary occasion and a great honour to Ireland.' When the ovation died down, Graves put his hand on Montague's shoulder and, with some mystery, fingered each of the six gem-like buttons on his own green velvet waistcoat. Then he opened the waistcoat to reveal another set of buttons inside, sewed into the scarlet lining. These, he explained, were diamonds; the ones on the outside were paste. They felt and tasted warm; the diamond ones were cold. To taste a poem, that was another thing, but similar. The crowd applauded this encore performance.

A dinner was held for Graves at the Oyster Tavern; the guests included the Lucys and Montagues, Tom McCarthy and Theo Dorgan. With Theo, a reader of *The White Goddess*, Graves 'exchanged a ceremonial rose'.[24] In the course of the meal, the old devil remarked to Tom McCarthy that he had been to heaven, in fact several times that very month. He paused for the shock of this claim to have its effect, then took out a little silver box with an emerald set in the lid. Inside were hallucinogenic mushrooms. He explained that he had been given them by Carlos Castaneda after a reading in Mexico. Beryl slapped her husband on the wrist – 'You mustn't ruin that young boy with your dirty mushrooms.'

Montague loved all the hocus-pocus. After a seminar at UCC, he suggested Graves anoint the young poets present. The old man duly patted Dorgan and McCarthy on the head, as he had long before been patted on the head by

Thomas Hardy, in an apostolic succession of English poets.[25] None of the young women writers in the room stepped forward for a blessing. Perhaps to them it looked like this particular masonic order was reserved for males.

4

In the third week of February 1975 Seamus Heaney called to 25 Grattan Hill, and the two poets sat down to a session over a bottle of Bushmills whiskey. One subject that came up that night was the schedule for the next Kilkenny Festival. The driving forces behind this festival were its founders, Barrie Cooke and Sonja Landweer. Typically, poets and artists featured heavily in the offerings. For the upcoming programme, Heaney had suggested inviting R.S. Thomas, a 62-year-old Welsh poet and Anglican priest. Thomas's poems are often harsh pastorals set in a bitter Welsh landscape pierced with spirituality, not a hundred miles from the Catholic mysticism of Patrick Kavanagh's Inniskeen.

A few years earlier Montague had been halfway into the composition of an unfinished article for *Poetry Wales* that argued that R.S. Thomas had in fact been heavily influenced by Kavanagh, even though the Welshman made much of his being utterly one of a kind.[26] Another factor underlying the conversation that night at 25 Grattan Hill was that, in an article in *The Listener*, Seamus Heaney had listed R.S. Thomas among the poets who had influenced him, along with Ted Hughes and Patrick Kavanagh, but, cagily (in John's opinion), he did not name a living Ulster rival, John Montague.

It is remarkable how much such slights, if a slight it was, mattered to Montague. He knew he ought to hide his resentment, but it still sprang up in conversation. On a late summer 1972 visit to Barrie Cooke in Kilkenny, Evelyn, who was inclined to fight John's fights, bitterly attacked in his absence Seamus Heaney. Barrie Cooke could not fall in with her attitude. On the spot, he said that he liked Seamus. To be honest, he had to admit that Seamus had lately replaced John as the man closest to his heart. A true follower of D.H. Lawrence, Cooke believed in the necessity of an intimate blood-brotherhood, like the one between Rupert and Gerald in *Women in Love*. Barrie confessed that he felt guilty that he had betrayed John, but there it was; he had done so; he was now very tight with Seamus. Montague was so shocked, he almost 'blacked out'. Cooke then led the Montagues outside to a mudflat next to the River Nore and, taking off his clothes, slid about in the slippery stuff. He called for John and Evelyn to join him. It was a joyous, disinhibited experience for them all, but Montague remained unsettled when he returned to Cork. In a follow-up letter, he apologized for Evelyn's personal attack on their common friend, but he admitted that he still had a beef with Seamus. In all Heaney's many interviews for the British press, Montague complained, 'I have never heard him speak well of another Irish poet where it would do him good.'[27]

Back in Cork, as the two poets drank one tumbler of Bushmills after another, John asked if Seamus would please for once admit in public that he borrowed from John's work.[28] Well able for this very Ulster 'passage at arms', Seamus in return told John his poetry did not on the whole 'cohere into a major status like Kinsella's'. Then Heaney gave his opinion that overall the poetry scene in Ireland was 'richer than anywhere in English-speaking lands'. That was a matter on which the two could agree.

A few weeks afterwards, Montague wrote a startling letter to R.S. Thomas that chews over the same issues of unacknowledged indebtedness:

> You may have wondered at my not sending *The Rough Field* as promised. What happened was that anticipating your making a record with Claddagh which people like MacDiarmid and Robert Lowell have been happy to do I read your work more closely. And I was shocked and startled to realize that a good deal of your early poem 'The Airy Tomb' is a reworking of Patrick Kavanagh's 'The Great Hunger'. I gather you acknowledged this somewhere (Kavanagh mentions it in his letters) but <u>not</u> very publicly. As you must know Patrick was very poor and little known for the larger part of his life so a little help from a more successful contemporary (especially one who had climbed on his shoulders, so to speak) would have been a minimal courtesy … I hope you will be prepared to answer me honestly on this. Did you write to Kavanagh or even perhaps meet him in Dublin? Remember this is not just to do with <u>your</u> prestige or place but with the memory of a very pitifully ignored poet.

Montague (himself 'pitifully ignored') sent a copy of this letter to Seamus Heaney and posted the original to the Welsh vicar. Predictably, R.S. Thomas was outraged by Montague's talk of a debt of honour. So this was the kind of treatment he could expect from poets in Ireland! He immediately wrote to Heaney in order to withdraw from the Kilkenny Festival. Heaney found the whole business hilarious. He forwarded to Brian Friel for his own entertainment both Montague's rude challenge and R.S. Thomas's indignant withdrawal.[29]

5

Montague was hardly two years into his UCC post before he became 'slightly bored with aspects of Cork teaching'.[30] Compared with creative-writing seminars in Berkeley, the Irish lecture system was a comedown. Lecturing was never Montague's forte. A student had to be interested in the subject to see the value of the remarks he made from the podium.[31] But most of all, he hated the marking. The Irish system of undergraduate education relies upon faculty primarily for one thing: to assign students various classes of degree on the basis of a final examination, consisting of a nearly unchanging set of questions. Students cram for a few weeks, then in a sweat of fear scribble into examination booklets their preconceived answers. Given the staff–student ratio, and prevailing system of double-marking, there are hundreds of papers for each teacher to assess. Marking them amounts to thirty days' solid work a semester, and very unpleasant work it is too, deciding the fates of the young. This was not only a bad way to go about educating people but it was, Montague felt, a waste of his precious time. Nonetheless, that was the job, and he needed to have a job.

After marking the autumn exams for 1973 Montague appealed to Robin Skelton. Would there be a chance of a visiting appointment in the new postgraduate writing programme at the University of Victoria in British Columbia? Not so fast, Seán Lucy warned Montague. He was not yet permanent at UCC.[32] By the summer of 1975 Montague was permitted to get away, provided that he got a plane back to Cork in order to mark autumn examinations.[33] Montague booked a summer of teaching in Toronto, then the 1975 autumn semester at University of Victoria, with an interval of marking in Munster. In total, he would be six months in Canada with his family.

Montague had friends in the wider Toronto area. Gregory O'Donoghue was doing an MA at Queen's University, Kingston; Maurice Riordan studied at McMaster University. David Lampe was just across the border at Buffalo State. The French poet Robert Marteau was now a short flight away in Montreal. Montague was close to Professor Ann Saddlemyer at the University of Toronto. Farther south were Thomas Redshaw, Montague's former UCD student, now doing a dissertation on the poet, and M.L. Rosenthal, director of that dissertation at NYU. But his primary contact in Toronto was the writer Barry Callaghan, whom he had known since 1963 and proved to be one of Montague's best friends over the following decades.

6

In 1963 Barry Callaghan had gone to London and Paris on his honeymoon. His father, the beloved Canadian fiction-writer Morley Callaghan, was published in the UK by MacGibbon and Kee. He gave Barry a letter of introduction to Tim O'Keeffe, who showed the boy a good time in London, and then sent him on to Montague in Paris.[34] Montague brought Barry around to the American Club where Morley Callaghan had boxed with Hemingway in 1929, to the Coupole bar in the hope of running into Beckett, and to the Montparnasse Cemetery to gaze at the grave of Baudelaire. In the course of this literary tourism, the two men bonded over their filial devotion to great writers, and to their pleasure in the good life, such as a bottle of Chambertin Grand Cru (Callaghan buying).

Three years later, the two again had 'a spry time' in Paris. Drink was consumed and money spent. Introduced to Bill and Désirée Hayter, Barry bought several engravings, the beginnings of a collection of the artist's work.[35] Callaghan left a vivid account of that night with Montague at the Hayters' Paris atelier:[36]

> We went to call on Montague's friend, William Hayter, the engraver and painter who had taught Giacometti, Tanguy, Masson, Nevelson, Ernest, Picasso, Miro and Calder …. He was compact and agile, his flesh tight about the bone for a man of sixty-five …. His jaw, cheekbones and nose were severe, chiselled. His eyes were almost pellucid, a crystal glint of light in them, and under the eyes, the lace lines of age in his skin …. His young west country Irish woman (he had left his wife to be with her) was standing barefoot on the tile floor, wearing a mini-sack shift, and – twenty-seven – she swung sensually about the room, laughing and prodding Montague in the ribs with her finger, her full breasts and buttocks straining against the cloth. Bill watched her, her wide-set eyes, aquiline nose, full mouth; a smiling taut man, possessive. Her name was Désirée … [After dinner] they were playing John Lee Hooker's music. *Boom boom boom boom, Gonna set you right down.* With her long hair swirling, Désirée pranced and kicked her legs and pulled her skirt high on her thighs. Montague

was up dancing with her and she looked powerful beside his long lean frame, grabbing him at the waist, spinning him around. Bill, smiling, moved around them, clapping, urging them on, but stalking them too … I saw that Bill and Montague were slouching toward the centre of the room, squaring off, pawing at each other. They circled warily, Bill intense, Montague a little bewildered, ham-fisted but reluctant. There were loud smacks: Bill was hitting Montague open-handed on the side of the jaw. He pursued the swaying, shying Montague.

Montague then uttered his spell to ward off harm:

> *One thing to do,*
> *Describe a circle*
> *Around, about me,*
> *Over, against you.*

Désirée blamed young Barry for the fisticuffs having turned rough; the trouble was all because he did not know how to play his part as a boxing referee.

Figure 49: S. W. ('Bill') Hayter and Désirée Moorhead Hayter.
Photographer Fiorenza Bassetti.

7

When Callaghan launched his literary magazine *Exile* in June 1972 ('an act of resistance against academic hegemony, which has turned writers into exiles'), Montague became a mainstay among its contributors. From publications in that top-flight magazine and Callaghan's articles in the *Toronto Telegram*, Montague began to be known by readers in Canada.[37]

During his summer in North America in 1975 John asked Barry Callaghan to be his best man. He and Evelyn were getting married. The ceremony was held on 15 August near Gloucester, Massachusetts, at the home of Laura and Norman Rasmussen, a tree-shaded house near the rocky Atlantic foreshore, within earshot of a sea bell that tolled 'sombre, friendly warnings'. John composed an elaborate wedding service in eight sections:

1. Address to Audience
2. Intention
3. Ceremony (in verse)
4. Prayer
5. Proclamation
6. Eyes (in verse)
7. The Seal (in verse)
8. Vows (in verse)

Figure 50: Evelyn, Oonagh, Norman Rasmussen and John Montague, at the wedding of John and Evelyn, 15 August 1975.

As opposed to the practices of the Catholic Church in County Tyrone, this matrimonial contract is fragrant of California and the sixties. The 'Address to Audience' (a handful of witnesses) explains that the couple, now with a child of two, are marrying after seven years together. During this time, their love has survived the frustrations of jealousy and separation, the pressures of society during a divorce, the fear of never being able to make a life of their own and consequent anguish and angers and the adjustment to cultural uprooting and parenthood under such conditions. Now, as well as requiring a legal bond, the address continues, they feel their love is strong enough to give a more permanent form to their relationship.

In the formulation of their common 'Intention', they acknowledge that each of them has 'a separate intellectual and emotional makeup'; the marriage aims to protect their individualities rather than to make them one. They promise 'to help each other towards fulfilment till death, or the death of love, do us part'.[38] In other words, the pact is not unconditional; it is a love relationship or nothing. In the 'Ceremony', they promise to 'exchange our freedom', not the same thing as agreeing to be bound. Theirs is 'an older form of espousal'. The 'Prayer' offered by the pastor is that the couple 'may have an active sexual life without narrow possessiveness', so that 'they not only exchange affection between themselves but also have affection and consideration for others'. Clearly, the rite was not a promise of constancy; it made provision for promiscuity. Their wish for 'a more permanent form to their relationship' stops short of being a vow to make the relationship permanent *tout court.*

Evelyn was a child of May '68. Since she first met John, she had had boyfriends in Paris and an older lover in Galway. However, a woman's attitude may change after going to live with a man in another country and bearing his child. Evelyn may not have been, at least subconsciously, as fully committed to the idea of an open and impermanent marriage as John was. Decades later, she recalled that the 'first crack in the golden bowl' occurred when John returned from a trip to London with Garech Browne and told her that he had had a novel adventure. Garech had brought him to meet an Indian Muslim woman named Farida who gave them a massage. The three did not have intercourse, but it was a completely sensual experience. At the time of this episode, John and Evelyn were at Roche's Point. They had lived together for a year. Evelyn had just had a baby. With an infant to care for, John had been underfoot and not really helpful, so Evelyn had urged him to accept Garech's offer of a London holiday. But she was rattled that this was how he had used his free time.[39]

Deep down, she did care about fidelity. One of the reasons she came along with John on his extended trips to Buffalo, Toronto and Vancouver was that she suspected that, as had been the case with Madeleine, he would see his duty of monogamy as applying only within his own postal code. In the years that John and Evelyn had lived together, he had not thus far been notably promiscuous, but what was tried and true in his character was that he was a flirt. He wanted the approval of women. He gave cause for jealousy. The idiosyncratic marriage contract made room for this dimension of his character, but it did not make equal provision for Evelyn's growing need for security. In that period, many people tried out new forms of marriage. The record of the non-binding unions is not great.

8

Bruce Arnold held an exhibition of S.W. Hayter's Irish work at the Neptune Gallery in Dublin on 13 June 1975. Montague provided a programme note for his Paris friend. He dropped the observation that Hayter was 'sensitive to a fault', but generously explained that the engraver had had a profound effect upon his own imagination: 'I learnt from him how to see the world as a complex of energies, a dance of chance and necessity.'[40]

On the night of the Dublin opening, Montague did not appear. This was a disappointment, as a special copy of Hayter's *Tides* design on handmade paper had been prepared as a gift for the poet. Evelyn, there on the night, made a remark that led Bruce Arnold to believe John had stayed away on account of some offence taken.[41] What was that offence? That remained unclear, but a degree of uneasiness was introduced in the old friendship of Montague and the Hayters.

Evelyn proposed a reprise of the Hayter exhibition at a friend's gallery in Cork. After some initial discussion of a show in 1976, Désirée Hayter did not follow up the possibility. Just back from Vancouver in January 1976, Evelyn, jet-lagged, showed her temper at this lapse.[42] Shocked, Désirée told John that she 'would in future decline to see him if [Evelyn] were to accompany him'. That was impossible, John loyally declared. Evelyn was his wife.

A letter of apology to Désirée was produced. Evelyn concluded it by saying, 'Let's keep our rapport or non-rapport separate but do please for old and future time's sake, contact John one way or another.'[43] Désirée replied with a newsy letter addressed to the couple and offered the Montagues use of the Hayters' newly acquired cottage in Kerry. However, John noted in the margin of Désirée's letter that a new heaviness had come into what had always been a sprightly friendship. But the Montague-Hayter friendship stood the course and eventually righted itself.

9

In late September 1975 after *A Slow Dance* was selected as a Christmas 'Recommendation', Montague chanced upon an appropriate setting in which to compose a note for the Poetry Book Society bulletin: a bar on Vancouver Island filled with Nootka people, one of the indigenous First Nations of North America.[44]

'An Irishman of Gaelic background is, in a sense,' Montague writes, 'a White Indian, sharing that affinity with nature celebrated in the opening title sequence of *A Slow Dance*. The poet-king Sweeney, who was translated into a bird, might be a figure – Raven, Crow – from Haida legend. And the green mitre of St Patrick, snakes writhing his Tallcrook, reappears as the Damballa of Haitian voodoo.'[45]

This world-religions quest for a discovery of a pre-Christian, localized, Neolithic belief system also characterizes Seamus Heaney's *North*, published at the same time. The bloody sectarianism of the Ulster conflict caused Heaney and Montague (there's a touch of this also, ironized, in 'Lives' by Derek Mahon) to give up trying to understand the violence in Christian terms. Something more primal and uncivilized was at work. In visionary lyrics, both poets set themselves up as time-travelling shaman figures. Heaney makes much of the ritual sacrifices to the Bog Queen in ancient Denmark and the Viking devotees of Thor. He compares the violence of those cultures with irrational murders in his home parishes of County Derry.

Montague turned to the Celtic gods vanquished by St Patrick. One was Anya, presiding goddess of Knockmany and Seskilgreen in County Tyrone. In the title sequence, the 'still/fragrant goddess' Anya is associated with the healing, slow, sexual rhythms of nature.[46] The other spirit is Crom Cruach, 'The Stooped One', worshipped at the Plain of Adoration, Magh Slécht, in County Cavan.

A kind of Moloch figure, Crom Cruach required a frenzied sacrifice of the firstborn.[47]

According to medieval legends, Crom Cruach was routed (or converted) by St Patrick. Iconic emblems of these two male cults of human sacrifice are interwoven in the cryptic 'The Hinge Stone and the Crozier'. On the facing page of the collection, in 'For the Hillmother', the poet offers up a Marian litany, praying for aid from the gentle, all-powerful Anya.[48]

In a review of *A Slow Dance*, Eiléan Ní Chuilleanáin identified 'the main note in Irish poetry at present' as 'melancholy: looking to the past but finding little comfort'.[49,50] Both Heaney and Montague in their new collections notably did not blame the sorrows of the province on the British or the colonists. Like anthropologists, they looked for the origins of violence within the ancient culture of the people in that place, long before entities such as nations had come into existence. The books turn away from anything to do with the language of political parties, whether Sinn Féin, the Social Democratic and Labour Party (SDLP), or Fianna Fáil, towards an atavistic world of myths.

The futility of militancy (IRA or otherwise) comes across in the opening image of Montague's anti-war sequence 'Wheels Slowly Turning', with its stanzaic captures of both world wars and the Troubles:[51]

> Seen, school years ago,
> on a summer morning
> an Army lorry
> like a beetle
> upside-down in a ditch
> wheels slowly turning.

In subsequent stanzas, those caught up in fighting are imagined as carried away by a hectic lust for a Black Widow goddess.

As opposed to the delicate rhythms and feminine endings of the title sequence, there are poems evoking the worst of the Troubles, such as 'Ratonnade', a French term for rat-hunt, also used for rampant attacks on ethnic minorities. Its surreal images and pounding trochees suggest a different kind of dance, not slow but wild and bloodthirsty, done to drumbeats.

Overall, *A Slow Dance* responds to the historical crisis, but a number of its poems fall outside this scheme and strike personal lyric notes. There are poems on family history, such as 'A Muddy Cup', one of the first fruits of Montague's attempt to deal with his mother's legacy that would culminate in *The Dead Kingdom*. Some of collection's best poems are the work of earlier years: 'Courtyard in Winter' is the collection's major achievement, an elegy for Joan Wardle (d. 1964), daring to sound like a Yeatsian meditation. 'Ó Riada's Farewell', not exactly an elegy, is Montague's response to the dreadful confrontation with the composer at Woodtown over the presence of Susan Hall Patron on the night of St Patrick's Day 1968.

What Eiléan Ní Chuilleanáin liked best in the collection was the sense of originality a reader gets from what the poet sees and feels, and the 'pronounced sense that what he sees and feels is all he's got': 'The body ... is the opaque limit of perception.' In 'Small Secrets', the slow-motion, up-close view of a snail inching across the poet's outdoor writing table recaptures a child's capacity for wonder. By means of its use of enjambement in the three- to four-syllable lines, the poem is a feat of formal mimicry of the snail's staggered progress over obstacles. Montague's sensitive register of touch, sight and sound also comes through in 'Windharp':

> The sounds of Ireland,
> that restless whispering
> you never get away
> from, seeping out of
> low bushes and grass,
> heatherbells and fern,
> wrinkling bog pools,
> scraping tree branches,
> light hunting cloud,
> sound hounding sight,
> a hand ceaselessly
> combing and stroking
> the landscape, till
> the valley gleams
> like the pile upon
> a mountain pony's coat.

Just a single sentence, the poem is alive and accurate in every phrase, intimate and intense, building up to a perfectly apt yet surprising simile.

10

John and Evelyn were pleased with the money earned and the natural grandeur of the Pacific Northwest, but the autumn semester at University of Victoria was not all that they hoped it would be. John, thinking of Wordsworth and Coleridge at Alfoxden, was looking for a period of serious exchanges with Robin Skelton and, as a couple, the Montagues had looked forward to the companionship of the Skelton family. However, John hardly saw Robin – for just one spell were the two closeted in Skelton's home library. Robin was drinking heavily, and he was much caught up in the troubles of chairing the writing programme at Victoria. John encouraged him to let it go – 'power is a bore, unless one is born to it' – but Robin did not want to give up captaining what he had constructed.[52] He was also more and more setting himself up as a West Coast magician. He had a following of people wearing pentagrams. His next book was to be *Spellcraft: A Manual of Verbal Magic* (1978). Left to himself, Montague took a friendly interest in the staff and students of the writing programme, such as the feminist poet Susan Musgrave.

On their return to Ireland, John hoped to break the long journey on the East Coast. He wanted to visit Galway Kinnell and his old friend Serge Fauchereau, then on the faculty at the State University of New York in Stonybrook. However, he did not want to be dragging Evelyn and Oonagh from pillar to post through the New England winter. Deirdre Bair, in the course of her research on Samuel Beckett (1978), had sought information from Montague. By way of courtesy, she would often say to her informants something to the effect of 'You really must visit us in Connecticut if you are ever in America – we have a lovely large house in the countryside, designed by my husband, with plenty of space for guests.' She was unpleasantly surprised that sometimes a past informant showed up at her door. In December 1977, it seemed to John that the Bair household at Woodbridge, near his alma mater, Yale University, would be perfect as a family shelter for the days before the Montagues' flight home. It was within easy reach of Stonybrook, so he could run down to meet Galway Kinnell. Evelyn herself was looking forward to some extended conversation with another young mother who reportedly shared her interest in feminism.

Figure 51: Galway Kinnell and John Montague, December 1975, New York state.

In 2019, a few years before her death, Deirdre Bair published a memoir of her time in Paris as a biographer of Beckett and Simone de Beauvoir.[53] In her introduction she reasons that most of her informants are now dead, so she can settle scores with a clear conscience (and no fear of contradiction). Many of her anecdotes are stories of impatience with those sources upon whom she depended for her books – they drink, they don't split the cheque at lunchtime, they are self-important, they come on to her sexually and finally they drop in on her at home. Pat Magee and Jackie MacGowran, Bill Hayter and A.J. 'Con' Leventhal (two great actors, a famous artist and a don from Trinity College) are dubbed the 'Becketeers', on the pattern of the fan club of Mickie Mouse on an American TV show in Bair's youth, *The Mouseketeers*. They are male idolators, hangers-on, nobodies; she is the iconoclast. The most offensive of all these Becketeers, according to Bair's memoir, is John Montague, and the most horrible thing he did was drop in on her during the winter holidays of 1975 without telling her he was coming with a wife and child, or that he would be leaving them behind for a day or two to see about his own business. In *Parisian Lives* Bair turns the short Montague visit into an entire indignant chapter.

Before the publication of Bair's memoir, Evelyn Montague was insistent that her own memories of that stay in Connecticut be heard, no matter how tangential they might be to a literary biography of her husband.[54] According to Evelyn's account, no sooner had John left for Stonybrook than Deirdre Bair explained that she was heading off to her university office to work. She had deadlines to meet. Would Evelyn look after the Bair children, she asked as she was leaving the house. However, the Bair children did not want to take orders from this Frenchwoman with a toddler. Upon Bair's return at the end of what was a long day for everyone, they complained of the bossy intruder. They could not take it another day. Deirdre Bair then surprised Evelyn with the news that the Bairs had a prior engagement to visit distant friends. She turned off the heat in the house. Evelyn, alone with Oonagh in a strange place, had to find somewhere else to stay and find it quickly.

What goes unmentioned in the various scornful mentions of Montague's name in *Parisian Lives* is that her Beckett biography had been reviewed by him in *The Guardian*. Before doing graduate study in literature, Bair had been a *Newsweek* reporter, and she was tireless in her pursuit of a scoop, particularly family scandal or irregularities in a person's sex life. This focus did not bother Montague, because, he says in his review, 'the only good biography is an indiscreet one'. But he goes on to admit that all who collaborated in the book, himself included, 'let Beckett down'.[55] They had confided his secrets to an untrustworthy biographer. The book, he said, was frequently inaccurate, simply to judge by those passages in which he himself appeared. The real problems with the book were *not* that it was indiscreet, but that it was imprecise and shed hardly any light on Beckett's writings. This particular biographer appeared to have very little interest in literature.

Getting a nasty review is rotten, and it was Bair's first book. Stung, she wrote a letter to the editor of *The Guardian* claiming that her quotations were absolutely accurate, because she always used a tape recorder. Montague, given right of reply, pointed to instances in which she did not use such a device, such as when he had dinner at her house in Connecticut. That *Guardian* review left a score still to be settled with Montague.

II

In a lengthy interview with Mary Leland, 'John Montague in Cork' (23 November 1976), the poet looked back over his life.[56] Things seemed to be working out all right for him. He had received a £2,500 prize from the Irish American Cultural Institute. It even seemed possible to take an understanding view of his mother's choice not to reclaim her youngest son upon her return to Ireland. She left him where he was, he supposed, because he was 'the chief object of love' for his aunts and well settled in Garvaghey. She wanted her child back as any mother would, and it was for his own sake, he suggested, that she did not take him away from Freda and Brigid.

He also brought up the subject of his stammer and admitted that he was still teased about it. One UCC professor spoke of him as 'Poor Montague' and quoted Garrick's epitaph on Oliver Goldsmith 'who wrote like an angel, but talked like Poor Poll'. The impediment had got better since he was twenty-five, Montague told Mary Leland. Before that time, he was dumbstruck. Still, it was to his stammer, he suspected, that he owed his poetry. 'The best way to deal with [a psychic wound] was to recognize it and to speak in public … one's strengths are born of one's weaknesses, when the weakness is recognized.'

His return from France appeared to him now as having been necessary. Being in Ireland during the Troubles was heart-rending, but had he remained in France, it would have been worse: he would have been 'raging and helpless'. His identity was not just as poet, but Irish poet.

Mary Leland looked about at 25 Grattan Hill, with its pictures by le Brocquy, Barrie Cooke and Bill Hayter, and observed that 'his physical surroundings bear witness not just to a sympathetic domestic aura but to the best parts of an already long and restless artistic life'.

Asked what he understood to be the nature of his vocation, Montague considered the question, then replied: 'Poetry is the best way of getting in at the point where the body and the soul meet, where one is most alive and most threatened. That is what I am for.'

TIRED OF 'THE TROUBLES' BUT TRYING TO GET TO THE BOTTOM OF *THE DEAD KINGDOM*

I

In 1976 Seamus Heaney and Barrie Cooke wanted advice about selecting a contemporary French poet to read alongside Montague at the Kilkenny Festival. John provided an overview of the possibilities:[1]

> There are three older poets of international stature in France (Jouve and Perse just died) at the moment, [Francis] Ponge, René Char, & André Frénaud. Char is in poor health and rarely travels, Ponge is conceited to a difficult degree, I think, while Frénaud is very pleasant company, a delight. As it happens, Evelyn and I have been translating a good deal of Frénaud, which could be made available for the Festival.
>
> What do you think of the idea? As he is a personal friend of ours we could give him enough hospitality to compensate for the discrepancy, alas, between the pound & the fat franc he is used to getting.

A visit by Frénaud in the summer of 1976 turned out to be impossible. In its place, an elaborate tour of Ireland was organized for the spring of 1977, to accompany a selection of his poems, translated by John and Evelyn and published by their Golden Stone private press.

André Frénaud (1907–93) was born in Montceau-les-Mines, a coal-mining region near Dijon. After studying philosophy and law at a Polish university, he entered the French civil service in 1937 and, apart from the war years, he remained in the job until his retirement in 1968; he was a lifetime bureaucrat. Early in the war Frénaud was captured and spent two years in a detention camp in Germany. After his escape he began publishing in Paul Éluard's Resistance journals. The view of life taken in the poetry is, by his own telling, of a piece with that of Sartre and Camus – one in which religious hopes are illusions and the only meaning to be found is of human manufacture. Unlike much of the French poetry written in the thirties and forties, Frénaud's poems are neither surreal nor semantically opaque; often they are simply stories of the defeat of the desire for transcendence, with death victorious. In 1973, just a few years before John and Evelyn began to translate him, Frénaud was awarded le Grand Prix de poésie de l'Académie française.

The Montagues' fifteen-page selection of Frénaud's poems, *November*, was conceived as a tribute on the poet's seventieth birthday, as well as a creative enterprise John and Evelyn could share.[2] Evelyn had an appetite for philosophy and theology; she took to Frénaud's work. She did the initial translations into English. John came in afterwards and 'gave the final polish'.[3]

As with the royal visit of Robert and Beryl Graves to Ireland, André Frénaud and his wife were given ceremonial treatment. Readings were scheduled over the third and fourth weeks of April 1977 at universities in Galway, Belfast and Cork, with another session at the Alliance Française in Dublin. Evelyn was his driver from city to city. At the Dublin event, Evelyn wittily noted in the crowd a rank of 'serious diplomats, forever dreaming of Claudel'.[4] That night, John explained that the impressive thing about Frénaud's lyrics was their wry courage of acceptance in the face of disillusionment.

As the two-week visit by Monsieur and Madame Frénaud passed day by day, the retired civil servant turned out to be not the delightful person they remembered from Paris but a truly 'nasty man'. Frénaud had nothing good to say about any of their common friends: 'Marteau is a peasant who married a bitch';[5] Serge Fauchereau's translations of Montague's poems were dull. In fact, the Montagues' translations in *November* were, Frénaud said, inaccurate (this was infuriating, because he had no English at all). The overall sense of insult built up. On the way into Belfast, Evelyn's car was hit by a truck. She was badly shaken; her car was a write-off. Frénaud's first reaction was to cry out (in French), 'My briefcase! My papers!' Evelyn was fed up with him. She gave him a curt introduction to the students at Queen's University: 'This is André Frénaud, one *élevé* fucker' [*élevé* = academic, superior]. Michael Longley got a laugh out of that. He agreed with the assessment.[6]

Even though the honoured guest made it known that he was dissatisfied with Ireland, Evelyn had a good time on the circuit. Her stop with the Longleys in Belfast had been particularly fun. Learning that they were thinking of interviewing the singer and actor Hedli Anderson in Kinsale for a biography of her late husband Louis MacNeice, Evelyn offered Michael and Edna the use of 25 Grattan Hill. The Longleys took up the offer and spent three weeks that summer in Cork while the Montagues were away. After a scouting expedition to Kinsale, they decided to do a MacNeice anthology rather than a biography.

2

On 25 April 1977 Montague opened the Barrie Cooke exhibition at the Cork Arts Society. He described Barrie Cooke as 'obsessive, obstinate, asocial, intuitive but not intellectual, in short, a true artist'. Of the four elements (water, earth, fire and air), water was dominant in his work:[7]

> Lake & rivers (fishing & hunting),
> Stone & bone (root & flower),
> Water & women, preferably nude,
> Seamus Heaney's 'the wet centre',
> Rain & heat,
> The boy & the jungle …
> The wet heart of the universe.

Cooke's paintings are, Montague said, his 'private diary of his preoccupation with the power of life itself'. In his own turn to speak at the opening, Cooke recalled his childhood years in Southeast Asia and the return visits to Malaysia and Borneo, which inspired the tropical paintings in the show. Montague, listening, jotted down phrases. They wound up in this 'found poem':

> Having lived out there
> it's the colour of tropics
> I miss part of my first life there,
> my lost life.
> What do I miss? The wet heat,
> The humid climate. When you're
> Living in that wet heat

You long for the wet coolness
of Ireland. When you're back
buried among coltsfoot leaves
and buttercups, you long for the heat.

The incredible noise, of course, is missing –
Crickets, [illeg], and monkeys –
But the smell is still there,
The smell of the forest. Decay
and growth; everything springing up
& dying in a single day

The friendship between the painter and the poet had rebalanced itself when Cooke stayed with the Montagues during the hanging of the show. He was at 25 Grattan Hill just before another house guest, Ciaran Carson, arrived on 29 March 1977.

3

Carson, then twenty-nine years old, was in Cork to read from his first collection, *The New Estate* (1976), alongside Paul Durcan, thirty-three years old, whose second collection, *O Westport in the Light of Asia Minor* was published in 1975. Montague admitted to Barrie Cooke that he was worried it was going to be a tense evening: 'You know how young men are!' Cooke ought to have understood, remembering how Montague fretted about Seamus Heaney and how Richard Murphy gave out about Montague.

Durcan, doing graduate work at UCC on Patrick Kavanagh, suspected there were conspiracies at work among the city's gang of poets.[8] He was nervous about his public appearance alongside Ciaran Carson before a large Cork audience. For the sake of the double bill, Michael Hartnett made the trip from County Limerick. Harnett (b. 1941) had published *A Farewell to English* in 1975, his declaration that his future works would be in Irish; he was done as an English poet. These people – Durcan, Carson, Hartnett and Montague – when they were drinking, were heavy drinkers, and when they were not drinking were sometimes hospitalized as patients in a treatment programme. There was a destructive intensity to the drinking life of poets in the period.

Just days before the reading, Montague and Durcan went 'on the batter'. Afterwards, Durcan declared he would not be able to do the reading. He was going on the wagon; no more drink for him.[9] That left Montague to take Durcan's place alongside Ciaran Carson.

This was a shaky pairing. Both Carson and Montague had a stammer. Each was sometimes just not able to do the business on the night in question. The young Belfast poet had found a personal remedy: he brought along his flute, which he played for little spells when the words would not come. Montague had no flute. He mistakenly placed his trust in his father's silver flask. Evelyn reported afterwards to the Longleys that everyone in the audience nearly had 'heart failure as [Montague] paused for longer and longer intervals between words'.[10] But he got through, this time, in the end.

4

John Montague is an autobiographical poet of an unusual kind. He strives to make narrative sense out of the whole body of his poetry, with individual collections following one another like chapters in a carefully plotted story. In actuality, several collections were in progress at a single time. *The Great Cloak* (1978), *The Dead Kingdom* (1984) and *Mount Eagle* (1989) were all three at least partly in manuscript in 1977. The first of these collections was complete and awaiting publication; the second had been mapped out and largely drafted; the third was just beginning to come into view.

In May 1977 Montague got a start on what was to become 'Harvest' in *Mount Eagle*. It revisits the theme of an old poem for Evelyn, 'A Dream of July', nine years after their first meeting, in an anniversary renewal of vows.[11]

> That first wild summer
> we watched each other,
> my greying hair and
> wary eyes slowly drawn
> to be warmed by your
> flaring hair, abundant body.
>
> No ice princess, you called
> me down from my high tower –
> on our first night together,

> I awoke, to watch over
> your rich shape, a shower
> of gold in the moonlight.

She remains for him an embodiment of Ceres, Roman goddess of the harvest. In its final two stanzas, the poem shifts to his childhood in Garvaghey, a dreamlike scene of a boy gathering in the corn, then tenting the sheaves into stooks, his hopes fulfilled. *Mount Eagle* was from the beginning envisioned as a book about Montague's own family, and the good things of life coming to the couple as a result of their work together. In some ways, it is a tribute to Evelyn in particular. Tom Redshaw, a family friend, observed that there was a second sense to the fact that, John never taking the wheel, Evelyn was a pilot force in their lives. She was the driver.[12]

5

On 7 September 1977 I called upon the Montagues at 25 Grattan Hill. A graduate student at Washington University in St Louis, Missouri, I had left my wife and two children behind for two weeks in order to interview poets and collect material for a special issue of *The Literary Review* on 'Irish Poetry after Yeats'. Five years earlier I had met John Montague for the first time. After arriving in Ireland for study at Trinity College, I happened to come across the poet and Garech Browne in The Bailey off Grafton Street. Montague was pleased to see in my possession a Swallow Press edition of *Tides*. Where had I come by that volume? In a bookstore in Claremont, California, while an undergraduate at Pomona College. Montague wanted news of Darcy O'Brien, a Pomona professor of English, and the Ulster poet W.R. Rodgers who spent his final years in Claremont.

So I was already acquainted with the poet's curiosity about everything to do with the making of literature. I had the same appetite if not the same talent. At Grattan Hill, we sat under the window at the kitchen table. He asked what Brendan Kennelly had had to say for himself in his interview, and what Eavan Boland had revealed in hers. He was intrigued by her distinctions between writing as an Irish person, as a woman, and the relations between the two types of identity, already an abiding interest of this poet. He wondered what books I had in my knapsack. In Dublin I had done the rounds of the old bookstores – the Eblana, Greene's, Hodges Figgis and Fred Hanna's. I put a stack of slender volumes on the table. Opening one, he started up discussion of a poem, apparently not to shape my opinion but to elicit what the views of a visitor might be.

He gave me tips about people to meet in Cork. On his advice I went to UCC to meet Seán Lucy and later knocked on the door of Seán Dunne, a thin-faced, pale fellow with long black hair, kindly and open-hearted. Neither, however, gave me anything to publish. On a walk that evening up Montenotte, a steep area above Grattan Hill, we met Paul Durcan, a nervous-looking man. His eyes never left John's. He did not take me in at all – so, no poems from him. John later passed along the postal address of Gregory O'Donoghue, then at Queen's University, Ontario; five of his poems appeared in the issue.

For his own part Montague offered something from *The Great Cloak* six months before that volume's publication. One of the pieces was a four-part sequence called 'Tearing'. The title may be a pun – primarily it means ripping apart, but it may also suggest the welling up of tears. The poet attempts to hear out the grief of his first wife as their marriage comes to pieces, and to accept responsibility for what he has done. The shockingly intimate view is wide-eyed, quiet, mostly unclouded by tropes:

> In the gathering dark
> I caress your head
> as you thrash out
> flat words of pain:
> 'There is no way back.
> I can feel it happening:
> we shall never be
> what we were, again.'

> *Never*, a solemn bell
> tolling through
> that darkening room
> where I cradle your head,
> only a glimmer left
> in the high window
> over what was once
> our marriage bed.

Like the film by Ingmar Bergman, it is a scene from a marriage – early evening, downstairs at 11 rue Daguerre. The woman's pain is unshielded. Her unanswerable words, meant only for him, are transmitted directly to the reader, as in Robert Lowell's *For Lizzie and Harriet* (1973). While heart-breaking and frightening, it makes a reader ask if it is right that a poem should be this revealing. I was impressed.

Montague did not agree immediately to do an interview for publication. He wanted first to get a sense of my enterprise. In fact, I was doing more than a special issue of an American literary quarterly; I was also at work on a dissertation on the history of Irish poetry after Yeats, with chapters on Beckett, Clarke, Kavanagh, Kinsella, Montague and Heaney – the obvious choices at that time. He wanted to know just what questions he would be asked in an interview. A full list was typed out.

Evelyn asked me to stay for dinner, a rabbit stew. Over the meal she explained her growing interest in quilt-making, newly re-conceived as a feminist artform. As it happened, my ancestors on our Missouri farm made quilts, once used as bedspreads, now heirlooms. A few were elaborate productions, friendship quilts made by women in the nineteenth century who belonged to the same reading group, and met monthly to talk about books and embroider a collaborative design. After my return to Missouri, I posted a few examples of local handiwork back to Evelyn.

The following morning, 8 September, I came to Grattan Hill to see about doing the interview, only to find that John was laid up with stomach trouble. But he had decided to go ahead with the recording, so long as he did not have to leave his bed.

My interview questions were intended to provide information about the degree of national unity in the tradition of modern Irish poetry and the ways it was affected by the English, American, or continental poetries. My thesis question was whether there was something new, continuous and valuable in Irish poetry, passing from Yeats through Clarke and Kavanagh and into those now writing.

Montague had had a night to think over these matters, and his answers were considered and subtle. At the time, I did not appreciate the way he had reframed the whole issue. Poetry, in his view, was connected to place and family, to the language (or languages) with which one grows up, to history as it tells upon the growth of the individual, and to the literature of one's land, but also to the canons of achieved masterpieces in the craft and contemporary developments worldwide. These must inevitably interest those whose chief interest was poetry. The title he gave the interview – 'Global Regionalism' – significantly leaves out one word, nation.[13] In regard to poetry, he declined to be an Irish nationalist.

The business of the interview wrapped up, Montague rang Edna and Michael Longley in Belfast. He had a young fellow there from America who was putting together a volume on contemporary poetry in Ireland. Would they show him around and put him right when he arrived in Belfast? And when they were done with him, could they send him along to James Simmons and Derek Mahon in Portrush, County Derry? After he put down the telephone receiver, Montague gave me the address of the Arts Council of Northern Ireland where I could find Michael Longley and Ciaran Carson. A very professional piece of business, that telephone call proved to be an immense help.

6

Given Montague's wariness about being defined in terms of the nation state, and his recent poems on the futility of the physical-force campaign (such as 'Wheels Slowly Turning' in *A Slow Dance*), it is surprising that he continued sometimes to stand up as a representative of Irish republicanism. Yet Montague had warned in his interview that it was a mistake to draw no distinction between the two sides of a person, the citizen and the poet. The latter was wiser than the former. Poetry was inherently an 'appeal from Philip drunk to Philip sober'.[14]

In February 1978 Montague attended a conference on 'Canada and the Celtic Consciousness' in Toronto. John Wilson Foster, a literature scholar and liberal Protestant from Ulster, kept a diary of the proceedings. There were two major events in the conference. The first was an evening 'Festival of Celtic Poetry', chaired by Barry Callaghan, at which Sorley MacLean, Thomas Kinsella, Roland Mathias and Montague all read. The following afternoon was the second key event, a symposium of historians on the subject of Irish republicanism, featuring Owen Dudley Edwards and Conor Cruise O'Brien (both anti-Republican).

Jack Foster sensed that the entire conference was building towards a showdown between the first and the second events, republican poets versus revisionist historians. To him, Montague's reading was designed to be a 'pre-emptive strike' on Conor Cruise O'Brien:[15]

> Gone [was] Montague's sportive Celticness of last year's Hamilton conference ... Even the stutter, a useful source of humor last year, was in this reading a source of vague menace, the wanted word dropping at long last like a fulfilled threat – a small depth charge. He elected to read the most controversial canto of *The Rough Field* – 'A New Siege', dedicated to Bernadette Devlin. Bernadette Who? We were back again in 1969 at the barricades in the Catholic ghettos of Derry and Belfast and it was *déjà vu*. There was to be no compromise with O'Brien. The rough fields of Tyrone, of the North, of republicanism were offered as an alternative to the polished lawn of O'Brien's oration next day.

Although an admirer of Montague's poetry, Jack Foster felt that 'the day had caught up with "A New Siege": it *spoke* outdatedly, and however well it might still work on the printed page'.

The following day Conor Cruise O'Brien gave a speech that dismantled the myths of Irish republicanism. The real causes of Irish independence were, he explained, the Famine and the subsequent Land Acts. 'Easter 1916 and the Troubles were the superfluous in pursuit of the unobtainable.' And the least acceptable face of the fantasies of romantic Ireland was the Provisional IRA.

When the chairperson, Norman Jeffares, called for questions, Montague was the first to take the microphone. 'Philip drunk' took the floor. Jack Foster reported what happened next:

> He began well if not wisely. When he closed his eyes as Conor Cruise O'Brien was speaking, he said, he imagined himself in the British House of Commons. When he closed his eyes as Owen Dudley Edwards was speaking, he said, he imagined himself hearing the rolling periods of Macaulay. What he meant was this: logic, clarity, and measured tones are Sassenach and alien vices, and when cultivated by Irishmen, signal the presence within the national gates of a fifth columnist ....

He spoke of Ireland as a natural unit unnaturally severed. He spoke of Seamus Heaney's sexual imaging of Ireland's relationship to England and rejected it. He spoke of bigotry in the Belfast shipyard. He spoke of the Provisional IRA as defenders of Ulster Catholics and as having been created by the British government. He spoke of the RUC. He spoke of ....

Behind me I heard [Proinsias] MacAonghusa say in quiet frustration to Seán MacBride, 'he's losing his drift'. But haven't most of us in Ireland, save O'Brien and a scant few like him?

Montague's was the old and failed rhetoric of republicanism. And I wanted to tell him: 'If you wish to speak to me of Irish unity you will have to do so, not through the medium of republican mythology (much less through the medium of gunplay), but through the language of O'Brien and Edwards, the language of reason and realism and multi-culturalism. Any other language is unacceptable.'

Conor Cruise O'Brien was a dangerous man with whom to debate. He made short work of Montague in his riposte.[16] He ironically exclaimed at the paradox that those who insist Ireland is a natural unit happily still call for the break-up of the states in the neighbouring island (Montague supported Hugh MacDiarmid's campaign for Scottish independence). Ireland's attempt under de Valera to isolate itself from Britain had been insane. O'Brien's most wounding strike concerned Montague's use of the word 'genocide' for the treatment of Catholics in the North: 'That word, the ex-UN intermediary told us, ought not, in light of what befell European Jewry some years ago, to be used lightly. Especially by a poet. He resumed his seat to huge applause.' Jack Foster felt sorry for Montague. He had spoken well and out of conviction. Even O'Brien acknowledged that fact, just before putting in the knife.

In a subsequent exchange of letters, Jack Foster and John Montague returned to the subject of that Toronto debate. The poet wanted the scholar to understand that he was not a sectarian. His point had been that outsiders – even those just across the border like Conor Cruise O'Brien – did not appreciate the tormented entanglement of people in the North, the familial intricacy of their quarrels. That might be so, Foster replied, but Ulster people like themselves 'seem to have ... our impulses and our public utterances ... cross-wired'.

That conflicted state could be a source for future poems, or instead a dry well, drilled as deep as it could go, exhausted. More and more, Montague himself wanted to move on from the subject of the Troubles. However, his public performances pulled him back to the recitation of former feelings. He wore a mask that no longer fit his face.

7

The launch of *The Great Cloak* in Cork was, for good luck, held on Montague's forty-ninth birthday, 28 February 1978, well before The Dolmen Press got the book into shops. The first review arrived in April, when John Jordan gave the volume careful consideration in the *Irish Independent*. It was nineteen years since he had reviewed Montague's first collection. Jordan mischievously declared Montague to be the best of the Irish poets from the North. This collection was his best, 'exquisitely shaped' and 'nakedly personal'.[17]

The Great Cloak was publicly presented as part of the Dublin Arts Festival at the Players Theatre, Trinity College. Montague's was one in a series of five readings from 25 to 29 April. The line-up is an indication of the strength of Irish writing at the time: Eavan Boland, Seamus Heaney, John McGahern, John Montague and Richard Murphy, all in one week.

At the reading Montague noticed his niece Blanaid Montague in the audience, one of Turlough's children. She was doing English and French at Trinity. John pushed past everyone to greet her. He knew so little about her – he begged her to write to him and tell him everything. Within a week, Blanaid sent a long letter. She recalled as a child practising her French with her sister Dara before John and Madeleine arrived in Fintona. Years later, along with her older sister, Sheena, she got to hear her famous uncle read at Loreto Convent in Omagh; she was so proud of him. In her final year, the class studied Irish poetry, and she was asked to interpret his poems, as if being his niece gave her a special insight. At Trinity, Brendan Kennelly, seeing Blanaid's address on a registration form, guessed she might be one of those Montagues. Kennelly cryptically remarked of her Uncle Johnnie, 'He's some boy!'

Blanaid Montague took *The Great Cloak* seriously as a statement about John's controversial divorce and remarriage. It showed, she told him, 'You had to do what you did and now you have to live with what you've done.' To her, the book seemed a justification of the ways of the poet to his family. As for her father, Blanaid could only tell him what she had heard from Sheena: that her dad believed John owed her mum an apology: 'The mate's hackles are up.'[18]

Given that in 1986 Irish people voted against liberalizing divorce laws by a 25 per cent margin, it is surprising that the local reception of *The Great Cloak* was favourable. The book plainly justifies divorce. Partly, its warm reception may have been the result of unusually friendly reviewers, Thomas McCarthy in *The Irish Times* (6 May 1978) and Paul Durcan in the *Cork Examiner* (1 May 1978).

In the *Sunday Press* Brian Lynch asked some tough questions.[19] The collection might be Montague's best, he supposed, but wasn't its language sometimes 'literary in the worst sense'? 'Redolent of roses', 'stately glory', 'tenebrous' ought to have been excised. Beyond that problem, there was something cold about the treatment of the first wife, even repellent. And really, is it harder to leave than to be left, as the poet claims? Brian Lynch did not think so. But Lynch accepted that a poet did not have to make himself out to be an admirable person in order to write an admirable poem. Readers, he concluded, should have a look and judge for themselves.

8

In the summer of 1978 the Montagues took in Derek Mahon. Over a lonely winter in Portrush teaching at the New University of Ulster, separated from wife and children, Mahon had been drinking himself to death.

A few years earlier John had already appealed to Seamus Heaney, then in California:[20] 'I am basically very worried about [Derek]: he doesn't drink for pleasure like us, but extinction, as if he couldn't stand the dishonesties of our world .... He has a sweet & delicate intelligence which is somehow in more danger than ours, being more absolute in its choices.' By September 1976 Montague knew that Mahon's financial and moral situation had become 'catastrophic', even though his writing kept getting better.[21] Midway through 1978, desperate for a cure, Mahon went on Antabuse, a drug regimen that makes the consumption of any amount of alcohol a serious emergency.[22] It was in this hyper-medicated state that he arrived at 25 Grattan Hill that June.

Besides offering shelter to his friend, Montague's contribution to the case was to write a poem, an Ovidian sonnet entitled 'Survivor'.[23] It draws upon a story from the *Annals of the Four Masters*. In biblical times, some women who were not allowed on Noah's Ark set sail for 'Inis Fail'. No humans having yet lived in Ireland, the island was believed to be free from the curse of God. After seven years at sea, their ship arrived, carrying fifty women and three men. One of the men was Fintan MacBochra. When the other two men died, Fintan, faced with so many women, ran away. An Irish Methuselah, he lived on for centuries. He saw the history of Ireland unfold before him. He became a famous bard and counselled the kings of Ireland, including the Firbolgs, before they fought the Tuatha de Danann in the battle of Moytura. Fintan departed from this life only upon the arrival of St Patrick.

The significance of the mythical bard Fintan to the case of Derek Mahon is that he survived the Flood, the curse of God. In Montague's poem Fintan lives to be an Irish hero by means of his metamorphosis into a fish:

> Under his high cliff, Fintan waited.
> He watched as the floods rose, rose,
> Never fell. He heard the women wail,
> Wail, and accept. He only felt the change
> Through his nostrils, flattening to gills,
> His arms thinning to fins, his torso
> Tightening into a single thrash:
> The undulating flail of a great fish.
>
> Nothing human would last. For centuries
> He slept at the bottom of the world,
> Currents stroking his sleek, strong back.
> Slowly, the old bare, earth reappeared,
> Barren, but with a rainbow brightened.
> Life might begin again. He lunges upwards.

Ovid was one of Mahon's favourite poets, and 'Afterlives' was one of his key motifs – Rip Van Winkle stories of people who went away, or fell asleep, before returning to a world completely different. Montague's offering – inscribed *'malgré lui'* – was a tribute to the way a person's transformative talents, in spite of his conduct, could carry him through a period of suffering. The poem was a sensitive, encouraging gesture of friendship.

Derek Mahon slept in the attic room at Grattan Hill, next to John's study. Evelyn made his meals, brewed him cups of tea and listened to his tales of trouble. Even allowing for Mahon's personal charm, it was not that easy on her, somewhat like having one more child in the house, a very large one. In July John was away in County Kerry, trying to write poems, so it helped when Tom Redshaw arrived at Grattan Hill. Redshaw, a New Englander, had become a family friend. He took some of the pressure off, just by being easy company.

It was up in the attic room at 25 Grattan Hill that Derek Mahon wrote one of his best-loved poems, 'Everything Is Going To Be All Right':

> I lie here in a riot of sunlight
> watching the day break and the clouds flying.
> Everything is going to be all right.

It is a poem that springs from hitting the bottom, then rising up from the depths to take a fresh breath of air.

At the end of July, Evelyn wrote to John, 'We have succeeded in healing Derek.'[24] She believed that, like it or not, he was fit to be discharged:

> I am a bit ashamed to find out that generosity isn't at all endless and that, at least, it has kept me so far from waving the broomstick towards the door .... I also worry about the effect on you though I trust you are now a much tougher crocodile. You usen't to be ten years ago. What happened, was it [Oonagh] who brought it out? Anyhow I think you should stop giving for the moment. Great Scottish projects and French contacts are being planned, but in as much as it's nice to know one's friends well, it shouldn't be too well. Something must be said or done ... all in calmness and propriety but I know not what. What if a real poet, as Derek is, pretends not to understand what any poet knows in his own heart? In any case, he is making me into your very debilitated muse!

Derek Mahon had a talent, as Evelyn noticed, for getting himself looked after by others. Delicately eased out, he left 25 Grattan Hill in August still on good terms with the Montagues.

Derek and John stayed in touch. They were soon collaborating on a dramatization of Montague's story 'The Cry' for Paul Muldoon. Muldoon was not just an emergent 27-year-old poet, but a BBC producer in Broadcasting

House, Belfast.[25] The interlacement of poets within the country, the day-to-day reality of the literary community, is notable.

9

Montague's American publisher for *A Chosen Light* and *Tides*, The Swallow Press, ran into financial trouble in late 1973. It was unable to take copies of The Dolmen Press's *The Rough Field* for US distribution.[26] In January 1975 Liam Miller suggested they offer American rights for that volume to Wake Forest University Press. That imprint had started a new line in contemporary Irish poetry under the editorship of Dillon Johnston. Thereafter, Wake Forest UP became Montague's main American publisher and Johnston a key counsellor and friend.

Wake Forest took a thousand copies of *The Great Cloak*. To launch the book, Johnston helped set up a reading tour taking Montague to a dozen American colleges. Altogether, the fees amounted to over $3,500 (about $15,000 in current money). The readings were scheduled on either side of an American Conference of Irish Studies held at St Mary's College in South Bend, Indiana, in the third week of October 1978.

A reading tour in America for Montague could wind up in a spiral of dissipation. There were many flights, taxis, nights in motels and the ever-present possibility of being incapacitated by his stammer when standing up in front of a crowd. He believed that a certain quantity of spirits imbibed beforehand settled his nerves, but it was important that it be not too much and not too little. If the nostrum did not work, he concluded the quantity on that night was just a little off.

Whether the event went well or not, he felt the need of more drink afterwards.[27] Hosts (sometimes with stereotyped notions of Irish poets) generally obliged with bottles ready to hand. By the time Montague got to South Bend, Indiana, he was in a ragged state.

His minder from 20 to 22 October was the young Irish scholar-poet Seán Golden, a junior faculty member at Notre Dame University. John loved being driven around by Golden in his red Triumph convertible.[28] The two made a stop at the Kit Kat strip club, where Montague was delighted with an artiste named Virginia; she herself was interested only in his young companion. To Golden, Montague passed along a secret of success with women that he had learned from an ugly-looking Dubliner who still had a great reputation as a Lothario: do to them whatever they ask you to do, and let them do to you whatever they want to do.

Taken to see the university chapel, Montague insisted on getting up into the pulpit, where he recited Yeats poems. In class with Catholic students of the university, he appeared to make a point of saying embarrassing things. Late one night at the American Conference for Irish Studies conference, Montague propositioned one of the participants, Professor Anthony Bradley; how seriously was unclear.[29] This was not the only time the poet, not wanting to go to bed alone, did not mind whether his companion was male or female. He had already damaged his reputation in Presbyterian Scotland with that kind of carry-on.[30]

The tour wound up in Milwaukee, where Montague's host was the homosexual poet James Liddy, once a habitué of McDaid's, now a professor at the University of Wisconsin. John enjoyed his time there. The reading went smoothly, the party at Liddy's house was riotous, and the interview with two of Liddy's students (Christopher Griffin and Nuala Archer) proved interesting.[31]

Nuala Archer lit into Montague with a spirited feminist critique. She started with *The White Goddess*. Graves had written that it was difficult for a woman to become a poet because society pressed her into domesticity. Now that social roles were changing, could men and women, she asked, 'integrate service to the muse and domesticity'?

Montague ignored the subject of shared housework and backed away from his past allegiance to Graves. He evasively said the muse was just 'whatever you most believe in and are touched by'. As for whether the life of a poet was easier for a man than for a woman, Montague claimed that problem did not arise in Ireland, where there had been many great poets who were women. Why then, Nuala Archer asked, hadn't he named any women writers in his lecture the night before? He did name a few women, he answered back; anyway, didn't it diminish the power of poets to think of themselves as female, or Irish, or Black, or gay? As for himself, he had feminine and homoerotic dimensions to his character, so he was not just a heterosexual male. Archer said she had not heard him read any poems about his love for another man. She kept right at him. Montague had a hard time dancing away from her pointed questions.

The interview is his first recorded confrontation with a contemporary feminist. He appears to have experienced it as a new kind of flirtation.

Afterwards, he sent via James Liddy his 'especially warm greeting to Nuala, whose gentle insistence made me consider seriously things that I may have been a little defensive about: I wish we could have talked longer next morning, though a small arrow may have grazed my heart, a vulnerable organ, always'.[32]

10

On the earnings from the American tour, John and Evelyn were able to make a trip to India in February and March 1979.[33] They did not have a lot of money for travel; they carried backpacks and took buses.

It was on this journey that their second child was conceived. Evelyn, believing in a multiplicity of spiritual determinants, reflected that conception was likely to have occurred on one of two occasions. The first possibility was after their visit to the Taj Mahal. This was in Agra, a Muslim-majority city. She wore a long dress, but no head scarf. On their way back to the hotel, some boys began to throw stones at them; one hit Evelyn in the spine. John spoke to an elder, who made the boys stop. Both John and Evelyn were rattled by the experience. Safely back in the hotel, John began to drink one beer after another. Evelyn was angry that he was just thinking of himself; he ought to have been comforting her. They quarrelled, then made love, roughly. Maybe it was then. Or maybe it was near the end of their trip when, having cash to spare after their frugality, the couple treated themselves to a night in the former palace of a Raj. That could have been when their second child, Sibyl, was conceived.

11

In 1979 John began to take part in Evelyn's Rudolf Steiner reading group. It is difficult to summarize the ideas of Steiner (1861–1925) without making him sound like a gifted crackpot. After publishing academic papers on Goethe's scientific beliefs, Steiner became an early follower of the thought of Friedrich Nietzsche and a favourite of the philosopher's sister.[34] His chief conclusion from reading Nietzsche's manuscripts was that the individual, once freed from instincts and social morality, could become conscious of his or her most original spiritual self. Steiner's intellectual path then took him away from Nietzsche's scepticism to beliefs in common with theosophy – reincarnation, the activity of the soul and the influence of spiritual beings on evolution. In 1899, age thirty-eight, he had a personal experience of Christ, though his thinking about Christianity was unorthodox. For him, all religions were valid, but Christ was central to each of them.

Steiner called his new belief system 'anthroposophy'. He attracted followers of many kinds. An industrialist invited him to start a school. The Waldorf system of childhood education sprang from Steiner's model school, with its attention to the body and the whole person, not just to the rational faculty. A league of farmers sought his advice, and he proposed a 'biodynamic' system, without fertilizers or pesticides. He started a pharmaceutical company featuring organic medicines. Steiner medical clinics employed extra-scientific and occult practices, particularly massage and dietary discipline. In every sphere, he proposed alternative ways of doing things. Respect for the soul was his key principle.

Evelyn took seriously the study of anthroposophy, as did various friends of the Montagues. The Hagues of Shanagarry participated in a Steiner reading group. Barrie Cooke's wife, the ceramicist Sonja Landweer, was another anthroposophist. Montague participated in the reading group for two years, 1979 to 1981. According to Evelyn's recollection, he was not a conscientious pupil. He would breeze into a meeting halfway through, and then remark of some anthroposophical notion that poets had always known that kind of thing.[35]

It is possible that there is some direct influence of Rudolf Steiner's writing on Montague's poetry, particularly in *The Dead Kingdom*. 'Deities' and 'Invocation to the Guardian' are both in line with Steiner's syncretic approach to world religions.[36] There may be cases of particular borrowings. For instance, Steiner made much of a line in Nietzsche's *Untimely Meditations*: 'No one can construct for you the bridge on which you must cross the stream of life, no one but you alone' ('Schopenhauer as Educator', Section 1). This sounds quite like 'A New Litany' from *The Dead Kingdom*:[37]

> That we are here
> for a time, that
> we make our lives
> carelessly, carefully,
> as we are finally
> also made by them;
> a chosen companion,
> a home, children;

> on such conditions
> I place my hopes
> beside yours, Evelyn,
> frail rope-ladders
> across fuming oblivion.

The theology of Teilhard de Chardin also interested Montague. He liked the idea of the evolution of the spirit over time. How many of the Catholic philosopher's books he read is uncertain (possibly *Man's Place in Nature*, in René Hague's 1966 translation). While at Vassar College on the 1978 reading tour, he was delighted when a local priest brought him to see the grave of the French priest. Montague left this lyric memorandum of his visit:[38]

> A Jesuit graveyard is like a military cemetery, small granite stones marching in order, as on the Somme. Between McQuaid and Reilly, you lie, earth's theologian, servant of the evolving *logos*, who attempted to read the book of this universe. A Calvary, gaunt and grey, broods on a hillock above you and your Jesuit comrades, the long sad Christ and the three mourning women. In winter you can see the tracks through the snow to your grave and in summer the flowers. In the evening the last rays of the sun seem to strike your grave above the lordly Hudson.

While post-Catholic, Montague was sensitively aware of the possibility of dimensions of life beyond the positivist and secular.

He was delighted to contribute when Kathleen Raine started *Temenos*, a journal devoted to 'the place of the imagination (or, if you like, the sacred dimension) in the arts'.[39] Robert Duncan, Robin Skelton and David Gascoyne were other poets associated with this celebration of the arts as an extension to 'the spirituality of the sacred traditions'.[40] The particular way Kathleen Raine married ancient wisdom with mysticism appealed to Montague:[41]

> It seems, John, that we are sent here for very specific reasons, both to learn something and to accomplish something. My life is, as you know, a 'write-off'. I have made every possible mistake and hurt and harmed many people who loved me. But each day dawns anew and one just has to go on and not let the accusers stop us from living *Ad Majoram Dei Gloriam*; though not as the Church Temporal sees these things.

Figure 52: Kathleen Raine and John Montague.

After reading her autobiography, Montague felt that Kathleen Raine, though a wise woman, was wrong to believe she had made a mess of her personal life. She thought that she had been cursed by the man she loved most. That was no curse, John wrote to Kathleen:[42] 'People in love [curse one another] again & again; someone, like Evelyn, whose whole being is love, does it twice a week, ignoring Sundays, clawing the air and scaring us all back to saving our souls. It could be easier but it is not genuine malevolence, not even bitterness.' In fact, Montague was worried that he himself, like Kathleen, was losing his way.

In the autumn of 1979 he unburdened himself to Robin Skelton: at the age of fifty, he felt himself to be undergoing a midlife crisis.[43] His drinking was out of control. Both his doctor and a psychiatrist had warned him that he must stop.

He was going to pieces. He had tinnitus, his back hurt and his knee clicked when he walked. Were these problems the result of the hard psychological work of investigating his feelings about his mother for *The Dead Kingdom*? Or his fights with Evelyn? Or was it just the drink itself? He did not know, but he was trying to adapt a regimen to steady himself: no bottles of whiskey in the house until Christmas, do the three kilometres to university on foot every day and swim laps whenever he had time to get to a pool.[44]

12

On 11 October 1979 Montague received a letter about a reading to the UCD English Literature Society.[45,46] On its back, he drafted a poem about being haunted. It had been six years since his mother was laid to rest, but still

> There is no noise/stir/I make that does
> not bring her before me
> like a living person

He felt the room quivering with her anger. Don't listen, he told himself; that's just death talking.

Yet all this late autumn, life was knocking on the door. When Evelyn's time came, 3 December 1979, the foetus was in the breech position, and the umbilical cord was wrapped around its neck. A Caesarean section was necessary, but their second daughter, Sibyl, was safely delivered.

Two months later, in February 1980, Montague participated in 'The Sense of Ireland' festival in London with a score of other Irish writers, an extravagant attempt at Troubles-era cultural diplomacy. One result of the trip was that he was back drinking again after his intermission the previous autumn. Celebrating the birth of Sibyl on his fifty-first birthday (28 February), he got drunk, fell down, gashed his eyebrow and broke four ribs.

'Yet I drink on, unwilling to decide,' he admitted to Robin Skelton in early May.[47] Following a reading with Michael Longley in Newcastle upon Tyne and 'a lunatic party at the end', he spent a few days exploring the Lake District.[48] He told Tom McCarthy he had a vision while he was there. A tree had spoken to him. It told him to give up the drink. And for the length of his conversation in the Long Valley with Tom McCarthy, he continued to take nothing but coffee.[49]

13

Montague finished a draft of *The Dead Kingdom* in June 1980. He wanted to let the subject of the North alone, but it did not leave him alone. In the early hours of Saturday, 21 June 1980, a young Provisional IRA man drove a Datsun sedan loaded with a 500-pound bomb into Main Street, Fintona, parked it in front of the chemist's shop and ran away. The explosion destroyed ten buildings and severely damaged thirty. The public house and original home of Montague's mother was wrecked – all the windows blown out, just the walls and the stairway left.[50] The devastation occasioned 'Cassandra's Answer'. The Greek prophetess of doom wearily complains of having 'one subject only' and being fated never to be heard. The last of the poem's two sections turns explicitly autobiographical:[51]

> To step inside a childhood home,
> tattered rafters that the dawn
> leaks through, brings awareness
>
> Bleaker than any you have known.
> Whole albums of Births, Marriages,
> roomfuls of tears and loving confidences
>
> Gone as if the air has swallowed them;
> stairs which climb towards nothing,
> walls hosed down to flaking stone:
>
> you were born inside a skeleton.

Still perfecting the poem, Montague went to Fintona for Easter 1981 (19 April).[52] That was during the hunger strike by IRA prisoners seeking 'political status' (recognition that they were soldiers, not mere criminals). On 9 April one of the prisoners, Bobby Sands, was elected to Parliament for South Tyrone, the Montagues' electoral district. Even John's brothers, usually SDLP supporters, voted for Bobby Sands.[53]

It was fifty days since Sands had had food by the time Montague came to Fintona to see the bombed premises of the Carney family. The present owner told him they had discovered old bullets under the floorboards below what had been his mother's bed. It was as if politically nothing had changed in sixty years.

On 2 May Montague flew to Toronto where he was scheduled to perform in an international poetry festival. Three days later, on the sixty-sixth day of his hunger strike, Bobby Sands died. Prime Minister Margaret Thatcher declined to express regret for the voluntary death of a man she defined as an ordinary criminal. Nine more hunger-strikers were to die, one by one until the end of August, a horribly newsworthy drama.

Around the world, expatriate Irish people protested. Montague went to a funeral mass for Sands at a basketball stadium in Toronto, conducted in Irish, with music by Seán Ó Riada. Asked to say something, he recited Yeats's most republican poem, 'The Rose Tree'. During the service, on the back of a flyer he then jotted down these verses:[54]

> There is a song of silence
> There is the song of the bone
> breaking through the skin
> of a slowly dying man;
> this is the song of his death
> but also of his living on.

David Lampe wanted to publish the lines right away, and White Pine Press printed a postcard entitled 'Hungerstriker'. Montague was afterwards taken to task by some literary critics for feeding the flames with this publication. Certainly, the poem is caught up in the wave of sympathy for the IRA caused by the hunger strikes and gives expression to that surge of sorrow and political anger.

While doing research for this biography, I met Father Joe McVeigh having his Saturday lunch in a hotel outside Enniskillen, County Fermanagh.[55] A patient of Seamus Montague, and present for the wedding of Turlough Montague Jr, Father McVeigh had been given a copy of the 'Hungerstriker' postcard by the poet. The priest then posted it to Gerry Adams, the head of Sinn Féin, who added his own autograph and returned it to McVeigh. The priest took it out of his wallet to show me. The death of Bobby Sands had been for him a nearly sacred event, a man who died for his beliefs, and this poem was a treasured memorial.

After ten years at UCC, Montague was happy to get away in January 1982 for a semester in Paris at the Sorbonne. His duties were light – a seminar on Samuel Beckett for the Institut d'Études Anglaises et Nord-Americaines.[56] The family stayed at first with Evelyn's mother in Neuilly on the far side of the Bois de Boulogne before they moved, in February, to a sublet on the ninth floor of a tower block at 7 rue Nicolas-Houël in the 5th arrondissement, with a panoramic view of the city.

Montague invited Beckett to come along to his birthday party there. Stephen Joyce and Maria Jolas would be among the guests. But Beckett was 'on a downer', and anyway, did not like crowds.[57] The two met up for a drink in Montparnasse on 25 May, along with Serge Fauchereau. Montague inscribed copies of his *Selected Poems* to his friends.[58] The conversation turned to James Joyce, and Beckett remarked that the novelist had great objectivity. 'The fall of a leaf, the fall of a child, the fall of an empire, it was all one to him.'[59]

Figure 53: John Montague and Samuel Beckett, Paris, May 1982.
Photographer Serge Fauchereau.

Professor Jacqueline Genet invited Montague to give a reading along with Seamus Deane at Université Caen Normandie. Montague offered the Derry writer lodging when he passed through Paris. Deane got on well with Evelyn and John, although he was annoyed by their obsession with the disproportionate success of Seamus Heaney. John repeated his laboured literary squib about Heaney's 'pommes de terre' (potatoes/poems), an allusion to the correspondence of Flaubert: '*O pauvre Olympe. Ils sont capable de faire sur ton sommet une plante de pommes de terre.*'[60] Not very funny and poorly calculated: Heaney and Deane had been schoolfellows at St Columb's College, Derry. After Caen, Montague and Deane again appeared on the same bill in Burlington, Vermont, at the ACIS Conference, 1–3 April 1982. John read well at Caen, but the performance in Vermont was ruinous: the stammer completely got the better of him.[61]

The Montagues had recently bought Letter Cottage, a two-storey farmhouse in a valley between Schull and Ballydehob, west Cork. It was lying empty while they were in Paris, so Evelyn offered the use of it during Easter to Seamus Deane and his family. She provided a detailed description of the house:[62]

> There is the usual large farmhouse room in which there is a good stove and a storage heater which are sufficient to warm the 3 tiny rooms upstairs. One double one with 2 bunks for smaller children, one with a single bed. There are two additional single beds in the living room. In addition there is a kitchen and bathroom. These two were added by the previous owner who was quite a tasteful modernizer.
>
> The farmhouse is in a field, probably of no interest at this time of year. But the region is wonderful and as the two of you like restaurants, they are everywhere. You could also call on all the West Cork craftsmen, they all live there and are friends of ours.
>
> I hope you can take up this very very late proposition. You needn't feel any gratitude, quite on the contrary because I bless the name of whoever airs the place.

To judge by the notes in the margin of Evelyn's letter, the Deanes took up the offer. Letter Cottage was to become a beloved second home for the Montague family. The bright garden was a relief from the steep gloom of Grattan Hill. There were kindly neighbours, particularly Mary Kate in the farm down the road, who became like a granny to the Montague girls.[63]

15

At end of May, the Montagues left Paris for Greece. With Evelyn at the wheel, they passed through Switzerland and, crossing Italy, stopped in Parma, Verona, Ravenna and Bergamo. In Greece, they visited Olympia, before getting a boat to the Cyclades islands in the Aegean.[64] On the island of Paros, they met Derek Mahon for a few days.[65]

Figure 54: Derek Mahon and John Montague, Paros, Greece; June 1982.

The journey continued onward by boat to Crete. On their return, they rested a while in the medieval city of Carcassonne, in the French Languedoc. The whole trip amounted to an odyssey.

The long tour was meant to be revitalizing, but, back in Cork that August, as John began preparing *The Dead Kingdom* for publication, he found himself still struggling. For the past year, he had suffered periods of despondency, blackouts, the return of his stammer and arthritis in his neck. His collection of poems had been conceived as a Freudian quest into the deep past for what ailed him, but, rather than knowledge setting him free, he felt like its prisoner. In her book on psychoanalysis, Janet Malcolm points out that in a breakthrough therapeutic hour, the subject often experiences a sense of doubt and defeat. That mood mirrors the patient's emotional reluctance to revisit 'the long-gone but never dead days of his parents' well-meaning, disastrous early dealings with him and with each other'.[66]

The narrative arc of *The Dead Kingdom* follows the drive northwards of Brendan O'Meara and Montague to the funeral of his mother in Fintona. As they pass through Longford, there are dreamy, reflective meditations on John's boyhood summers in Abbeylara with the O'Meara family. Going through Cavan, the poet reflects on the history and mythology of the border and, once in Tyrone, on the town of Fintona itself ('*What a View*'), as the stages of the journey trigger memories of the past.

Passing Enniskillen, County Fermanagh, his final visit to his mother in the hospital comes back to him. He 'might have/sought to explain;/but gentleness forbade' that he tell her that he had left Madeleine for Evelyn and was soon to be a father. His first child remained 'unacknowledged, unknown' ('Gravity'). In this book of poems, there was to be no shying away from painful subjects. One after another, he faces into them. He deals with his teenage period of courting his mother, bringing her on dates to the Fintona movie theatre, in an effort to win her love and find out about his past. 'Molly Bawn' treats directly of the time the Carney brothers, Frank and Tom, were interned during the War of Independence. After the border was set up and the Civil War broke out, they emigrated as soon as possible, part of 'the embittered diaspora of/dispossessed Northern Republicans'.

Of Molly's time in America, John could not get his mother to speak, though it was what he most wanted to know. For her it was 'a muddy cup' from which she refused to drink. The poet sought an impossibly historical answer to what was a psychiatric question: was he a child of love, or was he conceived accidentally and came into the world unwanted? Why did she leave 'the runt' 'to be fostered/ in Garvaghey'?

Once the poem visits those early years, it inevitably comes upon James Montague. The story of his father in Brooklyn is stitched together from scraps of information John has picked up from his brothers, mother and uncle. Fired from his job, 'angry/living off charity', 'Sunny Jim' depended on work in his brother's speakeasy. He still loved to sing, and when he had drink taken, he sang a lot. John could remember songs his father sang to him. Section four, 'The Silver Flask', hurls four elegies at the problem of honouring the sad figure of James Montague, who, living alone in a Brooklyn boarding house, worked on through the war years, sometimes sending money home, before returning to die in Fintona.

The dramatic crisis of the collection is Section five, 'A Flowering Absence':

Taut with terror, I rehearse a time
when I was taken from a sick room:
as before from your flayed womb.

And given away to be fostered
wherever charity could afford.
I came back, lichened with sores
from the care of still poorer
immigrants, new washed from the hold.

I bless their unrecorded names,
whose need was greater than mine,
wet nurses from tenement darkness
giving suck for a time,
because their milk was plentiful

Or their children gone.
They were the first to succour
that still terrible thirst of mine,
a thirst for love and knowledge,
to learn something of that time

Of confusion, poverty, absence.
Year by year, I track it down
intent for a hint of evidence,
asking to manage the pain –
how a mother gave away her son.

The naked pathos is startling: 'the pain – /how a mother gave away her son'. He was bound to face up to the fact (if it was a fact): 'All roads wind backwards to it./ An unwanted child, a primal hurt.' He acknowledges his alcoholism, his promiscuity and implicitly too his jealousy of luckier men. But his 'terrible thirst' is also what he believes drives his genius: the longing for truth, no matter the cost, and the desire for a beautiful reconciliation, through pain to beauty.

The session – a 'good analytic hour' – brings him next to the problem of his stammer. That had come about, the poem says, when the hurt of his abandonment 'ran briefly underground' only to surface when he was taunted for his accent by his teacher in Garvaghey School:

> 'So this is our brightest infant!
> Where did he get that outlandish accent?
> What do you expect, with no parents,
> sent back from some American slum:
> none of you are to speak like him!'

This explanation of his disability allows for two causes – his deep feeling of abandonment by his mother and the subsequent hostility on the part of one particular mother figure, his schoolteacher.

When John showed the draft of the collection to Evelyn and Désirée Moorhead, they told him it was whingy. Too much self-pity and putting the blame on women. Evelyn went so far as to say that 'A Flowering Absence' was 'spiritually wrong' because it sought vengeance on Celia MacMahon, the teacher who just possibly caused his stammer.

His confidence shaken, he appealed to Robin Skelton. A few years earlier Skelton had gone through his own midlife crisis.[67] Was the poem, John asked, a 'spiritual victory' in dealing with his Achilles heel, or actually a defeat? He was ready to delete the stanzas about the teacher in Garvaghey school, if that would help.

The following month Montague admitted himself to the Park Attwood Clinic, a Steiner-based residential treatment centre in England. It worked 'primarily through the soul element'. The initial diagnosis was gout, and he was prescribed a vegetarian diet. Montague was not long in hospital before he was bored and begged for company; Evelyn came over to join him. She was taught a technique of rhythmical massage that was meant to help. He certainly needed assistance. *The Dead Kingdom* had cost him all that he had to give.

Seven months later, at the end of April 1983, Montague took charge of the Seventh National Writers' Workshop at University College Galway. One of the students in Montague's workshop was the poet Eva Bourke. She recalled that Montague told the participants that they must deal honestly with their lives in their work. He himself, he confessed, had done some terrible things, things of which he was ashamed. These could not be kept out of the work; they had to be faced. Writing was not a means of self-promotion.[68]

16

In July 1983 I was back in Ireland, gathering material for review essays on contemporary poetry. Montague invited me to stop in to Letter Cottage. Derek Mahon, temporarily reunited with his wife Doreen and their children, was also there. The day was warm, and we drove to the coast for a swim. John waded immediately in, snorting like a horse, and Derek was not far behind him, soon floating on his back with his belly to the sun. After putting a foot in and finding the water cold, I was slow to take the plunge. Just what a critic needs, Montague shouted, a bath in the cold Irish sea.

Over dinner, we were talking about Tom Paulin's book on the poetry of Thomas Hardy. I thought it to be an effort to make a case for writing completely inimical to transcendence. Doreen found this line of thinking to her liking. Poets thought too much of themselves; they ought to give reality a look-in now and then. 'But what is reality?' Derek asked. 'Transcendence or solipsism is not a choice; it may simply be a condition of life.' John took this up: no writer wants to escape the conditions of his life; writers address what immediately presses upon them in the world – that is their reality. 'Well, still,' Doreen came back, 'poets need to give a hint now and then that they know the world and others have an equal existence to them ….' 'Of course, they should!' Evelyn added. 'Like right here in Ballydehob.'

The three men at the table were made to think again about their afternoon swim; their indifference to the squabbles of children, the order of the house and the preparation of the meal we were just then eating. John rose to the occasion and addressed me: 'See here, even in a cottage in west Cork, on the hip of Catholic Ireland, we live out the great conflicts of the age – what it is to be a man in the twentieth century, what new place woman will make for herself.'[69] The next day, the three men looked after the children, while Evelyn and Doreen collaborated in a quilting session, as members of the Patchwork Artists Guild of Ireland.

Figure 55: Oonagh Montague, Katie Mahon, Rory Mahon, Sibyl Montague; Letter Cottage, Ballydehob.

Late one night, John and I took a walk down the road. I questioned the jacket copy for *The Dead Kingdom*. It did not seem correct to suggest that the book was in any real way a response to the Troubles. The book mainly had to do with family not nation, psychology not ideology. John did not like this way of stating the matter. The simplifications of antitheses ran counter to his effort to see life whole. The book was meant to be poetry in Patrick Kavanagh's sense of the word, 'Justice ... without her sword.' As for it being about his mother, not his country, 'Well, my mother is Ireland.' That did not settle matters for me. There are a million mothers in Ireland, each different; his alone could not stand in for the rest. The conversation concluded with John saying that the important thing about the collection is that it is a warrant of his decision to write for happiness. He wanted the book to have a healing power.

HOME TRUTHS AND UNPRINTABLE POEMS

I

After their July 1983 in Ballydehob, the Montagues spent a month in France. They stayed for the first time in La Cure, the former mansion of a parish priest in Mauriac, near Saint-Émilion. Many aspects of the place pleased Montague: he got to sleep with Evelyn in a priest's bed, to read François Mauriac in a town named Mauriac and to spot vestiges of Celtic culture in the Auvergne, including Sheela-na-Gigs in Romanesque churches.[1] It was Bordeaux wine country; all around the farmers worked away as the grapes ripened. Montague liked to see them go by on their Massey Ferguson tractors, just like the ones farmers began to use in Tyrone when he was young. The heat was sometimes tremendous.[2] During the days, he worked at a writing table outside under a lime tree, with his papers scattered across it, dressed in shorts, a hat on his head. Mauriac suited Evelyn too. They returned in August year after year until 1991.

In August 1983 Montague brought along a folder of draft poems, the themes of which had not fitted into *The Dead Kingdom*. It was his plan to make *Mount Eagle* an expression of openness, peace and freedom – no focus on the North, no tortured investigation of the self, no wild subjection to an adulterous muse. Keeping to this resolution, however, was difficult. 'I dream of becoming easy-going, the perfect paterfamilias,' he wrote to Derek Mahon, 'but look at me!' Doreen and Derek had been spectators to a theatrical row between John and Evelyn at Letter Cottage, just before the Mahons had their own 'whopper of a quarrel'.

Instead of new poems of family life, in Mauriac John turned to prose. *The Lost Notebook* was an account of his first experience of sexual intercourse with a woman. That was in Florence just after his trip to Rome for Anno Santo, 1950, as a young Catholic reporter representing Ireland. When writing stories for *Death of a Chieftain*, he had considered treating this episode in his life.[3] But, asking himself, 'How much of one's life can go into one's art?' he shied away from the subject.[4] He was still worried twenty years later about how people would receive a true story about errant sexual behaviour. But he reminded himself that 'McGahern never gave a fuck'. One of his narrators can only manage to have sex with his girlfriend when outdoors under an umbrella.[5] Maybe everyone was abnormal in some fashion. The question was, just in what way had his own sexual self been developmentally disordered? The narrative opens the door on Montague's timidity around women, his ignorance of them, his adolescent male-male sexual experimentation, and his fear that he was an inadequate performer in bed.[6]

2

Back in Cork, Montague replied to a question from Dillon Johnston about his poetry. In addition to being his publisher at Wake Forest University Press, Johnston was writing *Irish Poetry After Joyce* (published in 1985). He noted a new 'mythic mode' in 'Mount Eagle', but Montague denied there was any such thing. During a 1978 stay in Ballyferriter, County Kerry, he had merely watched the mountain of that name 'until it spoke to me'.[7]

This is unconvincing. Plainly, that poem invents a parable about the relationship between the eagle and the mountain. It associates the eagle with a period before the loss of language, when there was a vibrant community of fishermen along the coast. Since that era eagles had literally disappeared from Ireland. It is important to the poem's autobiographical significance that the eagle once enjoyed the 'slight, drunk lurch' of the fishing fleet; he had liked taking to the skies in stormy weather; he had enjoyed being 'angry in the morning, calmed/ by midday, but brooding again in/the evening'. But that period had come to an end; there would be no more roaming and tumult in the air. He 'had to enter the mountain'. His destiny henceforth was to be fixed in one place, remote, lofty and admired. This new existence was, he was told, a greater service than the fleeting life he had lived before.

Basically, the poet's duty was now to be a famous man and a father, a public figure with only a public existence, living for the sake of others. Yet 'he sighs for lost freedom'. The poem is a mythic expression of Montague's ambivalence about sticking to a life decision to become a settled and respectable family man. 'Mount Eagle' is not a description of a mountain in Kerry but a meditation on his own life crisis. As Dillon Johnston detected, it is a poem in a new mode, rather like that practised by Eastern European poets (e.g., Miroslav Holub) and currently being imitated by Seamus Heaney in poems like 'The Mud Vision' from the forthcoming *The Haw Lantern.*

Nowadays when he climbed up to his attic study at Grattan Hill, Montague was depressed, not motivated to take up an old unfinished project.[8] There was a big table under the skylight with bookshelves behind it. Around under the eaves were suitcases full of papers – folders of drafts, copies of past publications bearing pencilled revisions, bundles of correspondence, each in a separate valise, unzipped, the tops open.[9] A fine dust lay over everything. He went back downstairs.

Figure 56: John Montague at work.

Sometimes Montague did get stuck into a poem or story, but it was in the living room that he did his writing. His filing system, his daughter Sibyl remembers, was 'horizontal'. He spread his newspaper clippings, notebook pages and drafts all around him. He still had the ability to lose himself in his work. He would forget about everything else but it. He had to be reminded to get a haircut, or before going out, to change out of the jumper with the holes in the sleeves.

He could be, Sibyl recalls, a 'very funny rascal'. When telling a joke, he would crack up laughing well before he got to its punchline.[10] A UCC colleague remembers Montague affectionately calling Sibyl, when still a baby, 'The Monster'. The Monster did this, The Monster did that. She was his 'heart's needle'.[11] Evelyn got a good laugh over his poem 'Sibyl's Morning', particularly the lines about her infant bouquet:[12]

> Lift her up, warm and close
> or held at arm's length –
> that smell, like a sheep pen,
> a country hedge steaming after rain.

3

In December 1983 Montague went north to attend the filming of Derek Mahon's BBC teleplay of Montague's 'The Cry', starring Adrian Dunbar as a young Catholic journalist, on a visit home from his job with a blue-ribbon London paper. At night soon after his arrival, a man is beaten up in the street by the B-Specials. Hearing the noise, the journalist looks out his window and sees down below the attack taking place; other people are watching too. Everyone in town soon knows what has happened. Challenged by his elderly nationalist father to do something about the injustice, the journalist investigates. But every door is shut in his face. He gets no co-operation from the priest, the victim's family, the local newspaperman, a teacher, or his past girlfriend. The townspeople are divided between the intimidators and the intimidated. Being neither, he is a misfit. He doesn't belong there anymore. Even the village idiot knows enough to tell him, 'Nosy Parker go home!' (which is no longer Tyrone).

The authenticity of the performances is remarkable; so is the pointedness of each story beat, as the film forensically explores sectarianism in Northern Ireland. A narrator makes the political message explicit. Unlike the English bobby, the viewer is told, the Royal Ulster Constabulary carry revolvers and sometimes Sten guns. The force is supplemented 'by 13,000 reservists exclusively drawn from the Protestant majority, who are over armed and undertrained. All the elements of a police state are present, not in Spain or South Africa, but in the British Isles.'

Off-duty, members of this same police force obstructed the filming of scenes in Staid, County Antrim in early December 1983. Representatives of the 'Ulster Special Constabulary Association' threatened to sue the BBC.[13] Changes were demanded to the script, to reflect recent steps to modernize the security services of Northern Ireland. Montague was highly agitated about the possibility that the BBC would make concessions that would blunt the point of the story. A sur-title was in fact added as a result of police pressure: it gives the date of the events as 1959, as if the political lesson of the film were no longer applicable.[14]

Derek Mahon was staying at Michael and Edna Longley's Belfast home during the completion of the film; the Longleys themselves were away. Mahon and Montague threw a 'wrap party' for the cast and crew of the teleplay; they also invited a number of Belfast poets, including Paul Muldoon and Medbh McGuckian.

Early that night John rang his brother Turlough in Fintona to ask if his daughter Blanaid had received the wedding gift John sent, a set of silver spoons. Turlough cut him short, perhaps because John had failed to attend the ceremony in Sligo, or maybe because he had still not apologized to Bridie, Turlough's wife, as he had been asked to do. John was stung.[15] He had hoped for a reconciliation.

Before the party Mahon asked the director, Chris Menaul, if he would mind for the duration of the evening not mentioning his last name. Montague was still worked up about censorship of 'The Cry'; he might jump to a sectarian conclusion if he learned Chris's surname. All evening, Menaul, while meeting so many new people, poets and their companions, was unable to say who he was. He finally went outside into the street to scream, 'Damn all these Irish poets! They're crazy.'[16]

That night Montague himself felt like a bull in a corrida, stuck with banderillas. He made notes afterwards about an exchange with one of guests, a young poet, who noticed 'a poet stranger in town, an old 'un,/with a reputation he wants/to gut, for his own satisfaction'. He told off the older poet: 'It's about time/someone should put you right/For twenty years you've been writing shite.'[17]

It was a Dionysian crowd, with a lot of drink taken. Like the protagonist of 'The Cry', Montague did not belong there anymore and was relieved to get out of Ulster once again.

4

The launch date for *The Dead Kingdom* was set for John's fifty-fifth birthday, 28 February 1984. The Poetry Book Society 'recommended' the book in its spring list, but it was not a 'Choice', reconfirmation of Montague's belief that he did not get fair treatment by the English juries of the PBS. After a study of their decisions, Dillon Johnston agreed with him. Between 1954 and 1993 the Poetry Book Society chose 156 books, twenty-one of them by poets from the North or the Republic: one each by Austin Clarke, Paul Durcan, Patrick Kavanagh, Michael Longley, Hugh Maxton, Richard Murphy, Tom Paulin and Matthew Sweeney; two by Eavan Boland, Derek Mahon, Paul Muldoon and Frank Ormsby; and four by Seamus Heaney. Not once was Montague a 'Choice'. Neither *The Rough Field* nor *The Great Cloak* were even recommended. The decisions 'seem inexplicable', but probably, Dillon Johnston surmised, they had more to do with English disapproval of the American aspects of Montague's poetic than with his republicanism. Another factor may have been that the poet had been a reviewer for many years in *The Spectator* and *The Guardian*, where he wrote as one standing outside metropolitan alliances. People never forget being slighted in the public prints. He may have had more silent enemies than friends in the London literary world.[18]

Montague, unfortunately, had at the least every writer's portion of neediness for public acclaim. He also lacked, or rather rejected as false, British graciousness, the 'good loser' gentleman jockey's code of conduct. He thought the race was fixed against him.[19]

5

Montague's Aunt Freda fell ill in May 1984 and died before John could get to see her one last time in Omagh Hospital. Evelyn drove John north from Cork for the funeral at Garvaghey Church, the only time Patsy Kelly (John's long-time friend and proprietress of Kelly's Bar) met Evelyn.

Having produced an elegiac portrait of Brigid ('Postmistress'), John owed one to Freda, to make a diptych for the two aunts who raised him. He had believed himself too dismayed by the 'dragging chain of nearly untranslatable events' to write anything further about the Troubles. Nonetheless, he turned his celebration of Aunt Freda into a political comment.[20] Once a 'girl courier of Cumann na mBan' during the War of Independence, in her last years Freda had lost all signs of contrariness and greeted everyone alike, without regard to religion or politics. His poem concludes: 'Such rich acceptance might take care/ Of our little local spot of bother.'[21]

6

There was one time, Evelyn Montague recalled, when she got her own back at John for his escapades.[22] Ted Hughes had come to Ireland to go fishing with Barrie Cooke and then give a reading at Listowel Writers' Festival. Since Evelyn was already booked to attend a Steiner seminar in anthroposophy with Sonja Landweer at Kilkenny, she agreed to collect Hughes at Cork Airport and drive him to the Cookes'.

She was not alone in the car with Hughes; Oonagh and Sibyl were in the back seat. Hughes asked her one question after another and showed interest in all that she had to say. She told him a story of having her fortune read by a witch on Vancouver Island. They talked, it seemed to her, as if they had known one another a long time. Not insensitive to his sexual appeal, during the Steiner conference the idea occurred to her that maybe she ought to go find him and enjoy a brief encounter; however, no sooner did she have the thought than she dismissed it. It would be rude to abandon the other anthroposophists and besides, her two daughters were nearby. At the end of the session, Hughes noticed Evelyn making preparations to go, and he seemed unhappily surprised. 'If only I had known you were leaving so soon ....'

On her return to Grattan Hill, John wanted to hear if she had any news of the big English poet. She said that he appeared to have fallen in love with her, at least a little bit. John did not believe it. Impossible! Still, he wanted to hear all the details.

At the end of May 1984 John Montague and Ted Hughes were both on the bill of the Listowel Writers' Festival. Nuala Ní Dhomhnaill drove John to the festival. She was a bit ashamed by the way her former lecturer danced attendance upon the British poet.[23] He ought to have had more self-respect, she thought. But Greg Delanty and his friend John Bourke were very pleased when

Montague brought Hughes to meet them for an hour in a quiet Listowel pub. Montague let them chat away uninterruptedly with the famous visitor.[24]

On his return to Grattan Hill, it was Evelyn's turn to ask if John had any news of Ted Hughes. You were right, he replied. He does find you attractive. He asked all sorts of questions about you.

7

John was apparently not worried that Evelyn loved another, but he did worry about whether or not she loved him. He never ceased to doubt it. He admitted in a letter to Robin Skelton that his course in life was wobbling, knocked this way and that by his own drinking and by Evelyn's temper.[25] The two of them, John and Evelyn, had 'egos that were simultaneously robust and fragile'.[26] The discord in their marriage worried them both. Montague drafted three painfully self-questioning stanzas:

> There is a white light in the room.
> It is anger. He is angry or
> She is angry. To them it is total.
> It is everything but to the visitor
> It is the usual, it is the absurd.
> If they did not love each other
> Why should they pay heed to a word?
> But now blows are struck.
> *
>
> Another sad goodbye at the airport;
> Neither has much to say, *en garde*,
> Lest a chance word turn barbed.
> You bring me, collect me, each journey
> Not winged as love, but heavy as duty;
> Lohengrin's swan dipping to Charon's ferry.
> *
>
> A last embrace at the door,
> Your lovely face made ugly
> By a sudden flush of tears
> Which tell me more than any phrase,
> Tell me what I most need to hear,

> Wash away and cleanse my fears:
> You have never ceased to love me.

In these verses, the only thing that proves to the couple that they continue to feel for each other is that they can still be hurt by one another. The surviving sign of love is sadness. Each wants the love of the other; neither can provide it. And the final phrase of the first section – 'blows are struck' (by whom?) – is a terminal omen.

They sought help from more than one therapist. One problem, from Evelyn's point of view, was that John was selfishly dominating. He did not, she felt, really treat her artistic practice as equal to his own and that undermined her. The first therapist they consulted, once the problem had been explained, said if the two of them were competitive with one another for public esteem, there was no hope for the marriage.[27]

Evelyn believed that, essentially, the cause of their trouble was John's alcoholism. She wanted him to join Alcoholics Anonymous. She herself joined a support group for families of alcoholics (in the archive, there are drafts of Montague poems on the back of the organization's flyers). While he did not join AA, he accepted that he had a drinking problem. He tried schemes of abatement: no drink until Christmas, or no spirits but just wine, or wine only at weekends. But even during those periods of rationing, he was sporadically tempted into frolics with lively companions, to take a 'cure' before a reading, or to drown his sorrows after a fight with Evelyn.

John believed that his drinking would be manageable were it not for Evelyn's violence. She did not hit him every time she was angry with him, but she hit him sometimes, and those occasions made each future explosion of temper carry an implicit physical threat. Most horrible of all, he could find himself, a big, tall, heavy man, hitting her back – inexcusable, disgraceful. How did they find themselves in this state? They spent several years in therapy trying to get out of it.

8

In the summer of 1984 Montague returned to his work-in-progress, *The Lost Notebook*. Among the Montagues' friends in west Cork were the painters William Crozier and John Verling. In 1982 Verling had done pen-and-ink drawings to illustrate a new translation of *The Midnight Court*, the satiric masterpiece by

Brian Merriman (c. 1747–1805). It tells the story of the poet, after falling asleep, being dragged away by a giantess to a trial by the Queen of Faeries. A young woman brings a case against the men of Ireland for refusing to have sex; as a result, Irish people are going to become extinct. The tale afforded Verling ample opportunities for pictures of naked women in the Irish countryside lusting after a man, any man, or whipping the daylights out of a celibate male. He would be just the man, Montague thought, to illustrate his novella.[28]

Evelyn hated the whole project. It was an embarrassment to her. Her husband, a UCC professor, writing erotic memoirs of his polymorphous perversity and commissioning nude pictures to illustrate it! Worse yet, the book was to be brought out in their home town by Mercier Press. John appeared indifferent to how she felt about it. *The Lost Notebook* was deliberately eroticised – he meant it to be a liberating stroke for Cork, with himself in his old role as bearer of the message of free love to Ireland.

In September Montague left for a reading tour in America. The seasonal migrations of the *spailpín* (wandering worker) became a strategy of domestic crisis management. The Montagues had, furthermore, developed a way of life that far outran what his Cork salary could support – a second house in west Cork, a month each summer in France, upkeep on 25 Grattan Hill, and frequent meals in restaurants. His annual salary was just £15,000, from which 40 per cent of the first £5000 was deducted as income tax and 58 per cent of the remainder.[29] He had to go on the road simply to pay the family bills.

9

On Montague's return to Ireland there was a big event in Monaghan to commemorate Patrick Kavanagh. Edna Longley, Tony Cronin, Paul Durcan, James Simmons and Sydney Bernard Smith were all performing.[30] Montague had turned against Kavanagh's concept of the parish, which he thought was being used in the North as a political front for Unionism and a refusal of international modernism. His talk, aggressively entitled 'The Parish or the Roots Racket',[31] argued that while parochialism had been 'adopted as a battle cry by the new or Neo-Northern writers', it would be difficult to call Belfast a parish (news to Ciaran Carson). All this talk of roots was, he claimed, ridiculous.

Edna Longley was dismayed by Montague's intervention. In a follow-up letter, he admitted to her that he had been cantankerous, but wasn't truculence fitting for an event commemorating Kavanagh? He continued to think that the concept of the parochial was nonsense. Garvaghey was not his single parish – 'I am the laureate also of Abbeylara .... and when I go through New York I stay in Brooklyn, where I have many friends. Any place where you have lived, loved and suffered is your parish .... Garvaghey gave me a glimpse of the old agricultural pattern but I am not going to lie and say <u>that</u> life is still going on; it is a travesty ... a pastoral lie.'[32] At whom was he drunkenly bristling here? Perhaps Seamus Heaney as much as Michael Longley, Frank Ormsby, or James Simmons. The Northern poets were riding the crest of a wave, but Montague was not being lifted up along with them.

10

Evelyn and John tried again and again to 'reset' their relationship. John sometimes appealed to his wife with a love poem, such as 'Matins', 'Crossing' and 'Harvest', each one a sentimental reprise of Evelyn's favourite, 'A Dream of July', about their first encounter.[33]

For her own part, Evelyn gave a long interview with the *Sunday Tribune* (14 April 1985), in which she talked for the entire time about her husband; she said nothing about her own artistic enterprises. She recalled their first meeting at 11 rue Daguerre, every detail of it still clear in her mind. She even stood up as a feminist character witness for him. He was 'one of the very few men I know who really loves women for themselves. He actually likes them. Not only as mothers, lovers, scrubbers, problem-solvers, not as women with something to offer to a particular man, but as human beings more often than not deeper and more interesting than men.' He was not educated into being a feminist; 'he was just born that way'.

Her husband was not a person easy to know, she explained, 'because he doesn't produce opinions; he asks for other people's and doesn't comment. He is not being cagey; he never stops reflecting.' When she was away, it had to be said, he was not a good housekeeper and never bothered to be a decent cook. She usually returned to a mess. But 'my life became easier the day I realized he is unchangeable; it was up to me to grow, and why not? Besides what I feared most in life is boredom, and John Montague is still keeping me interested.'

That interview was an honourable reaffirmation of vows in the most public of settings, an Irish Sunday newspaper. The pair of them made an effort, but the drinking and fighting went on. Only a few months after the *Sunday Tribune* article, John wrote a letter to Kathleen Raine despairing of the marriage.[34]

In the summer of 1985 Tom Smith and his partner Barbara Weiner visited Montague in Ballydehob, where they found him alone. With the backing of William Kennedy, the 1984 winner of the Pulitzer Prize for *Ironweed*, Smith was starting up the Writers Institute at the State University of New York in Albany. Montague and William Kennedy, age-mates, had met at a writers' conference in Belgrade in 1983 and again in Ireland during 1984.[35] Tom Smith asked John to be a visiting professor at SUNY that September and October, before his month-long stay at University of California Berkeley. This was a trial period, to see how Montague liked Albany, and how Albany liked Montague. A relocation from Cork to the USA, at least on a seasonal basis, after the pattern of Seamus Heaney's appointment at Harvard, was Montague's goal. On the heel of Montague's September 1985 stay in Albany, another visit was arranged for early 1986, following which the poet suggested to William Kennedy that they finalize an annual arrangement for seasonal teaching.[36]

The tension with Evelyn had not relaxed. John poured out his troubles to Barry Callaghan. Evelyn, he said, had offered to bring him to a sea cliff from which to jump.[37] In fairness, this could have been a loving rhetorical appeal. If he planned to drink himself to death, she might as well drive him to a cliff and let him do it cleanly. However, he adds that she attacked him with the car jack (the blow failed to land when she slipped and fell). Hard to believe.

They could not go on this way, but they did, doing what they could.

II

In mid-April 1986 John got a letter from Bridie, Turlough's wife, with bad news.[38] Turlough had fallen sick the previous month, retching all night. When brought to the hospital, he was diagnosed with inoperable cancer. He was now home. The family was praying that the pain could be controlled. There was no more to hope for.

John tried to get a ride to Fintona from Brendan O'Meara, the station master, but it turned out that he was stricken too, cancer of the bladder, so John drove up with two other O'Meara cousins.

In Fintona, he found Turlough in the conservatory of Drewsheen, his house above the golf course. Several of his children were present. John described the scene in a letter to Seamus Montague:[39]

> He declared that he had never been so happy in his life but did not believe in the Resurrection, certainly not of the Body, and thought that the idea of meeting your family in the next life as absurd .... Nor did he believe in a Judgment; 'all nonsense'. Nevertheless, I had hurt our mother's pride, and not understood their motives. I had the impression that he had read, or reread *The Dead Kingdom*, in preparation for my coming. Then he informed me that I had made the same mistake twice, in marrying outside the tribe; you needed a companion who thought and felt like you. I placed a picture of our happy children under his nose, but after a glance, he handed it back to me ....
>
> I found him quite lucid, unemotional, stoically brave, like an ancient Roman. The interview over, he said goodbye, stood up and walked through his family towards bed. I have the impression he was determined to show them how to die, with dignity, as his last testament to them.

John accepted the reproof in silence – you don't argue with a dying man – yet he was silently indignant.

In first week of July John was in Florence, Italy, for a week. He was the guest of his friend Alessandro Gentili, formerly of UCC, while attending the Congresso Internazionale dei Poeti. Evelyn rang with the news that Turlough had passed away. She wanted to know if she must drive the two girls north for the funeral; they were both busy with summer activities. Alessandro remembers John saying, 'Two young girls are more important than a dead body. Our business is with the living.'[40] While in some sense the truth of that statement is obvious, in terms of Irish Catholic norms, particularly those of Northerners, to whom attendance at funerals is a primary social obligation, it is a shockingly insensitive thing to say.

In Fintona a great crowd gathered to mourn the loss of one of the most respected figures in the legal profession.[41] Turlough Montague had been president of the Fermanagh Bar Association, captain of the Fintona Golf Club and a governor of the Showjumping Association. The Lord Chief Justice led the cortège of prominent figures in law, commerce and politics. But his famous youngest brother wasn't there.

It is likely that it was while the Montague family were in La Cure that August that John meditated on his relationship with Turlough by means of composing 'The Last Court', a poem not published until many years later. Stylistically, the poem belongs to the 1980s; it is of a piece with the candid reflections of *The Dead Kingdom*. Rather than being solely an elegy for Turlough, dead at sixty-two, it is a defence of John's own life. It was sensible as well as tactful to hold it back.

Instead, John published a tribute to Turlough in a book on the Easter Rising, *16 on 16: Letters from the New Island* (1988). He explained that his brother had been a key influence on his decision not to make an idol of 1916 in *A Patriotic Suite*. In 1966, the fiftieth anniversary of the Rising, Turlough had brought John along to a political meeting held to choose a nationalist candidate for Stormont:[42]

> Unexpectedly, my freckled brother rose to speak …. He said, very slowly, that although he was from a strong Republican background and proud of his ancestry, it was time, perhaps, for a change of emphasis. We should forget, surely, about all such old divisions, and strike a new note, by campaigning in the name of Social Justice, like the people in Dungannon. If we could break from the stranglehold of the past, then perhaps we might ask some local Protestants of goodwill to join us; they lived in Tyrone and Fermanagh as well.

This speech met with cold silence. Then a senior figure in the party declared he had never expected to hear talk of that kind – the speaker was a disgrace to the dead generations and a traitor to the ideals of 1916. In the tea room afterwards, the Montague brothers were shunned until 'one of the Charltons of Irvinestown' approached them. Turlough had made a moving speech, Mr Charlton said, then added a word to John, 'You must be proud of your brother' and he declared in his article that he certainly was.

12

In September and October 1986 Montague made a run to upstate New York and southern Ontario. He had several tasks: to give readings and seminars, to solidify his relationship with the Writers Institute in Albany and to negotiate the sale of his archive to the Poetry Collection at SUNY Buffalo. In closing the deal for his papers, John got considerable assistance from friends. David Lampe, a friend of Robert Bertholf, director of the Poetry Library, was helpful by being on the scene. Barry Callaghan came down from Toronto when the price for the papers was hammered out. Back in Cork, Tom Redshaw handled the job of cataloguing the contents of John's attic study.

Montague returned to Cork in time to see his 13-year-old daughter Oonagh play Ophelia in a production of *Hamlet* on 4 December. Seamus Heaney was going to be in town, and John looked forward to talking with him about their works-in-progress, but he told Heaney he would not be able to do so if the date of his visit was the night of Oonagh's performance.[43] He was properly proud of her.

Family life during the Christmas holiday season of 1986 turned calamitous. Tom Redshaw had come along with the Montagues to Letter Cottage; Derek Mahon was there too. Things began well, with a Christmas Eve service in the Ballydehob Church of Ireland and a dinner in the cottage. Over dessert and more wine, Evelyn remarked of something Derek had said, 'You can take the boy out of Belfast, but you can't take Belfast out of the boy.' Offended, Derek demanded that she explain herself. John attempted to calm the situation, but Evelyn thought he was in fact taking Derek's side against her. There was shouting, banging, recriminations fired back and forth. It seemed it would never end, so Tom Redshaw put the two girls to bed. On Christmas Day, Derek Mahon left before noon. Five days of marital discord followed, as rain poured down outside without cease. Redshaw brought the girls for walks, just to get them out of the stormy house. Finally he announced he was bringing Oonagh and Sibyl back to Grattan Hill on the bus and leaving John and Evelyn to their mutual mischief. Redshaw was fond of all the Montagues, but he concluded that John and Evelyn really ought not to be together.[44]

John, being the kind of poet he was, could not help but write about what was happening. In 'Lullaby', he tried to give a jolly music to the representation of their rows, as if John and Evelyn were just a funny old pair, a bit rough. It is the echo of 'The Night Before Christmas':[45]

NO LULLABY
It was the night before a quarrel
and all through the house everything
was stirring, including the mice,
and the children were startled
awake in their beds, because
downstairs their parents
were banging their heads.

And the shoes they are flying,
and the chairs thrown flat,
and saucepans and dishes,
and blows after that …

An ironically merry view of their brawls was impossible to sustain. The children were upset by them. In 'Entreaties', his daughters:

try to intercede with simple pleas
(scrawled aloft on crayoned posters)
Stop it, you two, please!
or, most heart-breaking of all, *Don't behave*
like children: think of us!
But the parents fail to register
their frail entreaties, seized in a kind of lust.

In 'Pure Rage', the woman stands over a man's body holding a bloody weapon. Afterwards,

Only the startled animals snuffle around
as audience, and nose the stained ground.

A marginal note on the draft indicates that by 'startled animals' he primarily means 'TDR', Thomas Redshaw, present at Letter Cottage in Christmas 1986.

All told, Montague wrote twenty-six lyrics upon a household shaken by domestic violence.[46] Entitled *Home Truths*, the sequence explores the couple's shame, sorrow, despair, desire for reconciliation, self-pity, crimes against each other and injury to their children's sense of security. Tastes in poetry may differ, but few could read these poems without being jolted by their terror and force.

However, the sequence was unpublishable at that time, or at perhaps any time before years put a distance between the poems and the people they first concerned. Even now, *Home Truths* has not appeared as a whole, although Montague offered it both to his Irish and American publishers in the late 1990s. The book-length sequence constitutes an essential chapter in his lifelong verse autobiography, but it was judged unfit for publication.[47] This created an impasse in his conception of himself as an author. He was not allowed to be himself in his poetry.

An important question is whether the unpublished sequence blames the woman or takes responsibility for the author's participation in the melees. The impression is given by some poems that he was more often fending off blows than smacking his wife, but Montague does not hide the fact that there were two of them in it. His heavy drinking is tackled in several poems. In one, it is seen as part of the cycle of violence:

Barred

Her insults dinning, dwindling in his ears,
He seeks a dark pub, down that burrow disappears.
There he huddles for hours, smouldering,
Brooding, or trying to read but
Also steadily sinking glass after glass until
Like a caricature (the offended male!)
He heads back, steaming, uphill.
Violence: the snake that eats its tail.

The whole situation was pitiful and unsightly, yet it cannot be overlooked.

13

In early March 1987, three months after that dreadful Christmas, John was invited to participate in a Temenos Conference in New Delhi, India, organized by Kathleen Raine. Evelyn wanted to come as well. Some of her recent quilt designs were in perfect sympathy with the goal of Temenos, the marriage of sacred traditions in spiritualist works of art. However, she was not, like John, a frequent contributor to *Temenos* (the journal) and had not been invited to the conference. So soon after their Christmas squalls, John refused to bring her along. Enraged, she threatened to throw his manuscripts into the fire. They struggled and, drunk, he struck her in the face. Their daughters ran into the room and saw what he had done.[48]

Once in New Delhi, remorseful and distressed, John told Kathleen Raine and Morris Graves how much Evelyn had wanted to be there. He urged them to write to her, not as his wife, but as an artist, and passed around a postcard of her quilted wall-hanging 'The Third Eye'. 'It should have been shown here at the Conference,' Graves wrote to Evelyn, 'because its image was deeply important to so many of the discussions.'[49] Kathleen Raine sent Evelyn an invitation to visit her in London. In New Delhi, John was not fit for public speaking; his stammer overwhelmed him. Desolate in his room, he worked on the poems of *Home Truths*. He hoped they might prove to be his 'Purgatorio', suffering with a goal in sight.[50]

He got a cold welcome on his return to Cork. Sibyl, just seven, said, 'At least the dog was glad to see you, Daddy.' Evelyn then left for a stay with her mother, who was turning seventy-nine years old. After that, she was going to America to give a masterclass in quilting. The couple's lives were drawing apart.

14

On 6 April 1987 Elizabeth Sheehan, a graduate student from New York in her mid-thirties, got the bus from Dun Laoghaire to Cork in order to interview John Montague, for her anthropology dissertation on Irish intellectuals' roles in political and social debate. She taped interviews with people and also kept field notes, recording every detail that seemed possibly significant in the day's events.[51]

When Montague came to meet her at Jurys Inn, she recognized him from his jacket photograph. They walked to his office at UCC, and in the course of a chat, she chanced a suggestive remark: 'Well, you are Ireland's leading erotic poet.' There was a meaningful exchange of looks.

Figure 57: Elizabeth Sheehan.

At the end of his work day, Elizabeth Sheehan accompanied John from the university towards Grattan Hill, stopping for a pint at Henchy's. When they arrived at the house, Sibyl was doing her homework. Oonagh then returned from school – 'very, very beautiful, clear face & eyes, beautiful girl', Sheehan wrote in her field notes; 'a late nineteenth-century porcelain face'. Oonagh was solicitous – offered tea, etc. – a very grown-up thirteen year old. Elizabeth and John then did their hour-long interview in the sitting room. At its conclusion, he came round to kiss her and, slightly shy, she kissed him back.

John asked Elizabeth if she knew how to cook a chicken, but she declined to be pushed into the role of mother and cook. She left the house to check into the Glenvara Hotel, a kilometre down Wellington Road, before returning for dinner. When the children went to bed, the two watched a movie on television. Afterwards, kissing her, John asked what she liked. It was time to leave for the hotel down the road.

However, the woman at the desk in the Glenvara stopped John from going upstairs with Elizabeth. So, reluctantly, they retraced their steps to Grattan Hill and to what John called 'the marital bed'.

There were no promises of fidelity in John and Evelyn's marriage, but there were tacit understandings between the couple. One was no mistresses in Cork, much less in the family home. This was a violation of an unspoken understanding. It was the custom of John and Evelyn that he would tell her of his affairs, as if candour made them tolerable and no threat to her. But they did matter to her; they made her impatient with him and intolerant of his affection when it was offered. Now he had abandoned concern for her feelings by making love to another woman in their own bedroom. When Evelyn returned to Cork, she soon detected that something of the sort had happened there.

15

In his time with Elizabeth Sheehan, Montague talked intimately about his life, and she recorded things he said in her field notes. He told her that 'Chronology keeps us from being lovers, but we can be friends' and 'Do not fall in love with me.' She kidded him 'about having hosts of adoring post-grads around ready to go to bed with [you]'. He did not do that anymore, he told her; she was the first person with whom he had misbehaved in a long time. This 'nice thing' between them was a surprise to him.

The next day, Elizabeth Sheehan returned by bus to her flat in Dun Laoghaire. Before meeting Montague she had been lonely, but she was not looking for an ongoing relationship. She had a husband and loved him, but this adventure was compelling. John was 'a complicated man, usually warm and charming, but distant when he felt threatened or diminished'.[52] She saw that he was plunged into sorrow over the impending crack-up of his marriage and the deaths of his brother Turlough and cousin Brendan. Now his publisher and friend Liam Miller was fatally ill. Naturally, she would have preferred that he pay some attention to herself and her history, but he was miserably self-absorbed and needy. She understood all that.

His notions of 'the muse' disgusted her. Such idealizations of women, she thought, stood in the way of their gaining basic rights in Ireland.[53] However, his company was wonderful, and she wanted more of it. On 24 April 1987 she wrote to her mother that while John Montague had an 'enormous ego', he was living his life with a genuinely artistic vision.

They met again when John came up to Dublin for the Seán Ó Riada memorial performance on 26 April at the National Concert Hall. There were to be readings by Cyril Cusack of Heaney's 'In Memoriam Seán Ó Riada' and of Montague's 'Ó Riada's Farewell'. John was booked into Buswells Hotel on Molesworth Street, and Elizabeth joined him there. Montague was going to have to read bits of the poem on the concert stage, and he was apprehensive. Before he left for the performance, they went upstairs together at Buswells.

While Montague was in Dublin, Elizabeth Sheehan attended an event honouring Francis Stuart.[54] Elizabeth could not understand why people would wish to celebrate a Nazi. John told her that as a reader for MacGibbon and Kee, he had rejected *Black List Section H* in manuscript when it was written in the first person (as autobiography). It was, apparently, much improved by the subsequent translation into the third person and thus becoming 'auto-fiction'. Montague told her that Stuart was admirable because he 'had the strength to experience what he sought, seeking immolation & total self-abnegation, etc. – most artists will not face up to this'. She was not convinced that this rationale justified Stuart, an antisemite supporter of Hitler, being elected to the highest honour of Aosdána, *An Saoi* ('Wise One').[55]

Elizabeth Sheehan's next encounter with Montague was 20 May, after the funeral of Liam Miller, dead at just sixty-three years old.[56] Tom Redshaw remembers Montague being reluctant to go to the wake. During his recent visit to Dublin, he had called to see Liam Miller in the hospice, and had found the suffering of the dying man frightful. But Redshaw kept at him, and Montague did his duty. He was a prominent mourner at what amounted to a national funeral, with representatives of the churches, universities, museums, libraries and departments of State in attendance, as well as writers and publishers. At the burial in Cluain Enaigh, Mountrath, Thomas Kinsella spoke over the grave. Afterwards, the chief mourners retired for the wake at Carton House, County Kildare.

Montague left for another trip to the USA in late May. He was to be named the State Poet by the Governor of New York, Mario Cuomo. The Writers Institute in Albany then made him a formal offer of a half-year position.[57] While he was in America, he rang Elizabeth Sheehan several times, a gratifying surprise to her. The two met a fourth time at the American Conference of Irish Studies in Dublin at the beginning of July. He showed Elizabeth a poem about Evelyn that, he said, she struck him for writing. Elizabeth did not want to hear about his wife. Frustrated with his lack of knowledge of just who she was, Elizabeth told him she had never 'had a day in [her] life when [she] felt economically & domestically secure'. That caught his attention. He was surprised, and interested.

Figure 58: William Kennedy, novelist, and John Montague, in Albany, New York.

She was a sympathetic witness to Montague's anxiety about performance. It struck him when he had to give a reading, sometimes a spectacle of breathtaking public failure, but it also visited him in the bedroom. He was driven to seek approval from women, but once in bed, he feared failure and humiliation and often experienced it. He tended to think that having a few drinks would put to rest his demons, but in fact, drink was the opposite of helpful. It occurred to Elizabeth that perhaps he wanted to fail – to be punished by a woman and have his hauteur undermined. He was often a passive partner. He liked both the rough and the tender sides of lovemaking. Once he asked to be strangled. Elizabeth enjoyed the shifting power play of their relations. She had a more liberated, mature sense of human sexuality than he did. Once he playfully cuffed her on the cheek during lovemaking, and it later occurred to her that he may have wished to explore sadomasochism, and discover if he had an appetite to humiliate and be humiliated, to hurt and yet still be loved, but their time together was short. He may have had in the past a number of partners, but he was not the most skilful or learned lover. He did not know enough to provide first for a woman's pleasure before seeking his own. He admitted to Elizabeth Sheehan that he had a 1950-ish notion that the man and woman would naturally climax together. After all, he was an old fellow.

When she saw Montague for the last time at the ACIS conference in July, she thought she had closed the book on the affair. He had exploited her, she supposed, but she had exploited him too, a brief romance with a troubled and fascinating Irish poet. To her surprise, afterwards, she retained a tender regard for him. As for Montague, he was seeking the companionship, affection and intimacy that were no longer possible within his marriage.

16

While in Dublin for the ACIS conference, Montague set up a meeting with Peter Fallon, editor of The Gallery Press.[58] Now that Liam Miller had passed away, it was very unlikely that Dolmen would continue. Derek Mahon had already shifted from Oxford University Press to Gallery simply because he wanted to be published from Ireland.[59] Gallery had developed a very strong list and the design of its books by 1987 was first-rate. John Montague and Peter Fallon were never to become close friends, as Montague had been with his other publishers,

Tim O'Keeffe, Liam Miller, Barry Callaghan and Dillon Johnston, but they developed a sound working relationship.

A year later, Peter Fallon set to work on producing *Mount Eagle*.[60] He was keen for Gallery Press to launch the poetry of Montague's 'golden years'.[61] Following the publication of *The Dead Kingdom*, Montague had formed the idea that his next collection would be brighter, freer and reflective of the life of a settled family man. His life had not turned out to be what he had then imagined. However, for the manuscript of *Mount Eagle* he filleted out the poems of *Home Truths* and others like them, about the woe that had engulfed his marriage. When he showed this selection to Dillon Johnston and Peter Fallon, they remarked on its 'mellowness, richness, maturity', 'a new note of ease'. There are some fine poems in *Mount Eagle* – 'The Well Dreams', 'Mount Eagle', 'The Hill of Silence' and 'The Well-Beloved' – but the overall tone of the book is a deliberate fiction. In truth, he was going through the most troubled time of his life.

13

COMING APART IN AMERICA: THE STATE
POET OF NEW YORK

I

Since 1985 Barry Callaghan had organized annual celebrations to honour the February birthdays of his father, Morley, and his friend John Montague. Each event was announced by a printed handbill and held at Barry's Sullivan Street house in Toronto. Musicians were engaged to play and a restaurant chef employed to prepare the food. Sometimes, Montague's Albany friends, such as William and Dana Kennedy and Joe and Vera Gagen would drive up for the occasion.[1]

For the February 1988 celebrations of Morley's eighty-fifth birthday and John's fifty-ninth, spirits were high. Montague was now State Poet of New York; the sale of his archive to SUNY Buffalo was soon to be publicly celebrated, and Barry Callaghan circulated the story that the poet had been nominated for the Nobel Prize.

Both Morley and Barry Callaghan enjoyed sparring with Montague. 'Your son is hopeless,' Montague ventured to the old novelist, with Barry standing by; 'He doesn't seem to be able to write a poem unless he believes he's fallen in love.' "Oh, the young in one another's arms ..." Morley replied, quoting Yeats's poem from the point of view of a writer getting old.[2]

To mark the sale of Montague's archive, an entire week of events (21–28 March 1988) was scheduled – readings at schools and colleges, a videotaped interview, a reception with the university board of trustees, and a formal dinner with Robert Creeley, the university's poet-in-residence. It was heavy work.

Barry Callaghan helped out; he sometimes accompanied John to readings, and himself recited the poems, while John provided commentary, so the threat of the stammer was kept at bay.

Figure 59: Montague and Barry Callaghan; Reception, SUNY Buffalo, March 1988.

It was impossible for John to hide his problem with drink from Bill Kennedy. He explained about the trouble at home. Evelyn was in 'a physical and psychological bind of a frightening nature'. He was trying to hold her together, but it was terrifying 'to see someone you love pulled apart'. He was not 'diviner enough to eradicate/anoint/heal a stricken childhood', Montague wrote to Kennedy, 'but I must do what I can'.[3]

In Cork Seán Lucy was away on sabbatical. His home life was in tatters too – he was drinking too much and had gotten involved with a visiting American student. Lucy's plan was to follow the student back to Chicago, where he had the shaky promise of a post in the English department of Loyola University.[4] While Lucy was away, Montague was meant to shoulder the burden of his courses. However, he himself was so often in New York or Toronto, he cannot have made a good fist of the job.

On 4 May 1988 the *Cork Examiner* carried the news that Professors Seán Lucy and John Montague were both taking early retirement; 'Brain Drain at UCC' was the headline. To a newspaper reporter, Montague blamed their departures on recession-driven cuts in university funding, leading to large classes.

Some of his colleagues in the English department were not sad to see Montague go.[5] As student numbers grew, Montague resented the expectation that he should do more work than in the past. Over the years his interest in the job had essentially boiled down to two things: it was permanent and pensionable. He was not the teacher he had been upon his arrival in Cork.[6] He accepted the wider civic duties that fell to him as a result of his post. He opened art exhibitions, introduced untold numbers of visiting poets, and supported the Everyman Theatre, the Triskel Arts Centre, the Cork Jazz Festival and the Cork Film Festival. In the Cork arts scene, he was a model citizen as well as a leading performer – a lot of work. However, his main task in life, as he understood it, was to write, and the basics of his salaried job – lecturing, marking and administration – were irritating distractions. This attitude did not ingratiate him with his English department colleagues. They had to take up the burdens he dropped. In addition, there were new women in the department, such as Patricia Coughlan. They might well have been impatient with the expressions of male privilege on the part of the two poet professors, Seán Lucy and John Montague.

In late September 1988 Montague returned from the family holiday in Mauriac to clear out his UCC office in Brighton Villas. Tom McCarthy came along to give him a hand with the boxes of papers. McCarthy insightfully observed in his journal that, more than Tom's help, John wanted his company during this important step in his life: 'he was not a loner ... but, rather, [had] the <u>constant need for company</u> – not necessarily witnesses, but human company. He couldn't be alone and certainly never at an important moment of transition in his life.' As they filled the nineteen boxes, John sometimes stopped and asked, 'What am I doing? Am I doing the right thing?'

Montague had just come back from Derry where he attended the Field Day Theatre production of Brian Friel's *Making History*, the occasion for a great gathering of 'the Ulster uber-Catholic community', including SDLP leader John

Hume and a number of Catholic bishops; the turnout was nearly as grand as at a prominent Ulster Catholic funeral. As the two poets carried out one box after another from Brighton Villas, John passed along the latest Field Day gossip: the board planned to expand the company's activities beyond theatre into academic publishing. With Seamus Heaney as a Trojan horse, Seamus Deane as theorist, and Faber as a publisher, they planned to take over the syllabus of English literature in British universities. Ireland's leading intellectuals were transferring 'their struggle from the field of battle (civil rights, politics) to the higher court of literature'.[7] Montague and McCarthy were sceptical. John thought the Northern writers were only reading one another's books; they did not realize that 'the new clutch of English poets' – James Fenton, Tony Harrison, Carol Ann Duffy, Craig Raine, Carol Rumens and others – were formidable figures in their own right. It was not going to be easy to push them aside.

By the time they finished, it was nearly midnight. John was 'speechless with emotion ('What can I say? What is there to say?')'. It was the end of sixteen years working in Cork. While John looked back on them despondently, Tom thought in fact those years were 'the happiest and most fulfilling of his life, and to say otherwise was a calumny against the generous city of Cork and its big-hearted University'.[8]

2

During the autumn in Mauriac, Montague suffered a dry spell. He had the time and the will to write poetry, but not the way forward. Instead, he engaged himself with a number of publishing projects.

One was a new anthology of Irish poetry, picking up where his *Faber Book of Irish Verse* (1974) left off. In 1982 an American publisher, Macmillan (New York), expressed interest in an updated volume.[9] Montague focused his attention on pulling a contemporary anthology together in the summer of 1988, contacting the authors and publishers for permissions. Macmillan provided a budget of just $2000 to cover the rights. Right away, Richard Murphy asked for $300 for three poems, and Faber put the price of four Heaney poems at $700.[10] That was half the budget gone on two poets. Everyone thought there was big money to be gotten from Americans for Irish poetry.

Montague's original impulse was simply to exhibit the fact that a number of remarkably good poems, some by a new crop of writers, had been written in

Ireland in the previous fifteen years. So, in just two hundred pages he included the work of forty-five poets. The table of contents takes the emphasis off the 'Ulster Renaissance' by adding young women poets, poets from Cork and poets from Dublin. However, the unappetizing title, *Bitter Harvest*, and Montague's brief introduction, both call attention to the Troubles. Published only in hardback, the book had poor sales.

A second project was translation into, and out of, French poetry. Two selections of Montague's own poems were published in France in 1988: *Amours, marées* by William Blake publishing company in Bordeaux and *La Langue Greffée* by Belin in Paris.[11] One of the translators for this second volume, Michel Deguy, appeared with Montague on 17 June 1988 at the South Bank Poetry Festival in a seminar chaired by Stephen Romer. Each poet talked about translating and being translated: Deguy by Montague, Montague by Deguy.

The third project of that period was an edition of Montague's selected prose. This volume had been 'in preparation' since 1961.[12] Since neither Liam Miller nor Montague had got round to putting together a text for the next twenty years, in 1981 Montague gave the job to an American graduate student he had taught at UCC, Mark Waelder.[13] Waelder's preface and organization, however, did not pass muster with the reader for Wolfhound Press.[14] In 1984 Liam Miller and Montague reworked the manuscript with a view to co-publications with Blackstaff Press and Notre Dame University Press.[15] But Liam Miller then fell ill, and the project passed to Antony Farrell and The Lilliput Press. Farrell thought a better book could be made of the material, so Antoinette Quinn, a Trinity College lecturer, was recruited to take the job in hand.[16] It was she who finally brought to a close the long process of publishing the selected essays of John Montague, *The Figure in the Cave* (1989). At the end of September 1988, while in Mauriac, Montague provided an introductory 'Chapter from an Autobiography', the backward look of one in his 'golden years' on his critical writings of the 1950s and '60s.

In recognition of Montague's sixtieth birthday in 1989, several publications were in the works. At UCD, Christopher Murray was editing a special issue of the *Irish University Review* devoted to Montague, and in America Thomas Redshaw was putting together a festschrift of poems, memoirs and tributes, entitled *The Hill Field*. These volumes came out alongside *Mount Eagle* and *The Figure in the Cave*, so there was bound to be some stock-taking on Montague's lifetime achievement by the end of that year.

3

Just because the crack of doom had sounded more than once over the marriage of John and Evelyn did not mean the two never again had a pleasant day of companionship and hope for a future together. They still searched for a path to understanding and (that therapeutic hope!) the consequent resolution of their troubles. The autumn in Mauriac in 1988 appears to have passed peacefully, and John departed for Albany in the New Year with the beginning of an idea for a new book of poems.

In late October he had begun to think back over the events behind 'That Dark Accomplice', a short story about his schooldays. Out of what had come his horror of (and attraction to?) hitting and being hit? How, after a loving childhood with his aunts, had he lost his easy, mutually gratifying relationship with women? Maybe the answers were to found in his time in Armagh at St Patrick's College. He began to write to old schoolfellows and shared his own recollections with them, then asked if they could add their own. He was again groping his way back into the past in hope of answers.[17]

4

In March 1989 I organized a reading by Montague at Union College in Schenectady, New York. It was not the first time he had read there. In 1985, while still a visiting instructor at Union, I had introduced the poet to my colleagues. At the end of that reading, a sandy-haired co-ed came up to compliment him. He invited her to join him later in his hotel room. She happened to be the daughter of a senior colleague in the department. I was not in a position, or of a mind, to laugh it off. John may not have understood how much had changed at American colleges with respect to staff/student relationships since the Free Love movement at Berkeley; indeed, he may even have believed drunken lechery was expected of him. But by the mid-1980s, such conduct could get a visiting speaker barred from campus in perpetuity.

Still, I liked John Montague. It was not in spite of his gaffes, but in some way because of them, that I could relate to him – although our chief connection remained an intense interest in literature. Whenever he was in Albany, John would ring me. Not only did he have no car, he did not know how to drive. In most of the United States, this put one in the class of the fundamentally disabled. He could not get groceries or buy drink.

Furthermore, as Tom McCarthy noticed, Montague had a need for company, and not any company, but someone interested in what he was interested in: poetry and free speculation about the nature of human life. Having landed in upstate New York, consulting his address book, he could sometimes do no better than me. So, during his visits to Albany, I often drove the fifteen miles from Schenectady to keep him company on the weekends, to take him to the grocery store or to a swimming pool, where he did laps while I marked first-year essays. The visits were always interesting. I never regretted taking the time to see John Montague.

Yet when we met at dinner before his reading in March 1989, it was mainly my colleague Peter Heinegg with whom Montague talked. Peter had been a Jesuit seminarian before doing a PhD at Harvard. The seminary was largely populated with homosexuals, and Peter himself was desperate for women and pure academic inquiry. This caught Montague's attention, and Peter followed up by sending him his unpublished memoir.

The reading that night at Union College was a disaster. So many people had showed up that we had to move to a larger room. John took a few swallows from 'the Silver Flask' before he stepped up to the podium. Attempting the first line of the first poem, he began to stammer, starting again and again at the first word, sometimes getting through to the second word but never managing a meaningful phrase. Between times, he could talk about his poems and even talk about his stammer, embarrassed but fluent; however, he never got through one single, complete line of poetry, and he tried for more than an hour. It took the heart out of all of us in the room. It was, weirdly, a more powerful emotional experience for some than if he had read his poems perfectly, but horrible nonetheless.

Afterwards we gathered in the home of a colleague, well-stocked with spirits. There were six or seven people present, comforters. The atmosphere was like that after a car accident. Everyone was wrecked and a bit frightened. Montague sank one glass of spirits after another. He tried to make sense of what had just happened. He went through his folder trying, in these different circumstances, to read a poem. He failed time and again. Finally, he was able to give voice to one lyric – 'Honey Harbour', an etymological litany of synonyms (like a medieval kenning) for the word *cunt*.

The following month Montague was scheduled to read along with Bernard MacLaverty at the American Conference of Irish Studies convention in Syracuse,

New York (12–15 April 1989). It was the main event of the Thursday night; the conference delegates all gathered in the hotel ballroom. When Montague thought about poetry readings, he was reminded of the Queen in *Alice's Adventures in Wonderland*: 'Give your evidence and don't be nervous, or I'll have you executed on the spot.'[18] It was painful to watch him struggle and fail in front of a broad cross-section of Irish studies scholars. He delivered a truly inglorious performance. It is a wonder that he was able to carry on through the remaining days of the conference, but he had no choice in the matter; he had lived with this impediment since childhood and humiliation was not new to him.

As delegates were beginning to leave a reception in the convention hotel, Lucy McDiarmid, a distinguished scholar and officer of the ACIS, was just arriving. Montague, noticing her on his way out, without so much as a 'how do you do', kissed her on the mouth. It could have been just another offensive sign of male entitlement, or else that plus an unconscious search for reassurance after his Thursday display of impotence, but it was not an action that was going to improve his reputation. He was not just self-destructive; he was being a public pest.

5

On 11 June 1989 Theo Dorgan, then director of Poetry Ireland, provided a boost for Montague. He booked the Gate Theatre in Dublin for a joint birthday celebration of Montague's sixtieth and Seamus Heaney's fiftieth, on 11 June 1989. The pairing with Seamus was a lift for John. There was a decorated cake for both men and a concert on the pipes by Liam Ó Flynn, played as if for the two of them. The success of the event delighted Dorgan and Montague too.[19]

Figure 60: John Montague, Seamus Heaney, and Liam Ó Floinn, Poetry Ireland celebrations of Montague's sixtieth and Heaney's fiftieth birthdays.

Figure 61: John Montague, Seamus Heaney, Poetry Ireland celebrations of Montague's sixtieth and Heaney's fiftieth birthdays.

Theo Dorgan had another ingenious publicity project in the works: *The Great Book of Ireland*, a volume including 121 artists, 143 poets and 9 composers, who each wrote directly on vellum pages, destined to be bound up in a single volume and auctioned. What Dorgan wanted Montague to secure was a page written upon by Samuel Beckett, then fatally unwell.[20]

Montague was to be in Paris at the beginning of December for a festival of ten Irish writers; he planned to make an effort to see Beckett then. However, in early November while in Galway on a *Mount Eagle* reading tour, he broke his leg, badly – a pin had to be surgically inserted before the cast could be put on. He was on crutches for months.

Nuala Ní Dhomhnaill, also at the Les Belles Étrangères festival, recalls Montague hobbling into her room at the Paris hotel, a small cubicle and nearly all bed. He had drink taken and she poured him some more, a glass of Black Bush. He told Nuala that his wife hated her. And why was that? John said it was because Nuala did not respect Evelyn's art. Her art! What was it she made – bedspreads? Nuala said she had never even seen one of them, so how could she have disrespected Evelyn's work? John made no reply. He had passed out at the end of the bed. Nuala had to get help from Derek Mahon and John McGahern (with rooms nearby) to hoist Montague and help him back to his own room.[21]

Still, the day after, he roused himself to pay his respects to Samuel Beckett. Critics often accused Montague of vainglory and name-dropping, as if he invented his friendships with famous writers. Admittedly something of a fanboy, as a matter of fact Montague became a witness to the lives of many writers of his time and they often enjoyed his company. That Beckett, a most private person, allowed Montague an hour in the last month of his life is simply a fact.[22] After his visit to the nursing home, Montague wrote down what had been said:

Ah, John. He rises to embrace me, on both cheeks. His eyes are watery but briefly bright: It was good of you to come. How's the leg? And solicitous, he starts to shuffle, and, like one of his own characters, intent on finding me a place to sit.

And how are you?

I'm done. Again the eyes focus on me, and I am astounded, as always, by their large size, like blue marbles. But waiting now, not watchful. I'm done. But it lasts such a long time. He pauses. Sat with my own father when he was dying. Fight, fight, fight, he said. But I've no fight left.

As if to [contradict] himself he turns towards his second little desk. Now you're here there's a job to be done. He pulls out a cylinder from Poetry Ireland. This Dorgan man, is he all right? Ah, yes, your name is on the masthead.

Baffled, he wrestles with the vellum, as I set out the small black ink bottle, & the shining nib. Finally, I held down the furling corners of the paper, and he strove to write what would be his last writing.

That done, we relax a little afterward. I got your new book. I see you sent it to me. The prose is good.

I didn't [dare] ask what he thought of the context but I did mention something he told me. Is it true you are dictating something autobiographical?

Ah, no, no, just tidying up the letters. Getting things straight … And only the professional details, nothing personal.

And where do you want to be when you go? Who's looking after things, the other things.

Edward, he's very good. He's in the XXX at the moment. He'll do everything that has to be done. Would you like a drink?

I rise to help but he waves me down, walking across the room again to a cupboard, to come back with a litre bottle of Bushmills malt whiskey. He splashes it out and leaves the bottle beside me.

And where do you want to be?

Ah, Montparnasse. With the wife. We knew each other for fifty years. We played tennis together when we met. And then after the stabbing she came back. Ah, yes, with the wife.

Thoughts tumble through my head. Shall I ask him again what he thinks about [love and fxxx?] I have another whiskey and [mention] the funeral of a former friend.

No, I didn't go. A bit of sharpness ... I took that as my cue for silence. He shows me the books he has been reading, old friends, *The Oxford Book of Irish Verse*, *The Penguin Book of English Verse*.

... I was reading Keats's 'Ode to a Nightingale' again. It's very beautiful.

I never heard him use that word beautiful, except in connection with Yeats. I mention that to him, and he nods.

Yes, yes, beautiful too. Have some whiskey.

He will not let me pour. I watched both my parents die ...

We sit together for what is clearly the last time.

I'm done, he said again, reflectively. And to my astonishment, tries a stave of an old Protestant hymn. Do you know that one? I have to join in, as a Catholic, lack of knowledge of the words does not help my share of the duet. We limp to a halt. I rise to go. We have been over an hour together. I help to tidy the desk, [illeg] He stands up.

Ah, John. He kisses me. We both kiss each other's cheeks, for the second time. Hail and farewell.

I do not look back.

Every phrase of the conversation was worth recording; what Beckett says has a sort of 'last words' sanctity. Just weeks later, on 22 December, he died. *The Guardian* asked Montague to write the obituary. He offered an entirely personal memoir, his own encounters with Beckett, a reverie composed amidst his own grief. He managed just one summary statement: 'Withal, he seemed to me deeply Irish, with his control masking volatile swings of mood from unshakable gloom about the human condition through ferocity at any surrender to lower standards; and underlying all, the quick redeeming flash of humour, the sudden surge of generosity.'[23]

6

In February 1990, back in the deep snows of Albany, Montague rang and asked me to visit. I found him annotating an article from the 28 January 1990 *Sunday Independent*, a sensationalist Dublin newspaper. The article was based on an interview by Sandra MacLiammoir, a young journalist, with Evelyn Montague in the 'Living and Leisure' section of the paper. The focus of the story – at least at its start – was the recent success of Evelyn's work as a textile artist. She had had a show the previous August at Riverrun Gallery in Limerick that was favourably reviewed by Hilary Pyle, the doyen of Irish art historians, and in December she staged an exhibition of French quilts at the Crawford Gallery in Cork.[24] However, the subheading of the *Sunday Independent* article, in large print at the top, was about her husband: 'It is amazing how much poets attract groupies.'[25]

The interviewer drew Evelyn into confidences about the mercantile provincialism of people in Cork. The Parisian explained that she had been able to introduce a bit of sophistication to the city. In Cork she was sometimes blamed for John having divorced, but that was not her fault. At the time of their getting together, she explained, she just thought herself lucky as a literature student to 'snaffle a writer', even if he was pretty old. She herself was 'never comfortable' with his being a divorced man. What had really made her happy at last was the independence she had achieved by virtue of her dedication to her own artistic practice. It gave her a path to equality with her husband. People always wanted to know if she was flattered by being the inspiration of his poetry. Not at all. Maybe for 'about half a day' she was taken with the first one he wrote for her, 'A Dream of July', but after that, she was unmoved. 'It's just someone else's vision, and I don't think men can describe women. It is a good thing that women now write.'

She went on to add that she used to be bothered by groupies, 'spiritually hungry' women, 'usually American'. They even came into her house. And the poets themselves 'like that sort of attention'. Now, however, it was not such a problem for her. John, as he grew older, no longer attracted interest from such women. While marriage as an institution had lasted a long time, she was not sure it had a future: 'Men will have to adjust to women insisting on their rights.

Women will have to achieve them without becoming bullies.' It would be easier, she concluded, if they had not had children.

John thrust the newspaper into my hands. Various sentences were underlined, and comments were scribbled in the margins. He was upset, slightly panicked. He could not wait for me to read the whole article before he started to talk about its contents. How could she do this? It was a betrayal of their private relationship! And not just with one outsider, but in a Sunday newspaper! When I got to the end of the article, it did not seem to me that he was exaggerating. The interview was like a public declaration of divorce. She had to have known that it would hurt him, and she did not care. I asked what Evelyn herself had said to him about the publication. Her explanation was that she had been tricked into confidences. The interview had slipped into being a girl-girl coffee klatch, both of them slagging off men. She was apologetic.

7

The *Sunday Independent* article was part of what was to be a year of reckoning with contemporary Irish feminism. Antoinette Quinn's essay in the Montague issue of the *Irish University Review* (Spring 1989), while warmly appreciative, was too intelligent not to state the limitations, from a feminist perspective, of the poet's 'obsession with the eternal feminine':[26]

> Apart from his resentment at the contemporary feminist's preference for equality of treatment over apotheosis, the bemused poet of 'The Well-Beloved' is markedly ambivalent in his attitude to womanhood. He proclaims himself a worshipper of the female and pays tribute to her strange sorcery; yet he also affirms that the Muse is a male creation – the outcast filial poet's ultimate revenge on matriarchy.

In her round-up review of books by and about Montague in 1989, Eiléan Ní Chuilleanáin, Quinn's TCD colleague, was also respectful of the poetry. She observed that Montague's erotic poems, such as 'Tracks', were not really about sexuality but about 'loneliness and vulnerability'; this was insightful when she might have chosen to be withering. However, she also let fly a zinger that found its target: 'About the politics of private life … what he has to say seems totally contained within a masculine convention which sees the other sex as the cannibal sees his dinner – raw material.'[27]

Montague had a dogged devotion to two historical conventions of poetic inspiration: the Provencal courtly love tradition and the Gaelic genre of the *aisling* (the visionary manifestation of Ireland as a woman). Modern feminist criticism judged both to be sexist and outworn. This climate of opinion inevitably was going to cast its shade over Montague's work. The first thorough-going application of the critique was by a former colleague at UCC, Patricia Coughlan, in her 1991 article '"Bog Queens": Representations of Femininity in the poetry of Seamus Heaney and John Montague'.[28] Although the rhetoric of its Lacanian 'gynocriticism' has dated, the general thrust of the article soon became orthodoxy. Both Heaney and Montague, by imagining the poet as male and the land as female and passive, were deemed responsible for 'oppressive allocations of gender positions'.

8

When Montague gave a talk at McMaster University to the students in Brian John's graduate seminar on 'The Erotic Poetry of John Montague', he might have been (but was not) on his guard about feminist criticism of his love poems. The class turned out to be group of enthusiastic admirers. He became aware of a tall young woman at the far end of the table, 'dark-haired and discreet and smiling, dipping her head like a black swan', as he later wrote. She was Janet Somerville.[29] At the conclusion of the seminar, he asked her and her friend Lauren if they would like to come along to his birthday party in Toronto on 3 March 1990. That was not an occasion they intended to miss.

At the time, Janet Somerville kept a memoir of events. When she arrived at 69 Sullivan Street, Toronto, Barry Callaghan's home, there was a jazz quartet playing. She recognized among the guests various Canadian poets, sculptors and novelists. People gathered to watch Montague blow out the candles on the cake. 'Montague was being ogled by many women (being a birthday boy and all),' she noted, but, plucking up her courage, she approached him. Although at first shy, he soon asked her to dance. She was attracted to him; he was 'bright, sensitive, charming and articulate'. By the end of the evening, the pair were wrapped up in one another on the sofa in the front room, and she found herself unashamedly half-undressed.

A few days later, Montague rang Janet Somerville to ask if she would like to come to a St Patrick's Day party in Albany; he would see what flights were available. On their next telephone call, 6 March 1990, he talked of an upcoming appointment to have the pin removed from his broken leg. On 10 March he rang back to report that the surgery had not gone well; he was back on crutches. Instead of being greeted by Lancelot, he joked, she would have to settle for the Fisher King, the legendary figure whose wounded thigh magically brought barrenness to his lands. Well up on T.S. Eliot's *The Waste Land*, she found the allusion hilarious.

On 16 March Janet Somerville settled into Montague's faculty apartment near SUNY Albany. She worked on her seminar paper while he typed up an article on Barry Callaghan. He reminisced about being lonely in America. When he first came to Yale, he told her, he had been terribly melancholy until he met his first wife, Madeleine. The next day, Phil Brady, an American poet John had taught at UCC, arrived for the weekend. They all went to see the film *My Left Foot* before a heavy-drinking dinner party at Joe and Vera Gagen's. Saturday night Janet got little sleep, 'since John was delighted by my female companionship and not as interested in sleeping as in lovemaking. I certainly can't complain. He is a gentle and compassionate lover despite his doom and gloom moods.'

Those moods partly had to do with anxiety about an upcoming visit by Evelyn. They were trying once again to reconcile, but he was not sure it was possible. Their relationship, he said, had been based on passion, and it had never grown into a warm friendship. He was at ease with Janet; she could tell that he genuinely liked her.

They continued to talk by telephone after her return to Canada. She made reservations to return in ten days, when John said another poet, Derek Mahon, would be in Albany. Barry Callaghan was coming down too, in order to put together a collection of John's love poetry. On this visit, Janet stayed for four days. She wrote in her diary, 'he makes me feel so good about myself'. One morning, she pinned him to the bed. When the two arrived for breakfast with Barry, John joked that no one had ever done to him what she had. Barry exclaimed, 'Did she get you out of the missionary position?'

Figure 62: John Montague and Janet Somerville, Saratoga Springs, New York 25 May 1990.

After John returned to Ireland in June, he wrote Janet a long, warm letter. She was considering a trip to Germany in October, and he said that it was possible he could meet her there. He was joining a delegation of Irish writers (including Nuala Ní Dhomhnaill and Joseph O'Connor) to Pankow, in former East Germany. However, he warned her not to become 'an Emily Hale'. This was another T.S. Eliot reference: Emily Hale was an American love-interest from before Eliot's marriage and, with his encouragement, she kept a flame alight for him for over thirty years, only to be disappointed in the end. Montague added that he was still trying to turn things around in his marriage:

> It is not easy to work or to live without love, or at least respect and affection. I am not saying my wife does not love me but she feels she has to defend herself against me, to the point of hostility. And there is the old psychological problem and patterns of the abused child, which took me so long to understand.

He had begun this reply on 16 June and did not post it until 30 July. He apologized: 'I find it hard these days to write honestly.'[30] It was a tribute to Janet Somerville that he tried to do so. He let down his defences with her; he sensed that she would not hurt him.

9

After August in Mauriac with his family, Montague returned to Ireland. On 28 September 1990 he was awarded the O'Shaughnessy Prize for *The Figure in the Cave*. The family came along to the ceremony at the National Concert Hall. John was delighted that his daughters appeared to be proud of him and told others about it – their pride, not his award.

In October he sent William Kennedy a 'progress report'. That summer in France he thought he might have discovered 'a *modus vivendi* with Evelyn which is not [merely] a stand-off'. She had not been as sharp with him as in the past, and he therefore had 'less reason to drink for the wrong reasons, hurt pride and incomprehension'. He had sobered up, relatively speaking. While he did not see why he should have to 'pay for what her father did to her', what his own mother had done to him had led him to endlessly woo other women.[31] They both carried burdens from childhood that made each a difficult partner.

A December 1990 letter to Janet Somerville returns to this subject. He has continued to try, by not responding to sharp remarks, to keep his marriage on an even keel. Evelyn was practising a similar discipline, learnt from a cognitive therapist: 'consider that your husband might be right in his criticism'.[32] After a pause, taking up again his letter to Janet, John reports there has just been a 'domestic storm'.[33] Perhaps Christmas would ease things, but he was now looking forward to being in New York.

10

In late November Seamus Heaney was in Cork for a performance of his Field Day play *The Cure at Troy*. He left tickets for John and Evelyn at the Everyman Palace Theatre. Afterwards, Seamus sent the family a Christmas postcard of 'The Field of Vision', illustrated by his daughter Catherine, about a woman who 'sat for years/In a wheelchair, looking straight ahead/Out the window at sycamore trees …' 'Face to face with her was an education/Of the sort you got across a well-braced gate.' It might well have reminded Montague of 'The Wild Dog Rose', his own lesson from a cailleach.

Seamus next posted John a typescript of a new poem, 'Wheels within Wheels', with the comment, 'More heavy greenness!' indicating that the poem was a spin-off of 'The Water Carrier', always a fertile gene for replication by the younger poet. It made things easier between the two poets when Heaney privately acknowledged that Montague's work had been a platform for his own.

Although Heaney found Montague a prickly character – 'gilt, jaggy, springy, frilled', like a whin bush – the two enjoyed one another's company during the May 1990 readings at the 92nd Street YMCA in New York.[34] Derek Mahon, Paul Durcan, Nuala Ní Dhomhnaill, Eavan Boland and Paul Muldoon also read at the three-day occasion. The event was another high point for Irish poetry in America.[35]

11

In August 1990 M.L. Rosenthal wrote to Montague asking for a contribution to a special issue of *Ploughshares* dedicated to poetic sequences. In Sally Gall and Rosenthal's *The Modern Poetic Sequence: The Genius of Modern Poetry* (Oxford University Press, 1983), Montague had been treated as a leading light in the form.

In one chapter, *The Rough Field* is examined alongside David Jones's *Anathemata* and Geoffrey Hill's *Mercian Hymns*.

In December Montague sent a section of *Time in Armagh*; Rosenthal was delighted to have it. The publication appears to have spurred the poet to complete the collection.[36] On the back of a letter from the *Ploughshares* editor, he drafted 'Peeping Tom'; on a Christmas circular from the United Arts Club, he began another: 'Did they beat courtesy out of us/As they beat the fear of God into us?' Further progress had to wait for the end of his teaching term in Albany. He typed out a draft of 'Goals' on the back of a May 1991 royalty statement from Mercier Press; and on a 27 May note from an Aix-en-Provence hotel manager, he scribbled an additional stanza for 'Peeping Tom'. On a poster advertising a September 1991 poetry reading in London by Robert Bly, Montague wrote out the opening lines of 'Screwy', concerning schoolboy nicknames. By the summer of 1992 he showed the manuscript of a complete collection to participants in his writing workshop at the Yeats Summer School in Sligo and invited them to respond.[37]

Time in Armagh drags back into the light one scene after another from the painful past – priests spying on boys through a judas hole, beating boys with a leather strap, wringing from boys confessions of masturbation, recruiting favoured boys into their clerical ranks, the bigger boys ganging up on the smaller, the old boys hazing the new ones, the herd picking on boys for their oddities (like a stammer, or a big nose), the hounding by frightened, repressed boys of any boy who showed some sign of tenderness, the secret longing for contact with the gentle spirit of a girl and the loneliness of incarceration.

The book is in verse, but it has something of the breadth and gravity of a public inquiry. The final angry verdict is plainly stated:

> The guilt givers who know what is right,
> they can shove their rules. A system
> without love is a crock of shite.

Generally, reviewers took the book in the right spirit. The poems, as poems, are not landmark achievements, but the volume is 'a deeply felt, serious attempt at truth-telling'.[38] Montague began with a desire to find out about the damage done to his own psyche, but, long before the Ryan Report (2009), *Time in Armagh* exploded the 'culture of self-serving secrecy' in Irish schools run by the Church.

12

In Montague's archive is a transcript of an interview, dated 30 March 1991, with an unnamed Washington DC psychiatrist, a man raised in the 1930s. Their conversation focuses on the feminist critique of the courtly love tradition of poetry. Montague had been distressed to hear the psychiatrist agree with that critique and declare the tradition finished. 'How can I go on?' Montague asked himself. It was not just him and Robert Graves, but poets such as Petrarch, Dante, Shakespeare, Donne and Yeats who belonged to the tradition. They were all inspired by dominant, unpossessable women to undertake a pursuit of beauty that ultimately turned philosophical. To understand the Other, in a spirit of love, was surely every poet's business.

He threw out a theory that there were four methods of experience:
1) Cult of the Warrior.
2) The Slope of Loneliness (O'Rahilly wrote a poem about it), familiar to exiles in the twentieth century: remake your spirit in a hard, lonely place.
3) The Hard Way: you endure the calamities that happen to you. Ramshackledom.
4) The Way that I prefer, the way that I was properly born to, I think, is what we call The Sweet Way.

The Sweet Way, he explained, had existed in the Tantric sects of ancient India and was recorded in the sculptures of the ruined temple at Konarak. 'The expression on those faces, the expressions of these people who indulged in what seem to us quite monstrous actions, was an expression of bliss.' People who love one another, or just feel tenderly towards one another, can, he believed, enter a zone where nothing is forbidden, so long as it is mutually desired:

> In this bed, which is as large as a battlefield, and which is a force-field in which all the energies of disappointment, all the frustrations, all the desires you have are slowly expressed, you are absolved of all things. And you come from this bed, you come from this area of love as refreshed as you would when you were a child and you had a glass of water. You've been reborn through the act of expressing all that was ailing in you.

It is as utopian a conception of human relations as any dreamed of by Gary Snyder or Allen Ginsberg, but it was still animating Montague at sixty-two.

He believed women had now stepped into the warrior class. They wanted to combat the male and gain back territory. He accepted that change was necessary. It would be good for men to give ground. They should become tender, as women had once been. They should cook, spend time with their children, do the laundry, be fully present in the household and drop the burden of being the single earners. But he did not approve of the operations of the new 'thought police' in the universities, who read literary works judgmentally, not in the ways in which they were conceived by their creators, but according to what was now 'politically correct'. By those standards, everyone who had ever been would be condemned.

Still, he did not believe the courtly love tradition was dead; it had simply switched genders. He himself was hearing it revived on the radio in the latest songs by Sinéad O'Connor.

13

Figure 63: Oonagh, Evelyn, and John Montague, Grattan Hill, Cork. Photograph by Barry Callaghan. He is being, in the eyes of Oonagh, funny. Evelyn is sceptical.

In August 1991 while the Montagues were in west Cork, Evelyn had an exhibition in Castletownshend, a haut-bourgeois seaside village. The show was widely covered in the national press as the work of an artist of international reputation, who was practising, according to Evelyn herself, 'the only artistic expression of the Women's Movement'.[39]

One series in the show was called '*Puer in Tenebris*' (Child in Darkness). Evelyn described it as 'an attempt to contemplate the emotions of a damaged childhood, how it really was, and how it lives on'. 'I didn't know how to speak about this (her self, her life, her pain) until I did it with my hands first.'[40]

At these exhibitions John appears to have played the part of proud and supportive husband, keeping out of the limelight. However, one journalist covering the Castletownshend show, the same who interviewed Evelyn in the January 1990 *Sunday Independent*, described him as the artist's 'paramour' (illicit lover, kept man). A correction was demanded, and the newspaper, in fear of a libel suit, printed an apology in which it was stated that John and Evelyn were in fact husband and wife. The wording gave legalistically equal status to the artistic reputations of husband and wife.[41]

Late that autumn Evelyn spotted Aidan Higgins at a party and, according to him, 'hurled accusations' in public. Higgins wrote to Montague to protest: 'I believe we are dealing here with imaginary slights, perhaps the most dangerous kind. At all events it has nothing to do with me.' He assumed that long ago, in Seamus Heaney's house, the two had settled their 'tiff'. Now Aidan 'would be most obliged if you would ask [Evelyn] to desist in future'.[42] It is a strange request – one man asking another to instruct his wife to shut up.

Whatever the private troubles between John and Evelyn, they were still publicly standing up for one another as husband and wife. John replied by not just defending Evelyn, but redoubling her critique of Higgins. Several drafts of the letter are in the archive:

> My wife's accusations were not preposterous, as you say, but accurate, although vehemently phrased. You know well that I have been encouraging and friendly towards you over the years, from *The Dolmen Miscellany* (that famous first chapter, accompanied by a very positive review, to create a context for same). Whether in Dublin or in Paris, I doubt if you remember an unfriendly word on my part! I assumed we were, as the French say, *confrères*, with different literary

ambitions but a common cause in which I was glad to give you what little help I could.

When we arrived in Muswell Hill that evening, we were high and happy: we had discovered that morning that Evelyn was pregnant ....

You say that you were on speed and booze but your attack on me was prolonged and detailed, as if you had been spoiling for a long time (I was dimly aware that there was some tension on your side, because of a resemblance to some brother of yours, and also perhaps because of the running around poets do, in the hope of reaching some kind of paying audience. But nothing serious.)

Evelyn actually begged me to leave as the aggression grew, but I could not believe my ears. Finally you said that 'if someone had said to you what you'd been saying to me', you'd have hit them. Whereupon, with a total reversal of logic, you struck me in the face, and Evelyn says, reached for a bottle. Donal O'Farrell was an unwilling witness to all this and tried to stop you. Evelyn persuaded the neighbours not to call the police which she now regrets. You were in a very violent mood, and might well have done harm if I had responded in kind.

You apologised for the incident chez Heaney (but not for going to my first wife in Paris to get money for gossip about myself and Evelyn!). Since then I have seen no indication of change, only a continuing obsession. At Evelyn's opening in Castletownshend you boasted to my friend, Professor Gerry Wrixon, about beating me up and offered to show how it was done. Fisticuffs at forty is bad enough; over sixty it seems pathetic. And professionally you never lost a chance to do me down. Your review of *The Lost Notebook* was unprofessional in its tone, a contrast to my scrupulous dealings with you. But why go on? I have no rancour against you whatsoever although I remain justifiably wary. Years ago I learnt boxing at school in order to ward off bullies but I observe over the years that I seemed to lack aggression. It takes a lot to rile me.

Did it actually, as he says here, take a lot to rile Montague? Or Aidan Higgins? The epistolary exchange ended in a stand-off.

14

For St Patrick's Day in 1992 the Writers Institute organized a reading at Page Hall in the downtown Albany campus, with Montague reading alongside Eiléan Ní

Chuilleanáin and Nuala Ní Dhomhnaill. I was present in the vast auditorium. It was not full, but there were plenty in the audience. Both women, according to Nuala, were annoyed at having to divide the first half of the programme between themselves, before Montague took up the second half with recitations from the newly published *Love Poems*.[43] I winced when from the podium Montague spoke of the guest poets as two of his many UCC students who had made good. Not only was this a lame attempt to appropriate the success of the two women for his own glory, it was not true. Eiléan Ní Chuilleanáin grew up in Cork, but she was long gone by the time Montague came to the city. As for Nuala Ní Dhomhnaill, Montague had in fact been helpful to her over the years (for instance, he took a weekend to give advice on how to structure the contents of her first collection), but she was in UCC only a short time before leaving for eight years in Turkey, so his statement was not exactly true of her either. Montague's splashy, nervous egotism on the podium spoiled the goodwill created by his invitation to two women poets to come all the way from Ireland for the reading. Often, Montague acted with natural grace; at other times he did not.

During a Sunday visit to Montague's faculty apartment not long after that reading, John showed me a long letter he had received from Nuala Ní Dhomhnaill. He was astonished – it was a diatribe. Nuala said his Irish was poor (deepest of insults from a *gaeilgeoir*). What's more, she wrote, it was nonsense for him to claim there had been a long tradition of poetry by women in Ireland. Even 'The Lament for Art O'Leary' was just an oral keen; Eibhlín Dubh Ní Chonaill had never put pen to paper. And Montague had not been much help to Nuala's own career, which was now flying. Her best translators were from the North, particularly Paul Muldoon.

While it seemed to me clearly the letter of a woman breaking loose from patriarchy, I did not at the time dare tell John that although what she said was impolite, he had it coming after his comments in Page Hall.

15

In April 1992 Montague was on a reading tour organized by the Irish-American poet Sabra Loomis. One engagement was on 3 April, at a venue in Manhattan managed by the crime novelist Walter Mosley.[44] Beforehand, Mosley rang a young friend, Elizabeth Wassell (who had a degree in writing from City College), to ask if she would help out by serving drinks at the after-party. According to Elizabeth's recollection, John came into the room laughing and spreading laughter around him. She instantly liked the look of the man.

When he came up to the bar, she told him she would be his Ganymede for the evening and 'replenish his flagons'. Her hair was short; thirty five years old, she had an attractively boyish look and was obviously bright. Next to him, she was tiny. When he asked for it, she was glad to give him her telephone number.

They agreed to meet on Easter Sunday evening. Over drinks at an Irish bar on 2nd Street, she told him hers was a bookish disposition. He explained that he was married, but the marriage had grown bitter; his wife battered him. Elizabeth herself had been married twice, once to the son of a real-estate magnate and once to a rock-and-roll musician. That second marriage ended in 1987. She had since then pursued her ambition to become a writer.

The next day John was off to read at Emory University. He rang Elizabeth every night. He admitted to being already half in love with her. They met next in Toronto, at the launch of *The Love Poems*. They stayed together at Barry Callaghan's home and reunited in Toronto on other weekends that spring. She wrote to John on 6 May after returning to NYC, tucking into the letter her repayment of a loan:[45]

> Here's your five bucks, you big dumb parsimonious Irish cluckhead. There, I've been caustic – which I think earns me the right to be romantic in this paragraph. I miss you so dreadfully, I am all yearning and loneliness ....

Over the summer and autumn, Elizabeth took transatlantic flights to meet John in Caen, in Paris, in Rome and in Ireland at summer schools. He told her, 'perplexedly', 'it seems to be you, and no one else'.

In January 1993 when John returned to Albany, Elizabeth moved into his faculty apartment. At first, she recalled, John thought he could manage a double life, with wife and daughters in Cork, and his 'congenial girlfriend' everywhere else. Gradually, they realized that a double life was not a life enriched, but a life torn in pieces.

Elizabeth's mother was a psychiatrist, and Elizabeth sought her advice. Elizabeth explained that she loved John, but he had had many girlfriends and was an errant husband. To give herself to him was a big risk. Dr Wassell said she should put the case to him honestly and say that she would go with him in life only on terms of mutual fidelity. Over lunch at Stuyvesant Plaza in Albany, Elizabeth asked if he would commit to their being a monogamous couple. He thought about it a moment, then agreed.

Some months afterwards, Elizabeth came to understand from John that he and Evelyn had come to an agreement to separate. That may not have been so clearly settled as she was given to believe. John had had a hard time finally leaving Madeleine, even under constant pressure to do so from a young Evelyn. It was not easy for him to end a long-standing relationship. No doubt, he was loath to leave his daughters behind.

Montague often rewrote the poem 'The Leap', about, as a boy, after many feints, taking a running jump across the Garvaghey river and landing safely on the other side.[46] The poem celebrates a successful leap, but it also registers the anxiety that comes from having landed on earlier attempts in the wet slime and sharp rocks of the streambed and then coming home to his aunts with his clothes in a shameful state. He was worried about taking the final jump.

Figure 64: Elizabeth Wassell and John Montague in Florida, March 1993.

In August Evelyn and the girls took the boat to Roscoff, France; John was to meet them there. However, when Evelyn arrived, John was not in Roscoff, but 130 kilometres away in a village close to St-Malo. Oonagh and Sibyl had come down with measles, so Evelyn had to leave them with a childminder while she went to collect John. She was angry at having had to make the long drive; he was disagreeable too. The holiday was unhappy. Later, Donnchadh Ó Corráin's wife tattled to Evelyn that the UCC historian had seen John with a young woman on the ferry to France. Evelyn found letters from Elizabeth to John. One, signed 'Pixie', said he ought to know how to manage his domestic obligations and to see her at the same time.[47] The two women in John's double life were heading for a collision.

In September 1993 Elizabeth booked into a bed and breakfast opposite Kent Station, just down the hill from Grattan Place. Evelyn was in Paris at the time, so John was able to visit freely; less so, after Evelyn returned. Elizabeth understood lawyers to be working on the separation agreement. Evelyn was to get Grattan Place and its contents; John would have the house in Ballydehob. Evelyn would get his UCC pension until he turned seventy. The bank balance would go to Evelyn; he would have to live off current earnings.

On 22 October, the opening day of the Cork Jazz Festival, Evelyn collected John from the municipal swimming pool and told him that she wished to be introduced to Elizabeth, about whom she was well aware. She dropped John at Elizabeth's B&B and said she would meet them in the pub. The two lovers entered like 'chastened children'. They had been behaving in a furtive way, but they had not been successfully secretive. Everyone was in pain.

In the pub Evelyn was soft-spoken. She would never break down, she said; she was a lady. She upbraided John for sleeping with a previous girlfriend in the marital bed. That was to let Elizabeth know what to expect from him in future. She warned Elizabeth that there would always be other women, and he would 'always be divisive about them'.[48] Then Evelyn told John she wanted him to leave the family home and leave Cork too.[49] It was an elegant dismissal.

In the following days and weeks, Evelyn allowed her anger to have its course. She put John's things out of the house onto the front steps. Cork was well notified of the scandal. John and Elizabeth found refuge in various places – Tom and Cathy McCarthy's home, then in one or another B&B, before flying off to Poitiers for a literary festival. Their life for some time was distracted and peripatetic, from one reading or launch to another. They imagined themselves as like Diarmuid and Gráinne, lovers in flight from wrath, sleeping each night in a different bed.

On 27 November 1992 John came to Galway in fulfilment of a promise to launch Mary O'Malley's second book of poems. He told Mary how delighted he was that her book was so good. This was not just *plámás*, Irish flattery; he had said the same before to Elizabeth. At their joint reading, John stopped after a few minutes – 'I'm reading badly tonight,' he explained. 'I know why, but I won't go into it.'[50]

The couple stayed on in Galway at Frenchville House, Grattan Road. John had come down with a urinary tract infection, caused by an inflamed prostate. He was referred to the hospital for a biopsy. The couple waited for the news, which, when it came at last, indicated no cancer.

At New Year the writer-broadcaster David Hanly and his companion Yvonne collected John and Elizabeth from Mary O'Malley's care and drove them to Renvyle House, Oliver Gogarty's former home on the Connemara coast, now a hotel. John kept a file of Hanly's columns from the *Sunday Tribune*, scores of them; he loved his work. John and Elizabeth seemed 'shell-shocked' in Galway, Hanly remarked. It had been John's first Christmas apart from Oonagh and Sibyl. Having forgotten all about Letter Cottage, they felt themselves to have no home in the world. Rather than being ecstatic at being at last together, they felt lost and distraught.

Evelyn was publicly working through her anger at the split-up. She wrote to common friends in west Cork to request that they not cut her off. She made a long-distance call to the wife of the director of the SUNY Writers Institute to express outrage at her complicity in John's affair.[51] She contacted the people whom she knew mattered most to John to tell them about his disgraceful conduct – his Aunt Eileen in New York City, Madeleine in Paris and Seamus Montague in County Fermanagh. She did not want him to be able to hide from what he had done. The waves of distress were spreading far and wide.

16

John knew that his very Catholic brother Seamus was bound to be disappointed at this development in his life – not just one divorce but two! And the desertion of his long-sought children. Would Seamus ever be able to forgive him? John might wind up with effectively no brother at all.

John's concern about the reaction of Seamus Montague caused him to finally complete a poetic sequence begun many years before, *Border Sick Call*. The essential scenario of the poem – the speaker alongside his medic brother, a snowy landscape, a remote farmhouse in which lay an ailing man, a dog barking –

was sketched in January 1963.[52] In the early 1970s Montague started collecting clippings from newspapers of snow-covered villages and farms in Ireland. In March 1973 he managed a stanza about the feeling of bewilderment that falls upon the two men as they pass through a snowy, liminal borderland. Then in October 1974 he began to treat the subject in a dreamlike narrative form. By that date, he had the title fixed. When Seamus retired from his medical practice, John considered trying to finish the sequence in time for the honorary dinner, 5 November 1986. Ultimately it took the fresh impetus of concern for the survival of his relationship with Seamus for John to complete the poem in February 1994 amid the heavy snows of Albany, New York.

On 24 February John wrote Seamus Montague a chatty letter accompanying a fair copy of *Border Sick Call*.[53] He asked if there were any corrections that needed to be made, and whether or not Seamus would allow John to dedicate the poem to him. The letter did not mention his parting from Evelyn. In the long run the poem failed to bring about genuine forgiveness on the part of Seamus for John's un-Catholic behaviour.

This is the last major sequence in Montague's work. He sent it off to James Olney, editor of *The Southern Review*. Olney immediately recognized its value: 'it is a tremendous poem, really terrific, and I cannot thank you enough for sending it to us'.[54] The border was of course a Republican shibboleth. The actuality of the division of the country in 1920 had a baleful effect upon the lives of Northern Catholics. But in this poem, those unmentioned political realities are made to appear small, because the poem ascends to high, snowy metaphysical places, where this earth and human mortality stand out vividly in themselves as ultimate facts. In that respect, it is very much a Good Friday Agreement poem ahead of its time. The sequence was one of Eiléan Ní Chuilleanáin's favourites:[55]

> If at first we saw the poem as a glittering snowy presence, its light and colour John Montague's favourite monochrome, its surface reflecting scraps of the landscape of Irish poetry (and prose and translation) of its time, we could also hear in it echoes that prompted listening for another note, the noise of geological time which speaks in the poet's ear often at the most human moments: 'a gross carapace sliding down the face of Europe ... bequeathing us ridges of stone, rubble of gravel, eskers of hardness: always within us – a memory of coldness'.

But more turns of narrative, as satisfactory as a romance revelation, awaited: the vision of the boat in the descent, the sudden gracious intrusion of the hare, before the doctor's grim account of rural death, his almost proverbial summation 'the real border is not between/ countries, but between life and death.' There is another border in the poem, between the known and the mystery.

Of the *navicella* the poet asks 'Why could I not see it on the way/ up, only on the journey home', and leaves the word 'home' twanging like a question to match the acceptance of limit in the final section: 'how little we know of each other! ... in what country have we been?'

A few years earlier, after a consultation with Dillon Johnston about the shape of his *Collected Poems* (published in 1995), Montague had wondered whether he ought now to shut up shop, quoting Patrick Kavanagh: 'Old cunning silence might be a better bet than poetry.'[56] It was not possible to continue his autobiography in poetry because *Home Truths* was unpublishable. Furthermore, the critical climate for male muse-poets was poisonous. Maybe, he thought, his work was done, and he should henceforth stay shtum. It is a good thing that Montague, pressed by urgent emotional demands, brought *Border Sick Call* to a conclusion. It is an honourable addition to his lifework.

17

On 18 February 1995, a year after the completion of *Border Sick Call*, John and Elizabeth were again in the faculty apartment at SUNY Albany, when Gerry Wrixon called in the middle of the night.[57] He had been contacted by the staff of a Dublin hospital. Evelyn had 'taken a turn'. At a quilting workshop in Navan she had stumbled, fallen and lay in need of assistance. Brought by ambulance to Beaumont Hospital, it was deemed necessary to relieve the pressure on her brain and then to do surgery to repair the aneurysm. The extent of the damage could not yet be determined.

The surgery was successful, but then Evelyn contracted septicaemia; her life was again at risk. She overcame that affliction and was moved to Cork University Hospital; and after a time to a rehabilitation clinic. Her left side remained partially paralyzed, a catastrophe for a handicraft artist.

From the time he received the telephone call, John was in torment about whether or not to fly back to Ireland. Some Cork friends admonished him to 'return to your wife'. Divorce still being illegal in Ireland, though formally separated, that was what Evelyn remained to him, his wife. He was told that Oonagh, just twenty-two, required his support during the crisis. Of course she did. The responsibility for decision-making during the whole crisis had fallen on her. Oonagh herself said, reportedly, that John was the last person her mother wanted to see. Elizabeth did not want him to go.[58] In the end, John waited until the end of the semester to return to Ireland.

When he did return, John called to see Evelyn. Her first words to him were 'You did this to me.'[59]

John entertained hypotheses that an abnormally fragile blood vessel to her brain was responsible for Evelyn's bouts of wrath, or that the wrath was responsible for the thinness of the blood vessel, which had finally burst. Both his theory and Evelyn's for why she had suffered a stroke are at the least unscientific; however, they do indicate the monstrously powerful emotions set off by this medical crisis. Guilt and anger ruled the day.

18

Early that summer Peter Fallon and Dillon Johnston, Montague's Irish and American editors, came to Ballydehob to work on the contents and design for the *Collected Poems*. John's initial preference was a book including all the poems in chronological order. Fallon thought a better collection would drop the weakest poems and lead off with the three great long poems: *The Rough Field*, *The Great Cloak* and *The Dead Kingdom*, which make up a nearly continuous story. Thereafter, poems from the remaining volumes could be printed in chronological order.

Elizabeth made a few suggestions. One was to insert 'The Huntsman's Apology' into the first section of *The Great Cloak*, to illustrate the casual cruelty of the libertine male. To the third section, about the early days of his union with Evelyn, 'Plea' was added, to temper the idealizations and take account of the troubles that in historical terms lay ahead for the marriage.[60]

Pat Mantle, a local photographer, shot the black-and-white portrait of Montague on the cover, standing on a misty Letter Road, Ballydehob, next to a big whin bush, with Mount Gabriel in the background.

There was a very quick turnaround between the agreement on contents and the publication of the volume. In the first week of October John and Elizabeth went up to Dublin for the launch. When they walked down Dawson Street, copies of the *Collected Poems* filled the windows of Hodges Figgis on the left and Waterstone's on the right. They returned to the Shelbourne Hotel to have a celebratory drink. At the bar, Elizabeth ran into John Hurt's partner, Sarah Owens. She said, 'Have you heard the news? Seamus Heaney has been awarded the Nobel Prize.' John took it calmly, but it was terrible news for him. When the two went back down Dawson Street, all the copies of the *Collected Poems* had been removed from the display windows, to make room for titles by Seamus Heaney.

By the time RTÉ broadcaster Mike Murphy dedicated an episode of the *Arts Show* to the *Collected Poems*, Montague had pulled himself together. In the meantime, Heaney had written John a note regretting the timing of the prize but reassuring John that his achievement would never be 'washed away'.[61] John had his answer ready when the predictable question came:

> Mike Murphy: Did you feel that your thunder was somewhat stolen by Seamus Heaney's Nobel Prize?
>
> JM: No, no, you have to take the long view. I've had to take the long view all my life, since I was four. When a green wave comes like that, the big boats get lifted up, but the little boats get swamped .... We have an extraordinary situation in Ireland. I said this once to Seamus. He was trying to define the situation in Ireland. I said not since the Elizabethan age have so many people been writing well.

John went on to name a number of the women poets he admired – Biddy Jenkinson, Nuala Ní Dhomhnaill, Paula Meehan and Eiléan Ní Chuilleanáin. It was the right thing to say at the time.

The coincidence of Heaney's prize with the publication of his own life's work was nightmarishly bad timing. As a result, Montague's *Collected Poems* did not get the attention it would otherwise have received. In July 1996 John told Seamus Heaney he might give the poetry a rest for a while.[62]

What a year – the traumatic separation from his children, Evelyn's stroke, the disastrous launch of his *Collected Poems*, the crisis in the relationship with his surviving brother. Adversity had not fallen on him alone. Evelyn's hardship and that of his children outweighed his own misfortune. It was a hard time for a man of his years.

14

THE YEARS IN NICE AND VAGABONDING
WITH ELIZABETH

1

'What do you think of Elizabeth?' Derek Mahon asked me. We were driving over the mountains between Troy, New York and Williamstown, Massachusetts, in order to take in the Clark Art Institute.

'I like her. He needs someone to look after him. Evelyn doesn't want to do it anymore.' Derek laughed (he also needed someone to look after him). I added, 'He's getting old – he doesn't cook, can't drive, wants company all the time. And she loves him. He likes that. She can't drive either, or cook, but that doesn't matter. He wants love.'

Derek asked if I had read Elizabeth's draft novel, *The Honey Plain* (1997). I hadn't known anything about it. Derek expected it would not go down well in Ireland. Apart from treating divorce with levity, the main problem was that Evelyn would be taken as the original of the raging wife in the story. Elizabeth had promised Derek to do another draft.

2

In January 1997 I came along to the performance in Albany by Billie Whitelaw in a production of Samuel Beckett's *Not I*, just the mouth of the actress moving in a hole in the curtain and a spotlight on it in a theatre otherwise entirely black. She gave a heart-shaking performance. I did not tag along afterwards with John, Elizabeth, Billie Whitelaw and others as they went for dinner and drinks.

Billie Whitelaw as an actress had been a muse figure for Beckett, sometimes his lover too. It had been a little more than seven years since the playwright's death. Billie and John had a lot to talk about. Following the dinner, she wrote John a letter that caused a good deal of worry to Elizabeth. It included the phrase, 'Let's talk about sex.' John explained to Elizabeth that he did not have a history with Billie Whitelaw. That only suggested to Elizabeth that the actor thought she might have a future with him.

Elizabeth faced into the matter without anger and wrote out her thoughts to John.[1] She had not forgotten Evelyn's warning that there would always be other women and that John would use them in a 'divisive' manner. Elizabeth did not believe that had to be the case. Nonetheless, she was troubled by something that had happened at a party hosted by filmmaker John Boorman at his home in County Wicklow. Garech Browne had been treating his girlfriend Valentine badly. John tried to comfort her, and Valentine responded by sitting on his lap, right in front of Elizabeth. John may have laughed, but his merriment was hurtful to Elizabeth and the harm was not just from another woman, but also from John himself; he disregarded her feelings. He might feel 'obliged to rescue, to protect women, as a kind of penance, for hurting your mother and then being exiled from her', but he 'should consider that impulse in yourself'. If he was going to respond to every offering by a woman, their future together was in trouble. The unrelenting frankness and intelligence of this response gave John a lesson he needed to learn. He had linked himself permanently not only to a woman who loved him but to a highly skilled psychotherapist on duty twenty-four hours a day.

3

In May 1997 when John and Elizabeth returned to Ballydehob, the poet and college professor Philip Brady and his girlfriend Linda were already there. Brady was on sabbatical from Youngstown State University in Ohio. He had met John in 1975 while on a Junior Year Abroad at UCC and again in 1983 when he returned with a plan to do a doctorate on Heaney and Montague, while supporting himself as a semi-professional basketball player. Neither leg of the plan held up, but Brady got to know the Cork poets and took an informal tutorial in modern poetry with Montague in his attic study. Sometimes Philip babysat for the two girls, either at Grattan Hill or in Ballydehob. When John began to spend winters in Albany in the later 1980s, Philip was doing a PhD at SUNY Binghamton, not much more than an hour's drive away. John remained a helpful mentor.

One day in 1997 John brought Philip to Levis, a grocery store and pub in Ballydehob run by two sisters, Nell and Julia. As they sat with their drinks, John asked Philip, 'Who are your contemporaries?' By way of explanation, John said that when he himself was finding his feet as a poet in America[2]

> 'You had your New York poets – Ashbery and Merrill and O'Hara and that crowd due east ... And [Langston] Hughes in Harlem and Williams just beyond.' He thumbed two creamy circles on the bar. 'And Bishop up north in the woods ... and Lowell ... up in Cambridge.
>
> 'Then you had the Chicago gangs,' he tapped a matchbox ... 'Lee and Brooks and the other ones – Kunitz and Reznikoff – the Objectivists. And above,' he pointed toward the bar's laurelled mirror, 'there was that mad Protestant farmer Robert Bly and the Ohio footballer James Wright with their Deep Image.
>
> 'In the middle, the Iowa bowsers ... top-guns flown in from everywhere by Henry Pussycat ... Down here,' he snapped a pound coin on the bar, 'the Southern gentry – Penn Warren, Tate and Ransom.
>
> 'And out there,' he continued, 'The rebels and mumbo-jumbo mystics, Reed and Duncan, Rexroth, Snyder and Ginsberg – with one ear cocked to Nirvana and the other to Gotham.'

The poetry world had changed, Philip thought. There was no longer a single story of American poetry, even one that was very complex; nor could it be mapped; and the whole idea of a Parnassus was gone, one person higher than another.

Brady had a small used car, and he piloted it through the narrow lanes of west Cork as the two couples went on adventures in the area. In mid-summer he brought John and Elizabeth all the way up to Falcarragh, County Donegal, where John was to be in residence at the Poets' House, a kind of summer school for international creative-writing students, run by James Simmons and his third wife, Janice Fitzpatrick.

In the first week of August Montague went from Donegal to the William Carleton Summer School in the Clogher Valley, just over the hill from Garvaghey, County Tyrone. Montague loved staying at the Corick House Hotel and Spa above the River Blackwater. Parts of the house went back to the seventeenth century. The place now had a pool, a restored walled garden and pleasant walks. He became an annual presence at the Carleton school.

John and Elizabeth went west to Sligo for the Yeats Summer School, then south to open the Kerry International Summer School in Tralee. In some sense this was a book tour, since the *Collected Poems* was still in its first year of publication and Elizabeth's novel *The Honey Plain* had been released, but such peregrinations also became the pattern of John and Elizabeth's summers. Normally they would attend the Poet's House, the Carleton School and a few other summer schools. They both enjoyed the hospitality, the social whirl and the company of writers and scholars.

At the beginning of September 1997 the finalists for the Irish Literature Prize in Poetry were announced in *The Irish Times*: the selected poems of Paul Muldoon, the collected poems of Eavan Boland and Montague's *Collected Poems*. Books by Kinsella and Heaney did not even make the shortlist. It was not a jury any critic would want to be on. Two poets who deserved to win were going to lose whoever was selected. At the end of the month the judges declared the winner to be Paul Muldoon. Peter Fallon tried to put a good face on the result: 'I've known all along that the choice of your *Collected Poems* as the winner would have been the least surprising outcome.'[3] Montague had believed that he would be the sentimental favourite. His book was the work of a whole lifetime; the other two were updates on the progress of poets in their prime. Muldoon himself took this view of the matter and wished the prize had gone to the older poet.[4] Coming exactly a year after Heaney's Nobel Prize cleared copies of Montague's *Collected Poems* out of the shop windows, the loss hurt.

4

In June 1997 Elizabeth's novel *The Honey Plain* was published by Wolfhound Press. The launch at Waterstone's in Dublin, with David Hanly doing the introduction, drew a large crowd. Tony Cronin and Anne Haverty, Paula Meehan and Theo Dorgan, John Hurt and Sarah Owens and Derek Mahon were all there; the room was crowded with people in second relationships.[5]

In an interview with the *Irish Examiner*, the Cork newspaper, Elizabeth stressed that while the novel might appear to be autobiographical – since she, like its heroine, was an American living in Ireland and her partner, like its hero Dermot, was a lot older – really Dermot was based on herself more than anyone else. It was fiction, not memoir. This was an excellent phosphorous flare or countermeasure, because it could be anticipated that incoming missiles would be fired at the author for making light of real people's personal lives. Ireland's definition of the libellous is far broader than that in America.

The Honey Plain is a bit like Kingsley Amis's *Lucky Jim* and David Lodge's *Changing Places* in being a witty novel about academics behaving badly, although in her case the campus novel genre is married to a serious romance plot from a woman's point of view. It begins with Professor Dermot O'Duffy, an expert on love in medieval literature, coming to Galway to give a lecture on 'The Feminine Voice in Early Irish Poetry'. He is in flight from an unhappy marriage to Fiona. At his B&B is a young American apprentice painter, Grania, daughter of a US senator. He almost unconsciously begins to flirt with her. At the conference, while people are having drinks before his talk, Dermot discovers that Grania is employed behind the bar, pouring drinks. 'I will be your Ganymede tonight,' is her line. When the time arrives for Dermot to give his talk, he is suddenly nervous:

> It's always the same, Dermot thought, placing his sheets of inky foolscap on the lectern, and looking out at the rustling, expectant crowd. Always this nervousness, sudden shyness, his voice feeling tight and dry as if unconnected to him, always the conviction that he will fail, the whisper, curdled with contempt, in his head (his mother's whisper, he sometimes thought). *So, do you really think you have something valuable to say, to all these people?*

After his talk, a Professor Talon, a woman, attacks Dermot for being a defender of the 'narcissism of the patriarchy' and fostering the oppression of women. She announces the formation of the Sheela-na-Gig Society, to exalt the powers of women.

Following a sleepless night of going over his sorry marriage to Fiona and his betrayals of her, Dermot goes for a walk and runs into Grania, who eventually invites him into her bed. However, he cannot perform, not initially. She tells him of her own early marriage and divorce, then he discovers himself to be ready for love. Dermot's wife Fiona soon shows up in Galway with her father, and with revenge on her mind. She levels some reasonable accusations against Dermot: 'if you have truly devoted your life to love, then why do you trifle with *my* love, why do you abuse it …' Fiona also turns on Grania at the conference hotel:

> 'And you,' she continued in that same curiously fluent voice, as though she were reciting from a play, 'you, whoever you are. You should not have done this thing.' She indicated the spellbound crowd. 'These people are my husband's colleagues, whom he and I often meet, together, but, thanks to you, from now on all such meetings will be – will be *soiled* by humiliation. You have come into this place from another country, intruded into this world which does not belong to you, and you have humiliated me here, where I must live. You have damaged my world by engaging in a public affair with my husband.'

Certainly, a lot of this is fiction, just as some parts came straight from experience, which gives the novel interest to a biographer of John Montague. Elizabeth knew a lot about him, and she is a talented, intelligent writer. That speech by Fiona to Grania – whether or not based on things Evelyn said to Elizabeth – shows a willingness on the part of the writer to state things that from her point of view fall outside the circle of wish fulfilment. Although Patricia Coughlan might have had cause to contact a solicitor over the characterization of 'Professor Talon', the novel gives the betrayed wife Fiona a good outing. Some of the best lines are hers, aimed at the author-surrogate. Overall, one can tell that the novel was written in the damn-the-rest-of-the-world spirit of new love, but it is not utterly irresponsible. As a novel, it survives its *roman-à-clef* origins; it remains a lively book.

5

In October 1996 John and Elizabeth came up to Dublin and at a meeting with Derek Mahon things were said that resulted in a split between the friends. It has remained a mystery just what happened.[6]

On the train up to Dublin John could not help but notice a man in the carriage being very rough with a child – cursing and hitting the little one. Unable to stand for it, John remonstrated with the man, who promptly threatened to batter the ageing poet. There were no train attendants in the carriage. Although things simmered down, the experience left both John and Elizabeth rattled.

Meeting Derek and Tony Cronin for dinner at La Mère Zou on St Stephen's Green, John took to drink to settle his nerves. Derek mentioned that his mother was ill, maybe dying. John was going up to Bangor in Northern Ireland for a literary festival. Why didn't Derek come along? After all, if John could bear to venture into that Orange territory, surely Derek could visit his mother one last time. Derek was indignant: 'I don't mock your people; why do you mock mine!' Derek was so offended, he decided he was done with John and Elizabeth.

Within a month, Derek's mother died. John wrote him a thoughtful letter of condolence and added, 'Whatever misunderstandings may have occurred when we last met, remember that my friendship is still there, to be called upon, if needed, despite seeming differences. We should not be fighting at this time.'[7] Derek relented and met John and Elizabeth again at the Long Bar in the Shelbourne Hotel. Elizabeth remarked that Derek's son Rory had grown up to be a handsome man. John capped this flattery by joking that Doreen had improved the Mahon stock. Derek did not like these jokes about his people, his line, his stock. He beckoned Elizabeth out into the corridor, then said, 'Every time I see John, he says something that annoys the hell out of me. So I will not see him again.'[8]

Derek began gaily telling everyone he was never going to speak to Montague again. I found this strange and told Derek that it was ridiculous to bring an end to such a long friendship over a word spoken in a bar. Derek cut me short. So did John when I asked him what he had said. I was sometimes a witness but never an actor in the story of their lives.

A good while later, Derek, having inherited money from his parents' estate, asked me to dinner in Dublin. He was then living on Fitzwilliam Square. As we were walking along St Stephen's Green, he stopped and said, Let's go down here, and we dropped into a posh restaurant. The reservation, he told the maître d', is in the name of John Montague. He regularly made reservations all over town in Montague's name, Derek said, then picked one or another for his place to dine.

It is impossible to say just what went on in Derek Mahon's mind when, after decades of friendship, he abruptly cut off all contact with John Montague. Was it Montague's drinking (in front of an alcoholic), Elizabeth's novel, Evelyn's stroke, Derek's aversion to his own mother (so very like him, in her rage for order), John's needling sense of humour, the sectarian reference to the Orange suburbs of Belfast, John and Elizabeth's happiness together when he himself was stranded? These are just some possibilities of what may have triggered Derek's flare-up and the 'cutting' of Montague. While he was merry about the fact that he had done so, Derek was sore if you tried to find out why. As I began research for this biography, when I asked about it again, he said, 'You know, Evelyn has had a very hard row to hoe.' My conclusion is that in the parting of friends that occurs on the occasion of any divorce, John having touched a nerve somehow, Derek decided that he was going to side with Evelyn. After his move to Kinsale, Derek remained a friend to Evelyn but never repaired the breach with John.

6

Montague did not give up the practice of poetry in these years. Perhaps Tennyson is relevant:

> But, for the unquiet heart and brain,
> > A use in measured language lies;
> > The sad mechanic exercise,
> Like dull narcotics, numbing pain.

It was the habit of a lifetime to be turning verses; he could not just stop. For the time being, he took up translation.

In 1994 Neil Astley had proposed that Montague complete the version of Eugène Guillevic's *Carnac* that John had begun twenty years earlier for publication in the Bloodaxe Contemporary French Poets series; there would an advance of £1000.[9] Montague accepted the commission, but he then let the project drop until 1997. He had done a first draft in 1971 during a storm at sea, when his ferry from France was trapped in the Devil's Hole off Cornwall. He worked away in the ship's bar with occasional translation help from a French priest.[10] At the time, Montague was inspired by the idea of handling the work 'like a [Robert] Duncan poem', the page as a force field of vector-like phrases.

In 1997 Montague had, courtesy of Bloodaxe, the counsel of Professor Michael Worton of University College London, an expert in French literature. He suggested some changes, but also provided encouragement: 'On the whole [these versions] work very well indeed – and sometimes you took my breath away with the way in which you found/crafted an English phrase that encapsulated all the simple (but oh! so Gallically subtle) weight of Guillevic's French.'[11] The landscape of *Carnac* was sympathetic: the menhirs of Brittany are similar to the dolmens of Ireland, both expressions of Palaeolithic Atlantic seaboard culture. Montague loved the way Guillevic, a mathematician, was able 'to pare things back to an almost inhuman minimum'. That suited his own aesthetic. The finished translation was sent off in January 1998, along with a memoir of his Paris neighbour.

Montague then took up another volume of poems by Guillevic, *Les Murs* (1947), twelve of which had been illustrated by Jean Dubuffet. Montague's chaste and delicate translation would wind up as part of an exhibition of Dubuffet's lithographs by the Hayward Gallery in July 1999. The exhibition produced a fine publication, *Dubuffet's Walls*, with Montague's versions and a commentary by Harry Gilonis. In translating *Carnac* and *Les Murs*, Montague subdued himself to Guillevic's 'mystic materialism' and his 'sparse, gnomic style'.[12]

7

In the late 1990s Montague also put together a volume of memoirs. At first he called this his 'Lives of Poets' book; it was ultimately published as *Company: A Chosen Life* (2001).[13] He intended the volume to be the first in a trilogy, but the first part was never written. That volume was intended to deal, as Frank McCourt had done in *Angela's Ashes* (1996) with the hardships of an Irish childhood.[14] A second volume came out in 2007 from Liberties Press (Dublin) as *The Pear is Ripe*.

Company focused on literary life in the fifties and sixties in Dublin, Paris and Berkeley, California. Montague started off with a number of pieces he had already written for newspapers or magazines, particularly his recollections of Brendan Behan, Mrs George Yeats, Samuel Beckett and Theodore Roethke. He also had ready to hand a large back-catalogue of his book reviews of authors who appear in the memoirs. In stitching these pieces together, he introduced the theme of a young man, who having grown up mostly without parents or his brothers, then sought out father-figures in the older writers he admired, such as Austin Clarke and Samuel Beckett and older-brother surrogates in mentors like Thomas Parkinson. No effort was made to keep track of chronology, or to provide a continuous narrative of his own life, although the book includes a friendly soft-focus portrait of Madeleine. Reviewers were sometimes taken aback by all the famous people Montague writes about, as if he were just a braggart, but the book, particularly for an autobiography, is not self-promotional. It is about other people, not about himself. Overall, *Company* is kindly to his companions; it never flirts with libel.

Published in hardback by Duckworth in 2001 as a part of a two-book deal, *Company* was praised in major daily newspapers. However, the publisher began to go bankrupt in 2001, stopped paying its staff, closed its New York office and ultimately sold its list to another publisher, Overlook Books.[15] The second part of Montague's deal was dropped.

8

In February 1998 the Ireland Chair of Poetry was set up as a cross-border initiative between the two Arts Councils and three universities: Trinity, UCD and Queen's. A three-year post with residencies rotating between the universities was advertised. Each of the universities prepared a list of candidates. After twenty-five years in existence, the rotating Ireland Chair may now have come to seem, while still a great honour, just a spectacular turnstile. For the first occupant, it came with novelty as well as prestige. No one could have been happier to get it than John Montague. It made up for many second-place finishes. It was a major life event for him.

On 26 April 1998, just back in Ballydehob from Albany (to which, sigh of relief, he need not return), John wrote to thank Seamus Heaney, a member of the adjudicating panel. Another one to thank was Donnell Deeny QC, the chairman of the Northern Ireland Arts Council and chairman of the Board of Trustees of the Ireland Chair of Poetry. Announced a month after the Good Friday Agreement, the new All-Ireland post seemed a herald of a better century to come.

In his published remarks on the presentation of the award, Heaney recalled that he began reading Montague's work in 1962 and 1963, the same years in which he first tried to write poems of his own. That acknowledgement was profoundly satisfying to the older poet. At the same time Heaney registered the characteristics that made him associate Montague with a whin bush:[16]

I first met John in person, under the sponsoring eye of Mary and Pearse O'Malley in their house on Derryvolgie Avenue, and felt the reach of that long bony arm across my shoulder, and felt also the test and flush of his giddy, goading intelligence. Ten years older, farther travelled, more widely published, he arrived on the scene like a combination of talent scout and poetic D.I., a kind of government inspector from the government of tongue sent in by the *aos dana* of the day, that body of unacknowledged legislators legislating for all they were worth from Monaghan to McDaid's, from rue Daguerre to Baggot Street Deserta. But there is no need to wax nostalgic about those days: they generated intensity and energy and edge, a combination of circumstances that has continued through the decades and done us all good as individual poets.

A sharp acknowledgement of Montague's sharpness, it is a very Ulster congratulation, humorous and not unfriendly.

John and Elizabeth happened to be in my house in Galway on 15 August. He was in top form with his laureateship. News then arrived of the Omagh bombing. John turned pale with alarm. The explosion had occurred on a Saturday in Garvaghey's market town, just eleven miles up the Broad Road. Hundreds had been injured; more than twenty killed. Montague was bound to know some of the victims. We had dinner planned, but John and Elizabeth hurried off to get the first bus north.

Through the Arts Council John arranged to make an appearance in Omagh once things settled.[17] He read alongside members of the Omagh Writers Group and then spent time with the still shell-shocked schoolchildren, some of whom had lost brothers, sisters, parents, or grandparents. The day took a lot out of him.

John's daughter Sibyl was there for the Omagh reading.[18] Only thirteen when her father left and sixteen when her mother had a stroke, she had suffered her own form of bystander's trauma. Both daughters remained angry with their father. Sibyl asked her father to explain how it was that he could have diverted his affections away from his children and devoted them entirely to Elizabeth. It seemed to her that he lumped his daughters together with their mother and then left all three behind. Why had he not come back right away to help them when her mother had a stroke? Sibyl was too young to handle the situation; she needed him. After this confrontation, Sibyl came away with the feeling that her father had done an extremely poor job of explaining himself.[19]

John followed up with a long letter. He reminded his younger daughter that he himself had grown up without any help from father or mother. It is uncertain whether he meant that she should manage on her own, just as he had done, or that, lacking a father himself, he did not know what was expected of him; he was lost in the role.

As for her more pointed questions, he needed time to reflect – 'Hasty answers are often too [hotly] phrased.' It had been six years since the separation, but he was disturbed to see that her wounds had not healed. It would have been better, no doubt, he proposed, if at the time the parents' decision to separate had been gently explained to the children by both John and Evelyn. The blow-up in Cork had been the worst way to part. As for Sibyl's request for a year's support in Dublin (so she could get on her feet as an artist), he explained his whole financial situation in detail – his small salary, length of contract, lack of a pension, years before retirement – then said that, yes, he would support her, and he would also continue to provide for the upkeep of 25 Grattan Hill. It may well have seemed to Sibyl that her father had given a cautiously financial answer to an emotional question, and to John that Sibyl was asking for his money rather than for his love or his company.

But surely, Sibyl was right in part – he was indeed running away from anger and guilt, centred in his abandoned Cork home. It was unnerving when an emissary of that emotional damage came out looking for him. Defensiveness left his fatherly love bottled up.

9

In 1999 John and Elizabeth undertook took to write an article for *The New Yorker* on a sensational crime in west Cork.[20] The beautiful wife of a French film producer, Sophie Toscan du Plantier, was murdered on 23 December 1996 outside her holiday home. Her body was found on a rocky path just over three miles from Letter Cottage, Montague's home. One of the first people on the scene, Ian Bailey, soon made himself a suspect by means of his newspaper disclosures about the discovery. An English blow-in, Bailey worked locally as a gardener, part-time journalist and market-trader; he also fancied himself a poet. Montague had employed him to do yard work at Letter Cottage and then, at

Bailey's request, offered advice about his poetry. So Montague had a privileged perspective on a most spectacular crime in a country like Ireland, where murders do not happen every day. The magazine offered $10,000 for his article, entitled 'A Devil in the Hills'.[21] The Ireland Chair paid £20,000 for his half year's work. He had children; he needed the money.

Ian Bailey was the rare sort that revels in being a notorious suspect. The local police made a mess of developing the evidence (the story of their sleuthing later led to a podcast, television series and a movie). Because of weaknesses in the gardai's case, Bailey was never prosecuted in Ireland. He then initiated a libel case against six newspapers, and lost it in 2003, because, according to the verdict, he was accurately and in good faith described as the leading suspect. In 2019, Bailey was convicted in his absence of murder by the Cour d'Assises de Paris but was never extradited by Ireland; he died in 2024.

From the beginning 'Devil in the Hills' was a co-authored article, although the 'hook' for the *New Yorker* was the fact that John was both eyewitness reporter and current poet laureate of Ireland. The magazine declined to permit the two to sign as co-authors, although the text states that fact in its first paragraph. It is possibly to Elizabeth that credit is due for the paragraphs introducing the outside reader to the culture of west Cork and the background of Sophie Toscan du Plantier, highly competent reportage. The passage on Bailey's poetry presumably came from John:

> After he had been working for us for almost a year, Bailey showed me his collected works – scraps of songs and poem-ballads – and I encouraged him in his writing. There was a glimmer of talent there, but it needed a level of discipline which he seemed unprepared to give. He had made a minor reputation for himself, reciting poetry and banging the bodhran ... at O'Sullivan's Pub, in Ballydehob, and he seemed to prefer the immediate gratifications of the pub's indulgent audience to the tedious, concentrated work of a serious writer ....
> On one occasion, he borrowed a typewriter that had been gathering dust in our house since we'd switched to computers. I worried later that I might have lent my typewriter to Raskolnikov, but I felt a vaguely paternal affection for Bailey back then, and saw him as an older version of the troubled young men I had dealt with as a teacher. I also felt a kind of abashed concern for him as someone with high

aspirations but modest gifts: there, but for the grace of God, *et cetera*. Above all, I saw him as a victim of the English class system, a butcher's son educated at a 'good' grammar school where he learned to read Latin but lost his social moorings, who craved acceptance in the more bohemian society of west Cork.

The co-authors tell how Bailey sent them a letter to explain, in case they had heard rumours, how it was that he had beaten up his companion Jules so badly that she required reconstructive surgery. It was all owing to the drink. Still, they rehired him. The Montagues were not the only ones in west Cork who failed to escape the company of Ian Bailey. Long after the article was published, and even after losing in court, he never went away, and persisted in regarding himself as an anchor member of the west Cork bohemian community.

John and Elizabeth called upon Bailey in 1999 to tell him that they were writing this story. He was delighted – there had already been many articles in England and France, he said, but America was under-represented. The general thrust of 'The Devil in the Hills' is that Bailey was a kind of Raskolnikov, an under-talented man who kills someone out of the delusion that he is great, beyond good and evil, like Napoleon. His sickness is an overwhelming desire to be the centre of attention.

At the sixtieth birthday party for Gerry Wrixon, then president of UCC, on 26 May 2000 in Kinsale, there was a bizarre contretemps sparked by this *New Yorker* article. Wrixon had asked his friend Montague if he would read some poems on the occasion. When John and Elizabeth arrived, they found that Aidan Higgins and his partner Alannah Hopkin were also among the guests.

Elizabeth made an unsuccessful attempt to strike up a friendship with Alannah, both second partners of older Irish writers, and both writers themselves. Alannah (a close friend of Evelyn's) felt their situations were very different: she did not use her older partner's reputation to advance her own career, nor did she ghost-write articles that he signed. In fact Aidan Higgins attributed to his own writings an unmatchable superiority and was disdainful of the common reader. He even judged Alannah's own work to be 'not proof against the mildew of the stock phrase'.[22] John, on the other hand, did collaborate with Elizabeth, thinking himself lucky to have a partner who was like a human thesaurus, always quick to suggest an alternative when he was in search of a word. 'I am not always sure where my phrases end and hers begin,' he wrote in the preface to his second book of memoirs.[23] Both men in fact could not do without their partners and were lucky to be loved.

At Wrixon's birthday party, Alannah quizzed Elizabeth about whether it was not she who actually wrote that *New Yorker* piece on Ian Bailey. Later, seeing John, Alannah kissed him and put the same question. He agreed, saying, Yes, it was mostly Elizabeth's work. 'Thank you, John,' she said. 'I know you wouldn't write crap like that.' This was not a good start to the night.

John himself pursued Aidan around the room, with servers carrying drinks to them on trays. He kept asking Higgins whatever it was he had against him,[24] until the novelist finally blurted out a full charge-sheet of grievances: Montague's best college friend had committed suicide, he exploited his friendship with Beckett and he was mean – 'this to a man who had bought him drinks galore, sent and given him money and sheltered him and his family in Paris where I was his translator as well'. The night was a disaster. When Montague went up to his room, he became violently sick. In the intensities of that post-Joycean, post-Yeatsian period, Aidan Higgins and John Montague were two writers who were each well aware of the shortcomings of the other. Yet it is perplexing why Montague should have continued to care what Higgins thought of him, and why he was still irked by a moment's fisticuffs from thirty years before. It is possible that an explanation may have to do with John's relations with his brother Turlough, with whom he had once fought and whose respect he dearly desired, but failed to win.

10

The renown of being the first holder of the Ireland Chair of Poetry led to invitations to read around the world. In November 1999 Montague went to Moscow;[25] in January 2000 to Florence; in September and October 2000 to Melbourne. John made a point of Elizabeth travelling with him 'on all these jaunts as the consort of the geriatric bard'.[26] With her help, he made an effort to conduct himself in a manner suitable to his title, a person of state. Friends from the past who had been accustomed to taking liberties with John's dignity were sometimes dismayed to find him more distant, wearing the manner of the *grand maître*, the mischievous old scamp nowhere in sight, or reduced to a quick grin, rather than, as in the old days, ready for a long debauch.

Figure 65: Elizabeth and John Montague.

Elizabeth was key to this new deportment. Like her heroine in *Sleight of Hand* (1999), because she was small and pale, people often misjudged her and thought her 'very young and timid'.[27] Actually, she was past forty, had been married twice before meeting John and was 'not really timid at all'. She was, again like that heroine, eager, earnest, intelligent and highly educated. In addition to being his bed mate and collaborator (and a prolific novelist), Elizabeth took on the parts of personal assistant and clinician. She kept track of the daily schedule, minded his diet (gently), monitored his drink intake and, to some degree, guided his social conversation. She cared for him in every way, and he showed every sign of being glad of the care. If it was cossetting, he liked it. Elizabeth was his 'Pocket Venus'.

Some past acquaintances regretted it was now difficult to get John away by himself for conversation, though that was his choice too.[28] His daughters particularly felt it hard that they did not have his company entirely to themselves (they wished Elizabeth to go away). Subsequently, Oonagh tried to organize get-togethers, and John tried to enable his daughters to trust in his assurances of love and support.[29] He did help out with things such as Oonagh's trip to Australia and her postgraduate study in Galway, as well as art colleges in Limerick and London for Sibyl. One difficulty with re-establishing family relationships was that after the millennium John was rarely in Cork city and often not even in Ireland. His usual globetrotting had slowed to a more sedentary life in France.

II

In December 1998 John and Elizabeth found a room at the Hotel Maison Durante, 16 Avenue Durante, in Nice. For an extended stay they paid €30 a night for a double room on the top floor. The room had a tiny kitchenette, but it was not so large as to make possible the entertainment of guests.

They soon became fond of the *quartier*, largely Arab, and wound up returning each winter, until Nice became their home base from which they visited Ireland, particularly Ballydehob, in the summertime.

Figure 66: 31 rue d'Angleterre, Nice. Photographer Howard Davies. In 2004 the Montagues bought a garret flat there; earlier, they stayed in the Hotel Maison Durante.

In their quartier, they dined regularly at the Restaurant d'Angleterre, a place that offered large portions at low prices.[30] Before dinner, they would call in to La Cave Romagnan. The proprietor was an Algerian named Manon. There were wine racks and bookshelves on one side; the other wall was available to artists to display their works. Most customers sat outside on white plastic chairs around three-legged, round metal tables. The seating area was on the broad footpath and just inside a row of potted plants. John and Elizabeth came to be on first-name terms with a former paratrooper, an actress, a painter, a photographer, a journalist and a film-maker.[31] People played dice or simply chatted. It became John and Elizabeth's 'local'; they were regulars. On Fridays, there was jazz, so on that night, John would arrive early, have his drink and leave when the music started.

Figure 67: La Cave Romagnan, Nice.

Another haunt was Le Toscan, a restaurant with a remarkable assembly of regular guests: a retired French opera singer, several poets and an international businessman. Through their literary agent Jonathan Williams, the couple met Howard Davies, who like Jonathan was a singer in the Dublin Welsh Male Voice Choir. He had retired from a Dublin advertising firm and spent part of each year in Villefranche, near Nice. John and Elizabeth brought this new friend along to Le Toscan. Amid so glittering a cast of clients, Howard felt embarrassed to be what he was, merely a highly cultured and very successful businessman, with a taste for poetry.[32]

Steadied by these habits of life in Nice, John and Elizabeth worked side by side in the little room at the Hotel Maison Durante. As the winters went by, the books and articles kept coming. Elizabeth published *The Thing He Loves* in 2001, *Dangerous Pity* in 2010 and *Sustenance* in 2011.

John began the second volume of his memoirs, *The Pear is Ripe*, in 2000, covering 'The Madeleine Years', 1956 until his return to Ireland in 1972.[33] He thought of it as his 'sixties memoir'.[34] It turned out to be a difficult book to write. He needed to deal with the period of 'free love' in California, but sexual politics had changed over the previous forty years; it was difficult to find the right way to present his promiscuity.[35]

He had begun with Elias Canetti's *The Tongue Set Free* as his stylistic model: 'revelation by anecdote'.[36] But Canetti is bitchy and cruel about his famous friends; he is even venomous about the women he loved and draws not the slightest veil over their persons. The more Montague read of Canetti, the less he liked his approach. Montague recoiled from saying cruel things about his contemporaries, or causing embarrassment to lovers of long ago. Both too many, and not enough, years had passed. In dealing with the living, he believed, 'the pattern is still not discernible; and, of course, you may cause hurt, which may fuel further uneasiness'.[37] He wrote to those about whom he was writing to solicit their help, and then showed them what he had written. His caution was admirably fair-minded, but it made composition difficult, and the final product (published in 2007) wound up just a bit toothless. Peter Fallon warned him, after reading a draft, that 'there's a general rosy warmth applied from without'. 'Everyone's either handsome or romantic or eloquent … Everyone!'[38]

For the purpose of writing his memoirs, Montague consulted his library – books, letters and past publications. Following the separation, these had been moved from Grattan Hill to a basement room in Cork. When the River Lee flooded, the boxes were drenched. The books and papers had to be transported to Letter Cottage for drying.[39] Maybe €20,000 of valuable material was irretrievably damaged. Montague had banked on selling the archive to keep himself and Elizabeth afloat in Nice.

He was able to fish out from this archive a number of draft poems. These, when polished, were added to new collections. In *Smashing the Piano* there are sentimental affectionate poems to his daughters, written when they were small. A half-dozen of the poems arose from festschrifts, birthdays, or other occasions, tributes to Edward McGuire, Robert Greacen, Robert Graves, Seán Ó Riada, Seán Ó Ríordáin and Gerry Wrixon. Looking into old diaries and letters inspired reveries in which the past returned with its sensations quickened again, as in 'Paths' and 'Still Life, with Aunt Brigid', a Rembrandt-like memory flash of the old woman, holding a storm lamp, as she crosses the haggard at night time. Some poems from the section 'Dark Rooms' go very far back, to the 1960s. 'Stand In' is a poem of jealousy written during Montague's affair with Susan Hall Patron. In the same section can be found 'Wrath', about the sad state of his marriage in the mid-1980s and plucked from the manuscript of the unpublished *Home Truths*. The book ends with a more recent public declaration, 'Landing', 'for Elizabeth', 'my late, but final anchoring'.[40]

Reviewers were kind to the latest offering from the new holder of the Ireland Chair of Poetry. It was said that there was no falling off in his work; indeed, some reviews claimed the poems were better than ever. This over-valuation of what were mostly leftovers hardly made up for the under-appreciation in Britain of books like *A Chosen Light*, *Tides* and *The Rough Field* at the times of their first publication; nonetheless, it was soothing.

Drunken Sailor (2004) was also steadied by ballast from the notebooks. 'The Hag's Cove', from the 1980s, is a particularist description of decay and wreckage around Cork harbour, with allusions to historic shipwrecks, but it is also an indirect meditation on his alcoholism, his marriage on the rocks and his despair-unto-death. The two poems that follow it – 'Roethke's Ghost at Roche's Point' and 'Hermit' – come from the autumn of 1973. The most powerful poem in the book is the angry elegy for his brother Turlough, 'Last Court', in which the poet defends his uncatholic way of life. Much of that great poem was written in 1986, but publication was held up out of respect for Turlough's children. When it was published, eighteen years later, its indignation still caused pain to the family; it showed their beloved father in a bad light.[41]

Among Montague's archives, there sat two complete versions of *Home Truths*. He picked out a few more poems for publication in *Chain Letter*, in the 1997 'Poetry Ireland Pamphlets' series, not widely circulated:

Cassandra's Lover

You were angry when I met you.
Somehow, it made you seem more beautiful,
Radiant, a glorious maenad!

But sometimes, with hair streaming,
Great sorrowful eyes, tears spattering,
You seemed the ugly duckling.

And I dreamt in loving vanity
That I might heal and comfort you:
Set old childhood wound aright.

But I could never get it straight;
They ran so deep. So with
Faltering courage I now fear

That I myself will drown there:
Unless our love steals out of this eclipse,
Gleams on us again with mild strength.

He wanted to get out the whole of *Home Truths* in order to ventilate the locked room of his own past. He submitted the sequence to Dillon Johnston, his American publisher. After talking over the drafts with his wife, Guinn Batten (herself a leading scholar of modern Irish poetry), Dillon wrote back in April 1998:[42]

> Guinn finds the poems both 'remarkably honest' and 'very well written.' She says they are wonderfully free of the self-pity we so often find in reports from the victim, 'which he is in this case.' She feels that regardless of any questions arising in the name of political correctness, the poems should be published. Evelyn's condition, however, does, she believes, make publication now inappropriate …. I wondered, and Guinn agreed, if you might not share the poems with your daughters.
>
> I admire the poems, even more on third and fourth reading than on first. They are very lean and well-tuned, so they resonate.

Near the end of John's life, Peter Fallon, when he read the sequence, took a similar view.[43] The time was not right. Publication would be terrible for John's Irish reputation, and hurtful to his children and their mother.

Reluctantly, Montague agreed. His experience with Evelyn was possibly unapproachable even before her stroke; afterwards, that was certainly the case. He told Barry Callaghan in 1999: 'It is a drastic and painful situation which probably cannot change and cannot easily be written about.'[44] Six years later, he was stuck in the same spot: 'A big block [to writing more poetry] would be the near impossibility of writing about the years with Evelyn, which were not easy, especially within earshot of the children.'[45]

The safest bet was to stick with translation. He was flushed with enthusiasm when he discovered his old friend from the rue Daguerre, Claude Esteban, had been writing excellent poems, meditations on *King Lear*. The theme of an old man having trouble with his daughters may have been part of the appeal to Montague. He worked away at his translations from 2002 to 2005, when he read alongside Esteban at the Poetry Now Festival in Dun Laoghaire. Caroline Walsh, Books Editor of *The Irish Times*, reported on the performance: 'Coming onstage to read with Esteban his long, King Lear-inspired poem *A Smile Between the Stones*, Montague provided one of the highlights of the festival, and possibly of the festival's 10-year history, with his spirited, passionate reading – more a performance, really, swerving powerfully between poignancy and comedy; Montague as Lear (and, indeed, as the Fool), was a sight to enjoy.' In June, *The Irish Times* printed an excerpt from the Esteban translation:[46]

> It will be evening the same
> evening hour, the doves
>
> will begin to settle on the branches,
> someone will say, how
>
> the grass has grown, come let us sit,
> and tell us
>
> to pass the time, a slightly daft story,
> that of a king
>
> who thought he knew everything and who lost
> everything, someone
>
> will say, that's enough of sad tales,
> forget them,
>
> as the sun slowly sets.

The poem is, at two removes of translation, King Lear in Act V talking to Cordelia. The fading light makes a new picture of the scene. A year later, Esteban was dead.

At seventy-seven, Montague was feeling his years. He had had prostate surgery in early 2004, then cataract surgery performed by his old UCC student Dr Eamon O'Donoghue later that year. Amidst such signs of bodily decrepitude, he realized that the time had come to put his affairs in order. He explained to his daughters that he loved them and wished to continue to provide support when they needed it. However, his regular income was small, less than €15,000 a year from Aosdána. It was not going to be possible for him, old as he was, to continue to make use of Letter Cottage. It was his intention that after his death, the house would be Elizabeth's to live in, should she choose to do so; afterwards, it would pass to the children.[47] At present, however, he thought he would have to sell a field in order to have money to buy a flat in Nice or Dublin.

That was hard news for his daughters. Oonagh replied with a long, thoughtful email on 21 February 2006.[48] She said she loved her father for thinking ahead and taking his children into account. She had, however, understood from him that Letter Cottage would come to his daughters immediately upon his death. All their childhood memories were there – Easter egg hunts in the garden, the best hideouts when hide-and-seek was played; she knew every inch of the fields. Still, she understood Elizabeth would need a place to live. Oonagh also put in a fervent request to be named (in place of Elizabeth) literary executor upon her father's death.

In the end, the sale of the field in Ballydehob did not go through, and John and Elizabeth did not at the time buy that city flat. Letter Cottage remained a beloved resort to Sibyl and Oonagh until his death, after which it was sold.

12

From 2002 Caroline Walsh sent books for review to Montague, with the understanding that he had free play and plenty of space to write about them. She was a wise editor to catch him at this point in his life. He had been a leading reviewer for *The Spectator* and *The Guardian* decades earlier. The opportunities she now gave him were both a lifeline and a forum. Ultimately, these reviews will be collected in book form, the reflections of a master poet who knew everyone in his time. They cover modern French poetry, the memoir of Richard Murphy,

Irish poets' versions of Dante, the importance of James Clarence Mangan to contemporary poets, Ezra Pound (a fracture line in Irish poetry), Thomas Moore, Sartre and de Beauvoir ('Is an open marriage possible, even when the game of love is played by French rules?'), T.S. Eliot, Arthur Koestler, Benedict Kiely and Christopher Isherwood. Montague loved literary biography. What was the life of an artist? How should it be lived?

The shadow of Yeats hung over all these reflections. In the 29 November 2003 *Irish Times*, Montague told of his delight when Seamus Heaney passed on a proof copy of the second volume of Roy Foster's biography *The Arch Poet*. The volume bears this inscription, with a fragment of Yeats:[49]

> For John
> 'who swerved in nought ...'
> le meas agus le grá [with respect and love],
> Seamus

John knew word for word the writings of Yeats and could immediately complete the fragmentary quotation: '... but something to perfection brought'. It is Seamus Heaney's tacit tribute to Montague's life work.

In his *Irish Times* review Montague compared Yeats's work to the collected poems of Robert Lowell and Ted Hughes. What did they not have, that Yeats did possess? Control over the story of their lives – that was Montague's conclusion. Yeats was the ultimate Sartrean poet, a person who took it upon himself his own life to create, unsupported by metaphysical absolutes, undeterred by vices, mental instability, or bad luck. The master poet was the person who made his or her own biography.

On 3 November 2010 Montague was made a Chevalier de la Légion d'Honneur, one of France's highest honours. Montague's primary contribution to France was the translation of twentieth-century French poetry – works by Verlaine, Apollinaire, Jouve, Aragon, Ponge, Follain, Guillevic, Cadou, Marteau, Jaccottet, Koltz, Deguy, Stéfan, Lasnier and his old friend Claude Esteban. The recognition was as well-deserved as it was enjoyable to its recipient. The good news was redoubled when the following week Montague was awarded an honorary doctorate by the Sorbonne.

One of the first to congratulate Montague for such recognitions was Seamus Heaney.[50] The two ageing poets often wrote back and forth in these years, trading poems and geriatric woes. Each had had cataract operations. Seamus had a stroke. John had two prostate operations and skin cancer surgery. John had to give up swimming in the Mediterranean because now the waves knocked him over. After the publication of *Human Chain*, Seamus fell into a slough of despond. John then wrote a brotherly letter to buck him up, reminiscing about his own depression after finishing *The Dead Kingdom*.[51] In a lengthy notice of *The Human Chain*, John saluted the 'exemplary run' of Seamus's career as a poet. He credited him with having the one thing necessary, what Patrick Kavanagh called 'the touch'.[52] 'What is truly dazzling in Heaney is his descriptive power, his almost hymn to a Conway Stewart fountain pen, or glimpses of his father performing a farmyard task, wrought to a hallucinatory, Van Gogh-like intensity.' In the past, John had sometimes been jealous of Seamus; but jealousy, as R.L. Stevenson said, is just admiration in warpaint. There is no warpaint here, no holding back, peace has been declared. Seamus wrote John to thank him for the candid tribute.

When Seamus died on 30 August 2013, John was not totally surprised. He had noticed premonitions in *The Human Chain* – 'again and again he returns to church and the graveyard'. But he had not wanted to recognize the signs. 'A benign father,' John noted, Seamus had truly 'fulfilled himself.'[53]

Figure 68: John Montague in churchyard.

13

When the poet Mary O'Malley visited John Montague in Nice in 2013, she thought he had changed. 'It wasn't that he had overcome his problems, but that his problems had left him, and left him with a degree of wisdom and peace.'[54] At a Yeats commemoration in the National Concert Hall, Nuala Ní Dhomhnaill noticed that Montague seemed 'more at ease and generous, bestowing kindness on all'.[55] James Harpur saw something new in *Speech Lessons* (2012): 'an ease and gentleness, a warmth'.[56] Harpur was particularly struck by the Christianity of *Baldung's Vision*:

> I saw a tiny Christ
> caper on the cross
>
> silent as a salamander
> writhing in fire
>
> or a soldier triumphant
> when the battle's lost;
>
> *wine bursts from*
> *his body's grapeskin*:
>
> The suffering you see
> is our daily mystery,
>
> so follow my body
> as it sings mutely
>
> (a lantern, a ladder,
> a window, a pathway)
>
> of pain calcined away
> in a dance of ecstasy.

In fact, John's relationship to Christianity, while it had not quite come full circle, had returned to something 'near belief'.[57] He was not again the little Roman Catholic boy who on Christmas Eve would put on a soutane and surplice and sing the *Adeste Fideles*, but he and Elizabeth quietly attended Sunday services at Holy Trinity, the Anglican church in Nice, a ten-minute walk from their flat.[58] To kneel, to sing hymns, to listen to scripture, to pray for grace – he found comfort in these rites. The chaplain Peter Jackson, Oxford graduate and author, was a gay man in a settled relationship. John and Elizabeth became friends to the chaplain and his partner, Joseph Voelker, and frequently enjoyed their company in the church rectory. I must say it surprised me to learn that at the end of his days the old sinner was breaking bread with a pair of true Christians.

On 2 October 2016 I was driving north to Bellaghy, County Derry, where Montague and Paddy Moloney of The Chieftains were to do a performance to mark the opening of The Home Place, the new Seamus Heaney centre. An RTÉ episode of *Sunday with Miriam* came on the car radio, featuring Montague. John and Miriam O'Callaghan, both Northerners, knew one another well; she had been married to his friend the poet Tom McGurk. Both were aware that he was living out his last days. Miriam reminded John of a piece he had written about his final conversation with Samuel Beckett.

> MO'C: You asked him, 'Now that's it's nearly over, Sam, was there much of the journey you found worthwhile?' And what did he reply?
> JM: 'Precious little!'

She then turned the subject around to John. What would he say now that his own life was coming near its end? Not skipping a beat, he replied, 'Give me more! Give me more!' But Miriam was not done yet. Did he believe that after this life we go on to somewhere else, or is this it?

> JM: We come to the arena of the grand questions. Some days I do, sometimes I don't. Depends on how I slept the night before.
> MO'C: Just not sure?
> JM: Who is?

Still sensing there is more to come, Miriam pressed on: 'Do you think you've had a good life? A happy life? A lucky life?

> JM: Confession time!
> MO'C: I'm interested. Tell me.

JM: I went through a period of time when I was into Buddhism. I was intrigued also by Mr Yeats and his communion with magic. There are days when I believe in one and not the other, and there are days when I believe in both, and in them all.

It's not easy to have certainty in this life, except for some people, generally not too bright.

I believe you asked me as to my attitude to life. I'd like to experience all the emotions, except if they are too painful. I'm always increased and pleased by the attitude of Shakespeare, who seems to have been the greatest man who ever lived, and who seems to have experienced all the emotions, including jealousy, 'envying this man's art and that man's scope, with what I most enjoy contented least'... Imagine Shakespeare, having written *King Lear*, thinking that Marlowe is much better!

After the Bellaghy event, John and I met for an hour back at his country-house hotel near Upperlands. We had been corresponding about this book, but we had been together on only a handful of occasions in the previous several years. His voice was faint, and my hearing had become poor, but we managed. He wanted to tell me something, and he also had a question.

The question was, how did I mean to handle the matter of sex? I said that the thing that made his life worth reading about was the poetry he had written, so the main focus would be on the work and how it came to be, but a fundamental aspect of a human being, and therefore of an author, it seemed to me, was the sexual life, so I would treat that subject frankly – as a matter of public interest, not as gossip. He nodded, apparently satisfied.

What he wanted to tell me now was that he was not finished with trying to understand what had happened to him as a boy in school. How did he come to have a stammer? There was a day when going to school in the morning, he was the best reader in the class, and then coming home after school that day, he could hardly speak at all. What had happened? He had been asked to read out in front of the class from a book, a strange book, with a picture of a naked girl dancing under the moon and a boy in animal skins. It began at that moment, and it dogged him afterwards through all his days. The stammer had ruined his life. He had heard that a child who was in his class remembered the moment; her name was Elizabeth Curley; she was now an elderly woman in

Clones, south of the border. She had told someone that the teacher had been very cruel to him that day. But the two times he had gone to Clones to look in on her, she was away from home. He had also made a search for the original of that strange book through the Linen Hall Library in Belfast, but with no luck. It was a mystery.

Once back in France, John met with his nephew Andrew Montague who happened to be in Nice. On 23 November the two met at Le Circuit, the café where John took his morning coffee. Would you look after me when I die? John asked. He did not want to be buried in France, but in the Garvaghey churchyard. So Andrew would have to seek permission from Father O'Dwyer for John to be buried there. And he wanted the McAtee brothers of Fintona to be the undertakers. They had been drinking pals in his youth. It would not be long before Andrew would have to carry out his mission. Strange, John had not attended either of his brothers' funerals, but he wanted an Ulster funeral for himself, and he relied on Turlough's sons to organize it. They were without question ready to do so, and pay for it too.[59]

By 28 November John had been sent to the hospital, suffering from a twist in his intestine. It had been a recurrent problem. Now the doctors decided that surgery, although risky, was necessary. He came through the procedure, but on 9 December he developed a post-operative infection, and had to be put on a respirator, and was sinking fast. His daughter Sibyl arrived in time to see him still alive; Oonagh made it to the hospital that Saturday morning, 10 December 2016, just hours after her father had passed away.

The phones were then ringing all over Ireland, and through France, and beyond to America, to those who particularly cared: John Montague had died. Each friend who got the news told three or four others who had not yet heard. The next day it was all over the national newspapers in Ireland. 'Another great tree has fallen!' was *The Irish Times* headline, alluding to the fall of the first tree, Seamus Heaney, three years before.

A service for friends was held at Newman Chapel on St Stephen's Green in Dublin. Nuala Ní Dhomhnaill, Turlough Montague and Oonagh Montague spoke. Paddy Moloney provided music. John's 1960s companion Richard Ryan (later Irish ambassador to the United Nations) then stepped up to give the eulogy. In early November John had sent Richard Ryan a poem about the time they climbed Knockmany Hill together in 1969, forty-seven years earlier:

And in that instant
Did I become a poet?
I was struck down
As by lightning's
Fierce flash, a
Savage music.

And all the confusions
Of my childhood,
A small boy launched
Into the empyrean,
Catapulted back to
Where we had come from:

A timid deer peering
From the hazel forest of
Our holy mountain,
The saddle shape of
Knockmany Hill,
Its magic stones.

Before it was too late, Richard had replied, and John, reading his letter, wept. Richard saw in this last poem:

> ... that clear identifying stamp that was there from the earliest poems onward – light as leaves floating on air or water, but crafted to increasingly supple strength, able to carry their burdens. It really is all so clear, looking backward, visible from the beginning, the long search for a voice to comprehend baffled hurt, missing components of childhood, what that causes. As the years have passed and, now here again, I think, you have been bringing those hurts to account with increasingly tender understanding, achieving at last a rare, exemplary settlement with them – all those shadowy figures. Your hard-won late gift ... is a sense of release, at last, from all that unintended, long-buried hurt ... a fragile reconciliation with the life lived, and sketching this with that leaf-light lyric crafting that hallmarks your life's poems.

Following the service at Newman Chapel, the cortège left for Tyrone, led by the hearse carrying his body. At the ceremony in St Matthew's Church, Garvaghey, John's nephew Turlough Montague KC recited from the poetry. Turlough is tall, slim and handsome, with the slightly reddish, faintly freckled complexion of the Montagues. Eerily, his voice is exactly that of John Montague – except that there is one difference: he has not the slightest hint of a stammer. It was spooky, like having the dead poet stand up in the family chapel, younger, in full possession of his health, now cured of his affliction.

After the service Father O'Dwyer led the family, followed by friends and other parishioners, down the sloping graveyard – everyone walking carefully over the frozen ground – to the poet's open grave. It would be some time before the headstone that John requested would be in place: a white, unpolished standing stone, with a rough cross-like outline toward the top, taller than the black headstones in the rest of the churchyard, but not flagrantly out-sized. At the graveside when he was buried, these verses were read that by his wish were inscribed on that headstone:

> So, for myself, I would seek
> no other final home, than
> this remote country hiding place,
> which gave me gentle nourishment
> when I was most in need of it
> and still gives solace.

Figure 69: Pallbearers, left to right, are Ciaran Montague, Turlough Montague, Paul Muldoon and Andrew Montague; on the far side of the coffin were Theo Dorgan, Ciaran Carson and Aidan Kelly; Garvaghey churchyard, 2016.

These Wordsworthian lines are taken from 'First Landscape, First Death', published in *Drunken Sailor* (2004). It is remarkable that a dozen years before his actual death, John Montague envisioned the day on which he would be buried, declared his wishes for the manner of that burial, and plainly stated his final understanding of his life. It is further remarkable that his Tyrone nephews and nieces, his spouses and daughters, scrupulously carried out his wishes.

A year later an anniversary mass was organized by his family in Garvaghey church. Snow lay several inches over the hillside pastures in December 2017, but the nave and transept were full for the weekly mass at five o'clock on a very dark evening. Afterwards, there was a dinner in Kelly's Bar next door. At the bar, Frank Horisk passed around a 'Christmas letter' John had written to his father Barney over thirty years earlier, reminiscing about people and events along the Omagh Road. Old-timers gathered around to peer at the words, and they nodded as it was read out. The mention of each name brought a chuckle, or slow shake of demurral. Aiden Kelly, married to the owner of the bar, took out his glasses and had a careful look at the letter. Then he reminisced about how John would for many years on his returns to Garvaghey stay with the Kellys at the Inn. They gave him a room for free, and he would settle in to meet at the bar all the locals for a good long gossip, a flood of reminiscence, and sharing of stories, rhymes and songs. Now, no more circling, he had come home to stay.

14

A full statement of the value of John Montague's poetry, or an interpretation of its effect on others, is matter for other books. But something needs to be said at the end of even a plain account of his life. Much depends upon whether you think that poetry can be important. In the period of Ireland's break from the British Empire, it was very important, even to political leaders – Thomas MacDonagh, Patrick Pearse and Joseph Plunkett were poets and also were executed for their parts in the Easter Rebellion. Yeats created a poetry of worldwide impact after mixing his materials in the crucible of that Irish revolutionary history.

Montague grew up with that heritage. He also belonged to the generation of post-World War II writers. A whole fleet of them, some of the best and the brightest of their time, took to poetry to put the human condition on record, what still remained of value after war had done its worst. Their vision of life was profoundly influenced by Sartre and Freud. So was that of John Montague.

When he attended the Salzburg Conference in 1950, with US army jeeps still racing around the city, Montague was at one with his European generation, on the side of America, but with a view of communism just over the border. He met Saul Bellow, John Berryman and Robert Lowell; he was a classmate of Harold Bloom, Robert Bly and Allen Ginsberg. These were gifted people who gave their lives to literature, as if to a very demanding god.

That professional seriousness about literature was something new to the contemporary Irish scene in the 1950s. After his return from postgraduate study in the USA, Montague's zeal shook up the literary life in the Ireland of his time. He did not do it alone – Kinsella, Liam Miller and many others were part of the reawakening from neutrality and the frozen hegemony of the Catholic Church. Just being infuriated with Denis Donoghue for overlooking contemporary Irish writers was a characteristic step of his cultural activism. The honours Montague organized for Patrick Kavanagh, John Hewitt and Austin Clarke taught the Irish public to regard its senior writers as people to be proud of. Bringing the best contemporary French poets to Dublin for dual-language readings was an early sign of Irish membership in Europe. Montague's welcome to Ireland of Roethke, Berryman and Tom Parkinson was a step towards levelling up to international standards. Montague was an Irish nationalist, but one with a global measure of achievement.

The autobiographical impulse in his work – the imperative to tell the most intimate truths – may have begun with D.H. Lawrence, so important to his generation. The risk and challenge of that kind of writing Montague encountered in contemporaries like Robert Lowell and Sylvia Plath. Poetry asked everything of a person. The pressure on Freudian-age poets was excruciating in a post-Christian period: nailed to your own cross, suffering, forsaken by God – now what do you have to say for yourself? Montague was the Irish poet who laid down the gauntlet for this kind of autobiographical poetry in Ireland and Britain.

His early experience of human intimacy came from the coarse lingo of the farmyard and the racecourse. It gave rise to a search for tenderness in the words for love and scholarly attention to courtly traditions of address to the beloved.

One aspect of Montague's achievement is underappreciated. He combined two sides of his American influences – confessional poetry and Bay Area anti-war poetry – into autobiographical quest narratives with a political aim. The imperative of truth-to-life, death-bed honesty led Montague to be for his country another kind of singing bird, the canary in the coal-mine, whose sensitivity alerts others to danger. Long ahead of the public acknowledgement of such issues, he wrote personally about abortion, divorce, alcoholism, domestic violence and clerical abuse in education. That is not even to touch upon his representation of living with a disability – which is what his stammer was. He shoved into the face of Irish readers what his life – and if they were to be honest, their own lives – had been.

In 1960 he had a vision of a Modernist epic set in his home place, Garvaghey – childhood, family, neighbours, landscape and history. It would be his equivalent of William Faulkner's Yoknapatawpha County in Mississippi, seemingly a backward area but examined with an array of Modernist techniques, in order to explore both national and universal concerns. He treated the poem as if it were a symphony, but one that had to be entirely played by himself, so first he had to learn each of the different instruments. It took him twelve years to complete. The variety of technical skills displayed in *The Rough Field* often goes unnoticed; each of the forms is handled with ease. As the poem approached completion Montague and Liam Miller, his publisher, issued sections as single publications. They both felt that what was being said was of immediate importance to the emergency unfolding in the North. The poem is at once high Modernist art and *littérature engagée*, committed literature.

When the British army moved into the North, because he was from that area and because his family had been caught up in the War of Independence and Civil War, Montague was emotionally a participant in the conflict. To be nearer the scene was a reason (though not the main reason) that he left his life in Paris to return to Ireland: he had to take part in what he was part of. He was far out in front in meeting the issue in his work and challenged 'the comitatus of poets' to respond to the alarming events.

Individual lyrics came to Montague as to another poet, 'as naturally as leaves to a tree', but he also continued after the publication of *The Rough Field* to conceive book-length works. Drawing upon his skills as writer of fiction, they were volumes to be read from beginning to end, with a plot, characters, a story arc and a resolution. *The Great Cloak*, *The Dead Kingdom* and *Border Sick Call* are successive chapters in a lifelong project of verse autobiography. In the late

1980s, with two children and a marriage in crisis, he came up against a dilemma. He had to write about what was happening (his marital trouble dominated his life), but he could not publish *Home Truths* out of consideration for others. That brought to an end his unique scheme of narrative autobiography in lyric sequences. He turned in his last decades to the translation of French poets, the publication of stories and the composition of memoirs, with the occasional poems still coming, as the leaves to the tree.

In the end, as he told his friends, he felt lucky to have been part of a great period of poetry in English, occurring in his own small country, a flowering to compare with the Elizabethans, the Metaphysicals and the Romantics. Thinking back upon the harsh relations among Dublin writers in the 1950s, he was delighted to find himself in 2010 in the Green Room of the Abbey Theatre, celebrating the fortieth anniversary of The Gallery Press. Eiléan Ní Chuilleanáin, Derek Mahon, Gerald Dawe, Medbh McGuckian and Seamus Heaney (the genial master of ceremonies) glided around the room like exotic fish in a large aquarium, never colliding, with the distant, excited sound of the full house like that of an inland sea. What a wonderful thing to be part of![60]

HOME TRUTHS

[an unpublished sequence]

Do not always believe
In my always coming back
No matter what words are said
No matter what blows are struck
There is also the going down
And the running out of luck.

Cassandra's Lover

You were angry when I met you.
Somehow, it made you seem more beautiful,
Radiant, a glorious maenad!

But sometimes, with hair streaming,
Great sorrowful eyes, tears spattering,
You seemed the ugly duckling.

And I dreamt in loving vanity
That I might heal and comfort you:
Set old childhood wounds aright.

But I could never get it straight;
They ran so deep. So with
Faltering courage I now fear

That I myself will drown there:
Unless our love steals out of this eclipse,
Gleams on us again with mild strength.

Plea

A dream of final ease, final understanding,
And then you make your staged entrance.

Medusa: eyes swollen, snake hair astray,
Why will you not allow us some peace
Before this long-sought house
Your furies also clamour to destroy,
Lashed by your divisive ecstasy?

Buckler bright, I stand ready to defy.

Re-Entry

Poised, hand on the door,
He wonders what reception is waiting for
Him, who has improbably dreamt of flying
All night across the globe
In white tennis shoes.

Charm

Child, may you never know
What your mother has known,
Harsh words, blows,
Night's silence overthrown.

Violence of word, of action,
All our century sways towards it.
But remember the lesson of the storm,
Bend: do not break under it.

No Lullaby

It was the night before a quarrel
and all through the house everything
was stirring, including the mice,
and the children were startled
awake in their beds, because
downstairs their parents
were banging their heads.

And the shoes they are flying,
and the chairs thrown flat,
and saucepans and dishes,
and blows after that ...

Entreaties

Through shrinking walls children hear
the harsh cries of their squalling parents
and try to intercede with simple pleas
(scrawled aloft on crayoned posters)
Stop it, you two, please!
or, most heart-breaking of all, Don't behave
like children: think of us!
But the parents fail to register
their frail entreaties, seized in a kind of lust.

Busy Bee

Busy as a bee, bearing its sting,
his dear wife, occupied with everything
he was too eager to give her:
townhouse, country house,
their vivid extensions; gardens,
offerings towards that irredeemable dream,
that ultimate healing home or scheme.

His best efforts fruitless, to be
answered only with a scream
of rage, which all the good will
in the world might not assuage,
snarled up as she always seemed
in her harsh childhood's theme,
the brutal father, the lost manoir,
her broken dream.

Pure Rage

Pure rage: a shining, something total
like a block of glittering crystal,
dry ice hissing, maniacal,
which only the other's death can heal.

You sigh with satisfaction as you stand
over the ruined body, in your hand
a bloodied weapon, which you raise
wearily, in a gesture of self-praise.

Only the startled animals snuffle around
as audience, and nose the stained ground.
In the emptied aftermath, the silence,
you contemplate your achieved victim
who now lies blessedly deaf and dumb

to the words and blows you hurl at him.

Surprise

A man, she says fiercely,
stomping, so to speak,
her pretty foot, should never
strike a woman, even
with a flower, or
the petals of one!

Then, as an afterthought,
seeing his guard is down,
she takes him by surprise,
and whirls and whams him one
right between the two surprised
and slowly blackening eyes.

Molly

My mother's name was Molly,
she complained all the time;
But I sought to use the bridle
when I had cause to complain.

All great tunes being simple,
when the pulse beats the time:
We must learn what our parents
Were surprised to go through, again.

Together

Someone has fastened to a door
two creatures, Bosch-monstrous,
(Like clothes on a hanger,
clinging intimately together):

Condemned to eat each other
ceaselessly, without rest,
clutched in the matching
tensions of their embrace.

The smaller, more tenacious
hangs above, ferret-fierce,
while the larger, more formidable
hugs bloodily from beneath.

Wrath

Lying in the darkness, grim with anger

against the one lying by your side,
herself grim with anger
at your lying
so grim with anger by her side.

This night only absence will be her love,
only wrath will be your bride.

Weather Vain

These changing skies we dwell under,
Shine shifting to rain, driving sleet.

The continuous electricity of storms
which obscure, then clear;

Hatred sparkling along the bones,
the drenching release of tears,

The following calm. For a minute's miracle
I discern, as down a leaf-choked well

the drowned glory of your face.

Paradox

Your touch on my spirit,
so fierce, so precise:
as chilling as fire,
as warming as ice.

Gorgon

How can I bend to kiss
that mouth that, all
too soon, will hiss
its terrible truths
against me?

Nature

Walking that morning
we found a trapped
animal that had gnawed
off half its leg
to escape and did
with a final thrust
as we approached,
but couldn't hobble far
before it was caught
and savaged by our terrier.

I rescued it from
her trained mouth
and held it up.
Now an eye was gone
as well as a hind leg.
The natural world has
no begging bowl and
our bitch was waiting.
I let it fall back.

Barred

Her insults dinning, dwindling in his ears,
He seeks a dark pub, into that burrow disappears.
There he huddles for hours, as down a tunnel.
Smouldering, brooding, or reading, but

Also steadily sinking glass after glass until
Like a caricature (the offended male!)
He heads back, steaming, uphill:
Violence, the snake that eats its tail!

Storm Warning

For years he tried to ignore the warning signs,
Believing it his duty to appease, to ease
The great drooping sadness in her eyes.
But he bolts from the home he bought
To shelter them, seeks the lowliest bar,
To hide, to heal the shame, the scar
Of his bruised pride, his bloodied face.
No questions asked in this tolerant space:
Why can't he handle his trouble and strife?
How can he thole this hole-in-corner life?
A solitary puzzles over his ritual crossword,
Railway men mock-battle a game of cards.
Their tactful silence in this homely place
A lost blessing, a forgotten grace.

Moments

Moments of sweetness.
A temporary blessing
Like a slant of light
Falling in a bedroom.
Rare days when I brought
A wintry smile to your face.

Shame

An ignominious memory, expunged

His bloodied face, which once
the kindly barman sponged

(After stumbling down the hill;
Golgotha hath reversed itself!)

with a towel and warm water
in a chipped metal basin
while half-daft, he mutters to himself,

A male Veronica, an uxorious Jesus!

ILLUSTRATIONS

BIBLIOGRAPHY

Algren, Nelson. 1960. *Who Lost an American?* London: Andre Deutsch.

Bingham, Alice, and Penelope Schmidt, editors. 1990. *Morris Graves: Vessels of Transformation 1932–1986*. New York: Schmidt-Bingham Gallery.

Allen, Michael. Autumn 1989. 'Celebrations, review of Mount Eagle, Irish University Review Special Issue on John Montague, etc'. *The Irish Review* 97–102.

— . 2015. Ed. Fran Brearton. *Michael Allen: Close Readings: Essays on Irish Poetry*. Dublin: Irish Academic Press.

Alvarez, Al. 1999. *Where Did It All Go Right?* New York: Simon and Schuster.

Armstrong, Robert. 1970. '*Threshold*, edited by John Montague'. *The Guardian*, August 20: 7.

Arnold, Bruce. 1993. *Haughey: His Life and Unlucky Deeds*. London: Harper Collins.

— . 1970. 'The factors of change'. *Irish Independent*, January 1: 24.

Bair, Deirdre. 2020. *Parisian Lives: Samuel Beckett, Simone de Beauvoir and Me – a Memoir*. London: Atlantic Books.

Bakewell, Sarah. 2016. *At The Existentialist Café: Freedom, Being, and Apricot Cocktails*. London: Chatto and Windus.

Barber, David. June 1994. 'Body and Soul: Review of *About Love*'. *Poetry* 157–61.

Bardon, Carol, and Anthony Weir. 1970. '"Why is it that most of the poets here are Catholic?" Review of "Northern Crisis" issue of *Threshold*'. *Fortnight*, October 9.

Barr, Rebecca Anne, Sean Brady, and Jane McGaughey, editors. 2019. *Ireland and Masculinities in History*. London: Palgrave Macmillan.

Barry, Peter. 2006. *Poetry Wars: British Poetry of the 1970s and the Battle of Earl Court.* Cambridge: Salt Press.

Batten, Guinn. 1998. *The Orphaned Imagination: Melancholy and Commodity Culture in English Romanticism.* Durham, North Carolina: Duke University Press.

Bayley, Sally and Tracy Brain, editors. 2011. *Representing Sylvia Plath.* Cambridge: Cambridge University Press.

Beckett, Samuel, John Montague, Barney Rosset and Michael Brodsky. Summer 1995. '*Eleutheria*, Notes by John Montague and Barney Rossett'. *Grand Street* 75–113.

Beer, Patricia. 1973. 'Donald Davie and British Poetry'. *The Listener*, March 1: 280.

Bernard, Philippa. 2009. *No End to Snowdrops: A Biography of Kathleen Raine.* London: Shepheard-Walwyn Publishers.

Bizot, Richard. Spring 1995. 'The Homing Instinct in the Poetry of John Montague'. *Eire Ireland* 167–76.

Bloom, Harold. 2015. *The Daemon Knows: Literary Greatness and the American Sublime.* New York: Spiegel & K. Grau.

Blunk, Jonathan. 2019. *James Wright: A Life in Poetry.* New York: Farrar, Straus and Giroux.

Bly, Robert. April 2000. 'The Art of Poetry: The Bly Interview'. *The Paris Review.*

Boland, Eavan. 1970. 'Irish Literary Magazines: An Assessment'. *The Irish Times*, February 17: 12.

— . 1968. 'Living Art of Poetry: Montague's Reading'. *The Irish Times*, September 11: 10.

— . 1970. 'Love Story, *Tides*'. *The Irish Times*, October 3: 8.

— . 1966. 'Poetic Advances: *Wormwood* and *All Legendary Obstacles*'. *The Irish Times*, April 2: 8.

— . 1970. 'Provincials and Exiles: *Atlantis*'. *The Irish Times*, April 18.

— . 1973. 'The Tribal Poet: John Montague'. *The Irish Times*, March 20: 10.

Boland, Eavan, Liam Miller, Seamus Heaney, Michael Hartnett. 1970. 'The Future of Irish Poetry'. *The Irish Times*, February 5: 14.

Boland, John. 1970. 'Evening of Music, Poetry: The Chieftains'. *The Irish Press*, July 6: 12.

Boston, Richard. 1989. 'Literary Establishments … London'. *The Guardian*, July 24.

Bowers, Paul. December 1994. 'John Montague and William Carlos Williams: Nationalism and Poetic Construction'. *The Canadian Journal of Irish Studies* 29–44.

Bradley, Anthony. Autumn 1996. 'The Politics of Irishness'. *Contemporary Literature* 481–91.

Brearton, Fran, and Alan Gillis. 2012. Editors. *The Oxford Handbook of Modern Irish Poetry*. Oxford: Oxford University Press.

Brearton, Fran, and Michael Longley. 2012. Editors. *Incorrigibly Plural: Louis MacNeice and His Legacy.* Manchester: Carcanet Press.

Brennan, Rory. May 1992. 'U2 to Utopia, review of *Born in Brooklyn*'. *Books Ireland* 109–11.

Brown, Terence. Summer 1981. 'An Ulster Renaissance?' *Concerning Poetry* 5-23.

— . 1975. *Northern Voices*. Dublin: Gill & Macmillan.

Brown, Terence and Alec Reid. 1975. *Time Was Away: The World of Louis MacNeice.* Dublin: The Dolmen Press.

Brumming, Alison, and Sara Crangle, Keston Sutherland, J. H. Prynne, Craig Dworkin. 2007. *Complicities: British Poetry 1945–2007*. Prague: Litteraria Pragensia.

Buckley, Vincent. 1985. *Memory Ireland: Insights into the Contemporary Irish Condition.* London: Penguin.

Callaghan, Barry. 1998. *Barrelhouse Kings: A Memoir.* Toronto: McArthur & Company.

Canetti, Elias. 1999. *The Memoirs of Elias Canetti.* New York: Farrar, Straus and Giroux.

Chambers, Harry. 1974. 'The Ulster Poets'. *Fortnight*, April 5: 12–13.

Clark, Heather. 2006. *The Ulster Renaissance: Poetry in Belfast 1962–1972.* Oxford: Oxford University Press.

Clarke, Austin. 1967. 'Poet in politics: Montague's Patriotic Suite'. *The Irish Press*, February 4: 10.

Clyde, Tom. Summer 1990. 'Epic and Lyric; review of The Figure in the Cave'. 105–6.

— . Spring 1994. 'Time in Armagh, a review'. *Honest Ulsterman.*

Collins, Lucy, Editor. Spring/Summer 2012. 'Irish Poetry Cultures'. *Irish University Review.*

Coughlan, Patricia. 1986. '"The Whole Strange Growth": Heaney, Orpheus and women'. *The Irish Review* 25–45.

— . 1997. '"Bog Queens": The Representation of Women in the poetry of John Montague and Seamus Heaney' by Michael Allen. London: Palgrave Macmillan.

Creeley, Robert. With Linda Wagner and Lewis MacAdams. Fall 1968. 'The Art of Poetry: Robert Creeley Interview'. *The Paris Review.*

Cronin, Anthony. 1999, first published 1976. *Dead as Doornails.* Dublin: The Lilliput Press.

— . 1975. 'The Harp of Our Country: Four anthologies'. *The Irish Times*, April 11: 10.

— . 1996. *Samuel Beckett: The Last Modernist.* New York: Harper Collins.

— . 2010; first pub, 1964. *The Life of Riley.* Dublin: New Island.

Crotty, Patrick. 1986. 'Cunning Ampersands: Review of *Collected Poems*'. *The Irish Review* 136–43.

— . Spring 1990. 'Harmonisations, Review of The Figure in the Cave and other works'. *The Irish Review* 106–10.

Dana, Robert, ed. 1999. *A Community of Writers: Paul Engle and the Iowa Writers' Workshop.* Iowa City: University of Iowa Press.

Darcy, Ailbhe, and David Wheatley, editors. 2021. *A History of Irish Women's Poetry.* Cambridge: Cambridge University Press.

Davenport-Hines, Richard. 1999. *Auden.* New York: Knopf.

Davison, Peter. 1994. *The Fading Smile: Poets in Boston, 1955–1960 from Robert Frost to Robert Lowell to Sylvia Plath.* New York: Knopf.

Dawe, Gerald. January 1990. 'Circle of Conceit, Review of *The Figure in the Cave and other works*'. *Fortnight* 26.

— . May 1993. 'False Faces: conflicting responses to the peace movement'. *Fortnight* 34–5.

— . 2017. Editor. *The Cambridge Companion to Irish Poets.* Cambridge: Cambridge University Press.

— . 2018. *The Wrong Country: Essays on Modern Irish Writing.* Dublin: Irish Academic Press.

Deane, John F. 1984. 'Montague's Journey into the past, *The Dead Kingdom*'. *Irish Independent*, April 28.

Deane, Seamus. 1977. 'John Montague: Native and Foreigner'. *Hibernia*, June 10.

— . 1976, Spring. 'The Appetites of Gravity: Contemporary Irish Poetry'. *The Sewanee Review* 199–208.

— . 1985. *Celtic Revivals: Essays in Modern Irish Literature, 1880–1980*. London: Faber & Faber.

Delanty, Greg. 2005. 'Gregory O'Donoghue 1951–2005'. *The Poetry Ireland Review* 109.

Denman, Peter. 2007. 'John Jordan as Critic'. *Poetry Ireland* 116-18.

— . Spring 1994. 'The Muse of Memory, review of Time in Armagh'. *Irish Literary Supplement*.

Dickstein, Morris. 1977. *Gates of Eden: American Culture in the Sixties*. New York: Basic Books.

Dilworth, Thomas. 2017. *David Jones: Engraver, Soldier, Painter, Poet*. Berkeley: Counterpoint Publishers.

Dodsworth, Martin. 1973. '"Hoping for the Best": HD, Montague, MacBeth, Brownjohn, Hollander, and Rich'. *The Guardian*, March 15: 18.

— . 1978. 'Image and Accuracy, Poems by Montague and Wainwright'. *The Guardian*, July 20: 14.

— . 1976. 'With heart and mind: *A Slow Dance*'. *The Guardian*, January 29: 9.

— . 1984. 'Wrought and Overwrought: poems by Montague, McGuckian, and Selma Hill'. *The Guardian*, October 11: 22.

Donoghue, Denis. 1955. 'Mummy Truths to Tell: *The Permanence of Yeats*'. *The Irish Times*, September 24: 6.

— . Winter 1960/61. 'Dublin Letter'. *The Hudson Review* 579–85.

— . 1974. '"Icham of Irlaunde": *The Faber Book of Irish Verse*'. *The Spectator*, April 5: 11.

— . 1976, Winter. 'Being Irish Together'. *The Sewanee Review* 129–33.

Dorgan, Theo. 2017. 'John Montague: The Influence of Anxiety'. *Poetry Ireland Review 121* 79–84.

— . Autumn 1995. 'Seán Dunne 1956–95'. *The Poetry Ireland Review* 4.

Doty, Mark. 2010. *The Art of Description: World into Word*. Minneapolis: Graywolf Press.

Dove, Rita. 18 March 2001. '"Poet's Choice"'. *The Washington Post* 12.

Duncan, Robert. 2014. *The Collected Later Poems and Plays*. Berkeley and Los Angeles: University of California Press.

Dunn, Douglas. 1984. 'The dance of discontent, Montague's *The Dead Kingdom*'. *The Times Literary Supplement*, October 5: 1124.

Dunne, Seán. 1982. 'A Generous Light, Montague's *Selected Poems*'. *The Cork Review* 54.

— . Autumn 1989. 'History Lessons: A Note on John Montague's relationship with the past'. *The Poetry Ireland Review* 6–14.

Durcan, Paul. 1978. 'Montague's Achievement, The Great Cloak'. *Irish Examiner*, May 1: 8.

Eagleton, Terry. 1973. 'The State of Ireland: Poems by Montague and Deane'. *The Times Literary Supplement*, February 16: 183.

Ellmann, Richard. Summer 1974. 'The Garden Party: *The Faber Book of Irish Verse*'. *The New Review* 70–71.

Ennis, Stephen. 2014. *After the Titanic: A Life of Derek Mahon*. Dublin: Gill and Macmillan.

Faas, Ekbert. 1983. *Young Robert Duncan: Portrait of the Poet as Homosexual in Society*. Santa Barbara: Black Sparrow Press.

Faas, Ekbert with Maria Trombacco. 2001. *Robert Creeley: A Biography*. Montreal and Kingston: McGill-Queen's University Press.

Faller, Kevin. 1966. 'Would Silence be Safer? Montague's Patriotic Suite'. *Irish Independent*, December 17: 10.

Felix. 1970. 'The Planter and the Gael'. *Fortnight*, December 4: 10.

Fiacc, Padraic. 2002. 'Name Droppings: From the Unpublished Autobiography'. *Fortnight*, June: 19-22.

— . 1974. 'An Ulsterman's Search for Identity: John Hewitt'. *Hibernia*, April 26: 11.

— . 1974. 'Violence and the Ulster Poet'. *Hibernia*, December 6: 19.

Finneran, Richard. Spring 1974. '"Modern Irish Literature"'. *James Joyce Quarterly* 293–6.

Fitzsimons, Andrew. 2008. *The Sea of Disappointment: Thomas Kinsella's Pursuit of the Real*. Dublin: UCD Press.

Foster, John Wilson. June 1978. 'The Celtic Arts, CAIS Conference – A Personal Report'. *The Canadian Journal of Irish Studies* 62–5.

— . November 1975. 'The Landscape of the Planter and the Gael in the Poetry of John Hewitt and John Montague'. *The Canadian Journal of Irish Studies* 17-33.

Frazier, Adrian. Winter 1979. 'Global Regionalism: Interview with John Montague'. Winter 1979. *The Literary Review* 153–74.

— . December 1983. 'John Montague's Language of the Tribe'. *The Canadian Journal of Irish Studies* 57–75.

— . Winter 1985. 'Pilgrim Haunts: Montague's *The Dead Kingdom* and Heaney's *Station Island*'. *Éire-Ireland* 134–43.

— . 2004. 'A poet in his prime: *Drunken Sailor* and *Well Dreams*'. *The Irish Times*, September 25: 13.

Fredman, Stephen, and Steve McCaffrey, editors. 2010. *Form, Power, and Person in Robert Creeley's Life and Work*. Iowa City: University of Iowa Press.

Gallant, Mavis. 1968. 'The Events in Paris'. *The New Yorker*, September 14 and 21.

Gardner, Raymond. 1977. 'Far from the city sandbags, Frank Ormsby'. *The Guardian*, December 7: 10.

— . 1970. 'Seigemograph: A New Siege'. *The Guardian*, January 10: 8.

Gelpi, Albert. 2015. *American Poetry after Modernism: The Power of the Word*. Cambridge: Cambridge University Press.

Ginsberg, Allen. 2009. Edited by Bill Morgan. *Selected Letters of Allen Ginsberg and Gary Snyder*. Berkeley: Counterpoint.

— . 2008. Selected by Mark Ford. *Allen Ginsberg*. London: Faber & Faber.

— . 1995 Edited by Gordon Ball. *Allen Ginsberg: Journals Mid-Fifties 1954–1958*. New York: Harper Collins.

Gitlin, Todd. 1987. *The Sixties, Years of Hope, Days of Rage*. New York: Bantam.

Graecen, Robert. 1997. *The Sash My Father Wore: An Autobiography*. Edinburgh: Mainstream Publishing.

Graves, Robert. 2003. *The Complete Poems*. London: Penguin Classics.

— . 1948. *The White Goddess: A Historical Grammar of Poetic Myth*. London: Faber & Faber.

Grennan, Eamon. 1990. 'Illuminations: review of *The Figure in the Cave*'. *Agni*, 292–5.

Grigson, Geoffrey. 1974. 'The Face of Irish Poetry'. *The Irish Times*, March 9: 10.

Grubgeld, Elizabeth. January 1989. 'Topography, Memory, and John Montague's "The Rough Field"'. *The Canadian Journal of Irish Studies* 25–36.

Haas, Robert. 2017. *A Little Book on Form: An Exploration into the Formal Imagination.* New York: Ecco Press.

Hacker, P.M.S. 1988. *The Renaissance of Gravure: The Art of S.W. Hayter.* Oxford: Clarendon Press.

Haffenden, John. 1980. *John Berryman: A Critical Commentary.* London & Basingstoke: Macmillan.

Hall, Donald. 2010. *Unpacking the Boxes: A Memoir of a Life in Poetry.* Boston: Houghton Mifflin Harcourt.

Hamilton, Ian. 2002. *Against Oblivion: Some Lives of the Twentieth-Century Poets.* New York: Viking.

— . 1994. *Walking Possession: Essays and Reviews, 1968–1993.* London: Bloomsbury.

Harmon, Maurice. 1971. 'Post-war Poets had a new vision'. *The Irish Press*, May 24.

— . Editor. Spring 1989. 'Special Issue on John Montague'. *Irish University Review.*

Heaney, Seamus. 2003. *Finders Keepers: Selected Prose 1971–2001.* New York: Farrar, Straus and Giroux.

— . 1973. 'Lost Ulstermen: The Rough Field'. *The Listener*, April 26: 550.

— . With Dennis O'Driscoll. 2009. *Stepping Stones.* London: Faber & Faber.

Hegarty, Peter. 1999. *Peadar O'Donnell.* Mercier Press: Cork and Dublin.

Hennigan, Aidan. 1969. 'Kavanagh Tribute'. *The Irish Press*, December 12: 13.

Higgins, Aidan. 2001. *The Whole Hog.* London: Vintage.

Hogan, Jeremiah J. Autumn 1976. 'Michael Tierney 1894–1975'. *Studies: An Irish Quarterly Review* 177–91.

Holland, Jack. 1975. 'A Phonetic Imagination: Seamus Heaney'. *Hibernia*, June 13: 22.

Hopkin, Alannah. 2021. *A Very Strange Man: A Memoir of Aidan Higgins.* Dublin: New Island.

Horgan, John. 1970. 'American Academics Look at Ireland'. *The Irish Times*, May 16: 10.

Howard, Jane. 1967. 'Whiskey and Ink: Berryman in Dublin'. *Life Magazine*, July 21.

Howard, Paul. 2016. *I Read the News Today, Oh Boy: The short and gilded life of Tara Browne, the man who inspired The Beatles' greatest song.* London: Picador.

Hutchinson, Pearse. Spring 1997. 'Drowning in the Aesthetic: interview'. *The Poetry Ireland Review* 22-33.

— . 1962. 'An Irish Poet: *Poisoned Lands'*. *Irish Independent*, January 13: 7.

— . 1959. 'First book by a young Irish poet: *Forms of Exile'*. *The Irish Press*, March 28.

Harper, Vicki and Lawrence Fong. 2013. *Morris Graves: Selected Letters.* Seattle & London: University of Washington Press.

Jamison, Kay Redfield. 2017. *Robert Lowell, Setting the River on Fire: A Study of Genius, Mania, and Character.* New York: Knopf.

Jarnot, Lisa. 2012. *Robert Duncan: The Ambassador from Venus.* Berkeley and Los Angeles: University of California Press.

Jeffries, Stuart. 2016. *Grand Hotel Abyss: The Lives of the Frankfurt School.* London: Verso.

John, Brian. June 1986. 'The Healing Art of John Montague'. *The Canadian Journal of Irish Studies* 35–52.

Johnston, Dillon. 1985. *Irish Poetry After Joyce.* Notre Dame: Notre Dame University Press.

— . 2001. *The Poetic Economies of England and Ireland, 1912–2000.* London: Palgrave.

Johnstone, Robert. 1976. 'What's on: John Montague's A Slow Dance'. *Fortnight*, September 10: 15.

Jones, David. Edited by René Hague. 1980. *Dai Greatcoat: A Self-Portrait of David Jones in his Letters.* London: Faber & Faber.

Jordan, John. 1975. '*Remembering How We Stood'*. *Hibernia*, September 19: 20.

— . 1978. '*The Great Cloak'*. *Irish Independent*, April 1: 8.

— . 1970. 'Magazine Scene'. *The Irish Press*, October 7: 13.

— . 1984. 'This ground it mined, THE DEAD KINGDOM'. *The Irish Press*, May 26.

— . Ed. Hugh McFadden. 2006. *Crystal Clear: Selected Prose of John Jordan.* Dublin: The Lilliput Press.

Kavanagh, Patrick. 1952. 'Graftonia'. *Kavanagh's Weekly*, June 14: 5.

Kennedy, Maurice. 1964. 'Breakthrough: *Death of a Chieftain'*. *The Irish Times*, September 24: 9.

Kennedy-Andrews, Elmer. 2006. 'John Montague: Global Regionalist?' *The Cambridge Quarterly* 31–48.

Kennelly, Brendan. 1972. 'Three Poets on the Tragedy of our Times: Montague, Watters, Tessier'. *Sunday Independent*, December 10: 16.

— . 1961. '*Poisoned Lands*'. *The Dubliner*, November/December.

Kern, Robert. Spring 1977. 'Recipes, Catalogues, Open Form Poetics: Gary Snyder's Archetypal Voice'. *Contemporary Literature* 173–97.

Kerouac, Jack. 1958. *The Dharma Bums*. New York: Viking Press.

Kersnowski, Frank. 1974. *John Montague*. Lewisburg: Bucknell University Press.

Kiely, Benedict ('Patrick Lagan'). 1959. 'An Irish poet born in New York in 1929'. *The Irish Press*, February 26.

— . 2004, first pub. 1945. *Counties of Contention*. Cork and Dublin: Mercier Press.

Kilroy, Thomas. Winter 1967. '*A Chosen Light, Good Souls to Serve*, and *New Territory*'. *Irish University Review* 302–6.

Kinsella, Thomas. 1976. 'The Cantos'. *Hibernia*, June 4: 23.

— . 1990. 'So That: The Cantos'. In *Poetic License: Essays on Modern and Postmodern Lyric*, 133-34. Evanston: Northwestern University Press.

— . 2009. *Prose Occasions 1951–2006*. Edited by Andrew Fitzsimons. Manchester: Carcanet Press.

Kinsella, Thomas and John Montague, eds. 1962. *The Dolmen Miscellany of Irish Writing*. Dublin: The Dolmen Press.

Knowles, John. 2004. 'Encounter with the Pagan'. *Fortnight* 24.

Knowlson, James. 1996. *Damned to Fame: The Life of Samuel Beckett*. London: Bloomsbury.

Kramer, Jane. 1969. *Allen Ginsberg in America*. New York: Random House.

Lalor, Brian. 2011. *Ink-Stained Hands: Graphic Studio Dublin and the Origin of Fine Art Printmaking in Ireland*. Dublin: The Lilliput Press.

Lattimore, Richard. Autumn 1971. 'Poetry Chronicle: Galway Kinnell, *Book of Nightmares*; John Montague, *Tides*'. *The Hudson Review* 499–510.

Leader, Zachary. 2016. *The Life of Saul Bellow: To Fame and Fortune, 1915–1964*. London: Cape.

Lee, J.J. 1989. *Ireland 1912–1985*. Cambridge: Cambridge University Press.

Legler, Philip. 1961. 'Forms of Exile'. *Poetry*, December.

Leland, Mary. 1975. '"I, Robert": Graves in Cork'. *The Irish Times*, May 16: 10.

— . 1976. 'John Montague in Cork'. *The Irish Times*, November 23: 6.

Lennon, Peter. 1994. *Foreign Correspondent: Paris in the Sixties.* London: Picador.

Lessing, Doris. 1962. *The Golden Notebook.* London: Michael Joseph.

Levine, Philip. 2016. *My Lost Poets: A Life in Poetry.* New York: Knopf.

— . Summer 1988. 'The Art of Poetry: The Philip Levine Interview'. *The Paris Review.*

Liddy, James, edited by Eamonn Wall. 2013. *On Irish Literature.* Dublin: Arlen House.

— . 1982. *This Was Arena.* Naas, County Kildare: The Malton Press.

Logan, William. 2005. *The Undiscovered Country: Poetry in the Age of Tin.* New York: Columbia University Press.

Longley, Edna. 1975. 'Letter to the editor, regarding Anthony Cronin's Viewpoint'. *The Irish Times*, November 1: 16.

— . 1976. 'Private Areas: A Slow Dance'. *The Irish Times*, January 17: 8.

— . 1974. 'Recent Poetry: The Cave of Night'. *The Irish Times*, April 20: 10.

— . July 1966. 'The Heroic Agenda: The Poetry of Thomas Kinsella'. *Dublin Magazine* 61–78.

— . 1986. *Poetry in the Wars.* Newcastle upon Tyne: Bloodaxe Books.

— . 1994. *The Living Stream: Literature and Revisionism in Ireland.* Newcastle upon Tyne: Bloodaxe Books.

Longley, Michael. 1970. 'Poetry to Link the Two Communities: Montague and Hewitt'. *The Irish Press*, December 7: 13.

— . Summer 1985. With Robert Johnstone. Summer 1985. 'The Longley Tapes'. *The Honest Ulsterman* 13–31.

Lowell, Robert, and Elizabeth Hardwick, edited by Saskia Hamilton. 2019. *The Dolphin Letters, 1970–1979: Elizabeth Hardwick, Robert Lowell and their Circle.* New York: Macmillan.

Lucy, Seán. 1977. 'Irish Writing: A New Criticism'. *Hibernia*, April 1: 18.

— . 1973 Autumn. '"Three Poets from Ulster"'. *Irish University Review* 179–93.

— . 1974. 'What about Ó Riada?' *Hibernia*, September 13: 25.

Lynch, Brian. 1978. 'Poet's Honesty Comes Through, Montague's *The Great Cloak*'. *Sunday Press*, May 28: 21.

Lyons, F.S.L. 1974. 'Two Traditions in One: *The Faber Book of Irish Verse*'. *The Times Literary Supplement*, July 19: 763.

Lynan, Siobhan, John O'Meara, Con Leventhal, John Montague. 1969. 'French TV viewers bewildered'. *The Irish Times*, February 14.

MacDonald, Peter. 1997. *Mistaken Identities: Poetry and Northern Ireland*. Oxford: Clarendon Press.

MacInerney, John. 1972. 'Montague's Irish Dimension: *The Rough Field*'. *Hibernia*, December 15: 12.

Mahon, Derek. 1996. *Journalism*. Oldcastle: The Gallery Press.

— . 2012. *Selected Prose*. Oldcastle: The Gallery Press.

Malcolm, Janet. 2019. *Nobody's Looking at You*. New York: Farrar, Straus and Giroux.

— . 1981. *Psychoanalysis*. New York: Knopf.

Mangan, Gerald. 2002. 'Cows Have No Religion'. *Parnassus: Poetry in Review* 247–63.

Mariani, Paul. 1990. *Dream Song: The Life of John Berryman*. Amherst: University of Massachusetts Press.

Martin, Augustine. Summer 1963. '*The Dolmen Miscellany and Poetry Ireland*'. *Studies: An Irish Quarterly Review* 222–4.

— . Autumn 1974. '*The Faber Book of Irish Verse*'. *Studies: An Irish Quarterly Review* 311–14.

— . 1967. 'The Northern Muse'. December 23: 11.

Maxwell, D.E.S. June 1973. 'The Poetry of John Montague'. *Critical Quarterly*.

McCarthy, Patricia, editor. 2004. *Agenda: John Montague – 75th Birthday Supplement*. Volume 40, Nos. 1–3.

McCarthy, Thomas. Autumn 2019. 'Journals 1974–2014'. *New Hibernia Review* 9–34.

— . September 2015. 'Poetry and the Memory of Fame'. *Poetry* 517–26, 539.

— . 'The Years of Forgetting'. *Irish Pages:* vol. 6, no. 1., 20–38.

— . Winter 2010. 'We Stayed Up Late: Remembering Vincent Buckley'. *New Hibernia Review* 125–8.

McCormack, W.J. 2015. *Northman: John Hewitt (1907–87)*. Oxford: Oxford University Press.

— . 1976. 'Rural past, urban present'. *The Times Literary Supplement*, March 19: 324.

McDonald, Ronan. 2005. 'Strategies of Silence: Colonial Strains in Short Stories of the Troubles'. *The Yearbook of English Studies* 249–63.

McDowell, Tara. 2019. *The Householders: Robert Duncan and Jess*. Cambridge, Massachusetts: MIT Press.

McFarland, James. 1976. 'Poetasters and Poseurs: *A Slow Dance*'. *Hibernia*, April 23: 2.

McIlroy, Brian. July 1990. 'Poetic Imagery as Political Fetishism; The Example of Michael Longley'. *The Canadian Journal of Irish Studies* 59–64.

Meenan, James. Editor. 1955. *Centenary History of the Literary and Historical Society of University College Dublin 1855–1955*. Dublin: A&A Farmar.

Menand, Louis. 2021. *The Free World: Art and Thought in the Cold War*. New York: 4th Estate.

Merwin, W.S. Spring 1987. 'The Art of Poetry: W. S. Merwin Interview'. *The Paris Review*.

Middlebrook, Diane. 2003. *Her Husband: Ted Hughes and Sylvia Plath – A Marriage*. New York: Penguin Books.

Miller, J. Hillis. 2001. *Speech Acts in Literature*. Stanford: Stanford University Press.

Miller, Karl. 2013. *Tretower to Clyro: Essays*. London: Quercus.

Mills, Barry. 1989. *Ginsberg: Beat Poet*. Penguin: London.

Mole, John. 1978. 'The relief of solitude: Montague's *The Great Cloak*'. *The Times Literary Supplement*, August 11: 906.

John Montague, interview with Stephen Arkin. Autumn/Winter 1982. 'John Montague interview'. *New England Review* 214–41.

John Montague, interview with Timothy Kearney and John Hewitt. 1981. 'The Planter and the Gael'. *The Crane Bag* 85–92.

John Montague, Publications. The first publications of poems in periodicals and newspapers, and occasional prose pieces, were too numerous to include in this incomplete but serviceable bibliography.

— . 1949. 'A Summer in Italy: Seán O'Faoláin'. *Catholic Standard*, November 25: 6.

— . 1949. 'Cartoons and Morality'. *Catholic Standard*, November 18.

— . 1949. 'The Genius of John Ford'. *Catholic Standard*, December 2: 6.

— . 1949. 'Something Rare in Modern Fiction: Benedict Kiely'. *Catholic Standard*, November 18.

— . 1950. '"The Yeats Film", and other film reviews, during this year'. *Catholic Standard*, January 13.

— . 1950 June. 'Evening in Austria'. *The National Student* 8–10.

— . 1951 June. 'Fellow Travelling with America'. *The Bell*.

— . 1951 July. 'George Moore: The Tyranny of Memory'. *The Bell*.

— . 1951 October. 'The Young Writer and *The Bell*'. *The Bell*.

— . 1952 January, February, March. 'Theatre'. *The Bell*.

— . 1952 February. 'The Theatre'. *The Bell*.

— . 1952 April. 'Tribute to William Carleton'. *The Bell* 13–19.

— . 1952. 'The English Legend'. *The Irish Times*, July 12: 6.

— . 1952. 'Four Poems'. *The Bell*, October: 275–7.

— . 1952. 'The Theatre'. *The Bell*, May: 111–14.

— . 1956 December. 'Return to Europe'. *Poetry* 203–4.

— . 1957. 'Sante Fe'. *The Irish Times*, March 9: 6.

— . 1957 July. 'First Week in Lent – A Political Snapshot'. *Threshold* 69–72.

— . 1957 August. 'Letter from Dublin'. *Poetry* 310–15.

— . 1957. 'An End to Innocence: USA 1945–1955'. *The Irish Times*, July 13: 6.

— . 1957. 'Portrait of the Enemy: Wyndham Lewis'. *The Irish Times*, August 10: 6.

— . 1958 Winter. 'Contemporary Verse: A short chronicle'. *Studies: An Irish Quarterly Review* 441–9.

— . 1958. 'Snopes for President: William Faulkner's *The Town*'. *The Irish Times*, March 8: 6.

— . 1958. 'The Modern Novel: *Craft and Character in Modern Fiction*'. *The Irish Times*, January 11: 6.

— . 1959 July. 'Isolation and Cunning: Recent Irish Verse (Clarke, Colum, Kavanagh and Kinsella)'. *Poetry* 264–70.

— . 1959 Winter. 'Review of John Press, James Harrison, Christopher Fry, and Edwin Muir'. *Studies: An Irish Quarterly Review* 481–2.

— . 1960 Spring. 'Penguin anthologies of verse'. *Studies: An Irish Quarterly Review* 102–4.

— . 1960 Spring. 'The Tragic Picaresque: Oliver Goldsmith, the Biographical Aspect'. *Studies: An Irish Quarterly Review* 45–53.

— . 1960. 'The Mother Country: *Alienation*'. *The Irish Times*, October 1: 6

— . 1960 Winter. 'Dobree's *English Literature in the Early Eighteenth Century*'. *Studies: An Irish Quarterly Review* 203–5.

— . 1961 Spring. 'Alspach, Irish Poetry to 1798'. *Studies: An Irish Quarterly Review* 97–9.

— . 1961. *Poisoned Lands and other poems*. London: MacGibbon and Kee.

— . 1962. *The Dolmen Miscellany of Irish Writing*. Edited, with Thomas Kinsella. Dublin: The Dolmen Press.

— . 1962. 'Menaced Mildness: Vernon Scannell'. *The Spectator*, August 10: 21.

— . 1962. 'Responsibilities: Yeats and Macmillan publisher'. *The Guardian*, June 22: 10.

— . 1962. 'True Observation: Blunden and Tremayne'. *The Spectator*, September 28: 25.

— . 1962. 'Post-atomic French writing'. *The Guardian*, June 15: 7.

— . 1962. 'Un-English Urges: Poems by Tony Connor, Christopher Logue and Robin Skelton'. *The Spectator*, December 7.

— . 1963. 'Letter from Paris: Early Middle-Age Wave'. *The Irish Times*, July 13: 10.

— . 1963. 'Mental Fire: Harold Bloom's *Blake's Apocalypse*'. *The Irish Times*, October 30: 9.

— . 1964. *Death of a Chieftain*. London: MacGibbon and Kee.

— . 1964. 'Expressing and explaining: Mary Lavin's stories'. *The Guardian*, August 28: 7.

— . 1964. 'A cowboy Casanova: Frank Harris'. *The Guardian*, November 13: 9.

— . 1965. 'Shall we overcome? *Three Lives for Mississippi*'. *The Irish Times*, November 13: 8.

— . 1965. 'The Trinity Scholard: Beckett's *Proust*'. *The Guardian*, November 26: 17.

— . 1966. *All Legendary Obstacles*. Dublin: The Dolmen Press.

— . 1966. 'Louis le Brocquy: A painter's interior world'. *Hibernia*, December: 29.

— . 1966. 'Snapshots and Towards a New Novel: Robbe-Grillet'. *The Guardian*, February 4: 8.

— . 1966. 'Poet and peasants: Muriel Rukeyser'. *The Guardian*, April 7: 10.

— . 1966. 'Living under Ben Bulben'. *Kilkenny Magazine*, July.

— . 1966. 'The end of Brendan: Rae Jeffe's *Brendan Behan*'. *The Guardian*, November 4: 6.

— . 1966. *All Legendary Obstacles*. Dublin: The Dolmen Press.

— . 1967. 'A Home in Kildare: Langrishe, Go Down'. *The New York Times*, April 16: 144.

— . 1967. 'Irish revaluations: A Golden Treasury and The Backward Look'. *The Guardian*, May 26: 7.

— . 1967. 'Less tactual than the male, Clara Malraux's memoirs'. *The Guardian*, September 22: 7.

— . 1967. 'The Hungry Years, review of *Realities of Irish Life*'. *Hibernia*, January: 24.

— . 1967/68. 'Hugh MacDiarmid: The Seamless Garment and the Muse'. *Agenda*.

— . 1968. 'And an Irishman: Kinsella's *Nightwalker*'. *The New York Times*, August 18.

— . 1968. '"I survive you": Berryman's Sonnets'. *The Guardian*, April 26: 7.

— . 1968. 'Painter's Problem: Barrie Cooke'. *The Irish Times*, May 11: 6.

— . 1969. '"Earth House Hold: Technical Notes and Queries to Fellow Dharma Revolutionaries"'. *Chicago Tribune*, October 19.

— . 1969. 'Hymn to the New Omagh Road'. *The Irish Press*, March 8: 9.

— . 1969. 'Le Cri'. Trans. Serge Fauchereau. *Les Lettres Nouvelles*, Juin–Juillet: 91–116.

— . 1969. 'Laying Rough Hands on the Well-wrought Urn'. *Chicago Tribune*, August 17: 5.

— . 1969. 'The Last Performance: Frank O'Connor'. *The Guardian*, April 10: 9.

— . 1969. 'Wilful Wilde: review of Julian's *Oscar Wilde*'. *The Guardian*, May 29: 9.

— . 1969. 'Ulster bull fight'. *The Guardian*, November 27: 15.

— . 1970. *Tides*. Dublin: The Dolmen Press.

— . 1970. 'A Lost Tradition'. *The Irish Press*, March 27: 9.

— . 1970. 'The prize-winner: André Maurois'. *The Guardian*, April 2: 9.

— . 1970. 'A poet's manifold world: Pablo Neruda'. *Chicago Tribune*, May 17: 267.

— . 1970. 'Black Catholics, Liam de Paor's *Divided Ulster* and Owen Dudley Edwards' *The Sins of our Fathers*'. *The Guardian*, June 18: 11.

— . 1970. 'A Primal Gaeltacht'. *The Irish Times*, July 30.

— . 1970. 'Brendan's Being: Ulick O'Connor's *Brendan Behan*'. *The Guardian*, July 30: 7.

— . 1970. 'Like the Mother of God: Lady Gregory'. *The Guardian*, August 8: 7.

— . 1970. 'The Young Campaigner: Yeats's *Uncollected Prose*'. *The Guardian*, September 3: 7.

— . 1970. 'Village Bard: Joel Oppenheimer'. *Chicago Tribune*, February 15.

— . 1970. 'A Man's World: The Táin'. *Fortnight*, November 20: 22–23.

— . 1970. 'Kinsella's *Táin*'. *Fortnight*, November 20: 22–3.

— . 1971. *Tides*. Chicago: Swallow Press.

— . 1971. 'Past Master: A Bash in the Tunnel'. *The Guardian*, March 25: 7

— . 1971. 'Collapsing Suns: The Four Sons, The Heroic Triad, and Documentary History of Mexican Americans'. *The Guardian*, July 22: 12.

— . 1971. 'Master of Britain: David Jones'. *The Guardian*, September 9: 9.

— . 1971. 'Today and Yesterday in Northern Ireland'. *BBC Radio Magazine*, October: 16.

— . 1972. *A Fair House: Versions of Irish Poetry*. Dublin: Cuala Press.

— . 1972. *The Rough Field*. Dublin: The Dolmen Press.

— . 1972. 'Order in Donnybrook Fair'. *The Times Literary Supplement*, March 17: 289.

— . 1972/73 Autumn/Winter. 'A Note on Rhythm'. *Agenda*.

— . 1973 March. With Serge Fauchereau. 'Hymne à la nouvelle route d'Omagh'. *Les Lettres Nouvelles*.

— . 1974. 'John Berryman's Exile'. *Hibernia*, May 24.

— . 1974 July. 'The Philosophical Vagabond: Oliver Goldsmith'. *Ireland of the Welcomes*.

— . 1974. 'In the Irish Grain', *The Faber Book of Irish Verse*. London: Faber & Faber.

— . 1974. 'Reply to Denis Donoghue's review of *The Faber Book of Irish Verse*'. *The Spectator*, May 3: 5.

— . 1975. *A Slow Dance*. Dublin: The Dolmen Press, and Oxford: Oxford University Press.

— . 1975. 'Ulster Poetry, regarding Edna Longley's review'. *The Irish Times*, January 31: 11.

— . 1975. '"Poor Noll": Oliver Goldsmith'. *The Guardian*, February 27: 9.

— . 1976. 'Kinsella's Clarke'. *The Irish Times*, July 17: 8.

— . 1976. 'Domestic Sphinx: Emily Dickinson'. *Hibernia*, July 30: 23.

— . 1977. 'Doomed Intelligence: *Letters to W.B. Yeats*'. *The Guardian*, December 15: 9.

— . 1977. *Poisoned Lands, revised edition*. Dublin: The Dolmen Press and Oxford University Press.

— . 1977. *November: a choice of translations from Andre Frénaud*. Cork: Golden Stone Press.

— . 1977. 'The Melancholy Beauty of Banks'. *The Irish Times*, October 20: 1.

— . 1982. 'ReJoyce: see how he rises'. *The Guardian*, October 21: 10.

— . 1978. *The Great Cloak*. Dublin: The Dolmen Press, and Oxford: Oxford University Press.

— . 1978. 'Beckett's privacy breached, Deirdre Bair's biography'. *The Guardian*, September 14: 9.

— . 1978. 'Jaweyes'. *The Crane Bag* 9–10.

— . 1978. 'Mystic Materialist: Hugh MacDiarmid'. *The Guardian*, November 30: 14.

— . 1979. *The Leap*. Deerfied: Deerfield Press; and Oldcastle: The Gallery Press.

— . 1979. 'Irish doom: Berleth's *The Twilight Lords*'. *The Guardian*, February 8: 16.

— . 1980. 'Patrick Kavanagh: A Speech from the Dock'. *The Irish Times*, July 5 and 8.

— . 1981. 'Invitation to a poet's workshop, Heaney's *Preoccupations*'. *The Guardian*, January 4: 21.

— . 1982. *Selected Poems*. Dublin: The Dolmen Press.

— . 1982 July. 'James Joyce: Work Your Progress'. *Irish University Review* 48–52.

— . 1983. 'To make up a good yarn, Kenner's *A Colder Eye*'. *The Guardian*, July 28: 8.

— . 1984. *The Dead Kingdom*. Dublin: The Dolmen Press.

— . 1984. 'What to Make of W.B. Yeats, Finneran's *Poems* and Jeffares' *Commentary*'. *The Guardian*, July 2: 21.

— . 1984. 'Writer's Ireland, William Trevor'. *The Guardian*, April 5: 18.

— . 1985. 'A Poet Remembers'. *Newsday*, October 14: 4.

— . 1985. 'In anger and affection, review of Maurice Harmon's book on Seán O'Faoláin'. *The Times Literary Supplement*, September 6: 980.

— . 1985. 'Worshipping the White Goddess'. *Encounter*, March: 65–70.

— . 1987. *The Lost Notebook*. Cork & Dublin: Mercier Press.

— . 1988. *Mount Eagle*. Oldcastle: The Gallery Press.

— . 1988. 'Robert Duncan, obituary'. *The Guardian*, February 13: 39.

— . 1988. *Amours, marées*. Bordeaux: William Blake and Co.

— . 1989. *The Figure in the Cave and Other Essays*. Edited by Antoinette Quinn. Syracuse: Syracuse University Press, and Dublin: The Lilliput Press.

— . 1989. *Bitter Harvest: An Anthology of Contemporary Irish Verse*. Selected and introduced. New York: Scribner's.

— . 1989. 'Cryptic, Celtic, review of Maurice Harmon on Austin Clarke'. *Irish Independent*, July 29: 6.

— . 1989. 'The Gloom and Glory of Beckett'. *The Guardian*, December 27: 13.

— . 1989. *The Figure in the Cave: and Other Essays*. Dublin: The Lilliput Press.

— . 1991. *Born in Brooklyn*, edited by David Lampe. Fredonia: White Pine Press.

— . 1991. 'A Literary Gentleman: Seán O'Faoláin'. *The Cork Review* 53–4.

— . 1992. *An Occasion of Sin*. Toronto: Exile Editions.

— . 1992. *The Love Poems*. Toronto: Exile Editions.

— . 1993. *Time in Armagh*. Oldcastle: The Gallery Press.

— . 1995. *Collected Poems*. Winston-Salem: Wake Forest University Press, and Oldcastle: The Gallery Press.

— . 1995, Autumn. 'A Strategic Snarl, Review of Kinsella, The Dual Tradition'. *The Poetry Ireland Review* 34–7.

— . 1995. 'The poet and his muses: Robert Graves'. *The Guardian*, June 24: 10.

— . 1997. *A Love Present & Other Stories*. Dublin: Wolfhound Press.

— . 1999. [Translator] *Dubuffet's Walls*, 'Les Murs' by Eugène Guillevic. London: Hayward Gallery National Touring Exhibitions.

— . Translator. *Carnac* by Eugène Guillevic. Newcastle upon Tyne: Bloodaxe Books.

— . 1999. *Smashing the Piano*. Oldcastle: The Gallery Press.

— . 2001. *Company: A Chosen Life*. London: Duckworth.

— . 2002. 'The French muse', *The Irish Times*, June 1: 60.

— . 2003. 'A kick out of you: Richard Murphy', *The Irish Times*, June 22: 57.

— . 2002. 'A towering inferno'. *The Irish Times*, November 23: 59.

— . 2003. 'No buck-lepping here'. *The Irish Times*. June 27: 9.

— . 2003. 'Monuments to Mangan'. *The Irish Times*. April 26: 59.

— . 2004. *Drunken Sailor*. Oldcastle: The Gallery Press.

— . 2005. 'The Gaul of them'. *The Irish Times*. January 22: 13.

— . 2005. 'An Ulster Tandem'. *Irish Pages* 162–8.

— . 2005. 'Has He the Touch?'. *The Poetry Ireland Review* 86–8.

— . 2005. 'Words of a grumpy old man: Elias Canetti'. *The Irish Times*, October 8: 12.

— . 2006. 'John Milton, "Paradise Lost"'. *Poetry Ireland Review* 52–3.

— . 2006. 'Stricken blackbird: Gregory O'Donoghue'. *The Irish Times*. January 28: 10.

— . 2007. *The Pear is Ripe: A Memoir*. Dublin: Liberties Press.

— . 2007. 'The early years of Ezra Pound'. *The Irish Times*. December 22: 10.

— . 2008. 'The man and his Melodies: Thomas Moore'. *The Irish Times*. April 26: 11.

— . 2008. 'Complicated Conquests'. *The Irish Times*. May 31: 10.

— . 2009. 'Poet far from Paradise'. *The Irish Times*. December 19: 10.

— . 2010. 'Koestler's melancholic mind'. March 13: 12.

— . 2010. '*The Human Chain*'. *Dublin Review of Books*.

— . 2010. 'Beach, boys, and the swami'. *The Irish Times*. November 20: 12.

— . 2011. *Speech Lessons*. Oldcastle: The Gallery Press.

— . 2017. *Second Childhood*. Oldcastle: The Gallery Press.

— . 2018. *A Spell to Bless the Silence: Selected Poems*. Winston-Salem: Wake Forest University Press.

Montague, John and others. 2013. *Chosen Lights: Poets on Poems*. Oldcastle: The Gallery Press.

Murphy, Gerry. 2007. *End of Part One: New and Selected Poems*. Dublin: Dedalus Press.

Murphy, Hayden. 1983. *Broadsheet 1967–1978, Poetry, Prose, and Graphics*. Edinburgh: National Library of Scotland.

Murphy, Richard. 2003. *The Kick: A Life Among Writers*. London: Granta Books.

Nelson, Maggie. 2022. *On Freedom*. London: Penguin.

Ní Chuilleanáin, Eiléan. Autumn 1989. 'A Festive Note, review of *Hill Field, Irish University Review*: John Montague Special Issue, and *The New Oxford Book of Irish Verse* by Thomas Kinsella'. *The Poetry Ireland Review* 66–69.

— . 1976. 'A Joyous Suite: A Slow Dance'. *Hibernia*, March 12: 18.

Ní Dhomhnaill, Nuala. Autumn 1992. 'What Foremothers?' *The Poetry Ireland Review* 18–31.

Ní Ríordáin, Clíona. 2020. *English Language Poets in Cork 1970–1980*. London: Palgrave Macmillan.

O'Brien, Paddy. 1964. 'A Dublin Literary Pub, interview'. *Hibernia*, August: 12–13.

O'Brien, Seán. 1990. 'Elevating Identity: review of *Mount Eagle*, *The Figure in the Cave*, and *The Hill Field*'. *The Times Literary Supplement*, April 27: 443.

O'Donnell, Mary. Winter 1992. 'Montague's Love Poetry'. *The Poetry Ireland Review* 51–9.

O'Driscoll, Dennis. October 1995. 'A Map of Contemporary Irish Poetry'. *Poetry* 94–106.

— . Winter 1991. 'Poet as Civil Servant: Thomas Kinsella'. *The Poetry Ireland Review* 57–64.

O'Driscoll, Dennis and Seamus Heaney. 2009. *Stepping Stones: Interviews with Seamus Heaney*. London: Faber & Faber.

O'Faolain, Nuala. 1996. *Are You Somebody? The Accidental Memoir of a Dublin Woman*. Dublin: New Island.

Olney, James. Summer 1995. *The Southern Review: A Special Issue: Contemporary Irish Poetry and Criticism*. Volume 31, No. 3.

O'Malley, Mary. 1990. *Never Shake Hands With the Devil*. Dublin: Elo Publications.

Orsmby, Frank. 1970. 'The Tide Man Cometh: Montague's *Tides*'. *Fortnight*, December 18: 19.

— . 1974. 'Faber's List'. *Fortnight*, April 5: 16–17.

O'Shea, Edward. v. 98, no. 2. 'Seamus Heaney at Berkeley 1970–71'. *Southern California Quarterly* 157–93.

O'Sullivan, Michael. 1999. *Brendan Behan: A Life*. Boulder: Roberts Rinehart; Dublin: Blackwater Press.

O'Sullivan, Philip. 1969. 'Juanita Casey's *Horse by the River* and John Montague's *The Bread God*'. *Irish Independent*, January 11.

Paor, Liam de. 1971. 'The Growth of a Myth: The Planter and the Gael Tour'. *The Irish Times*, January 6: 10.

Parker, Michael. 2007. *Northern Irish Literature: the imprint of history*, 2 vols. London: Palgrave Macmillan.

Parkin, Andrew. 1977. 'Tenth Annual Seminar of CAIS at McMaster University'. *The Canadian Journal of Irish Studies*, June: 80–3.

Parkinson, Thomas. 1957. 'Letter from Dublin'. *The Nation*, October 5: 227–30.

Payne, Basil. Summer 1968. '*A Chosen Light* and *Patriotic Suite*'. *Studies: An Irish Quarterly Review* 209–12.

— . 1970. 'Aspects of Irish Culture: Poetry Readings'. *The Irish Press*, July 8: 10.

Porter, Peter. 1971. 'Floundering: Allen Tate, Tom Raworth, and John Montague'. *Guardian*, February 4: 7.

Pratt, William. Winter 1997. 'Montague's Collected Poems'. *World Literature Today* 155.

Quidnunc. 1959. 'An Irishman's Diary: Wandering Scholar (John Montague)'. *The Irish Times*, March 2.

Quinn, Antoinette. 2001. *Patrick Kavanagh: A Biography*. Dublin: Gill and Macmillan.

— . Spring 1989. '"The Well-Beloved": Montague and the Muse'. *Irish University Review* 12–43.

Quinn, Justin. 2003. 'The Weather of Irish Poetry'. *The Sewanee Review*, July: 486–92.

Qwarnstrom, Loretta. 2004. 'Travelling through Liminal Spaces: An Interview with Nuala Ní Dhomhnaill'. *Nordic Irish Studies*, 65–73.

Rafferty, Oliver P. 2015. *Irish Catholic Identities*. Manchester: Manchester University Press.

Raine, Craig. 2013. *More Dynamite: Essays 1990–2012*. London: Atlantic Books.

— . 2012. *The Divine Comedy*. London: Atlantic Books.

Raine, Kathleen. Spring 1987. 'Waiting for Grace, report on New Delhi Temenos Conference'. *India International Centre Quarterly* 91–4.

Randolph, Jody Allen. 2004. 'Michael Longley in Conversation with Jody Allen Randolph'. *The Poetry Ireland Review*, 78–89.

Redshaw, Thomas Dillon. 1974 Summer. '"Ri" as in Regional'. *Éire-Ireland* 41–64.

— . 1976 Winter. 'John Montague: An Appreciation'. *Éire-Ireland* 122–33.

— . 1982 Summer. 'The Surviving Sign: John Montague's *The Bread God*'. *Éire-Ireland* 56–91.

— . 1988, January. 'Books by John Montague: A Descriptive Checklist, 1958–1988'. *Irish University Review.*

— . 1989. *Hill Field: Poems and Memoirs for John Montague on His Sixtieth Birthday.* Minneapolis: Coffee House Press, and Oldcastle: Gallery Books.

— . 2004. *The Well Dreams: Essays on John Montague.* Edited. Omaha: Creighton University Press.

— . 2009. 'Undertow: John Montague's 'Sea Changes' (1981)'. *The Canadian Journal of Irish Studies.*

— . 2016, Fall. 'Cuimhneachán 1966: Song, Setting, and Satire in John Montague's *Patriotic Suite*'. *South Carolina Review* 20–38.

Rexroth, Kenneth. 1984. *Selected Poems.* New York: New Directions.

Riordan, Maurice. Autumn 1982. 'John Montague's Selected Poems'. *Irish University Review* 152–6.

Robinson, Peter. 2013. *The Oxford Handbook of Contemporary British and Irish Poetry.* Oxford: Oxford University Press.

Rosenfeld, Ray. 1970. 'Ulster's Two Cultures in Poetry'. *The Irish Times*, December 3: 10.

Rosenthal, M.L. 1971. 'Poet of Brooklyn, Ulster, & Paris'. *The Nation*, May 17: 632–3.

— . With Sally Gall. 1983. *The Modern Poetic Sequence: The Genius of Modern Poetry.* Oxford: Oxford University Press.

— . Editor. Spring, 1991. 'Works-in-Progress'. *Ploughshares.*

Rubin, Ida E. 1974. *The Drawings of Morris Graves, with comments by the Artist.* Boston: New York Graphic Society.

Rudolf, Anthony. 1973. 'Grim Ambitious Poet: The Rough Field'. *Tribune*, July 6.

Rumaker, Michael. 2013. *Robert Duncan in San Francisco.* San Francisco: City Lights/Grey Fox.

Rushe, Desmond. 1970. 'Two Poets Talk About Themselves: Hewitt and Montague'. *Irish Independent*, November 20: 12.

Ryan, John. 2008; first publication 1975. *Remembering How We Stood: Bohemian Dublin at the Mid-Century.* Dublin: The Lilliput Press.

Saroyan, Aram. 1979. *Genesis Angels: The Saga of Lew Welch and the Beat Generation.* New York: William Morrow.

Scammell, Vernon. 1971. '"A Chosen Light"'. *The Hudson Review.*

Schneider, D. 2015. *Crowded by Beauty: The Life and Zen of Poet Philip Whalen*. Berkeley and Los Angeles: University of California Press.

Seager, Allan. 1968. *The Glass House: The Life of Theodore Roethke*. New York: McGraw-Hill.

Sealy, Douglas. 1966. 'Irish Poets of the Sixties'. *The Irish Times*, January 24: 8.

— . 1969. 'Poetry and Documenta: *The Bread God*'. *The Irish Times*, January 4: 11.

— . 1967 July. '"Patriotic Suite"'. *The Dublin Magazine* 99–100.

— . 1972. 'Appearance and Reality: *The Rough Field* and *Wintering Out*'. *The Irish Press*, November 25.

Shapiro, Karl. 1990. *Reports of My Death: A Distinguished American Poet Looks at the Literary Life of Our Times*. Chapel Hill: Algonquin Books.

Sheridan, Jean. 1975. 'The Graves touch delights UCC'. *The Irish Press*, May 14: 4.

Shovlin, Frank, editor. 2021. *The Letters of John McGahern*. London: Faber & Faber.

Sigal, Clancy. 2019. *The London Lover: My Weekend that Lasted Thirty Years*. London: Bloomsbury.

Simmons, James. 1972. 'Field and River: The Rough Field, Omen of Lagan'. *Fortnight*, December 15: 16–17.

— . 1976. '*A Slow Dance*'. *Books Ireland*, July/August: 126–27.

— . 1976. 'Saintly Poets'. *Hibernia*, May 7: 3.

— . 1976. 'The Credible Dancing Montague'. *The Honest Ulsterman*, May: 68–71.

— . 1978. 'Triad of Love, *The Great Cloak*'. *Books Ireland*, April: 53.

— . 1994, Spring. 'Poetry: Review of Mahon, *Selected Poems*, and Montague, Time in Armagh'. *The Linen Hall Review* 18–20.

Simpson, Eileen. 1982. *Poets in Their Youth: A Memoir*. New York: Random House.

Skelton, Robin, ed. 1963. *Six Irish Poets*. Oxford: Oxford University Press.

— . March 1983. 'Montague's Selected Poems'. *Concerning Poetry* 87–9.

Skloot, Floyd. 2003. 'The Simple Wisdom: Visiting Thomas Kinsella'. *New Hibernia Review*, July: 9–18.

Smee, Sebastian. 2017. *The Art of Rivalry: Four Friendships, Betrayals, and Breakthroughs in Modern Art*. New York: Random Housse.

Smith, Rod, Peter Baker, & Kaplan Harris, eds. 2014. *The Selected Letters of Robert Creeley.* Berkeley and Los Angeles: University of California Press.

Snodgrass, W.D. Spring 1994. 'The Art of Poetry: The Snodgrass Interview'. *The Paris Review.*

Spicer, Jack, and Peter Gizzi. 1998. 'The California Lecture, Poetry & Politics, July 14, 1965'. *American Poetry Review*, January/February: 28–32.

Spivack, Kathleen. 2012. *With Robert Lowell and His Circle: Sylvia Plath, Anne Sexton, Elizabeth Bishop, Stanley Kunitz & Others.* Boston: Northeastern University Press.

Sullivan, Kevin. 1973. '"The Rough Field"'. *Nation*, June 25: 821–2.

Swift, Patrick, and David Wright, eds. 1988. *An Anthology from X: A Quarterly Review of Literature and the Arts, 1959–1962.* Oxford: Oxford University Press.

Terdiman, Richard. 2010. 'Memory in Freud'. In *Memory: Histories, Theories, Debates*, by Bill Schwarz, editor Susannah Radstone. New York: Fordham University Press.

Tomlinson, Charles. Winter 1998. 'The Art of Poetry: Tomlinson Interview'. *The Paris Review.*

Tracy, Robert. 1979. 'An Ireland the Poets have Imagined: *The Rough Field*'. *The Crane Bag* 82–8.

Vance, Norman. July 1996. 'Catholic and Protestant Literary Visions of "Ulster": Now You See It, Now You Don't'. *Literature and Religion in Ireland* 127–40.

Wall, Barbara. 1989. *René Hague: A Personal Memoir.* Upton, Cheshire: Aylesford Press.

Wallis, William. Fall 1971. 'Notes on Five Poets'. *Prairie Schooner* 278–9.

Wassell, Elizabeth. 1997. *The Honey Plain.* Dublin: Wolfhound Press.

— . 1999. *Sleight of Hand.* Dublin: Wolfhound Press.

— . 2001. *The Thing He Loves.* Dingle: Brandon.

— . 2010. *Dangerous Pity.* Dublin: Liberties Press.

— . 2011. *Sustenance.* Dublin: Liberties Press.

Waterman, Andrew. Autumn 1989. 'Golden Girls: review of *Mount Eagle* and *The Mirror Wall*'. *PN Review.*

— . 1979. 'Ulsterectomy'. *Hibernia*, April 26: 16–17.

Welch, Robert. 2003. 'Faultlines, Limits, Transgressions'. *Éire-Ireland*, March: 161–80.

Wheatley, David. 2001. '"That Blank Mouth": Secrecy, Shibboleths, and Silence in Northern Irish Poetry'. *Journal of Modern Literature* 1–16.

Wilson, Frances. 2021. *Burning Man: The Trials of D.H. Lawrence.* London: Bloomsbury Circus.

Wooten, William. 2015. *The Alvarez Generation: Thom Gunn, Geoffrey Hill, Ted Hughes, Sylvia Plath, and Peter Porter.* Liverpool: Liverpool University Press.

Young, Vernon. Winter 1976/77. 'Poetry Chronicle, including review of *A Slow Dance*'. *The Hudson Review* 615, 630, 632, 634, 636.

Yueh, Norma N. 1969. 'Alan Swallow, Publisher 1915-1966'. *The Library Quarterly: Information, Community, Policy*, July: 223–32.

ENDNOTES

CHAPTER ONE

1. Verso of typed pages describing a Glencull (County Tyrone) church service, a memoir of the Atlantic crossing with his brothers; UCC.

2. Hoot of a tender

   in the grey darkness

   after the gaiety

   of an ocean voyage

   a child changes hands

   [illeg.] of a strange house

   observes what

   he must grow old

   to understand

undated draft verses, Buffalo B74, F1; Incoming Passenger Lists, 1878–1960, www.ancestry.Countyuk

3. 'Garvaghey Man's Death in Brooklyn', *Strabane Chronicle* (8 April 1933).

4. *Irish University Review* (Spring 1989), 74.

5. Much of the information about the boys' arrival is from Turlough Montague's son Andrew, the chief informant for family history for this biography.

6. Memoir on checked paper in pencil, c. 1959; NLI.

7. My thanks to Peter Montague for this family tree.

8. *Ulster Herald*, 23 March 1907.

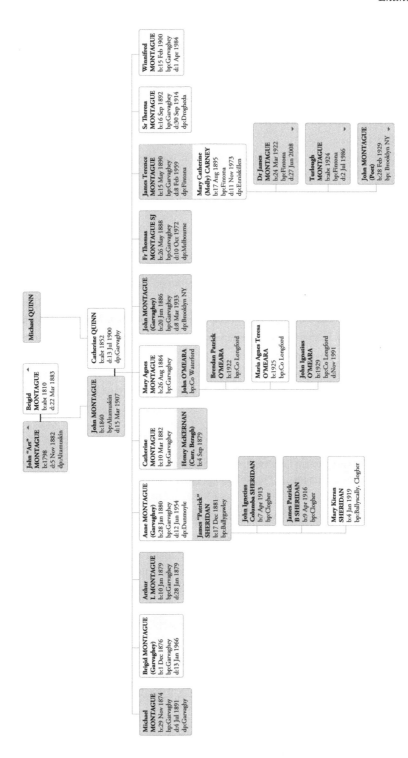

Michael QUINN

John "Art" MONTAGUE
b:1798
d:5 Nov 1882
dp:Altamuskin

Brigid MONTAGUE
b:abt 1810
d:22 Mar 1883

Catherine QUINN
b:abt 1852
d:13 Jul 1900
dp:Garvaghy

John MONTAGUE
b:1840
bp:Altamuskin
d:15 Mar 1907

Michael MONTAGUE
b:29 Nov 1874
bp:Garvaghy
d:4 Jul 1891
dp:Garvaghy

Brigid MONTAGUE (Garvaghey)
b:1 Dec 1876
bp:Garvaghey
d:13 Jan 1966

Arthur L MONTAGUE
b:10 Jan 1879
bp:Garvaghey
d:28 Jan 1879

Anne MONTAGUE (Garvaghey)
b:28 Jan 1880
bp:Garvaghey
d:12 Jun 1954
dp:Dunmoyle

James "Patrick" SHERIDAN
b:17 Dec 1881
bp:Ballygawley

John Ignatius Columba SHERIDAN
b:7 Apr 1913
bp:Clogher

James Patrick B SHERIDAN
b:9 Apr 1916
bp:Clogher

Mary Kieran SHERIDAN
b:4 Jan 1919
bp:Ballyscally, Clogher

Catherine MONTAGUE
b:10 Mar 1882
bp:Garvaghey

Henry McKERNAN (Curr, Beragh)
b:4 Sep 1879

Mary Agnes MONTAGUE
b:26 Aug 1884
bp:Garvaghey

John O'MEARA
bp:Co Waterford

Brendan Patrick O'MEARA
b:1922
bp:Co Longford

Maria Agnes Teresa O'MEARA
b:1925
bp:Co Longford

John Ignatius O'MEARA
b:1929
bp:Co Longford
d:Nov 1991

John MONTAGUE (Garvaghey)
b:20 Jun 1886
bp:Garvaghey
d:8 Mar 1933
dp:Brooklyn NY

Fr Thomas MONTAGUE SJ
b:26 May 1888
bp:Garvaghey
d:10 Oct 1972
dp:Melbourne

James Terence MONTAGUE
b:15 May 1890
bp:Garvaghey
d:8 Feb 1959
dp:Fintona

Mary Catherine (Molly) CARNEY
b:17 Aug 1895
bp:Fintona
d:11 Nov 1973
dp:Enniskillen

Dr James MONTAGUE
b:24 Mar 1922
bp:Fintona
d:27 Jun 2008

Turlough MONTAGUE
b:abt 1924
bp:Fintona
d:2 Jul 1986

John MONTAGUE (Poet)
b:28 Feb 1929
bp: Brooklyn NY

Sr Theresa MONTAGUE
b:16 Sep 1892
bp:Garvaghey
d:30 Sep 1914
dp:Drogheda

Winnifred MONTAGUE
b:15 Feb 1900
bp:Garvaghey
d:1 Apr 1984

9. John Montague JP owned several parcels of land in Garvaghey, according to the Valuation Revision Books for 1910 in the Public Record Office of Northern Ireland. He had parcels of 100, 11, and 6 acres.

10. *Occasions of Sin*, 20.

11. Undated draft verses, Buffalo B74, F1.

12. 'The hours I remember most are those from six o'clock onward', John Montague Papers; MS 50,718/2; NLI.

13. Note at top of page – 'Give Auden's density'. John Montague Papers, NLI MS 50, 718/3.

14. Buffalo, Notebook 1960–1, B71F1.

15. 'Return', draft memoir, c. 1950; UCC.

16. 'Postmistress: A Diptych', *Collected Poems*, p. 300.

17. John Montague, *Occasions of Sin*, 16; 'Brigid Montague (1876–1966)', *Collected Poems* (1995), p. 300.

18. Interview Seamus Rogers, 5 February 2017; interview, Frank Horisk, 4 February 2017.

19. 'Beragh Gaelic Festival', *Ulster Herald* (26 July 1919); 'Concerts at Errigal', *Ulster Herald* (2 March 1935); '*The New Gossoon*, A Brilliant Production', *Ulster Herald* (4 January 1936), an article that includes the double-edged compliment that 'Miss Freda Montague was true to life as Mag Kehoe, the sharp-tongued servant maid.' See also 'Winifred Montague (1900–1983)', *Collected Poems* (1995), p. 300.

20. Information from Frank Horisk, 4 February 2017; and Seamus and Frank Rogers, 5 February 2017. John Montague, *A Love Present and Other Stories* (Wolfhound Press: Dublin, 1997), 48.

21. Unpublished draft lyrics; no date; UCC.

22. Montague, *The Figure in the Cave*, Loc. 415.

23. *Irish University Review* (Spring 1989): 80.

24. Draft of 'A Love Present', in pencil, on checked paper; NLI; John Montague, *A Love Present and Other Stories* (Wolfhound Press: Dublin, 1997).

25. *A Love Present*, p. 50.

26. William Wordsworth, *The Prelude* (1805), Book XII, ll. 208–15.

27. David L. Smith, 'The Mirror Image of the Present: Freud's Theory of Retrogressive Screen Memories', *Psychoanalytische Perspectiven*, 2000, nr. 39.

28. Email from JM and Elizabeth Montague to author; 6 October 2016.

29. It has proved impossible to pin down the date of the onset of his stammer. Montague's various memoirs suggest anything from age six to age nine.

30. 'Obsession', *Massachusetts Review* (Winter 1967): 205.

31. Conversation with JM and Elizabeth Montague, Ardtara Country House, Upperlands, near Bellaghy, after Seamus Heaney Home Place reading, 2 October 2016; email from JM and Elizabeth Montague, 6 October 2016.

32. Mary ('Molly') Montague arrived on the *California* on 29 September 1935; Passenger Lists, ancestry.co.uk.

33. Molly liked to tell the story, unsettling to her youngest son, of his hard birth, how he 'brought the calf bed with him' (email from Elizabeth Montague, 26 May 2019). This misfortune lies behind the poetic diction of 'her flayed womb'.

34. 'All roads wind backwards', *Sunday Independent* (1 April 1984).

35. Old school notebook paper, ballpoint; also typed draft entitled 'Ledger', NLI.

36. Draft verses for 'Like Dolmens Round My Childhood', 1959 notebook; Buffalo.

37. *Irish University Review* (Spring 1989): 87.

38. Notebook (30 December 1962); 'Death of Minnie'.

39. Conversation with Frank Horisk, 4 February 2017.

40. T.P. MacDevitte to JM; 21 October 1975; Buffalo, B30.

41. Montague, 'The Poet and His Community', *Fortnight*, n276 (February 1999), pp. 19–22.

42. The schoolmate was Pat O'Neill; information from Andrew Montague, 4 February 2017.

43. Patsy Kelly, conversation, 5 February 2017.

44. *A Love Present*, pp. 65–7.

45. Andrew Montague to JM, 8 December 2016; telephone conversation with Andrew Montague, 2 April 2017.

46. 'Death of Very Rev. Dr Montague', *Freeman's Journal* (31 October 1845): 3.

47. Conversation with Pat Montague, whose family are from Altamuskin; 22 October 2017.

48. Draft 'Death of a Dignitary', possibly 1961; notebook, NLI.

49. The poet's uncle was not, but is sometimes mistaken for, the Frank Carney (1896–1933) who was the Officer Commanding the 1st Northern Division of the IRA in the War of Independence, later a member of Dail Eireann. 'DOC series: Ballykinlar Internment Camp'.

    There were two Frank Carneys in Ballykinlar Internment Camp, one from Enniskillen, the other from Fintona. Andrew Montague: 'My granny, Molly (Frank and Tom's sister) told me that on the evening of Bloody Sunday, Frank was arrested as he had been identified as being at a meeting that morning in the Davenport Hotel but the hotel receptionist was not able or perhaps didn't want to identify him, and he was released at that time, although he was later interned' (email 27 February 2022). My thanks to Andrew Montague, Mary Montague and Brian Crowley.

50. John Montague, *The Pear Is Ripe*, 98; conversation with Andrew Montague, 18 October 2018. JM to Turlough Montague, 6 April 1976; NLI; Turlough Montague to JM, 30 April 1976; UCC. Bloody Sunday was 21 November 1920, a year before the marriage of Jim Montague and Molly Carney, so Molly's story is not exactly true.

51. Dara Montague, email, 7 February 2016.

52. 'A Poet Remembers', *Newsday* (14 October 1985): Sec. 2, p. 4. 'Siegemograph', *Guardian* (10 November 1970): 8.

53. 'Stele for a Northern Republican', *John Montague: Collected Poems* (Wake Forest UP: 1995), 40.

54. 'Shooting in Ballygawley Sunday', *Irish News* (26 January 1921).

55. Still, Andrew Montague points out that his grandfather James left Tyrone in odd circumstances, more than a year after his older brother. He sailed from Cork for New York on the *President Polk* in September 1923, when his wife Molly was more than four months pregnant; her second son Turlough, Andrew's father, was born in Fintona on 11 February 1924. At Ellis Island, under 'employment', James listed himself as a commercial traveller. He was held there for a time to

check his bona fides. (So, after settling in Brooklyn, James never saw his second child until the boy was four years old.)

This all has the appearance to Andrew Montague of a sudden, unplanned and compulsory departure, perhaps under threat from the Ulster police, in the aftermath of civil war.

Roy Foster's comparison of Irish emigrants' stories of why they left, first taken at the time of departure, second years later, may be relevant. Asked why they are leaving, they typically say it is because of a poor harvest, family quarrels, difficulty with neighbours, or joblessness; then when asked a second time years later, they say they were forced into exile by the British. See Foster, *The Irish Story.*

56. Conversation with Seamus and Frank Rogers, GAA centre, Garvaghey, 5 February 2017.

57. 'Anglo-Celt Statement Causes Sensation', *Anglo-Celt* (20 August 1921): 1; 'Horses for Greece', *Irish News* (25 November 1921): 4; '1000 Irish Horses', *Belfast Newsletter* (31 March 1922): 12.

58. Andrew Montague to JM, 8 December 2016.

59. *Collected Poems*, 47.

60. The memory on which 'The Letters' is based was first jotted down in a notebook from August 1968 (Buffalo). The story was published in *Born in Brooklyn* (1991).

61. 'A Brilliant Production', review of *The New Gossoon, Ulster Herald* (4 January 1936); 'Entertainment in Ballygawley', *Ulster Herald* (3 April 1937).

62. Conversation with Frank Horisk, 4 February 2017.

63. John Montague Papers, UCC.

64. 'The Road's End', *Collected Poems* (1995), 32.

65. Seamus Heaney to Michael Parker, [2 November 1985]; *The Letters of Seamus Heaney* (Faber & Faber: London, 2023), p. 264: 'I must have read the Montague *Poisoned Lands* round about 1962/3 also. 'The Water Carrier' was the poem of his that touched me – the shape of "Mid-Term Break" was suggested or informed by it.'

66. Conversation with Elizabeth (Wassell) Montague, 20 January 2019.

CHAPTER TWO

1. JM to M. Riordain, late October 1989; ALS; NLI.

2. JM to Evelyn Montague, 2 May [1981]; NLI Ms 50,718/1003.

3. John Montague, *Irish University Review* (Spring 1989), 74.

4. 'A Love Present', p. 45.

5. *Time in Armagh*, p. 33.

6. Single page from a notebook, 'Why do my best friends not appear', NLI.

7. JM to Paul Muldoon, May 1993; Emory.

8. *Chosen Lights: Poets on Poems by John Montague*, Loc. 310–13.

9. Conversation with Tom McGurk, 3 January 2017.

10. *The Figure in the Cave: and Other Essays*, Loc. 879–89.

11. JM to Seán O'Boyle, 3 December 1963.

12. Seán O'Boyle wrote to JM thanking him on 5 February 1973: 'It was very gratifying, especially in my last year of teaching' (NLI).

13. JM to M. Riordain, late October 1989; NLI.

14. Undated notebook, from time in Iowa (approx. autumn 1954); verso of draft of 'Nursery Rhyme'; Buffalo.

15. JM to M. Riordain, late October 1989; NLI. The person who reportedly 'fell in love with Frank Lenny' is still alive, and therefore not named.

16. *Collected Poems*, 331.

17. 'Love Along the Waterside', draft memoir, 1968 Notebook; Buffalo.

18. 'The Current', *Smashing the Piano*, 29.

19. 'Waiting', *Collected Poems*, 337.

20. 'United States Armed Forces in Northern Ireland during World War II', *New Hibernia Review*, p. 35.

21. *The Figure in the Cave*, Loc. 476.

22. *The Figure in the Cave,* Loc. 587.

23. Single-spaced, typed memoir of St Patrick's during the war; draft; 1 page; NLI. Inscribed by JM '1946'. Belfast was bombed in April and May 1941.

24. '*Professor Tim* in Ballygawley', *Ulster Herald* (15 April 1944).

25. *The Figure in the Cave*, Loc. 499. For this idiom, see the satirical article about a new course in Dungannon for teenagers 'on all aspects of Codology including modules called 'Acting The Clift', 'Bollocksing About', and 'Eejit Studies' (Tyrone Tribulations website).

26. 'The Locket', *Collected Poems*, 183.

27. *Irish University Review*, p. 75

28. Molly's letters are in the NLI, MS 50,718/1000.

29. 'Absence', *Collected Poems*, 341.

30. 'Deo Gratias', *Collected Poems*, 339.

31. 'At Newry last night Tony Mackie remembered John Montague "could sing like a lark",' Illeg. to JM, on *Hibernia* stationery (24 November 1966), NLI.

32. 'Speech Lesson', *NCP,* 480–2.

33. 'A Chapter of Autobiography', *Irish University Review* (Spring 1989).

34. Draft of 'A Welcoming Party' (sometimes-titled 'Auschwitz, Mon Amour' or 'The last newsreel of the war'), [April 1960], Notebook 1960–61, Buffalo, B71, F1; and *NCP*, 360. 'Terrible, shy' are also the words used to describe the voice of the ghost in the cellar, in the unpublished early poem about childhood night terrors, quoted above.

CHAPTER THREE

1. *Irish University Review* (Spring 1989): 76.

2. Maurice Harmon, Review of 'UCD: A National Idea' *Books Ireland* (March 2000): 69–71. John O'Meara, a professor and contemporary at UCD, described Monsignor Horgan 'as a ready vehicle for Archbishop [McQuaid]'s purposes. Horgan was a tall man in black with a stalking gait; he had a conspicuous bald dome under which his blue green eyes glanced

furtively. He haunted the College and liked to engage in confessional-type conversations with younger staff.' 'Guardians of the Truth', *Irish University Review*, Vol. 26, No. 1 (Spring–Summer 1996), 10.

3. John O'Meara, 'Guardians of the Truth', *Irish University Review*, Vol. 26, No. 1 (Spring–Summer 1996), 8–9.

4. 'Report of the President of University College Dublin for the session 1949–1950', December 1950. Part I, p. 18. UCD Library.

5. Donal McCartney, *UCD: A National Idea* (Gill and Macmillan: Dublin, 1999), 163.

6. 'College Questionnaire', *The National Student*, May 1948.

7. Roger McHugh, Foreword, *The National Student*, April 1947.

8. 'Society News', *The National Student*, May 1946.

9. The elaborately phrased and preposterous proposal, launched from near the crowded doorway, was O'Nolan's specialism, rousing the crowds to gales of chaotic laughter; see Anthony Cronin, *No Laughing Matter*, p. 64.

10. James Meenan (ed.), *Centenary History of the Literary and Historical Society of University College Dublin 1855–1955* (A & A Farmar, 1955, reprint, 2005), 236.

11. In 1948 'Donat O'Donnell' (Conor Cruise O'Brien, then a student at Trinity College) gave a penetrating analysis of young Irishmen's timid paralysis in relation to the Church. The father of the Irish family 'tries to bring up his children in the ways of righteousness, beats them, teaches them respect for their pastors and masters, and checks all manifestations of the sin of pride – as for the sin of lust, that knows better than to manifest itself in his presence. He is a worried and unimposing martinet .... But behind him, insignificant and insecure as he is, is something enormous and seemingly impregnable: the Catholic Church .... In the family, the nightly Rosary, and through the land, as far as sound can carry, the music of the Church-bells reminds the mutinous adolescent that in revolting against his family he will be alone against a people, fighting a flagless war against a unanimous acceptance.'

   The Irish rebels of the nineteenth century, so regularly condemned by the Catholic hierarchy, were inevitable heroes for the spirited son of a pious and 'loyal family', 'The Parnellism of Seán O'Faoláin', *Irish Writing* (July 1948): 65–6.

12. *No Laughing Matter*, p. 68.

13. *No Laughing Matter*, p. 72.

14. *The National Student* (December 1946): 5–6; 29. Cronin repeated his depressed estimate of the intellectual climate in Ireland, for example, in 'A Dream of 50 years Ago' (*The Irish Times*, 7 April 1978). There had been, and would be, he declared, no new Irish Renaissance. That could come about, he argued, only by state management and support of leading artists. He said this years after the publication of Seamus Heaney's *North*, John Montague's *The Rough Field*, Brian Friel's *Philadelphia, Here I Come!*, John McGahern's *The Barracks*, and so on and so forth. It was an absurd underestimate of the achievements of his contemporaries. By way of explanation, it should be noted that Cronin was strategically concerned at the time to propagandize for Aosdána, the state scheme for honouring and subsidizing selected artists.

15. *Irish University Review* (Spring 1989), 78.

16. This companion is unidentified, but appears to be the 'Seamus', who wrote to Montague in 1956 from Derry, where he taught in the famous Christian Brothers School, 'the Brow on the Hill' (Seamus to Dear John; 33 Marlboro Avenue, Derry; Montague Family Correspondence, NLI, MS 50,718/999).

17. *Irish Examiner* (22 October 2011). See also *The Figure in the Cave*, Loc. 409, and *The Bag Apron* (The Lilliput Press: Dublin, 2008).

18. 'All these days', John Montague Papers, NLI MS 50, 718/3. Wordsworth defined poetry as 'the spontaneous overflow of powerful feelings', but added, 'recollected in tranquillity' (Preface, *Lyrical Ballads*, 1801).

19. 'I am glad for the gift of youth,' John Montague Papers, NLI MS 50, 718/3.

20. 'The flea of Gide's intellect hopping', John Montague Papers, NLI MS 50, 718/3.

21. 'It suddenly struck me', Red copybook, John Montague Papers, NLI MS 50, 718/3.

22. 'My First Job', John Montague Papers, UCC. My thanks to Martin Carney for his reminiscences of the customs then prevailing at Dublin ballrooms.

23. 'Jazz – Dance as often as dance you can', John Montague Papers, NLI MS 50, 718/3.

24. '*Je Vais Dévoiler Tous Les Mystères*, Rimbaud', *The National Student* (February 1949); 33; 'To a Dead Poet Friend', *The National Student* (May 1948), p. 17; 'Sermon for Sunday', *The National Student* (May 1949), p. 21. It is doubtful if Montague had a dead poet friend in 1948, but the Housman-like yearning for a young man, with sexual fulfilment baffled by early death, was a popular mode of poeticism, and a safety valve for the expression of male-male desires.

25. Pearse Hutchinson, 'The River', *The Bell* (March 1945): 472.

26. For a sample of Jordan's verse from this period, see 'Second Letter. To Patrick Swift' in *A Raft from Flotsam* (The Gallery Press: Loughcrew, Co. Meath, 1975).

27. John Montague, *Company: A Chosen Life* (Duckworth: London, 2001), 113.

28. Email, Denis Donoghue to AF.

29. Email, Colm Tóibín to AF; 27 June 2019.

30. Montague, 'My First Job', draft memoir, John Montague Papers, UCC.

31. See Jordan's diary for 14 August 1951; NLI MS 35,118 John Jordan papers, diaries.

32. See Jordan's diary entries for 23 August and 17 September 1947, and for July 1950; NLI MS 35,118 John Jordan papers, diaries.

33. The Foreword of *Envoy* (n. 9; 1950) regretted Clarke's disparagement of modernism, insistence on the 'Irish mode', and overall lack of enthusiasm for younger poets: 'In most other countries, the new generation is helped and encouraged by the older. Here, to-day, however, little encouragement is given and a young writer has to battle his way through a network of hostility and disparagement which more often than not finally dries up his talent' (p. 6).

34. Antoinette Quinn notes that Kavanagh could easily have taken a bus, or bicycled. Going by foot was peasant cunning, a deliberate exhibition of his 'authenticity,' for the benefit of AE.

35. Antoinette Quinn, *Patrick Kavanagh: A Biography* (Gill and Macmillan: Dublin, 2001), p. 247.

36. Patrick Kavanagh to Peter Kavanagh, 8 April 1947; *Lapped Furrows: Correspondence 1933–67* (Peter Kavanagh Hand Press: NY, 1969), p. 150.

37. Patrick Kavanagh, *The Irish Times* (19 December 1947).

38. 'Meet Mr Patrick Kavanagh', *The Bell* (April 1948): 5–8.

39. James Liddy, *The Doctor's House* (Salmon Press: Cliffs of Moher, 2004), 61.

40. Anthony Cronin, *The Life of Riley* (New Island: Dublin, 2010; first published, 1964), pp. 13–14.

41. James Liddy, *The Doctor's House* (Salmon Press: Cliffs of Moher, 2004), p. 62. In fact, Liddy was happily uncloseted.

42. To Thomas Kinsella, there was nothing funny about social life in McDaid's. In the satiric couplets of 'Open Court', he gives a steely-eyed survey of the scene: the 'ruined Arnold', 'ruined Auden' and 'ruined Wilde' are, respectively, Jordan, Cronin and Hutchinson, while the 'ruined Anonymous' is of course Kavanagh (*Collected Poems 1956-2001*; Carcanet Press: Manchester, 2001; pp. 315–17.)

43. John Montague, 'Wonder', *Dublin Magazine* (July–September 1949): 7–8; Montague, 'Discovery', 3pp draft article on Austin Clarke; NLI.

44. Montague, 'It's a bloody disgrace', A4 handwritten drafts, possibly for MA; NLI.

45. John Montague to Adrian Frazier, 21 May 2015. My thanks to Dáibhí Ó Cróinín.

46. In the same 18 November 1949 issue of the *Catholic Standard* is his review of Ben Kiely's novel *In a Harbour Green*, a prompt payback for Kiely's help with getting the job. Rules of the game exemplified.

47. Not to mention a chance to play 'Casanova of the cinema cafés', John Ryan, *Remembering How We Stood*, Loc. 1481.

48. Patrick Kavanagh to Peter Kavanagh, 12 July 1949; *Lapped Furrows*, 155.

49. Conversation with Frank Horisk, 4 February 2017.

50. 'The Seventh Art', *Catholic Standard* (25 November 1949).

51. 'The Genius of John Ford', *Catholic Standard* (2 December 1949): 6. Montague cited recent articles by Lindsay Anderson, the director and film historian.

52. NLI MS 50,718/3.

53. 'Something Rare in Modern Fiction', *Catholic Standard* (18 November 1949). Montague was not wholly convinced by the right-wing French school: Péguy, he noted, was a propagandist, not an artist, and Mauriac was more Catholic than man.

54. Anthony Cronin, 'Some Notes on Evelyn Waugh', *National Student* (December 1949): 10–11.

55. Montague, Notebook from 1960, Buffalo, B7, F1.

56. Out of kindness, Montague sometimes gave a streetwalker a bed for the night, then made her breakfast in the morning. Brendan Behan stopped by, and was impressed: 'You're a quare one. Film critic for the *Catholic Standard* and running a whores' hostel' (*Company*, p. 49).

57. 'Climbing the stiffer mountains', typed in red on *Catholic Standard* stationery, NLI MS 50,718/2.

58. 'The Yeats Film', *Catholic Standard* (6 January 1950).

59. *The Figure in the Cave*, Loc. 3245. For the required writing sample, he 'produced a fervid essay on [Hart] Crane with suitable reference … to Melville, Whitman, Emily Dickinson and the Book of Job … side-stepping exact knowledge as the mouse does the trap'.

Pearse Hutchinson, who had been living in Vienna that summer, showed up for the Salzburg Seminar that year too, and joined the classes; in fact, he was shown particular favour by Saul Bellow. It is possible that Pearse, however, did not apply in the usual way, and that is why Montague could correctly write that he had been the only Irish applicant. Still, it is odd that in his recollections of the Salzburg Seminar, he never mentions his friend Pearse Hutchinson.

60. John Montague, *The Lost Notebook* (Mercier Press: Cork & Dublin, 1987), p. 13.

61. *Quidnunc*, 'Invasion of Europe', *The Irish Times* 21 March 1950): 5.

62. John Montague, 'Evening in Austria', *The National Student* (June 1950): 8–10.

63. And woman with woman – the female students of the Seminar were roughly equal in number to the males. Henry Nash Smith, 'The Salzburg Seminar', *American Quarterly* (Spring 1949): 30.

64. Louis Menand notes that in these campaigns for 'cultural freedom' the values held by intellectuals were indistinguishable from those of the modern state. They were examples of what Herbert Marcuse called 'repressive tolerance' (*The Free World: Art and Thought in the Cold War*, p. 716).

65. Montague, 'Fellow Travelling with America', *The Figure in the Cave*, Loc. 3265, first published in *The Bell*, June 1951.

66. 'Fellow Travelling', Loc. 3180.

67. Interview by Stephen Arkin, *New England Review* (Autumn/Winter 1982), p. 230.

68. Typed draft; pub dialogue in the North; UCC.

69. Montague, 'The Distracted Shepherd: (Rome: Anno Santo)', *Threshold* (Spring 1958): 12.

70. Draft of 'Virgo Hibernica', 20 October 1964; Montague papers, NLI; see also draft letter to Robin Skelton, 10 August 1965; Notebook for 1965; B75, F1, Buffalo.

71. Montague, 12 August 1968; notebook; Buffalo.

72. Montague, *The Lost Notebook* (Mercier Press: Cork & Dublin, 1987), p. 27.

73. John Jordan, diary, 1 August 1950; John Jordan papers, NLI. The 'Donal' is presumably Donal Barrington, lawyer and UCD friend of Jordan and Montague.

74. Tony Bradley, Lionel Pilkington, and Seán Golden are among those Montague surprised by propositioning in the 1980s. One time in Albany, he even asked the present writer to join him in the bedroom for 'a roll in the hay'. 'Are you mad?' I said, being not that way inclined. I did not at the time believe he could have been serious.

75. Montague, 'Patrick Oliver', a mixed prose & verse comedy; draft; [1962]; NLI Ms 50,718/2.

76. Ibid.

77. Montague, 'The dark days', notebook for 1958; John Montague Papers, NLI MS 50, 718/3. JM to Richard Ryan, 20 December 1968; private collection.

78. Unpublished; Montague, 'For Suzanne', 19 December; 1963 notebook; Buffalo.

79. 'The Young Writer and *The Bell*', *The Figure in the Cave*, Loc. 3100. Without naming them, he criticized the spitefulness of Kavanagh and the McDaid's crowd too: 'the failed or faded writer taking it out on his more successful contemporaries'.

80. Patrick Kavanagh, 'Irish Stew', *Collected Poems* (Allen Lane: London, 2004), p. 202.

81. Montague, 'A Tribute to William Carleton', *The Bell* (April 1952): 18.

82. Even Kavanagh liked the Carleton essay, with its emphasis on natural talent and authenticity. Montague, *The Pear Is Ripe* (Liberties Press: Dublin, 2007), p. 82.

83. Jordan wrote in his diary on 11 January 1952, 'So much work to do, so much that my courage fails. And if I do not get this studentship I shall torment myself for not having thrown … human respect to the winds and been a mummer.' (John Jordan papers, NLI).

84. Montague, 'Paradise Lost', *The Poetry Ireland Review* (May 2006), 52–3.

85. JM to Roger McHugh; draft letter, (after 15 December 1952 – see mention of McHugh's second narrow defeat in a Senate election), from 103 Seville Place; NLI.

86. 'In Her Service', *The Dublin Magazine* (October 1952): 276–7.

87. Interview with Denis O'Driscoll, *Agenda* (v40, No 1–3): 57.

88. 'A confused and destructive future', typed, with pen additions, nd, NLI.

89. Montague, preface, *Poisoned Lands* (Dolmen Press: Dublin, 1977).

90. See Sheila Iremonger to JM, 26 April 1954, for an example of her witty nature; UCC.

91. JM to Tim O'Keeffe, 19 June [1961], and JM to Tim O'Keeffe, 10 July [1961]; Tulsa.

92. *Peadar O'Donnell*, p. 261.

CHAPTER FOUR

1. 'The Oklahoma Kid', *Occasions of Sin*, 20.

2. *Occasions of Sin*, 21.

3. JM to Barry Callaghan; January 1996; Buffalo (Barry Callaghan folder).

4. Turlough Montague to JM; 13 January 1947; NLI; and Mother to JM [December 1950?], UCC. My thanks to Andrew Montague for the story of the brothers' effort to bring their father home from NYC.

5. 'Midnight Mass', draft for 'At Last', Notebook 1965, B75, F1, Buffalo.

6. One of the poems, dedicated to Suzanne, describes the four levels of the passenger ship as a beehive; another, imagining a shipwreck, is entitled 'Death by Fire or Water', and the third is about people drinking themselves to death at the ship's bar. None was finished. (UCC).

7. Draft memoir, in folder of materials from his time at Iowa; NLI.

8. 'Old English, Pope', UCC.

9. Montague to John Kelleher; nd; draft, from School of Letters, Indiana University; UCC.

10. Montague, 'Mental Fire', review of Harold Bloom's *Blake's Apocalypse*, *The Irish Times* (30 November 1963): 9.

11. 'deaf mute with flow signals', page of calendar, 10 May [1954]; UCC.

12. Elizabeth Montague to AF, 5 February 2022.

13. 'With a sudden rush of memory Yale all comes back,' Notebook 1963 (approximately 13 March); Buffalo.

14. Elizabeth Montague, email, 5 February 2022.

15. JM to Kenneth; nd; draft letter, fragment; UCC.

16. JM to Tony, from 2993 Yale Station; frag; UCC.

17. JM to Brigid and Freda; 2773 Yale Station; fragment; [late March 1954]; UCC.

18. 'Storm Coming Up', NLI; published as 'Downtown, America', in *Born in Brooklyn*, p. 65.
19. 'Badly dressed ...', UCC.
20. 'The jet planes cross ...' fragmentary verses, on a mimeographed course hand-out, entitled 'Object and Image in Modern Art and Poetry', 2773 Yale Station; UCC. Dogwood blooms in late March or early April in Connecticut.
21. 'During my year at Yale', nd [February 1961?]; NLI.
22. It has not been possible to fix a date on Montague's psychological crisis. It could have been soon after his disembarkation in New York in July 1953. If so, it put him in a tailspin from which he failed to recover through his whole year at Yale. Or it is possible that the loneliness and sense of alienation at the university built up over the year, and the crisis peaked with the events in the Greyhound bus station, the strip joint, and the queer bar in New York City in mid-1954.
23. After a summertime binge in sailors' bars in New York, the narrator finds himself locked up in Bellevue mental hospital. Around him are criminally insane patients who will never leave the institution.
24. 'It all comes flooding back', 13 March 1963; Notebook for 1963; Buffalo.
25. Regarding Montague's return to a Catholic understanding of his condition, consider the line cited earlier in 'Storm Coming Up': 'back are driven to confession of our sins', and see the use of the term 'evil' in the following draft verses, entitled 'Nervous Breakdown', from mid-winter 1954 (NLI).

> In ordinary conversation a mood develops
> As of danger or evil,
> A current floating under the words,
> Moving towards fulfilment,
> Towards something terrible:
> And laughing we turn from each other,
> Who have learned to forget,
> Without knowing more than that we do forget,
> Turning from the sentence
> To something we knew before and are safe with,
> Speaking of what we already know of,
> And are glad to forget,
> Though knowing, without being the less certain,
> That this current will flood over us yet.

In 1970 Montague spoke of his crisis at Yale not in religious, but in diagnostic, terms: it was 'a developing schizophrenia': 'those were darker days (McCarthyism and the BOMB), and young Irishmen were less adjusted sexually' (JM to Richard Ryan, September/October 1970; private collection).

26. 'Indiana Summer School', Notebook for 1958; B69, F1; Buffalo.

27. Mary [McAllister] to JM, 28 July 1956; NLI, Montague Family Corr. MS 50,718/1001

28. Empson absentmindedly left his battered brown hat behind, and Montague claimed it as a trophy; JM to Dear Tony; unstamped, perhaps unsent postcard, Dundas Street, Toronto; UCC.

29. Stephen Arkin, Interview with John Montague, *New England Review* (Autumn/Winter 1981), p. 231.

30. Robert Lowell, 'For John Berryman (*After reading his last* Dream Song)', *New York Review of Books* (23 June 1977); *Day by Day* (Farrar, Straus, & Giroux, 1977), p. 27.

31. Robert Dana, *A Community of Writers: Paul Engle and the Iowa Writers' Workshop*, p. 42.

32. W.D. Snodgrass, Interview, *Paris Review* (Spring 1994).

33. Philip Levine, Interview, *Paris Review* (Summer 1988).

34. Ian Hamilton, *Against Oblivion: Some Lives of the Twentieth-Century Poets*, Loc. 4110; Peter Davison, *The Fading Smile*, Loc. 118; Loc. 3986.

35. 'Soliloquy on a Southern Strand', comment on proofs for *Forms of Exile*, Buffalo, B2, F9; see also TS, dated April 30, 'This is meant to be a long meditative poem', Buffalo.

36. *Poisoned Lands* (MacGibbon and Kee: London), 1961; p. 27.

37. 'Advance proof, 11/58', [*Forms of Exile*], pencil note on 'Soliloquy on a Southern Strand'.

38. 'Children are afraid in the night', undated notebook; Buffalo.

39. Personal communication, Philip Brady.

40. Montague, notes on a photocopy of Michael Longley's *Selected Poems of Louis MacNeice* (1990).

41. Herbert Leibowitz, '*Something Urgent I Have to Say to You': The Life and Works of William Carlos Williams*, Loc. 7584

42. 'William Carlos Williams, 1955', *A Chosen Light*, 4 (proudly composed in Montague's version of the Williams metric); Interview, *New England Quarterly*, p. 233; and Lucien Stryk to JM, 22 September 1968; NLI: 'I read your fine piece on WC Williams, remembering the day.'

43. Montague, *Company: A Chosen Life*, 21.

44. Madeleine to AF, 13 March 2022.

45. Montague's passport was stamped on 6 September 1955 as he left Mexico; UCC.

46. My thanks to John Ridland, husband of Muriel Thomas, for this story.

47. Barry Miles, *Ginsberg: Beat Poet* (Penguin: London, 1989), 192. See also David Schneider, *Crowded by Beauty: The Life and Zen of Poet Philip Whalen* (University of California Press: Berkeley, 2015), 12.

48. Jack Kerouac, *The Dharma Bums* (Penguin Modern Classics), Loc. 591.

49. Gordon Ball (ed.), *Allen Ginsberg, Journals Mid Fifties 1954–1958* (HarperCollins: NY, 1955), 167.

50. *Company*, p. 175.

51. Miles, 240.

52. Donald Fanger to JM, 11 April 1966; personal collection.

53. John Montague, 'Comedy: The Other Side of the Mirror', 21-page typescript; Donald Fanger correspondence with John Montague, personal collection.

54. JM to Donald Fanger; 8 November 1961; personal collection.

55. James Montague wrote to JM on 11 January 1956 about these heavy rains, news of which had reached Fintona: 'You had great floods in California. I told Mother they were not near you … Turlough told her they wouldn't reach your neck.' (NLI MS 50,718/998).

56. Interview with Denis O'Driscoll, *Agenda*, v. 40, n.13, p. 61. If so, then the journeying Madeleine is the Orpheus figure, and Montague the one in Hell, and needing rescue.

57. Roger McHugh to JM, 20 July [1956]; NLI MS 050, 718/1007.

CHAPTER FIVE

1. Madeleine's grandfather, Louis Nicolas d'Avout, duc d'Auerstadt, had inherited from his forbear the Maréchal d'Avout, both his name and his title. He married in 1902 the wealthy heiress of the Bellozanne estate. Their first child (out of fourteen) was Madeleine's mother. She married Leopold de Brauer, Madeleine's father, in 1925, and followed him in a garrison life. When retired, he and Madeleine's mother chose to live in one of the many elegant houses on the estate, rather than in the castle (too big and much damaged by the war), which is now the property of their grandchildren, Madeleine's nephews. One cannot say that Madeleine is titled a countess like her mother; her sisters, however, are titled as a result of their marriages. (Madeleine to AF, 13 March 2022).

2. 'Some Poets on Their Travels: Robert Fitzgerald, Harold Norse, John Montague, Charles Tomlinson, Harry Roskolenko, Kimon Friar and William Jay Smith', *Poetry* (December 1956): 176–92.

3. Donald Fanger to JM; 5 October 1956; JM's notes in margin toward a reply. If Fanger finds moving from Berkeley to Harvard an adjustment, a 'much more risking proposition' is 'introducing M. to Ireland'. Private collection.

4. *Company*, 112. My thanks for help on this point to Madeleine Mottuel, 13 March 2022.

5. Montague, October 20, Notebook for 1956, Buffalo.

6. Notebook for 1956, p. 5; Buffalo.

7. 'Emigrants' was published in *Poisoned Lands* (1961), 31.

8. Montague, 'Honeymoon', Buffalo, Box 53.

9. *Company*, 22.

10. In his preface to Brian Lalor's *Ink-Stained Hands*, Colm Tóibín lists the addresses of prominent artists and writers who lived in the area, pp. 6–7. Additions to the list have been made by the author.

11. *Company*, 51.

12. In *Company* (p. 71), Montague says he first met Liam Miller in 1956 in his basement offices at Upper Mount Street. That is inaccurate, because The Dolmen Press did not move to Mount Street from Glenageary until mid-1957. My thanks to Thomas Redshaw.

13. My thanks to Thomas Redshaw for an advance look at his yet-to-be-published 'Liam Miller (1924–1987): A Published Life.' I rely on his account.

14. Thomas Redshaw, '"The Dolmen Poets": Liam Miller and Poetry Publishing in Ireland, 1951–1961', *Irish University Review* (Spring/Summer 2012), pp. 141–54.

15. JM to Thomas Parkinson, 19 December [1957]; Buffalo, B92, F10.

16. Denis Donoghue, review of *The Permanence of Yeats*, *The Irish Times* (24 September 1955): 6.

17. See Denis Donoghue's articles on Wyndham Lewis in *The Irish Times* for 5 November 1955 and 31 December 1955. In 1957 Montague gave a corrective assessment of Lewis, lamenting the 'viciousness of Lewis and Eliot', and the way younger critics (i.e., Donoghue) had been infected with 'presuppositions from ... Maurras', the far-right French Catholic ('Portrait of the Enemy', *The Irish Times*, 10 August 1957 p. 6).

18. JM, Letter to the Editor, *The Irish Times* (19 January 1957).

19. JM to Thomas Parkinson, 19 February 1957; Buffalo.

20. 'Change of Management', *An Occasion of Sin*.

21. See 'Journalists', *Connaught Tribune* (20 June 1959): 8.

22. The Newry bombings were reported in *The Irish Times* on 12 August 1957. The recollection of Parkinson's visit is from JM, 'A Poet at Croke Park', written after 25 September 1960; NLI, Box 22.

23. Interview with Elizabeth Healy, 14 October 2017; Seapoint, Co. Dublin.

24. *Poisoned Lands*, 52, 23.

25. Nelson Algren, 'The Banjaxed Land', *Who Lost an American* (André Deutsch: London, 1960), pp. 50–65. *The Vanishing Irish* by Rev. John O'Brien was published in 1954.

26. Margaret Drabble's summary of Lessing's attitude, in 'Who am I? Who do I want to be?' *The Guardian* (7 April 2012): 2.

27. JM to Thomas Parkinson, [10 December 1958]; Buffalo.

28. Ibid.

29. *Collected Poems*, 220. 'That Room' was written in 1962.

30. Montague's resignation from Bord Fáilte did not take effect until 1 July 1959.

31. 'Moral for Cosmonauts', *Poisoned Lands* (1961), p. 59.

32. Among other bits of evidence for Madeleine's role in planning their future is her letter to Thomas Parkinson, 2 July 1959: 'John intends a whole year of reflection and writing, including his thesis. I am very adamant about that, it seems the *sine qua non* condition of leaving his job.'

33. Paul Howard, *I Read the News Today, Oh Boy: The short and gilded life of Tara Browne, the man who inspired The Beatles' greatest song*, Picador, 2016, p. 85.

34. 'Notice of Intended Libel Action Granted', *The Irish Times* (18 April 1959): 9.

35. Madeleine Montague to Thomas Parkinson, 2 July 1959; Buffalo; Share certificate, 3 August 1965 (UCC).

36. 'Soirée in Quinn's Lane', *The Irish Times* (12 December 1959).

37. Michael O'Sullivan, *Brendan Behan: A Life* (Roberts Rinehart: Boulder, Colorado, 1999; first published, Blackwater Press, Dublin).

38. This account is largely dependent on *I Read the News Today*, p. 102.

39. JM to Tim O'Keeffe, [11 January 1960]; Tulsa.

40. Morris Graves and his partner, Richard Svare, had drinks with the former King of England and his American wife on 21 November 1957 in Paris; *Morris Graves: Selected Letters*, p. 78. Svare

(1930–2004) was an actor and singer. After his years with Graves, he became the administrator of the Merce Cunningham dance company.

41. Morris Graves, letter of reference for Montague's proposal for a Ford Foundation Grant, [March 1959]; my thanks to Lawrence Fong.

42. Morris Graves to Dan Johnson, 7 September [1958]; *Morris Graves: Selected Letters*, ed. Vicki Harper and Lawrence Fong (University of Washington Press: Seattle & London, 2013); see also pp. 177, 180.

43. *Morris Graves: Selected Letters*, edited by Vicki Harper, and Lawrence Fong, University of Washington Press, 2013.

44. *Morris Graves: Selected Letters*, p. 80.

45. 'Woodtown Manor (for Morris Graves)', *Studies: An Irish Quarterly Review*, vol. 49, no. 195 (Autumn, 1960): 278; *Collected Poems*, 207. I have dropped the third section, with its too obvious echo of Wallace Stevens's 'Sunday Morning' in the final line.

46. Madeleine and JM to Thomas Parkinson, 22 February [1960]; Buffalo, B91, F10. In NYC, Morris Graves met many celebrities – Mark Rothko, Truman Capote, the theologian Paul Tillich, and, happily for Graves, the mythographer Joseph Campbell: 'Many times I've painted from Joe Campbell's writings but had never met him. It was like meeting part of yourself outside of yourself'; *Morris Graves: Selected Letters*, p. 82.

47. Notebook for 1957/58; p. 50; Buffalo.

48. JM to Thomas Parkinson, 19 December [1957]; Buffalo, B92, F10.

49. 'Martin Gerard', 'Goodbye to All That: A Child's Guide to Two Decades', *An Anthology from X* edited by Patrick Swift and David Wright (Oxford University Press: Oxford, 1988), pp. 52–8. The fiction of John McGahern was first published in 'X'; the editor Patrick Swift and his brother Jimmy were close friends of McGahern. See John McGahern to Mary Keelan, 3 February 1964; *The Letters of John McGahern* (Faber & Faber: London, 2022), pp. 10–13.

50. JM to Tim O'Keeffe, 19 June [1961]; Tulsa.

51. The *Dictionary of Irish Biography* for John Jordan states that he left Oxford and returned to Dublin and UCD in 1955; however, Pearse Hutchinson is still writing to Jordan at various street addresses in Oxford in March and August 1956, and September 1958; John Jordan Papers, NLI Ms 35,080.

52. See the letters page of *The Irish Times* for 16 July, 30 July and 5 August 1958.

53. Quidnunc, 'Discussion of Poetry', *The Irish Times* (13 February 1960): 6.

54. Notebook for 1960–61. Buffalo.

55. Notebook for 1960–61, p. 19; Buffalo, B71, F1.

56. Notebook for 1960–61, p. 211. Buffalo.

57. JM to Dear Denis; 22 June 1960; Typed letter, frag.; Buffalo, B71.

58. JM to Thomas Parkinson [ah 10 December 1958]; Buffalo.

59. Pearse Hutchinson, 'First book by a young Irish poet', *The Irish Press* (28 March 1959); John Jordan, *Crystal Clear: Selected Prose of John Jordan* (Lilliput: Dublin, 2006), pp. 62–3; John Hewitt, *Threshold* (July 1959).

60. Leonora Leet to JM; 18 October 1959; UCC; JM notes, 'gentleness in the voice.'

61. Mary O'Malley, *Never Shake Hands with the Devil* (Elo Publications: Dublin, 1990), pp. 89–93.

62. Mary O'Malley to JM, 19 February [1957]; Hardiman Library, Galway; T4/850.

63. JM, 'The First Week in Lent: A Political Snapshot', *Threshold* (July 1957): 70–71.

64. The *Threshold* (and Lyric Theatre) fundraiser was held on 7 June 1960; it raised £220 (Mary O'Malley to John Hewit; 13 June [1960]; Hardiman.

65. John Hewitt was not thrilled about Montague's 'Rome: Anno Santo', but he accepted it for publication in the Spring 1958 issue. He loved 'That Dark Accomplice', Montague's short story then entitled 'Rebellion'. John Hewitt to Mary O'Malley, 14 October [1958]; Hardiman. 'This … shows how a story shd be written. A really powerful piece of work. Indisputably Irish in its nature. Brutal, harsh, malicious, clearly observed. If we cd get more of this quality it would be wonderful.'

   Montague's article on Hewitt's poetry was eventually published as 'John Hewitt: Regionalism into Reconciliation' in *Poetry Ireland* (Spring 1964). Thanking Montague, Hewitt wrote, 'I doubt if there's another mortal who has taken so much trouble to grasp its tendency.'

66. JM to Thomas Parkinson, 6 February [1958]; Buffalo, B92, F5; *Company*, p. 14.

67. Ezra Pound, *The Cantos*, LXXXI.

68. The original for 'Maggie Owens' appears to have been Minnie Kearney, or MacKearney. See drafts for 'The Wild Dog Rose', Buffalo B33, and B72, F1, where she is named.

69. 'I must place a few things on record. My feeling is for the weak', [c. 1949?]; UCC.

70. JM to Austin Clarke [November 1958]; draft; Buffalo; Box 2. It was in, then it was out. The editors made 'public apologies at the big dinner of OUP – the whores', (JM to Fanger [October 1958], UCC]. The first drafts of 'The Sean Bhean Bhoct' appear to belong to May 1957 (Buffalo, B1, F5).

71. On a rough draft of 'Like Dolmens', JM indicated it was written in August 1959, while staying at Rossdohan in County Kerry.

72. JM to Robin Skelton; 16 May 1960; University of Victoria.

73. Significantly, of course, there was a publisher by that name. 'Like Dolmens' is clearly a Liam Miller poem, even though he was not the first to publish it.

74. JM, *Collected Poems*, p. 22.

75. Notebook, 1960; p. 107; Buffalo.

76. Maebh Long, ed., *The Collected Letters of Flann O'Brien* (Dalkey Archive Press: Victoria, TX, 2018), p. 229.

77. Tim O'Keeffe to editor, MacGibbon and Kee; 24 December 1960; Tulsa. 'Williams' may be Desmond Williams, History Department, UCD.

78. Tony Carroll, a UCD medical student, was introduced to Patrick Kavanagh by James Liddy in 1962, after *Poisoned Lands* was published. Kavanagh declared that 'the trouble with Montague's book is that it's too much like him'. By that, Carroll understood Kavanagh to mean too spiffy, cosmopolitan and trendy. Kavanagh's 'ace in the hole' was that his poems were those of a truly authentic, unimproved country man; Tony Carroll message to AF, 31 October 2019.

79. JM to John L. (Jack) Sweeney, 22 August 1960; Papers of John L. (Jack) Sweeney and Máire MacNeill Sweeney; UCD Special Collections. It may have been at this launch that the conversation with MacNeice occurred later recalled by Montague:

> JM: You are the best Ulster Protestant poet.
>
> LM: [Sheepish nod.] You are the best Ulster Catholic poet?
>
> JM: There are none.
>
> LM: [Brightens.] You are the best poet from County Tyrone!

This conversation startles one into an awareness of Montague's role in 1961 as a lonely forerunner of Catholic poets from the North, before the flourishing of Heaney, Carson, McGuckian and Muldoon. Much was later made of how MacNeice showed Northern Irish Protestants how to be both inside and outside an Irish identity, and both modern and classical. Yet he had also been an important influence on Kinsella (particularly upon the satirical passages of his meditative poems) and on Montague, in regard to the shared themes of the lost mother and the disturbed childhood.

80. Denis Donoghue, letter to the editor, *The Irish Times* (30 July 1958): 5.

81. JM to Davie; draft; nd; Buffalo.

CHAPTER SIX

1. Richard Murphy, *The Kick: A Life Among Writers*.

2. 'An Irishman's Diary', *The Irish Times* (24 January 1961): 6.

3. Richard Murphy, *The Irish Times* (15 December 2016).

4. 'Old Mythologies', *TLS* (17 February 1961): 98.

5. 'a sort of strictness', 1959 notebook, p. 196; Buffalo.

6. Thomas Kilroy, review of *A Chosen Light*, *University Review* (Winter 1967): 302–6.

7. 'Poet's Mission', *The Irish Press* (20 January 1961).

8. 'Hibernian Hotel Reading', notebook, 19 March 1963 (Buffalo).

9. JM to Liam Miller; 7 June 1961; Dolmen Archive, Wake Forest.

10. Richard Murphy, Loc. 3430; p. 199.

11. JM to Kinsella; 17 December 1961; Buffalo.

12. JM's note on a Kinsella to Montague letter, 3 January 1962; Buffalo.

13. Thomas Redshaw, 'Liam Miller (1924–1987): A Published Life', p. 102.

14. JM to Liam Miller, 27 February 1961; Wake Forest.

15. Michael P. Farrell, *Collaborative Circles: Friendship Dynamics and Creative Work* (University of Chicago Press: Chicago, 2001).

16. The manner in which Murphy functioned as a boundary-marking scapegoat is apparent in a controversy over the draft review John Jordan wrote of collections by Kinsella, Montague, Desmond O'Grady and Murphy for *The Dolmen Miscellany*. Montague was shocked by the draft. It was, he told Jordan, 'terribly biased' and 'manifestly unfair' to Murphy. Montague argued point-by-point with the arch, snide critique of 'The Last Galway Hooker'. He admitted that he shared Jordan's indignant Catholicism, but 'because we – the real Murphies – are in

control now, we must handle such Kenya Highlanders with a firm but tactful kindness: not like an enemy but a child'. At Montague's request, and with the support of Kinsella, Jordan dropped the whole section from his poetry chronicle (JM to John Jordan, 7 May 1962; Ms 35 098 John Jordan papers, NLI). In this way, the second Irish Revival defined itself as a literary movement in which discernibly sectarian literary evaluation was forbidden.

17. Anthony Cronin, *The Life of Riley* (New Island: Dublin, 2010), p. 90. Cronin later explained that O'Donnell 'didn't want to know what the younger generation thought. He wanted to tell them what to think ... I didn't think there were that many young writers around that needed a special issue of *The Bell* to have their say. I didn't approve of the majority of the people that Peadar wanted in, etc. I'm afraid I was a very very severe critic at that time,' (Interview with Carolyn Meyer, Willowdale, Ontario; Cronin papers AC 5719; NLI). O'Donnell did not tell Montague and Kinsella what to think; he left them free to edit the *Miscellany* as they pleased.

18. Mary O'Malley to John Hewitt, 22 February 1961; Hardiman Library, NUI Galway.

19. JM to Mary O'Malley, 3 March 1961; Hardiman Library, NUI Galway.

20. JM to Robin Skelton, 1 February 1961; University of Victoria.

21. Notebook, 7 February [1961]; NLI.

22. 'Inside me I sometimes feel', Notebook for 1963; Buffalo.

23. JM to Tim O'Keeffe; 11 January 1960; Tulsa.

24. JM to Professor Hogan; 17 November 1959; UCC.

25. JM to Donald Fanger, 8 November 1961; personal collection.

26. JM to Barrie Cooke, 8 October 1970; NLI.

27. JM to Thomas Parkinson, 6 January 1962; Buffalo.

28. 'The projected story book', Box 9, Buffalo.

29. JM to Tim O'Keeffe, 19 June 1961; Tulsa.

30. When Montague visited the family in Fintona before Christmas 1964, his brothers Turlough and Seamus gave him a good ribbing over his collection of stories. By its publication, he had 'done slut on his own doorstep' just as when, back from university, he once paired up for a night with a girl from the cottages their mother rented in the Back Lane. Irritated by his brothers' sharply humorous rebuke, Montague undertook to write a story about that episode, 'Sugarbush, I love you so', which culminates in Turlough (once a member of the Queen's University boxing team) punching him in his mother's kitchen. Upon further reflection, he decided not to publish anything about Fintona so long as Molly was alive (Molly to JM, Christmas 1964; UCC; and 'Fragment', [January 1965], Buffalo notebook).

31. JM to Thomas Parkinson, 21 September 1961; Buffalo.

32. See articles in the *Belfast Telegraph* for 2 and 3 December 1983.

33. JM to Donald Fanger; 8 November 1961.

34. Draft letter to Donal O'Sullivan, journal for August/September 1961; NLI. Draft letter, possibly to J.J. Hogan [September? 1961]; UCC.

35. JM to Tim O'Keeffe, 2 August 1961; Tulsa.

36. JM to John Jordan, 19 December 1961; NLI 35 098 John Jordan papers.

37. JM to Tim O'Keeffe, 1 December 1962; Tulsa.

38. Unlike his protagonist, Montague did not himself want to work at Bord Fáilte under a new efficient manager, and when Niall Sheridan was moved out, Montague felt the time had come to resign. 'Clohessy' may be a construct of Tim O'Driscoll, a lofty senior civil servant who was director general of the tourist board, and Michael Whelan, who came into the board from Aer Lingus, and had a research-based approach to the job. Kevin Barry suggests, 'perhaps "John O'Shea" is modelled on my father elsewhere described as "Kevin Barry", a top aide to O'Driscoll at Bord Fáilte, and who was an independent architect but chose, anxious for a securer living, to join the *Bord*'. My thanks to Kevin Barry, James Larkin and Mary O'Sullivan Long for background on Bord Fáilte.

39. By the mid-1960s Montague was friends with Patrick Pye, Barrie Cooke, Louis le Brocquy, Patrick Scott and Seán Sweeney; closer to them, possibly, than to contemporary Irish writers.

40. 'An Occasion of Sin' was republished in David Marcus's *Bodley Head Book of Irish Short Stories* (1980).

41. JM to Liam Miller, 13 June 1964.

42. My thanks to Thomas Redshaw for clarification of this point.

43. An event recollected in JM's letter to Tim O'Keeffe of 5 February 1969; Tulsa.

44. Maurice Kennedy, 'Breakthrough' (review of *Death of a Chieftain*), *The Irish Times* (24 September 1964), p. 9; Notebook, [7 November?] 1963; Buffalo.

45. Montague collected McGahern from the Paris airport in August 1962, and together, for a lark, they visited an Indian yogi in Dublin in November.

46. Loose page in notebook, with list of those to receive gratis copies of *Poisoned Lands*; September 1961; NLI; and 'That Room', notebook for c. 20 March 1962; Buffalo.

47. John McGahern to JM, before Christmas 1961; Victoria; Yeats, *Collected Works of W.B. Yeats*, v3; p. 147.

48. JM to John Jordan, 13 April 1961; NLI Ms 35,098.

49. Aidan Higgins to JM, 27 October 1961; University of Victoria.

50. Aidan Higgins to JM, 23 March 1963; University of Victoria.

51. 'Glancing at Aidan Higgins' book …', 14 July 1963, Notebook; Buffalo.

52. Madeleine to Thomas Parkinson, 19 November 1959; Buffalo.

53. Notebook, November 1959; Buffalo.

54. Kinsella to JM, 3 January 1962; 9 February 1962; Buffalo.

55. 'For Tom', notebook, c. 3 February 1962; Buffalo; JM to Robin Skelton, 12 March 1962; Victoria.

56. JM to Liam Miller, 18 July 1962; Dolmen archive.

57. Kinsella to JM, 16 April 1962; Buffalo.

58. Notebook, c. 10 November 1962; 6 December 1962; Buffalo.

59. Draft letter, JM to Kinsella; 28 February 1963.

60. 'Apology, explanation', notes toward a letter to Kinsella, 10 January 1963. Notebook, Buffalo.

61. 'I do observe in myself a failure', Notebook, c. 29 January 1963; Buffalo.

62. Kinsella to JM, no date, poor-quality photocopy; Buffalo.

63. JM to Tim O'Keeffe, 30 October 1961; Tulsa; JM to Tim O'Keeffe, 13 May 1963; Tulsa.

64. JM to Tim O'Keeffe, 10 March 1963; Tulsa. In truth, the last two weren't quite 'Beats', though they were friendly with them.

65. Antoinette Quinn, *Patrick Kavanagh: A Biography* (Gill and Macmillan: Dublin, 2001), p. 404.

66. 'Writer in Profile', Tim O'Keeffe on RTÉ; 16 February 1971.

67. Montague, *The Pear Is Ripe*, 84.

68. Martin Green, letter to the editor, *The Guardian* (8 October 2005): 8.

69. Fiona Green remembers Martin going to Dublin three times for the purpose (conversation with Fiona Green, 18 October 2019). Tony Carroll met Martin Green on one of these trips. He stayed two weeks, and succeeded in gathering some manuscripts; conversation with Tony Carroll, 7 November 2019.

70. JM to Tim O'Keeffe, [July 1962]; Tulsa.

71. Barrie Cooke to JM, 23 February [1963]; NLI.

72. *The Pear Is Ripe*, 86.

73. Patrick Kavanagh, 'I May Be Wrong', *Hibernia* (December 1964): 24.

74. JM, 2 December, 4 December, and 9 December 1964; Notebook for 1964, B74, F1; *Company*, 131. In *The Pear Is Ripe*, JM says that Kavanagh mauled *The Death of a Chieftain* not because he did not know he was indebted to Montague for *The Collected Poems*, but because he did know (p. 90).

75. 'Try to make myself into a Laurentian', NLI, Montague archive.

76. JM, 'The Lawrence Phenomenon', *The Irish Times* (3 June 1961): 3.

77. 'The Lawrence mood', 17 January 1963, notebook; Buffalo.

78. Barrie Cooke to JM; 2 April 1961; NLI.

79. Barrie Cooke to JM, 28 November 1961; NLI.

80. 'Death of Minnie', 30 December 1962; notebook; Buffalo. My thanks to Frank and Seamus Rogers, and to Frank Horisk, for information about Jim McKillion and his crimes. For at least one of his assaults, he did serve time in a Belfast prison.

81. *Ulster Herald*, 22 May 1965; Montague papers, NLI.

82. Freda Montague to JM, 5 July 1960; B71; Buffalo.

83. Jonathan Blunk, *James Wright: A Life in Poetry*, (Farrar, Straus and Giroux: 2019), p. 143.

84. Kinsella noticed this feature of Montague's lyrics too, and helpfully brought it to his attention: 'Your signature tune is the break-off toward the end of the poem & the change of direction, whether toward epigram, a new direction, or distanced (cinematic) point of view, & c. It is in a great number of them. Do you know; do you mind? No. You feel a need to look hard at it and inquire from yourself whether (in some instances) it is not a dubious way of pulling your poem to a halt, avoiding certain depths which I feel must sooner or later be plunged into, ballock-naked, for good or ill – even at the cost of losing control over form, tone, & (i.e., to get the thing explored & said <u>completely</u>: are there not limits to the achievement you can get with this 'wry' effect, like allusiveness.) Poem by poem, it has no detrimental effect, but cumulatively: like a lot of short stories with surprise endings: you grow to predict the surprises', Kinsella to JM, 4 April 1966; Buffalo. The difference between the advice of

Bly and Kinsella about closure is that Bly thought JM should trust in the images alone to carry the poem, and Kinsella thought the journey should go farther and deeper, even if there was less and less light to see by. Bly was against abstract statement; Kinsella was against neat enclosures of the comprehensible. 'Message from Paris', Box 17, Buffalo. In a notebook entry for December 1964 (Buffalo), Montague reminds himself to bring the sections of the *A Chosen Light* manuscript 'to Bob Bly as they are done'.

85. 'Message from Paris', Box 17, Buffalo. In a notebook entry for December 1964 (Buffalo), Montague reminds himself to bring the sections of the *A Chosen Light* manuscript 'to Bob Bly as they are done'.

86. *Chosen Lights: Poets on Poems by John Montague*, Loc. 442.

87. JM to Parkinson, 16 July 1963; B92, F18; Buffalo.

88. *The Kick*, Loc. 4170.

89. Diary of May Monaghan, *Journal of Modern Literature* (April 1975): 855.

90. *Company*, p. 184.

91. 'not a smooth-faced young philanderer', 20 March 1964; notebook, Buffalo; *Company*, p. 186.

92. The notebook page with the first draft of 'The Blow' mentions a long conversation with the UC Berkeley poet Louis Simpson about Lawrence. 'Fierce awareness' is a symptomatic 'transferred epithet'; literally, it is awareness of ferocity. Donald Fanger wisely expressed reservations before the publication of 'The Blow': 'The situation … is less common, and more specific, and altogether more problematical' than that of the other poems in *All Legendary Obstacles* (Fanger to JM, 23 December 1964; personal collection).

93. My thanks to Tom Burns (email 6 March 2017), a student in the workshop, for his recollections.

94. John de St Jorre, 'The poet and his muses', *The Guardian* (24 June 1995).

95. Written in Mallorca on 17 August 1953; Ekbert Faas, with Maria Trombacco, *Robert Creeley: A Biography* (McGill-Queen's University Press: Montreal and Kingston, 2001), 124.

96. Montague, published in revised form as 'No More Than a Parable', *The Bell* (October 1952): 276.

97. JM to Thomas Parkinson, 27 September [1958?]; Buffalo; Robert Graves to JM, 23 May 1959; B65; Buffalo;.

98. Robert Graves to JM, 22 November 1960; Buffalo.

99. Montague, 'An Old Story' [later entitled 'Beyond the Liss'], 4 September and 7 September, 1963; Notebook, Buffalo.

100. 'Looking at the poems, I see an absence of pressure', 21 March 1964; notebook; Buffalo.

101. *Company*, 187.

102. 'The intense reality of a love affair', 24 April 1964; Notebook; Buffalo.

103. 'Clear Sight', 'actually E. who says this', 27 April 1964; Notebook; Buffalo.

104. JM to Carolyn Kizer, 5 June [1964]; *Poetry Northwest* Papers at the University of Washington, Seattle; my thanks to Marian Janssen.

105. Montague, notebook, 17 August 1964; Buffalo.

106. 'Awaiting the letter from Lena', 4 November 1964; notebook; Buffalo.

107. The quotation was used as an epigraph to the Dolmen edition of *All Legendary Obstacles* (February 1966), p. 26.

108. 'My love, while we talked', with passage from Camus [JM translation]; B15, Buffalo. The date of composition for 'Postscript'. It was first published in May 1966; there is a typescript with '1965' written at the top. My guess is Autumn 1965.

109. JM to Madeleine, nd, fragment; between pp. 42 and 43, notebook for 1965; B75aF10, Buffalo

CHAPTER SEVEN

1. Jack Weinberg had heard Hal Draper's critique of *The Uses of the University*, 'The Mind of Clark Kerr', the day before his arrest; see Max Heinrich, *The Beginning: Berkeley, 1964* (Columbia University Press: NY, 1968, 1970), p. 80, 103.

2. Heinrich, p. 86.

3. *The Pear Is Ripe*, 15.

4. Jack Kerouac, *The Dharma Bums*, Loc. 760.

5. 'The howling day ...', notebook entry for 18 March 1965; B75, F1; Buffalo. The draft lines are also like Snyder's poetry in its outward-looking style, locating 'the self ecologically in its actions with the environment', minute by minute in the physical world; see Robert Kern, 'Recipes, Catalogues, Open Form Poetics: Gary Snyder's Archetypal Voice', *Contemporary Literature* (Spring 1977): 187.

6. J.J. Lee, *Ireland 1912–1985* (Cambridge University Press: Cambridge, 1989), 646.

7. Notebook entry, 9 February 1965; B75, F1; Buffalo.

8. 'She is no liar', notebook for 24 March 1965; Buffalo; Robert Graves, *Complete Poems* (Carcanet Poems: Manchester, 1999), p. 65.

9. 'To have five women fighting over me ...', notebook entry for 25 March 1965; Buffalo.

10. 'On not fully believing in the imagination', notebook entry for 13 January 1965; Buffalo.

11. The description is derived from Michael Rumaker, *Robert Duncan in San Francisco* (City Lights/Grey Fox: San Francisco, 2013), p. 21.

12. Montague, obituary for Robert Duncan, *The Guardian* (13 February 1988); Thom Gunn, *The Letters of Thom Gunn*, p. 40.

13. Robert Duncan, *The Collected Later Poems and Plays*, ed. Peter Quartermain (University of California Press: Berkeley & Los Angeles, 2014), pp. 753; 751–2.

14. JM to Robert Duncan, 22 March 1965; Robert Duncan papers; Buffalo. It is not clear what 'proofs' these would have been. Parts of the 'H.D. Book' were published in journals, but the manuscript as a whole did not appear until 2011; see Robert Duncan (author), Michael Boughn and Victor Coleman (editors), *The H.D. Book* (University of California Press: Berkeley and Los Angeles, 2011).

15. Notebook, 'Supper with Robert and Jess', 19 April 1965; Buffalo.

16. Tara McDowell, *The Householders: Robert Duncan and Jess* (MIT Press: Cambridge, Mass., 2019), p. 48. The Stan Brakage quotation is on page 50.

17. Madeleine and John Montague to Robert and Jess; 9 April 1967; Robert Duncan papers; Buffalo.

18. Donald Fanger to JM, 24 July 1960; private collection.

19. JM to Donald Fanger, 6 May 1965; private collection; Robert and Rebecca Tracy to Adrian Frazier, email, 19 October 2018; *The Hill Field* (Coffee House Press, Minneapolis; The Gallery Press, Oldcastle: 1989), p. 70.

20. JM to Madeleine, 21 May 1965; *The Pear Is Ripe*, 40.

21. Montague began drafting 'The Siege of Mullingar' on 3 June 1963, immediately following the Fleadh Cheoil; notebook, Buffalo.

22. JM to Donald Fanger; 19 May 1965; personal collection.

23. Peter Whitehead, 'Wholly Communion', documentary film; available on YouTube.

24. 'Notes for August', 31 August 1965; notebook, Buffalo.

25. JM to Liam Miller, 18 September 1965; Dolmen Archive; Wake Forest.

26. Lena to JM; 25 August [1965]; Buffalo.

27. 'The Pale Light', *Tides*, 27.

28. '… in the pale light', [6 September 1965]; notebook; Buffalo.

29. JM to Barrie Cooke; draft letter; [8 September 1965]; notebook; Buffalo.

30. 'Milligan and Company Enjoy Themselves', *The Irish Times* (4 October 1965): 11.

31. 'Coming Events', *Tides*, 26. The painting is panel two of *The Judgment of Cambyses*.

32. 'Marriage …. If I lose her, I lose everything', 18 October 1965; notebook; Buffalo.

33. The phrase 'nothing left to desire' is a bit misleading. John and Lena continued to correspond in 1966, and even arranged a rendezvous in late February and another in mid-April. She thought of him as her own sexual Ferris wheel, or pedal boat. But in August she became pregnant by her husband. The marriage was mended, and the affair came to an end.

34. 'When have you taken to reading my notebooks', 16 November 1965; Buffalo.

35. 'Special Delivery', *Tides*, 29–30.

36. 'A Private Reason', *A Chosen Light*, 24. Published in *The Irish Times* on 12 March 1966.

37. Irving Wardle email to AF, 20 February 2017, quoting JM to Irving Wardle (2012); JM to 'Dark One', draft letter; notebook; Buffalo. 'Courtyard in Winter' was written over a long period. It began as simply a winter scene in 1963, before the suicide of Joan Wardle. The suicide of Sylvia Plath may have had an impact on it. In 1970 Montague told Tom Redshaw the poem was a response to the cancer diagnosis of *amhránaí* (traditional singer) Dolly MacMahon. Clearly, the poem drew its life from several roots, and was at once personal and abstract. He did not get a complete draft until early 1971.

38. 'It dawns on me …', notebook 10 September 1965; Buffalo; JM to Liam Miller, 24 November [1965], Wake Forest.

39. Clipping of 'Digging', Montague papers, NLI; 'perfect arrogance', JM's marginalia in Faber first edition of *Death of a Naturalist* (NLI).

40. JM to Tim O'Keeffe, 1912-2000 [c. 19 January 1966]; Tulsa.

41. JM to Liam Miller, 24 November [1965]; Wake Forest.

42. Dillon Johnston, *The Poetic Economies of England and Ireland*, p. 140.

43. JM to Serge Fauchereau, 7 May 1966; Bibliothèque S. et Y. Fauchereau, Musée de L'Abbaye Sainte-Croix, Les Sables-d'Olonne.

44. JM to Serge Fauchereau, 18 November 1965; Musée de L'Abbaye Sainte-Croix.

45. Liam Miller to JM, 20 November [1965]; Wake Forest.

46. JM to Liam Miller, 8 December 1965; Wake Forest.

47. 'A Charm' was written during a visit by Lena to Paris; 'a shadow at the corner of my mind'; her proximity caused Montague to feel threatened by sexual obsession (Notebook 23 December 1965; Buffalo).

48. *The Pear Is Ripe*, p. 47; JM to [Roger McHugh], draft letter, c. 13 November 1965; notebook; Buffalo; JM to Dear Roger, nd; draft letter; between pp. 362 and 363, 1965 notebook; Buffalo. The strange thing is, as soon as Montague joined the UCD faculty, John Jordan took a job at Memorial University in Newfoundland, Canada.

49. JM to Liam Miller, 26 February 1966; Wake Forest.

50. Montague, *The Figure in the Cave*, Loc. 862–7.

51. 'On the morning of 14 April 1965', translation; memoir of John Montague by Serge Fauchereau; Bibliothèque S. et Y. Fauchereau, Musée de L'Abbaye Sainte-Croix.

52. Serge Fauchereau, 'Renaissance poétique en Irlande', *Les Lettres Nouvelles* (July–September 1966).

53. JM to Serge Fauchereau, 16 February 1966; and 28 March 1966; Bibliothèque S. et Y. Fauchereau. Later, James Dickey dropped out and Serge Fauchereau became a full partner in the proposed anthology.

54. Richard Loftus, *Nationalism in Modern Anglo-Irish Poetry* (University of Wisconsin Press: Madison, 1964); JM to Serge Fauchereau, 'April/May '66', Bibliothèque S. et Y. Fauchereau.

55. Adrian Frazier, 'Global Regionalism: Interview with John Montague', *Literary Review* (Winter 1979): 152–74.

56. Madeleine to Donald Fanger, 13 May 1966; personal collection.

57. An Irishman's Diary, *The Irish Times*, (20 July 1967): 9.

58. Paul Mariani, *Dream Song: The Life of John Berryman*, *8731–33* (University of Massachusetts Press, 1990); JM to Liam Miller, 'Stop Press', [June? 1966]; Wake Forest; *The Pear Is Ripe*, p. 110.

59. JM to Serge Fauchereau, December 1966; Bibliothèque S. et Y. Fauchereau. 'Beyond the Gentility Principle' is the title of Al Alvarez's introduction to his anthology *The New Poetry* (Penguin: London, 1962, 1966).

60. *The Pear Is Ripe*, p. 110.

61. Jane Howard, 'Whiskey and Ink', *Life Magazine* (21 July 1967).

62. Nuala O'Faolain, *Are You Somebody?*, p.101.

63. JM to Thomas Parkinson, 8 April 1967; Buffalo.

64. This paragraph relies on an email from Tom Redshaw, 19 May 2022.

65. H.C. [Harry Chambers?], 'John Berryman reading from Dream Songs', *The Irish Times* (21 June 1967): 7.

66. JM, 'Afterwards you came to Paris', NLI.

67. Interview with Serge Fauchereau, Paris.

68. Tim O'Keeffe to JM, 9 March 1967; Tulsa.

69. Louis le Brocquy to Tim O'Keeffe, 15 April 1967; Tulsa.

70. JM to Tim O'Keeffe, 2 November 1967; Tulsa.

71. Michael Longley, review of *A Chosen Light*, *The Dublin Magazine* (Spring 1968): 93–4. The 9 November 1967 review of *A Chosen Light* in the *TLS* found the influence of the Black Mountain poets, and did not like it (p. 1059).

72. Kinsella to JM, 15 October 1967; Buffalo.

73. Padraic Fiacc, 'Name Droppings: From the Unpublished Autobiography', *Fortnight* (June 2002): 19–22.

74. 'Laid to Rest in Native Soil', *Sunday Independent* (3 December 1967): 8; Antoinette Quinn, *Patrick Kavanagh*, p. 463. Seamus Heaney, David Wright and Richie Riordan also read at the graveside.

CHAPTER EIGHT

1. JM to Liam Miller, 23 June 1964; Dolmen.

2. JM to Liam Miller, 7 June 1961; Dolmen.

3. JM to Liam Miller, 25 February 1963; 11 March 1964. Dolmen.

4. 'Who died of booze in Brooklyn', draft notes for 'The Country Fiddler', B16, Buffalo.

5. In May 1967, JM brought Berryman to Woodtown Manor in order to record his poems, with John Hurt in attendance. A record from the session was never released. See *The Pear Is Ripe*, p. 116.

6. An early draft of 'Konarak' appears in a notebook for November 1963 (Buffalo).

7. JM to Madeleine [c. 14 January 1968]; B84; Buffalo.

8. *The Pear Is Ripe*, p. 121.

9. By August 1973 Montague had decided Whaley 'himself is of no real interest I feel – rakes rarely are – but his actions are symbolic of a people who have lost a sense of decorum. In a certain sense, I think this is happening again which is why I find the Buck interesting. Some of my friends would behave like him, if they dared,' JM to Sybil le Brocquy [August 1973]; NLI.

10. Barrie Cooke to JM, 8 September 1965; NLI.

11. JM to Barrie Cooke, 3 January 1969; Cambridge.

12. JM to Barrie Cooke, 1 January 1968; Cambridge.

13. Notebook, c. 8 April 1968; Buffalo.

14. JM to Barrie Cooke, 1 January 1968; Cambridge.

15. *The Collected Works in Verse and Prose of William Butler Yeats*, Vol. II, preliminary poem (1908). Information from Montague's student at UCD in 1967, Thomas Redshaw.

16. *The Pear Is Ripe*, p. 122.

17. Conversation with Richard Ryan, 23 September 2017.

18. 'Say Seán is in town; he could bring her out', 16 February 1968; notebook; B84, F1; Buffalo.

19. JM to Susan, 14 September 1968; Buffalo. Perhaps unsent.

20. 'Must you know it again', 5 March 1968; notebook; Buffalo.

21. 'Susan: I want to make you as strong as I am', 8 April 1968; notebook; Buffalo.

22. Nuala O'Faolain, 'Enjoyable Session of Poetry', *The Irish Press* (16 March 1968).

23. JM, 'Swift Homage on a Canal Bank', *The Guardian* (18 March 1968): 6.

24. Notebook entry, 17 March 1968; Buffalo.

25. 'The wind testing the clasp of the shutters', draft poem, 23 May 1968; Buffalo.

26. *The Pear Is Ripe*, 200.

27. Samuel Beckett, *Murphy* (Faber & Faber: London, 2009), p. 5.

28. JM to Susan, 27 June 1968; Buffalo.

29. 'Writers Will Meet', *Ulster Herald* (4 May 1968): 1. The Belfast Group set up a conference as part of Dungannon Civic Week, featuring Heaney, Montague, Mary Lavin, and Patrick Boyle.

30. Lisa Jarnot, *Robert Duncan*, p. 280.

31. Francois Crouzet, 'A University Besieged: Nanterre, 1967–69', *Political Science Quarterly* (June 1969): 328–50.

32. Mavis Gallant, 'Reflections: The Events in May: A Paris Notebook', *The New Yorker*.

33. Sarah Bakewell, *At the Existentialist Café: Freedom, Being, and Apricot Cocktails* (Chatto and Windus, 2016), p. 22.

34. Montague, notebook for 25 May 1968; Buffalo. C. S. ('Todd') Andrews was chief executive of the Turf Development Board (later Bord na Mona), the Irish transport company CIE, and finally the national broadcaster RTÉ.

35. Montague, notebook for 20 May 1968; Buffalo.

36. *The Situationist International Anthology*, ed. Ken Knabb (Bureau of Public Secrets, 2007). The quotation is from the 1967 pamphlet 'On the Poverty of Student Life'.

37. Todd Andrews to Madeleine Montague, 18 July 1968; Buffalo.

38. 'Love, oh my love, it will come', verse fragment, Notebook, 28 June 1968; Buffalo.

39. 'Faithless', Notebook, 27 April 1968.

40. 'The rain falls flatly', Notebook, 27 May 1968; Buffalo.

41. T.S. Eliot, 'Gerontion'.

42. 'Are you to become a burden to me?' Notebook, 30 June 1968.

43. 'The dreams xxx through the night', Notebook, 15 May 1968; Buffalo.

44. 'a childlike mother', Notebook, 26 July 1968.

45. Interview with Evelyn Montague, 19 February 2017.

46. Frank Kersnowski to Adrian Frazier, 2 February 2016.

47. 'No choice …' Notebook, 24 July 1968; Buffalo.

48. 'The wall around …' Notebook, 28 July 1968; Buffalo. This notebook entry is the germ of the poem 'Mosquito Hunt' [part of 'Summer Storm'], *Collected Poems*, 242.

49. 'That helpful goodness', Notebook, 30 July 1968; Buffalo.

50. 'Have I never really swallowed suffering?' Notebook, 1 August 1968; Buffalo.

51. Valentin Iremonger had originally agreed to do the Faber anthology, but his diplomatic postings took him far from the National Library of Ireland, a necessary resource for the job. On 19 January 1967 he suggested to Faber that they ask Montague to take over (Iremonger to Dear Colin, Buffalo, B42). On 17 February, Montague met with Faber in London to come to an agreement (17 February 1967; Buffalo, B42). From the start, Montague introduced the idea of including translations from the Irish, starting very early.

52. Eavan Boland, 'Living Art of Poetry: Montague's Reading', *The Irish Times* (11 September 1968): 10. In the *Irish Times* Eavan Boland also acclaimed 'The Hag of Beare' as the best of all the poems Montague had read at the Living Art Exhibition.

    Antoinette Quinn provides a penetrating appreciation of Montague's translation in the Spring 1989 issue of the *Irish University Review*: 'His version of the lament of the Cailleach Berri, from the ninth century Irish, transcends the barriers of gender, age, history and language to achieve imaginative empathy with this celebrated hag. She lives and breathes as in no previous translation, resurrected in the present tense, not as the *puella senilis* of Irish myth, but as a tragic figure, a lonely, aged, post-sexual woman. The sea floods and ebbs throughout the poem, tidal images and rhythms recreating the diastole and systole of the human cycle: life at the full, beautiful and sensual and its inevitable decline into dearth and death. Montague has proclaimed that "Puritan Ireland" is now "dead and gone" but the Gaelic Ireland glimpsed in his versions of Irish poetry enjoys an almost uninterrupted sexual frolic …. Unlike "The Wild Dog Rose", "The Hag of Beare" ends bleakly and negatively; its disconsolate speaker eludes Montague's healing vision and proffers no redemptive symbols of her own.' (p. 34).

53. 'A Last Drink', Notebook, 21 September 1968; Buffalo.

54. John Montague, 'Hugh MacDiarmid: The Seamless Garment and the Muse', *Agenda* 5 (1967–8).

55. *The Irish Times* (16 November 1968): 6; and *The Irish Times* (18 November 1968): 12. The proposed university merger was effectively an engulfment of Trinity by UCD. At the debate, UCD English lecturer Augustine Martin spoke against any steps that would remove the Bishop's ban on Catholics studying at Trinity, a prohibition that was bleeding Trinity dry, and reserving for UCD many of the best Irish students. Montague did not commit a great deal of energy to the debate, but he was in favour of a single metropolitan university like the Sorbonne in Paris, with TCD and UCD as affiliates rather than rivals.

56. Montague quoting MacDiarmid, 'MacDiarmid Explains Purpose', *The Irish Times* (18 November 1968): 12.

57. JM to Tim O'Keeffe, 29 October 1967; Tulsa.

58. See Montague's article on Hugh MacDiarmid and 'The Drunk Man Looks at a Thistle', 'The Seamless Garment and the Muse', *Agenda* (Autumn–Winter, 1967–8): 27; and Thomas Dillon Redshaw, 'John Montague's the "Rough Field": Topos and Texne', *Studies: An Irish Quarterly Review* (Spring 1974), p. 29–46.

59. JM to Serge Fauchereau; nd; Buffalo, Box 31.

60. 'Poetry and Documenta', *The Irish Times* (4 January 1969): 11.

61. JM to David Marcus, 6 February 1969; it is possible this letter was never sent; Buffalo, B30.

62. Turlough Montague to JM, 11 April 1969; Buffalo, B21; conversation with Elizabeth Montague, 20 December 2019.

63. Interview with Andrew, Sheena, and Dara Montague, 4 February 2017.

64. Conversation with Richard Ryan, 1 September 2017.

65. Richard Ryan to JM, 3 November 2016; private collection – a letter recalling this occasion.

66. 'Message', *Collected Poems*, p. 259.

67. JM to Richard Ryan, 26 January 1970; private collection. At the time, Ryan showed the pebble to a fellow UCD student, Kevin Barry (conversation with Kevin Barry, 4 January 2017).

68. Richard Ryan to JM, 3 November 2016; private collection.

69. 'Return', *Second Childhood*, p. 25.

70. JM to John Jordan, 7 April 1969; John Jordan Papers, NLI.

71. Information from Kevin Barry who was present, conversation, 4 January 2017.

72. Conversation with Evelyn Montague, 25 March 2017.

73. Conversation with Hayden Murphy, Galway, 30 September 2023; Liam Miller to JM, 5 May 1969; Wake Forest. This find led to some unpublished draft (and homophobic) verses dedicated to 'Hayden, who recovered certain manuscripts':

> Mutual Mutilation: Have Another
> A praise of feeding flies
> celebrates the rare ditch
>
> in which, they breed
> deformed feet & hands
>
> claw through soft mud
> sphincter muscles

74. JM to Tim O'Keeffe, 15 May 1969; Tulsa; Michael [Anania] to JM, 24 July 1968; NLI.

75. JM to Donald Fanger, 10 July 1969; JM to Richard Ryan, July 1969; private collection.

76. 'I was in Dungannon a few weeks ago', a note alongside draft lines for *A New Siege*, Buffalo.

77. 'Butcher's Gate: Londonderry', dated in JM's hand, 1969; Buffalo B32.

78. Note on draft of 'A New Siege', Buffalo, B31.

79. JM to Frank Ormsby, 9 January 1971; NLI. Hughes made the observation after Montague's reading at the Institute of Contemporary Arts in London.

80. This emphasis on physics originated in Montague's discussions with Stanley William Hayter, a major influence on *Tides*: 'I learnt from him how to see the world as a complex of energies, a dance of chance and necessity. He was always fascinated by wind and wave, down to the minutest detail, busily explaining, for example, how a stone in a pool creates a "standing wave",' (*The Pear Is Ripe*, pp. 67–8).

81. *Ulster Herald* (15 August 1970): 8; *Irish Independent* (13 August 1970): 6; typescript draft of 'Outside Armagh Jail', NLI.

82. Madeleine to JM, 16 November [1968]; Buffalo.

83. 'Lady, how stern and strange', draft poem, dated in JM's hand 1969; NLI.

84. Edward O'Shea, 'Seamus Heaney at Berkeley, 1970–71', *Southern California Quarterly*, Vol. 98, No. 2, pp. 157–93; JM to Parkinson, 12 November 1969; Buffalo B80. Montague had decided against a return to Berkeley, but the same thing that made him want to stay, the situation in the North, made Seamus Heaney want to leave, so Parkinson offered the visiting writer

post to the younger poet. In 1971 Montague once again wanted a position at the University of California at Berkeley.

85. Parkinson to JM, 4 January 1970; Buffalo, B80.
86. Parkinson to JM, 14 February 1971; Buffalo, B80.
87. Barrie Cooke to JM, 2 April 1976; NLI.
88. Frank Kersnowski to Adrian Frazier, 2 February 2016.
89. Evelyn to Robin Skelton, 4 June 1970; Victoria.
90. Conversations with Evelyn Montague, 25 March 2017; 9 March 2019; conversation with Sybil Montague, 23 February 2019.
91. JM to Adrian Frazier, 5 October 2016; private collection.
92. JM to Richard Ryan, 9 February 1971; private collection. 'The Hero's Portion' (*CP*, 280) was first published in *A Slow Dance* (1975).
93. JM to Robin Skelton, 30 July 1971; Victoria.
94. See Robin Skelton, 'Among the Stones', *The Collected Shorter Poems, 1947–1977*.
95. JM to Robin Skelton, 15 June 1970; Victoria.
96. Robin Skelton to JM, nd; Victoria.
97. Evelyn Robson to Robin Skelton, 17 October [1970]; Victoria.
98. JM to Tim O'Keeffe, 9 October 1969; Tulsa.
99. Jeremy Lewis to JM, 23 February 1970; Buffalo, B22.
100. JM to Liam Miller, 14 January 1970; Wake Forest.
101. Eavan Boland, 'Love Story', *The Irish Times* (3 October 1970): 8.
102. JM to John F. Deane, 3 November 1969; John F. Deane Papers, Boston College.
103. Peter Porter, 'Floundering', *The Guardian* (4 February 1971): 7.

CHAPTER NINE

1. John Hewitt, 'The Colony', *Collected Poems*, p. 79.
2. Thomas Kinsella, *The Táin* (Dolmen Press: Dublin, 1970), p. 61.
3. *The Pear Is Ripe*, p. 160–1; John Horgan, 'American Academics Look at Ireland', *The Irish Times* (16 May 1970): 10.
4. JM to Mary O'Malley, 2 March 1970, and 22 March 1970; Hardiman Library, Galway. Brian Friel was one of those to decline.
5. Brendan Kennelly to JM, 3 September 1970; JM to Brendan Kennelly, [September? 1970]; Buffalo, B31. W.J. McCormack and Frank Ormsby were also angered by *A New Siege*; JM to Liam Miller, 8 September 1970; Dolmen Archive. (19 October 1970; Buffalo B31). The jeering remarks about JM's dedications apparently refers to his letter to *The Irish Times* of 29 August 1970, which somewhat laboriously explains why *A New Siege* is dedicated to both Mary Holland (journalist covering the North) and Bernadette Devlin MP.
6. Montague to Kennelly: 'The Penguin book was probably the worst anthology of Irish verse ever produced, the most obviously venal' (September 1970).

7. JM to Brendan Kennelly [September 1970]; Kennelly to JM, 3 September 1970; 19 October 1970; Buffalo B31; Peggy O'Brien to author, 26 November 2017; Montague to Richard Ryan, 20 December 1968, private collection. Montague continued the feud in the *TLS* on 17 March 1972 where he wrote that it was sad to see Patrick Kavanagh 'celebrated by Brendan Kennelly, the last in our long line of professional Irishmen', and confirmation that 'what Kavanagh called "buckleppin" is a disease endemic in our literature'. (313).

8. John Hewitt, 'The Scar', *Collected Poems* (Blackstaff: Belfast, 1991), p. 177. See Britta Olinder, 'Inclusion and Marginalisation: John Hewitt as an Ulster Protestant in Opposition', *Nordic Irish Studies*, Special Issue: Discourses of Inclusion and Exclusion: Artistic Renderings of Marginal Identities in Ireland (2016), pp. 89–104

9. 'The Planter and the Gael, Excellent Entertainment', *Ulster Herald* (5 December 1970): 11.

10. John Hewitt, interview by Timothy Kearney, *The Crane Bag* (February 1981): 86.

11. Montague, 'The Impact of International Modern Poetry on Irish Writing', *The Figure in the Cave*, pp. 208–20.

12. Seán Lucy to JM, 4 May 1971; NLI.

13. Seán Lucy, 'A short note on John Montague', Boston College.

14. *The Pear Is Ripe*, p. 202.

15. Madeleine to JM, 5 November 1971; Buffalo, B51.

16. JM to Madeleine, January 1972; Buffalo, B52, and JM to Robin Skelton, nd, from UCC, 5 January 1982.

17. Désirée Moorhead to JM, 29 November 1972; Buffalo, B52.

18. JM was a long time bringing himself to compose 'Herbert Street Revisited'; see JM to Robin Skelton, 24 September 1976; Victoria.

19. JM to Evelyn [May? 1998], perhaps unsent; UCC.

20. Kevin O'Sullivan, review of *The Rough Field*, *Nation* (31 January 1978): 821.

21. 'Court Scenes', *The Irish Press* (7 March 1972).

22. *The Pear Is Ripe*, 209.

23. *The Pear Is Ripe*, 211; JM to Turlough, 29 July 1974; NLI.

24. JM to Robin Skelton, 15 March 1972; Victoria.

25. Skype conversation with Patrick Crotty, 27 August 2019; conversation with Nuala Ní Dhomhnaill, 30 December 2016.

26. *The Pear Is Ripe*, 214.

27. 'Belfast Evening of Poetry and Music', *The Irish Times* (10 May 1972): 10.

28. Interview with Patrick Crotty, 30 August 2019; Heaney, *Stepping Stones*, Loc. 3305.

29. Seamus Heaney, *The Guardian* (25 May 1972).

30. Kinsella to JM, 11 October 1971; Buffalo, B41; JM to Kinsella, draft letter, 5pp; Buffalo, B41. The commemorative service for MacNeice seems to have occurred in late March 1965, when Kinsella and Hedli Anderson went to Belfast for a performance at the Lyric Theatre (*Belfast News Letter*, 29 March 1965). Although the event is not recorded in John Stallworthy's biography of MacNeice, the interment of the poet's ashes at Carrowdore Churchyard, Co. Down, probably took place at this time. Heaney, Longley and Mahon all came along in

Heaney's Volkswagen, and each of the three contemplated writing an elegy. Only Mahon finished a poem that found a place in the collected poetry, 'In Carrowdore Churchyard'.

31. JM to Liam Miller, 1 June ny; Wake Forest; JM to Robin Skelton, 27 April 1972; Victoria.

32. Michael Devenish, editor, Oxford University Press, to Liam Miller, 29 November 1972; Buffalo, B34.

33. Thomas Redshaw, 'John Montague's *The Rough Field*: Topos and Texne', *Studies* (Spring 1974): 29–46. Redshaw drafted the article in a seminar for Roger McHugh's department of Anglo-Irish Literature at UCD in the spring of 1971.

34. Brendan Kennelly, 'Three Poets on the Tragedy of Our Times', *Sunday Independent* (10 December 1972): 16.

35. Eavan Boland, 'The Tribal Poet: John Montague', *The Irish Times* (20 March 1973): 10; in this interview, Montague's definition of the poet's role reflects his reading about shamanism in Siberia.

36. 'The State of Ireland', review of poetry collections by Montague and Seamus Deane, *The Times Literary Supplement* (16 February 1973): 183. Montague wrote to Deane on 1 April 1973: 'I am still angry over the reception of *The Rough Field* in England. Not for sales but because it shows a lack of comprehension of the subject. Who do you think did us both in the TLS?' (Emory).

37. Heaney to Michael Longley, 16 May 1973; *Letters of Seamus Heaney*, 104.

38. John Montague, 'An Gaeltacht Inniu' ['A Primal Gaeltacht'], *The Irish Times* (30 July 1970); see also, Michael Parker, 'Gleanings, Leavings: Irish and American Influences on Seamus Heaney's *Wintering Out*', *New Hibernia Review* (Autumn 1998): 16–35.

39. Seamus Heaney, 'For John Montague', 15 November 1972; inscription in copy of *Wintering Out*, Montague archive, NLI; Montague, 'Beyond the Liss', *Collected Poems*, p. 239.

40. The 'rough field' reference is perhaps not to the book title but to the phrase as it appears in 'A Lost Tradition', *CP*, 33, earlier published in *The Irish Press* on 27 March 1970 (p. 9).

41. Another copy of *Wintering Out* than the one bearing Heaney's versified dedication, Montague archive, NLI.

42. Higgins to JM, 3 January 1992; JM to Aidan Higgins, 'Samhain 1992'; NLI; conversation with Evelyn Montague, 11 March 2019; JM to Robin Skelton, 24 April 1977, Victoria.

43. Alannah Hopkin, *A Very Strange Man* (New Island: Dublin, 2021), p. 131: 'He and John had come to blows some years earlier in London, in the apartment at Muswell Hill, and had avoided each other ever since. Aidan admitted he had been taking some kind of speed, and had just flipped when Montague turned up yet again to have supper and stay the night without contributing a bottle, and could not resist the compulsion to punch him in the face. I thought it a strange way for grown men to behave. I neither liked nor disliked John Montague; he had always been polite and helpful to me.'

44. Evelyn Montague to Robin Skelton, 4 September 1973; Victoria.

45. Dennis O'Driscoll, Interview with John Montague, *Agenda*, v. 40, No. 1–3; pp. 52–74.

46. Antoinette Quinn insightfully observes of *The Great Cloak* that 'it is surely not insignificant that in its concluding poem, "Edge", Montague insistently employs positive imagery of

anchorage, refuge, harbouring, shelter in describing his home and home life, deliberately ignoring the precariousness and marginalization implicit in his choice of location and locution: on the edge is best', *Irish University Review* (Spring 1989): 40.

47. Danny Weissbort to Evelyn Montague, 18 February 1974; NLI.

48. Fiona MacCarthy, 'Witty, drunk, holy, bawdy', *The Guardian* (2 January 1990).

49. Barbara Wall, *René Hague: A Personal Memoir* (Aylesford Press: Upton, Cheshire, 1989), p. 29.

50. Interview with Evelyn Montague, 9 March 2019.

51. See Philippa Bernard, *No End to Snowdrops: A Biography of Kathleen Raine* (Shepheard-Walwyn: London, 2009).

52. JM to Robin Skelton, 21 December 1969; Victoria.

53. Thomas Dilworth, *David Jones: Engraver, Soldier, Painter, Poet* (Jonathan Cape: London, 2017), 91; see also René Hague, editor, *Dai Greatcoat: A Self-Portrait of David Jones in his Letters* (Faber & Faber: London, 2017).

54. JM to Turlough Montague [September/October 1973], NLI; Turlough to JM, 8 November 1973, NLI. It was Freda herself who told JM that Bridie had given her the news of John's separation from Madeleine and relationship with Evelyn; see JM to Turlough, 29 July 1974; conversation with Andrew Montague, 2 April 2017.

55. Madeleine to JM, 2 December 1973; Buffalo, B51. John and Madeleine's divorce became final on 17 April 1974.

56. Turlough to JM, 13 March 1974 (private collection, Andrew Montague); JM to Turlough, 26 May 1974; JM to Turlough, 29 July 1974; Turlough to JM, 20 August 1974; NLI.

57. Denis Donoghue, 'Icham of Irlaunde', *The Spectator* (5 April 1974): 11. 'pretended to be': because it is an impossible position for a person of Denis Donoghue's intelligence to hold, given his awareness of the intertextuality of all great literary works. Donoghue also made the extraordinary charge that Montague, while selecting his own best poems for inclusion, churlishly put in the lesser works of his contemporaries. Montague replied in the 3 May issue of *The Spectator* that this was a 'demonstrably dishonest accusation' because he had checked his choice of poems with their authors. The spats between the head boys in English at UCD thus continued twenty-five years after their graduation.

58. Augustine Martin, review of *Faber* anthology, *Studies* (Autumn 1974), p. 312.

59. Geoffrey Grigson, 'The Face of Irish Poetry', *The Irish Times* (9 March 1974): 10. Grigson's review is blatantly anti-Irish.

60. Montague, *Faber Book of Irish Verse*, p. 22.

61. See Máirín Ní Dhonnchadha, 'Women in the Medieval Poetry Business', *A History of Irish Women's Poetry*, ed. Ailbhe Darcy and David Wheatley (Cambridge University Press: Cambridge, 2021), pp. 40–56.

62. In the case of Nuala Ní Dhomhnaill, the reason may have been that she was not prominently as yet in print. Montague regarded Nuala Ní Dhomhnaill as the brightest of his UCC students in 1973. See JM, letter of recommendation, for Nuala Ní Dhomhnaill, Summer Term 1973; Boston College. It is possible that at the time of the Faber selection Montague had seen only Ní Dhomhnaill's academic work, but he knew enough of her poetry by 1974 to ask Evelyn

Montague to seek contributions to the 'Celtic Poetry' issue of *Modern Poetry in Translation*. Contributions to that issue were also sought from Máire Mhac an tSaoi.

Nuala Ní Dhomhnaill told the author that one time Montague asked her how she was going to proceed as a poet – would she not have to become a lesbian? Because great poetry depended on the relationship to the Moon-goddess, as discovered within an individual woman! In fairness, one must allow for the possibility that Montague may have been (as often) just teasing (conversation 30 December 2016).

It is noteworthy that Thomas Kinsella's *New Oxford Book of Irish Verse*, although published twelve years later, included even fewer women poets born after 1920; Kinsella did not choose a single woman. Not until the 1991 protest at the poor accounting of women's writing in *The Field Day Anthology* did gender balance become a standard concern of editors in Ireland.

CHAPTER TEN

1. JM to Turlough, cc to Seamus; 26 May 1974; NLI.
2. Evelyn to JM, 28 June [1974]; NLI.
3. Evelyn to JM, [July 1974]; NLI. 'Wheels Slowly Turning', a poem that relates the violence in the North to a war goddess, was later published in *A Slow Dance* (pp. 39–40).
4. David Lampe to Adrian Frazier, 20 August 2018.
5. 'Buffalo State College: Literary Series Brought Hundreds of Esteemed Poets, Writers to Campus', *Targeted News Service* (3 December 2020).
6. See Thomas Redshaw, 'Altar Books: Liam Miller and the Visit of John Paul to Ireland, 1979', *The South Carolina Review*, 46, 1 (Fall 2013).
7. Kevin Etchingham to JM; 11 January 1973; UCC. Talbot Press offered to bring out both a Goldsmith anthology and a critical volume by Montague.
8. Thomas McCarthy to JM, 6 December 1975; Buffalo, B42.
9. Clíona Ní Ríordáin, pp. 28, 31.
10. Thomas McCarthy, Facebook post, 10 April 2019.
11. Conversation with Pat Crotty, Skype, 27 August 2019.
12. Conversation with Greg Delanty, Cork, 18 February 2017.
13. Conversation with Nuala Ní Dhomhnaill, Galway, 30 December 2016.
14. JM to Serge Fauchereau, 18 May 1972; Bibliothèque S. et Y. Fauchereau, Les Sables-d'Olonne.
15. Patrick Crotty, 'How the Sailor Got Drunk: The Poetry of John Montague 1958-2004', typescript of lecture-review of *The Drunken Sailor*, Montague papers, UCC.
16. Conversation with Eamonn O'Donoghue, 8 January 2017.
17. Thomas McCarthy, 'The Years of Forgetting, 2006–2011', *Irish Pages* (v.6, n.1): 37.
18. Conversation with Greg Delanty, 12 January 2019.
19. Thomas McCarthy, 'Journals, 1974–2014', *New Hibernia Review* (Autumn 2019): 11.
20. Theo Dorgan, 'John Montague: The Influence of Anxiety', *Poetry Ireland Review*, n.121 (2017): 81.

21. Christopher Grieve to JM, 19 December 1973; Buffalo; *The Pear Is Ripe*, p. 217.

22. Robert Graves to JM, 10 December 1974; Buffalo, B65.

23. Jean Sheridan, 'The Graves Touch Delights UCC', *The Irish Press* (14 May 1975): 4.

24. *The Pear Is Ripe*, p. 217.

25. McCarthy, Facebook post, 10 April 2019.

26. JM to Meic Stephens, editor *Poetry Wales*; 18 March 1972.

27. JM to Barrie Cooke, [October/November 1972], draft letter, fragment; NLI.

28. JM to Serge Fauchereau, 25 February 1975; Musée de L'Abbaye Sainte-Croix, Les Sables-d'Olonne.

   Montague finally got the sort of acknowledgement he wanted from Heaney's schoolmate Seamus Deane. In a 1977 review of the revised edition of *Poisoned Lands*, Deane observed that 'Heaney's Derry carries Montague's Tyrone like a watermark'; i.e., it underlies everything (*Hibernia*, 10 June 1977: p. 20).

29. Roy Foster to Adrian Frazier, 25 November 2018; Heaney to Friel, NLI 37,247; folder 4.

30. JM to Robin Skelton, 31 August 1973; University of Victoria.

31. See Thomas McCarthy, 'Journals 1974–2014', *New Hibernia Review*, for a sensitive response to Montague's lecture on Alexander Pope, on 12 October 1974 (p. 14); *The Years of Forgetting*, p. 29. The subtlety of McCarthy's response could hardly have been matched by many in the class.

32. JM to Robin Skelton, 30 January 1974; University of Victoria.

33. On Montague's return trip to mark exams in August 1974, Seán Lucy made the job of marking pleasant for him by collecting him at the airport and driving him to Sligo for the Yeats Summer School. There they encountered 'an aggressive Longley, an affectionate Mahon, and a subdued Simmons' (JM to Evelyn, 24 August 1975; NLI). Afterwards, Lucy and Montague went on a ramble through Sligo and Cavan trying to find 'The Plain of Blood' (Magh Slecht) and the chief idol of Crom Cruach, male deity of pre-Christian Ireland. According to legend, he required the sacrifice of the first-born. This jaunt led to Montague's poem 'The Hinge Stone and the Crozier', *A Slow Dance*, p. 13.

34. Barry Callaghan, *Barrelhouse Kings: A Memoir* (McArthur & Company: Toronto, 1998), 125.

35. JM to Barry Callaghan, 6 November 1966; Callaghan papers; my thanks to Janet Somerville.

36. *Barrelhouse Kings*, 127–8.

37. See for instance Callaghan's full-page review of *A Chosen Light*, 'Poet John Montague: The Falcon Under the Hood', *Toronto Telegram* (9 March 1968): 27.

38. Wedding service of John Montague and Evelyn Robson, one of three privately printed copies, Barry Callaghan papers.

39. Conversation with Evelyn Montague, 25 March 2017; conversation with Elizabeth Montague, 20 January 2019.

40. 'Work in Progress', Exhibition of work by S.W. Hayter, catalogue, Neptune Gallery, 13 June–19 July 1975; Buffalo, B22.

41. Bruce Arnold to JM, 13 June 1975; Buffalo, B22.

42. Désirée Moorhead Hayter to Mairead Murphy; 6 January 1976; Buffalo, B22.

43. Evelyn to Désirée Hayter, 20 April 1976; Buffalo, B22.

44. Montague's note was drafted on the *verso* of a 25 September 1975 letter from the Poetry Book Society; Buffalo, B42. Christmas, 1975. See Elmer Kennedy-Andrews, 'John Montague: Global Regionalist?' *Cambridge Quarterly*, v. 35, n. 1 (2006): 31–48, for a discussion of the parallels between *A Slow Dance* and *North*.

45. 'John Montague writes', Bulletin, Poetry Book Society, Christmas 1975.

46. *A Slow Dance*, p. 11.

47. Kevin White, 'The Plain of Blood: A Study of the Ritual Landscape of Magh Slécht', (MA thesis: IT Sligo, 2013).

48. *A Slow Dance*, pp. 12–13. Crom Cruach also presides over 'The Cave of Night', a sequence on violence in the North (pp. 29–35).

49. Eiléan Ní Chuilleanáin, 'A Joyous Suite', *Hibernia* (12 March 1976): 18.

50. Some reviewers from Northern Ireland, affiliates of the Belfast Group, were vexed by Montague's continuing practice of organizing his poems into sequences. For them, poetry was just lyric poetry, discrete, free-standing, well-made formal entities. Edna Longley called the mounting of *A Slow Dance* 'overdone' and 'fussy' (*The Irish Times*, 17 January 1976, p. 8). James Simmons said the sequences were 'willed constructions', not the results of authentic 'inspiration' (*Honest Ulsterman*, May/October 1976, pp. 68–71); Robert Johnstone sneered at Montague's 'poetic-posing' (*Fortnight*, 10 September 1976, p. 15). Yet other Irish poets also began to compose in sequences; witness Heaney's *North*, Kinsella's *Notes from the Land of the Dead*, and Eavan Boland's *In Her Own Image* (1980) and *Night Feed* (1982).

These Northern critics did not credit the way a sequence could provide an interpretative context for the poems within it, so that, for instance, 'Killing the Pig', by virtue of its place in 'The Cave of Night', is more than a description of barnyard butchery on an Ulster farm; it is intended to be a reflection on the brutalization of the people and the Troubles (*A Slow Dance*, p. 34). Terence Brown spotted the shortcomings of the *bien fait* canon in 'An Ulster Renaissance?' (*Concerning Poetry*, October 1981): pp. 5–23. Yes, he explained, there was a local renaissance of a particular kind of poem, the well-made poem, which the local context has inflected with 'tense astringency'. Brown noted the recent popularity of a motif of a journey to a different poetic territory, which 'widens horizons without great risk'. When poems by authors associated with the Group inspect more disturbing local scenes, it is from a distance, as in the dedicatory poem for *Wintering Out*, where the Long Kesh detention camp is seen from 'a dewy motorway'.

51. *A Slow Dance*, pp. 29–40.

52. Evelyn and JM to Robin Skelton; 24 September 1976; Victoria.

53. Deirdre Bair, *Parisian Lives* (Atlantic: London, 2019), especially pp. 178–83.

54. Conversation with Evelyn Montague, 25 March 2017.

55. Montague, review of biography of Beckett, *The Guardian* (14 September 1978): 9.

56. Mary Leland, 'John Montague in Cork', *The Irish Times* (23 November 1976).

CHAPTER ELEVEN

1. JM to Barrie Cooke, 9 April 1976; Barrie Cooke archive. Montague met Frénaud in 1968 when he was gathering poems for an anthology of modern French poetry with Serge Fauchereau: 'I don't like most of what I have read of him but recently I met Frénaud, & rather like him. He said <u>you</u> were very intelligent, so he has good taste!' (JM to Fauchereau, 1 May 1968; Les Sables-d'Olonne).

2. Evelyn Montague to Robin Skelton, 11 February 1977; University of Victoria.

3. JM to Serge Fauchereau, 26 October 1977; Les Sables-d'Olonne.

4. Evelyn Montague to Michael and Edna Longley, 2 May 1977; Emory.

5. JM to Serge Fauchereau, 26 October 1977; Les Sables-d'Olonne.

6. Conversation with Michael and Edna Longley, 9 February 2019.

7. Montague, notes for Barrie Cooke opening at Cork Arts Centre, Lavitt Quay; NLI 50 718/937.

8. Edna Longley to Paul Durcan; Durcan papers, NLI.

9. JM to Michael and Edna Longley, 2 May 1977; Emory.

10. Evelyn Montague to Michael and Edna Longley, 2 May 1977; Emory.

11. *CP*, 312.

12. Redshaw to author, email August 2023: 'Evelyn was willing to travel, to go along with JM, even when she was also establishing herself in the small society of educated Cork. But I also think that her presence "drove" him to finish projects, books, collections, and not just in the sense that he had to "provide", but in the dreaded "Muse" sense. Relations with her were sometimes painful, but always eventful, intellectually and emotionally stimulating.' And she got tired of driving. And he got tired of being 'driven'.

13. JM, 'Global Regionalism', interview with Adrian Frazier, *The Literary Review* (Winter 1979): 153–74.

14. The original source of this popular maxim is Valerius Maximus, *Facta et Dicta Memorabilia* (*Memorable Deeds and Sayings*), Book 6, chapter 2.

15. John Wilson Foster, 'The Celtic Arts, CAIS Conference – A Personal Report', *Canadian Journal of Irish Studies* (June 1978), pp. 62–5.

16. Montague knew that he had lost the debate with Conor Cruise O'Brien; he reported to Robin Skelton that because of the Troubles, 'We are torn, bad-tempered, disconsolate, our psyches turned every which way. The main psychic event of Toronto seemed to be my confrontation with Conor Cruise which I found necessary but painful; he is as unscrupulous as Cuchulain, and rhetorically reduced me to shreds, although many approved my stand' (JM to Skelton, 24 April 1978; Victoria).

17. John Jordan, review of *The Great Cloak*, *Irish Independent* (1 April 1978): 8. Montague was 'immensely touched' by his old classmate's salute; JM to John Jordan, 2 April 1978; John Jordan papers, NLI.

   Strangely, during this same April, Anthony Cronin published an article on the present condition of the arts, saying 'There has been, and will be, no new Irish Renaissance.' That would come only with government investment ('A Dream of Fifty Years Ago', *The Irish Times* (7 April 1978). The article was part of Cronin's ultimately successful campaign for Aosdána, an Irish organization founded in 1981 which honours outstanding artists and financially assists members in need.

18. Blanaid Montague to JM, 5 May 1978; NLI, Ms 50,718/999.

19. Brian Lynch, 'Poet's Honesty Comes Through', *The Sunday Press* (28 May 1978): 21.

20. JM to Heaney, May 1976; Emory.

21. JM to Skelton, 24 September 1976; Victoria.

22. Stephen Enniss, *After the Titanic: A Life of Derek Mahon*, Gill and Macmillan: Dublin, 2014), p. 145.

23. The first extant version of 'Survivor' (*CP*, 321) was typed on the back of letter to JM from Garech Browne's secretary, Mary Rose Cahill, dated 21 June 1978.

24. Evelyn to JM, 27 July 1978; NLI; quoted in Enniss, *After the Titanic*, 146.

25. JM to Paul Muldoon, 14 September 1978; Emory; Thomas Redshaw to JM, 12 December 1973; NLI.

26. JM to Michael [Anania], November 1973; Buffalo, B34.

27. Montague reported to James Liddy, 'I stammered through "A Courtyard in Winter" at Boston College (too much emotion and the wrong season for reading it) but came on strong at Harvard the next day, ending up in a jazz joint listening to a sax playing bluesman called Clean Head Johnson' (8 November 1978; James Liddy Papers, University of Wisconsin, Milwaukee).

28. Seán Golden to AF, email, 14 October 2016.

29. Anthony Bradley to AF, email, 12 October 2016.

30. Interview with Pat Crotty.

31. My thanks to Christopher Griffin for a transcription of this interview; Christopher Griffin to AF, 22 February 2017.

32. JM to James Liddy, 8 November 1978; University of Wisconsin Milwaukee, Mss 300, Box 8, Folder 30001.

33. JM to Seamus Heaney, 25 February 1979; Emory; interview with Evelyn Montague, 25 March 2017.

34. Christoph Lindenberg, *Rudolf Steiner: A Biography*.

35. Conversations with Evelyn Montague, 19 February and 25 March 2017.

36. *Collected Poems*, 158, 134.

37. *Collected Poems*, 132, 184.

38. JM made a copy of the passage on the back side of a letter to Evelyn [October 1978]; NLI. The first mention in Montague's notebooks of Teilhard de Chardin is in June 1963; Buffalo.

39. Kathleen Raine to JM, 20 February 1980; NLI.

40. Philippa Bernard, *No End to Snowdrops*, p. 151.

41. Kathleen Raine to JM, 30 March 1982; NLI.

42. JM to Kathleen Raine [March 1981?]; NLI; Montague had recently read Raine's autobiography, *The Lion's Mouth* (1977).

43. JM to Robin Skelton, Samhain 1979; Victoria.

44. The actress Fiona Shaw sometimes kept him company on these walks across Cork to the university; see *The Sunday Times* (26 February 2017): 9.

45. There are other drafts from this month on the back of an AIB bank statement and an advertisement for an exhibition by T.P. Flanagan. As one who grew up in the Depression and amid the paper shortages of the war years, Montague never wasted a sheet of paper. He reused one sheet after another that arrived in the post.

46. Desmond McCabe to JM, 11 October 1979; NLI.

47. JM to Robin Skelton, May 1980; Victoria.

48. 'John Montague reads his work', *Newcastle Evening Chronicle* (2 May 1980); JM to Michael Longley, May 1980; Emory.

49. Thomas McCarthy, 'Journals 1974–2014', *New Hibernia Review* (Autumn 2019): 21.

50. JM to Derek Mahon, 27 November 1982; Emory; *Belfast Telegraph* (21 June 1980): 1.

51. 'Cassandra's Answer', *CP*, 301–2. The poem was drafted on the backs of March 1981 letters from scholar Mark Waelder and the Vancouver poet Mary Barnard, NLI. Edna Longley objected to the appearance in the poem of 'well-worn Montague adjectives: "fatal", "gaunt", "fierce", "bleak"' (*London Review of Books*, 22 March 1990, p. 22). Those words are indeed key notes in Montague's verbal palette, but there can be little doubt of the sincerity of his shock at the destruction of his mother's home.

52. John Montague interview, with Stephen Arkin, *New England Review* (Autumn/Winter 1982): 214–41.

53. Conversation with Andrew, Sheena and Dara Montague, 4 February 2017.

54. JM, 'Hungerstriker', draft on verso of flyer for Ben Wicks Restaurant, Toronto; NLI; another typed draft is entitled 'Sands'.

55. Conversation with Fr Joe McVeigh, 4 February 2017. My thanks for this encounter to Andrew Montague.

56. Montague admitted to Richard Ryan that he was weary of teaching at Cork, depressed by 'male menopause' and worried by 'things I can't solve, like Ulster'; JM to Richard Ryan, 26 January 1982; private collection.

57. JM to Samuel Beckett [February 1982], NLI; JM and Evelyn to Seamus Deane [March? 1982]; Emory.

58. In the library of Serge Fauchereau, Les Sables-d'Olonne.

59. JM, 'Rejoyce: see how he rises', review of Richard Ellmann's *James Joyce*, revised edition, *The Guardian* (21 October 1982).

60. Flaubert, *Correspondence*, I, 321 (18 September 1846).

61. Seamus Deane to AF, email, 22 October 2017.

62. Evelyn to Seamus Deane, 19 March [1982]; Emory.

63. Tom Redshaw to AF, 12 November 2022.

64. JM to Liam Miller, July 1982; Wake Forest.

65. On the beach in Paros, Montague also ran into John Peter, who was writing a book on Beckett, *Vladimir's Carrot: Modern Drama and the Modern Imagination* (1987). He joined the Mahons and Montagues for dinner, at which John and Derek did an impression of Ian Paisley being heckled at a public meeting; John Peter to JM, nd; NLI, f. 1026.

66. Janet Malcolm, *Psychoanalysis: The Impossible Profession* (Knopf: NY, 1981), Loc. 1800.

67. JM to Robin Skelton, 27 August 1982; Victoria.

68. Conversation with Eva Bourke, 3 October 2016.

69. AF, diary, July 1983; 'Leaves from a Guestbook', *Hill Field: Poems & Memoirs for John Montague*, ed. Thomas Redshaw, (Coffee House Press: Minneapolis; Gallery Books: Oldcastle, 1989), pp. 80–5.

CHAPTER TWELVE

1. JM to Derek Mahon, August 1983; Emory.

2. JM to Seamus Montague, August 1986; NLI, f.1027; *The Figure in the Cave*, Loc. 409.

3. Notebook for 10 July 1963; Buffalo. He already had the title 'The Lost Notebook' then.

4. Notebook for 31 August 1964; Buffalo.

5. JM to Seamus Heaney, July 1984; Emory.

6. 'Poetry flourishes from broken places', Montague's phrase, from conversation with Elizabeth Montague, 20 December 2019.

7. JM to Dillon Johnston [September 1983?]; NLI, f.1477. The letter also takes issue with the title of Johnston's study: '*Irish Poetry After Joyce* – don't fall for that Dublin fallacy – … Yeats still shows the way, beyond the boredoms of Irish Catholicism – no one has grasped more than a bit of the mantle yet. Clarke got stuck in detail – the wary Heaney knows Yeats is there, Kavanagh and Kinsella bounce off him.' For a letter from this period in Kerry, see JM to Seamus Heaney, 12 July 1978; Emory. At the time that Derek Mahon was drying out at Grattan Hill, Montague reflected that he too must change his life.

8. JM to Robin Skelton, 10 November 1983; Victoria.

9. My thanks to Tom Redshaw; this description adapts his message of 17 October 2022.

10. Interview with Sibyl Montague, 23 February 2019.

11. Interview with Alessandro Gentili, 2 March 2019.

12. *CP*, 316; Evelyn Montague, 'Raver Reviewed', *Sunday Tribune* (14 April 1985).

13. *Belfast Telegraph* (2 and 3 December 1983).

14. This is speculation. The sur-title is there, but it may not have been added because of police pressure in 1983, but in order to reflect accurately the time of the actual events that inspired the writing of the original story.

15. JM to Paul Muldoon, 10 September 1984; Emory; Blanaid to JM and family, 29 November 1983; NLI.

16. Conversation with Edna and Michael Longley, 9 February 2019.

17. Verse notes written on the back of a 14 December 1983 letter from John Hughes, editor of *North Magazine* (Belfast), NLI; JM to Paul Muldoon, 10 September 1984; Emory.

    Michael Foley (co-editor, *The Honest Ulsterman*) was there for the party: 'And I was fortunate to witness an exchange between John and Paul Muldoon, so passionate and eloquent that I commemorated it in verse:

    Your work's a load of shite, snarled Muldoon to Montague.

    But John bounced back

> With the witty crack,
>
> I think yours is a load of shite too.

(Email message from Michael Foley, 22 April 2020).

18. See Dillon Johnston, *The Poetic Economies of England and Ireland, 1912–2000* (Palgrave: London, 2001) for a thorough analysis of the decisions of the Poetry Book Society. The 'literary establishment' of London was tightly knit, as explained by Richard Boston in *The Guardian* on the occasion of 1989 dispute between Blake Morrison and Michael Horovitz. Horovitz had complained that many were locked out of prizes, reviews, and publishing contracts by a *quadrumvirate* of Blake Morrison (*The Observer*), Andrew Motion (Chatto and Windus) Craig Raine (Faber's poetry editor), and Christopher Reid (also Faber), none of whom had much of a taste for international modernism.

    Boston named other members of the ruling elite: 'The editor of *The Times Literary Supplement*, Jeremy Treglown, came from University College London (which is where Morrison did his post-graduate studies) and that at UCL the Northcliffe Professor of English Literature is Karl Miller, formerly literary editor of *The Spectator* and the *New Statesman*, editor of *The Listener* and now of the *London Review of Books*. Treglown's predecessor at the *TLS* was John Gross who had also been literary editor of the *New Statesman*, as was Martin Amis, who came from Oxford (as did Horovitz) via the *TLS* to *The Observer*. Other *New Statesman* alumni included Anthony Thwaite (*Encounter*), Claire Tomalin (then literary editor of *The Sunday Times*), and there was Julian Barnes (*New Statesman, The Sunday Times, The Observer*). Craig Raine's route was Oxford, *New Review, Quarto*, and *New Statesman* to Faber ('Literary Establishments ... London', *The Guardian* [24 June 1989]).

    Not a single one of these influential persons was among Montague's close acquaintances or correspondents. Seamus Heaney was, to judge by his recently published letters, pals from early on with Karl Miller, Charles Monteith, Blake Morrison, Andrew Motion and Christopher Reid, a considerable swathe of this 'literary establishment'.

19. Yet most reviewers judged it one of the best books of the season; see, for instance, John Jordan, 'The ground it mined', *The Irish Press* (26 May 1984) and Douglas Dunn, 'The dance of discontent', *The Times Literary Supplement* (5 October 1984): 1124. However, Martin Dodsworth, normally an admirer of Montague's work, thought that in this case the subject was 'too much for him' (*The Guardian*, 11 October 1984; p. 22).

20. JM, draft card, 20 May 1984; NLI, B5, F24.

21. *CP*, 300.

22. Conversation with Evelyn Montague, 25 March 2017.

23. Conversation with Nuala Ní Dhomhnaill, 30 December 2016.

24. Conversation with Greg Delanty, 28 October 2022.

25. JM to Robin Skelton, 10 November 1983; Victoria.

26. The observation is by Patrick Crotty (Skype conversation, 31 August 2019).

27. Conversation with Evelyn Montague; and Kathleen Raine to JM, 5 August 1985; Raine, more a spiritualist than a feminist, tried to comfort Montague: 'Why have women ceased to love their men and to give the support of womanhood, and instead refused to be woman and

gone into competition? No country is free from it, although in India one sees how wonderful the women can be without renouncing their womanhood. But then the Goddess still is worshipped there ....' (NLI).

28. John Verling's illustrations of *The Lost Notebook* were not, like those for *The Midnight Court*, done with a fine-tipped pen, but with a messy brush, quickly. They are not collector's items.

29. The tax figures and salary scale are from an Irish government website. However, in her 'field notes' for 20 May 1987 Elizabeth Sheehan says that JM told her that he made £28,000, of which £11,000 was taken in taxes. The difference may be due to Montague's promotion to Associate Professor and an 'added years bonus'.

30. 'Weekend of Events to Commemorate Patrick Kavanagh', *Dundalk Democrat* (24 November 1984).

31. 'The Parish or the Roots Racket', NLI. In 1985 Michael Longley was still saying that American free verse, such as the work of William Carlos Williams, was 'poetry-less poetry'. He continued to believe that the pentameter was the 'natural breath length' and that speech was 'mainly iambic' ('The Longley Tapes', interview with Robert Johnstone, *The Honest Ulsterman* (Summer 1985): 19.

32. JM to Edna Longley, draft letter, perhaps unsent [December 1984]; NLI.

33. *CP*, 310. Some of these poems, it appears, were inspired by extramarital affairs, even though they re-enact the original lyric acclamation of Evelyn.

34. JM to Kathleen Raine, 5 August 1985; NLI.

35. Message from William Kennedy, 11 May 2017; conversation with Barbara Weiner, 9 May 2017.

36. JM to William Kennedy, 21 May 1986; SUNY Albany.

37. JM to Barry Callaghan, 31 March 1986; NLI.

38. Bridie Montague to JM, 15 April 1986; NLI.

39. JM to Seamus Montague [August 1986]; NLI, F.1027.

40. Alessandro Gentili to AF; 4 April 2017.

41. 'Death of Distinguished Solicitor', *Fermanagh Herald* (12 July 1986).

42. John Montague, 'Living for Ireland', *16 on 16: Letters from the New Island* (Raven Arts: Dublin, 1988), p. 17.

43. JM to Seamus Heaney, November 1986; Emory.

44. Tom Redshaw to AF, 12 November 2022.

45. JM, 'Home Truths', unpublished sequence of poems; my thanks to Elizabeth Montague.

46. There are three extant manuscripts for the unpublished sequence *Home Truths*. The number of poems varies between manuscripts from twenty-one to twenty-four. The titles of some poems also vary. The appendix reproduces what appears to be the most recent typescript. It does not include the poems 'Respite', 'After Rain' or 'Chain Letter' (this last poem is printed in *New Collected Poems*, p. 396).

47. A few of the lyrics – 'Wrath' and 'Chain Letter' – are scattered through *Smashing the Piano* (1999), but in a manner that makes biographical inferences unlikely.

48. JM to Kathleen Raine [no date].

49. Morris Graves to Evelyn Montague, 5 March 1987; NLI, F.960.

50. JM to Kathleen Raine, May 1987; NLI.

51. The following account of Elizabeth Sheehan's meetings with John Montague is based on the field notes kept at the time, her commentary on them, and discussion via email with the author; my thanks to Elizabeth Sheehan.

52. Elizabeth Sheehan, draft article; email, 20 November 2018.

53. Sentence paraphrased from Elizabeth Sheehan's dissertation.

54. A celebration of Francis Stuart's 85th birthday, held at Trinity College, on 7 May 1987.

55. Elizabeth Sheehan, notes on JM's comments about Francis Stuart, 20 May 1987; private collection.

56. 'Liam Miller, publisher, dies at 63', *The Irish Times* (18 May 1987): 9; Tom Redshaw to AF, 12 November 2022.

57. Elizabeth Sheehan, field notes, 10 June 1987, p. 2.

58. Elizabeth Sheehan, field notes, 5 July 1987.

59. Derek Mahon to Jacqueline Simms, OUP, 21 May 1987; Enniss, *After the Titanic*, 211.

60. Peter Fallon to JM, 17 July 1988; NLI.

61. Peter Fallon to JM, 16 October 1988; NLI.

CHAPTER THIRTEEN

1. Gagen was a writer and film-maker who had worked with William Kennedy on movie projects. He and Montague had grown to be drinking buddies during Montague's Albany visits.

2. Barry Callaghan, *Barrelhouse Kings*, p. 560.

3. JM to William Kennedy, April 1988; SUNY Albany Library.

4. Lucy had accepted as assurance of a position the informal enthusiasm of an Irish-American professor at Loyola, but this professor was not on the faculty of the English Department, and therefore not in a position to offer Lucy a job.

5. In fact, harsh words were exchanged in the course of Montague's departure from UCC; Thomas Kinsella to JM, 5 August 1988; NLI; JM to Gerry Dawe, 5 September 1988, NLI; Ger Fitzgibbon to AF, 3 August 2021; Conversation with Evelyn Montague, March 2019.

6. Conversation with Louis de Paor, 8 January 2017.

7. For documentation of this development at Field Day, see the Thomas Kilroy papers at the Hardiman Library, University of Galway; e.g., Matthew Evans, Faber editor, to Brian Friel, 8 March 1989 and Seamus Deane to board members, 13 November 1990.

8. Thomas McCarthy, Facebook post, 13 March 2019, based on his diary entry of the time.

9. JM to Michael Longley, 19 July 1982; Emory; JM to Derek Mahon, August 1982; Emory.

10. Richard Murphy to JM, 7 May 1988; NLI. Seamus Heaney persuaded his publisher to reduce the charge, because 'My relations with John involve the *comitatus* of poets and the *pietas* of a shared background in the North, as well as a twenty-five-year friendship', Seamus Heaney to Dear Michael, 12 September 1988; NLI.

11. Thomas Redshaw, 'Undertow: John Montague's "Sea Changes" (1981)', *Canadian Journal of Irish Studies* (Fall 2009): 18.

12. JM to Liam Miller, 30 December 1961; Wake Forest; JM to Robin Skelton, 6 June 1964; Victoria.

13. Mark Waelder to JM; 20 March 1981; NLI.

14. Mark Waelder to JM, 1 July 1981, NLI.

15. Liam Miller to JM, 10 May 1984; Wake Forest.

16. Antony Farrell to JM, 1 July and 2 September 1987; NLI.

17. JM to [Monsignor Ó Riordain]; late October 1989; NLI.

18. JM to Janet Somerville, 16 June 1990; Buffalo.

19. Theo Dorgan to JM; 16 June 1989; NLI.

20. Samuel Beckett to JM, undated [October 1988?]; NLI.

21. Conversation with Nuala Ní Dhomhnaill, 30 December 2016.

22. It hardly needs saying, but Deirdre Bair was not called to the bedside of Beckett.

23. JM, 'An Appreciation of Samuel Beckett', *The Guardian* (27 December 1989).

24. Hilary Pyle, 'Startling Effect of Patchwork', *Irish Examiner* (5 August 1989): 13; 'A Revolution in Quilts', *Irish Examiner* (22 December 1989): 3.

25. Sandra MacLiammoir, 'Living and Leisure', *Sunday Independent* (28 January 1990): 20.

26. Antoinette Quinn, "The Well Beloved': Montague and the Muse', *Irish University Review* (Spring 1989): 43.

27. Eiléan Ní Chuilleanáin, 'A Festive Note', *Poetry Ireland Review* (Autumn 1989): 68.

28. Patricia Coughlan, '"Bog Queens": Representations of Femininity in the Poetry of Seamus Heaney and John Montague', *Gender and Irish Writing*; David Cairns and Toni O'Brien Johnson, eds. (Open University Press: London, 1991).

29. 'Dark-haired and discreet', from an impromptu poem Montague wrote for Janet Somerville on the back of an Aer Lingus boarding pass; my thanks to Janet Somerville.

30. JM to Janet Somerville [pm 30 July 1990]; my thanks to Janet Somerville.

31. JM to William Kennedy, October 1990; Albany.

32. Conversation with Evelyn Montague, 19 March 2017.

33. JM to Janet Somerville, 7 December 1990; Buffalo, Barry Callaghan folder in Montague papers.

34. Seamus Heaney, 'Whinlands', *Door into the Dark* (Faber: London, 1969), p. 48.

35. 'Contemporary Irish literature', *The New York Times* (11 May 1990); 'Two Evenings of Irish Poetry', *The New Yorker* (14 May 1990).

36. M.L. Rosenthal to JM, 22 December 1990; NLI; *Ploughshares* (Spring 1991): 107–10.

37. Joan McBreen to JM, 15 August 1992; NLI; David Coleman to JM, 2 September 1992; NLI.

38. Tom Clyde, review of *Time in Armagh*, *Honest Ulsterman* (Spring 1994).

39. 'Exhibition of Quilts', *Irish Examiner* (27 July 1991); see also Stan Gébler Davies, 'Carbery Diary', *Independent* (London), (10 August 1991); 'Works that cover fabric of life', *Irish Independent* (12 August 1991): 8.

40. Jackie Keogh, 'Evelyn Gets Straight to the Point', *Southern Star* (18 August 1991): 2.

41. 'Apology', *Sunday Independent* (8 September 1991): 22.

42. Aidan Higgins ('Rory of the Glens') to JM, 3 January 1992; NLI.

43. Interview with Nuala Ní Dhomhnaill, 30 December 2016.

44. The following account relies heavily on Elizabeth Montague's unpublished memoir 'John & Me', sent to the author.

45. Elizabeth to JM, 6 May [1992]; NLI.

46. John Montague, *The Leap* (Deerfield Press: Deerfield, Massachusetts; The Gallery Press: Oldcastle, 1979). The poem was originally inspired by his flight from his first marriage to be with Evelyn.

47. Evelyn Montague made copies of one or more of the letters from 'Pixie' and later used them in the construction of a quilt, a unique adaptation of the women's handiwork for feminist artistic revenge. The quilt appeared in exhibitions of Evelyn's work in Minneapolis/St Paul and elsewhere.

48. Elizabeth Montague to JM, 24 February 1997; NLI.

49. This account relies on Elizabeth Montague's memoir.

50. Frances Lynn, letter to AF, 20 November 2016. A visitor from Oregon, Frances Lynn wrote that she fell in love with John Montague on that night, and later acquired all his works: 'I only hope to live long enough, Adrian Frazier, to read your biography of my favourite poet.'

51. Conversation with Barbara Weiner (widow of Tom Smith), 9 May 2017. See also Evelyn Montague to Katherine and Bill Crozier, 30 January 1994; NLI.

52. Parts of *Border Sick Call* appear in draft in JM's notebooks from 4, 5 and 7 January 1963 (Buffalo); 25 January 1972; 30 March 1973; 22 October 1974 (NLI).

53. JM to Seamus Montague, 24 February 1994; my thanks to Mary Montague. Elizabeth Montague observed that when he was troubled about someone, John tended to idealize them, and does so with Seamus in this poem, and with Evelyn in *The Great Cloak*.

54. James Olney to JM, 18 April 1994; NLI, f301. The poem appears in *The Southern Review* (July 1995): 409–24.

55. Eiléan Ní Chuilleanáin, '*Border Sick Call*', *Chosen Lights Poets on Poems by John Montague*, Loc. 1571–86.

56. JM to Janet Somerville, 16 June 1990; Buffalo.

57. Conversation with Elizabeth Montague, 20 December 2019.

58. Conversation with Barbara Weiner, 9 May 2017.

59. Katherine Crouan, 'Memoir of Crozier & Montague', estate of William Crozier.

60. Elizabeth Montague, 'John & Me, 1995'; email to AF.

61. Seamus Heaney to JM, 12 November 1995; NLI.

62. JM to Seamus Heaney, 11 July 1996; Emory.

CHAPTER FOURTEEN

1. Elizabeth Wassell Montague to JM, [February 1997]; NLI.

2. Philip Brady to AF, 10 October 2016; Philip Brady, 'Ginsberg in Ballydehob', *The Ohio Writer* (Spring 2001).

3. Peter Fallon to JM, 30 September 1997; NLI. Montague blamed the Corkman on the jury, John A. Murphy, but another member told Elizabeth that it was A.S. Byatt who cast the deciding vote; JM to Peter Fallon, draft letter; NLI.

4. Paul Muldoon to JM, 9 October 1997; NLI.

5. 'Tales of Summer Schools', *The Irish Times* (21 June 1997): 2; Katie Donovan, 'Ignited by Ireland', *The Irish Times* (10 June 1997): 13.

6. For another account, see Enniss, *After the Titanic*, p. 246.

7. JM to Derek Mahon, [November 1996]; Emory. With a PS by Elizabeth: 'Please come back to us. We miss and love you.'

8. Elizabeth Montague to AF, 27 December 2022.

9. Neil Astley to JM, 18 January 1994; NLI.

10. There is a draft of *Carnac* in the NLI from June 1971. The comparison with a Robert Duncan poem appears to come from a draft made in June 1973; NLI.

11. Michael Worton to JM, 6 March 1997; NLI.

12. John Montague, trans., *Guillevic/ Carnac* (Bloodaxe Books: Newcastle upon Tyne, 1999), p. 28. Kevin McGrath called Montague's 'certainly the best version currently available of one the finest poems of twentieth-century European poetry' (*Harvard Review* [Spring 2001]: 154).

13. Montague showed chapters to the editor of *Grand Street* in 1995 under the title 'Lives of Poets', Deborah to JM, 10 July 1995; NLI.

14. *Sunday Independent* (24 June 2001).

15. Thomas J. Hedley (an editor at Duckworth) to JM; 1 February 2001; NLI.

16. *The Poet's Chair: The First Nine Years of the Ireland Chair of Poetry* (The Lilliput Press: Dublin, 2008), pp. vii–x.

17. 'Omagh launches Christmas programme in bid to move forward', *Ulster Herald* (19 November 1998): 3.

18. Before John went to Belfast to take up the duties of his Ireland Chair, he became anxious about the many occasions when he would be required to perform in public, in front of a crowd that was not always full of friends. Sometime in the early 1990s, before their separation, Evelyn had asked John to hand over his big silver gannet ring; caught off guard, he did so, and she kept it. Montague did not wear so many magical rings as Robert Graves, nor was he so superstitious as W.B. Yeats, but he did tend to credit certain things and places with spiritual power, particularly this gannet ring which Madeleine had given him after he had left for Cork. Whatever power it may have had, he believed he had lost, and that unnerved him as he prepared to go North. He appealed for its return to Evelyn, twice, and she gave it to Sibyl to carry back to him. The saga does not end there. John later returned the ring to Madeleine, because she had originally been given it by a Cambridge lecturer when she was at the University of Illinois in the mid-1950s (Madeleine Montague to AF, 7 January 2023).

19. Conversation with Sibyl Montague, 23 February 2019.

20. Contract, *The New Yorker*, for 'A Devil in the Hills', NLI.

21. John Montague, 'A Devil in the Hills', *The New Yorker* (10 January 2000): 40.

22. *A Very Strange Man*, (New Island: Dubin, 2021), p. 27.

23. Strangely enough, John Carey in his *Sunday Times* review of *Company* quoted two phrases, one to praise and the other to scorn. Each of them was in fact written by Elizabeth (report from Tom McCarthy's *Poetry, Memory, and the Party*, pp. 310–11).

24. Letters associated with Gerry Wrixon birthday, NLI 50,718/1007; email, Alannah Hopkins to AF, 7 June 2021; Elizabeth Montague to AF, 9 June 2021. Who the college friend was who committed suicide is unknown.

    By this stage in his life, Aidan Higgins was beginning to suffer dementia, and may have been locked into old memories, and unable to deal diplomatically with an aggressive interrogation; see Alannah Hopkin, *A Very Strange Man* (New Island: Dublin, 2021), p 225.

25. 'Irish Poetry Travels East', *Moscow Times* (5 November 1999).

26. JM to Barry Callaghan, 1 October 1999; NLI.

27. Elizabeth Wassell, *Sleight of Hand* (Wolfhound Press: Dublin, 1999), p. 37.

28. Seán Lysaght to AF, 8 December 2016.

29. Oonagh Montague to JM, 21 February 2006; UCC.

30. Liam Mansfield to AF, January 2017.

31. *The Irish Times* (22 March 2014).

32. Conversation with Howard Davies, 14 December 2017. My thanks for his description of La Cave Romagnan.

33. JM to Serge Fauchereau, January 2000; NLI.

34. JM to Garech Browne, August 2002; NLI.

35. JM to Jonathan Williams, 2 February 2002; private papers.

36. *The Memoirs of Elias Canetti* (Farrar, Straus and Giroux: New York, 1999); Montague, 'Words of a grumpy old man', *The Irish Times* (8 October 2005): 12; JM to Jonathan Williams, 15 April 2002: 'a style I adapted from Canetti' (private papers).

37. JM to Désirée Moorhead, 17 March 2003; NLI.

38. Peter Fallon to JM, 10 April 2004; NLI.

39. JM to Barry Callaghan, January 1996; Buffalo.

40. John Montague, *Smashing the Piano* (The Gallery Press: Oldcastle, 1999), p. 32.

41. Conversation with Andrew Montague, 5 January 2022.

42. Dillon Johnston to JM, 2 April 1998; UCC.

43. Peter Fallon to JM, 19 July 2014; UCC.

44. JM to Barry Callaghan, 1 October 1999; Buffalo.

45. JM to Barrie Cooke, [May? 2005], Barrie Cooke Archive, Cambridge.

46. JMO, 'A Smile Between the Stones', *The Irish Times* (25 June 2005).

47. As it turned out, Montague in his will left Letter Cottage to Elizabeth, and the house was sold following his death, to the disappointment of his daughters.

48. Oonagh Montague to JM, 21 February 2006; UCC.

49. John Montague, 'Since I am …' *The Irish Times* (29 November 2003): 59. The proof copy of Foster's biography is in the Montague papers of the NLI.

50. Seamus Heaney to JM, 22 October and 28 October 2010; UCC.

51. JM to Seamus Heaney, August 2011; UCC.

52. JM, review of *The Human Chain*, *Dublin Review of Books* (2010); Seamus Heaney to JM, 4 January 2011, UCC.

53. Notes on the occasion of the death of Seamus Heaney, written on a document about 'Cengage Learning'; my thanks to Elizabeth Montague.

54. Conversation with Mary O'Malley, 10 December 2016.

55. Conversation with Nuala Ní Dhomhnaill, regarding a 15 September 2015 event at the National Concert Hall; conversation, 30 December 2016.

56. James Harpur, review of *Speech Lessons*, *The Poetry Ireland Review* (April 2012): 90–92.

57. Lara Marlowe, profile of John Montague at 85, *The Irish Times* (22 March 2014).

58. Freda Montague to JM, Christmas 1970; NLI.

59. Between hotels for the widows, undertaker, gravediggers, priests, reception, transport, there were many bills for the funeral, amounting to about £4,000, paid for by Turlough and Andrew Montague.

60. John Montague, review of *The Human Chain*, *Dublin Review of Books* (2010).

INDEX